EFFECTIVE WRITING FOR THE COLLEGE CURRICULUM

EFFECTIVE WRITING FOR THE COLLEGE CURRICULUM

Robert Atwan
Seton Hall University

William Vesterman
Rutgers University

McGRAW-HILL BOOK COMPANY

New York • St. Louis • San Francisco • Auckland • Bogotá • Hamburg
Johannesburg • London • Madrid • Mexico • Milan • Montreal
New Delhi • Panama • Paris • São Paulo • Singapore
Sydney • Tokyo • Toronto

EFFECTIVE WRITING
FOR THE COLLEGE CURRICULUM

1 2 3 4 5 6 7 8 9 0 DOCDOC 8 9 2 1 0 9 8 7

ISBN 0-07-002439-1

This book was set in Electra by Better Graphics.
The editors were Emily G. Barrosse and James R. Belser;
the designer was Jo Jones;
the production supervisor was Diane Renda.
The cover was designed by Joseph Gillians.
The drawings were done by Voll Information Sciences.
R. R. Donnelley & Sons Company was printer and binder.

See Acknowledgments on pages 777–781.
Copyrights included on this page by reference.

Library of Congress Cataloging-in-Publication Data
Effective writing for the college curriculum.

   1. College readers.   2. English language—Rhetoric.
3. Interdisciplinary approach in education.   I. Atwan,
Robert.   II. Vesterman, William.
PE1417.E36   1987   808'.0427   86-18588
ISBN 0-07-002439-1

C·O·N·T·E·N·T·S

PART FOUR   BUSINESS AND ECONOMICS
Careers/Finance/Corporate Management/
Retailing/Marketing/Ethics

P·R·E·F·A·C·E

Effective Writing for the College Curriculum is a reader for freshman composition that provides lively essays of high quality in a broad range of topics from the many disciplines that make up today's college curriculum. The collection includes a wide variety of effective twentieth-century writing on subjects well within the freshman student's own range of experience, areas of interest, and powers of judgment—writing that clearly shows the ways in which accomplished writers achieve clarity, organization, and forcefulness of expression in contemporary expository prose throughout the spectrum of specialized fields. The essays also show how and why skill in expository writing is a practical requirement not only for every major area of study but also for the businesses and professions that lie beyond college.

This anthology is designed to work in many different composition courses. The book attempts to provide help in a variety of programs and to the students they serve by presenting several specific aspects of design—many of them—in the areas of contents, organization, and special features.

The contents of *Effective Writing for the College Curriculum* are distinctive in providing:

- A full and serious treatment of the business and economics major—one of the largest in the country—along with representative articles in and on other neglected areas of study, such as agriculture.
- A special subsection of essays called Academic and Professional Discourse included within each general area of study. This breakdown allows the freshman student to become familiar with the kinds of specialized writing done *in* the various disciplines of a college curriculum and the various occupations of its graduates as well as with writing addressed to a general audience *on* many of the topics of current concern to those disciplines and occupations.

- A special section on Mass Communications and Popular Culture containing examples of topics of interest to contemporary students, whatever their career goals might be.

  The organization of *Effective Writing for the College Curriculum* is designed for flexibility.

- A functional Table of Contents reflects a rhetorical organization within each of the five sections, an organization that moves from simpler to more complex prose forms. The first group in each section contains the forms often used at the beginning of a composition course and emphasizes personal observation and narration. The next group provides examples of the more complex methods involved in analysis and explanation, while the last group contains essays with a special emphasis on advocacy and argument.
- Linked selections allow a fuller discussion of an individual writer, such as Stephen Jay Gould, or of a particular topic, such as the cultural impact of Joe Louis.
- Thorough headnotes trace the career and mark the general achievements of each writer, while introducing that writer's particular essay.
- *Organized* discussion questions and suggestions for writing are broken down into four categories for each selection:
  Summarizing main points
  Analyzing methods of discourse
  Focusing on the field
  Writing assignments

Effective Writing for the College Curriculum also provides several special features to enhance the book's usefulness:

- A special appendix on the process of writing. Student writers first respond to one of the writing assignments in the book, e.g., on the essay by John Kenneth Galbraith, "How to Get the Poor off Our Conscience." In interviews the students then describe the ways in which they came to compose their essays, giving specific examples of problems they encountered and revisions they made. A parallel interview raises the same questions with one of the professional authors from the section on Science and Technology. William Tucker tells how he came to write his controversial environmental article, "Conservation in Deed."
- Each Section: Humanities, Social Sciences, Science and Technology, Business and Economics, Mass Communications and Popular Culture

is introduced by quotations from distinguished writers who testify to the universal value of good writing and discuss its principles.
- Two alternate tables of contents provide course organizations by compositional techniques and by themes and issues.
- A Teacher's Manual organizes possible responses to the discussion questions within the book itself into class plans and suggested syllabi, with a special emphasis on essays usefully taught together.

Taken as a whole, the contents, organization, and special features of *Effective Writing for the College Curriculum* attempt to foster reading and writing skills through the variety of interests and goals that characterize the students who take freshman composition today. From Russell Baker on the making of a writer to Tracy Kidder on the making of a fortune; from John McPhee on the making of an ice pond to Calvin Trillin on the making of an ice cream empire; from James Baldwin on black English to Thomas Sowell on the language of race; from Stephen Jay Gould on Darwin and Mickey Mouse to Philip Roth on literature and baseball; from Ada Louise Huxtable on the architecture of Houston to Stan Luxenberg on the structure of a McDonald's franchise; from Nora Ephron on the morality of photographs to Ann Hollander on the morality of women's dress—*Effective Writing for the College Curriculum* offers students high-quality writing on a range of interesting topics within contemporary fields of study, writing that neither talks down to nor is over the heads of the aspiring majors who need to learn to write for all the fields of activity they will come to explore in college and beyond.

ACKNOWLEDGEMENTS

Many people helped us to do this book. We would like to thank Helene Atwan and Susan Vesterman. Jack Roberts and Laura Parkington helped us through various stages of manuscript production. John Wright brought us to Emily Barrosse who, along with James R. Belser at McGraw-Hill, took the book through development and production. Along the way, we received valuable comment and counsel from John Hanes, Duquesne University; Anne Herrington, University of Massachusetts; Bruce Herzberg, Bentley College; Frank Hubbard, Cleveland State University; Edward Jennings, State University of New York at Albany; Mane Logue, Rutgers University; Thomas Martinez, Villanova University; Roger Mergendahl, University of Wisconsin; Thomas J. Morrissey, State University of New York at Plattsburg; Robert Reising, Pembroke State University; Judith Stanford, Rider College; Jan Stanhope, American University; Christopher J. Thaiss, George Mason

University; and Dora Tippens, McHenry County College. We especially thank Lisa Honaker and Michael Arnold for their invaluable help in producing this book and the Teacher's Manual that accompanies it.

Robert Atwan

William Vesterman

LEARNING
TO WRITE EFFECTIVELY:
A REQUIREMENT
FOR COLLEGE AND BEYOND

Writing is a vital task in all disciplines and professions. Even fields we may not think demand verbal skills often require a great deal of writing. As Dr. Gerald Weissmann, a professor of medicine at the New York University Medical Center, puts it: "Like other professionals—football scouts, diplomats, and underwriters come to mind—doctors write many words, under pressure of time and for a limited audience." Dr. Weissmann refers here to the writing that goes into the medical charts of patients. Although the everyday on-the-job writing required of practicing doctors does not ordinarily demand a high level of articulation, Weissmann nevertheless believes that the writing of physicians is extremely important: "The opening sequence of a medical record is," he maintains, "unique, and when well written, there's nothing quite like it." In his essay, "The Chart of the Novel" (see p. 315), he examines some of the literary styles of "clinical prose" and concludes that "when we fail at words, we fail to understand, we fail to feel."

Dr. Weissman's essay—it appropriately appeared in *Hospital Practice* magazine—should make it clear to all students that intelligent reading and good writing are not required only of English majors. All professions involve writing; in most of them, writing well, as Dr. Weissmann suggests, displays our competence and success in the field. One purpose of this text is to expose readers to a large, representative sample of effective writing on a broad range of topics from all the major disciplines and professions.

Besides offering a wide variety of authentic models from most major areas of college study, this collection also introduces students to several common categories of composition relevant to all writing, regardless of the writer's special interest. No matter what course a student writes for, certain organizational patterns and mental approaches will come into play. All disciplines require us to make independent observations, to describe a sequence of events, to analyze information and formulate explanations, to take a position and argue a point. Whether we are writing a business analysis, a scientific report, a study of popular music, or a personal reminiscence, these patterns and approaches often establish our focus and set our direction.

This is not to say that the various disciplines and professions do not have differences in methods and techniques. We soon learn that every field we study in college has a fairly specialized vocabulary: "value" means something different in art, economics, and mathematics; a "wash" is one thing in painting and another in business. An important part of learning any profession is learning to speak its language. As William Howarth says of the noted nonfiction writer, John McPhee (see p. 307): "A good part of his style rests on knowing the professional 'lingo' of a subject. He masters its vocabulary and syntax, even the jargon of atomic destruction—ploot, shake, jerk, kilojerk, megajerk."

A specialized vocabulary, technical terms, and jargon represent only one aspect of writing within a discipline. Many courses require that we learn certain procedures and conventions, that we adhere to prescribed formats, such as we see in scholarly articles, lab and business reports, case studies, and legal briefs. Nevertheless, despite visible differences in style and format throughout the various disciplines, much professional writing is generated out of similar patterns of thinking and forms of discourse. The critical analysis of a poem differs noticeably from the case analysis of a business firm, yet both literary critic and management consultant are similarly engaged in trying to understand the structure of a whole by examining its separate parts. A lab report does not resemble a sociological essay, yet both chemist and sociologist will have based their work on close firsthand observation. A legal brief sounds quite different from an essay on painting, yet both attorney and art critic advocate positions and construct arguments to support their cases.

The selections in this book, though intended to represent the various types of writing found throughout the college curriculum, also reflect several basic modes of discourse. These have been conveniently divided into three categories that pertain to most of the writing ordinarily conducted in every field of study: personal observation and narration, analysis and explanation, and advocacy and argument. Students can thus move from one field to another while maintaining a common focus on how observation (and description), narration, exposition, and argument remain crucial to the processes of writing within all disciplines. (These forms of discourse represent a complex field of study in themselves. Entire books have been written on each of them, and their significance in composition can only be surveyed here.) We have included in each chapter a fourth category, academic and professional discourse, to show how all these modes and patterns are reflected in the specialized writing performed by experts within the various fields.

PERSONAL OBSERVATION AND NARRATION

All disciplines depend on observation: A civil engineer carefully surveys a stretch of land to determine the necessary banking of a highway, a physician notices black gangrene on a patient's fingertips and deduces severe circulatory illness, a marketing analyst notices how children affect purchasing decisions in a supermarket, a journalist meticulously describes the key witness in a murder trial. Accurate observation is the bedrock of all scientific and humanistic inquiry. It provides the basis for our sense of reality, much of our language, and our acceptance or rejection of many ideas.

In any subject, good writers are good observers. They have learned to be attentive to details, to notice things that a less careful observer may miss. Give two students an assignment to describe an instructor's office and one will see only bland generalities ("Plenty of books . . . a cluttered desk . . . a sofa . . . pictures on the wall") while the other will notice things in a greater specificity ("books ranging from Boswell's *Life of Johnson* to a special history of the machine gun . . . a desk piled with papers from various projects . . . a black sofa with work shoes underneath . . . pictures of favorite authors on the wall"). The first office could be anyone's—it is practically generic; the other begins to suggest a real individual.

Detail and specificity will keep a writer's observations from being general and abstract. Much of the ineffective writing in any discipline works at the level of minimal detection ("a tree," "a bird") rather than at precise recognition ("a Dutch elm," "a cardinal"). Though concrete writing often demands a knowledge of specific terms, it also demands that as observers we develop the habit of viewing the world and events with greater attention to detail. Here are a few techniques, which are fully exemplified throughout the book, that can help writers become better observers, and observers better writers.

1. **Learn to see beyond convenient generalizations.** Most people tend to see the objects around them in generic terms. Students, for example, can spend four years at a college and never notice what the major buildings on campus actually look like. Someone who develops good habits of observation will not see merely "buildings" but particular types of buildings—made out of various materials and designed according to specific architectural styles. (For an example of a keen architectural eye, see Ada Louise Huxtable's observations of Houston, p. 38.)
2. **Choose descriptive terms carefully.** A danger in descriptive writing is the careless adjective. In lazy writing there is often an abuse of synonyms, as though the writer assumed that closely related words mean more or less the same thing. Yet, a careful writer, who consults a dictionary, will find a wealth of distinctions among words he or she might have used indis-

criminately. For example, in describing the reflection of light, it is useful to know that "glittering," "glimmering," and "glistening" have different shades of meaning. A good dictionary, remember, is not merely a place to check spelling and isolated definitions; it can disclose a wide spectrum of important distinctions among seemingly similar words. Awareness of such distinctions will help give any writing clarity, accuracy, and force.

3. **Be aware of your own predispositions and expectations.** As social scientists consistently warn, what we see is frequently determined by what we expect to see. A careful observer takes such expectations into account. A sociologist, for example, fascinated by criminal subcultures (urban street gangs, for instance) might easily convey a distorted, romanticized view of the subculture's behavior. Journalists, too, may find their objectivity compromised by biases and preconceptions. If the writer, however, does not intend to advocate a position, but intends to be intellectually objective and neutral, then potentially distorting, preexisting attitudes toward the subject need to be carefully considered before writing.

4. **Consider your standpoint as observer.** Our perceptions are often determined by our particular position as observers. Where are you in location to an object or event? Are you close or far? Are you at the game or watching it on television? Are you a participant, an observer, or both? Whether writing in the arts or sciences, a consideration of our own physical point of view is extremely important. For example, in the sociological paper "Stepping Aside: Correlates of Displacement in Pedestrians" (see p. 249), note how the writers are careful to provide specific information about where and how they conducted their observations of sidewalk behavior.

5. **Be selective in the use of detail.** Though personal observations cannot exist without detail, some details are always more significant than others. We have all been bored by speakers who do not make distinctions between the significant and the trivial, who cannot tell us about a tour of Europe without dragging us through every airport along the way. Good observers, of course, do notice minutiae and small events. In "The Making of a Writer" (see p. 5), Russell Baker describes in careful detail the manager of the grocery store where he worked as a boy. Yet Baker does not wallow in specificity; he makes each detail contribute to his portrayal of the manager's personality.

6. **Learn to see what is *not* there.** All good observers develop the habit of noticing missing details. A detective at the scene of a serious automobile accident might wonder why he finds no skid marks in sight. An ecologist may discover that the absence of a particular species signals a significant environmental change. Scientists especially learn to pay attention to the absence of phenomena, knowing that sometimes negative results can lead to positive discoveries. They know, too, that much valuable knowledge derives from inferring what is not seen from what is.

Much of the effective writing in this collection grew out of careful observation. Within each discipline, you will find a vital interaction between solid observation and good writing. What Daniel E. Garvey and William L. Rivers say in their book *Newswriting for the Electronic Media* applies to writing across the curriculum: "Observing . . . is a double process. It is seeing things with as little distortion as possible and describing what you see with as much verbal precision as your abilities permit. Verbal precision is useless without good observation, and good observation can be crippled by imprecise writing."

Writers commonly develop their observations in a narrative format. Accurate observation plays an important role in all types of writing, but without personal observation, narrative could hardly function. In most narratives, the writer not only tells what happened but builds into the account a wealth of descriptive detail. Writers in every field rely on narration to unfold a sequence of events. As an expository mode of writing, narration appears (as many of the selections in this book clearly demonstrate) throughout scientific studies, business reports, historical accounts, journalism, and broadcasting. The literary uses of narrative, moreover, are especially complex, and many scholarly studies have focused exclusively on the function and meaning of narration in fiction and poetry.

In its most elementary forms, narration records a straightforward chronological series of events: "A happened, then B happened, then C, etc." But such storybook narration is seldom useful in expository writing, where the interdependency of events—their logical development—is more important than simple sequential order. In other words, in most college and professional writing, consequence is more important than sequence: "B occurred because of A, which then led to C, and so on." Note in Steven Levy's scientific detective story, "My Search for Einstein's Brain" (see p. 271), the interlocking of events—how each personal experience logically builds to another.

One difficulty in composing narration is that writing is a linear activity, while much of what happens in our personal experience happens all at once. Anyone who has tried to describe a fairly complicated event or process—recounting the plot of a spy movie or hitting a baseball—knows how easily we get sidetracked by simultaneous activities. The narrator is often forced into a sequence of "A happened, which led to B, and then resulted in C, D, and E simultaneously." Clearly, we can't write about (or read about) C, D, and E all at the same time. In such cases—and these are common in expository narration—the writer needs to organize the events in a hierarchical order. Without a clear structure, the most significant events may get buried in digressions, and insignificant occurrences may receive disproportionate coverage. What helps the writer most in recording complicated sequences is a clear sense of purpose (ask: what is my main reason for writing?) and a strong sense of direction (ask: where is my narrative ultimately heading?).

A clear sense of purpose and direction is also important in maintaining an effective balance between the narrative's forward movement and the inclusion of personal observations. When we tell a story we almost always add description or commentary. Relating the process of his religious "salvation" (see p. 22), the poet Langston Hughes combines narration and description: "A great many old people came and knelt around us and prayed, old women with jet-black faces and braided hair, old men with work-gnarled hands." Hughes's purpose in his essay, however, is not to describe the people or setting around him but rather to give a step-by-step account of an unforgettable experience. The narrative thrust of the passage can be clearly seen by examining the opening words of nearly every paragraph ("Still," "Finally," "Then," "Now," "Suddenly," "When," "That night"). Yet, even with an undeviating sense of narrative direction, Hughes manages to include vivid observations so that we obtain a picture of the dramatic event along with the main action.

Whether you are writing in the first-person singular of your experiences (as does Langston Hughes) or reporting events in third-person expository prose (as does Calvin Trillin in "Competitors: The Great Ice Cream War" [on p. 439], narration and description often proceed hand in hand. In the section Personal Observation and Narration, you will see how writers working in a variety of disciplines effectively integrate descriptive details into well-regulated and carefully developed narrative.

ANALYSIS AND EXPLANATION

At Harvard Business School, all first-year students are required to take a course in the written analysis of cases (see p. 427); in literature courses students are routinely expected to analyze the works of major writers; broadcasting students must learn how to analyze the news as well as report it; social scientists spend enormous amounts of time analyzing data. Analysis is a key term in science, philosophy, psychology, mathematics, art, medicine, and law. In fact, analyzing information is perhaps the most commonly required writing task throughout the disciplines and professions.

Though each discipline may use different analytical techniques, "analysis" generally refers to a method by which something is broken down into its separate elements. The separate parts are then rigorously examined with respect to each other and to the organization of the whole. Thus a chemist can analyze a substance not only to discover what elements it contains but also to learn the exact proportions of each element and the molecular arrangement of the whole. So, too, a psychoanalyst will often work with a patient's dream by dividing the dream into separate parts and then examining the interrelations of each part.

Most analysis involves four phases: (1) identifying the separate parts, (2) examining each part, (3) determining the relations of part to part, and (4) determining the relations of the parts to the whole. All these activities can be clearly seen in Aaron Copland's essay "How We Listen to Music" (see p. 32), which moves from a consideration of separate notes to the effects of an entire musical composition. One could also apply analytical methods to understand the writing process: We could (1) break it down into three stages—prewriting, writing, and revision; (2) examine the distinctive features of each stage; (3) look at how any one stage in the process is connected to the others; and (4) determine how the distinctive features of each stage affect the entire process of composition.

Learning analytical methods in some fields, especially the humanities, may seem cumbersome at first and may also seem to interfere with an instinctive appreciation. "I don't want to analyze the poem, I just want to enjoy it," students often say, employing a false distinction, since the appreciation of any art form or performance is enhanced—not diminished—by our ability to understand what went into its composition or achievement. Someone who does not understand the often intricate patterns of play in football will most likely watch a game simply by focusing only on the ball, thus missing about 75 percent of the real action on the field. So, too, someone who reads a novel simply to find out what happens at the end—or perhaps to acquire a "big idea" or two—will miss all the verbal artistry that went into its production.

Analysis is not often intended to be an end in itself nor meant only to enhance our appreciation; it is throughout the disciplines an aid to explanation. In most college assignments, students will be asked to analyze information for the purpose of explaining something significant about it. The child psychiatrist Robert Coles (see p. 178), for example, analyzed the language and behavior of affluent children to see how important notions of social "entitlement" take root. The art historian, Anne Hollander (see p. 167), analyzed contemporary styles of dress to explain a new trend in adolescent sexual identity.

Analysis for the purpose of explaining the meaning of objects, ideas, or events can follow several common patterns of development. These patterns can be used to organize paragraphs within an essay or sometimes an entire essay. A working knowledge of these patterns is fundamental to writing within all disciplines:

1. **Definition.** Explaining thoroughly what something is can be accomplished through extended definition. This is especially important when attempting to explain abstract or complex ideas for which a single dictionary definition would be inadequate. Extended definitions are often necessary when a writer attempts to refine or expand our understanding of a subject about which we may not have considered as carefully as the writer. Such is the case in John Canaday's "What Is a Painting?" (see p. 26) and Ernest Hartmann's "What Is a Nightmare?" (see p. 240)

2. **Illustration.** Elucidating a general point by offering concrete examples is one of the most commonly used methods of explanation. There is scarcely a page in this collection that doesn't itself offer an example of using examples. By means of carefully selected examples the writer can show familiarity with the topic, give the statements clarity, and support his or her arguments. When confronted with general statements and assertions in writing, we almost instinctively want examples, and when they are not offered, we feel the writer has not properly prepared the material. How convincing would Joan D. Lynch's study of music videos be if she had neglected to offer any specific examples of the form to support her contention that the videos are a contemporary version of surrealistic art? (see p. 727)

3. **Classification.** Explaining something by placing it within a larger category or dividing it into smaller categories can be done through classification. In attempting to understand human gesture, for example, Desmond Morris (see p. 659) first examined gesture within the larger category of communication (gesture then becomes like language), then classified gesture into all the various types ("the thumb up," etc.) he could find in use. Yet, another anthropologist might have devised a different system of classification, dividing gestures into facial gestures, hand gestures, arm gestures, etc.

4. **Comparison and Contrast.** In many instances explanation can be usefully achieved by means of comparison and contrast. The writer explains a subject or idea by demonstrating how it either resembles or differs from another subject or idea. A student who wants to write about his love of baseball might do so by showing either (a) how closely baseball resembles something else of value (as Philip Roth does in comparing the pleasures of baseball to the enjoyment of literature (on p. 612) or (b) by contrasting it to another sport he finds inferior (e.g., the precision of baseball versus the clumsy violence of ice hockey). Comparison and contrast essays are commonly used for evaluative purposes throughout the disciplines: a critic will establish the importance of a movie by comparing it favorably to an undisputed film classic; a business writer will show the superior quality of one fast food franchise by contrasting it with another. Comparison and contrast also help sharpen distinctions between similar concepts, as Bruno Bettelheim shows in his essay "Fairy Tale versus Myth" (see p. 154).

5. **Cause and Effect.** An important method of explaining why something happened or may happen is causal analysis. Historians and social scientists often attempt to determine the causes behind events, ideologies, or prevailing attitudes and behavior. In science, technology, business, and economics, writers examine causative factors in order to predict effects. Cause-and-effect relations are critical to marketing decisions, as James Atlas demonstrates in "Beyond Demographics: How Madison Avenue

Knows Who You Are and What You Want" (see p. 514). Though effective when causes and effects are carefully linked, causal analysis can lead to numerous intellectual pitfalls. "Because" is a very tricky term in any subject. No matter which discipline we work in, we always need to ask ourselves if we are making a correct distinction between what we perceive as a cause and what we see as an effect. Did the President improve the performance of the economy, or did the economy improve the performance of the President?

6. **Analogy.** Explaining an abstract topic or one that is unfamiliar to readers can be achieved by means of analogy. In most expository writing, analogy works as an extended comparison, in which the writer points out a number of similar features between two things, e.g., the brain and a computer, corporate life and warfare. As a way of visualizing one thing in terms of another, analogy often lends concreteness to subjects that may be difficult to follow. Also, by explaining one thing in terms of another, analogy can offer new ways of considering a subject: e.g., Gerald Weissmann's depiction of hospital medical charts as though they were parts of novels (see p. 315), Jay Haley's analysis of psychotherapy in terms of gamesmanship (see p. 188).

The above patterns of development can be used to stimulate our thinking (How can I define W?" "What caused X?"), to direct our planning ("Can I list three examples of Y?"), and to organize paragraphs or even entire essays ("Suppose I contrast Z with A throughout the paper?"). Though the patterns are fundamental to writing in all disciplines, they rarely appear in isolated form in any one paper. Writers naturally and frequently combine several patterns in a single essay. In "What Is a Painting?" (see p. 26), note how John Canaday uses illustration in conjunction with comparison and contrast to formulate his definition of a painting.

ADVOCACY AND ARGUMENT

Besides having to prepare reports on personal observations and to analyze information, college students are also commonly required to perform a third type of writing—arguing a position. Throughout various courses, students will customarily be asked to advocate an idea or support an issue (e.g., supply-side economics, capital punishment, the right to abortion). Later, when on the job, the defense of ideas becomes almost an occupational necessity, as people are often required to put into writing their suggestions and proposals. Engineers with a good argument for how to speed up a plant's production methods will certainly be required not only to express the idea in writing but also to make a strong case for its implementation. Rarely can important professional recommendations or policy decisions be made without argument.

The poet Robert Frost once said that most people tend to confuse thinking with voting. That is, they feel that a stance for or against something—without supplying reasons—is sufficient in itself. A show of hands may be acceptable in an assembly, however, or a ballot in a voting booth, but in argumentative writing we must give convincing reasons for our positions and opinions. It is not enough in an essay to assert that we are for or against the death penalty; we must make a case for our position. Doing so—constructing well-ordered argumentative essays—is among the most practical and satisfying verbal skills we can learn in a writing course.

Though effective argumentation is a complex topic, with numerous categories and subcategories, there are five important matters to keep in mind when we advocate a position or make a claim. These are:

1. **The assertion.** This is the main proposition—the point—of our argument. Though it may take the form of a thesis statement ("I intend to show that pornography is not protected by the First Amendment"), the main point could also be implied throughout an essay. Whether the assertion is about meaning or values or policy, the writer should first make sure that the assertion is truly an arguable point. Many argumentative-sounding essays are constructed around personal opinions that no one would object to ("Pets Can Be Fun") or matters of taste ("Why I Prefer Tulips to Roses") that barely constitute a basis for legitimate debate. A good example of a strong assertion based on a clear arguable point is James Baldwin's "If Black English Isn't a Language, Then Tell Me, What Is?" (see p. 101).

2. **Evidence.** To make a convincing argument, writers need to back up their assertions with evidence. Most evidence used in argumentative essays takes the form of relevant examples, carefully validated observations, facts and figures, and authoritative testimony. All these evidentiary techniques can be seen, for example, in Isaac Asimov's historical essay on scientific method, "Pure and Impure: The Interplay of Science and Technology" (see p. 342). Since a writer's space is often limited, evidence must be selected carefully and used economically. A multiplication of examples is not necessary (in fact, it may backfire) if one or two instances will adequately make the point. Also, the writer should only worry about supporting those statements required to make the point; not every statement in an argument requires evidence.

3. **Anticipating Objections.** In most arguments, especially those involving popular controversies (abortion, euthanasia, freedom of speech, etc.), the writer should be familiar with the objections that will be raised by opposing points of view. If writers know in advance the criticism that will most probably be brought against their argument, they will be better prepared to defend it. Including objections to our arguments—as long as we summarize them fairly—is always a good strategy. Not only can we

show that we are aware of other positions, but we may possibly beat our opponent to the punch. In "The Boston Photographs" (see p. 693), Nora Ephron effectively demonstrates a way of handling an abundance of strong objections to her case.

4. **Reasoning.** The heart of any argument is, of course, its method of reasoning. Put briefly, reasoning is the means by which we use portions of information to yield new portions of information. In an argument we try to convince someone that something we say *must* be valid because our conclusion or position logically follows other statements that are also valid. Logicians make a distinction between two types of reasoning—deductive and inductive. In deduction, we reason from a premise to a conclusion; if the method of reasoning is valid, the conclusion necessarily follows from the premise. For example, we argue that all literature is composed of words, but since Professor Cal Culus's mysterious composition "AC(903)X" in the latest issue of *Integer* contains no words, it cannot be called literature. In induction, on the other hand, we infer a general conclusion from the evidence of particulars: We notice all the automobiles on the street have flat tires and infer vandalism. Induction is crucial to scientific method, where it is often used to determine causation: A large number of cigarette smokers have contracted lung cancer, therefore medical investigators conclude inductively that cigarette smoking can lead to cancer.

5. **Organization.** An argumentative essay is not the skeletal outline of our reasoning process, nor is it a simple sequence of premises and conclusions. To be effective, our argument must be structured effectively. Most of the arguments that we will construct in college courses need to be organized so that our conclusions do not seem "jumped to," and our reasons appear integrated and related to our main point. Depending on our subject and the nature of our evidence, we can usually build two types of arguments: essays in which our conclusion is arrived at after following a close chain of interdependent reasons, and essays in which an assertion is supported by a well-organized set of independent reasons.

ACADEMIC AND PROFESSIONAL DISCOURSE

Students who learn how to report personal observations in a narrative format, who can write expository prose that is at once analytical and informed, and who can convincingly advocate a course of action or argue a position will be equipped to handle any writing task they will encounter in college and beyond. The main purpose of this book—the reason for its selections, organization, and apparatus—is to show college students how such writing is achieved throughout the courses they will take, the fields they will major in, and the various professions they will pursue.

To further illustrate the writing and reading required of specialized study in the various disciplines, each section of the book contains two essays that demonstrate "academic and professional discourse." For the most part, these essays demand more of readers; they require a patience with unfamiliar methods or scientific techniques and a willingness to understand a technical vocabulary. These essays not only clearly demonstrate the particular format (style, footnotes, and organization) expected of writers within a profession, but they also indicate the level of writing and thinking required. The academic and professional essays have a further educational value. In reading them the student can observe how all of the compositional skills outlined above—the emphasis on accurate observation, clear narration, careful analysis, and well-rounded argument—form a consistent basis for effective writing across all the college disciplines.

O·N·E

HUMANITIES
Literature/Language/ Autobiography and Biography/History/Philosophy/ Religion/Fine Arts and Architecture

If you wish to be a writer, write.

Epictetus, *Discourse II*

The desire to write grows with writing.

Erasmus, *Adagia*

The greatest part of a writer's time is spent in reading in order to write.

Samuel Johnson, from Boswell's *Life*

But literature is stern; it is no use being charming, virtuous, or even learned and brilliant into the bargain, unless, she seems to reiterate, you fulfil her first condition—to know how to write.

Virginia Woolf, "The Modern Essay"

Sometimes I work for months and have to throw everything away, but I don't think any of that was time wasted. Something goes on that makes it easier when it does come well. And the fact is if you don't sit there every day, the day it would come well, you won't be sitting there.

Flannery O'Connor, *Letters*

. . . American historians, in their eagerness to present facts and their laudable anxiety to tell the truth, have neglected the literary aspects of their craft. They have forgotten that there is an art of writing history.

Samuel Eliot Morison, "History as a Literary Art"

. . . That's what a writer is: Someone who sees problems a little more clearly than others.

Eugene Ionesco

I write to find out what I'm thinking about.

Edward Albee

When I write, I like to have an interval before me when I am not likely to be interrupted. For me, this means usually the early morning, before others are awake. I get pen and paper, take a glance out the window (often it is dark out there), and wait. It is like fishing. But I do not wait very long, for there is always a nibble—and this is where receptivity comes in. To get started I will accept anything that occurs to me. Something always occurs, of course, to any of us. We can't keep from thinking. Maybe I have to settle for an immediate impression: it's cold, or hot, or dark, or bright, or in between! Or—well, the possibilities are endless. If I put down something, that thing will help the next thing come, and I'm off. If I let the process go on, things will occur to me that were not at all in my mind when I started. These things, odd or trivial as they may be, are somehow connected. And if I let them string out, surprising things will happen.

William Stafford, "A Way of Writing"

There is much to suggest to us that without language there is no thought—at least no cognitive, discursive thought as it has taken shape in all developed human cultures. To begin with the most simplistic example, consider the familiar pseudo-joke

(E. M. Forster recorded it) about the old lady on the train. On being accused of illogicality and wandering inconsistency in her conversation, she protests: "How can I tell what I think till I see what I say?" The implication is straightforward: vague affective rumination does not constitute thought. Verbal utterance alone can shape and certify obscure mental interchanges which, without speech, remain subcognitive.

Roger Shattuck

Whether in biography or straight history, my form is narrative because that is what comes naturally to me. I think of history as a story and myself as a storyteller, and the reader as a listener whose attention must be held if he is not to wander away. Schererazade only survived because she managed to keep the sultan absorbed in her tales and wondering what would happen next. While I am not under quite such exigent pressure, I nevertheless want the reader to turn the page and keep on turning to the end. Narrative, if the action is kept moving through every paragraph, has the power to accomplish this. It also has inherent validity: it is the spine of history and the key to causation. Events do not happen in categories—economic, intellectual, military—they happen in sequence. When they are arranged in sequence as strictly as possible down to month, week, and even day, cause and effect that may have been previously obscure, will often become clear, like secret ink.

Barbara Tuchman, "Biography as a Prism of History"

Russell Baker

THE MAKING OF A WRITER

"I didn't set out to be a humorist," Russell Baker once claimed, "I set out in life to be a novelist, and I look like a novelist. Art Buchwald looks like a humorist . . . I don't look like him and most of the time I don't even look like myself." Indeed, the following chapter from Baker's Pulitzer Prize–winning autobiography, *Growing Up* (1982), illustrates both the truth and irony of Baker's ambitions as he describes the preliminary stages of a calling in which talent, chance, and his mother's prayers and determination all had a part.

Born in rural Virginia in 1925, he moved frequently with his mother and sister after his father's death. He spent his adolescence in Baltimore, Maryland, where he attended Johns Hopkins University, taking a B.A. in 1947, the same year he became a reporter for the *Baltimore Sun*. In 1953, he became the *Sun's* London bureau chief, foreshadowing later interests and accomplishments with a lively weekly series for that paper called "From a Window on Fleet Street." In 1954, he moved back to the United States, covering politics in Washington for the *New York Times,* an eight-year stint that yielded his first three books: *Washington: City on the Potomac* (1958), *An American in Washington* (1961), and *No Cause for Panic* (1964).

It was in 1962, in order to keep him with the paper, that the *Times* offered Baker the "Observer" column, which he still writes. According to one critic, in his column "Baker walks the high wire between light humor and substantive comment." Over the years, Baker has collected these columns in *Baker's Dozen* (1964), *Poor Russell's Almanac* (1972), and *So This Is Depravity* (1980). He received a Pulitzer Prize for distinguished commentary in 1979.

"Something will come along."

That became my mother's battle cry as I plowed into the final year of high school. Friends began asking her what Russell planned to do when he graduated, and her answer was, "Something will come along." She didn't know what, and nothing was in sight on the horizon, but she'd survived so long now on faith that something always came along for people who did their best. "Russ hasn't made up his mind yet, but something will come along," she told people.

I saw no possibilities and looked forward to the end of school days with increasing glumness. It was assumed I would get a job. Boys of our economic class didn't ordinarily go to college. My education, however, hadn't fitted me for labor. While I was reading the Romantic poets and learning Latin syntax, practical boys had been taking shop, mechanical drawing, accounting, and typing. I couldn't drive a nail without mashing my thumb. When I mentioned my inadequacies to my mother she said, "Something will come along, Buddy."

If, gloomily, I said, "Fat chance," she snapped at me, "For God's sake, Russell, have a little gumption. Look on the bright side."

I didn't mind the prospect of working. Having worked since I was eight, I had acquired the habit of work, but I was stymied about what kind of full-time work I might be fit for. That winter I was trying to muster enthusiasm for a career in the grocery business. Moving from Lombard Street to Marydell Road, I had lost my newspaper route. To make up the lost income I'd taken a Saturday job at a large grocery in the Hollins Market, which paid $14 for twelve hours' work. It was a "self-service" store, a primitive forerunner of the supermarket, the first expression of an idea whose time had not yet come. Situated in a dilapidated old building where groceries had once been sold, old-style, across the counter, it bore little resemblance to the bulging supermonuments to consumption that were to rise after World War II. There was no air-conditioning in summer and little heat in winter. Under the cellar's cobwebbed rafters an occasional rat scurried among sacks of cornmeal and hundred-pound bags of flour. As a stock clerk, I toted merchandise from the cellar, marked its price in black crayon, and stacked it on shelves for Saturday shoppers. The flour sacks were slung over the shoulder and lugged upstairs to be dipped from with an aluminum scoop on demand.

The manager was Mr. Simmons, a bawdy, exuberant slave driver who had learned the business in the days of over-the-counter selling, when a manager's personality could attract customers or turn them away. Simmons was a tall, square-shouldered man who affected the breezy style, as though he'd studied his trade under burlesque comedians. His head was as round and hairless as a cannon ball. He wore big horn-rimmed glasses and bow ties, and his mouth, which was wide and frequently open from ear to ear, displayed dazzling rows of teeth so big they would have done credit to a horse.

Throughout the day the store was filled with his roars, guffaws, shouted jokes, and curses. He romped the aisles in Groucho Marx lope, administering tongue lashings when he discovered empty shelves where the canned tomatoes or the Post Toasties or the Ovaltine were supposed to be. Spotting a handsome woman at the meat counter, he might glide behind the hamburger grinder to whisper sotto voce some dirty joke at the butcher's ear, then glare at the woman, part his mouth from ear to ear, and display his magnificent ivory. The store was his stage, and he treated it as if he were its star, director, producer, and owner.

If there was a dull half hour he might creep up behind one of the stock clerks hoisting oatmeal from crate to shelf, goose him with both thumbs, then gallop away roaring with laughter. Many of the customers were black and poor and arrived late on Saturday nights hoping to have their paychecks cashed. With them Simmons played Simon Legree, examining their checks suspiciously, demanding identification papers, then rejecting some damp proffered document as inadequate. "That damn thing is so dirty I don't even want to touch it. You open it up and show it to me." Or, if the credentials were in order: "I don't know whether I'm going to cash this check or not. How much do you want to buy here?"

Simmons boasted of being a great lecher. In the cellar ceiling he had drilled a small hole through which he could look up the skirts of women customers standing at the cash register overhead. When a woman who pleased his fancy entered the store, he ostentatiously departed for the cellar with some such cry as "Hot damn! I've got to see more of this." Rolling his eyeballs and smacking his lips he plunged into the cellar and could be found there standing on a pile of flour sacks, one eye glued to his peephole.

I wasn't exhilarated by the grocery business, but at least I was getting experience I thought might help me get full-time work at it after high school. For this purpose I wanted to learn to work the cash register so I could become a checker, the most glamorous job in the store except for the manager's. Simmons withheld this prize. At some point I'd made the mistake of trying to show him I was fancily educated, thinking this would move him to promote me from cellar labor. Whether he took me for an overeducated young fool or whether he resented my failure to laugh loudly enough at his jokes, I don't know. Whatever the reason, I waited in vain for my chance to work the cash register. I knew I would never get it when Simmons, desperate one day for help at the cash registers, came down to the cellar, passed me by, and called on Earl to do the job. Earl was black, and black people were contemptible to Simmons but still preferable to me. It made me wonder if I was cut out for the grocery business. But on the other hand, what else was there?

The only thing that truly interested me was writing, and I knew that sixteen-year-olds did not come out of high school and become writers. I thought of writing as something to be done only by the rich. It was so obviously not real work, not a job at which you could earn a living. Still, I had begun to think of myself as a writer. It was the only thing for which I seemed to have the smallest talent, and, silly though it sounded when I told people I'd like to be a writer, it gave me a way of thinking about myself which satisfied my need to have an identity.

The notion of becoming a writer had flickered off and on in my head since the Belleville days, but it wasn't until my third year in high school that the possibility took hold. Until then I'd been bored by everything associated with English courses. I found English grammar dull and baffling. I hated the assignments to turn out "compositions," and went at them like heavy labor, turning out leaden, lackluster paragraphs that were agonies for teachers to read and for me to write. The classics thrust on me to read seemed as deadening as chloroform.

When our class was assigned to Mr. Fleagle for third-year English I anticipated another grim year in that dreariest of subjects. Mr. Fleagle was notorious among City students for dullness and inability to inspire. He was said to be stuffy, dull, and hopelessly out of date. To me he looked to be sixty or seventy and prim to a fault. He wore primly severe eyeglasses, his wavy hair was primly cut and primly combed. He wore prim vested suits with neckties blocked primly against the collar buttons of his primly starched white shirts. He had a primly pointed jaw, a primly straight nose, and a prim manner of speaking that was so correct, so gentlemanly, that he seemed a comic antique.

I anticipated a listless, unfruitful year with Mr. Fleagle and for a long time was not disappointed. We read *Macbeth*. Mr. Fleagle loved *Macbeth* and wanted us to love it too, but he lacked the gift of infecting others with his own passion. He tried to convey the murderous ferocity of Lady Macbeth one day by reading aloud the passage that concludes

> . . . *I have given suck, and know*
> *How tender 'tis to love the babe that milks me.*
> *I would, while it was smiling in my face,*
> *Have plucked my nipple from his boneless gums.* . . .

The idea of prim Mr. Fleagle plucking his nipple from boneless gums was too much for the class. We burst into gasps of irrepressible snickering. Mr. Fleagle stopped.

"There is nothing funny, boys, about giving suck to a babe. It is the—the very essence of motherhood, don't you see."

He constantly sprinkled his sentences with "don't you see." It wasn't a question but an exclamation of mild surprise at our ignorance. "Your pronoun needs an antecedent, don't you see," he would say, very primly. "The purpose of the Porter's scene, boys, is to provide comic relief from the horror, don't you see."

Late in the year we tackled the informal essay. "The essay, don't you see, is the . . ." My mind went numb. Of all forms of writing, none seemed so boring as the essay. Naturally we would have to write informal essays. Mr. Fleagle distributed a homework sheet offering us a choice of topics. None was quite so simpleminded as "What I Did on My Summer Vacation," but most seemed to be almost as dull. I took the list home and dawdled until the night before the essay was due. Sprawled on the sofa, I finally faced up to the grim task, took the list out of my notebook, and scanned it. The topic on which my eye stopped was "The Art of Eating Spaghetti."

This title produced an extraordinary sequence of mental images. Surging up out of the depths of memory came a vivid recollection of a night in Belleville when all of us were seated around the supper table— Uncle Allen, my mother, Uncle Charlie, Doris, Uncle Hal—and Aunt Pat served spaghetti for supper. Spaghetti was an exotic treat in those days. Neither Doris nor I had ever eaten spaghetti, and none of the adults had enough experience to be good at it. All the good humor of Uncle Allen's house reawoke in my mind as I recalled the laughing arguments we had that night about the socially respectable method for moving spaghetti from plate to mouth.

Suddenly I wanted to write about that, about the warmth and good feeling of it, but I wanted to put it down simply for my own joy, not for Mr. Fleagle. It was a moment I wanted to recapture and hold for myself. I wanted to relive the pleasure of an evening at New Street. To write it as I wanted, however, would violate all the rules of formal composition I'd learned in school, and Mr. Fleagle would surely give it a failing grade. Never mind. I would write something else for Mr. Fleagle after I had written this thing for myself.

When I finished it the night was half gone and there was no time left to compose a proper, respectable essay for Mr. Fleagle. There was no choice next morning but to turn in my private reminiscence of Belleville. Two days passed before Mr. Fleagle returned the graded papers, and he returned everyone's but mine. I was bracing myself for a command to report to Mr. Fleagle immediately after school for discipline when I saw him lift my paper from his desk and rap for the class's attention.

"Now, boys," he said, "I want to read you an essay. This is titled 'The Art of Eating Spaghetti.' "

And he started to read. My words! He was reading *my words* out loud to the entire class. What's more, the entire class was listening. Listening attentively. Then somebody laughed, then the entire class was laughing, and not in contempt and ridicule, but with openhearted enjoyment. Even Mr. Fleagle stopped two or three times to repress a small prim smile.

I did my best to avoid showing pleasure, but what I was feeling was pure ecstasy at this startling demonstration that my words had the power to make people laugh. In the eleventh grade, at the eleventh hour as it were, I had discovered a calling. It was the happiest moment of my entire school career. When Mr. Fleagle finished he put the final seal on my happiness by saying, "Now that, boys, is an essay, don't you see. It's—don't you see—it's of the very essence of the essay, don't you see. Congratulations, Mr. Baker."

For the first time, light shone on a possibility. It wasn't a very heartening possibility, to be sure. Writing couldn't lead to a job after high school, and it was hardly honest work, but Mr. Fleagle had opened a door for me. After that I ranked Mr. Fleagle among the finest teachers in the school.

My mother was almost as delighted as I when I showed her Mr. Fleagle's A-Plus and described my triumph. Hadn't she always said I had a talent for writing? "Now if you work hard at it, Buddy, you can make something of yourself."

I didn't see how. As the final year of high school neared its end and it began to seem that even the grocery business was beyond me, my mother was also becoming worried. She'd hoped for years that something would come along to enable me to go to college. All those years she had kept the door open on the possibility that she might turn me into a man of letters. When I was in eighth grade she'd spent precious pennies to subscribe to mail-order bargains in the classics. "World's Greatest Literature," retailing at 39 cents a volume, came in the mail every month, books that stunned me with boredom. *The Last of the Mohicans, Ben Hur, Westward Ho, Vanity Fair, Ivanhoe.* Unread, her attempts to cultivate my literary tastes gathered dust under my bed, but it comforted her to know I had them at my fingertips.

She also subscribed on my behalf to the *Atlantic Monthly* and *Harper's.* "The best magazines in America," she said. "That's where you'll find real writers." The best magazines in America also piled up unread and unreadable in my bedroom. I seemed cut out to serve neither literature nor its bastard offspring, journalism, until my great coup in Mr. Fleagle's English class. Then her hopes revived.

"If only something would come along so you could go to college . . ." became, "For somebody with grades as good as yours, Buddy, there must be some way of getting into college."

Delicately, she spoke to Herb [Baker's stepfather]. She could push and haul Herb on matters of household management, but she could scarcely ask him to finance college for me. Grand though his income seemed after her years of poverty, it wasn't big enough to put a boy through college without great sacrifice. There was also a question of taste. I'd done nothing to endear myself to Herb, and she knew it. What's more, with his few years of elementary school education, Herb would have been flabbergasted by the suggestion that a healthy young man should idle away four years in college at vast expense instead of making his own way in the world as he had done.

Still, my mother did speak to Herb, and Herb listened sympathetically. She told me about it next day. "Herb says he thinks he can get you a job as a brakeman on the B&O," she reported.

"Well," I said, "railroad men make good pay."

"Maybe something will come along before school's out," she said.

The idea of becoming a railroad brakeman entertained me for a while that winter. Any job prospect would have interested me then. I was becoming embarrassed about being one of the few boys in class with no plan for the future. The editors of the high-school yearbook circulated a questionnaire among members of the senior class asking each student to reveal his career ambition. I could hardly put down "To be a writer." That would have made me look silly. Boys of the Depression generation were expected to have their hearts set on moneymaking work. To reply "Ambition: None" was unthinkable. You were supposed to have had your eye on a high goal from the day you left knee pants. Boys who hadn't yet decided on a specific career usually replied that their ambition was "to be a success." That was all right. The Depression had made materialists of us all; almost everybody wanted "to be a success."

I studied the yearbook questionnaire with deepening despair. I wanted the yearbook to record for posterity that I had once had flaming ambition, but I could think of nothing very exciting. Finally I turned to my friend Bob Eckert in the desk behind me.

"What are you putting down for ambition?" I asked.

"Foreign correspondent," Eckert said.

I loved it. It sounded dashing, thrilling. Unfortunately, it was so different, so exciting an "ambition," that I couldn't copy Eckert without looking like a cheat. And so, turning my mind to journalism, I ticked off other glamorous newspaper jobs and after a moment's reflection wrote down, "To be a newspaper columnist."

In fact I hadn't the least interest in journalism and no ambition whatever to be a newspaper columnist. Though City College published an excellent weekly newspaper, during my four years there I was never interested enough to apply for a job, never knew where its office was located, and never cared enough to find out.

Having solved the problem of finding an "ambition" elegant enough for the yearbook, I returned to reality. Was I really sharp enough to make it in the retail grocery business? Should I become a railroad man?

Matters were at this stage in the spring of 1942 when I discovered my great friend and classmate Charlie Sussman filling out a sheaf of forms between classes one day. Sussman was a prodigious bookworm and lover of education. I admired him greatly for the wide range of his knowledge, which far exceeded mine. He understood the distinction between fascism and communism, subjects on which I was utterly ignorant. He was interested in politics and foreign policy, subjects that bored me. He listened to classical music, to which I was completely deaf. He planned to become a teacher and had the instinct for it. It bothered him that there were such great gaps in my education. Like my mother, Sussman wanted to improve me. He tried to awaken me to the beauties of music. "Start with Tchaikovsky," he pleaded. "Tchaikovsky is easy. Everybody likes Tchaikovsky. Then you'll discover the beauty of Beethoven and Mozart."

Now, finding him bent over a strange batch of papers, I asked, "What're you doing, Suss?"

"Filling out college application forms," he said.

"What college are you going to?"

"Johns Hopkins," he said.

I knew that Johns Hopkins was a hospital and produced doctors.

"I didn't know you wanted to be a doctor. I thought you wanted to teach."

"Hopkins isn't just for doctors," he said.

"No kidding."

"It's a regular college too," he said. "What college are you going to?"

"I'm not going to college."

Sussman was shocked. Dropping his pen, he glared at me in amazement. "Not going to college?" He said it in outrage. He refused to tolerate this offense to education. "You've got to go to college," he said. "Get some admission forms—they've got them downstairs at the office—and we'll go to Hopkins together."

That would be great, I said, but my family couldn't afford it.

"Apply for a scholarship," he commanded.

"What's that?"

Sussman explained. I was astonished. It seemed that this college, of whose existence I had just learned, was willing to accept a limited number of students absolutely free if they could do well on a competitive examination. Sussman himself intended to take the test in hope of reducing the cost to his parents.

"I'll get you a set of application forms," he said, and he did. He was determined that education would not lose me without a struggle.

My mother was as surprised as I'd been. Just when she had begun to lose faith that something would come along, providence had assumed the shape of Charlie Sussman and smiled upon us. The day of the examination she stopped me as I was going out the door and kissed me.

"I've been praying for you every night," she said. "You'll do great."

She'd been doing more than praying. For three weeks she'd worked with me every night on a home refresher course in mathematics, my weakest subject. Night after night she held the math books and conducted quizzes on geometry and algebra, laboriously checking my solutions against those in the back of the books and, when I erred, struggling along with me to discover where I'd gone wrong. Afterwards, when we were both worn out, she went to bed and prayed. She believed in prayer, in the Lord's intercession, but not in the Lord's willingness to do it all. She and I together had to help. The Lord helped those who helped themselves.

The examination was held on a Saturday in May. I hadn't been to Johns Hopkins before, so I gave myself an extra hour against the possibility of getting lost on the streetcar trip to North Baltimore. My mother had written the directions and put them in my pocket, just in case, but the trip went smoothly, and when I reached the campus I was directed to a huge lecture hall reeking of chemicals. I was dismayed to find the hall filled with boys, each of whom probably wanted one of the few available scholarships as desperately as I did.

Unlike my mother, I had no faith in prayer. From early childhood I had thought of God as a cosmic trick player. Though I'd never told this to my mother and went to church regularly to please her, I'd grown up a fatalist with little faith. Now, though, as I counted the boys in the room and realized the odds against me, I decided it was foolish to leave even the remotest possibility untouched. Closing my eyes, I silently uttered the Lord's Prayer in my head and, to leave no base untouched, followed it with the only other prayer I knew, the one my mother had taught me years ago when putting me to bed in Morrisonville. And so, as the examination papers were being distributed, I sat at my desk silently repeating, "Now I lay me down to sleep, I pray the Lord my soul to keep . . ."

At the end I improvised a single line of my own and prayed, "Dear God, help me with this test." It lasted four hours.

My mother was waiting on the porch when I came back down Marydell Road that afternoon. "How'd it go, Buddy?"

"Don't know," I said, which I didn't.

Two weeks crept slowly past and May neared its end. I had only three weeks left of high school when I arrived home one afternoon to find my mother sitting expressionless in the glider on the front porch. "You got a letter from Hopkins today," she said. "It's in on the table."

"Did you open it?"

"I'm not in the habit of opening other people's mail," she said. "You open it and tell me what it says."

We went inside together. The envelope was there on the table. It was a very small envelope. Very small. Hopkins had obviously decided I was not worth wasting much stationery on. Picking it up, I saw that it was also very thin. The message was obviously short and probably not sweet if it could be conveyed in such flimsy form. I ripped the end off the envelope, slid out a piece of note-sized paper, and unfolded it. I saw it was a form letter on which someone had typed a few words in the blank spaces. I read it to myself.

"Well, what does it say?" my mother asked.

I read it aloud to her:

> Sir: I am pleased to inform you that you have been awarded a Hopkins Scholarship for two terms of the academic year 1942–43. This award will entitle you to remission of tuition fees for this period. Please let me know at once if you will accept this award.
>
> Yours very truly,
> Isaiah Bowman
> President

"Let me read it," my mother said. She did, and she smiled, and she read it again; then she said, "Herb is going to be proud of you, Buddy."

"What about you?" I asked.

"Well, I always knew you could do it," she said, heading for the kitchen. "I think I'll make us some iced tea."

She had to do something ordinary, I suppose, or risk fainting with delight. We had helped ourselves, the Lord had helped us in return, and one of her wildest dreams had come true. Something had come along.

QUESTIONS FOR READING, RESPONDING, AND WRITING

Summarizing Main Points

1. To what—or whom—does Baker attribute his writing career? Do you believe that Baker's college scholarship answered one of his mother's "wildest" dreams? Baker describes himself as a "fatalist with little faith." What does he mean by this? According to Baker, is his mother a "fatalist"? Does she have faith? If so, in what?

2. What is Baker's attitude toward Mr. Simmons? What relationship do you see between Mr. Simmons's egocentric personality and Baker's own need for the limelight? What does Baker learn about himself and Mr. Simmons both from his informal essay for Mr. Fleagle and from writing the essay presented here?

Analyzing Methods of Discourse

1. Baker describes his essay for Mr. Fleagle as "hardly honest work." Do you suppose this is because his essay violated "all the rules of formal composition"? Does Baker violate any rules for formal composition in this essay? If so, list them and explain why they are violations *and* why they still might deserve a passing grade.

2. Baker's essay is a kind of personal reminiscence, just as the informal essay he writes for Mr. Fleagle is. Does it matter that at first the reader is not entirely clear as to who "Herb" is? What does the reader find out about Herb? How does the seemingly random method that Baker uses to convey these details contribute to the personal or familiar feeling the reader gets from Baker's essay?

Focusing on the Field

1. Baker spent half a night writing his informal essay for Mr. Fleagle. Do you feel that writing is "work" for Baker? Support your assertion with evidence from the essay. Baker took obvious pleasure in the results of his labors. Was that pleasure entirely caused by the essay's reception by the class? Again, support your answer with evidence from the essay.

2. At the time of the essay, what was Baker's attitude toward the "World's Greatest Literature"? What was Baker's attitude toward journalism? Support your claim with evidence from the essay. Baker is now a journalist. Judging from the essay, how do you account for this? Do you suppose Baker's attitude toward literature has changed?

Writing Assignments

1. Using Baker's essay as a model, write an informal, reminiscent essay of your own that violates "the rules of formal composition." Be prepared to read your essay aloud and to defend the violations as essential to achieve a particular effect on your audience (e.g., to be humorous or dramatic).

2. Baker obviously learned many things about himself and others—his mother, Sussman, Mr. Simmons—both from writing his informal essay for Mr. Fleagle and later from writing about the entire incident in the essay presented here. Study Janet Emig's "Writing as a Mode of Learning." In a short essay, describe the "learning strategies," as Emig presents them, that Baker's essay embodies.

Richard Rodriguez

MEMORIES OF A BILINGUAL CHILDHOOD

The son of Mexican-American immigrants who wanted their children to become integrated into American life so that they could "go far," Richard Rodriguez was born in 1944 in San Francisco and grew up in Sacramento, California. Rodriguez apparently fulfilled his parents' dreams, receiving his B.A. in English from Stanford University in 1967 and his M.A. in English from Columbia University in 1969. He went on with graduate study in English Renaissance literature at the University of California, Berkeley, and at the Warburg Institute in London, England, on a Fulbright Fellowship In 1972. But during his time in London, Rodriguez abruptly left academia when, ironically enough, he discovered that his overwhelming success in overcoming problems of cultural assimilation as a non-English-speaking child meant he had become "the beneficiary of truly disadvantaged Mexican-Americans." He went on to turn down several university-level teaching jobs because he "could not withstand the irony of being counted a 'minority' when in fact the irreversibly successful effort of his life had been to become a fully assimilated member of the majority." Rodriguez set out to earn his living as a writer, subsidizing himself with a National Endowment for the Humanities fellowship and a variety of jobs. In 1982, Rodriguez published his autobiography, *Hunger of Memory: The Education of Richard Rodriguez*, in which he charts his alienation not only from American culture but from his own family as well.

His struggles revolved around language, and, in the following essay, Rodriguez describes the difficulties he encountered in relinquishing his private language— Spanish—in order to learn the public language—English.

Supporters of bilingual education imply today that students like me miss a great deal by not being taught in their family's language. What they seem not to recognize is that, as a socially disadvantaged child, I regarded Spanish as a private language. It was a ghetto language that deepened and strengthened my feeling of public separateness. What I needed to learn in school was that I had the right, and the obligation, to speak the public language. The odd truth is that my first-grade classmates could become bilingual, in the conventional sense of the word, more easily than I. Had they been taught early (as upper-middle-class children often are taught) a "second language" like Spanish or French, they could have regarded it simply as another public language. In my case, such bilingualism could not have been so quickly achieved. What I did not believe was that I could speak a single public language.

Without question, it would have pleased me to have heard my teachers address me in Spanish when I entered the classroom. I would have felt much less afraid. I would have imagined that my instructors were somehow "related" to me; I would indeed have heard their Spanish as my family's language. I would have trusted them and responded with ease. But I would have delayed—for how long?—learning the great lesson of school: that I had a public identity.

Fortunately, my teachers were unsentimental about their responsibility. What they understood was that I needed to speak public English. So their voices would search me out, asking me questions. Each time I heard them I'd look up in surprise to see a nun's face frowning at me. I'd mumble, not really meaning to answer. The nun would persist. "Richard, stand up. Don't look at the floor. Speak up. Speak to the entire class, not just to me!" But I couldn't believe English could be my language to use. (In part, I did not want to believe it.) I continued to mumble. I resisted the teacher's demands. (Did I somehow suspect that once I learned this public language my family life would be changed?) Silent, waiting for the bell to sound, I remained dazed, diffident, afraid.

Three months passed. Five. A half year. Unsmiling, ever watchful, my teachers noted my silence. They began to connect my behavior with the slow progress my brother and sisters were making. Until, one Saturday morning, three nuns arrived at the house to talk to our parents. Stiffly they sat on the blue living-room sofa. From the doorway of another room, spying on the visitors, I noted the incongruity, the clash of two worlds, the faces and voices of school intruding upon the familiar setting of home. I overheard one voice gently wondering, "Do your children speak only Spanish at home, Mrs. Rodriguez?" While another voice added, "That Richard especially seems so timid and shy."

That Rich-heard!

With great tact, the visitors continued, "Is it possible for you and your husband to encourage your children to practice their English when they are home?" Of course my parents complied. What would they not do for their children's well-being? And how could they question the church's authority, which those women represented? In an instant they agreed to give up the language (the sounds) that had revealed and accentuated our family's closeness. The moment after the visitors left, the change was observed. "*Ahora,* speak to us only *en inglés,*" my father and mother told us.

At first, it seemed a kind of game. After dinner each night, the family gathered together to practice "our" English. It was still then *inglés,* a language foreign to us, so we felt drawn to it as strangers. Laughing, we would try to define words we could not pronounce. We played with strange English sounds, often over-anglicizing our pronunciations. And we filled the smiling gaps of our sentences with familiar Spanish sounds. But that was cheating, somebody shouted, and everyone laughed.

In school, meanwhile, like my brother and sisters, I was required to attend a daily tutoring session. I needed a full year of this special work. I also needed my teachers to keep my attention from straying in class by calling out, "*Rich-heard!*"—their English voices slowly loosening the ties to my other name, with its three notes, *Ri-car-do*. Most of all, I needed to hear my mother and father speak to me in a moment of seriousness in "broken"—suddenly heartbreaking—English. This scene was inevitable. One Saturday morning I entered the kitchen where my parents were talking, but I did not realize that they were talking Spanish until, the moment they saw me, their voices changed and they began speaking English. The gringo sounds they uttered startled me. Pushed me away. In that moment of trivial misunderstanding and profound insight, I felt my throat twisted by unsounded grief. I simply turned and left the room. But I had no place to escape to where I could grieve in Spanish. My brother and sisters were speaking English in another part of the house.

Again and again in the days following, as I grew increasingly angry, I was obliged to hear my mother and father encouraging me: "Speak to us *en inglés.*" Only then did I determine to learn classroom English. Thus, sometime afterward it happened: One day in school, I raised my hand to volunteer an answer to a question. I spoke out in a loud voice, and I did not think it remarkable when the entire class understood. That day I moved very far from being the disadvantaged child I had been only days earlier. Taken hold at last was the belief, the calming assurance, that I *belonged* in public.

Shortly after, I stopped hearing the high, troubling sounds of *los gringos*. A more and more confident speaker of English, I didn't listen to how strangers sounded when they talked to me. With so many English-speaking people around me, I no longer heard American accents. Conversations quickened. Listening to persons whose voices sounded eccentrically pitched, I might note their sounds for a few seconds, but then I'd concentrate on what they were saying. Now when I heard someone's tone of voice—angry or questioning or sarcastic or happy or sad—I didn't distinguish it from the words it expressed. Sound and word were thus tightly wedded. At the end of each day, I was often bemused, and always relieved, to realize how "soundless," though crowded with words, my day in public had been. An eight-year-old boy, I finally came to accept what had been technically true since my birth: I was an American citizen.

But diminished by then was the special feeling of closeness at home. Gone was the desperate, urgent, intense feeling of being at home among those with whom I felt intimate. Our family remained a loving family, but one greatly changed. We were no longer so close, no longer bound tightly together by the knowledge of our separateness from *los gringos*. Neither my older brother nor my sisters rushed home after school any more. Nor did I. When I arrived home, often there would be neighborhood kids in the house. Or the house would be empty of sounds.

Following the dramatic Americanization of their children, even my parents grew more publicly confident—especially my mother. First she learned the names of all the people on the block. Then she decided we needed to have a telephone in our house. My father, for his part, continued to use the word gringo, but it was no longer charged with bitterness or distrust. Stripped of any emotional content, the word simply became a name for those Americans not of Hispanic descent. Hearing him, sometimes I wasn't sure if he was pronouncing the Spanish word *gringo,* or saying gringo in English.

There was a new silence at home. As we children learned more and more English, we shared fewer and fewer words with our parents. Sentences needed to be spoken slowly when one of us addressed our mother or father. Often the parent wouldn't understand. The child would need to repeat himself. Still the parent misunderstood. The young voice, frustrated, would end up saying, "Never mind"—the subject was closed. Dinners would be noisy with the clinking of knives and forks against dishes. My mother would smile softly between her remarks; my father, at the other end of the table, would chew and chew his food while he stared over the heads of his children.

My mother! My father! After English became my primary language, I no longer knew what words to use in addressing my parents. The old Spanish words (those tender accents of sound) I had earlier used—*mamá* and *papá*—I couldn't use any more. They would have been all-too-painful reminders of how much had changed in my life. On the other hand, the words I heard neighborhood kids call their parents seemed unsatisfactory. "Mother" and "father," "ma," "papa," "pa," "dad," "pop" (how I hated the all-American sound of that last word)—all these I felt were unsuitable terms of address for *my* parents. As a result, I never used them at home. Whenever I'd speak to my parents, I would try to get their attention by looking at them. In public conversations, I'd refer to them as my "parents" or my "mother" and "father."

My mother and father, for their part, responded differently as their children spoke to them less. My mother grew restless, seemed troubled and anxious at the scarceness of words exchanged in the house. She would question me about my day when I came home from school. She smiled at my small talk. She pried at the edges of my sentences to get me to say something more. ("What . . . ?") She'd join conversations she overheard, but her intrusions often stopped her children's talking. By contrast, my father seemed to grow reconciled to the new quiet. Though his English somewhat improved, he tended more and more to retire into silence. At dinner he spoke very little. One night his children and even his wife helplessly giggled at his garbled English pronunciation of the Catholic "Grace Before Meals." Thereafter he made his wife recite the prayer at the start of each meal, even on formal occasions when there were guests in the house.

Hers became the public voice of the family. On official business it was she, not my father, who would usually talk to strangers on the phone or in stores. We children grew so accustomed to his silence that years later we would routinely refer to his "shyness." (My mother often tried to explain: both of his parents died when he was eight. He was raised by an uncle who treated him as little more than a menial servant. He was never encouraged to speak. He grew up alone—a man of few words.) But I realized my father was not shy whenever I'd watch him speaking Spanish with relatives. Using Spanish, he was quickly effusive. Especially when talking with other men, his voice would spark, flicker, flare alive with varied sounds. In Spanish he expressed ideas and feelings he rarely revealed when speaking English. With firm Spanish sounds he conveyed a confidence and authority that English would never allow him.

The silence at home, however, was not simply the result of fewer words passing between parents and children. More profound for me was the silence created by my inattention to sounds. At about the time I no longer bothered to listen with care to the sounds of English in public, I grew careless about listening to the sounds made by the family when they spoke. Most of the time I would hear someone speaking at home and didn't distinguish his sounds from the words people uttered in public. I didn't even pay much attention to my parents' accented and ungrammatical speech—at least not at home. Only when I was with them in public would I become alert to their accents. But even then, their sounds caused me less and less concern. For I was growing increasingly confident of my own public identity.

I would have been happier about my public success had I not recalled, sometimes, what it had been like earlier, when my family conveyed its intimacy through a set of conveniently private sounds. Sometimes in public, hearing a stranger, I'd hark back to my lost past. A Mexican farm worker approached me one day downtown. He wanted directions to some place. "*Hijito*, . . ." he said. And his voice stirred old longings. Another time I was standing beside my mother in the visiting room of a Carmelite convent, before the dense screen that rendered the nuns shadowy figures. I heard several of them speaking Spanish in their busy, singsong, overlapping voices, assuring my mother that, yes, yes, we were remembered, all our family were remembered in their prayers. Those voices echoed faraway family sounds. Another day, a dark-faced old woman touched my shoulder lightly to steady herself as she boarded a bus. She murmured something to me I couldn't quite comprehend. Her Spanish voice came near, like the face of a never-before-seen relative in the instant before I was kissed. That voice, like so many of the Spanish voices I'd hear in public, recalled the golden age of my childhood.

QUESTIONS FOR READING, RESPONDING, AND WRITING

Summarizing Main Points

1. In this essay, Rodriguez recalls his difficult, emotionally trying transition from Spanish to English. What particularly made that transition so painful for Rodriguez? What changes occurred in his "private" life? In his "public" life?
2. Describe how, at this time, Rodriguez suggests his attitude toward his mother and father changed. Did his mother or father change or was it simply Rodriguez's attitude toward them that changed? Support your answer with examples from the essay.

Analyzing Methods of Discourse

1. When Rodriguez's teachers visit his home they call him "Richard." Rodriguez hears his name as *"Rich-heard."* What is the difference, and how do you account for it? Later, the reader discovers that Rodriguez's "other name" is *"Ri-car-do."* How does Rodriguez prepare the reader for this information? List any other examples of Rodriguez's or his parents' confusion over the transition from Spanish to English.
2. Rodriguez ends his essay with the sentence, "That voice, like so many of the Spanish voices I'd hear in public, recalled the golden age of my childhood." Perhaps everyone's transition from childhood to adulthood is painful and tinged with a sense of loss. In what ways does Rodriguez make it clear that, for him, the loss was greater? According to Rodriguez, is that greater loss partly his own fault?

Focusing on the Field

1. Rodriguez is not entirely happy about his "public success." Why not? Could Rodriguez have presented his essay as a formal study of public versus private language or as a study of bilingual education? Would it have been more or less effective? Why?
2. Early in his essay, Rodriguez says, "Fortunately, my teachers were unsentimental about their responsibility." Should Rodriguez's teachers have been so unsentimental? How else might they have handled the situation?

Writing Assignments

1. Using "Memories of a Bilingual Childhood" as a model, describe an incident in your own life that had consequences beyond those your reader might have expected. Make sure you describe details. Do not merely generalize.
2. In James Baldwin's "If Black English Isn't a Language, Then Tell Me, What Is?" he says, "Language, incontestably, reveals the speaker. Language, also, far

more dubiously, is meant to define the other—and, in this case, the other is refusing to be defined by a language that has never been able to recognize him." Later, Baldwin claims that language "reveals the private identity, and connects one with, or divorces one from, the larger public, or communal identity." Would Rodriguez agree or disagree with Baldwin? Support your answers in a short essay that draws on both Rodriguez and Baldwin for evidence.

Langston Hughes

SALVATION

A prominent poet of the "Harlem Renaissance" of the 1920s, (James) Langston Hughes differed from his contemporaries and predecessors, "in that he addressed his poetry to the people, specifically to black people." Not only in his poetry, such as *Fine Clothes for the Jew* (1926) and *The Panther and the Lash* (1960), but also in novels, such as *Not Without Laughter* (1930) and *Tamborines to Glory* (1958), short stories, such as "The Ways of White Folks" (1934) and "Simple Speaks His Mind" (1950), nonfiction, such as *The Sweet Flypaper of Life* (1955) and *Fight for Freedom: The Story of the NAACP* (1962), plays, such as *Joy to My Soul* (1937) and *Black Nativity* (1961), and numerous children's books, essays, and lectures, Hughes's main goal was "to explain the Negro condition in America" as he had seen and lived it. Much to the consternation of both black and white critics and intellectuals, Hughes wrote about ordinary black people. As he explained: "I didn't know the upper-class Negroes well enough to write about them. I knew only the people I had grown up with, and they weren't people whose shoes were always shined, who had been to Harvard, or who had heard of Bach. But they seemed to me good people, too." In the following essay from his autobiography, *The Big Sea* (1940), Hughes gives the reader a sample of the style and character of those people and their importance in his own life.

Born in Joplin, Missouri in 1902, Hughes attended Columbia University from 1912–1922 and received his B.A. from Lincoln University in 1929. He supplemented his formal education with a variety of jobs in a variety of countries. By the time he was 24, Hughes had worked as a truck farmer, a cook, a laundryman, a busboy, a doorman at a Paris nightclub, and a sailor on voyages to Europe and Africa. Such diversity set a pattern for the rest of his life. By the time he died at the age of 65 of congestive heart failure, he had won numerous awards, including Guggenheim and Rosenwald Fellowships, an honorary doctorate from Lincoln University, an American Academy of Arts and Letters grant, and the Spingarn Medal from the NAACP. His more than sixty books, of which the former list provides a small sampling, attest to a lifetime of immense literary productivity, which one critic has called "as full, as varied, as original as Picasso's, a joyful honest monument of a career [which had] no noticeable sham in it, no pretension, no self-deceit, but a great, great deal of delight and smiling irresistible wit."

I was saved from sin when I was going on thirteen. But not really saved. It happened like this. There was a big revival at my Auntie Reed's church. Every night for weeks there had been much preaching, singing, praying, and shouting, and some very hardened sinners had been brought to Christ, and the membership of the church had grown by leaps and bounds. Then just before the revival ended, they held a special meeting for children, "to bring the young lambs to the fold." My aunt spoke of it for days ahead. That night I was escorted to the front row and placed on the mourners' bench with all the other young sinners, who had not yet been brought to Jesus.

My aunt told me that when you were saved you saw a light, and something happened to you inside! And Jesus came into your life! And God was with you from then on! She said you could see and hear and feel Jesus in your soul. I believed her. I had heard a great many old people say the same thing and it seemed to me they ought to know. So I sat there calmly in the hot, crowded church waiting for Jesus to come to me.

The preacher preached a wonderful rhythmical sermon, all moans and shouts and lonely cries and dire pictures of hell, and then he sang a song about the ninety and nine safe in the fold, but one little lamb was left out in the cold. Then he said: "Won't you come? Won't you come to Jesus? Young lambs, won't you come?" And he held out his arms to all us young sinners there on the mourners' bench. And the little girls cried. And some of them jumped up and went to Jesus right away. But most of us just sat there.

A great many old people came and knelt around us and prayed, old women with jet-black faces and braided hair, old men with work-gnarled hands. And the church sang a song about the lower lights are burning, some poor sinners to be saved. And the whole building rocked with prayer and song.

Still I kept waiting to *see* Jesus.

Finally all the young people had gone to the altar and were saved, but one boy and me. He was a rounder's son named Westley. Westley and I were surrounded by sisters and deacons praying. It was very hot in the church, and getting late now. Finally Westley said to me in a whisper: "God damn! I'm tired o' sitting here. Let's get up and be saved." So he got up and was saved.

Then I was left all alone on the mourners' bench. My aunt came and knelt at my knees and cried, while prayers and song swirled all around me in the little church. The whole congregation prayed for me alone, in a mighty wail of moans and voices. And I kept waiting serenely for Jesus, waiting, waiting—but he didn't come. I wanted to see him, but nothing happened to me. Nothing! I wanted something to happen to me, but nothing happened.

I heard the songs and the minister saying: "Why don't you come? My dear child, why don't you come to Jesus? Jesus is waiting for you. He wants you. Why don't you come? Sister Reed, what is this child's name?"

"Langston," my aunt sobbed.

"Langston, why don't you come? Why don't you come and be saved? Oh, Lamb of God! Why don't you come?"

Now it was really getting late. I began to be ashamed of myself, holding everything up so long. I began to wonder what God thought about Westley, who certainly hadn't seen Jesus either, but who was now sitting proudly on the platform, swinging his knickerbockered legs and grinning down at me, surrounded by deacons and old women on their knees praying. God had not struck Westley dead for taking his name in vain or for lying in the temple. So I decided that maybe to save further trouble, I'd better lie, too, and say that Jesus had come, and get up and be saved.

So I got up.

Suddenly the whole room broke into a sea of shouting, as they saw me rise. Waves of rejoicing swept the place. Women leaped in the air. My aunt threw her arms around me. The minister took me by the hand and led me to the platform.

When things quieted down, in a hushed silence, punctuated by a few ecstatic "Amens," all the new young lambs were blessed in the name of God. Then joyous singing filled the room.

That night, for the last time in my life but one—for I was a big boy twelve years old—I cried. I cried, in bed alone, and couldn't stop. I buried my head under the quilts, but my aunt heard me. She woke up and told my uncle I was crying because the Holy Ghost had come into my life, and because I had seen Jesus. But I was really crying because I couldn't bear to tell her that I had lied, that I had deceived everybody in the church, that I hadn't seen Jesus, and that now I didn't believe there was a Jesus any more, since he didn't come to help me.

QUESTIONS FOR READING, RESPONDING, AND WRITING

Summarizing Main Points

1. Though Hughes never sees Jesus, what does he come to recognize? Why does he cry?

2. What was Hughes's attitude toward his aunt before the revival meeting? How does his attitude change?

Analyzing Methods of Discourse

1. Read the third paragraph of Hughes's essay out loud. How does Hughes's choice of words and sentence structure reflect the "rhythmical sermon" of the preacher? Does the last sentence of the paragraph change that rhythm? Why or why not?
2. The last sentence of Hughes's essay is in some ways much like the paragraph about the preacher and in other ways much different. Consider, for instance, the use of pronouns and conjunctions, the sentence structures, and the repetition of words. How do these similarities and differences reflect the changes that Hughes has or has not undergone?

Focusing on the Field

1. The "rounder's son named Westley" is obviously not "saved" in any way. How does Hughes make sure that the reader knows this?
2. After studying Richard Rodriguez's "Memories of a Bilingual Childhood," describe how Hughes's essay distinguishes between private and public selves.

Writing Assignments

1. Langston Hughes is reflecting back on what was then a painful experience. Compare his account of his rite of passage from childhood to adulthood with Richard Rodriguez's account of his childhood in "Memories of a Bilingual Childhood." In a short essay, decide which experience you think would be the more traumatic. Support your choice with examples from both essays.
2. Describe a moment in your emotional life when its public setting made a difference.

ANALYSIS
AND· EXPLANATION

John Canaday

WHAT IS A PAINTING?

Born in Fort Scott, Kansas, John Edwin Canaday (1907–1985) graduated from the University of Texas in 1925, and received an M.A. from Yale University in 1932. He taught art history for many years, and from 1952 until 1959 he was chief of the division of education for the Philadelphia Museum of Art. In the 1940s, Canaday's own wish to read a mystery novel that explored its characters in depth prompted him to write *The Smell of Money* (1943). Canaday has said that he wrote this mystery under the pseudonym Matthew Head—the name has a "faintly sinister" look to it, according to its author—because "I didn't know whether it would be a success, and if it wasn't a success I didn't want my name on it." His novel *was* successful, as were the six that followed it. Critics called it "the detective-literary find of 1943" and the "finest in detective fiction."

Yet Canaday gave up fiction and began writing about art history. His twelve-volume *Metropolitan Seminars in Art* (1958) was not only well received critically but also sold well—over 5 million copies. Canaday went on to become art critic for the *New York Times,* where he argued that most abstract expressionists were frauds. Canaday's criticism resulted in a collaboration with his wife, Katherine, entitled *Embattled Critic: Views on Modern Art,* a collection of his controversial essays and responses to them. The book only extended the argument. The *New York Times Book Review* said that Canaday was "justified" in his investigation of abstract expressionism but that he failed to prove his claims, while the *Chicago Tribune* called his work "inspired" and said that Canaday wrote "perceptively and beautifully." His introduction to art appreciation, *What Is Art?,* from which the following selection is taken, provides a sensible, honest, accessible, concrete, yet comprehensive guide to art.

A painting is a layer of pigments applied to a surface. It is an arrangement of shapes and colors. It is a projection of the personality of the artist who painted it, a statement—or at least a partial statement—of the philosophy of the age that produced it, and it can have meanings beyond anything

26

concerned with the one person who painted it or the one period in which it was created.

For something like fifteen or twenty thousand years—that is, until our century and the revolution called modern art—a painting was also a picture *of* something, whether it was the work of Rembrandt or the sorriest hack alive, even though Rembrandt's painting of, say, an old beggar would be a profound philosophical comment on the human condition, and the hack's would be the tritest kind of picturesque sentimentality. In the nineteenth century, when art exhibitions first became a form of popular entertainment, art's new audience was not up to making that kind of distinction and felt safe enough in enjoying a painting simply as a picture (the words were virtually synonymous) *of* something—a man, a dog, a vase of flowers, the Madonna, a battlefield (in France, preferably Napoleonic), a small boy stealing cookies—and that was that.

To judge the merits of a painting by this standard was a simple affair. A picture was good first to the extent that the objects represented in it "looked real," and second to the extent that the artist's interpretation of the subject conformed to established ideas of what was entertaining (the small boy stealing cookies), or beautiful (the vase of flowers), or uplifting (the Madonna), or simply informative.

We like to think that all that has changed, and to a certain degree it has; but the twentieth century cannot look back smugly on the popular taste of the nineteenth. In spite of our proliferated museum and art education programs, this limited response to painting—not to esthetic qualities but to subjects that in themselves are entertaining, beautiful, uplifting, or informative in the most obvious ways—is not only persistent today but remains dominant outside a relatively limited circle. The American art public since about 1950, after decades of exposure to evangelism for modern art, is no doubt the most sophisticated in the world, yet the only artist to receive front-page headlines two days in a row in *The New York Times* on the occasion of his death was not Picasso but Norman Rockwell.

Norman Rockwell has been without doubt the general public's most beloved painter in the history of American art. Whether offering a humorous subject such as *No Swimming* or the piously folksy Thanksgiving scene *Freedom from Want* [see illustration], Rockwell's pictures are always easy to read, either as images, which are affectionately commonplace, or as ideas, which are so standard that preconditioned response is automatic. At this level of conception it makes no difference—in truth, it is a help—that the expressions on faces are just as posed, as self-consciously assumed, as are the bodily attitudes, and that any stimulation of the imagination, any extension or enlargement of experience, is rigorously avoided.

Norman Rockwell, *Freedom from Want,* 1943. Oil on canvas, 45½ by 35½ inches. Estate of Norman Rockwell. © 1943 Curtis Publishing Co.

Pictures of this kind are easily derided—too easily perhaps, in view of one important virtue: they please and art is meant to be enjoyed. The trouble is that enjoyment at their level is nothing more than a stirring up of stock responses to stock subjects, a form of picture enjoyment unrelated to the inexhaustible pleasures offered by exploration of the art of painting—deeper pleasures that can often be discovered beneath popular surface attractions.

Take, as an elementary exercise, a painting that has become so barnacled with Rockwellesque associations that its true character has become obscured—the painting universally but incorrectly known as *Whistler's Mother* [see illustration]. It comes off very well by the standards we have just mentioned. It "looks real" to such a degree that it suggests soft-focus photography. Its subject immediately calls into play the double reverence we feel for motherhood and old age. These associations are stirred up even more vigorously because this picture of a mother

James Abbott McNeill Whistler, *Arrangement in Gray and Black,* No. 1, 1871–1872. Oil on canvas, 56 by 64 inches. The Louvre, Paris.

in her old age was painted by her son, adding filial devotion to the already impressive sum of virtues tied in with the subject. With such admirable connections, *Whistler's Mother* might have found its way into popular favor even if it had been a very bad painting. It happens to be a very fine painting, but *not* because it is a lifelike portrait of an old lady by her son.

The correct title is still the one Whistler gave it and always insisted upon: *Arrangement in Gray and Black.* And the real subject is a mood, a mood compounded of gentleness, dignity, reflection, and resignation. This mood may be suggested by the quiet pose of the old lady, but it is completed by the shapes and colors Whistler chose to use and the relationships he established among them. The disposition of form and color, termed "composition"—that is, the way a picture is put together—can be, as here, the most important single factor in the expressive quality of a painting.

Surely it is obvious that the quiet and tender mood Whistler had in mind could not be relayed through vivid colors and jagged shapes in complex or agitated relationships to one another. Hence the artist reduces the background to a few subtly spaced rectangles of subdued neutral tones, and against this background the figure of the old lady is reduced to a silhouette nearly as geometrical and just as uneventful. The head, the hands, and the scattering of luminous flecks on the curtain serve as relieving accents, lighter in tone and livelier in shape, in a scheme that might otherwise have been monotonous and melancholy.

At the risk of being unfair to an honest and proficient illustrator who never pretended to be more than he was, and in the certainty of offending his enormous public, let us imagine how Norman Rockwell might have gone about painting *Whistler's Mother*. In the first place, the picture would not be an arrangement in gray and black but a lively conglomeration of objects painted in cheerful colors, and the old lady would be *doing something*—not just sitting there. She might be knitting, in which case the immediate associative pictorial response of a kitten playing with a ball of yarn on the floor would be incorporated. A rag rug, affording an opportunity for maximum display of the artist's talent for precisely detailed description, might be included among other homely accessories in the sunny room to show how happy the old lady is in the modest family home where she lives. The pictures on the wall would lose their function as compositional elements and become narrative aids; perhaps the old lady's wedding photograph would be there, with some affectionately humorous pictorial comment on the groom's dandified moustaches. Any possible vestiges of the Whistlerian mood of loneliness and resignation would be removed by the introduction of a small boy or girl—or one of each—peeking into the room from behind the curtain at the left, and the whole thing would be polished off by a pair of granny-type spectacles over which the old lady would beam at her grandchildren. The fact that none of this would have anything much to do with life as it is has everything to do with why a vast audience would love *Rockwell's Mother*.

Why this same public loves *Whistler's Mother* must be explained on another basis. We have said that even if this had been a bad picture, it might have been a popular one. But it would never have become as widely known and loved as it is now, because even people who never doubt that their enjoyment comes from the subject matter of *Whistler's Mother* are being affected, whether they realize it or not, by the expressive composition of *Arrangement in Gray and Black*.

Composition affects our reaction to a picture, regardless of whether we think of it in compositional terms. If the arrangement of shapes and colors is successful, we respond as the artist intended us to, without asking ourselves why. But once we are aware of composition as an element in painting, we have the additional pleasure of discovering how the artist goes about evoking the response he is after. These two pleasures

[handwritten margin notes: "Two pleasures", "blocking of to see the picture within a picture"]

are perfectly compatible. In the same way, we may be moved by a great performance in the theater while simultaneously, quite aside from our emotional participation, we admire the actor's skill.

The structure of a composition can be tested by blocking off different areas with pieces of paper. Effective little pictures-within-pictures may be isolated in this way, but the fragments can never say the same thing as the total of a good composition, not because part of the subject matter is eliminated but because the relationships of shapes and colors have been disturbed. If everything in *Arrangement in Gray and Black* is blocked off except the central figure, you still have a picture of an old lady sitting in a chair. Nothing has been eliminated that tells part of a story or adds to what we know about this particular woman. But the picture's mood is gone. This picture, in fact, suffers in countless cheap reproductions where it is chopped off along the edges for convenience in putting it into a frame or onto a page.

[handwritten margin note: "Mood"]

QUESTIONS FOR READING, RESPONDING, AND WRITING

Summarizing Main Points

1. According to Canaday, what different methods of expression does a painter have available? List the three methods of enjoying a painting that Canaday analyzes.
2. In his description of the imagined painting *Rockwell's Mother*, Canaday tells the reader that "the pictures on the wall would lose their function as compositional elements and become narrative aids." Explain this statement and support your explanation with evidence from elsewhere in Canaday's essay.

Analyzing Methods of Discourse

1. Canaday introduces James Whistler's most famous painting by the title *Whistler's Mother*. Shortly thereafter, Canaday insists that "the correct title is still the one Whistler gave it and always insisted upon: *Arrangement in Gray and Black*." Why do you suppose Whistler insisted on this title? In what ways do this title and Whistler's insistence on it support Canaday's analysis? Why do you suppose Canaday introduces it incorrectly first?
2. Canaday suggests that *Arrangement in Gray and Black* "comes off well" in that it pleases by "stirring up . . . stock responses to stock subjects." He says, "It 'looks real' to such a degree that it suggests soft-focus photography." Why does Canaday enclose the words "looks real" in quotation marks? Does Canaday believe that *Arrangement in Gray and Black* "looks real"? Is that its primary pleasure, according to Canaday? Do you agree or disagree with his analysis?

Focusing on the Field

1. Canaday chooses to analyze only two paintings. Do you feel that they are sufficient evidence to make his point? Would two other paintings have done as well?

2. Though Canaday never discusses abstract art in this essay, what methods of enjoying it do you suppose Canaday might advocate? Can abstract art be representational? Support your answer with evidence from Canaday's essay.

Writing Assignments

1. Choose a painting you like and, using Canaday's essay as a model, define its mood and describe how that mood is achieved.
2. Canaday explains that there are three ways to look at a painting: for its pictorial element, for its composition, and for the way the artist achieves a response. Compare and contrast Canaday's analysis of paintings with Aaron Copland's analysis of "How We Listen to Music" in the following essay.

Aaron Copland

HOW WE LISTEN TO MUSIC

Born in 1900 in Brooklyn, New York, Aaron Copland has composed music that is both well-respected and popular. One of the first classical composers to incorporate homespun American music—jazz, folk, blues, cowboy ditties, and church tunes—into orchestral arrangements, Copland gained fame among the musically sophisticated and the general public. A teacher as well as a composer, Copland has become an unmistakable influence in American music. Although most famous, perhaps, for his Pulitzer Prize–winning score for the ballet *Appalachian Spring,* most of his compositions are familiar to the American people, if not by name, then almost certainly by their distinctive sound. They include *Concerto* (1926), *Short Symphony* (1933), *Billy the Kid* (1938), *Rodeo* (1942), and *Third Symphony* (1946). Appropriately enough, given his innovative approach, Copland also composed the scores for several popular films, including *Of Mice and Men* (1939), *Our Town* (1940), and *The Heiress* (1949). Copland has also written several books that help make music more accessible to the general public, including *New Music* (1941), *Music and Imagination* (1952), and *Copland on Music* (1960). In the following selection from *What We Listen to in Music* (rev. 1957), Copland suggests that we can deepen our appreciation for music by not "just listening but . . . listening *for* something."

We all listen to music according to our separate capacities. But, for the sake of analysis, the whole listening process may become clearer if we break it up into its component parts, so to speak. In a certain sense we all listen to music on three separate planes. For lack of a better terminology, one might name these: (1) the sensuous plane, (2) the expressive plane, (3) the sheerly musical plane. The only advantage to be gained from mechanically splitting up the listening process into these hypothetical planes is the clearer view to be had of the way in which we listen.

The simplest way of listening to music is to listen for the sheer pleasure of the musical sound itself. That is the sensuous plane. It is the plane on which we hear music without thinking, without considering it in any way. One turns on the radio while doing something else and absent-mindedly bathes in the sound. A kind of brainless but attractive state of mind is engendered by the mere sound appeal of the music.

You may be sitting in a room reading this book. Imagine one note struck on the piano. Immediately that one note is enough to change the atmosphere of the room—proving that the sound element in music is a powerful and mysterious agent, which it would be foolish to deride or belittle.

The surprising thing is that many people who consider themselves qualified music lovers abuse that plane in listening. They go to concerts in order to lose themselves. They use music as a consolation or an escape. They enter an ideal world where one doesn't have to think of the realities of everyday life. Of course they aren't thinking about the music either. Music allows them to leave it, and they go off to a place to dream, dreaming because of and apropos of the music yet never quite listening to it.

Yes, the sound appeal of music is a potent and primitive force, but you must not allow it to usurp a disproportionate share of your interest. The sensuous plane is an important one in music, a very important one, but it does not constitute the whole story.

There is no need to digress further on the sensuous plane. Its appeal to every normal human being is self-evident. There is, however, such a thing as becoming more sensitive to the different kinds of sound stuff as used by various composers. For all composers do not use that sound stuff in the same way. Don't get the idea that the value of music is commensurate with its sensuous appeal or that the loveliest sounding music is made by the greatest composer. If that were so, Ravel would be a greater creator than Beethoven. The point is that the sound element varies with each composer, that his usage of sound forms an integral part of his style and must be taken into account when listening. The reader can see, therefore, that a more conscious approach is valuable even on this primary plane of music listening.

The second plane on which music exists is what I have called the expressive one. Here, immediately, we tread on controversial ground. Composers have a way of shying away from any discussion of music's expressive side. Did not Stravinsky himself proclaim that his music was an "object," a "thing," with a life of its own, and with no other meaning than its own purely musical existence? This intransigent attitude of Stravinsky's may be due to the fact that so many people have tried to read different meanings into so many pieces. Heaven knows it is difficult enough to say precisely what it is that a piece of music means, to say it definitely, to say it finally so that everyone is satisfied with your explanation. But that should not lead one to the other extreme of denying to music the right to be "expressive."

My own belief is that all music has an expressive power, some more and some less, but that all music has a certain meaning behind the notes and that that meaning behind the notes constitutes, after all, what the piece is saying, what the piece is about. This whole problem can be stated quite simply by asking, "Is there a meaning to music?" My answer to that would be, "Yes." And "Can you state in so many words what the meaning is?" My answer to that would be, "No." Therein lies the difficulty.

Simple-minded souls will never be satisfied with the answer to the second of these questions. They always want music to have a meaning, and the more concrete it is the better they like it. The more the music reminds them of a train, a storm, a funeral, or any other familiar conception the more expressive it appears to be to them. This popular idea of music's meaning—stimulated and abetted by the usual run of musical commentator—should be discouraged wherever and whenever it is met. One timid lady once confessed to me that she suspected something seriously lacking in her appreciation of music because of her inability to connect it with anything definite. That is getting the whole thing backward, of course.

Still, the question remains, How close should the intelligent music lover wish to come to pinning a definite meaning to any particular work? No closer than a general concept, I should say. Music expresses, at different moments, serenity or exuberance, regret or triumph, fury or delight. It expresses each of these moods, and many others, in a numberless variety of subtle shadings and differences. It may even express a state of meaning for which there exists no adequate word in any language. In that case, musicians often like to say that it has only a purely musical meaning. They sometimes go farther and say that *all* music has only a purely musical meaning. What they really mean is that no appropriate word can be found to express the music's meaning and that, even if it could, they do not feel the need of finding it.

But whatever the professional musician may hold, most musical novices still search for specific words with which to pin down their musical reactions. That is why they always find Tschaikovsky easier to "understand" than Beethoven. In the first place, it is easier to pin a meaning-word on a Tschaikovsky piece than on a Beethoven one. Much easier. Moreover, with the Russian composer, every time you come back to a piece of his it almost always says the same thing to you, whereas with Beethoven it is often difficult to put your finger right on what he is saying. And any musician will tell you that that is why Beethoven is the greater composer. Because music which always says the same thing to you will necessarily soon become dull music, but music whose meaning is slightly different with each hearing has a greater chance of remaining alive.

Listen, if you can, to the forty-eight fugue themes of Bach's *Well Tempered Clavichord*. Listen to each theme, one after another. You will soon realize that each theme mirrors a different world of feeling. You will also soon realize that the more beautiful a theme seems to you the harder it is to find any word that will describe it to your complete satisfaction. Yes, you will certainly know whether it is a gay theme or a sad one. You will be able, in other words, in your own mind, to draw a frame of emotional feeling around your theme. Now study the sad one a little closer. Try to pin down the exact quality of its sadness. Is it pessimistically sad; is it fatefully sad or smilingly sad?

Let us suppose that you are fortunate and can describe to your own satisfaction in so many words the exact meaning of your chosen theme. There is still no guarantee that anyone else will be satisfied. Nor need they be. The important thing is that each one feel for himself the specific expressive quality of a theme or, similarly, an entire piece of music. And if it is a great work of art, don't expect it to mean exactly the same thing to you each time you return to it.

Themes or pieces need not express only one emotion, of course. Take such a theme as the first main one of the *Ninth Symphony*, for example. It is clearly made up of different elements. It does not say only one thing. Yet anyone hearing it immediately gets a feeling of strength, a feeling of power. It isn't a power that comes simply because the theme is played loudly. It is a power inherent in the theme itself. The extraordinary strength and vigor of the theme results in the listener's receiving an impression that a forceful statement has been made. But one should never try to boil it down to "the fateful hammer of life," etc. That is where the trouble begins. The musician, in his exasperation, says it means nothing but the notes themselves, whereas the nonprofessional is only too anxious to hang on to any explanation that gives him the illusion of getting closer to the music's meaning.

Now, perhaps, the reader will know better what I mean when I say that music does have an expressive meaning but that we cannot say in so many words what that meaning is.

The third plane on which music exists is the sheerly musical plane. Besides the pleasurable sound of music and the expressive feeling that it gives off, music does exist in terms of the notes themselves and of their manipulation. Most listeners are not sufficiently conscious of this third plane. It will be largely the business of this book to make them more aware of music on this plane.

Professional musicians, on the other hand, are, if anything, too conscious of the mere notes themselves. They often fall into the error of becoming so engrossed with their arpeggios and staccatos that they forget the deeper aspects of the music they are performing. But from the layman's standpoint, it is not so much a matter of getting over bad habits on the sheerly musical plane as of increasing one's awareness of what is going on, in so far as the notes are concerned.

When the man in the street listens to the "notes themselves" with any degree of concentration, he is most likely to make some mention of the melody. Either he hears a pretty melody or he does not, and he generally lets it go at that. Rhythm is likely to gain his attention next, particularly if it seems exciting. But harmony and tone color are generally taken for granted, if they are thought of consciously at all. As for music's having a definite form of some kind, that idea seems never to have occurred to him.

It is very important for all of us to become more alive to music on its sheerly musical plane. After all, an actual musical material is being used. The intelligent listener must be prepared to increase his awareness of the musical material and what happens to it. He must hear the melodies, the rhythms, the harmonies, the tone colors in a more conscious fashion. But above all he must, in order to follow the line of the composer's thought, know something of the principles of musical form. Listening to all of these elements is listening on the sheerly musical plane.

Let me repeat that I have split up mechanically the three separate planes on which we listen merely for the sake of greater clarity. Actually, we never listen on one or the other of these planes. What we do is to correlate them—listening in all three ways at the same time. It takes no mental effort, for we do it instinctively.

Perhaps an analogy with what happens to us when we visit the theater will make this instinctive correlation clearer. In the theater, you are aware of the actors and actresses, costumes and sets, sounds and movement. All these give one the sense that the theater is a pleasant place to be in. They constitute the sensuous plane in our theatrical reactions.

The expressive plane in the theater would be derived from the feeling that you get from what is happening on the stage. You are moved to pity, excitement, or gayety. It is the general feeling, generated aside from the particular words being spoken, a certain emotional something which exists on the stage, that is analogous to the expressive quality in music.

The plot and plot development is equivalent to our sheerly musical plane. The playwright creates and develops a character in just the same way that a composer develops a theme. According to the degree of your awareness of the way in which the artist in either field handles his material will you become a more intelligent listener.

It is easy enough to see that the theatergoer never is conscious of any of these elements separately. He is aware of them all at the same time. The same is true of music listening. We simultaneously and without thinking listen on all three planes.

In a sense, the ideal listener is both inside and outside the music at the same moment, judging it and enjoying it, wishing it would go one way and watching it go another—almost like the composer at the moment he composes it; because in order to write his music, the composer must also be inside and outside his music, carried away by it, and yet coldly critical of it. A subjective and objective attitude is implied in both creating and listening to music.

What the reader should strive for, then, is a more *active* kind of listening. Whether you listen to Mozart or Duke Ellington, you can deepen your understanding of music only by being a more conscious and aware listener—not someone who is just listening, but someone who is listening *for* something.

QUESTIONS FOR READING, RESPONDING, AND WRITING

Summarizing Main Points

1. Copland describes many of the elements of music that the reader should listen for. List them in the order of importance that you feel Copland might attach to them.
2. Copland warns the reader "not to get the idea that the value of music is commensurate with its sensuous appeal or that the loveliest sounding music is made by the greatest composer." Explain what Copland means by this statement. What does Copland say the "value" of music is? Do you agree or disagree?

Analyzing Methods of Discourse

1. Copland often uses words descriptive of emotion in his essay, most frequently to describe music, but often to describe the listener's state. For example, he suggests listeners may "lose themselves," they may be "frustrated" or "satisfied." Do his descriptions strike familiar notes for you? How do they work to make Copland's advice more believable?
2. Toward the end of his essay, Copland describes the "ideal listener." List the ways that Copland allows the reader to move from "the man in the street" who "absentmindedly bathes in the sound" of music to that "ideal state."

Focusing on the Field

1. Which plane of listening do you think Copland values most? Support your answer with evidence from Copland's essay.

2. Copland is most famous for his innovative use of American folk music in orchestral arrangements. List the ways that this essay seems appropriate to such innovations—that is, how does Copland incorporate homespun American virtues into his analysis of "How We Listen to Music"?

Writing Assignments

1. In a short essay, apply Copland's advice about listening to music to an aspect of contemporary music with which you are familiar. Make sure you consider whether listening to contemporary music more than once affects your enjoyment of it, and, as Copland suggests, "pin down the exact quality" you feel the music expresses.
2. In a brief essay, describe the difficulties inherent in teaching someone about an art whose experience you value highly. You should draw upon Copland's essay for evidence of that difficulty, and you may wish to consider Reuben Brower's "Reading in Slow Motion" and John Canaday's "What Is a Painting?" as well.

Ada Louise Huxtable

HOUSTON

Ada Louise Huxtable's distinctive critical style and architectural acumen have garnered her numerous awards and honors, among them the first Pulitzer Prize for distinguished criticism. As the following essay on Houston, selected from *Kicked Any Buildings Lately?* makes clear, Huxtable's architectural vision combines plain common sense with equal doses of incisive historical scholarship in a style that is at once accessible and learned.

Born in New York City in 1921, Huxtable studied at both Hunter College and New York University. Awarded both a Fulbright and a Guggenheim fellowship early in her career, Huxtable has since received numerous honorary degrees and, most recently, the prestigious McArthur Foundation award. For ten years (1963–1973) the architecture critic for the *New York Times,* Huxtable received the American Association of University Women "Woman of the Year" Award in 1974. Aside from *Kicked Any Buildings Lately?* (1976), Huxtable has written many well-respected books on architectural styles, among them, *Pier Luigi Nervi* (1960) and *Classic New York* (1964).

This is a car's-eye view of Houston—but is there any other? It is a short report on a fast trip to the city that has supplanted Los Angeles in current intellectual mythology as the city of the future. You'd better believe. Houston is the place that scholars flock to for the purpose of seeing what modern civilization has wrought. Correctly perceived and publicized as freeway city, mobile city, space city, strip city, and speculator city, it is being dissected by architects and urban historians as a case study in new forms and functions. It even requires a new definition of urbanity. Houston is *the* city of the second half of the twentieth century.

But what strikes the visitor accustomed to cities shaped by rivers, mountains, and distinguishing topography, by local identity and historical and cultural conditioning, is that this is instant city, and it is nowhere city.

Houston is totally without the normal rationales of geography and evolutionary social growth that have traditionally created urban centers and culture. From the time that the Allen brothers came here from New York in 1836 and bought the featureless land at the junction of two bayous (they could not get the site they really wanted), this city has been an act of real estate, rather than an act of God or man. Houston has been willed on the flat, uniform prairie not by some planned ideal, but by the expediency of land investment economics, first, and later by oil and petrochemical prosperity.

This is not meant to be an unfavorable judgment. It is simply an effort to convey the extraordinary character of this city—to suggest its unique importance, interest, and impact. Its affluence and eccentricities have been popularly celebrated. It is known to be devoutly conservative, passionately devoted to free enterprise and non-governmental interference. It is famous, or notorious, for the fact that, alone among the country's major cities, it has no zoning—no regulations on what anyone builds anywhere—and the debate rages over whether this makes it better or worse than other cities. (It's a draw, with pluses and minuses that have a lot to do with special local conditions.)

Now the fifth largest city in the country, Houston has had its most phenomenal expansion since the Second World War. At last count, it covered over 500 square miles and had a population of 1.4 million, with a half million more in surrounding Harris County. A thousand new people move in every week. This record-setting growth has leap-frogged over open country without natural boundaries, without land use restrictions, moving on before anything is finished, for the kind of development as open-ended as the prairie. It has jumped across smaller, fully incorporated cities within the vast city limits. The municipality can legally annex 10 percent of its urban area in outlying land or communities every year, and the land grab has been continuous and relentless.

Houston is a study in paradoxes. There are pines and palm trees, skyscrapers and sprawl; Tudor townhouses stop abruptly as cows and prairie take over. It deals in incredible extremes of wealth and culture. In spite of its size, one can find no real center, no focus. "Downtown" boasts a concentration of suave towers, but they are already challenged by other, newer commercial centers of increasing magnitude that form equally important nodes on the freeway network that ties everything together. Nor are these new office and shopping complexes located to serve existing communities in the conventional sense. They are created in a vacuum, and people come by automobile, driving right into their parking garages. They rise from expressway ribbons and seas of cars.

Houston is all process and no plan. Gertrude Stein said of Oakland that there was no there, there. One might say of Houston that one never gets there. It feels as if one is always on the way, always arriving, always looking for the place where everything comes together. And yet as a city, a twentieth-century city, it works remarkably well. If one excepts horrendous morning and evening traffic jams as all of Houston moves to and from home and work, it is a lesson in how a mobile society functions, the values it endorses, and what kind of world it makes.

Houston is different from the time one rises in the morning to have the dark suddenly dispelled by a crimson aureole on a horizon that seems to stretch full circle, and a sun that appears to rise below eye level. (New Yorkers are accustomed to seeing only fractured bits and pieces of sky.) From a hotel of sophisticated excellence that might be Claridge's-on-the-prairie, furnished with an owner-oilman's private collection of redundant boiserie and Sevres, one drives past fountains of detergent blue.

Due north on Main Street is "downtown," a roughly 20-block cluster of commercial towers begun in the 1920s and thirties and doubled in size and numbers in the 1960s and seventies, sleek symbols of prosperity and power. They are paradigms of the corporate style. The names they bear are Tenneco, Shell Plaza, Pennzoil Place, Humble, and Houston Natural Gas, and their architects have national reputations.

In another paradox, in this country of open spaces, the towers are increasingly connected by tunnels underground. Houston's environment is strikingly "internalized" because of the area's extremes of heat and humidity. It is the indoors one seeks for large parts of the year, and that fact has profoundly affected how the city builds and lives.

The enclosed shopping center is Houston's equivalent of the traditional town plaza—a clear trend across the country. The Post Oak Galleria, a $20-million product of Houston developer Gerald Hines and architects Hellmuth, Obata and Kassabaum, with Neuhaus and Taylor, is characteristically large and opulent. A 420,000-square-foot, 600-foot long, three-level, covered shopping mall, it is part of a 33-acre commercial, office, and hotel complex off the West Loop Freeway, at the city's western edge.

The Galleria is the place to see and be seen: it is meeting place, promenade, and social center. It also offers restaurants, baubles from Tiffany and Nieman-Marcus, a galaxy of specialty shops equivalent to Madison Avenue, and an ice-skating rink comparable to Rockefeller Center's, all under a chandelier-hung glass roof. One can look up from the ice-skating to see joggers circling the oblong glass dome. The Galleria is now slated for an expansion larger than the original.

These enterprises do not require outdoor settings; they are magnets that can be placed anywhere. In fact, one seeks orientation by the freeways and their man-made landmarks (Southwest Freeway and Sharpstown, West Loop and Post Oak Tower) rather than by reference to organic patterns of growth. Climate, endless open topography, speculator economics and spectator consumerism, and, of course, the car have determined Houston's free-wheeling, vacuum-packed life and environment.

For spectator sports, one goes to the Astrodome to the southwest which has created its own environment—the Astrodomain [sic] of assiduously cultivated amusements and motels. Popular and commercial culture are well served in Houston. There is also high, or middle, culture, for which the "brutalist" forms of the Alley Theater by New York architect Ulrich Franzen, and the neutral packaging of Jones Hall for the performing arts, by the Houston firm of Caudill, Rowlett, Scott, have been created. They stand in the shadow of the downtown oil industry giants that have provided their funding.

Farther south on Main are the Fine Arts Museum, with its handsome extension by Mies van der Rohe, and the Contemporary Arts Association building, a sharp-edged, metal trapezoid by Gunnar Birkets. They cling together among odd vacant lots in a state of decaying or becoming, next to a psychoanalytic center.

Because the city has no zoning, these surreal juxtapositions prevail. A hamburger stand closes the formal vista of Philip Johnson's delicate, Miesian arcade at St. Thomas University. Transitional areas, such as Westheimer, not only mirror the city's untrammeled development in ten-year sections, but are freely altered as old houses are turned into new shops and restaurants, unhampered by zoning taboos. (Conventionally zoned cities simply rezone their deteriorating older residential neighborhoods to save their tax base and facilitate the same economic destiny. The process just takes a little longer.)

Houston's web of freeways is the consummate example of the twentieth-century phenomenon known as the commercial strip. The route of passage attracts sales, services, and schlock in continuous road-oriented structures—gas stations, drive-ins, and displays meant to catch the eye and fancy at 60 miles an hour. There are fixed and mobile signs, and signs larger than buildings ("buildingboards," according to students of the Pop environment). Style, extracted as symbols, becomes a kind of sign in itself, evoking images from Rapunzel to Monticello. There are miles of fluttering metallic pennants (used cars), a giant lobster with six shooters, cowboy hat, and scarf (seafood), a turning, life-size plaster bull (American International Charolais Association), and a revolving neon piano. The strip is full of intuitive wit, invention, and crass, but also real creativity—a breathtaking affront to normal sensibility that is never a bore.

Directly behind the freeways, one short turn takes the driver from the strip into pine and live oak-alleyed streets of comfortable and elegant residential communities (including the elite and affluent River Oaks). They have maintained their environmental purity by deed restrictions passed on from one generation of buyers to another.

Beyond these enclaves, anything goes. Residential development is a spin-the-wheel happening that hops, skips, and jumps outward, each project seemingly dropped from the sky—but always on the freeway. The southwest section, which was prairie before the 1950s, is now the American Dream incarnate. There is a continuing rivalry of you-name-it styles that favor French and Anglo-Saxon labels and details. If you live in Westminster, authentic-looking London street signs on high iron fences frame views of the flat Texas plains. You know you're home when you get to La Cour du Roi or Robin Hood Dell.

Because Houston is an urban invention, this kind of highly salable make-believe supplies instant history and architecture; it is an anchor to time and place where neither is defined. All of those values that accrue throughout centuries of civilization—identity, intimacy, scale, complexity, style—are simply created out of whole cloth, or whole prairie, with unabashed commercial eclecticism. How else to establish a sense of place or community, to indicate differences where none exist?

Houston is a continuous series of such cultural shocks. Its private patronage, on which the city depends for its public actions, has a cosmic range. There is the superb, *echt*-Houston eccentricity of Judge Roy Hofheinz's personal quarters in the Astrodome, done in a kind of Astro-baroque of throne chairs, gold phones, and temple dogs, with a pick-a-religion, fake stone chapel (good for bullfighters or politicians who want to meditate), shooting gallery, and presidential suite, tucked into the periphery of the stadium, complete with views of the Astros and Oilers. At the other end of the esthetic scale there is the Rothko Chapel, where the blood-dark paintings of the artist's pre-suicide days have been brought together by Dominique de Menil—a place of overwhelming, icy death. One welcomes the Texas sunshine.

Houston is not totally without planned features. It has large and handsome parks and the landscaped corridor of the Buffalo Bayou that are the result of philanthropic forethought. There are universities and a vast medical center.

But no one seems to feel the need for the public vision that older cities have of a hierarchy of places and buildings, an organized concept of function and form. Houston has a downtown singularly without amenities. The fact that money and population are flowing there from the rest of the country is considered cause for celebration, not for concern with the city's quality. This city bets on a different and brutal kind of distinction—of power, motion, and sheer energy. Its values are material fulfillment, mobility, and mass entertainment. Its returns are measured on its commercial investments. These contemporary ideals have little to do with the deeper or subtler aspects of the mind or spirit, or even with the more complex, human pleasure potential of a hedonistic culture.

When we build a new city, such as Houston, it is quite natural that we build in this image, using all of our hardware to serve its uses and desires. We create new values and new dimensions in time and space. The expanded, mobile city deals in distance and discontinuity; it "explodes" community. It substitutes fantasy for history. Houston is devoted to moon shots, not moon-viewing. The result is a significant, instructive, and disquieting city form.

What Houston possesses to an exceptional degree is an extraordinary, unlimited vitality. One wishes that it had a larger conceptual reach, that social and cultural and human patterns were as well understood as dollar dynamism. But this kind of vitality is the distinguishing mark of a great city in any age. And Houston today is the American present and future. It is an exciting and disturbing place.

QUESTIONS FOR READING, RESPONDING, AND WRITING

Summarizing Main Points

1. According to Huxtable, the absence of zoning laws and the plethora of freeways have been most responsible for Houston's distinctive style. Find examples of how these two factors have influenced the city. Is there a single feature of Houston that might be accounted for by both the absence of zoning laws and the many freeways?
2. List the ways that Houston is different from other American cities, according to Huxtable. How does Huxtable suggest it is similar to them?

Analyzing Methods of Discourse

1. "Houston is a study of paradoxes," according to Huxtable. What evidence does she present to support her claim? How do her sentence structure and choice

of details help suggest the contradictory nature of Houston? Find examples to support your statements.

2. What is Huxtable's attitude toward Houston? Would she live there? List the ways she lets the reader know what her attitude is.

Focusing on the Field

1. List the ways that Huxtable's knowledge of architecture helps her explain what is distinctive about Houston. Does she notice more than someone unfamiliar with architecture might? Or is she simply more concerned with the reasons behind Houston's distinctive features? What overriding reason for Houston's unique qualities does she offer? Is this reason a cultural or an architectural one?

2. Compare Huxtable's remarks about shopping centers to Joan Didion's in "On the Mall" and consider the difference in their approaches: Didion's is personal observation while Huxtable's is analysis and explanation. Why do you think each writer chooses her particular method of development?

Writing Assignments

1. Examine the city or town where you live now. Do you recognize any "paradoxes"? What would you consider the main feature of your area? Can you offer any reasons why this might be the main feature? Write an essay in which you describe your area and answer the questions above.

2. Write an essay in which you argue that Huxtable's description of Houston does or does not fit John A. Kouwenhoven's advocacy of "What's American about America?"

Barbara Tuchman

THE TROJAN HORSE

As a historian, Barbara Tuchman prides herself on being a good storyteller. Two Pulitzer Prize–winning histories, *The Guns of August* (1962) and *Sand Against the Wind: Stillwell and the American Experience in China, 1911–1945* (1971), both of which were also Book-of-the-Month Club selections, and the best-selling *A Distant Mirror: The Calamitous Fourteenth Century* (1978) attest to the accuracy of her self-assessment. Though she always does her own research and visits the appropriate sites, she believes that the result of such work—of which the following essay is a fine illustration—should always be a narrative "with a beginning, middle and end . . . plus an element of suspense to keep a reader turning the pages." She attributes her talent for history-writing to a lack of academic training in the subject. She explains, "I never took a Ph.D. It's what saved me, I think. If I had taken a doctoral degree, it would have stifled any writing capacity." Her writing capacity is unquestioned. In addition to the three books mentioned above, Tuchman has also published several other histories, which include *Bible and Sword: England and Palestine from the Bronze Age to Balfour* (1956), *The Proud Tower: A Portrait of the World Before the War, 1890–1914* (1966), and *Notes from China* (1972). She also contributes to such periodicals as *Harper's, American Scholar,* and *Foreign Affairs.*

Born in 1912 in New York City, Tuchman took a B.A. at Radcliffe in 1933, and went on to become a research and editorial assistant at New York's Institute of Pacific Relations. In 1935, she joined the *Nation* as a staff writer and foreign correspondent, eventually becoming an editor there from 1943 to 1945. She has also been a lecturer at Harvard University, University of California, and the U.S. Naval War College, and in 1980 became the first woman appointed as a Jefferson Lecturer by the National Endowment for the Humanities. She has also been president of the Society of American Historians and of the American Academy of Arts and Letters. In addition to her Pulitzer Prizes, she has been awarded a gold medal for history by the American Academy of Arts and Sciences and has accepted numerous honorary degrees.

The most famous story of the Western world, the prototype of all tales of human conflict, the epic that belongs to all people and all times since— and even before—literacy began, contains the legend, with or without some vestige of historical foundation, of the Wooden Horse.

The Trojan War has supplied themes to all subsequent literature and art from Euripides' heart-rending tragedy of *The Trojan Women* to Eugene O'Neill, Jean Giraudoux and the still enthralled writers of our time. Through Aeneas in Virgil's sequel, it provided the legendary founder and national epic of Rome. A favorite of medieval romancers, it supplied William Caxton with the subject of the first book printed in English, and Chaucer (and later Shakespeare) with the setting, if not the story, of Troilus and Cressida. Racine and Goethe tried to fathom the miserable sacrifice of Iphigenia. Wandering Ulysses inspired writers as far apart as Tennyson and James Joyce. Cassandra and avenging Electra have been made the protagonists of German drama and opera. Some thirty-five poets and scholars have offered English translations since George Chapman in Elizabethan times first opened the realms of gold. Countless painters have found the Judgment of Paris an irresistible scene, and as many poets fallen under the spell of the beauty of Helen.

All of human experience is in the tale of Troy, or Ilium, first put into epic form by Homer around 850–800 B.C. Although the gods are its motivators, what it tells us about humanity is basic, even though—or perhaps because—the circumstances are ancient and primitive. It has endured deep in our minds and memories for twenty-eight centuries because it speaks to us of ourselves, not least when least rational. It mirrors, in the judgment of another storyteller, John Cowper Powys, "what happened, is happening and will happen to us all, from the very beginning until the end of human life upon this earth."

Troy falls at last after ten years of futile, indecisive, noble, mean, tricky, bitter, jealous and only occasionally heroic battle. As the culminating instrumentality for the fall, the story brings in the Wooden Horse. The episode of the Horse exemplifies policy pursued contrary to self-interest—in the face of urgent warning and a feasible alternative. Occurring in this earliest chronicle of Western man, it suggests that such pursuit is an old and inherent human habit. The story first appears, not in the *Iliad*, which ends before the climax of the war, but in the *Odyssey* through the mouth of the blind bard Demodocus, who, at Odysseus' bidding, recounts the exploit to the group gathered in the palace of Alcinous. Despite Odysseus' high praise of the bard's narrative talents, the story is told rather baldly, as if the main facts were already familiar. Minor details are added elsewhere in the poem by Odysseus himself and in what seems an impossible flight of fancy by two other participants, Helen and Menelaus.

Lifted by Homer out of dim mists and memories, the Wooden Horse instantly caught the imagination of his successors in the next two or three centuries and inspired them to elaborate on the episode, notably and importantly by the addition of Laocoon in one of the most striking incidents of the entire epic. He appears earliest in *The Sack of Ilium* by Arctinus of Miletus, composed probably a century or so after Homer. Personifying the Voice of Warning, Laocoon's dramatic role becomes central to the episode of the Horse in all versions thereafter.

The full story as we know it of the device that finally accomplished the fall of Troy took shape in Virgil's *Aeneid*, completed in 20 B.C. By that time the tale incorporated the accumulated versions of more than a thousand years. Arising from geographically separate districts of the Greek world, the various versions are full of discrepancies and inconsistencies. Greek legend is hopelessly contradictory. Incidents do not conform necessarily to narrative logic; motive and behavior are often irreconcilable. We must take the story of the Wooden Horse as it comes, as Aeneas told it to the enraptured Dido, and as it passed, with further revisions and embellishments by Latin successors, to the Middle Ages and from the medieval romancers to us.

It is the ninth year of inconclusive battle on the plains of Troy, where the Greeks are besieging the city of King Priam. The gods are intimately involved with the belligerents as a result of jealousies generated ten years earlier when Paris, Prince of Troy, offended Hera and Athena by giving the golden apple as the award of beauty to Aphrodite, goddess of love. Not playing fair (as the Olympians, molded by men, were not disposed to), she had promised him, if he gave her the prize, the most beautiful woman in the world as his bride. This led, as everyone knows, to Paris' abduction of Helen, wife of Menelaus, King of Sparta, and the forming of a federation under his brother, the Greek overlord Agamemnon, to enforce her return. War followed when Troy refused.

Taking sides and playing favorites, potent but fickle, conjuring deceptive images, altering the fortunes of battle to suit their desires, whispering, tricking, falsifying, even inducing the Greeks through deceit to continue when they are ready to give up and go home, the gods keep the combatants engaged while heroes die and homelands suffer. Poseidon, ruler of the sea, who, with Apollo, was said to have built Troy and its walls, has turned against the Trojans because their first king failed to pay him for his work and further because they have stoned to death a priest of his cult for failure to offer sacrifices necessary to arouse the waves against the Greek invasion. Apollo, on the other hand, still favors Troy as its traditional protector, the more so because Agamemnon has angered him by seizing the daughter of a priest of Apollo for his bed. Athena, busiest and most influential of all, is unforgivingly anti-Trojan and pro-Greek because of Paris' original offense. Zeus, ruler of Olympus, is not a strong partisan, and when appealed to by one or another of his extended family, is capable of exercising his influence on either side.

In rage and despair, Troy mourns the death of Hector, slain by Achilles, who brutally drags his corpse by the heels three times around the walls in the dust of his chariot wheels. The Greeks are no better off. The angry Achilles, their champion fighter, shot in his vulnerable heel by Paris with a poisoned arrow, dies. His armor, to be conferred on the most deserving of the Greeks, is awarded to Odysseus, the wisest, instead of to Ajax, the most valorous, whereupon Ajax, maddened by insulted pride, kills himself. His companions' spirits fail and many of the Greek host counsel departure, but Athena puts a stop to that. On her advice, Odysseus proposes a last effort to take Troy by a stratagem—the building of a wooden horse large enough to hold twenty or fifty (or in some versions, as many as three hundred) armed men concealed inside. His plan is for the rest of the army to pretend to sail for home while in fact hiding their ships offshore behind the island of Tenedos. The Wooden Horse will carry an inscription dedicating it to Athena as the Greeks' offering in the hope of her aid in ensuring their safe return home. The figure is intended to excite the veneration of the Trojans, to whom the horse is a sacred animal and who may well be moved to conduct it to their own temple of Athena within the city. If so, the sacred veil said to surround and protect the city will be torn apart, the concealed Greeks will emerge, open the gates to their fellows, summoned by signal, and seize their final opportunity.

In obedience to Athena, who appears to one Epeius in a dream with orders to build the Horse, the "thing of guile" is completed in three days, aided by the goddess' "divine art." Odysseus persuades the rather reluctant leaders and bravest soldiers to enter by rope ladder during the night and take their places "halfway between victory and death."

At dawn, Trojan scouts discover that the siege is lifted and the enemy gone, leaving only the strange and awesome figure at their gates. Priam and his council come out to examine it and fall into anxious and divided discussion. Taking the inscription at face value, Thymoetes, one of the elders, recommends bringing the Horse to Athena's temple in the citadel. "Knowing better," Capys, another of the elders, objects, saying Athena had for too long favored the Greeks, and Troy would be well advised either to burn the pretended offering at once or break it open with brazen axes to see what the belly contains. Here was the feasible alternative.

Hesitant, yet fearful of desecrating Athena's property, Priam decides in favor of bringing the Horse into the city, although the walls must be breached or, in another version, the lintel of the Scean Gate removed to allow it to enter. This is the first warning omen, for it has been prophesied that if ever the Scean lintel is taken down, Troy will fall.

Excited voices from the gathering crowd cry, "Burn it! Hurl it over the rocks into the sea! Cut it open!" Opponents shout as loudly in favor of preserving what they take to be a sacred image. Then occurs a dramatic intervention. Laocoon, a priest of Apollo's temple, comes rushing down from the citadel crying in alarm, "Are you mad, wretched people? Do you think the foe has gone? Do you think gifts of the Greeks lack treachery? What was Odysseus' reputation?

> "Either the Greeks are hiding in this monster,
> Or it's some trick of war, a spy or engine,
> To come down on the city. Tricky business
> Is hiding in it. Do not trust it, Trojans;
> Do not believe this horse. Whatever it may be,
> I fear the Greeks, even when bringing gifts."

With that warning that has echoed down the ages, he flings his spear with all his strength at the Horse, in whose flank it sticks quivering and setting off a moaning sound from the frightened souls within. The blow almost split the wood and let light into the interior, but fate or the gods blunted it; or else, as Aeneas says later, Troy would still be standing.

Just as Laocoon has convinced the majority, guards drag in Sinon, an ostensibly terrified Greek who pretends he has been left behind through the enmity of Odysseus, but who has actually been planted by Odysseus as part of his plan. Asked by Priam to tell the truth about the Wooden Horse, Sinon swears it is a genuine offering to Athena which the Greeks deliberately made huge so the Trojans would *not* take it into their city because that would signify an ultimate Trojan victory. If the Trojans destroy it they will doom themselves, but if they bring it inside they will ensure their city's safety.

Swung around by Sinon's story, the Trojans are wavering between the warning and the false persuasion when a fearful portent convinces them that Laocoon is wrong. Just as he cautions that Sinon's tale is another trick put into his mouth by Odysseus, two horrible serpents rise in gigantic black spirals out of the waves and advance across the sands.

> *Their burning eyes suffused with blood and fire,*
> *Their darting tongues licking their hissing mouths.*

As the crowd watches paralyzed in terror, they make straight for Laocoon and his two young sons, "fastening their fangs in those poor bodies," coiling around the father's waist and neck and arms and, as he utters strangled inhuman cries, crush him to death. The appalled watchers are now nearly all moved to believe that the ghastly event is Laocoon's punishment for sacrilege in striking what must indeed be a sacred offering.

Troublesome even to the ancient poets, the serpents have defied explanation; myth has its mysteries too, not always resolved. Some narrators say they were sent by Poseidon at Athena's request to prove that his animus against the Trojans was equal to hers. Others say they were sent by Apollo to warn the Trojans of approaching doom (although, since the effect worked the other way, this seems to have a built-in illogic). Virgil's explanation is that Athena herself was responsible in order to convince the Trojans of Sinon's story, thus sealing their doom, and in confirmation he has the serpents take refuge in her temple after the event. So difficult was the problem of the serpents that some collaborators of the time suggested that Laocoon's fate had nothing to do with the Wooden Horse, but was owed to the quite extraneous sin of profaning Apollo's temple by sleeping with his wife in front of the god's image.

The blind bard of the *Odyssey*, who knows nothing of Laocoon, simply states that the argument in favor of welcoming the Horse had to prevail because Troy was ordained to perish—or, as we might interpret it, that mankind in the form of Troy's citizens is addicted to pursuing policy contrary to self-interest.

The instrumentality of the serpents is not a fact of history to be explained, but a work of imagination, one of the most forceful ever described. It produced, in agonized and twisted marble, so vivid that the victims' cries seem almost to be heard, a major masterpiece of classical sculpture. Seeing it in the palace of the Emperor Titus in Rome, Pliny the Elder thought it a work to be preferred "above all that the arts of painting and sculpture have produced." Yet the statue is dumb as to cause and significance. Sophocles wrote a tragedy on the theme of Laocoon but the text disappeared and his thoughts are lost. The existence of the legend can tell us only one thing: that Laocoon was fatally punished for perceiving the truth and warning of it.

While on Priam's orders ropes and rollers are prepared to pull the Horse into the city, unnamed forces still try to warn Troy. Four times at the Gate's threshold, the Horse comes to a halt and four times from the interior the clang of arms sounds, yet though the halts are an omen, the Trojans press on, "heedless and blind with frenzy." They breach the walls and the Gate, unconcerned at thus tearing the sacred veil because they believe its protection is no longer needed. In post-*Aeneid* versions, other portents follow: smoke rises stained with blood, tears flow from the statues of the gods, towers groan as if in pain, mist covers the stars, wolves and jackals howl, laurel withers in the temple of Apollo, but the Trojans take no alarm. Fate drives fear from their minds "so that they might meet their doom and be destroyed."

That night they celebrate, feasting and drinking with carefree hearts. A last chance and a last warning are offered. Cassandra, Priam's daughter, possesses the gift of prophecy conferred on her by Apollo, who, on falling in love with her, gave it in exchange for her promise to lie with him. When Cassandra, dedicating herself to virginity, went back on her promise, the offended god added to his gift a curse providing that her prophecies would never be believed. Ten years before, when Paris first sailed for Sparta, Cassandra had indeed foretold that his voyage would bring doom upon his house, but Priam had paid no attention. "O miserable people," she now cries, "poor fools, you do not understand at all your evil fate." They are acting senselessly, she tells them, toward the very thing "that has your destruction within it." Laughing and drunken, the Trojans tell her she talks too much "windy nonsense." In the fury of the seer ignored, she seizes an axe and a burning brand and rushes at the Wooden Horse but is restrained before she can reach it.

Heavy with wine, the Trojans sleep. Sinon creeps from the hall and opens the trap door of the Horse to release Odysseus and his companions, some of whom, cooped up in the blackness, have been weeping under the tension and "trembling in their legs." They spread through the city to open the remaining gates while Sinon signals to the ships with a flaming torch. In ferocious triumph when the forces are joined, the Greeks fall upon the sleeping foe, slaughtering right and left, burning houses, loot-ing treasure, raping the women. Greeks die too as the Trojans wield▨ swords, but the advantage has been gained by the invaders. Everyw▨ the dark blood flows, hacked corpses cover the ground, the crackle of flames rises over the shrieks and groans of the wounded and the wailing of women.

The tragedy is total; no heroics or pity mitigate the end. Achilles' son Pyrrhus (also called Neoptolemus), "mad with murder," pursues the wounded and fleeing Polites, Priam's youngest son, down a corridor of the palace and, "eager for the last thrust," hacks off his head in the sight of his father. When venerable Priam, slipping in his son's blood, flings a feeble spear, Pyrrhus kills him too. The wives and mothers of the defeated are dragged off in indignity to be allotted to the enemy chiefs along with other booty. Hecuba the Queen falls to Odysseus, Hector's wife, Andromache, to the murderer Pyrrhus. Cassandra, raped by another Ajax in the temple of Athena, is dragged out with hair flying and hands bound to be given to Agamemnon and ultimately to kill herself rather than serve his lust. Worse is the fate of Polyxena, another daughter of Priam once desired by Achilles and now demanded by his shade, who is sacrificed on his tomb by the victors. The crowning pity is reserved for the child Astyanax, son of Hector and Andromache, who on Odysseus' orders that no hero's son shall survive to seek vengeance, is hurled from the battlements to his death. Sacked and burned, Troy is left in ruins. Mount Ida groans; the river Xanthus weeps.

Singing of their victory that has ended the long war at last, the Greeks board their ships, offering prayers to Zeus for a safe return home. Few obtain it, but rather, through a balancing fate, suffer disaster parallel to that of their victims. Athena, enraged by the rapist's profanation of her temple, or because the Greeks, careless in victory, have failed to offer prayers to her, asks Zeus for the right to punish them and, given lightning and thunderbolts, raises the sea to a storm. Ships founder and sink or are smashed on the rocks, island shores are strewn with wrecks and the sea with floating corpses. The second Ajax is among those drowned; Odysseus, blown off course, is storm-tossed, shipwrecked and lost for twenty years; arriving home, Agamemnon is murdered by his faithless wife and her lover. The bloodthirsty Pyrrhus is killed by Orestes at Delphi. Curiously, Helen, the cause of it all, survives untouched in perfect beauty, to be forgiven by the bewitched Menelaus and to regain royal husband, home and prosperity. Aeneas too escapes. Because of his filial devotion in carrying his aged father on his back after the battle, he is allowed by Agamemnon to embark with his followers and follow the destiny that will lead him to Rome. With the circular justice that man likes to impose upon history, a survivor of Troy founds the city-state that will conquer Troy's conquerors.

How much fact lies behind the Trojan epic? Archeologists, as we know, have uncovered nine levels of an ancient settlement on the Asian shore of the Hellespont, or Dardanelles, opposite Gallipoli. Its site at the crossroads of Bronze Age trade routes would invite raids and sack and account for the evidence at different levels of frequent demolition and rebuilding. Level VIIA, containing fragments of gold and other artifacts of a royal city, and exhibiting signs of having been violently destroyed by human hands, has been identified as Priam's Troy and its fall dated near the end of the Bronze Age, around 1200 B.C. It is quite possible that Greek mercantile and maritime ambitions came into conflict with Troy and that the overlord of the several communities of the Greek peninsula could have gathered allies for a concerted attack on the city across the straits. The abduction of Helen, as Robert Graves suggests, might have been real in its retaliation for some prior Greek raid.

These were Mycenaean times in Greece, when Agamemnon, son of Atreus, was King at Mycenae in the citadel with the Lion Gate. Its dark remains still stand on a hill just south of Corinth where poppies spring so deeply red they seem forever stained by the blood of the Atridae. Some violent cause, in roughly the same age as the fall of Troy but probably over a more extended period, ended the primacy of Mycenae and of Knossus in Crete with which it was linked. Mycenaean culture was literate as we know since the script called Linear B found in the ruins of Knossus has been identified as an early form of Greek.

The period following the Mycenaean collapse is a shadowy void of some two centuries called the Greek Dark Ages, whose only communication to us is through shards and artifacts. For some unexplained reason, written language seems to have vanished completely, although recitals of the exploits of ancestors of a past heroic age were clearly transmitted orally down the generations. Recovery, stimulated by the arrival of the Dorian people from the north, began around the 10th century B.C. and from that recovery burst the immortal celebrator whose epic fashioned from familiar tales and legends of his people started the stream of Western literature.

Homer is generally pictured as reciting his narrative poems to accompaniment on the lyre, but the 16,000 lines of the *Iliad* and 12,000 of the *Odyssey* were certainly also either written down by himself or dictated by him to a scribe. Texts were undoubtedly available to the several bards of the next two or three centuries who, in supplementary tales of Troy, introduced material from oral tradition to fill in the gaps left by Homer. The sacrifice of Iphigenia, Achilles' vulnerable heel, the appearance of Penthesilea, Queen of the Amazons, as an ally of Troy and many of the most memorable episodes belong to these poems of the post-Homeric cycle which have come down to us only through summaries made in the

2nd century A.D. of texts since lost. The *Cypria,* named for Cyprus, home of its supposed author, is the fullest and earliest of these, followed by, among others, *The Sack of Ilium* by Arctinus and the *Little Iliad* by a bard of Lesbos. After them, lyric poets and the three great tragic dramatists took up the Trojan themes, and Greek historians discussed the evidence. Latin authors elaborated further both before and especially after Virgil, adding jeweled eyes for the Wooden Horse and other glittering fables. Distinction between history and fable faded when the heroes of Troy and their adventures splendidly filled the tapestries and chronicles of the Middle Ages. Hector becomes one of the Nine Worthies on a par with Julius Caesar and Charlemagne.

The question of whether a historical underpinning existed for the Wooden Horse was raised by Pausanias, a Latin traveler and geographer with a true historian's curiosity, who wrote a *Description of Greece* in the 2nd century A.D. He decided the Horse must have represented some kind of "war machine" or siege engine because, he argues, to take the legend at face value would be to impute "utter folly" to the Trojans. The question still provokes speculation in the 20th century. If the siege engine was a battering ram, why did not the Greeks use it as such? If it was the kind of housing that brought assaulters up to the walls, surely it would have been even greater folly for the Trojans to take it in without breaking it open first. One can be lured this way down endless paths of the hypothetical. The fact is that although early Assyrian monuments depict such a device, there is no evidence that any kind of siege engine was used in Greek warfare in Mycenaean or Homeric times. That anachronism would not have worried Pausanias, because it was normal in his, and indeed in much later, days to view the past dressed and equipped in the image of the present.

Ruse was indeed used in the siege of walled or fortified places in biblical lands in the warfare of the 2nd millenium B.C. (2000–1000), which covers the century generally given for the Trojan War. If unable to penetrate by force, the attacking army would attempt to enter by cunning, using some trick to gain the confidence of the defenders, and it has been said by a military historian that "the very existence of legends concerning the conquest of cities by stratagem testifies to a core of truth."

Although silent on the Wooden Horse, Herodotus in the 5th century B.C. wished to attribute more rational behavior to the Trojans than Homer allowed them. On the basis of what priests of Egypt told him in the course of his investigation, he states that Helen was never in Troy at all during the war, but remained in Egypt, where she had landed with Paris when their ship was blown off course following her abduction from Sparta. The local King, disgusted by Paris' ignoble seduction of a host's wife, ordered him to depart; only a phantom Helen came with him to

Troy. Had she been real, Herodotus argues, surely Priam and Hector would have delivered her up to the Greeks rather than suffer so many deaths and calamities. They could not have been "so infatuated" as to sustain all that woe for her sake or for the sake of Paris, who was anything but admired by his family.

There speaks reason. As the Father of History, Herodotus might have known that in the lives of his subjects, common sense is rarely a determinant. He argues further that the Trojans assured the Greek envoys that Helen was not in Troy but were not believed because the gods wished for the war and the destruction of Troy to show that great wrongs bring great punishment. Probing for the meaning of the legend, here perhaps he comes closer to it.

In the search for meaning we must not forget that the gods (or God, for that matter) are a concept of the human mind; they are the creatures of man, not vice versa. They are needed and invented to give meaning and purpose to the puzzle that is life on earth, to explain strange and irregular phenomena of nature, haphazard events and, above all, irrational human conduct. They exist to bear the burden of all things that cannot be comprehended except by supernatural intervention or design.

This is especially true of the Greek pantheon, whose members are daily and intimately entangled with human beings and are susceptible to all the emotions of mortals if not to their limitations. What makes the gods so capricious and unprincipled is that in the Greek conception they are devoid of moral and ethical values—like a man lacking a shadow. Consequently, they have no compunction about maliciously deceiving mortals or causing them to violate oaths and commit other disloyal and disgraceful acts. Aphrodite's magic caused Helen to elope with Paris, Athena tricked Hector into fighting Achilles. What is shameful or foolish in mortals is attributed by them to the influence of the gods. "To the gods I owe this woeful war," laments Priam, forgetting that he could have removed the cause by sending Helen home at any time (presuming that she was there, as she very actively was in the Homeric cycle) or by yielding her when Menelaus and Odysseus came to demand her delivery.

The gods' interference does not acquit man of folly; rather, it is man's device for transferring the responsibility for folly. Homer understood this when he made Zeus complain in the opening section of the *Odyssey* how lamentable it was that men should blame the gods as the source of their troubles, "when it is through blindness of their own hearts" (or specifically their "greed and folly" in another translation) that sufferings "beyond that which is ordained" are brought upon them. This is a notable statement for, if the results are indeed worse than what fate had in store, it means that choice and free will were operating, not some implacable predestination. As an example, Zeus cites the case of

Aegisthus, who stole Agamemnon's wife and murdered the King on his homecoming, "though he knew the ruin this would entail since we ourselves sent Hermes to warn him neither to kill the man nor to make love to his wife, for Orestes when he grew up was bound to avenge his father and desire his patrimony." In short, though Aegisthus well knew what evils would result from his conduct, he proceeded nevertheless, and paid the price.

"Infatuation," as Herodotus suggested, is what robs man of reason. The ancients knew it and the Greeks had a goddess for it. Named Atē, she was the daughter—and significantly in some genealogies, the eldest daughter—of Zeus. Her mother was Eris, or Discord, goddess of Strife (who in some versions is another identity of Atē). The daughter is the goddess, separately or together, of Infatuation, Mischief, Delusion and Blind Folly, rendering her victims "incapable of rational choice" and blind to distinctions of morality and experience.

Given her combined heritage, Atē had potent capacity for harm and was in fact the original cause, prior to the Judgment of Paris, of the Trojan War, the prime struggle of the ancient world. Drawn from the earliest versions—the *Iliad*, the *Theogony* of Hesiod, roughly contemporary with Homer and the major authority on Olympian genealogy, and the *Cypria*—the tale of Atē ascribes her initial act to spite at not being invited by Zeus to the wedding of Peleus and the sea-nymph Thetis, future parents of Achilles. Entering the banquet hall unbidden, she maliciously rolls down the table the Golden Apple of Discord inscribed "For the Fairest," immediately setting off the rival claims of Hera, Athena and Aphrodite. As the husband of one and father of another of the quarreling ladies, Zeus, not wishing to invite trouble for himself by deciding the issue, sends the three disputants to Mount Ida, where a handsome young shepherd, reportedly adroit in matters of love, can make the difficult judgment. This, of course, is Paris, whose rustic phase is owed to circumstances that need not concern us here and from whose choice flows the conflict so much greater than perhaps even Atē intended.*

Undeterred from mischief, Atē on another occasion devised a com-

---

*In other versions, the origins of the war are associated with the Flood legend that circulated throughout Asia Minor, probably emanating from the region of the Euphrates, which frequently overflowed. Determined to eliminate the unsatisfactory human species, or alternatively, according to the *Cypria*, to "thin out" the population, which was overburdening the all-nurturing earth, Zeus decided upon "the great struggle of the Ilian war, that its load of death might empty the world." He therefore contrived or took advantage of the goddesses' quarrel over the Apple to bring the war about. Euripides adopts this version when he makes Helen say in the play named for her that Zeus arranged the war that "he might lighten mother earth of her myriad hosts of men." Evidently, very early, there must have been a deep sense of human unworthiness to produce these legends.

plicated piece of trickery by which the birth of Zeus' son Heracles was delayed and an inferior child brought forth ahead of him, thus depriving Heracles of his birthright. Furious at the trick (which does indeed seem capricious even for an immortal), Zeus flung Atē out of Olympus, henceforward to live on earth among mankind. On her account the earth is called the Meadow of Atē—not the Meadow of Aphrodite, or the Garden of Demeter, or the Throne of Athena or some other more pleasing title, but, as the ancients already sadly knew it to be, the realm of folly.

Greek myths take care of every contingency. According to a legend told in the *Iliad*, Zeus, repenting of what he had done, created four daughters called *Litai*, or Prayers for Pardon, who offer mortals the means of escape from their folly, but only if they respond. "Lame, wrinkled things with eyes cast down," the Litai follow Atē, or passionate Folly (sometimes translated Ruin or Sin), as healers.

> *If a man*
> *Reveres the daughters of Zeus when they come near,*
> *He is rewarded and his prayers are heard;*
> *But if he spurns them and dismisses them*
> *They make their way back to Zeus again and ask*
> *That Folly dog that man till suffering*
> *Has taken arrogance out of him.*

Meanwhile, Atē came to live among men and lost no time in causing Achilles' famous quarrel with Agamemnon and his ensuing anger, which became the mainspring of the *Iliad* and has always seemed so disproportionate. When at last the feud which has so damaged the Greek cause and prolonged the war is reconciled, Agamemnon blames Atē, or Delusion, for his original infatuation for the girl he took from Achilles.

> *Delusion, the elder daughter of Zeus; the accursed*
> *Who deludes all and leads them astray. . . .*
> *. . . took my wife away from me.*
> *She has entangled others before me—*

and, we might add, many since, the Litai notwithstanding. She appears once again in Brutus' fearful vision when, gazing on the murdered corpse at his feet, he foresees how "Caesar's spirit, raging for revenge with Atē by his side, shall cry 'Havoc' and let slip the dogs of war."

Anthropologists have subjected myth to infinite classification and some wilder theorizing. As the product of the psyche, it is said to be the means of bringing hidden fears and wish fulfillments into the open or of reconciling us to the human condition or of revealing the contradictions and problems, social and personal, that people face in life. Myths are seen as "charters" or "rituals," or serving any number of other functions. All or some of this may or may not be valid; what we can be sure of is that myths are prototypes of human behavior and that one ritual they serve is that of the goat tied with a scarlet thread and sent off into the wilderness to carry away the mistakes and the sins of mankind.

Legend partakes of myth and of something else, a historical connection, however faint and far away and all but forgotten. The Wooden Horse is not myth in the sense of Cronus swallowing his children or Zeus transforming himself into a swan or a shower of gold for purposes of adultery. It is legend with no supernatural elements except for Athena's aid and the intrusion of the serpents, who were added, no doubt, to give the Trojans a reason for rejecting Laocoon's advice (and who are almost too compelling, for they seem to leave the Trojans with little option but to choose the course that contains their doom).

Yet the feasible alternative—that of destroying the Horse—is always open. Capys the Elder advised it before Laocoon's warning, and Cassandra afterward. Notwithstanding the frequent references in the epic to the fall of Troy being ordained, it was not fate but free choice that took the Horse within the walls. "Fate" as a character in legend represents the fulfillment of man's expectations of himself.

QUESTIONS FOR READING, RESPONDING, AND WRITING

Summarizing Main Points

1. According to Tuchman, what accounts for the popularity of the story of the fall of Troy?
2. Explain why the serpents who destroy Laocoon and his sons are "troublesome even to the ancient poets."

Analyzing Methods of Discourse

1. Tuchman, in her last sentence, says, " 'Fate' as a character in legend represents the fulfillment of man's expectations of himself." What specific sentences in the essay help prepare the reader for Tuchman's final conclusions?
2. List the ways that Laocoon and Cassandra are similar. Explain how those similarities reinforce Tuchman's main point.

Focusing on the Field

1. Tuchman makes every effort to be more than an armchair historian—that is, she has not only studied the literature surrounding the fall of Troy but she has quite obviously visited the area and studied what remains of Troy that she could find. List the examples she provides that suggest her personal involvement with her subject.

2. Tuchman, like all the best historians, does more than document the past. At what specific points in her essay does Tuchman allow the history of the Trojan Horse to reflect forward to events closer to our own time? Where exactly, during the course of her essay, does she support her contention that "all of human experience is in the tale of Troy"?

Writing Assignments

1. Read Samuel Eliot Morison's "History as Literary Art." In a short essay, argue that Tuchman's essay does or does not conform to Morison's standard of literary art.
2. Compare and contrast Tuchman's view of myths, as evidenced by "The Trojan Horse," with Bruno Bettelheim's in "Fairy Tale versus Myth." Consider in particular Tuchman's statement that "myth has its mysteries too, not always resolved."

Alan Bullock

THE YOUNG ADOLF HITLER

Born in England in 1914, Alan Louis Charles Bullock began his distinguished scholarly career at Oxford University where he graduated with first-class honors and a master's degree in arts (1938). He makes his home at St. Catherine's College, Oxford, where since 1960 he has been master of the college. In 1940, he married Hilda Yates Handy and began working as a diplomatic correspondent for the British Broadcasting Company. After five years with the BBC, Bullock became a fellow, dean, and tutor in modern history at Oxford.

The following selection comes from his influential book *Hitler, A Study in Tyranny,* first published in 1952 and since then revised several times. Bullock has also served as a general editor for *The Oxford History of Modern Europe* and has published works on Ernest Bevin, as well as *The Liberal Tradition* (1956). In *Hitler, A Study in Tyranny,* Bullock succeeds in providing a dispassionate study of one of history's leading monsters, a feat that doubtless tested Bullock's ability to remain objective to the fullest extent.

I

Adolf Hitler was born at half past six on the evening of 20 April 1889, in the Gasthof zum Pommer, an inn in the small town of Braunau on the River Inn which forms the frontier between Austria and Bavaria.

The Europe into which he was born and which he was to destroy gave an unusual impression of stability and permanence at the time of his birth. The Hapsburg Empire, of which his father was a minor official, had survived the storms of the 1860s, the loss of the Italian provinces, defeat by Prussia, even the transformation of the old Empire into the Dual Monarchy of Austria-Hungary. The Hapsburgs, the oldest of the great ruling houses, who had outlived the Turks, the French Revolution, and Napoleon, were a visible guarantee of continuity. The Emperor Franz Joseph had already celebrated the fortieth anniversary of his accession, and had still more than a quarter of a century left to reign.

The three republics Hitler was to destroy, the Austria of the Treaty of St Germain, Czechoslovakia, and Poland, were not yet in existence. Four great empires—the Hapsburg, the Hohenzollern, the Romanov, and the Ottoman—ruled over Central and Eastern Europe. The Bolshevik Revolution and the Soviet Union were not yet imagined: Russia was still the Holy Russia of the Tsars. In the summer of this same year, 1889, Lenin, a student of nineteen in trouble with the authorities, moved with his mother from Kazan to Samara. Stalin was a poor cobbler's son in Tiflis, Mussolini the six-year-old child of a blacksmith in the bleak Romagna.

Hitler's family, on both sides, came from the Waldviertel, a poor, remote country district, lying on the north side of the Danube, some fifty miles north-west of Vienna, between the Danube and the frontiers of Bohemia and Moravia. In this countryside of hills and woods, with few towns or railways, lived a peasant population cut off from the main arteries of Austrian life. It was from this country stock, with its frequent intermarriages, that Hitler sprang. The family name, possibly Czech in origin and spelled in a variety of ways, first appears in the Waldviertel in the first half of the fifteenth century.

The presumed grandfather of the future chancellor, Johann Georg Hiedler, seems to have been a wanderer who never settled down, but followed the trade of a miller in several places in Lower Austria. In the course of these wanderings he picked up with a peasant girl from the village of Strones, Maria Anna Schicklgruber, whom he married at Döllersheim in May 1842.

Five years earlier, in 1837, Maria had given birth to an illegitimate child, who was known by the name of Alois. According to the accepted tradition the father of this child was Johann Georg Hiedler. However, although Johann Georg married Maria, then forty-seven in 1842, he did not bother to legitimize the child, who continued to be known by his mother's maiden name of Schicklgruber until he was nearly forty and who was brought up at Spital in the house of his father's brother, Johann Nepomuk Hiedler.

In 1876 Johann Nepomuk took steps to legitimize the young man who had grown up in his house. He called on the parish priest at Döllersheim and persuaded him to cross out the word 'illegitimate' in the register and to append a statement signed by three witnesses that his brother Johann Georg Hiedler had accepted the paternity of the child Alois. This is by no means conclusive evidence, and, in all probability, we shall never know for certain who Adolf Hitler's grandfather, the father of Alois, really was. It has been suggested that he may have been a Jew, without definite proof one way or the other. However this may be, from the beginning of 1877, twelve years before Adolf was born, his father called himself Hitler and his son was never known by any other name until his opponents dug up this long-forgotten village scandal and tried, without justification, to label him with his grandmother's name of Schicklgruber.

Alois left his uncle's home at the age of thirteen to serve as a cobbler's apprentice in Vienna. But he did not take to a trade and by the time he was eighteen he had joined the Imperial Customs Service. From 1855 to 1895 Alois served as a customs officer in Braunau and other towns of Upper Austria. He earned the normal promotion and as a minor state official he had certainly moved up several steps in the social scale from his peasant origins.

As an official in the resplendent imperial uniform of the Hapsburg service Alois Hitler appeared the image of respectability. But his private life belied appearances.

In 1864 he married Anna Glass, the adopted daughter of another customs collector. The marriage was not a success. There were no children and, after a separation, Alois's wife, who was considerably older and had long been ailing, died in 1883. A month later Alois married a young hotel servant, Franziska Matzelberger, who had already borne him a son out of wedlock and who gave birth to a daughter, Angela, three months after their marriage.

Alois had no better luck with his second marriage. Within a year of her daughter's birth, Franziska was dead of tuberculosis. This time he waited half a year before marrying again. His third wife, Klara Pölzl, twenty-three years younger than himself, came from the village of Spital, where the Hitlers had originated. The two families were already related by marriage, and Klara herself was the granddaughter of the Johann Nepomuk Hiedler in whose house Alois had been brought up as a child. She had even lived with Alois and his first wife for a time at Braunau, but at the age of twenty had gone off to Vienna to earn her living as a domestic servant. An episcopal dispensation had to be secured for such a marriage between second cousins, but finally, on 7 January 1885, Alois

Hitler married his third wife, and on 17 May of the same year their first child, Gustav, was born at Braunau.

Adolf was the third child of Alois Hitler's third marriage. Gustav and Ida, both born before him, died in infancy; his younger brother, Edward, died when he was six; only his younger sister, Paula, born in 1896, lived to grow up. There were also, however, the two children of the second marriage with Franziska, Adolf Hitler's half-brother Alois, and his half-sister Angela. Angela was the only one of his relations with whom Hitler maintained any sort of friendship. She kept house for him at Berchtesgaden for a time, and it was her daughter, Geli Raubal, with whom Hitler fell in love.

When Adolf was born his father was over fifty and his mother was under thirty. Alois Hitler was not only very much older than Klara and her children, but hard, unsympathetic, and short-tempered. His domestic life—three wives, one fourteen years older than himself, one twenty-three years younger; a separation; and seven children, including one illegitimate child and two others born shortly after the wedding—suggest a difficult and passionate temperament. Towards the end of his life Alois Hitler seems to have become bitter over some disappointment, perhaps connected with another inheritance. He did not go back to his native district when he retired in 1895 at the age of fifty-eight. Instead he stayed in Upper Austria. From Passau, the German frontier town, where Alois Hitler held his last post, the family moved briefly to Hafeld-am-Traun and Lambach before they settled at Leonding, a village just outside Linz, overlooking the confluence of the Traun and the Danube. Here the retired customs official spent his remaining years, from 1899 to 1903, in a small house with a garden.

Hitler attempted to represent himself in *Mein Kampf*[1] as the child of poverty and privation. In fact, his father had a perfectly adequate pension and gave the boy the chance of a good education. After five years in primary schools, the eleven-year-old Adolf entered the Linz Realschule in September 1900. This was a secondary school designed to train boys for a technical or commercial career. At the beginning of 1903 Alois Hitler died, but his widow continued to draw a pension and was not left in need. Adolf left the Linz Realschule in 1904 not because his mother was too poor to pay the fees, but because his record at school was so indifferent that he had to accept a transfer to another school at Steyr, where he boarded out and finished his education at the age of sixteen. A year

---

[1]The edition referred to throughout this book is the unexpurgated translation by James Murphy (Hurst & Blackett, London, 1939).

before, on Whit Sunday 1904, he had been confirmed in the Roman Catholic Cathedral at Linz at his mother's wish.

In *Mein Kampf* Hitler makes much of a dramatic conflict between himself and his father over his ambition to become an artist.

> I did not want to become a civil servant, no, and again no. All attempt on my father's part to inspire me with love or pleasure in this profession by stories from his own life accomplished the exact opposite. . . . One day it became clear to me that I would become a painter, an artist. . . . My father was struck speechless. . . . 'Artist! No! Never as long as I live! . . .' My father would never depart from his 'Never!' And I intensified my 'Nevertheless!'[2]

There is no doubt that he did not get on well with his father, but it is unlikely that his ambition to become an artist (he was not fourteen when his father died) had much to do with it. A more probable explanation is that his father was dissatisfied with his school reports and made his dissatisfaction plain. Hitler glossed over his poor performance at school which he left without securing the customary Leaving Certificate. He found every possible excuse for himself, from illness and his father's tyranny to artistic ambition and political prejudice. It was a failure which rankled for a long time and found frequent expression in sneers at the 'educated gentlemen' with their diplomas and doctorates.

Forty years later, in the sessions at his Headquarters which produced the record of his table talk, Hitler several times recalled the teachers of his schooldays with contempt.

> They had no sympathy with youth; their one object was to stuff our brains and turn us into erudite apes like themselves. If any pupil showed the slightest trace of originality, they persecuted him relentlessly, and the only model pupils whom I have ever known have all been failures in later-life.[3]

For their part they seem to have had no great opinion of their most famous pupil. One of his teachers, Dr. Eduard Hümer, gave this description of the schoolboy Hitler at the time of his trial in 1923:

> I can recall the gaunt, pale-faced youth pretty well. He had definite talent, though in a narrow field. But he lacked self-discipline, being notoriously cantankerous, wilful, arrogant, and bad-tempered. He had obvious difficulty in fitting in at school. Moreover he was lazy . . . his enthusiasm for hard

---

[2]*Mein Kampf*, p. 22.
[3]7 September 1942, *Hitler's Table Talk, 1941–4* (London, 1953), pp. 698–9.

work evaporated all too quickly. He reacted with ill-concealed hostility to advice or reproof; at the same time, he demanded of his fellow pupils their unqualified subservience, fancying himself in the role of leader. . . .[4]

For only one of his teachers had Hitler anything good to say. In *Mein Kampf* he went out of his way to praise Dr. Leopold Pötsch, an ardent German nationalist who, Hitler claimed, had a decisive influence upon him:

> There we sat, often aflame with enthusiasm, sometimes even moved to tears. . . . The national fervour which we felt in our own small way was used by him as an instrument of our education. . . . It was because I had such a professor that history became my favourite subject.[5]

When Adolf finally left school in 1905, his widowed mother, then forty-six, sold the house at Leonding. With the proceeds of the sale and a monthly pension of 140 kronen, she was not ill provided for and she moved to a small flat, first in the Humboldtstrasse in Linz, then in 1907 to Urfahr, a suburb of Linz. There is no doubt that Hitler was fond of his mother, but she had little control over her self-willed son who refused to settle down to earn his living and spent the next two years indulging in dreams of becoming an artist or architect, living at home, filling his sketch book with entirely unoriginal drawings and elaborating grandiose plans for the rebuilding of Linz. His one friend was August Kubizek, the son of a Linz upholsterer, eight months younger than Hitler, who provided a willing and awe-struck audience for the ambitions and enthusiasms which Hitler poured out in their walks round Linz. Together they visited the theatre where Hitler acquired a life-long passion for Wagner's opera. Wagnerian romanticism and vast dreams of his own success as an artist and Kubizek's as a musician filled his mind. He lived in a world of his own, content to let his mother provide for his needs, scornfully refusing to concern himself with such petty mundane affairs as money or a job.

A visit to Vienna in May and June 1906 fired him with enthusiasm for the splendour of its buildings, its art galleries and Opera. On his return to Linz, he was less inclined than ever to find a job for himself. His ambition now was to go back to Vienna and enter the Academy of Fine Arts. His mother was anxious and uneasy but finally capitulated. In the autumn of 1907 he set off for Vienna a second time with high hopes for the future.

---

[4]Quoted in Franz Jetzinger: *Hitler's Youth* (London, 1958), pp. 68–9.
[5]*Mein Kampf*, p. 26.

His first attempt to enter the Academy in October 1907 was unsuccessful. The Academy's Classification List contains the entry:

> The following took the test with insufficient results or were not admitted. . . .
> Adolf Hitler, Braunau a.Inn, 20 April 1889.
> German. Catholic. Father, civil servant. 4 classes in *Realschule*. Few heads.
> Test drawing unsatisfactory.[6]

The result, he says in *Mein Kampf*, came as a bitter shock. The Director advised him to try his talents in the direction of architecture: he was not cut out to be a painter. But Hitler refused to admit defeat. Even his mother's illness (she was dying of cancer) did not bring him back to Linz. He returned only after her death (21 December 1907) in time for the funeral, and in February 1908 went back to Vienna, to resume his life as an 'art student.'

He was entitled to draw an orphan's pension and had the small savings left by his mother to fall back on. He was soon joined by his friend Kubizek whom he had prevailed upon to follow his example and seek a place at the Vienna Conservatoire. The two shared a room on the second floor of a house on the Stumpergasse, close to the West Station, in which there was hardly space for Kubizek's piano and Hitler's table.

Apart from Kubizek, Hitler lived a solitary life. He had no other friends. Women were attracted to him, but he showed complete indifference to them. Much of the time he spent dreaming or brooding. His moods alternated between abstracted preoccupation and outbursts of excited talk. He wandered for hours through the streets and parks, staring at buildings which he admired, or suddenly disappearing into the public library in pursuit of some new enthusiasm. Again and again, the two young men visited the Opera and the Burgtheater. But while Kubizek pursued his studies at the Conservatoire, Hitler was incapable of any disciplined or systematic work. He drew little, wrote more and even attempted to compose a music drama on the theme of Wieland the Smith. He had the artist's temperament without either talent, training, or creative energy.

In July 1908, Kubizek went back to Linz for the summer. A month later Hitler set out to visit two of his aunts in Spital. When they said goodbye, both young men expected to meet again in Vienna in the autumn. But when Kubizek returned to the capital, he could find no trace of his friend.

In mid-September Hitler had again applied for admission to the

---

[6]Quoted in Konrad Heiden: *Der Führer* (London, 1944), p. 48.

Academy of Art. This time, he was not even admitted to the examination. The Director advised him to apply to the School of Architecture, but there entry was barred by his lack of a school Leaving Certificate. Perhaps it was wounded pride that led him to avoid Kubizek. Whatever the reason, for the next five years he chose to bury himself in obscurity.

II

Vienna, at the beginning of 1909, was still an imperial city, capital of an Empire of fifty million souls stretching from the Rhine to the Dniester, from Saxony to Montenegro. The aristocratic baroque city of Mozart's time had become a great commercial and industrial centre with a population of two million people. Electric trams ran through its noisy and crowded streets. The massive, monumental buildings erected on the Ringstrasse in the last quarter of the nineteenth century reflected the prosperity and self-confidence of the Viennese middle class; the factories and poorer streets of the outer districts the rise of an industrial working class. To a young man of twenty, without a home, friends, or resources, it must have appeared a callous and unfriendly city: Vienna was no place to be without money or a job. The four years that now followed, from 1909 to 1913, Hitler himself says, were the unhappiest of his life. They were also in many ways the most important, the formative years in which his character and opinions were given definite shape.

Hitler speaks of his stay in Vienna as 'five years in which I had to earn my daily bread, first as a casual labourer then as a painter of little trifles.'[7] He writes with feeling of the poor boy from the country who discovers himself out of work. 'He loiters about and is hungry. Often he pawns or sells the last of his belongings. His clothes begin to get shabby—with the increasing poverty of his outward appearance he descends to a lower social level.'[8]

A little further on, Hitler gives another picture of his Vienna days. 'In the years 1909–10 I had so far improved my position that I no longer had to earn my daily bread as a manual labourer. I was now working independently as a draughtsman and painter in water-colours.' Hitler explains that he made very little money at this, but that he was master of his own time and felt that he was getting nearer to the profession he wanted to take up, that of an architect.

This is a very highly coloured account compared with the evidence of those who knew him then. Meagre though this is, it is enough to make

---

[7]*Mein Kampf*, p. 32.
[8]ibid., p. 35.

nonsense of Hitler's picture of himself as a man who had once earned his living by his hands and then by hard work turned himself into an art student.

According to Konrad Heiden, who was the first man to piece together the scraps of the independent evidence, in 1909, Hitler was obliged to give up the furnished room in which he had been living in the Simon Denk Gasse for lack of funds. In the summer he could sleep out, but with the coming of autumn he found a bed in a doss-house [flop-house] behind Meidling Station. At the end of the year, Hitler moved to a hostel for men started by a charitable foundation at 27 Meldemannstrasse, in the 20th district of Vienna, over on the other side of the city, close to the Danube. Here he lived, for the remaining three years of his stay in Vienna, from 1910 to 1913.

A few others who knew Hitler at this time have been traced and questioned, amongst them a certain Reinhold Hanisch, a tramp from German Bohemia, who for a time knew Hitler well. Hanisch's testimony is partly confirmed by one of the few pieces of documentary evidence which have been discovered for the early years. For in 1910, after a quarrel, Hitler sued Hanisch for cheating him of a small sum of money, and the records of the Vienna police court have been published, including (besides Hitler's own affidavit) the statement of Siegfried Loffner, another inmate of the hostel in Meldemannstrasse who testified that Hanisch and Hitler always sat together and were friendly.

Hanisch describes his first meeting with Hitler in the doss-house in Meidling in 1909. 'On the very first day there sat next to the bed that had been allotted to me a man who had nothing on except an old torn pair of trousers—Hitler. His clothes were being cleaned of lice, since for days he had been wandering about without a roof and in a terribly neglected condition.'9

Hanisch and Hitler joined forces in looking for work; they beat carpets, carried bags outside the West Station, and did casual labouring jobs, on more than one occasion shoveling snow off the streets. As Hitler had no overcoat, he felt the cold badly. Then Hanisch had a better idea. He asked Hitler one day what trade he had learned. ' "I am a painter", was the answer. Thinking that he was a house decorator, I said that it would surely be easy to make money at this trade. He was offended and answered that he was not that sort of painter, but an academician and an artist.' When the two moved to the Meldemannstrasse, 'we had to think out better ways of making money. Hitler proposed that we should fake pictures. He told me that already in Linz he had painted small landscapes in oil, had roasted them in an oven until they had become quite brown

---

9Quoted in Rudolf Olden: *Hitler the Pawn* (London, 1936), p. 45.

and had several times been successful in selling these pictures to traders as valuable old masters.' This sounds highly improbable, but in any case Hanisch, who had registered under another name as Walter Fritz, was afraid of the police. 'So I suggested to Hitler that it would be better to stay in an honest trade and paint postcards. I myself was to sell the painted cards, we decided to work together and share the money we earned.'[10]

Hitler had enough money to buy a few cards, ink and paints. With those he produced little copies of views of Vienna, which Hanisch peddled in taverns and fairs, or to small traders who wanted something to fill their empty picture frames. In this way they made enough to keep them until, in the summer of 1910, Hanisch sold a copy which Hitler had made of a drawing of the Vienna Parliament for ten crowns. Hitler, who was sure it was worth far more—he valued it at fifty in his statement to the police—was convinced he had been cheated. When Hanisch failed to return to the hostel, Hitler brought a lawsuit against him which ended in Hanisch spending a week in prison and the break-up of their partnership.

This was in August of 1910. For the remaining four years before the First World War, first in Vienna, later in Munich, Hitler continued to eke out a living in the same way. Some of Hitler's drawings, mostly stiff, lifeless copies of buildings in which his attempts to add human figures are a failure, were still to be found in Vienna in the 1930s, when they had acquired the value of collectors' pieces. More often he drew posters and crude advertisements for small shops—Teddy Perspiration Powder, Santa Claus selling coloured candles, or St Stefan's spire rising over a mountain of soap, with the signature 'A. Hitler' in the corner. Hitler himself later described these as years of great loneliness, in which his only contacts with other human beings were in the hostel where he continued to live and where, according to Hanisch, 'only tramps, drunkards, and such spent any time'.

After their quarrel Hanisch lost sight of Hitler, but he gives a description of Hitler as he knew him in 1910 at the age of twenty-one. He wore an ancient black overcoat, which had been given him by an old-clothes dealer in the hostel, a Hungarian Jew named Neumann, and which reached down over his knees. From under a greasy, black derby hat, his hair hung long over his coat collar. His thin and hungry face was covered with a black beard above which his large staring eyes were the one prominent feature. Altogether, Hanisch adds, 'an apparition such as rarely occurs among Christians.'[11]

From time to time Hitler had received financial help from his aunt in

---

[10]Olden: p. 46.
[11]Olden: p. 50; Heiden: *Der Führer*, p. 61.

Linz, Johanna Pölzl and, when she died in March 1911, it seems likely that he was left some small legacy. In May of that year his orphan's pension was stopped, but he still avoided any regular work.

Hanisch depicts him as lazy and moody, two characteristics which were often to reappear. He disliked regular work. If he earned a few crowns, he refused to draw for days and went off to a café to eat cream cakes and read newspapers. He had none of the common vices. He neither smoked nor drank and, according to Hanisch, was too shy and awkward to have any success with women. His passions were reading newspapers and talking politics. 'Over and over again,' Hanisch recalls, 'there were days on which he simply refused to work. Then he would hang around night shelters, living on the bread and soup that he got there, and discussing politics, often getting involved in heated controversies.'[12]

When he became excited in argument he would shout and wave his arms until the others in the room cursed him for disturbing them, or the porter came in to stop the noise. Sometimes people laughed at him, at other times they were oddly impressed. 'One evening,' Hanisch relates, 'Hitler went to a cinema where Kellermann's *Tunnel* was being shown. In this piece an agitator appears who rouses the working masses by his speeches. Hitler almost went crazy. The impression it made on him was so strong that for days afterwards he spoke of nothing except the power of the spoken word.'[13] These outbursts of violent argument and denunciation alternated with moods of despondency.

Everyone who knew him was struck by the combination of ambition, energy, and indolence in Hitler. Hitler was not only desperately anxious to impress people but was full of clever ideas for making his fortune and fame—from water-divining to designing an aeroplane. In this mood he would talk exuberantly and begin to spend the fortune he was to make in anticipation, but he was incapable of the application and hard work needed to carry out his projects. His enthusiasm would flag, he would relapse into moodiness and disappear until he began to hare off after some new trick or short cut to success. His intellectual interests followed the same pattern. He spent much time in the public library, but his reading was indiscriminate and unsystematic. Ancient Rome, the Eastern religions, Yoga, Occultism, Hypnotism, Astrology, Protestantism, each in turn excited his interest for a moment. He started a score of jobs but failed to make anything of them and relapsed into the old hand-to-mouth existence, living by expedients and little spurts of activity, but never settling down to anything for long.

12Olden: p. 51.
13ibid.

As time passed these habits became ingrained, and he became more eccentric, more turned in on himself. He struck people as 'queer', unbalanced. He gave rein to his hatreds—against the Jews, the priests, the Social Democrats, the Hapsburgs—without restraint. The few people with whom he had been friendly became tired of him, of his strange behaviour and wild talk. Neumann, the Jew, who had befriended him, was offended by the violence of his anti-Semitism; Kanya, who kept the hostel for men, thought him one of the oddest customers with whom he had had to deal. Yet these Vienna days stamped an indelible impression on his character and mind. 'During these years a view of life and a definite outlook on the world took shape in my mind. These became the granite basis of my conduct at that time. Since then I have extended that foundation very little, I have changed nothing in it . . . Vienna was a hard school for me, but it taught me the most profound lessons of my life.'[14] However pretentiously expressed, this is true. It is time to examine what these lessons were.

III

The idea of struggle is as old as life itself, for life is only preserved because other living things perish through struggle. . . . In this struggle, the stronger, the more able, win, while the less able, the weak, lose. Struggle is the father of all things. . . . It is not by the principles of humanity that man lives or is able to preserve himself above the animal world, but solely by means of the most brutal struggle. . . . If you do not fight for life, then life will never be won.[15]

This is the natural philosophy of the doss-house. In this struggle any trick or ruse, however unscrupulous, the use of any weapon or opportunity, however treacherous, are permissible. To quote another typical sentence from Hitler's speeches: 'Whatever goal man has reached is due to his originality plus his brutality.'[16] Astuteness; the ability to lie, twist, cheat and flatter; the elimination of sentimentality or loyalty in favour of ruthlessness, these were the qualities which enabled men to rise; above all, strength of will. Such were the principles which Hitler drew from his years in Vienna. Hitler never trusted anyone; he never committed himself to anyone, never admitted any loyalty. His lack of scruple later took

---

[14]*Mein Kampf*, pp. 32 and 116.

[15]Hitler's speech at Kulmbach, 5 February 1928; G. W. Prange (ed.): *Hitler's Words* (Washington, 1944), p. 8.

[16]Hitler at Chemnitz, 2 April 1928, ibid.

by surprise even those who prided themselves on their unscrupulousness. He learned to lie with conviction and dissemble with candour. To the end he refused to admit defeat and still held to the belief that by the power of will alone he could transform events. . . .

QUESTIONS FOR READING, RESPONDING, AND WRITING

Summarizing Main Points

1. Characterize the main features of Hitler's youth. What was his family like? What were the places where he lived like? What was his academic life like? In what ways do these descriptions correspond to what we might expect Hitler's youth to be like? How did Hitler himself paint the picture of his youth?
2. List the ways that Bullock's description of Hitler's work history—or lack of it— reinforces his characterization of Hitler as a "combination of ambition, energy, and indolence." What, according to Bullock, did Hitler's youth teach him?

Analyzing Methods of Discourse

1. What is Bullock's attitude toward the controversy that surrounded—and still surrounds—Hitler's father's parentage? List the ways the reader discovers that attitude.
2. Bullock intercuts his chronological history of Hitler's youth with descriptions of the political climate of the cities in which Hitler lived during that time. How do these descriptions intensify Bullock's characterization of Hitler's youth?

Focusing on the Field

1. What is Bullock's attitude toward Hitler's autobiography *Mein Kampf?* How does Bullock make his attitude clear? Judging from the passages that Bullock includes from *Mein Kampf,* do you believe Bullock is fair as a historian in his presentation of the book?
2. Bullock also provides evidence from other sources. What is Bullock's attitude as historian toward the validity of each of these other sources, and how does he make this attitude clear?

Writing Assignments

1. Research a famous—or infamous—figure from history, paying particular attention to the details of the early life that may have been influential in creating the later life. Write an essay that demonstrates those influences.
2. Samuel Eliot Morison in "History as Literary Art" quotes Theodore Roosevelt as saying about historical writing that "no amount of dull, painstaking detail will sum up the whole truth unless the genius is there to paint the truth." After studying Morison's essay in full, write an essay that argues that Bullock's picture of Hitler either does or does not "paint the truth."

Samuel Eliot Morison

HISTORY AS A LITERARY ART

Samuel Eliot Morison (1886–1976) led a life of adventure and scholarship. His historical method, briefly exposed in the following essay, combined experience, observation, and research. Morison has, in his own words, "endeavored to live and feel the history I write." The title chosen by his daughter for a collection of his best work, *Sailor Historian: The Best of Samuel Eliot Morison,* sums up Morison's avid, life-long reverence for two things: sailing and history. For his Pulitzer Prize–winning *Admiral of the Ocean Sea: A Life of Christopher Columbus,* Morison traced Columbus's path across the Atlantic in ships much like the earlier vessels. A military historian under Roosevelt, Morison lived the naval battles of World War II, observing the battle for Okinawa from on board the flagship *Tennessee.* Morison would later record those observations, and the personal conclusions which he felt made history worth reading, in a fifteen-volume *History of United States Naval Operations in World War II.*

Morison also realized a distinguished academic career, studying at Harvard (Ph.D., 1912), Oxford, and L'École des Sciences Politiques. An award-winning teacher for many years at Harvard and elsewhere, Morison was commissioned a lieutenant commander during World War II. His extensive writings include *The Oxford History of the United States: 1783–1917, The Growth of the American Republic, Builders of the Bay Colony, Three Centuries of Harvard College, The European Discovery of America,* and *By Land and By Sea,* from which the following selection is taken.

Exploring American history has been a very absorbing and exciting business now for three quarters of a century. Thousands of graduate students have produced thousands of monographs on every aspect of the history of the Americas. But the American reading public for the most part is blissfully ignorant of this vast output. When John Citizen feels the urge to read history, he goes to the novels of Kenneth Roberts or Margaret Mitchell, not to the histories of Professor this or Doctor that. Why?

Because American historians, in their eagerness to present facts and their laudable anxiety to tell the truth, have neglected the literary aspects of their craft. They have forgotten that there is an art of writing history.

Even the earliest colonial historians like William Bradford and Robert Beverley knew that; they put conscious art into their narratives. And the historians of our classical period, Prescott and Motley, Irving and Bancroft, Parkman and Fiske, were great literary craftsmen. Their many-volumed works sold in sufficient quantities to give them handsome returns; even today they are widely read. But the first generation of seminar-trained historians, educated in Germany or by teachers trained there, imagined that history would tell itself, provided one were honest, thorough, and painstaking. Some of them went so far as to regard history as pure science and to assert that writers thereof had no more business trying to be "literary" than did writers of statistical reports or performers of scientific experiments. Professors warned their pupils (quite unnecessarily) against "fine writing," and endeavored to protect their innocence from the seductive charm of Washington Irving or the masculine glamour of Macaulay. And in this flight of history from literature the public was left behind. American history became a bore to the reader and a drug on the market; even historians with something to say and the talent for saying it (Henry Adams, for instance) could not sell their books. The most popular American histories of the period 1890–1905 were those of John Fiske, a philosopher who had no historical training, but wrote with life and movement.

Theodore Roosevelt in his presidential address before the American Historical Association in 1912 made a ringing plea to the young historian to do better:

> He must ever remember that while the worst offense of which he can be guilty is to write vividly and inaccurately, yet that unless he writes vividly he cannot write truthfully; for no amount of dull, painstaking detail will sum up the whole truth unless the genius is there to paint the truth.

And although American historians cannot hope as Theodore Roosevelt did to "watch the nearing chariots of the champions," or look forward to the day when "for us the war-horns of King Olaf shall wail across the flood, and the harps sound high at festivals in forgotten halls," we may indeed "show how the land which the pioneers won slowly and with incredible hardship was filled in two generations by the overflow from the countries of western and central Europe." We may describe the race, class, and religious conflicts that immigration has engendered, and trace the rise of the labor movement with a literary art that compels people to read about it. You do not need chariots and horsemen, harps and war-horns to make history interesting.

Theodore Roosevelt's trumpet call fell largely on deaf ears, at least in the academic historical profession. A whole generation has passed without producing any really great works on American history. Plenty of good books, valuable books, and new interpretations and explorations of the past; but none with fire in the eye, none to make a young man want to fight for his country in war or live to make it a better country in peace. There has been a sort of chain reaction of dullness. Professors who have risen to positions of eminence by writing dull, solid, valuable monographs that nobody reads outside the profession, teach graduate students to write dull, solid, valuable monographs like theirs; the road to academic security is that of writing dull, solid, valuable monographs. And so the young men who have a gift for good writing either leave the historical field for something more exciting, or write more dull, solid, valuable monographs. The few professional historians who have had a popular following or appeal during the last thirty years are either men like Allan Nevins who were trained in some juicier profession like journalism, or men and women like the Beards who had the sense to break loose young from academic trammels.

In the meantime, the American public has become so sated by dull history textbooks in school and college that it won't read history unless disguised as something else under a title such as "The Flowering of Florida," "The Epic of the East," or "The Growth of the American Republic." Or, more often, they get what history they want from historical novels.

Now I submit, this is a very bad situation. The tremendous plowing up of the past by well-trained scholars is all to the good, so far as it goes. Scholars know more about America's past than ever; they are opening new furrows and finding new artifacts, from aboriginal arrowheads to early twentieth-century corset stays. But they are heaping up the pay dirt for others. Journalists, novelists, and free-lance writers are the ones that extract the gold; and they deserve every ounce they get because they are the ones who know how to write histories that people care to read. What I want to see is a few more Ph.D.'s in history winning book-of-the-month adoptions and reaping the harvest of dividends. They can do it, too, if they will only use the same industry at presenting history as they do compiling it.

Mind you, I intend no disparagement of historians who choose to devote their entire energies to teaching. Great teachers do far more good to the cause of history than mediocre writers. Such men, for instance, as the late H. Morse Stephens, who stopped writing (which he never liked) as soon as he obtained a chair in this country, and the late Edwin F. Gay, who never began writing, inspired thousands of young men and initiated scores of valuable books. Thank God for these gifted teachers, I say; universities should seek out, encourage, and promote them far more than they do. My remarks are addressed to young people who have the urge to write history, and wish to write it effectively.

There are no special rules for writing history; any good manual of rhetoric or teacher of composition will supply the rules for writing English. But what terrible stuff passes for English in Ph.D. dissertations, monographs, and articles in historical reviews! Long, involved sentences that one has to read two or three times in order to grasp their meaning; poverty in vocabulary, ineptness of expression, weakness in paragraph structure, frequent misuse of words, and, of late, the introduction of pseudo-scientific and psychological jargon. There is no fundamental cure for this except better teaching of English in our schools and colleges, and by every teacher, whatever his other subject may be. If historical writing is infinitely better in France than in America, and far better in the British Isles and Canada than in the United States, it is because every French and British teacher of history drills his pupils in their mother tongue, requiring a constant stream of essays and reports, and criticizing written work not only as history but as literature. The American university teacher who gives honor grades to students who have not yet learned to write English, for industrious compilations of facts or feats of memory, is wanting in professional pride or competency.

Of course, what we should all like to attain in writing history is style. "The sense of style," says Whitehead in his *Aims of Education,* "is an aesthetic sense, based on admiration for the direct attainment of a foreseen end, simply and without waste. Style in art, style in literature, style in science, style in logic, style in practical execution, have fundamentally the same aesthetic qualities, namely attainment and restraint. Style, in its finest sense, is the last acquirement of the educated mind; it is also the most useful. It pervades the whole being. . . . Style is the ultimate morality of mind."

Unfortunately, there is no royal road to style. It cannot be attained by mere industry; it can never be achieved through imitation, although it may be promoted by example. Reading the greatest literary artists among historians will help; but do not forget that what was acceptable style in 1850 might seem turgid today. We can still read Macaulay with admiration and pleasure, we can still learn paragraph structure and other things from Macaulay, but anyone who tried to imitate Macaulay today would be a pompous ass.

Just as Voltaire's ideal curé advises his flock not to worry about going to heaven, but to do right and probably by God's grace they will get there;

so the young writer of history had better concentrate on day-by-day improvement in craftmanship. Then perhaps he may find some day that his prose appeals to a large popular audience; that, in other words, he has achieved style through simple, honest, straightforward writing.

A few hints as to the craft may be useful to budding historians. First and foremost, *get writing!* Young scholars generally wish to secure the last fact before writing anything, like General McClellan refusing to advance (as people said) until the last mule was shod. It is a terrible strain, isn't it, to sit down at a desk with your notes all neatly docketed, and begin to write? You pretend to your wife that you mustn't be interrupted; but, actually, you welcome a ring of the telephone, a knock at the door, or a bellow from the baby as an excuse to break off. Finally, after smoking sundry cigarettes and pacing about the house two or three times, you commit a lame paragraph or two to paper. By the time you get to the third, one bit of information you want is lacking. What a relief! Now you must go back to the library or the archives to do some more digging. That's where you are happy! And what you turn up there leads to more questions and prolongs the delicious process of research. Half the pleas I have heard from graduate students for more time or another grant-in-aid are mere excuses to postpone the painful drudgery of writing.

There is the "indispensablest beauty in knowing how to get done," said Carlyle. In every research there comes a point, which you should recognize like a call of conscience, when you must get down to writing. And when you once are writing, go on writing as long as you can; there will be plenty of time later to shove in the footnotes or return to the library for extra information. Above all, *start* writing. Nothing is more pathetic than the "gonna" historian, who from graduate school on is always "gonna" write a magnum opus but never completes his research on the subject, and dies without anything to show for a lifetime's work.

Dictation is usually fatal to good historical writing. Write out your first draft in longhand or, if you compose easily on the typewriter, type it out yourself, revise with pencil or pen, and have it retyped clean. Don't stop to consult your notes for every clause or sentence; it is better to get what you have to say clearly in your mind and dash it off; then, after you have it down, return to your notes and compose your next few pages or paragraphs. After a little experience you may well find that you think best with your fingers on the typewriter keys or your fountain pen poised over the paper. For me, the mere writing of a few words seems to point up vague thoughts and make jumbled facts array themselves in neat order. Whichever method you choose, composing before you write or as you write, do not return to your raw material or verify facts and quotations or insert footnotes until you have written a substantial amount, an amount that will increase with practice. It is significant that two of our greatest

American historians, Prescott and Parkman, were nearly blind during a good part of their active careers. They had to have the sources read to them and turn the matter over and over in their minds before they could give anything out; and when they gave, *they gave!*

Now, the purpose of this quick, warm synthesis between research, thinking, and writing is to attain the three prime qualities of historical composition—clarity, vigor, and objectivity. You must think about your facts, analyze your material, and decide exactly what you mean before you can write it so that the average reader will understand. Do not fall into the fallacy of supposing that "facts speak for themselves." Most of the facts that you excavate, like other relics of past human activity, are dumb things; it is for you to make them speak by proper selection, arrangement, and emphasis. Dump your entire collection of facts on paper, and the result will be unreadable if not incomprehensible.

So, too, with vigor. If your whole paragraph or chapter is but a hypothesis, say so at the beginning, but do not bore and confuse the reader with numerous "buts," "excepts," "perhapses," "howevers," and "possiblys." Use direct rather than indirect statements, the active rather than the passive voice, and make every sentence and paragraph an organic whole. Above all, if you are writing historical narrative, make it move. Do not take time out in the middle of a political or military campaign to introduce special developments or literary trends, as McMaster did to the confusion of his readers. Place those admittedly important matters in a chapter or chapters by themselves so that your reader's attention will not be lost by constant interruption.

That brings us to the third essential quality—objectivity. Keep the reader constantly in mind. You are not writing history for yourself or for the professors who are supposed to know more about it than you do. Assume that you are writing for intelligent people who know nothing about your particular subject but whom you wish to interest and attract. I once asked the late Senator Beveridge why his *Life of John Marshall*, despite its great length and scholarly apparatus, was so popular. He replied: "The trouble with you professors of history is that you write for each other. I write for people almost completely ignorant of American history, as I was when I began my research."

A few more details. Even if the work you are writing does not call for footnotes, keep them in your copy until the last draft, for they will enable you to check up on your facts, statements, and quotations. And since accuracy is the prime virtue of the historian, this checking must be done, either by the author or by someone else. You will be surprised by the mistakes that creep in between a first rough draft and a final typed copy. And the better you write, the more your critics will enjoy finding misquotations and inaccuracies.

The matter of handling quotations seems to be a difficult one for young historians. There is nothing that adds so much to the charm and effectiveness of a history as good quotations from the sources, especially if the period be somewhat remote. But there is nothing so disgusting to the reader as long, tedious, broken quotations in small print, especially those in which, to make sense, the author has to interpolate words in brackets. Young writers are prone to use quotations in places where their own words would be better, and to incorporate in the text source excerpts that belong in footnotes or appendices. Avoid ending chapters with quotations, and never close your book with one.

Above all, do not be afraid to revise and rewrite. Reading aloud is a good test—historians' wives have to stand a lot of that! A candid friend who is not a historian and so represents the audience you are trying to reach, is perhaps the best "dog" to try it on. Even if he has little critical sense, it is encouraging to him stay awake. My good friend Lucien Price years ago listened with a pained expression to a bit of my early work. "Now, just what do you mean by that?" he asked after a long, involved, pedantic, and quote-larded paragraph. I told him in words of one syllable, or perhaps two. "Fine!" said he, "I understand that. Now write down what you said; throw the other away!"

Undoubtedly the writer of history can enrich his mind and broaden his literary experience as well as better his craftsmanship by his choice of leisure reading. If he is so fortunate as to have had a classical education, no time will be better spent in making him an effective historian than in reading Latin and Greek authors. Both these ancient languages are such superb instruments of thought that a knowledge of them cures slipshod English and helps one to attain a clear, muscular style. All our greatest historical stylists—notably Prescott, Parkman, Fiske, and Frederick J. Turner—had a classical education and read the ancient historians in the original before they approached American history.

If you have little Latin and less Greek and feel unable to spare the time and effort to add them to your stock of tools, read the ancient classics in the best literary translations, such as North's Plutarch, Rawlinson's Herodotus, John J. Chapman's Æschylus, Gilbert Murray's Euripides, and, above all, Jowett's or Livingstone's Thucydides. Through them you will gain the content and spirit of the ancient classics, which will break down your provincialism, refresh your spirit, and give you a better philosophical insight into the ways of mankind than most of such works as the new science of psychology has brought forth. Moreover, you will be acquiring the same background as many of the great Americans of the past generations, thus aiding your understanding of them.

The reading of English classics will tend in the same direction, and will also be a painless and unconscious means of improving your literary style. Almost every English or American writer of distinction is indebted to Shakespeare and the English Bible. The Authorized Version is not only the great source book of spiritual experience of English-speaking peoples; it is a treasury of plain, pungent words and muscular phrases, beautiful in themselves and with long associations, which we are apt to replace by smooth words lacking in punch, or by hackneyed or involved phrases. Here are a few examples chosen in five minutes from my desk Bible: I Samuel i, 28: "I have lent him to the Lord." What an apt phrase for anyone bringing up their son for the Church! Why say "loaned" instead of "lent"? Isaiah xxii, 5: "For it is a day of trouble, and of treading down, and of perplexity." In brief, just what we are going through today. But most modern historians would not feel that they were giving the reader his money's worth unless they wrote: "It is an era of agitation, of a progressive decline in the standard of living, and of uncertainty as to the correct policy." Romans xi, 25: "Wise in your own conceits." This epigram has often been used, but a modern writer would be tempted to express the thought in some such cumbrous manner as "Expert within the limits of your own fallacious theories."

Of course much of the Biblical phraseology is obsolete, and there are other literary quarries for historians. You can find many appropriate words, phrases, similes, and epigrams in American authors such as Mark Twain, Emerson, and Thoreau. I have heard an English economist push home a point to a learned audience with a quotation from *Alice in Wonderland*; American historians might make more use of *Huckleberry Finn*.

The historian can learn much from the novelist. Most writers of fiction are superior to all but the best historians in characterization and description. If you have difficulty in making people and events seem real, see if you cannot learn the technique from American novelists such as Sherwood Anderson, Joseph Hergesheimer and Margaret Mitchell. For me, the greatest master of all is Henry James. He used a relatively simple and limited vocabulary; but what miracles he wrought with it! What precise and perfect use he makes of words to convey the essence of a human situation to the reader! If you are not yet acquainted with Henry James, try the selection of his shorter novels and stories edited by Clifton Fadiman, and then read some of the longer novels, like *Roderick Hudson* and *The American*. And, incidentally, you will learn more about the top layers of American and European society in the second half of the nineteenth century than you can ever glean from the works of social historians.

What is the place of imagination in history? An historian or biographer is under restrictions unknown to a novelist. He has no right to override facts by his own imagination. If he is writing on a remote or obscure subject about which few facts are available, his imagination may legitimately weave them into a pattern. But to be honest he must make clear what is fact and what is hypothesis. The quality of imagination, if properly restrained by the conditions of historical discipline, is of great assistance in enabling one to discover problems to be solved, to grasp the significance of facts, to form hypotheses, to discern causes in their first beginnings, and, above all, to relate the past creatively to the present. There are many opportunities in historical narrative for bold, imaginative expressions. "A complete statement in the imaginative form of an important truth arrests attention," wrote Emerson, "and is repeated and remembered." Imagination used in this way invests an otherwise pedestrian narrative with vivid and exciting qualities.

Finally, the historian should have frequent recourse to the book of life. The richer his personal experience, the wider his human contacts, the more likely he is to effect a living contact with his audience. In writing, similes drawn from the current experience of this mechanical age rather than those rifled from the literary baggage of past eras, are the ones that will go home to his reader. Service on a jury or a local committee may be a revelation as to the political thoughts and habits of mankind. A month's labor in a modern factory would help any young academician to clarify his ideas of labor and capital. A camping trip in the woods will tell him things about Western pioneering that he can never learn in books. The great historians, with few exceptions, are those who have not merely studied, but lived; and whose studies have ranged over a much wider field than the period or subject of which they write.

The veterans of World War II who, for the most part, have completed their studies in college or graduate school, should not regard the years of their war service as wasted. Rather should they realize that the war gave them a rich experience of life, which is the best equipment for a historian. They have "been around," they have seen mankind at his best and his worst, they have shared the joy and passion of a mighty effort and they can read man's doings in the past with far greater understanding than if they had spent these years in sheltered academic groves.

To these young men especially, and to all young men I say (as the poet Chapman said to the young Elizabethan): "Be free, all worthy spirits, and stretch yourselves!" Bring all your knowledge of life to bear on everything that you write. Never let yourself bog down in pedantry and detail. Bring History, the most humane and noble form of letters, back to the proud position she once held; knowing that your words, if they be read and remembered, will enter into the stream of life, and perhaps move men to thought and action centuries hence, as do those of Thucydides after more than two thousand years.

QUESTIONS FOR READING, RESPONDING, AND WRITING

Summarizing Main Points

1. What does Morison see as the "end" or goal of historical writing? What obstacles stand in the way of that end, according to Morison?

2. Morison provides "a few hints . . . to budding historians." List those hints in the order of importance that you feel Morison would assign them.

Analyzing Methods of Discourse

1. Morison writes that "similes drawn from current experience . . . are the ones that will go home to his reader." Morison himself compares the historian to "excavators" of different kinds at several points during his essay. Trace the development of that comparison throughout the essay.
2. How do the novelist and historian differ, according to Morison? More importantly, how does Morison suggest they are the same? List those similarities and differences.

Focusing on the Field

1. Why is it "significant that two of our greatest historians, Prescott and Parkman, were nearly blind"? How is their method a good model for all historians, according to Morison? List the "hints" that Morison supplies for historians elsewhere in his essay that reflect the qualities that characterize Prescott and Parkman.
2. Morison apparently intends his essay largely for historians. He says early on that some historians and teachers "went so far as to regard history as pure science and to assert that writers thereof had no more business trying to be 'literary' than did writers of statistical reports or performers of scientific experiments." Do you believe that Morison would be willing to expand his audience to include writers of such reports and experiments? Consider the essays in the section here or those in "Science and Technology." Do the writers in both sections take positions similar to Morison's? Do they demonstrate similar skills?

Writing Assignments

1. Choose an essay of your own (either an earlier English composition or a paper for another academic area). Revise and rewrite according to Morison's advice. Be prepared to read your essay aloud in class. Do not be alarmed if it is "listened to with pained expression" as Morison's early work was, but be encouraged, as Morison was, if your audience stays awake. Listen carefully to suggestions on how to improve your paper.
2. Read Malcolm Cowley's "Sociological Habit Patterns in Linguistic Transmogrification." Write an essay that argues that both Cowley and Morison are advocating the same points.

Tom Wolfe

THE WORSHIP OF ART
Notes on the New God

Famous as one of the creators of the "new journalism" and as the owner of at least nine $600 white suits, Tom Wolfe was born in Richmond, Virginia in 1931. He graduated cum laude from Washington and Lee University in 1951 and gained a Ph.D. from Yale University in 1957. Starting out as a reporter for the *Springfield Union* in Springfield, Massachusetts in 1956, Wolfe has been a reporter and Latin American correspondent for the *Washington Post,* a reporter and writer for the *New York Herald Tribune,* a contributing editor for both *New York* and *Esquire* magazines, and a contributing artist for *Harper's* magazine. His often credited creation of the "new journalism" took place in 1963 in the process of writing a magazine article—his first—for *Esquire* on the "strange subculture of west coast car customizers." Finding standard reportorial techniques inadequate for the bizarre collection of facts he had assembled and preparing to turn his material over to another writer to have a go at it, he wrote out a forty-nine page "stream-of-consciousness" memo to his editor, who merely struck the salutation from the top and published it verbatim.

Wolfe, himself, defines the "new journalism" as the "use by people writing nonfiction of techniques which heretofore had been thought of as confined to the novel or to the short story, to create in one form or another both the kind of objective reality of journalism and the subjective reality that people have always gone to the novel for." To match those two realities—to fit style to subject—is the goal Wolfe has sought in his work, beginning with his bizarre accounts of sixties trends and personalities in *The Kandy Kolored Tangerine Flake Streamlined Baby* (1965), *The Electric Kool-Aid Acid Test* (1968), *Radical Chic and MauMauing the Flak Catchers* (1970). He continued with his attacks on the worlds of modern art and architecture in *The Painted Word* (1975) and *From Bauhaus to Our House* (1981), from which the following essay takes its inspiration, and with his account of the beginnings of the American space program in *The Right Stuff* (1979), for which he won both the American Book Award and the National Book Critics Circle Award in 1980. The success of these various endeavors has made Wolfe the object of repeated imitation. Indeed, in 1979, Wolfe called himself "the most parodied writer of the last fifteen years."

Let me tell you about the night the Vatican art show opened at the Metropolitan Museum of Art in New York. The scene was the Temple of Dendur, an enormous architectural mummy, complete with a Lake of the Dead, underneath a glass bell at the rear of the museum. On the stone apron in front of the temple, by the lake, the museum put on a formal dinner for 360 souls, including the wife of the President of the United States, the usual philanthropic dowagers and corporate art patrons, a few catered names, such as Prince Albert of Monaco and Henry Kissinger, and many well-known members of the New York art world. But since this was, after all, an exhibition of the Vatican art collection, it was necessary to include some Roman Catholics. Cardinal Cooke, Vatican emissaries, prominent New York Catholic laymen, Knights of Malta—there they were, devout Christians at a New York art world event. The culturati and the Christians were arranged at the tables like Arapaho beads: one culturatus, one Christian, one culturatus, one Christian, one culturatus, one Christian, one culturatus, one Christian.

Gamely, the guests tried all the conventional New York conversation openers—real estate prices, friends who have been mugged recently, well-known people whose children have been arrested on drug charges, Brits, live-in help, the dishonesty of helipad contractors, everything short of the desperately trite subjects used in the rest of the country, namely the weather and front-wheel drive. Nothing worked. There were dreadful lulls during which there was no sound at all in that antique churchyard except for the pings of hotel silver on earthenware plates echoing off the tombstone facade of the temple.

Shortly before dessert, I happened to be out in the museum's main lobby when two Manhattan art dealers appeared in their tuxedos, shaking their heads.

One said to the other: "Who *are* these *unbelievable people?*"

But of course! It seemed not only *outré* to have these . . . these . . . these . . . these *religious types* at an art event, it seemed sacrilegious. The culturati were being forced to rub shoulders with heathens. That was the way it hit them. For today art—not religion—is the religion of the educated classes. Today educated people look upon traditional religious ties—Catholic, Episcopal, Presbyterian, Methodist, Baptist, Jewish—as matters of social pedigree. It is only art that they look upon religiously.

When I say that art is the religion of the educated classes, I am careful not to use the word in the merely metaphorical way people do when they say someone is religious about sticking to a diet or training for a sport. I am not using "religion" as a synonym for "enthusiasm." I am referring specifically to what Max Weber identified as the objective functions of a religion: the abnegation or rejection of the world and the legitimation of wealth.

Everyone is familiar with the rejection of the world in the ordinary religious sense. When I worked for the *Washington Post,* I was sent into the hills of West Virginia to do a story about a snake-handling cult—or I should say religion, since a cult is nothing more than a religion whose political influence is nil. The snake-handling religion is based on a passage in Mark in which Jesus, in the Upper Room, tells his disciples that those who believe in him will be able to "handle snakes" and "come to no harm." At the services, sure enough, there is a box or basket full of snakes, poisonous snakes, right before your eyes, and their heads poke out from under the lid and you can see their forked tongues. Snake-handling thrives only in mountain areas where the farmlands are poor and the people scrape by. The message of the preachers usually runs as follows: "Oh, I know that down there in the valley they're driving their shiny cars, yes, and smoking their big cigars, unh hunh, and playing with their fancy women, unh hunh, oh yes. But you wait until the Last Days, when it comes time to kiss the snake. *You* will ascend to the right hand of God and live in His Glory, and they will perish." There you have the religious rejection of the world.

Today there are a few new religions that appeal to educated people— Scientology, Arica, Synanon, and some neo-Hindu, neo-Buddhist, and neo-Christian groups—but their success has been limited. The far more common way to reject the world, in our time, is through art. I'm sure you're familiar with it. You're on the subway during the morning rush hour, in one of those cars that is nothing but a can of meat on wheels, jammed in shank to flank and haunch to paunch and elbow to rib with people who talk to themselves and shout obscenities into the void and click their teeth and roll back their upper lips to reveal their purple gums, and there is nothing you can do about it. You can't budge. Coffee, adrenaline, and rogue hate are squirting through every duct and every vein, and just when you're beginning to wonder how any mortal can possibly stand it, you look around and you see a young woman seated serenely in what seems to be a perfect pink cocoon of peace, untouched, unthreatened, by the growling mob around her. Her eyes are lowered. In her lap, invariably, is a book. If you look closely, you will see that this book is by Rimbaud, or Rilke, or Baudelaire, or Kafka, or Gabriel García Márquez, author of *One Hundred Years of Solitude*. And as soon as you see this vision, you understand the conviction that creates the inviolable aura around her: "I may be forced into this rat race, this squalid human stew, but I do not have to be *of* it. I inhabit a universe that is finer. I can reject all this." You can envision her apartment immediately. There is a mattress on top of a flush door supported by bricks. There's a window curtained in monk's cloth. There's a hand-thrown pot with a few blue cornflowers in it. There are some Paul Klee and Modigliani prints on the wall and a poster from the Acquavella Galleries' Matisse show. "I don't need your Louis Bourbon bergères and your fabric-covered walls. I reject your whole Parish-Hadley world—through art."

And what about the legitimation of wealth? It wasn't so long ago that Americans of great wealth routinely gave 10 percent of their income to the church. The practice of tithing was a certification of worthiness on earth and an option on heaven. Today the custom is to give the money to the arts. When Mrs. E. Parmalee Prentice, daughter of John D. Rockefeller Sr. and owner of two adjoining mansions on East Fifty-third Street, just off Fifth Avenue, died in 1962, she did not leave these holdings, worth about $5 million, to her church. She left them to the Museum of Modern Art for the building of a new wing. Nobody's eyebrows arched. By 1962, it would have been more remarkable if a bequest of that size had gone to a religion of the old-fashioned sort.

Today it has reached the point where there is a clear-cut hierarchy of museum bequests. Best of all is to found a new museum with your name on it, such as the Hirshhorn Museum in Washington, named for Joseph H. Hirshhorn, whose collection of modern art is the core of the museum's holdings. Next best is endowing a new wing, such as the new wing at the Museum of Modern Art. Next best, a big gallery on the first floor with sunlight; next best, other galleries on the first floor. Then you go up to the second floor, with the sunny corner rooms in front the first pick, and the rooms in the rear next best; then upward to the third floor, and the fourth, until there are no more upper floors and you are forced to descend into the cellar. Today it is not unusual to be walking along a basement corridor of a museum and come upon what looks like the door to a utility room with a plaque on it reading: "The E. Runcey Atherwart Belgian Porcelain Cossack Collection."

When the new Metropolitan Opera House was built, there were so many people eager to pour money into it that soon every seat in the orchestra had its own little plaque on the back reading "Sheldon A. Leonard and Family," or whatever. That was nothing more than the twentieth-century version of a traditional religious practice of the seventeenth and eighteenth centuries, when every pew in the front half of the main floor of the church had its own little plaque on the back with the name of the family that had endowed it—and sat in it on Sunday. At the Opera House, when they ran out of seats in the orchestra, they went into the lobbies. People endowed columns. And when I say columns, I'm not talking about columns with stepped pediments or fluted shafts or Corinthian capitals with acanthus leaves. I'm talking about I-beams, I-beams supporting the upper floors. When they ran out of columns, they moved on to radiator covers and water fountains.

There was a time when well-to-do, educated people in America adorned their parlors with crosses, crucifixes, or Stars of David. These were marks not only of faith but of cultivation. Think of the great homes, built before 1940, with chapels. This was a fashionable as well as devout use of space. Today those chapels are used as picture galleries, libraries, copper kitchens, saunas, or high-tech centers. It is perfectly acceptable to use them for the VCR and the Advent. But it would be in bad taste to use them for prayer. Practically no one who cares about appearing cultivated today would display a cross or Star of David in the living room. It would be . . . *in bad taste*. Today the conventional symbol of devoutness is—but of course!—the Holy Rectangle: the painting. The painting is the religious object we see today in the parlors of the educated classes.

There was a time, not so long ago, when American businesses gave large amounts of money to churches. In the Midwest and much of the South, areas dominated by so-called Dissenting Protestants, if any man wished to attain the eminence of assistant feed-store manager or better, he joined the Presbyterian or the United Brethren or the Lutheran or the Dutch Reformed church in his community. It was a sign of good faith in every sense of the term. It was absolutely necessary. Businesses literally prayed in public.

Today, what American corporation would support a religion? Most would look upon any such thing as sheer madness. So what does a corporation do when the time comes to pray in public? It supports the arts. I don't need to recite figures. Just think of the money raised since the 1950s for the gigantic cultural complexes—Lincoln Center, Kennedy Center, the Chandler Pavillion, the Woodruff Arts Center—that have become *de rigueur* for the modern American metropolis. What are they? Why, they are St. Patrick's, St. Mary's, Washington National, Holy Cross: the American cathedrals of the late twentieth century.

We are talking here about the legitimation of wealth. The worse odor a corporation is in, the more likely it is to support the arts, and the more likely it is to make sure everybody knows it. The energy crisis, to use an antique term from the 1970s, was the greatest bonanza in the Public Broadcasting Service's history. The more loudly they were assailed as exploiters and profiteers, the more earnestly the oil companies poured money into PBS's cultural programming. Every broadcast seemed to end with a discreet notice on the screen saying: "This program was made possible by a grant from Exxon," or perhaps Mobil, or ARCO. The passing of the energy crisis has been bad news for PBS. That resourceful institution would do well to mount an attack on real estate ventures, money-market funds, low-calorie beer, flea collars, antihistamines, videodisc racks, pornographic magazines, or some other prosperous enterprises. One of the pornography *jefes*, Hugh Hefner, has given his Chicago headquarters, known as the Playboy Mansion, worth an estimated $3 million, to the Chicago Art Institute. It is safe to predict that other pornographers will seek—and with some success—to legitimize their wealth by making devout offerings upon the altar of *Art*. To give the same offerings to a church would make them look like penitent sinners.

As you can imagine, this state of affairs has greatly magnified the influence of the art world. In size, that world has never been anything more than a village. In the United States, fashions in art are determined by no more than 3,000 people, at least 2,950 of whom live in Manhattan. I can't think of a single influential critic today. "The gallery-going public" has never had any influence at all—so we are left with certain dealers, curators, and artists. No longer do they have the servant-like role of catering to or glorifying the client. Their role today is to save him. They have become a form of clergy—or clerisy, to use an old word for secular souls who take on clerical duties.

In this age of the art clerisy, the client is in no position to say what will save him. He is in no position to do anything at all except come forward with the money if he wants salvation and legitimation.

Today large corporations routinely hire curators from the art village to buy art in their behalf. It is not a mere play on words to call these people curates, comparable to the Catholic priests who at one time were attached to wealthy European families to conduct daily masses on their estates. The corporations set limits on the curators' budgets and reserve the right to veto their choices. But they seldom do, since the entire purpose of a corporate art program is legitimation of wealth through a spiritually correct investment in art. The personal tastes of the executives, employees, clients, or customers could scarcely matter less. The corporate curators are chiefly museum functionaries, professors of art, art critics, and dealers, people who have devoted themselves not so much to the history of art as to the theories and fashions that determine prestige within the art world—that village of 3,000 souls—today, in the here and now.

Thus Chase Manhattan Bank hired a curator who was a founding trustee of the scrupulously devout and correct New Museum in New York. IBM hired a curator from the Whitney Museum to direct the art program at its new headquarters in New York. Philip Morris, perhaps the nation's leading corporate patron of the arts, did IBM one better. In its new headquarters in New York, Philip Morris has built a four-story art gallery and turned it over directly to the Whitney. Whatever the Whitney says goes.

For a company to buy works of art simply because they appeal to its executives and its employees is an absolute waste of money, so far as legitimation is concerned. The Ciba-Geigy agricultural chemical company started out collecting works of many styles and artists, then apparently realized the firm was getting no benefit from the collection whatsoever, other than aesthetic pleasure. At this point Ciba-Geigy hired an artist and a Swiss art historian, who began buying only Abstract Expressionist works by artists such as Philip Guston and Adolph Gottlieb.

These works were no doubt totally meaningless to the executives, the employees, and the farmers of the world who use agricultural chemicals, and were, therefore, a striking improvement.

If employees go so far as to protest a particular fashionable style, a corporation will usually switch to another one. Corporations are not eager to annoy their workers. But at the same time, to spend money on the sort of realistic or symbolic work employees might actually enjoy would be pointless. The point is to be acclaimed for "support of the arts," a phrase which applies only to the purchase of works certified by the curates of the art village. This was quite openly the aim of the Bank of America when it hired a curator in 1979 and began buying works of art at the rate of 1,000 a year. The bank felt that its corporate image was suffering because it was not among those firms receiving "credit for art support."

The credit must come from the art clerisy. It is for this reason that IBM, for example, has displayed Michael Heizer's *Levitated Mass* at its outdoor plaza at Madison Avenue and Fifty-sixth Street. The piece is a 25-foot-by-16-foot metal tank containing water and a slab of granite. It is meaningless in terms of IBM, its executives, its employees, its customers, and the thousands of people who walk past the plaza every day. Far from being a shortcoming, that is part of *Levitated Mass*'s exemplary success as a spiritual object.

It is precisely in this area—public sculpture—that the religion of art currently makes its richest contribution to the human comedy. A hundred years ago there was no confusion about the purpose of public sculpture. It glorified the ideals or triumphs of an entire community by the presentation of familiar figures or symbols, or, alternatively, it glorified the person or group who paid for it. The city where I grew up, Richmond, Virginia, was the capital of the Confederacy during the Civil War. After the war, Robert E. Lee ascended to the status of a saint in the South, and above all in Richmond. In 1888, a six-story-high statue of Lee on his horse was commissioned. In 1890, when it arrived by boat up the James River, the entire city turned out and went down to the harbor. The men of Richmond took off their seersucker jackets and rolled up their sleeves and, by sheer manpower, hauled the prodigious figures of Lee and his horse Traveller up a two-mile slope to the crest of Monument Avenue, where it now rests. Then they stepped back and cheered and wept. Such was the nature of public sculpture a century ago.

Other public sculpture, as I say, was created simply for the glory of whoever paid for the building it stood in front of. My favorite example is the statue of James Buchanan Duke of the American Tobacco Company that stands in the main quadrangle of the Duke University campus. He's leaning debonairly on his walking stick and has a great round belly and a jolly look on his face and a cigar in his left hand. The statue just comes right out and says: "He made a lot of money in tobacco, he gave you this place, he loved smoking, and here he is!"

That, too, was the nature of public sculpture up until World War II. Shortly before the war, the Rockefeller family erected a monument to itself known as Rockefeller Center, a great building complex featuring two major pieces of sculpture (and many smaller sculptures and bas-reliefs). One, at the skating rink, is a gilt statue of Prometheus, rampant, by Paul Manship. The other, on Fifth Avenue, is Lee Lawrie's highly stylized rendition of Atlas supporting the globe. The use of mythological imagery was typical of public sculpture at the time, and the local meaning was clear enough: the Rockefellers and American business were as strong as Atlas and Promethean in their daring.

But what did the Rockefellers commission in the way of public sculpture *after* World War II? The Rockefellers' Number One Chase Manhattan Plaza was the first glass skyscraper on Wall Street. Out front, on a bare Bauhaus-style apron, the so-called plaza, was installed a sculpture by Jean Dubuffet. It is made of concrete and appears to be four toadstools fused into a gelatinous mass with black lines running up the sides. The title is *Group of Four Trees*. Not even *Group of Four Rockefellers*. After all, there *were* four at the time: David, John D. III, Nelson, and Laurance. But the piece has absolutely nothing to say about the glory or even the existence of the Rockefellers, Wall Street, Chase Manhattan Bank, American business, or the building it stands in front of. Instead, it proclaims the glory of contemporary art. It fulfills the new purpose of public sculpture, which is the legitimation of wealth through the new religion of the educated classes.

Six years after Number One Chase Manhattan Plaza was built, the Marine Midland Bank building went up a block away. It is another glass skyscraper with a mean little Bauhaus-style apron out front, and on this apron was placed a red cube resting on one point by Isamu Noguchi. Through the cube (a rhombohedron, strictly speaking) runs a cylindrical hole. One day I looked through that hole, expecting at the very least that my vision would be led toward the board room, where a man wearing a hard-worsted suit, and with thinning, combed-back hair, would be standing, his forefinger raised, thundering about broker loan rates. Instead what I saw was a woman who appeared to be part of the stenographic pool probing the auditory meatus of her left ear with a Q-Tip. So what is it, this red cube by Noguchi? Why, nothing more than homage to contemporary art, the new form of praying in public. In 1940, the same sculptor, Noguchi, completed a ten-ton stainless steel bas-relief for the main entrance of Rockefeller Center's Associated Press building. It shows five heroic figures using the tools of the wire-service employee: the Teletype, the wire-photo machine, the telephone, the camera, and the pad and pencil. It is entitled *News*. Noguchi's sculpture in front of the Marine Midland building is entitled *Rhombohedron*. Even a title suggesting that it had anything to do with American banking would have been a gauche intrusion upon a piece of corporate piety.

No doubt some corporations find it convenient not to have to express what is on their minds, nor to have to make any claims about being Promethean or Atlas-like or noble or even helpful in any way. How much easier it is, surely, to make a devout gesture and install a solemn art icon by Jean Dubuffet or Isamu Noguchi or Henry Moore. Noguchi's solid geometries, lumps, and extruded squiggles, and Moore's hard boluses with holes in them, have become the very emblems of corporate devoutness.

This type of abstract public sculpture is known within the architectural profession, sotto voce, as the Turd in the Plaza school. The term was coined by James Wines, who said, "I don't care if they want to put up these boring glass boxes, but why do they always deposit that little turd in the plaza when they leave?"

We are long since past the age when autocrats made aesthetic decisions based on what *they* wanted to see in public. Today corporations, no less than individuals, turn to the clerisy, saying, in effect, "Please give us whatever we should have to certify the devoutness of our dedication to art."

If people want to place Turds in the Plazas as a form of religious offering or prayer, and they own the plazas, there isn't much anybody else can do about it. But what happens when they use public money, tax money, to do the same thing on plazas owned by the public? At that point you're in for a glorious farce.

The fun began with a competition for the Franklin Delano Roosevelt memorial. In 1955 Congress created a commission, which called in a jury composed of art curates, headed by an orthodox Bauhaus-style architect named Pietro Belluschi. By 1955 this seemed natural enough. In fact, it was a novel step, and an indication of the emerging power of the art clerisy. In the case of the Lincoln Memorial, completed in 1922, Congress appointed a commission, and the commission solicited entries from only two men, Henry Bacon and John Russell Pope, both classicists, and chose Bacon. To make sure that the Jefferson Memorial, completed in 1947, would match the Lincoln Memorial, another congressional commission chose Pope. In the case of the Roosevelt memorial—a project initiated just eight years after the completion of the Jefferson Memorial—neither Congress nor the public could figure out what hit them.

As soon as the idea of building a memorial was announced, every American who had lived through the Depression or World War II could envision Roosevelt's prognathous jaw and his grin with more teeth than a possum and his cigarette holder cocked up at a forty-five-degree angle. So what did they get? The jury selected a design by a devout modernist sculptor named Norman Hoberman: eight rectangular white concrete slabs—some of them as high as 200 feet. That was it: homage not to Franklin Roosevelt but to—of course!—Art. The Roosevelt family and Congress were nonplussed at first and, soon enough, furious. The press named the slabs Instant Stonehenge. Congress asked to see the designs of the other five finalists. But there was nothing to choose from. All five designs were abstract. To this day no Roosevelt memorial has been built, even though the project remains officially alive.

This *opéra bouffe* has been repeated with stunning regularity ever since. Our own period has been especially rich, thanks in no small part to the General Services Administration's Art-in-Architecture program and the Veterans Administration's Art in Public Places program, under which the federal government in effect gives the art clerisy millions of tax dollars for the creation of public sculpture.

In 1976, the city of Hartford decided to reinforce its reputation as the Athens of lower central midwestern New England by having an important piece of sculpture installed downtown. It followed what is by now the usual procedure, which is to turn the choice over to a panel of "experts" in the field—i.e., the clerisy, in this case, six curators, critics, and academicians, three of them chosen by the National Endowment for the Arts, which put up half the money. So one day in 1978 a man named Carl Andre arrived in Hartford with thirty-six rocks. Not carved stones, not even polished boluses of the Henry Moore sort—rocks. He put them on the ground in a triangle, like bowling pins. Then he presented the city council with a bill for $87,000. Nonplussed and, soon enough, furious, the citizenry hooted and jeered and called the city council members imbeciles while the council members alternately hit the sides of their heads with their hands and made imaginary snowballs. Nevertheless, they approved payment, and the rocks—entitled *Stone Field*—are still there.

One day in 1981, the Civil Service workers in the new Javits Federal Building in Manhattan went outside to the little plaza in front of the building at lunchtime to do the usual, which was to have their tuna puffs and diet Shastas, and there, running through the middle of it, was a wall of black steel twelve feet high and half a city block long. Nonplussed and, soon enough, furious, 1,300 of them drew up a petition asking the GSA to remove it, only to be informed that this was, in fact, a major work of art, entitled *Tilted Arc*, by a famous American sculptor named Richard Serra. Serra did not help things measurably by explaining that he was "redefining the space" for the poor Civil Service lifers and helping to wean them away from the false values "created by advertising and corporations." Was it his fault if "it offends people to have their preconceptions of reality changed"? This seventy-three-ton gesture of homage to contemporary art remains in place.

The public sees nothing, absolutely nothing, in these stone fields, tilted arcs, and Instant Stonehenges, because it was never meant to. The public is looking at the arcana of the new religion of the educated classes. At this point one might well ask what the clerisy itself sees in them, a question that would plunge us into doctrines as abstruse as any that engaged the medieval Scholastics. Andre's *Stone Field*, for example, was created to illustrate three devout theories concerning the nature of sculpture. One, a sculpture should not be placed upon that bourgeois device, the pedestal, which seeks to elevate it above the people. (Therefore, the rocks are on the ground.) Two, a sculpture should "express its gravity." (And what expresses gravity better than rocks lying on the ground?) Three, a sculpture should not be that piece of bourgeois pretentiousness, the "picture in the air" (such as the statues of Lee and Duke); it should force the viewer to confront its "object-ness." (You want object-ness? Take a look at a plain rock! Take a look at thirty-six rocks!)

Public bafflement or opposition is taken as evidence of an object's spiritual worthiness. It means that the public's "preconceptions of reality" have been changed, to use Serra's words. When George Sugarman's sculpture for the plaza of the new federal courthouse in Baltimore was protested by both the building's employees and the judges, Sugarman said: "Isn't controversy part of what modern art is all about?" These are devout incantations of the Turbulence Theorem, which has been an article of faith within the clerisy for the past forty years. It was originally enunciated by the critic Clement Greenberg, who said that all great contemporary art "looks ugly at first." It was expanded upon by the art historian Leo Steinberg, who said that the great artists cause us "to abandon our most cherished values." In short, if a work of art troubles you, it's probably good; if you detest it, it's probably great.

In such a situation, naturally you need expert counsel: i.e., the clerisy. The notion of "the art expert" is now widely accepted. The curators of programs such as Art-in-Architecture and Art in Public Places are contemptuous of the idea that politicians, civic leaders, or any other representative of the public—much less the people themselves—should determine what sculpture is installed in public. The director of the Art-in Architecture program, Donald Thalacker, once said: "You go to a medical expert for medical advice; you go to a legal expert for advice about the law. . . . Yet when it comes to art, it seems they want the local gas station attendant in on things." This is a lovely piece of nonsense—as anyone who sought to devise a licensing examination for an art expert or, for that matter, an artist, would soon discover. An "art expert" is merely someone who understands and believes in the tastes and values of the tiny art village of New York.

The public is nonplussed and, soon enough, becomes furious—and also uneasy. After all, if understanding such arcana is the hallmark of the educated classes today, and you find yourself absolutely baffled, what does that say about your level of cultivation? Since 1975, attendance at museums of art in the United States has risen from 42 million to 60 million people per year. Why? In 1980 the Hirshhorn Museum did a survey of people who came to the museum over a seven-month period. I find the results fascinating. Thirty-six percent said they had come to the museum to learn about contemporary art. Thirty-two percent said they had come to learn about a particular contemporary artist. Thirteen percent came on tours. Only 15 percent said they were there for what was once the conventional goal of museumgoers: to enjoy the pictures and sculptures. The conventional goal of museumgoers today is something quite different. Today they are there to learn—and to see the light. At the Hirshhorn, the people who were interviewed in the survey said such things as: "I know this is great art, and now I feel so unintelligent." And: "After coming to this museum, I now feel so much better about art and so much worse about me."

In other words: "I believe, O Lord, but I am unworthy! Reveal to me Thy mysteries!"

QUESTIONS FOR READING, RESPONDING, AND WRITING

Summarizing Main Points

1. Though "nonrepresentational" or "abstract" modern art, especially art purchased by corporations for public display, clearly "means" something, according to Wolfe, what does Wolfe claim such art tells the public? How does Wolfe say the public generally reacts?
2. Describe the comparison Wolfe makes between art today and religion in the past. List each similarity. Are there any other likenesses that you can think of that Wolfe never mentions?

Analyzing Methods of Discourse

1. Wolfe claims that the standard reaction of the public to art is to be "nonplussed and, soon enough . . . furious." What does it mean to be "nonplussed"? Is it the same as "public bafflement"? Wolfe repeats that standard reaction several times. What point is he trying to make by such repetition?
2. The last time Wolfe says that "the public is nonplussed and, soon enough, becomes furious," he adds "and also uneasy." Find this phrase in the essay and explain its relation to Wolfe's last sentence: "In other words: I believe, O Lord, but I am unworthy! Reveal to me Thy mysteries!"

Focusing on the Field

1. Wolfe says that "an 'art expert' is merely someone who understands and believes in the tastes and values of the tiny art village of New York." Who, according to Wolfe, should judge the value or worth of a piece of art? Do you agree or disagree? When the piece of art in question sits in a plaza where workers "have their tuna puffs and diet Shastas," who do you feel should decide on the worthiness of that art?
2. Wolfe's essay is rather informal. Do you believe that informality helps or hinders his argument? Does that informality suggest anything about Wolfe's attitude toward art in general? Is that informality an argument in itself?

Writing Assignments

1. Choose a work of art from your own community and in a short essay argue that it is or is not part of the "arcana of the new religion of the educated classes."
2. Consider what John Canaday says about art in "What Is a Painting?" In a brief essay drawing on both Canaday and Wolfe for evidence, argue that the two authors either agree or disagree as to what modern art is.

Czeslaw Milosz

ON VIRTUE

Born in Lithuania in 1911, Czeslaw Milosz spent his early childhood in Russia and later, after World War I, moved with his family to Wilno, Poland, where he attended Catholic schools. Milosz's college experiences introduced him to Marxist political philosophy and, during World War II, Milosz served secretly in Warsaw as an editor and writer for Polish resistance publications. After the war, Milosz continued to serve his socialistic ideals, working for the Polish diplomatic service until political upheaval eventually forced him to move to Paris in 1951. During all this time, Milosz had been writing poetry and intellectual essays of various sorts.

A professor of Slavic literature and languages at the University of California at Berkeley since 1961, Milosz was the winner of the 1980 Nobel Prize for Literature. At Berkeley, Milosz continues to translate and to write essays and poems. His nonfiction work has included a study of intellectuals and Communism, *The Captive Mind* (1953), an autobiographical history, *Native Realm* (1968), criticism of Russian and Polish literature, *Emperor of the Earth: Modes of Eccentric Vision* (1977), and a collection of philosophical essays, *Views from San Francisco Bay* (1982), which includes "On Virtue," reprinted below. Milosz has also published poetry, *Selected Poems* and *Bells in Winter,* and fiction. "On Virtue," at once deeply philosophical, yet entirely applicable to common experience, epitomizes Milosz's concerns.

> Appellata est enim ex viro virtus; viri autem propria maxime est fortitudo.
> [The word "virtue" derives from *vir*, man, while courage best characterizes
> man.] Cicero

Virtue, *virtus*, is that strength of character from whence arise the
qualities indispensable for standing up to the world—courage, resolve,
perseverance, control of the constantly changing emotions and impulses.
If I regarded nature sentimentally, I would treat virtue with less respect.
Since nature is not a loving mother but ravages and kills us without
qualms if we find ourselves in it without weapons or tools, virtue must be
held in high esteem, for it alone permits the effective use of weapons and
tools. The courage (*fortitudo*) of which Cicero speaks may reside in the
evil and the good, the wise and the foolish. It manifests itself in situations
that exist independent of our will, and it commands us to behave in one
definite way and no other. Where the struggle with nature has imposed
upon men the necessity of organization, thus dividing them into those
who give orders and those who carry them out, the oppressors and the
oppressed, the master cannot dispense with virtue without endangering
his position as master, while the slave is compelled to virtue by his desire
to survive and to outwit his master. The history of mankind is astonishing
in its endless examples of virtue keeping societies, nations, and civilizations alive—the virtue of leaders and soldiers, torturers and the tortured,
saints and criminals, captains and crews, owners and workers. No one
can deny strength of character to Genghis Khan and his commanders, or
to the knights of Cortes and Pizarro, or to the capitalist ascetics who
tormented themselves as much as they did others, or to the generations of
peasants who supported their families by hard labor on small plots of
land. The human being is worthy of admiration because he suffers so
much and remains undaunted in spite of it. If, for better or worse, our
planet has been subjugated by technology, this probably did not occur
because of some impersonal, inevitable laws of development, but because
of the virtue of the groups, nations, and classes whose self-discipline
created the appropriate conditions for it.

Until now, virtue had to be exercised in the struggle with nature and
the struggle among men in which the losers met with extermination.
Were it not for the abilities of self-discipline and self-denial, the conflicts
that pitted men against each other would not have been so merciless. The
greatest battlefields of our century—Verdun in World War I and the
Russian plains in World War II—are enduring testimony to the unbelievable courage of the most ordinary men, the most anonymous country
people and city dwellers who wore the uniform of the French and German, the German and Russian infantries. But, in times of peace as well,
these same farmers, workers, shopkeepers, and bookkeepers gave proof of
their merits, going to work each morning in acceptance of the rule "He

who doesn't work doesn't eat." It was also their hands that made the cannon, machine guns, tanks, and shells with which they were to slaughter each other.

Arguments can be set forth against virtue, for it fosters obedience and is an agent of order, whatever sort that order may be, splendid or sordid. Heretics, renegades, and revolutionaries have not been devoid of virtue, but on the whole, virtue does not coexist very well with the anxious mind and the restless imagination. The mind, always somewhat skeptical, whispers its various doubts concerning our goals, even the smallest of them, when all our efforts should be directed toward their fulfillment; the imagination throws bridges from the present to the next hour or day, which is not healthy. Perhaps virtue leans toward the conservative or reactionary. One Polish critic reproached Joseph Conrad for glorifying the heroism of the crew in his tales of the sea. His seamen do not hesitate to sacrifice their lives to do what must be done, and they do not reflect on what is served by their efforts. The ship, however, is the property of the shipowners, who sent it to sea with a cargo of goods to be sold for a profit. Thus, Joseph Conrad is, indirectly, a defender of the established order; that is, capitalism. This conclusion is not entirely without its logic, especially since the poverty of the lower classes in Conrad's England was truly horrendous, but that logic is none too exacting, either. Any social system must appeal to the virtue of its workers, sailors, and soldiers or cease to exist. If, in the countries that are called socialist, the workers, sailors, and soldiers were to perform their duties out of love for the national economy, nobody would lift a finger. The critic's conclusion seems simply to mean that the virtue in people working for my affairs is praiseworthy, whereas it merits disapproval in those who work for my competitors and opponents.

There is no doubt, however, that a writer whose principal concern is the manly *fortitudo* of his heroes remains more or less insensitive to revolutionary slogans. The practice of virtue is difficult, it demands great willpower, and, for that reason, the hatred of one's superiors, the mocking of them and the goals they set, and the incitement of rebellion are rejected as dissension, anarchy, weakness, a temptation that must be overcome if one does not wish to be derelict in one's duty. The virtuous do not question. Whoever their captain, leader, or monarch may be, they do what they are told because they must. This does not mean that they are simply robots. They act in this way because others like themselves are beside them and they must be loyal to them, in solidarity with them. This solidarity can also be called conformism.

The United States is a land of virtue. Through virtue it arose and achieved its technical might. The solidarity of the colonists proved stronger than their loyalty to the English king; here one should ponder how and when virtue, though basically indisposed to mutterings and seditious acrimony, gives itself, once past a certain threshold, into the service of revolution. But those were not simple decisions, and both sides displayed great fortitude in the War for Independence, just as both sides did later on in the Civil War, an especially bloody conflict for the nineteenth century. But is not the entire growth of America the quest for profit, the worship of the golden calf, the rule of the dollar? Undoubtedly. And is not money a quantitative standard of measure in the duels of men; is it not admitted that, empirically, the "best" man wins? Does not "best" mean the braver, the more competent, the more tenacious, the more industrious? And, above all, the one better able to repress his own momentary whims, fears, dreams, despair, cravings? Here virtue, unfortunately, seems to consist primarily of repression and renunciation. I would like to lie in the sun, but I get up and go because I must. I am afraid, but I forbid myself fear. I do not believe that what I am doing has any meaning, but I forbid myself to think that. I have worked enough, now I should take a rest, but I do not because I have, in advance, designated the hour, or the year, when I will be free to rest.

Repression. In the name of satisfying a need tomorrow, I deny myself its satisfaction today. Virtue, too, takes that form. Instead of enjoying a day off from work, I hit on the idea of devoting the day to fashioning a tool that will make my work easier tomorrow. The next day it occurs to me that it is worth devoting many days off to the making of a tool that will permit the fashioning of other tools in a shorter time, and so on. A parable of humanity producing machines that produce other machines that produce other machines. Or, in relation to an individual fate, a parable of someone who has toiled for decades, suppressed all his own needs, saving his money to someday finally "enjoy life," and who then realizes that it is too late, for he no longer has any desires. Or, to return to the literature of the sea, which always depicts the crew, a miniature society, pitted against an element representing the universe, Herman Melville's novel, *Moby Dick*, furnishes another example: Captain Ahab, obsessed by the pursuit of the white whale that gives him neither rest nor respite. Perhaps Ahab was insane, but he had, in its highest form, the virtue that represses its possessor as well as others.

Technology is virtue condensed, consolidated in tangible forms. Although technological progress can be imagined in a world of universal brotherhood, kindness, and peace, nothing of the sort has happened yet; any invention we can name was realized under conditions of more or less open and active force, compulsion, exploitation, with severe sanctions imposed on weakness. The two faces of technology, one beneficent, one malevolent, have their counterpart in the two faces of virtue, one of which is death's helper. For that simple reason, virtue has no love for squabblers and skeptics. One of the most virtuous peoples, the Germans, brought to power a madman more dangerous than Captain Ahab, for he was not commanding a ship but a nation that was obedient to him to the end, to the final catastrophe.

American virtue, primarily that of rural America, is nourished on naïveté, ignorance, ordinary dullness. The course of nearly every election leads one to suppose there is nothing so foolish that it cannot be used as bait, if only it is American enough—that is, is not marked as a foreign import. It would simply be light-mindedness not to see the seeds of destruction here, of the whole country by a new civil war, or of the whole world. The protest of the other America, now many millions strong, takes the form of hatred for virtue, for it is virtue which compels one to join the "rat race," to accept the given, to achieve, act, strive, to conform to the morals of one's neighbor.

To negate virtue, one must oppose industry with idleness, puritanical repression of urges with instant gratification, tomorrow with today, alcohol with marijuana, moderation in the display of emotion with shameless emotionality, the isolation of the individual with the collective, calculation with carelessness, sobriety with ecstasy, racism with the blending of the races, obedience with political rebellion, stiff dignity with poetry, music, and dance. In the background there is the permanent conviction that *we have gone too far*, that virtue has taken us too far; hence the readiness to smash machines, those guardians of the house of bondage. Among the revolt's many ingredients, the strongest is probably the dream of a return. The place of honor is given to primitive man, who has none of civilization's repressions, is not ashamed of his instincts, whose body rhythms are joined with those of nature. No one outside of America is aware how deeply the revolutionary gospel has been influenced by a religious admiration for nature and an obsessive guilt at its poisoning and pollution by business and industry.

The works of three American writers—Thoreau, Whitman, and Melville—sketched out (leaving room to grow) all the problems that torment their heirs. At a time when progress and Western civilization were being paid homage, Melville did not believe in the beneficial results of industry and commerce, and he rejected the Christianity which was then respected, sincerely or insincerely. The narrator of *Moby Dick* is set between Captain Ahab, in whom the virtue and madness of Western Christian man are fused, and the Polynesian, Queequeg. Victory falls (posthumously) to the latter, a pagan with no care for the morrow, who lives in an eternal now, devoid of any ambition to prove his worth here or in the hereafter, free of any impulse toward self-repression. Besides, for Melville, Queequeg had a different sort of *fortitudo* from the virtue of white men—the (Oriental) dissolution of the individual in the cosmic flow, in the universal cycle turning life into death and death into life, so that everything is accepted and actions are performed almost impersonally through submission to the great rhythm.

Virtue in the Western sense is now not only exposed to the malice of today's imitators of Queequeg, it is also subject to erosion from within, for, ultimately, it needs a certain complex of conventional beliefs to ensure its safety from the subversive whisperings of the mind and imagination. Literature and film have sufficiently acquainted us with the "breakdown" of the respectable citizen, who always did what was expected of him, worked from/until, earned a living, and then suddenly—often as a result of meeting a demon woman—discovers the emptiness, the absurdity of his way of life. This is a character invented by vindictive writers hostile to virtue. But breakdowns, though in somewhat less violent form, are not limited to individuals. The invisible withering of Christianity and the pressure of the myths of advertising (primarily the sexual myth or the myth of the Islands of Happiness, where what is natural is good) cannot help but weaken Puritanical restraint. The myths of advertising are in themselves contradictory. They create needs in order to stimulate ceaseless competition, which requires self-repression. At the same time its philosophy, opposed to the concept of Original Sin, deprives discipline of its basis and elevates today above a temporal or posthumous tomorrow.

There is a large element of uncertainty here; no one can measure the extent of the erosion or judge how today's virtue differs from the virtue of a hundred years ago. I have attended country fairs—in Oregon, for example, in the little town of Myrtle Point, Coos County. In that agricultural valley— not really rural, since there's so much smoke from sawmills and paper mills in the air—changing beliefs and convictions have been completely absorbed by the normal course of life, repeated from generation to generation.

The parade down Main Street, the American flag, the beautiful horses of the sheriff and his men, decorated saddles inlaid with silver. A band wearing false noses and Tyrolean hats goes by in a truck. The pom-pom girls, their ages ranging from sixteen to six, the smallest ones struggling awkwardly with their batons, sticking out their tongues. Floats with goddesses of plenty representing Progress or the blessing of Pomona. Clubs, associations, lodges. The Lodges of the Temple of the Orient: shopkeepers with painted-on mustaches, dressed up as Oriental kings in broad silk galligaskins, turbans, and slippers with pointed toes, pipe fifes and pound drums. Again, beautiful horses ridden by the children of farm families, boys and girls, long-legged, lean, straight in the stirrups, the costumes always changing, for one group follows another, the Caballeros, the River Rangers, the Coos Rangers. The cars of candidates running for local office or the state senate: "Vote for." A dragon that stretches out its neck every few seconds and belches smoke, an advertisement for a bulldozer company. Trucks, each carrying one felled tree more than a meter in diameter—the drivers are those who took first place in the professional competition, an event that makes sense in this region of sawmills. Much regal beauty—the queens of the melon growers, of the fishermen, of the county, the town. They throw kisses, smiles. A few girls are dressed up as squaws. There is even one genuine Indian leading a team of sheep dogs. Then the annual exhibits—stalls of cows, horses, sheep, pigs, domestic fowl, ribbons for first place, second, and honorable mention.

All this is quite typical and could be found in hundreds of small towns and counties across America. For a revolutionary, this is nothing more than the dull, insipid life of yokels and provincial boors. I, however, have a wonderful time at country fairs and applaud them. The difference between us is that, for me, all the frameworks that permit the daily practice of virtue are very fragile, it is easy to destroy them, as I saw for myself while observing ideologically planned regimes at close range. Virtue: to be thirteen years old, jump up every day at dawn to feed, water, and brush your own horse, bullock, ram, to learn everything that could ensure victory in the livestock competition. The long-haired revolutionary, usually raised in a big city in a well-to-do family, has no idea that a few thoughtless edicts are enough to ruin agriculture and set the lives of farm children on a completely different course, not necessarily a better one.

However, it is perfectly probable that a great change is gradually occurring and that there will be increasingly less virtue, simply because a smaller number of virtuous people will ensure the efficient functioning of society as a whole. If machines are virtue consolidated in matter, they can replace the efforts of the human will, and their cybernetic brains will not have to battle emotions, which do not exist in metal hearts. With the exception of a relatively small number of administrators, the remainder of the citizenry will be liberated from the afflictions and the triumphs *fortitudo* provides. Perhaps, but there is one other possibility that should not be excluded: perverse history, in order to check humanity's too-rapid progress, could throw its temporary support to systems that idolize economic inefficiency and privation, where everyone labors feverishly from morning till night with paltry results.

QUESTIONS FOR READING, RESPONDING, AND WRITING

Summarizing Main Points

1. Milosz says that courage "may reside in the evil and the good, the wise and the foolish." Explain this statement and provide examples of the courageous evil

man and the courageous foolish man. According to Milosz—and to Cicero—how is virtue different from courage?

2. List the human attributes that, according to Milosz, are necessary for virtue to exist. List those human attributes that Milosz says cannot be present side by side with virtue.

Analyzing Methods of Discourse

1. Basically, Milosz presents his argument by redefinition. At one point, he suggests that technology has "two faces." What are those two faces, and what relation does each have to Milosz's definitions of virtue?
2. Milosz's argument here is very complex. Rather than straightforwardly arguing for or against a particular kind of virtue, Milosz reviews the consequences of virtuous behavior in different circumstances. On reading the essay for the first time, was there any particular place where you were surprised by those consequences? How did that surprise work to reinforce Milosz's argumentative tactics?

Focusing on the Field

1. Milosz suggests that the Oriental sort of virtue is different from the Western sort. Choose a particular example of Western virtue as Milosz describes it and explain how it would be different in the East.
2. According to Milosz, what is the greatest danger for virtue—or salvation from it—in the United States today?

Writing Assignments

1. In an essay that works by way of redefinition and example as Milosz's does, advocate a particular point of view toward an abstract "idea," such as "courage," "loyalty," "faith," or "brotherhood."
2. Alan Bullock describes "the young Adolf Hitler" in an essay of the same name. Drawing on Bullock and Milosz for evidence, in a short essay argue that Bullock's portrait of Hitler does or does not embody "virtue" as Milosz defines it.

James Baldwin

IF BLACK ENGLISH ISN'T A LANGUAGE, THEN TELL ME, WHAT IS?

Born in Harlem in 1924, James Baldwin grew up surrounded by black English. The son of a minister and the oldest of nine children, Baldwin was himself a preacher at Harlem's Fireside Pentecostal Church in his early teens. His writing career likewise began early: "I began plotting novels at about the time I learned to read." Yet for many years, Baldwin only found time to write after more mundane duties were over: after high school, he worked as a dishwasher, waiter, and office boy in New York City. In 1945, a fellowship afforded Baldwin the opportunity to write full-time, but he still felt suffocated by a society that "seemed to lock every black writer into crude simplicities of propaganda and protests." In 1948, at the age of 24, Baldwin escaped to France where he lived in self-imposed exile for nearly ten years. In Paris, he found the time—and the distance—to explore his feelings about religion, sexuality, America, and race relations. Three of his most important works emerged, all of which are basically autobiographical: the novels, *Go Tell It on the Mountain* (1953) and *Giovanni's Room* (1956), and a collection of essays, *Notes of a Native Son* (1955). Since then, Baldwin has published other essays and works of fiction and drama, sometimes working in collaboration with other noted writers, such as Margaret Mead and Alex Haley.

The essay that follows suggests Baldwin's ability to ignore the simple, superficial, and too-pat answers often given to some of the hardest questions facing society today.

The argument concerning the use, or the status, or the reality, of black English is rooted in American history and has absolutely nothing to do with the question the argument supposes itself to be posing. The argument has nothing to do with language itself but with the *role* of language. Language, incontestably, reveals the speaker. Language, also, far more dubiously, is meant to define the other—and, in this case, the other is refusing to be defined by a language that has never been able to recognize him.

People evolve a language in order to describe and thus control their circumstances, or in order not to be submerged by a reality that they cannot articulate. (And, if they cannot articulate it, they *are* submerged.) A Frenchman living in Paris speaks a subtly and crucially different language from that of the man living in Marseilles; neither sounds very much like a man living in Quebec; and they would all have great difficulty in apprehending what the man from Guadeloupe, or Martinique, is saying, to say nothing of the man from Senegal—although the "common" language of all these areas is French. But each has paid, and is paying, a different price for this "common" language, in which, as it turns out, they are not saying, and cannot be saying, the same things: They each have very different realities to articulate or control.

What joins all languages, and all men, is the necessity to confront life, in order, not inconceivably, to outwit death: The price for this is the acceptance, and achievement, of one's temporal identity. So that, for example, though it is not taught in the schools (and this has the potential of becoming a political issue) the south of France still clings to its ancient and musical Provençal, which resists being described as a "dialect." And much of the tension in the Basque countries, and in Wales, is due to the Basque and Welsh determination not to allow their languages to be destroyed. This determination also feeds the flames in Ireland for among the many indignities the Irish have been forced to undergo at English hands is the English contempt for their language.

It goes without saying, then, that language is also a political instrument, means, and proof of power. It is the most vivid and crucial key to identity: It reveals the private identity, and connects one with, or divorces one from, the larger public, or communal identity. There have been, and are, times, and places, when to speak a certain language could be dangerous, even fatal. Or, one may speak the same language, but in such a way that one's antecedents are revealed, or (one hopes) hidden. This is true in France, and is absolutely true in England: The range (and reign) of accents on that damp little island make England coherent for the English and totally incomprehensible for everyone else. To open your mouth in England is (if I may use black English) to "put your business in the street": You have confessed your parents, your youth, your school, your salary, your self-esteem, and, alas, your future.

Now, I do not know what white Americans would sound like if there had never been any black people in the United States, but they would not sound the way they sound. *Jazz*, for example, is a very specific sexual term, as in *jazz me, baby*, but white people purified it into the Jazz Age. *Sock it to me*, which means, roughly, the same thing, has been adopted by Nathaniel Hawthorne's descendants with no qualms or hesitations at all, along with *let it all hang out* and *right on! Beat to his socks*, which was once the black's most total and despairing image of poverty, was transformed into a thing called the Beat Generation, which phenomenon was, largely, composed of *uptight*, middle-class white people, imitating poverty, trying to *get down*, to get *with it*, doing their *thing*, doing their despairing best to be *funky*, which we, the blacks, never dreamed of doing—we *were* funky, baby, like *funk* was going out of style.

Now, no one can eat his cake, and have it, too, and it is late in the day to attempt to penalize black people for having created a language that permits the nation its only glimpse of reality, a language without which the nation would be even more *whipped* than it is.

I say that this present skirmish is rooted in American history, and it is. Black English is the creation of the black diaspora. Blacks came to the United States chained to each other, but from different tribes: Neither could speak the other's language. If two black people, at that bitter hour of the world's history, had been able to speak to each other, the institution of chattel slavery could never have lasted as long as it did. Subsequently, the slave was given, under the eye, and the gun, of his master, Congo Square, and the Bible—or, in other words, and under these conditions, the slave began the formation of the black church, and it is within this unprecedented tabernacle that black English began to be formed. This was not, merely, as in the European example, the adoption of a foreign tongue, but an alchemy that transformed ancient elements into new language: *A language comes into existence by means of brutal necessity, and the rules of the language are dictated by what the language must convey.*

There was a moment, in time, and in this place, when my brother, or my mother, or my father, or my sister, had to convey to me, for example, the danger in which I was standing from the white man standing just behind me, and to convey this with a speed, and in a language, that the white man could not possibly understand, and that, indeed, he cannot understand, until today. He cannot afford to understand it. This understanding would reveal to him too much about himself, and smash that mirror before which he has been frozen for so long.

Now, if this passion, this skill, this (to quote Toni Morrison) "sheer intelligence," this incredible music, the mighty achievement of having brought a people utterly unknown to, or despised by "history"—to have brought this people to their present, troubled, troubling, and unassailable and unanswerable place—if this absolutely unprecedented journey does not indicate that black English is a language, I am curious to know what definition of language is to be trusted.

A people at the center of the Western world, and in the midst of so hostile a population, has not endured and transcended by means of what is patronizingly called a "dialect." We, the blacks, are in trouble, certainly, but we are not doomed, and we are not inarticulate because we are not compelled to defend a morality that we know to be a lie.

The brutal truth is that the bulk of the white people in America never had any interest in educating black people, except as this could serve white purposes. It is not the black child's language that is in question, it is not his language that is despised: It is his experience. A child cannot be taught by anyone who despises him, and a child cannot afford to be fooled. A child cannot be taught by anyone whose demand, essentially, is that the child repudiate his experience, and all that gives him sustenance, and enter a limbo in which he will no longer be black, and in which he knows that he can never become white. Black people have lost too many black children that way.

And, after all, finally, in a country with standards so untrustworthy, a country that makes heroes of so many criminal mediocrities, a country unable to face why so many of the nonwhite are in prison, or on the needle, or standing, futureless, in the streets—it may very well be that both the child, and his elder, have concluded that they have nothing whatever to learn from the people of a country that has managed to learn so little.

QUESTIONS FOR READING, RESPONDING, AND WRITING

Summarizing Main Points

1. Reread Baldwin's first paragraph. After reflecting on the rest of the essay, describe what Baldwin would consider the "use" of language. What would he say its "status" is? Its "reality"? List the examples of the "*role* of language" that Baldwin advocates.
2. According to Baldwin, black English has been "patronizingly called a 'dialect.' " Who has been patronizing and why? If black English were considered a "language," would black people gain anything, according to Baldwin? Would other people?

Analyzing Methods of Discourse

1. Baldwin provides several examples of other languages that "resist being described as . . . dialect[s]," languages that describe different realities. What common point do you see to Baldwin's choice of examples? How do these examples prepare the reader for Baldwin's main points?
2. Though Baldwin employs black language to help make his points, for the majority of his essay he uses standard English. Why do you suppose Baldwin proceeds in this manner? Later Baldwin says, "We, the blacks, are in trouble, certainly, but we are not doomed." Does Baldwin intend his audience to be limited to blacks? Support your answer with evidence from the essay.

Focusing on the Field

1. Baldwin says early on that because Provençal is not taught in French schools, it "has the potential of becoming a political issue." What does Baldwin mean by this statement? Is Baldwin discussing any other "political issues" either explicitly or implicitly?
2. Richard Rodriguez in "Memories of a Bilingual Childhood" states that "What I needed to learn in school was that I had the right, and the obligation, to speak the public language," and that standard English taught him that "I had a public identity." Would Baldwin agree with Rodriguez?

Writing Assignments

1. Most groups of people develop special "languages" to help them understand their particular worlds. In high school and college, cliques of students, for instance, use special words and phrases unique to their groups. Write an essay that identifies these words, the cliques that use them, and how those words function.
2. Study the functions of language that Janet Emig presents in "Writing as a Mode of Learning." In a short essay, argue that Baldwin's conception of the functions of language either does or does not fit the categories that Emig presents.

Flannery O'Connor

THE TEACHING OF LITERATURE

Though the quantity of her writing was limited by her early death from lupus, (Mary) Flannery O'Connor (1925–1964) is still considered by many critics to be the greatest short story writer of our time. Her reputation as a prose stylist has also continued to rise since the posthumous publication of her letters, collected in *The Habit of Being* (1979), and her nonfiction, collected in *Mysteries and Manners: Occasional Prose* (1969), from which "The Teaching of Literature" is taken. O'Connor felt that "the novel is an art form and when you use it for anything other than art, you pervert it. . . . If you do manage to use it successfully for social, religious, or other purposes, it is because you made it art first." Yet she also knew that to realize that art, a good writer must begin with "experience, not an abstraction." In her fiction—two novels, *Wise Blood* and *The Violent Bear It Away,* and two collections of short stories, *A Good Man Is Hard to Find* and *Everything That Rises Must Converge*—O'Connor blends humor and violence, creating boldly unique characters who come to find themselves and their redemption, as she suggests below, in "the experience of limitation."

Born in Savannah, Georgia, O'Connor studied English at the Women's College of Georgia and writing at the University of Iowa. A devout Roman Catholic, O'Connor spent most of her life at her family's home in Milledgeville, Georgia, where she wrote, cared for her prize-winning peacocks, and conducted a wide-ranging correspondence.

Every now and then the novelist looks up from his work long enough to become aware of a general public dissatisfaction with novelists. There's always a voice coming from somewhere that tells him he isn't doing his duty, and that if he doesn't mend his ways soon, there are going to be no more fiction readers—just as, for all practical purposes, there are now no more poetry readers.

Of course, of all the various kinds of artists, the fiction writer is most deviled by the public. Painters and musicians are protected somewhat since they don't deal with what everyone knows about, but the fiction writer writes about life, and so anyone living considers himself an authority on it.

I find that everybody approaches the novel according to his particular interest—the doctor looks for a disease, the minister looks for a sermon, the poor look for money, and the rich look for justification; and if they find what they want, or at least what they can recognize, then they judge the piece of fiction to be superior.

In the standing dispute between the novelist and the public, the teacher of English is a sort of middleman, and I have occasionally come to think about what really happens when a piece of fiction is set before students. I suppose this is a terrifying experience for the teacher.

I have a young cousin who told me that she reviewed my novel for her ninth-grade English class, and when I asked—without a trace of gratitude—why she did that, she said, "Because I had to have a book the teacher wouldn't have read." So I asked her what she said about it, and she said, "I said 'My cousin wrote this book.' " I asked her if that was all she said, and she said, "No, I copied the rest off the jacket."

So you see I do approach this problem realistically, knowing that perhaps it has no solution this side of the grave, but feeling nevertheless that there may be profit in talking about it.

I don't recall that when I was in high school or college, any novel was ever presented to me to study as a novel. In fact, I was well on the way to getting a Master's degree in English before I really knew what fiction was, and I doubt if I would ever have learned then, had I not been trying to write it. I believe that it's perfectly possible to run a course of academic degrees in English and to emerge a seemingly respectable Ph.D. and still not know how to read fiction.

The fact is, people don't know what they are expected to do with a novel, believing, as so many do, that art must be utilitarian, that it must do something, rather than be something. Their eyes have not been opened to what fiction is, and they are like the blind men who went to visit the elephant—each feels a different part and comes away with a different impression.

Now it's my feeling that if more attention, of a technical kind, were paid to the subject of fiction in the schools, even at the high-school level, this situation might be improved.

Of course, I'm in a bad position here. So far as teaching is concerned, I am in a state of pristine innocence. But I do believe that there is still a little common ground between the writer of English and the teacher of it. If you could eliminate the student from your concern, and I could eliminate the reader from mine, I believe that we should be able to find ourselves enjoying a mutual concern, which would be a love of the language and what can be done with it in the interests of dramatic truth. I believe that this is actually the primary concern of us both, and that you can't serve the student, nor I the reader, unless our aim is first to be true to the subject and its necessities. This is the reason I think the study of the novel in the schools must be a technical study.

It is the business of fiction to embody mystery through manners, and mystery is a great embarrassment to the modern mind. About the turn of the century, Henry James wrote that the young woman of the future, though she would be taken out for airings in a flying-machine, would know nothing of mystery or manners. James had no business to limit the prediction to one sex; otherwise, no one can very well disagree with him. The mystery he was talking about is the mystery of our position on earth, and the manners are those conventions which, in the hands of the artist, reveal that central mystery.

Not long ago a teacher told me that her best students feel that it is no longer necessary to write anything. She said they think that everything can be done with figures now, and that what can't be done with figures isn't worth doing. I think this is a natural belief for a generation that has been made to feel that the aim of learning is to eliminate mystery. For such people, fiction can be very disturbing, for the fiction writer is concerned with mystery that is lived. He's concerned with ultimate mystery as we find it embodied in the concrete world of sense experience.

Since this is his aim, all levels of meaning in fiction have come increasingly to be found in the literal level. There is no room for abstract expressions of compassion or piety or morality in the fiction itself. This means that the writer's moral sense must coincide with his dramatic sense, and this makes the presentation of fiction to the student, and particularly to the immature student, very difficult indeed.

I don't know how the subject is handled now, or if it is handled at all, but when I went to school I observed a number of ways in which the industrious teacher of English could ignore the nature of literature, but continue to teach the subject.

The most popular of these was simply to teach literary history instead. The emphasis was on what was written when, and what was going on in the world at that time. Now I don't think this is a discipline to be despised. Certainly students need to know these things. The historical sense is greatly in decay. Perhaps students live in an eternal present now, and it's necessary to get across to them that a Viking ship was not equipped like the *Queen Mary* and that Lord Byron didn't get to Greece by air. At the same time, this is not teaching literature, and it is not enough to sustain the student's interest in it when he leaves school.

Then I found that another popular way to avoid teaching literature was to be concerned exclusively with the author and his psychology. Why was Hawthorne melancholy and what made Poe drink liquor and why did Henry James like England better than America? These ruminations can take up endless time and postpone indefinitely any consideration of the work itself. Actually, a work of art exists without its author from the moment the words are on paper, and the more complete the work, the less important it is who wrote it or why. If you're studying literature, the intentions of the writer have to be found in the work itself, and not in his life. Psychology is an interesting subject but hardly the main consideration for the teacher of English.

Neither is sociology. When I went to school, a novel might be read in an English class because it represented a certain social problem of topical interest. Good fiction deals with human nature. If it uses material that is topical, it still does not use it for a topical purpose, and if topics are what you want anyway, you are better referred to a newspaper.

But I found that there were times when all these methods became exhausted, and the unfortunate teacher of English was faced squarely with the problem of having to teach literature. This would never do, of course, and what had to be done then was simply to kill the subject altogether. Integrate it out of existence. I once went to a high school where all the subjects were called "activities" and were so well integrated that there were no definite ones to teach. I have found that if you are astute and energetic, you can integrate English literature with geography, biology, home economics, basketball, or fire prevention—with anything at all that will put off a little longer the evil day when the story or novel must be examined simply as a story or novel.

Failure to study literature in a technical way is generally blamed, I believe, on the immaturity of the student, rather than on the unpreparedness of the teacher. I couldn't pronounce upon that, of course, but as a writer with certain grim memories of days and months of just "hanging out" in school, I can at least venture the opinion that the blame may be shared. At any rate, I don't think the nation's teachers of English have any right to be complacent about their service to literature as long as the appearance of a really fine work of fiction is so rare on the best-seller lists, for good fiction is written more often than it is read. I know, or at least I have been given to understand, that a great many high-school graduates go to college not knowing that a period ordinarily follows the end of a sentence; but what seems even more shocking to me is the number who carry away from college with them an undying appreciation for slick and juvenile fiction.

I don't know whether I am setting the aims of the teacher of English too high or too low when I suggest that it is, partly at least, his business to change the face of the best-seller list. However, I feel that the teacher's role is more fundamental than the critic's. It comes down ultimately, I think, to the fact that his first obligation is to the truth of the subject he is teaching, and that for the reading of literature ever to become a habit and a pleasure, it must first be a discipline. The student has to have tools to understand a story or a novel, and these are tools proper to the structure of the work, tools proper to the craft. They are tools that operate inside the work and not outside it; they are concerned with how this story is made and with what makes it work as a story.

You may say that this is too difficult for the student, yet actually, to begin with what can be known in a technical way about the story or the novel or the poem is to begin with the least common denominator. And you may ask what a technical understanding of a novel or poem or story has to do with the business of mystery, the embodiment of which I have been careful to say is the essence of literature. It has a great deal to do with it, and this can perhaps best be understood in the act of writing.

In the act of writing, one sees that the way a thing is made controls and is inseparable from the whole meaning of it. The form of a story gives it meaning which any other form would change, and unless the student is able, in some degree, to apprehend the form, he will never apprehend anything else about the work, except what is extrinsic to it as literature.

The result of the proper study of a novel should be contemplation of the mystery embodied in it, but this is a contemplation of the mystery in the whole work and not of some proposition or paraphrase. It is not the tracking-down of an expressible moral or statement about life. An English teacher I knew once asked her students what the moral of *The Scarlet Letter* was, and one answer she got was that the moral of *The Scarlet Letter* was, think twice before you commit adultery.

Many students are made to feel that if they can dive deep into a piece of fiction and come up with so edifying a proposition as this, their effort has not been in vain.

I think, to judge from what the nation reads, that most of our effort in the teaching of literature has been in vain, and I think that this is even more apparent when we listen to what people demand of the novelist. If people don't know what they get, they at least know what they want. Possibly the question most often asked these days about modern fiction is why do we keep on getting novels about freaks and poor people, engaged always in some violent, destructive action, when actually, in this country, we are rich and strong and democratic and the man in the street is possessed of a general good-will which overflows in all directions.

I think that this kind of question is only one of many attempts, unconscious perhaps, to separate mystery from manners in fiction, and thereby to make it more palatable to the modern taste. The novelist is asked to begin with an examination of statistics rather than with an examination of conscience. Or if he must examine his conscience, he is asked to do so in the light of statistics. I'm afraid, though, that this is not the way the novelist uses his eyes. For him, judgment is implicit in the act of seeing. His vision cannot be detached from his moral sense.

Readers have got somewhat out of the habit of feeling that they have to drain off a statable moral from a novel. Now they feel they have to drain off a statable social theory that will make life more worth living. What they wish to eliminate from fiction, at all costs, is the mystery that James foresaw the loss of. The storyteller must render what he sees and not what he thinks he ought to see, but this doesn't mean that he can't be, or that he isn't, a moralist in the sense proper to him.

It seems that the fiction writer has a revolting attachment to the poor, for even when he writes about the rich, he is more concerned with what they lack than with what they have. I am very much afraid that to the fiction writer the fact that we shall always have the poor with us is a source of satisfaction, for it means, essentially, that he will always be able to find someone like himself. His concern with poverty is with a poverty fundamental to man. I believe that the basic experience of everyone is the experience of human limitation.

One man who read my novel sent me a message by an uncle of mine. He said, "Tell that girl to quit writing about poor folks." He said, "I see poor folks every day and I get mighty tired of them, and when I read, I don't want to see any more of them."

Well, that was the first time it had occurred to me that the people I was writing about were much poorer than anybody else, and I think the reason for this is very interesting, and I think it can perhaps explain a good deal about how the novelist looks at the world.

The novelist writes about what he sees on the surface, but his angle of vision is such that he begins to see before he gets to the surface and he continues to see after he has gone past it. He begins to see in the depths of himself, and it seems to me that his position there rests on what must certainly be the bedrock of all human experience—the experience of limitation or, if you will, of poverty.

Kipling said if you wanted to write stories not to drive the poor from your doorstep. I think he meant that the poor live with less padding between them and the raw forces of life and that for this reason it is a source of satisfaction to the novelist that we shall always have them with us. But the novelist will always have them with him because he can find them anywhere. Just as in the sight of God we are all children, in the sight of the novelist we are all poor, and the actual poor only symbolize for him the state of all men.

When anyone writes about the poor in order merely to reveal their material lack, then he is doing what the sociologist does, not what the artist does. The poverty he writes about is so essential that it needn't have anything at all to do with money.

Of course Kipling, like most fiction writers, was attracted by the manners of the poor. The poor love formality, I believe, even better than the wealthy, but their manners and forms are always being interrupted by necessity. The mystery of existence is always showing through the texture of their ordinary lives, and I'm afraid that this makes them irresistible to the novelist.

A sense of loss is natural to us, and it is only in these centuries when we are afflicted with the doctrine of the perfectibility of human nature by its own efforts that the vision of the freak in fiction is so disturbing. The freak in modern fiction is usually disturbing to us because he keeps us from forgetting that we share in his state. The only time he should be disturbing to us is when he is held up as a whole man.

That this happens frequently, I cannot deny, but as often as it happens, it indicates a disease, not simply in the novelist but in the society that has given him his values.

Every novelist has his preoccupations, and none can see and write everything. Partial vision has to be expected, but partial vision is not dishonest vision unless it has been dictated. I don't think that we have any right to demand of our novelists that they write an *American* novel at all. A novel that could be described simply as an American novel and no more would be too limited an undertaking for a good novelist to waste his time on. As a fiction writer who is a Southerner, I use the idiom and the manners of the country I know, but I don't consider that I write *about* the South. So far as I am concerned as a novelist, a bomb on Hiroshima affects my judgment of life in rural Georgia, and this is not the result of taking a relative view and judging one thing by another, but of taking an absolute view and judging all things together; for a view taken in the light of the absolute will include a good deal more than one taken merely in the light provided by a house-to-house survey.

QUESTIONS FOR READING, RESPONDING, AND WRITING

Summarizing Main Points

1. List the variety of ways in which, according to O'Connor, "the industrious teacher of English could ignore the nature of literature, but continue to teach the subject."

2. According to O'Connor, what is the "business of fiction"? How does she think English teachers should approach it? How does she think novelists should approach it?

Analyzing Methods of Discourse

1. What point is O'Connor trying to make through the example of her cousin's review? Through the example of the teacher's experience with *The Scarlet Letter?*
2. At the end of her essay, O'Connor states: "So far as I am concerned as a novelist, a bomb on Hiroshima affects my judgment of life in rural Georgia, and this is not the result of taking a relative view and judging one thing by another, but of taking an absolute view and judging all things together; for a view taken in the light of the absolute will include a good deal more than one taken merely in the light provided by a house-to-house survey." In what way does this statement embody O'Connor's notion of the "business of fiction"?

Focusing on the Field

1. Who is O'Connor's audience here? How does she let the reader know that she has a very specific audience in mind? What is her attitude toward that audience?
2. Compare O'Connor's account of student attitudes toward "mystery" to her accounts of reader reaction to "the poor." What is the relationship between the two terms? Between the two attitudes? Between the two groups of people—students and readers? What is O'Connor's attitude toward students and readers?

Writing Assignments

1. Write an essay in which you apply O'Connor's remarks on literary education to your own literary education so far.
2. Read Reuben Brower's "Reading in Slow Motion." Using material from both Brower's and O'Connor's essays, write an essay of your own in which you argue that Brower's "Literature X" would or would not present the kind of literary education that O'Connor advocates.

ACADEMIC AND
PROFESSIONAL DISCOURSE

Reuben A. Brower

READING IN SLOW MOTION

Reuben Arthur Brower (1908–1975) was a master at "reading in slow motion" as his many distinguished explications of literature will attest, among them *Alexander Pope: The Poetry of Allusion* (1959) and *Hero and Saint: Shakespeare and the Graeco-Roman Tradition* (1971). As a respected editor of numerous editions of literary and critical works by such authors as John Dryden, Jane Austen, and Alexander Pope, Brower established himself not only as a scholar of the first rank, but also as a teacher par excellence. For his book *The Poetry of Robert Frost—Constellations of Intention,* Brower was presented the Explicator Award in 1964.

Brower was born in Lanesboro, Pennsylvania. His scholarly career began at Amherst College, where he graduated summa cum laude in 1930. He also attended Cambridge University (B.A., 1932; M.A., 1936), as well as Harvard (Ph.D., 1936). He was a fellow, master, and lecturer at Harvard and studied at the Center for Advanced Study in Behavioral Sciences in 1961–1962. A Fulbright senior scholar at Oxford in 1968–1969, Brower received throughout his career many awards, fellowships, and honors. This much revered teacher and scholar died of a heart attack in 1975.

The Question put to me at a conference on undergraduate education, "How shall we encourage and influence the lifetime reading habit?" brought to mind the words of Solon that Croesus recalled on the funeral pyre: "I shall not call you fortunate until I learn that the end of your life was happy too." Call no student a lifetime reader until . . . No teacher can be quite sure that he has a lifetime habit of reading, and if asked whether his students have acquired it or formed good reading habits, he will probably feel most uneasy about making an answer. But assuming that we could see each student's life as a whole, *sub specie æternitatis*, we should have to ask the further question: What reading habit are we evaluating? In the age of the New Stupid (a term Aldous Huxley once used for the age of mass literacy), nearly everyone has a reading habit of some sort. Everyone runs through the morning newspaper or *Time* and *Life* strictly as a matter of daily or weekly routine. Each social group has its "great readers," a term of admiration used to cover a wide range of activities that have little more than the printed page in common. There is, for example, reading as anodyne, and reading as extended daydream. There is reading as pursuit of fact or of useful technical knowhow, and reading that may or may not be useful, when we are interested solely in understanding a theory or a point of view. Still more remote from immediate usefulness comes reading as active amusement, a game demanding the highest alertness and the finest degree of sensibility, "judgment ever awake and steady self-possession with enthusiasm and feeling profound or vehement." Reading at this level—to borrow Coleridgean terms a second time—"brings the whole soul of man into activity." Coleridge was speaking of the poet and the power of imagination, but his words describe very well the way we read when we enter into, or rather engage in, experiences of imaginative literature. I say "amusement," not "pleasure," to stress the play of mind, the play of the whole being, that reading of this sort calls for. I am hardly suggesting that literary experience is not a "good," that it is not in some indirect and profound way morally valuable. But if it is to do us any good, it must be fun. The first line of a poem by D. H. Lawrence offers an appropriate motto for teachers and students of literature:

If it's never any fun, don't do it!

Active "amusement" is the reading habit I am concerned with here and more especially with the role played by the teacher of literature in encouraging students to acquire it. I prefer to speak of the "teacher of literature," not the "humanities," because that noble term has become so debased in current usage, and because teachers of texts in humanities courses are or should be teachers of literature. The teacher of Plato or Hobbes or Hume is not only interpreting a system but an expression, an expression that uses many resources of language and uses them in ways that profoundly influence how we take the writer's radical meaning. We cannot subtract from our interpretations the effect of Platonic comedy or of Hobbesian metaphor or of Hume's dispassionate irony. But it remains true that the teacher of literature in the conventional sense has a special interest in encouraging students to respond actively to all the uses of language, from the barely referential to the rhythmic. He is always more or less consciously urging his students to make themselves readers of imagination.

How will the teacher go about reaching this noble aim? By a method that might be described as "slow motion," by slowing down the process of reading to observe what is happening, in order to attend very closely to the words, their uses, and their meanings. Since poetry is literature in its essential and purest form—the mode of writing in which we find at the same time the most varied uses of language and the highest degree of order—the first aim of the teacher of literature will be to make his students better readers of poetry. He will try by every means in his power to bring out the complete and agile response to words that is demanded by a good poem.

But in order not to create a wrong impression, a word needs to be said here about method, a term liable to please some and displease others for equally bad reasons. There is certainly no single sacred technique for teaching reading at the level I have in mind. In teaching literature— unlike science, one may suppose—no holds are barred, providing they work and providing that the injury to the work and to the student does not exceed the limits of humanity. The most distinctive feature of the kind of literature course I am about to describe is that the teacher does have some "holds," some ways of reading that he is willing to demonstrate and that his students can imitate. In this respect "Literature X," as I shall call it, differs from the old-time appreciation course in which the teacher mounted the platform and sang a rhapsody which he alone was capable of understanding and which the student memorized, with the usual inaccuracies, for the coming examination.

But why a course in slow reading? The parent who has a son or daughter in college may well feel confused, since almost certainly he has at least one child with a reading difficulty, the most common complaint being that the child cannot read fast enough. As the parent himself watches the mounting lists of important books, and as he scans the rivers of print in the daily paper, he may well feel that like Alice and the Red Queen, he and his children are going faster and faster but getting nowhere.

The difficulties of parent and child point to conditions that have led to the introduction of how-to-read courses in our colleges and universities. We might note first the sheer mass of printed material to which we are exposed—not to mention the flood of words and images pouring through radio and television. If by temperament or principle we resist the distracting appeals of the press and other media, we must nevertheless read a great deal as we run if we are to perform our tasks as citizens and wage earners. Add to such facts the changes in family life that have altered reading habits of both parents and children. Memorization of Bible texts and poetry is hardly common in school or home, and the family reading circle where books were read aloud and slowly, has all but disappeared even from the idyllic backwaters of academic communities. Yet many if not all of the writers of the past, from Homer to novelists like Jane Austen and Dickens, have assumed reading aloud and a relatively slow rate of intellectual digestion. Literature of the first order calls for lively reading; we must almost act it out as if we were taking parts in a play. As the average high school student reads more and more with less and less wholeness of attention, he may become positively incapacitated for reading the classics of his own or any literature. Incidentally, the parent of the slow reader should take heart: his child may not be stupid, but more than ordinarily sensitive to words. He may in fact have the makings of a poet.

Another change in precollege education is almost certainly connected with the decline in the ability to read literature of the first quality, a change that points also to profound changes in the literary public of the past century and a half. Until thirty or forty years ago a high proportion of students of literature in our liberal arts colleges had received a considerable training in Latin or Greek. If we move back to the much smaller reading publics of the seventeenth and eighteenth centuries, the audiences for whom much of our greatest literature was written, the relative number of readers trained in the classics becomes much higher. The principal method of teaching the ancient languages, translation into English or from English into Latin or Greek, may have had disadvantages compared with the direct method of today, but as a basic preparation for the study of literature it can hardly be surpassed. It may be doubted whether learning of a foreign language can take place without some translation, at least into what experts in linguistics call the "meta-language" of the learner. To translate from Latin and Greek demanded close attention to the printed word, and since the ideas being communicated and the linguistic and literary forms through which they were expressed were often quite unlike those in English, translation compelled the closest scrutiny of meanings and forms of expression in both the ancient and the modern language. Although the old-time classicist may not always have been successful as a teacher of literature, he cannot often be accused of lacking rigor. His students had to spend a good many hours in school and college reading some pieces of literature very attentively. One purpose of a course in slow reading is to offer a larger number of present-day undergraduates an equivalent for the older classical training in interpretation of texts.

It might be noted that Coleridge, who harshly criticized the practice of Latin versemaking in English schools, paid the highest tribute to that "severe master, the Reverend James Bowyer":

> At the same time that we were studying the Greek tragic poets, he made us read Shakespeare and Milton as lessons: and they were the lessons too,

which required the most time and trouble to *bring up*, so as to escape his censure. I learned from him, that poetry, even that of the loftiest and, seemingly, that of the wildest odes, had a logic of its own, as severe as that of science; and more difficult, because more subtle, more complex, and dependent on more and more fugitive causes. In the truly great poets, he would say, there is a reason assignable not only for every word, but for the position of every word; and I well remember that, availing himself of the synonymes to the Homer of Didymus, he made us attempt to show, with regard to each, why it would not have answered the same purpose; and wherein consisted the peculiar fitness of the word in the original text.

In our own English compositions (at least for the last three years of our school education) he showed no mercy to phrase, metaphor, or image, unsupported by a sound sense, or where the same sense might have been conveyed with equal force and dignity in plainer words. *Lute, harp,* and *lyre, Muse, Muses,* and *inspirations, Pegasus, Parnassus,* and *Hippocrene* were all an abomination to him. In fancy I can almost hear him now, exclaiming: "Harp? Harp? Lyre? Pen and ink, boy, you mean! Muse, boy, Muse? Your nurse's daughter, you mean! Pierian spring? Oh aye! the cloister-pump, I suppose!"

The Reverend James Bowyer and not Coleridge, it appears, was the original New Critic, which is to say that much New Criticism is old criticism writ large. Bowyer's example suggests another important point to which I shall return: that teaching of reading is necessarily teaching of writing. The student cannot show his teacher or himself that he has had an important and relevant literary experience except in writing or in speaking that is as disciplined as good writing.

To teach reading or any other subject in the style of the Reverend Bowyer demands an attitude toward the job that is obvious but easily overlooked in our larger universities, where increasing numbers of students often impose mass production methods. The most important requirement for teaching an undergraduate course—beyond belief in what one is doing—is to keep this question in mind: What is happening to the student? Other questions soon follow: What do I want him to do and how can I get him to do it? Planning and teaching from this point of view makes the difference between a course that engages the student and one that merely displays the teacher. The perfect model for the teacher of literature as for the teacher of science is Agassiz, who would come into the laboratory, pour out a basket of bones before the student, and leave him alone to sort them out. We learn that after this introduction to the "material" of the course, Agassiz limited his teaching to infrequent visits, when he checked on the learner's progress by an occasional nod or shake of the head to say "That's right!" or "No, not that!" The great thing in teaching is to get the basket of bones before the student and get him to sorting them for himself as soon as possible. What we must avoid at all costs is sorting out all the bones in advance. Agassiz' principle is of great importance in the teaching of literature, where far too often we present the undergraduate with the end products of literary scholarship without being sure he has read or has the capacity of reading the works we are interpreting.

If we are interested in fostering a habit of reading well, we must set up our introductory courses on a principle very different from that underlying the older survey or the now more fashionable history-of-ideas course. We are not handing the student a body of knowledge, so much "material"—the history of the Romantic Movement or an anatomy of the concepts labeled "Romanticism"—however useful such knowledge may be at a later stage in literary education. Our aim rather is to get the student in a position where he can learn for himself. If we succeed, we have reason to believe that he may acquire a lifetime habit of learning independently. The teacher who is working toward this noble end will always be working *with* the student, not *for* him or *over* him. Whitehead used to say that the student should feel he is present while the teacher is thinking, present at an occasion when thought is in process. Those who knew Whitehead in the classroom will know what he meant and why he never seemed to be lecturing, even before a class of a hundred or two hundred students. His listeners never knew exactly where he was coming out. Not knowing where one is coming out is an essential part of the experience of thinking.

To get the student to a point where he can learn for himself requires therefore a redefinition of a "lecture." It asks the teacher to share his ignorance with his students as well as his knowledge. Or if professors shrink from admitting less than omniscience, it calls for at least a Socratic simulation of ignorance. What is wanted is the "nonlecture," to borrow E. E. Cummings's happy term, an action performed by the teacher but clearly directed to the next performance of the student. The ideal nonlecturer is setting a job for the student and showing him how he would go about doing it. If he is not in fact setting a job, he will clearly indicate a relevant kind of job to be done. A proper job means setting a question and offering a way, not a formula, for answering it. Student and teacher must clearly understand that a course in interpretation is a course in "right answering," not a course in "right answers."

Let me now attempt to describe Literature X, a course in slow reading that aims to meet the general requirements I have been outlining and that is designed also to meet the needs of young readers in our colleges and universities. I have said that we want students to increase their power of engaging in imaginative experience, and we assume—this was implied by our earlier reference to Coleridge—that a work of literature offers us an experience through words that is different from average, everyday experience. It is different in its mysterious wholeness, in the number of elements embraced and in the variety and closeness of their relationship. When Othello, just before Desdemona's death, says, "Put out the light, and then put out the light," we feel not only the horror of his intention but also a remarkable concentration of much that has gone on before: the moving history of the relations between the lovers and between them and Iago, the echoed presence of earlier moments of "lightness" and "darkness."

We all agree that such experiences in literature are wonderful, but what can a teacher do to guide a student to discover them? He will of course start from his own excitement, and he will do everything he can to infect his students with it: he will try to express in other words what Othello and the audience are experiencing; he will read the passage aloud or get a student to do it; he will exhort and entreat. But finally he cannot hand over his feelings to his students; he cannot force them to be more sensitive than they are. What can he do that the students may also do and that they can imitate when they read another scene or another play? He can do a great deal if he remembers that while he and his students do not have a common nervous system, they do have the same printed page and they share some knowledge of the English language. He will therefore direct their attention to the words, to what they mean and to their connection with other words and meanings. In considering the "put out the light" speech from *Othello*, the teacher may begin by asking what the words mean in terms of stage business. He may then call for a paraphrase: for "put out the light" someone may offer "bring darkness," or "put an end to." The class can next be asked to connect this expression with others used elsewhere in the play. Someone may recall Othello's earlier line associating Desdemona with darkness and death: ". . . when I love thee not,/ Chaos is come again." The reader can now begin to appreciate the poignancy and the irony of Othello's picturing his action as "putting out the light." So by directing attention to words, their meanings, and relationships, the teacher may put his students in a position where they too will feel the pity and terror of this moment in the play.

We might describe Literature X as a "mutual demonstration society," the work of the course being carried on mainly through student-teacher explorations of the kind I have been attempting to illustrate. For the students the most important and most strenuous demonstrations will be the exercises that they write on their own after being suitably prepared by the teacher. *Othello* may serve as an example once more. After several classes of reading aloud and exploring connections in the earlier acts of the play, an exercise will be set on a speech or scene from the last act. The students now have an opportunity to show whether they can practice independently the sort of interpretation they have been attempting in class. To guide them, they will be given an exercise sheet with a very carefully planned series of questions. Beginning with queries on words and phrases, the exercise goes on to ask about relationships of various kinds, and it concludes with a question demanding a generalization about the work as a whole or about a type of literature or experience. An exercise on *Othello* might finally call for a statement about the nature of Othello's tragedy and for a tentative definition of "tragic" as used in Shakespearean drama. But the words "tragic" or "tragedy" will not necessarily appear in the directions; rather, the students will be impelled to talk about these concepts because they are relevant. In the class on the exercise papers the student and his teacher will be admirably prepared to consider what is meant by tragic literature and experience. These discussions of the exercises should be among the most valuable classes in the course. Here the student can learn by comparing where he succeeded or failed as an interpreter, and frequently he may have the pleasure of finding that he has taught his teacher something, an event that can give satisfaction to both parties and that can take place more often in a course where the student is an active participant, not a passive member of an audience.

Literature X as a whole will consist of a series of these exercise waves, with some more terrifying than others, the seventh and last coming when the students are given two or more weeks without classes in which to read new material—poems, plays, or novels—with no teacher to guide them.

The course will not begin with Shakespeare, although Shakespeare is the necessary measure of imaginative experience and of the capacity to engage in it. We shall begin rather with the smaller model of the short poem, because as I have said it offers literary experience in its purest form. By beginning with poems we can be reasonably sure that the student learns early to distinguish between life and literature and not to be unduly distracted by questions of biography and history or by social and psychological problems of the type raised so often by the novel. Most important, the student will learn at the outset to deal with *wholes*, since within the limits of a class hour or a brief paper he can arrive at an interpretation of a whole literary expression. Poems may come to stand in his mind as Platonic forms of true and complete literary experience.

Beginning with poems has another advantage if students are to learn the value of attending closely to language and if they are to see the satisfactions that come from alert and accurate reading. In the small world of a sonnet, a reader can see how a single word may cause a shift in the equilibrium of feeling in the whole poem. So when Shakespeare says:

> *For thy sweet love remember'd such wealth brings*
> *That then I scorn to change my state with kings.*

"state" carries connotations of Elizabethan *state*, and as a result the speaker's voice takes on a tone of grandeur, a somewhat stagey grandeur that reminds us of gestures in a play. But the word "state" would hardly impart that quality without the reference to "kings." This fairly simple example brings home the importance in interpretation of considering the context. A course in interpretation is a course in definition by context, in seeing how words are given rich and precise meaning through their interrelations with other words. The student who acquires this habit of definition will be a better reader of philosophy or law or any other type of specialized discourse, and he may learn something about the art of writing, of how to control context in order to express oneself.

Reading poems also offers one of the best ways of lifting the student from adolescent to adult appreciation of literature. The adult reader realizes that reading a work of literature is at once a solitary and a social act. In reading we are alone, but we are also among the company of readers assumed by the poem or play or novel. The poem is more than a personal message, it invites us to move out of ourselves, to get into an "act," to be another self in a fictive drama. The sonnet of Shakespeare we have just quoted seems to call for a very simple identification of the actual reader with the imagined speaker,

> When in disgrace with fortune and men's eyes
> I all alone beweep my outcast state . . .

(Many will recall their own youthful readings of the poem.) Yet even this simple if not sentimental sonnet asks something more of us in the end; it asks us to take on the demonstrative air of the theatrical lover, to protest in language we would never actually use in our most romantic moments.

In Literature X we shall start by reading poems, and start with no apparent method or at least with method well concealed. We begin, as Frost says, with delight, to end in wisdom. "What is it *like*," we say rather crudely, "to read this poem?" "With what feeling are we left at its close?" "What sort of person is speaking?" "What is he *like*, and where does he reveal himself most clearly?" "In what line or phrase?" We may then ask if there is a key phrase or word in the poem, and we can begin to introduce the notion of the poem as a structure, as an ordered experience built up through various kinds of meaning controlled in turn by various uses of language.

Remembering our questions about the speaker, we first direct attention to dramatic uses of language, to the ways in which the words create a character speaking in a certain role. We may ask, for example, who is speaking in Keats's sonnet on Chapman's *Homer*. An alert student may point out that he is a traveler (many do not see this), and that he uses idioms with a medieval coloring: "realms," "goodly," "bards in fealty," "demesne." But the speaker does not continue to talk in this vein:

Till I heard Chapman speak out loud and bold.

He has changed, and the drama moves into a second act. We hear a voice that is powerful and young, the voice of the New World discoverer and the Renaissance astronomer. We now point out to our young reader (if he is still listening) that the poem is indeed an "act." The poet is speaking *as if* he were a traveler-explorer, and the whole poem is built on a metaphor. So, while reading many poems, we may introduce a few basic notions of literary design and some useful critical terms. But our emphasis will always be on the term as a tool, as a device for calling attention to the poem and how it is made. In time we can turn to study of the poem as an experience of ordered sounds, but not, we hasten to add, of sounds divorced from sense. Our aim in talking about rhythmic pattern, as in considering dramatic and metaphorical design, is to show how the poem "works" and what it expresses. We see, for example, that as Keats's sonnet moves from the medieval to the modern speaker, and as the metaphor also shifts, the rhythm changes from the "broken" couplets and inversions of the octave to the long and steady sweep of the sestet. The whole sonnet in its beautiful interaction of parts gives us the sense of discovery and release into a new world of literary and aesthetic experience.

Following a period of reading poems, the course will move ahead to a play by Shakespeare so that students can see at once that the way in which they have read poems works also for a poetic drama and that there are some basic similarities between the structure of these different types of literature. They may see, for example, that the man speaking in a poem corresponds to the character in a play, that Shakespeare has his large metaphors just as Keats has his smaller ones.

From drama we go to the reading of a novel, often via short stories. The short story like the poem gives us literary experience in microcosm and makes it easier to see analogies between fiction and poetry, to see that a tale by Hawthorne is the unfolding of a single metaphorical vision, or that the narrator in a story by Joyce controls our sense of being within the child's world, exiled from adult society. The novel, especially as we have it in its classic nineteenth century form in Dickens or George Eliot, demands a very different reading from a Shakespearean drama, but by putting the same questions to both genres their likeness and their unlikeness can be defined, and the exact quality of a particular work can be discovered. The student will find, for example, that the "marshes" and "mists" of *Great Expectations* are nearer to the fixed symbols of allegory than to the fluid metaphors of Shakespeare. But he can also see that in a novel as in a poem the narrative voice is of immense importance. Comparison of the opening scene in the film of *Great Expectations* with Dickens's telling shows that when the sanely humorous, entertaining voice of Dickens is removed, we are left with images of pure nightmare. The major themes of *Great Expectations*, guilt and innocence, justice and injustice, are not un-Shakespearean, but we can hardly read the novel without an awareness that unlike *King Lear* and *Macbeth* and like most novels, the imaginative world of *Great Expectations* has a date. Jaggers is an awesome symbol of the link between criminality and legal justice, but he also embodies a sharp criticism of the actual court and prison world of mid-nineteenth century England.

Reading a novel forcibly reminds us that literature is embedded in history, that the meaning of the work in itself changes when we view it in relation to other works and to the social situation in which it first appeared. Literature X will move on in its later phases to some experiments in historical interpretation, "historical" being used here to include the relation of a work to its time, especially to more or less contemporary works, and to literary tradition. If we return to *Othello* or *Coriolanus* after reading the *Iliad* and after gaining some familiarity with the heroic tradition in Renaissance epic and drama, we find that both plays are clearer and richer in their meaning. We see in *Coriolanus* what happens when an Achilles enters the Roman forum: the simple absolutes of the hero, the code that makes Coriolanus prefer a "noble life before a long" one, bring confusion in a civil society. The teacher of our ideal course will not merely lay a comparison of this sort before his students, he will try to get them into a position where they can make the comparison for themselves. He will use all the ingenuity he can muster to devise assignments in which the student can practice thinking historically about works of literature.

In a year in which the class has made some study of the hero in Homer and in the Renaissance, a project might be focused on Fielding's *Tom Jones*. While the students are reading the novel outside class (it takes time!), they would study with their teacher readings useful for interpreting the novel in relation to the heroic tradition and to the climate of moral opinion in the eighteenth century. They could observe in Dryden's *Mac Flecknoe* the shift from the Renaissance "heroick" to the mock-heroic, and in *The Rape of the Lock*, they could see how allusions to the ancient heroic world are used to satirize eighteenth century high society while giving the world of the poem splendor and moral seriousness. After comparing the mock-heroic in Pope and Fielding, they might attempt a definition of the hero in *Tom Jones*. By skillful prodding (in an exercise) they could be led to see that Fielding has created a new type of hero, a youth who is at once ridiculous and charmingly "good-natured," that although he finally gains a modicum of "prudence," he wins his way largely through "benevolence" and "goodness of heart."

As a final step in this experiment, there might be a series of readings in Chesterfield, Hume, and Dr. Johnson, all concerned with social "goodness," and more especially with "prudence" and "benevolence." The students would then be asked to define and place the moral attitudes expressed in *Tom Jones*, through comparing them with similar attitudes expressed in these eighteenth century moralists. By projects of this type undergraduates could be given some practice—at an elementary level— in writing intellectual history. At the same time their earlier practice in interpretation would protect them from reducing the experience of the novel to the abstracted idea. But they would also begin to see that a purely literary judgment is finally impossible, that we are impelled to move back from literature to life. Dr. Johnson's famous comparison of Fielding and Richardson might be used to show that "liking" or "disliking" a novel is an act of moral evaluation. At the end of Literature X, by returning to poetry we could make the point that a choice between poems is a choice between lives.

You may be asking by now what the connection is between our ideal course and the lifetime reading habits of undergraduates. I should reply that Literature X attempts to influence future reading habits by keeping to the principle of student activity. No test or exercise or final examination asks the student to "give back" the "material" of the course. On the contrary, each stage of the work is planned with a view to how the student reads the *next* work, whether poem or play or novel. At the end of the first half of the course the student is sent off to read and interpret on his own another play of Shakespeare and another novel. He is given leading questions that impel him to do likewise "differently." An appropriate midyear examination in the course might consist of a sight poem to interpret and an essay-exercise on a longer work read outside class. The test for the second half-year (whether an examination or a long essay) would ordinarily be based on a set of texts to be used in interpreting a work in the manner of the project on *Tom Jones*.

But the teacher of a course in slow reading will always be haunted by the question once asked by a colleague of mine: "Our students learn *how* to read, but *do* they read?" Do they, for example, ever read an author, read every one of his books they can lay their hands on, with an urge to know the writer's work as a whole? Can we do anything in our ideal course to stimulate this most valuable habit? Some modest experiments can be made, I believe, and with some assurance of success. A model can be set by reading generously in a single poet, preferably a contemporary, such as Frost, Yeats, or Eliot. Or the teacher can give the class a start by reading a few poems in each of a number of writers, and then send the students off to read one of the poets independently. After some weeks they might write an essay "On Reading So-and-So." The essay must have a point (surprisingly few students know what a point is) supported by deft and apt interpretation of particular poems. The novel, the most important form for habitual readers in this generation, presents a problem, since we can hardly read all or even several novels of the same writer within the limits of an introductory course. But two novels and some stories by a single writer may rouse some readers to go ahead on their own, and sometimes the discovery that a difficult writer—James or Joyce—is understandable and rewarding or that an old-fashioned writer—Fielding or Jane Austen—is amusing, will start a student along the right path. The best way to influence later habits is the natural way: recommending without system books we have read with pleasure and without ulterior motives. Students recognize the difference between love and duty, and they will respond to genuine enthusiasm and avoid books that they "ought to" read or—and this is the lowest of all academic appeals—that "fill a gap" in preparing for general examinations or graduate school placement tests.

If we turn our attention from lifetime reading habits to the larger educational influence of courses in slow reading, we can note some possible correlations between classroom and later performances. In this connection we should recall the value for close reading of practice in equally close writing. The student who looks at poems as carefully as we have suggested will understand that poetry begins in grammar and that to express a just appreciation of a poem demands fine control of grammar on the part of the appreciator. But to help the student make such discoveries calls for guidance in small classes or at least careful criticism of written exercises. Good writing is an art not amenable to mass production methods.

Attentive criticism of written work is almost certainly of much more value for teaching good reading and writing than the usual discussions or section meetings. The value of a discussion meeting does not depend primarily on size, as many assume, but on the planning that precedes the meeting and the direction of the conversation to a defined goal. In our course in slow reading the discussion is not an addendum, but the culminating act toward which the teacher's demonstration and the student's exercise have been directed. Under these conditions student and teacher are fully prepared to say something meaningful to each other, since they have before them well-defined questions to pursue and alternative expressed answers to compare and judge.

But discussion of this type need not be vocal. The student can carry it on internally during a lecture, if the lecture is an exercise in how to ask and answer a question of interpretation. The indispensable requirement for an active course in literature is not "sections," but some form of independent performance for an attentive critical audience of one. Here is where large-scale production methods break down, and limitations in size are necessary. Very few readers can handle more than twenty to twenty-five papers of the type I have been describing and maintain the necessary vigilance and the power of viewing them as individual performances. A reader can handle them in the usual fashion—grade them and add a complimentary or devastating comment—but he cannot give them critical attention at a high level. The student who is to rise to the kind of reading and writing called for in our ideal course must feel that he has a responsible reader, one who addresses himself to this essay and to this mind. The most valuable discussion a teacher can give is a comment surely directed to an individual written performance. Here we have the ideal section: two actors engaged in a Socratic dialogue. A teacher who is not bewildered and dulled by reading too many papers on the same topic will be able to judge the student's present achievement in relation to what he has done in the past. He can also help him keep track of his development and show him where he is going, and when he has failed, show him how to build on an earlier successful performance. Again Coleridge's Reverend Bowyer may serve as a guide:

> . . . there was one custom of our master's, which I cannot pass over in silence, because I think it imitable and worthy of imitation. He would often permit our exercises, under some pretext of want of time, to accumulate, till each had four or five to be looked over. Then placing the whole number abreast on his desk, he would ask the writer, why this or that sentence might not have found as appropriate a place under this or that other thesis: and if no satisfying answer could be returned, and two faults of the same kind were found in one exercise, the irrevocable verdict followed, the exercise was torn up, and another on the same subject to be produced, in addition to the tasks of the day. The reader will, I trust, excuse this tribute of recollection to a man, whose severities, even now, not seldom furnish the dreams, by which the blind fancy would fain interpret to the mind the painful sensations of distempered sleep; but neither lessen nor dim the sense of my moral and intellectual obligations.

The marker of an English paper, as Coleridge realized though with "painful sensations," is a very important person indeed; he becomes the higher literary conscience, the intellectual guardian angel of his students.

It is evident that education in literature of this kind must be personal, and expensive, though scarcely more expensive than education in the sciences. Let us have at least as generous a supply of readers and conference rooms as we have of laboratory assistants and laboratories. The Humanities cannot flourish without *humanitas*. A protest is in order against the inhumanity of the Humanities when in some of our larger institutions the study of Great Books is reduced to display lectures before audiences of five and six hundred, and when the individual performance is measured by machine-graded examinations.

The teaching of great literary texts in Humanities courses has also had other if less depressing results which the teacher of literature should note if he is to fulfill his proper educational role. Because many works are taught in translation and taught often by staffs including many non-specialists in language and literature, and because the texts are often presented in some broad historical framework, a work of imaginative literature tends to be treated either as a document for studying the history of ideas or as a text for illustrating and enforcing desirable moral and social attitudes. Though neither of these approaches is in itself harmful or inappropriate to a university, it may involve serious losses, especially in courses in which many students are reading for the first time—or for the first time at an adult level—masterpieces of European literature. There is a danger, which is increased by the large amounts of reading assigned in Great Books courses, that rich and special experiences will be too readily reduced to crude examples of a historic idea or a moral principle. Though the reductions may be necessary and useful for certain purposes, we must not let students make them too soon or too easily, not if we are seriously concerned with lifetime habits of reading. The undergraduate who masters the trick too early and too well may in the process suffer real damage. He may have acquired the dubious art of reading carelessly, of making the reduction *before reading,* and he may have lowered rather than increased his capacity for responding precisely to a particular work and for making fine discriminations between works.

Hence the special function of the teacher of literature, which is not to be confused with that of the historian or the moral philosopher. The teacher of literature in a Humanities course must feel he has betrayed a trust if he has not given the lay reader what he is best qualified to give: training in the literary disciplines of reading and writing. It is pertinent to recall the historic definition of the Humanities as it stands in the *Oxford English Dictionary:* "Learning or literature concerned with human culture, as grammar, rhetoric, poetry, and especially the ancient Latin and Greek classics." I suspect that some of the more enthusiastic general educators may be surprised by the words that follow "human culture": "as grammar, rhetoric, poetry . . ." (The order of items in the list is instructive, too.) The disciplines named are the ones that the teacher of literature has a special responsibility to impart. He is, like Horace's poet, a guardian of the language who shows (as Pope translates it) "no mercy to an empty line." His prime object is to maintain fineness of response to words, and his students rightly assume that he will be adept in discovering and illustrating refinements in writing whether in a great book or a student essay. This guardianship, once performed by teachers of the ancient Latin and Greek classics, now falls to the teachers of English and other modern literatures. Why is this so? Because they are committed to the principle that the study of letters is inseparable from the study of language.

Study of literature based on this principle can hardly be carried on in a course based mainly on texts in translation. Translations have their place in a course in interpretation, but only as ancillary to the main business of close reading in the original. The finer distinctions, the finer relationships which we are training our students to discover and make are almost invariably dulled or lost in the process of translation. We want the student to acquire the habit of recognizing and making such distinctions in his *own* language, and we can hardly teach him to do it if the examples before him are relatively crude. Whitehead once remarked when discussing Plato's cosmology, "After all, the translators of Plato have had B+ philosophic minds." With rare exceptions the translators of literature have had literary minds of similar quality. There are of course the handful of translations that are masterpieces, such as Pope's *Illiad*, North's *Plutarch*, and Dryden's *Aeneis*, texts that can bear the close study necessary for literary education. Ironically enough, these are the very translations avoided in most Great Books courses.

In speaking of the necessity for close attention to language, I am not forgetting that teachers of literature are also teachers of human culture and that they are therefore guardians of important values. But they do not set out to teach these values, although they inevitably impart them by the way they talk and act in the presence of works of literature. But they are especially concerned with another task, with teaching ways of discovering and experiencing values expressed through literary objects. The most precious thing they can give their students is some increase of power, some help however humble in getting into Shakespeare or Dr. Johnson or Joyce.

We may hope that a student who has learned how to get into these writers will go back for further experiences after he has left the classroom and the university. That he surely will we cannot say. Even if he does not return to Shakespeare or Johnson, the experiences in the classroom almost certainly have their value and their effect in determining the quality of his later reading. One play well read with a good teacher and well digested in a reflective essay may serve as a touchstone of what literary experience can be. But finally, our belief that students' habits of reading are permanently affected is Platonic. The model for most cultural education is to be found in the third book of the *Republic*:

> . . . our young men, dwelling as it were in a healthy region, may receive benefit from all things about them; the influence that emanates from works of beauty may waft itself to eye or ear like a breeze that brings health from wholesome places, and so from earliest childhood insensibly guide them to likeness, to friendship, to harmony with beautiful reason.

In the effort to realize this Platonic vision in a modern university the undergraduate library plays its part by surrounding our youth with fair works of literature through which they may come into "harmony with beautiful reason." No one knows how born readers are produced, but we can put books in their way and in the way of the less happily born in the hope that proximity will have its effect as it does in the formation of more mundane habits. Of one thing I am convinced: that a born reader on a library staff can have a tremendous effect on young readers who come his way. I remember with gratitude two librarians of that description, one in school and one in college, who led us to read books we might never have looked into by sharing their love for what they had read. If I were to found a library dedicated to influencing the reading habit, I should place a half-dozen of these enthusiasts at strategic points to ensnare wandering students. They would not necessarily be trained librarians, and they would surely waste students' time and occasionally disturb their colleagues, but like great authors they would create an ever-widening circle of readers. Mere teachers of literature could hardly hope to compete with them, and might in time quietly disappear from the academic scene.

QUESTIONS FOR READING, RESPONDING, AND WRITING

Summarizing Main Points

1. What sort of a student/teacher relation does Brower advocate? Locate and list the specific actions that Brower says a teacher must perform. Locate and list the specific actions that Brower says a student must perform. How are these actions different from typical classroom behavior?
2. What exactly does the teacher of literature teach, according to Brower? List the by-products of a good literary education, according to Brower. List the dangers that most frequently arise, according to Brower, in "Great Books" courses.

Analyzing Methods of Discourse

1. Why is the reference to *Alice in Wonderland* and the Red Queen especially appropriate to Brower's discussion of the difficulties in parent and child reading habits? How might a "slow-motion" reading of *Alice in Wonderland* alleviate those difficulties?
2. Brower quotes Coleridge's remarks on his teacher, the Reverend James

Bowyer, several times. How does the first quotation work as a summary of Brower's own essay? What points are especially pertinent to Brower's main ideas as evidenced by Brower's final quotation from Coleridge? How does the Reverend Bowyer handle the difficulty of "mass production" in literary courses?

Focusing on the Field

1. Brower provides several miniature studies of literary works within his essay. Study the discussion of "light" imagery in *Othello* that Brower presents. How is it especially appropriate to Brower's discussion? How does it fit the *Oxford English Dictionary*'s historic definition of "humanities" found near the end of this essay? How does Brower leave his discussion of *Othello* open-ended?
2. How does Brower's ordering of literary types—poems, short stories, novels—in literature courses reflect his understanding of what is important about literature? Is that the same order in which you have been taught literature? Considering the dangers of literature courses, why has your literary education reflected or not reflected Brower's ordering?

Writing Assignments

1. Read a short poem or short story or another essay from this anthology in the manner that Brower prescribes, that is, in "slow motion," paying particular attention to the words on the page, to their "grammar, rhetoric, poetry." In a short paper, illustrate your own "fineness of response to words" by "discovering and illustrating refinements in writing."
2. In a short paper, compare the dangers of the usual literary course as described by Flannery O'Connor in "The Teaching of Literature" with the dangers that Brower outlines here. Compare also the solutions each author advocates.

Janet Emig

WRITING AS A MODE OF LEARNING

A highly respected and innovative educator, Janet Ann Emig was born in Cincinnati, Ohio. After graduating magna cum laude from Mount Holyoke College in 1950, Emig furthered her studies at the University of Michigan (M.A., 1951) and Harvard (Ed.D., 1969). Currently a professor of English education at Rutgers University in New Brunswick, New Jersey, Emig has taught in public and private schools and colleges for over thirty years. A member of the National Conference on Research in English, where she has contributed essays to *New Directions in Composition Research* and *The Basics and Rhetoric,* Emig has also been a member of the editorial board of the *Harvard Educational Review.* The coeditor of *Language and Learning* (1966), Emig wrote *Writing as Process,* an influential study of writing and learning in 1977. A frequent contributor to language journals, Emig also finds time for poetry, some of which has been anthologized.

In the following lucid and direct essay previously published in *College Composition and Communications,* Emig argues that writing is a powerful learning tool.

Writing represents a unique mode of learning—not merely valuable, not merely special, but unique. That will be my contention in this paper. The thesis is straightforward. Writing serves learning uniquely because writing as process-and-product possesses a cluster of attributes that correspond uniquely to certain powerful learning strategies.

Although the notion is clearly debatable, it is scarcely a private belief. Some of the most distinguished contemporary psychologists have at least implied such a role for writing as heuristic. Lev Vygotsky, A. R. Luria, and Jerome Bruner, for example, have all pointed out that higher cognitive functions, such as analysis and synthesis, seem to develop most fully only with the support system of verbal language—particularly, it seems, of written language.[1] Some of their arguments and evidence will be incorporated here.

Here I have a prior purpose: to describe as tellingly as possible *how* writing uniquely corresponds to certain powerful learning strategies. Making such a case for the uniqueness of writing should logically and theoretically involve establishing many contrasts, distinctions between (1) writing and all other verbal languaging processes—listening, reading, and especially talking; (2) writing and all other forms of composing, such as composing a painting, a symphony, a dance, a film, a building; and (3) composing in words and composing in the two other major graphic symbol systems of mathematical equations and scientific formulae. For the purpose of this paper, the task is simpler, since most students are not permitted by most curricula to discover the values of composing, say, in dance, or even in film; and most students are not sophisticated enough to create, to originate formulations, using the highly abstruse symbol system of equations and formulae. Verbal language represents the most *available* medium for composing; in fact, the significance of sheer availability in its selection as a mode for learning can probably not be overstressed. But the uniqueness of writing among the verbal languaging processes does need to be established and supported if only because so many curricula and courses in English still consist almost exclusively of reading and listening.

WRITING AS A UNIQUE
LANGUAGING PROCESS

Traditionally, the four languaging processes of listening, talking, reading, and writing are paired in either of two ways. The more informative seems to be the division many linguists make between first-order and second-order processes, with talking and listening characterized as first-order processes; reading and writing, as second-order. First-order processes are acquired without formal or systematic instruction; the second-order processes of reading and writing tend to be learned initially only with the aid of formal and systematic instruction.

The less useful distinction is that between listening and reading as receptive functions and talking and writing as productive functions. Critics of these terms like Louise Rosenblatt rightfully point out that the connotation of passivity too often accompanies the notion of receptivity when reading, like listening, is a vital, construing act.

An additional distinction, so simple it may have been previously overlooked, resides in two criteria: the matters of origination and of graphic recording. Writing is originating and creating a unique verbal construct that is graphically recorded. Reading is creating or re-creating *but not* originating a verbal construct that is graphically recorded. Listening is creating or re-creating but not originating a verbal construct that is *not* graphically recorded. Talking is creating *and* originating a verbal construct that is *not* graphically recorded (except for the circuitous routing of a transcribed tape). Note that a distinction is being made between creating and originating, separable processes.

For talking, the nearest languaging process, additional distinctions should probably be made. (What follows is not a denigration of talk as a valuable mode of learning.) A silent classroom or one filled only with the teacher's voice is anathema to learning. For evidence of the cognitive value of talk, one can look to some of the persuasive monographs coming from the London Schools Council project on writing: *From Information to Understanding* by Nancy Martin or *From Talking to Writing* by Peter Medway.[2] We also know that for some of us, talking is a valuable, even necessary, form of pre-writing. In his curriculum, James Moffett makes the value of such talk quite explicit.

But to say that talking is a valuable form of pre-writing is not to say that writing is talk recorded, an inaccuracy appearing in far too many composition texts. Rather, a number of contemporary trans-disciplinary sources suggest that talking and writing may emanate from different organic sources and represent quite different, possibly distinct, language functions. In *Thought and Language*, Vygotsky notes that "written speech is a separate linguistic function, differing from oral speech in both structure and mode of functioning."[3] The sociolinguist Dell Hymes, in a valuable issue of *Daedalus*, "Language as a Human Problem," makes a comparable point: "That speech and writing are not simply interchangeable, and have developed historically in ways at least partly autonomous, is obvious."[4] At the first session of the Buffalo Conference on Researching Composition (4–5 October 1975), the first point of unanimity among the participant-speakers with interests in developmental psychology, media, dreams and aphasia was that talking and writing were markedly different functions.[5] Some of us who work rather steadily with writing research agree. We also believe that there are hazards, conceptually and pedagogically, in creating too complete an analogy between talking and writing, in blurring the very real differences between the two.

What are these differences?

1. Writing is learned behavior; talking is natural, even irrepressible, behavior.
2. Writing then is an artificial process; talking is not.
3. Writing is a technological device—not the wheel, but early enough to qualify as primary technology; talking is organic, natural, earlier.
4. Most writing is slower than most talking.
5. Writing is stark, barren, even naked as a medium; talking is rich, luxuriant, inherently redundant.
6. Talk leans on the environment; writing must provide its own context.
7. With writing, the audience is usually absent; with talking, the listener is usually present.
8. Writing usually results in a visible graphic product; talking usually does not.
9. Perhaps because there is a product involved, writing tends to be a more responsible and committed act than talking.
10. It can be said that throughout history, an aura, an ambience, a mystique has usually encircled the written word; the spoken word has for the most part proved ephemeral and treated mundanely (ignore, please, our recent national history).
11. Because writing is often our representation of the world made visible, embodying both process and product, writing is more readily a form and source of learning than talking.

UNIQUE CORRESPONDENCES BETWEEN LEARNING AND WRITING

What then are some *unique* correspondences between learning and writing? To begin with some definitions: Learning can be defined in many ways, according to one's predilections and training, with all statements about learning of course hypothetical. Definitions range from the chemophysiological ("Learning is changed patterns of protein synthesis in relevant portions of the cortex")[6] to transactive views drawn from both philosophy and psychology (John Dewey, Jean Piaget) that learning is the re-organization or confirmation of a cognitive scheme in light of an experience.[7] What the speculations seem to share is consensus about certain features and strategies that characterize successful learning. These include the importance of the classic attributes of re-inforcement and feedback. In most hypotheses, successful learning is also connective and selective. Additionally, it makes use of propositions, hypotheses, and other elegant summarizers. Finally, it is active, engaged, personal—more specifically, self-rhythmed—in nature.

Jerome Bruner, like Jean Piaget, through a comparable set of categories, posits three major ways in which we represent and deal with actuality: (1) enactive—we learn "by doing"; (2) iconic—we learn "by depiction in an image"; and (3) representational or symbolic—we learn "by restatement in words."[8] To overstate the matter, in enactive learning, the hand predominates; in iconic, the eye; and in symbolic, the brain.

What is striking about writing as a process is that, by its very nature, all three ways of dealing with actuality are simultaneously or almost simultaneously deployed. That is, the symbolic transformation of experience through the specific symbol system of verbal language is shaped into an icon (the graphic product) by the enactive hand. If the most efficacious learning occurs when learning is re-inforced, then writing through its inherent re-inforcing cycle involving hand, eye, and brain marks a uniquely powerful multi-representational mode for learning.

Writing is also integrative in perhaps the most basic possible sense: the organic, the functional. Writing involves the fullest possible functioning of the brain, which entails the active participation in the process of both the left and the right hemispheres. Writing is markedly bispheral, although in some popular accounts, writing is inaccurately presented as a chiefly left-hemisphere activity, perhaps because the linear written product is somehow regarded as analogue for the process that created it; and the left hemisphere seems to process material linearly.

The right hemisphere, however, seems to make at least three, perhaps four, major contributions to the writing process—probably, to the creative process generically. First, several researchers, such as Geschwind and Snyder of Harvard and Zaidal of Cal Tech, through markedly different experiments, have very tentatively suggested that the right hemisphere is the sphere, even the *seat*, of emotions.[9] Second—or perhaps as an illustration of the first—Howard Gardner, in his important study of the brain-damaged, notes that our sense of emotional appropriateness in discourse may reside in the right sphere:

> Emotional appropriateness, in sum—being related not only to *what* is said, but to how it is said and to what is *not* said, as well—is crucially dependent on right hemisphere intactness.[10]

Third, the right hemisphere seems to be the source of intuition, of sudden gestalts, of flashes of images, of abstractions occurring as visual or spatial wholes, as the initiating metaphors in the creative process. A familiar example: William Faulkner noted in his *Paris Review* interview that *The Sound and the Fury* began as the image of a little girl's muddy drawers as she sat in a tree watching her grandmother's funeral.[11]

Also, a unique form of feedback, as well as reinforcement, exists with writing, because information from the *process* is immediately and visibly available as that portion of the *product* already written. The importance for learning of a product in a familiar and available medium for immediate, literal (that is, visual) re-scanning and review cannot perhaps be overstated. In his remarkable study of purportedly blind sculptors, Géza Révész found that without sight, persons cannot move beyond a literal transcription of elements into any manner of symbolic transformation— by definition, the central requirement for reformulation and re-interpretation, i.e., revision, that most aptly named process.[12]

As noted in the second paragraph, Vygotsky and Luria, like Bruner, have written importantly about the connections between learning and writing. In his essay "The Psychobiology of Psychology," Bruner lists as one of six axioms regarding learning: "We are connective."[13] Another correspondence then between learning and writing: in *Thought and Language*, Vygotsky notes that writing makes a unique demand in that the writer must engage in "deliberate semantics"—in Vygotsky's elegant phrase, "deliberate structuring of the web of meaning."[14] Such structuring is required because, for Vygotsky, writing centrally represents an expansion of inner speech, that mode whereby we talk to ourselves, which is "maximally compact" and "almost entirely predicative"; written speech is a mode which is "maximally detailed" and which requires explicitly supplied subjects and topics. The medium then of written verbal language requires the establishment of systematic connections and relationships. Clear writing by definition is that writing which signals without ambiguity the nature of conceptual relationships, whether they be coordinate, subordinate, superordinate, causal, or something other.

Successful learning is also engaged, committed, personal learning. Indeed, impersonal learning may be an anomalous concept, like the very notion of objectivism itself. As Michael Polanyi states simply at the beginning of *Personal Knowledge:* "the ideal of strict objectivism is absurd." (How many courses and curricula in English, science, and all else does that one sentence reduce to rubble?) Indeed, the theme of *Personal Knowledge* is that

> into every act of knowing there enters a passionate contribution of the person knowing what is being known, . . . this coefficient is no mere imperfection but a vital component of his knowledge.[15]

In *Zen and the Art of Motorcycle Maintenance,* Robert Pirsig states a comparable theme:

> The Quality which creates the world emerges as *a relationship* between man and his experience. He is a *participant* in the creation of all things.[16]

Finally, the psychologist George Kelly has as the central notion in his subtle and compelling theory of personal constructs man as a scientist steadily and actively engaged in making and re-making his hypotheses about the nature of the universe.[17]

We are acquiring as well some empirical confirmation about the importance of engagement in, as well as self-selection of, a subject for the student learning to write and writing to learn. The recent Sanders and Littlefield study, reported in *Research in the Teaching of English,* is persuasive evidence on this point, as well as being a model for a certain type of research.[18]

As Luria implies in the quotation above, writing is self-rhythmed. One writes best as one learns best, at one's own pace. Or to connect the two processes, writing can sponsor learning because it can match its pace. Support for the importance of self-pacing to learning can be found in Benjamin Bloom's important study "Time and Learning."[19] Evidence for the significance of self-pacing to writing can be found in the reason Jean-Paul Sartre gave last summer for not using the tape-recorder when he announced that blindness in his second eye had forced him to give up writing:

> I think there is an enormous difference between speaking and writing. One rereads what one rewrites. But one can read slowly or quickly: in other words, you do not know how long you will have to take deliberating over a sentence. . . . If I listen to a tape recorder, the listening speed is determined by the speed at which the tape turns and not by my own needs. Therefore I will always be either lagging behind or running ahead of the machine.[20]

Writing is connective as a process in a more subtle and perhaps more significant way, as Luria points out in what may be the most powerful paragraph of rationale ever supplied for writing as heuristic:

> Written speech is bound up with the inhibition of immediate synpractical connections. It assumes a much slower, repeated mediating process of analysis and synthesis, which makes it possible not only to develop the required thought, but even to revert to its earlier stages, thus transforming the sequential chain of connections in a simultaneous, self-reviewing structure. Written speech thus represents a new and powerful instrument of thought.[21]

But first to explicate: writing inhibits "immediate synpractical connections." Luria defines *synpraxis* as "concrete-active" situations in which language does not exist independently but as a "fragment" of an ongoing action "outside of which it is incomprehensible."[22] In *Language and Learning*, James Britton defines it succinctly as "speech-cum-action."[23] Writing, unlike talking, restrains dependence upon the actual situation. Writing as a mode is inherently more self-reliant than speaking. Moreover, as Bruner states in explicating Vygotsky, "Writing virtually forces a remoteness of reference on the language user."[24]

Luria notes what has already been noted above that writing, typically, is a "much slower" process than talking. But then he points out the relation of this slower pace to learning: this slower pace allows for—indeed, encourages—the shuttling among past, present, and future. Writing, in other words, connects the three major tenses of our experience to make meaning. And the two major modes by which these three aspects are united are the processes of analysis and synthesis: analysis, the breaking of entities into their constituent parts; and synthesis, combining or fusing these, often into fresh arrangements or amalgams.

Finally, writing is epigenetic, with the complex evolutionary development of thought steadily and graphically visible and available throughout as a record of the journey, from jottings and notes to full discursive formulations.

For a summary of the correspondences stressed here between certain learning strategies and certain attributes of writing see Figure 1.

This essay represents a first effort to make a certain kind of case for writing—specifically, to show its unique value for learning. It is at once over-elaborate and under-specific. Too much of the formulation is in the off-putting jargon of the learning theorist, when my own predilection would have been to emulate George Kelly and to avoid terms like *reinforcement* and *feedback* since their use implies that I live inside a certain

FIGURE 1

UNIQUE CLUSTER OF CORRESPONDENCES BETWEEN CERTAIN LEARNING STRATEGIES AND CERTAIN ATTRIBUTES OF WRITING

Selected characteristics of successful learning strategies	Selected attributes of writing, process and product
1. Profits from multi-representational and integrative re-inforcement	1. Represents process uniquely multi-representational and integrative
2. Seeks self-provided feedback:	2. Represents powerful instance of self-provided feedback:
(a) immediate	(a) provides product uniquely available for *immediate* feedback (review and re-evaluation)
(b) long-term	(b) provides record of evolution of thought since writing is epigenetic as process-and-product
3. Is connective:	3. Provides connections:
(a) makes generative conceptual groupings, synthetic and analytic	(a) establishes explicit and systematic conceptual groupings through lexical, syntactic, and rhetorical devices
(b) proceeds from propositions, hypotheses, and other elegant summarizers	(b) represents most available means (verbal language) for economic recording of abstract formulations
4. Is active, engaged, personal—notably, self-rhythmed	4. Is active, engaged, personal—notably, self-rhythmed

paradigm about learning I don't truly inhabit. Yet I hope that the essay will start a crucial line of inquiry; for unless the losses to learners of not writing are compellingly described and substantiated by experimental and speculative research, writing itself as a central academic process may not long endure.

REFERENCES

1. Lev S. Vygotsky, *Thought and Language*, trans. Eugenia Hanfmann and Gertrude Vakar (Cambridge: The M.I.T. Press, 1962); A. R. Luria and F. Ia. Yudovich, *Speech and the Development of Mental Processes in the Child*, ed. Joan Simon (Baltimore: Penguin, 1971); Jerome S. Bruner, *The Relevance of Education* (New York: W. W. Norton and Co., 1971).
2. Nancy Martin, *From Information to Understanding* (London: Schools Council Project Writing Across the Curriculum, 11–13, 1973); Peter Medway, *From Talking to Writing* (London: Schools Council Project Writing Across the Curriculum, 11–13, 1973).
3. Vygotsky, p. 98.
4. Dell Hymes, "On the Origins and Foundations of Inequality Among Speakers," *Daedalus*, 102 (Summer, 1973), 69.

5. Participant-speakers were Loren Barrett, University of Michigan; Gerald O'Grady, SUNY/Buffalo; Hollis Frampton, SUNY/Buffalo; and Janet Emig, Rutgers.

6. George Steiner, *After Babel: Aspects of Language and Translation* (New York: Oxford University Press, 1975), p. 287.

7. John Dewey, *Experience and Education* (New York: Macmillan, 1938); Jean Piaget, *Biology and Knowledge: An Essay on the Relations between Organic Regulations and Cognitive Processes* (Chicago: University of Chicago Press, 1971).

8. Bruner, pp. 7–8.

9. Boyce Rensberger, "Language Ability Found in Right Side of Brain," *New York Times*, 1 August 1975, p. 14.

10. Howard Gardner, *The Shattered Mind: The Person After Brain Damage* (New York: Alfred A. Knopf, 1975), p. 372.

11. William Faulkner, *Writers at Work: The Paris Review Interviews*, ed. Malcolm Cowley (New York: The Viking Press, 1959), p. 130.

12. Géza Révész, *Psychology and Art of the Blind*, trans. H. A. Wolff (London: Longmans-Green, 1950).

13. Bruner, p. 126.

14. Vygotsky, p. 100.

15. Michael Polanyi, *Personal Knowledge: Toward a Post-Critical Philosophy* (Chicago: University of Chicago Press, 1958), p. viii.

16. Robert Pirsig, *Zen and the Art of Motorcycle Maintenance* (New York: William Morrow and Co., Inc., 1974), p. 212.

17. George Kelly, *A Theory of Personality: The Psychology of Personal Constructs* (New York: W. W. Norton and Co., 1963).

18. Sara E. Sanders and John H. Littlefield, "Perhaps Test Essays Can Reflect Significant Improvement in Freshman Composition: Report on a Successful Attempt," *RTE*, 9 (Fall, 1975), 145–153.

19. Benjamin Bloom, "Time and Learning," *American Psychologist*, 29 (September, 1974), 682–688.

20. Jean-Paul Sartre, "Sartre at Seventy: An Interview," with Michael Contat, *New York Review of Books*, 7 August 1975.

21. Luria, p. 118.

22. Luria, p. 50.

23. James Britton, *Language and Learning* (Baltimore: Penguin, 1971), pp. 10–11.

24. Bruner, p. 47.

QUESTIONS FOR READING, RESPONDING, AND WRITING

Summarizing Main Points

1. What makes writing a "unique" learning mode, according to Emig? Why do you suppose that Emig is so concerned with the fact that writing is a "unique" way to learn?

2. What "hazards, conceptually and pedagogically" might arise, according to Emig, "in creating too complete an analogy" between writing and talking?

Analyzing Methods of Discourse

1. Emig calls on a multitude of sources and authorities. Are there any that you recognize? List them. Does Emig's wide range of authorities, that is, authorities from outside her specialized field, make her argument more believable? If so, why?
2. Emig summarizes her results at the conclusion of her essay in a chart. Do you find that chart helpful? If so, why? Using the chart as an outline, go back over Emig's essay and fill in the details—the proof, as it were—for each item on the chart under the heading "Selected attributes of writing, process and product."

Focusing on the Field

1. Emig begins her essay with a disclaimer, that the notion of writing as a mode of learning is "clearly debatable." Where, exactly, in her essay does she address that debate?
2. Emig ends her essay with the "hope that the essay will start a crucial line of inquiry." To whom is this hope addressed? Can you imagine what sorts of lines of inquiry her essay might initiate?

Writing Assignments

1. Emig suggests that "writing, typically, is a 'much slower' process than talking. . . . This slower pace allows for—indeed, encourages—the shuttling among past, present, and future." After studying Reuben Brower's "Reading in Slow Motion," write a short essay of your own in which you argue that Brower advocates slow reading for the same reason. Support your argument with details from Brower's essay.
2. Write an essay in which you attack or defend the proposition by Samuel Johnson that "no one but a blockhead ever wrote for anything but money."

T·W·O

SOCIAL SCIENCES
Psychology/Sociology/ Anthropology/Political Science/ Law/Education

Modern English, especially written English, is full of bad habits which spread by imitation and which can be avoided if one is willing to take the necessary trouble. If one gets rid of these habits one can think more clearly, and to think clearly is a necessary first step towards political regeneration: so that the fight against bad English is not frivolous and is not the exclusive concern of professional writers.

George Orwell, "Politics and the English Language"

The ethnographer "inscribes" social discourse; *he writes it down.* In so doing, he turns it from a passing event, which exists only in its own moment of occurrence, into an account, which exists in its inscriptions and can be reconsulted.

Clifford Geertz, *The Interpretation of Cultures*

When I am lecturing to students and I get into technical terms, then I write their etymology on the blackboard. Once the students understand a word and know where it comes from, they better remember it.

Ashley Montague

. . . no matter how aseptic and odourless when first coined, psychological and sociological terms very quickly acquire undertones of praise or blame in accordance with whether the reality to which they refer is liked or not. For instance, who likes to be called a 'masochist' or a 'psychotic'? Yet these terms were invented for strictly clinical use, as near to objectivity as anything that we can imagine in the study of man.

Stanislaw Andreski, *Social Sciences as Sorcery*

Statistical data by themselves do not make sociology. They become sociology only when they are sociologically interpreted, put within a theoretical frame of reference that is sociological. Simple counting, or even correlating different items that one counts, is not sociology.

Peter L. Berger, *Invitation to Sociology:*
A Humanist Perspective

. . . Desire for status is one reason why academic men slip so readily into unintelligibility. . . . To overcome the academic *prose* you have first to overcome the academic *pose*. It is much less important to study grammar and Anglo-Saxon roots than to clarify your answer to these important questions: (1) How difficult and complex after all is my subject? (2) When I write, what status am I claiming for myself? (3) For whom am I trying to write?

C. Wright Mills, *The Sociological Imagination*

Lillian B. Rubin

WORLDS OF PAIN:
The Families

Lillian B. Rubin was born in Philadelphia, Pennsylvania, in 1924, and grew up in the Bronx, New York. After receiving a doctorate in sociology from the University of California, Berkeley, she began a practice in clinical therapy, with a speciality in family counseling. Currently a Senior Research Associate at the Institute for the Study of Social Change, Lillian Rubin has written many books in the fields of sociology and psychology: *Busing and Backlash: White Against White in an Urban School District* (1972), *Worlds of Pain: Life in the Working-Class Family* (1976), *Women of a Certain Age: The Midlife Search for Self* (1979), *Intimate Strangers: Men and Women Together* (1983), *Just Friends: The Role of Friendship in Our Lives* (1985), and *Quiet Rage: Bernie Goetz in a Time of Madness* (1986).

In *Worlds of Pain*, Lillian Rubin closely observed white working-class families from twelve communities in the San Francisco Bay area. Based on many hours of intensive interviews, the book attempts to render a "flesh-and-blood" portrait of blue-collar family life. How she met the people and conducted the interviews is the subject of the following selection.

As I drive through the streets, each with its row of neat houses sitting primly behind a small, struggling front lawn, I'm struck with the similarities between working-class neighborhoods in the twelve different communities I have now visited. In the newer tracts, the houses sit well back from gently curving, treeless streets; the tender young plantings at their bases are still too small to cover their naked cement foundations; and time has not yet softened the cruel mark the bulldozer left on the surrounding land. In the older neighborhoods, streets are straight; plantings are fuller, if less well tended; and the houses, like aging people trying to retain a semblance of youth, look tired with the effort.

An occasional tricycle, scooter, or rumpled doll give evidence that young children live and play on these streets. But at ten o'clock in the morning the streets are still, almost eerily void of life. The older children are off to school for the day; the younger ones are playing in fenced back yards; the youngest, in their cribs for the morning nap.

Their mothers are catching their first free breath of the day, perhaps perched on a stool in the kitchen, coffee in one hand, telephone in the other. Since five-thirty or six they have been up and about—preparing breakfast, packing lunches, feeding and changing a crying baby, scolding this child, prodding that one, brushing away a husband's hand unexpectedly on her breast as he moves toward the door. "Oh God," she thinks, "I can't say no *again* tonight; and already I'm tired."

Finally, the rush to clean up the house because this morning, for at least one of them, something different is about to happen. That lady from the university is coming to talk. She muses, "I wonder what she wants to know about me? She said she wants a few hours of my time. What could take *that* long? God, I hope the baby sleeps."

Juggling purse, tape recorder, and small briefcase, I climb out of my car into the morning sunshine. I've dressed casually but carefully for this meeting—none of my more "hip"-looking clothes, no threadbare jeans. I already know—partly because I was once a young working-class woman, partly because I've been doing research in working-class communities for years—that it's expected that I'll look like a professional woman ought to look. Anything else could be taken as a sign of disrespect, both for myself and my hostess. For those who have lived on the edge of poverty all their lives, the semblance of poverty affected by the affluent is both incomprehensible and insulting.

Across the quiet street, a camper is parked in the driveway of one house, a small boat in another. The garage is open in the house next door to the one I'm about to visit; in it a woman is stripping a table, preparing it for a new finish. A little further down the street a Sears truck, brakes squealing, stops; two men begin to unload a new washing machine. With one part of me I observe all this; with another, I become aware that, like the woman who waits inside, I feel some anxiety. "How can I make this stranger comfortable enough to talk openly to me?" I wonder. "And why is she letting me into her life at all?"

With that, I find myself facing the front door, looking around for the doorbell. Before I find it, the door opens; a young woman in her late twenties stands smiling shyly before me. I introduce myself. "Hi, I'm Lillian Rubin; you must be Mary Ann Corbett." She nods, opens the door wider, motioning me inside. "Come in," she says in the hushed voice of a mother whose baby has just been put down for a nap. Then, awkwardly, formally, "I'm glad to meet you."

As we step into the front room, she looks at the paraphernalia I carry, and asks, "Where would you like to sit? In here, or at the kitchen table?" It makes no difference to me; sometimes we stay in the living room; sometimes we go into the kitchen. This time I say, "This will be fine, if it's all right with you. I can just put my recorder on the table between those two chairs."

As I move forward to settle myself, she offers to get coffee. Mary Ann Corbett is a medium-sized, slightly round woman, with short, wavy brown hair, hazel eyes, and a self-conscious, relatively joyless smile. She is dressed neatly on this warm day—light cotton pants, a short-sleeved knit shirt, and sandals on her bare feet. As she turns and walks toward the kitchen, I have a sudden, clear image of what she will look like in twenty years. Although not yet thirty, the contours of the middle-aged woman to come are already apparent.

The room, like most I will go into, has the look of one that was tidied up for company. The furnishings are nondescript and of indeterminate age; it has a familiar look, a scene out of my girlhood. Once in a while, usually in a house in one of the newer tracts, the furnishings stand out in memory because they wear the decorator-matched and unlived-in look of the rooms on display at the local furniture store. No surprise! When a family has worked so hard, waited so long to acquire these goods, they are not treated lightly. Once in a while, the disorder is the dominant memory—yesterday's laundry spilling over the sides of a chair, unwashed dishes piling up in the sink, children's toys littering the floor, a vacuum, with its promise of cleanliness, propped against the wall. But mostly the houses look much like Mary Ann Corbett's—picked up, tucked in, well tended—a family still making do with a collection of hand-me-downs and cheap Ward's or Sears' specials bought expensively on credit when they were first married. For not only the poor, but those just up from poverty as well, always pay more. Without ready cash, they must rely on high-interest time payment purchases for all but their daily needs.

In this house, as in others, a large color television set dominates the room. Indeed, as flowers turn toward the light, so everything in the room is turned expectantly toward the darkened tube. "Does *everybody* have one of these things?" I wonder. I had not yet been in a home without one; nor, as it turns out, would I be.

I notice another common phenomenon: there's only one small lamp in this room that doesn't even have an overhead light fixture. Some homes have no lamps at all in the living room; only a few have anything that approaches adequate reading light. I shrug, impatient with myself, trying to shake off my intellectual's bias. "So why," I ask myself, "should people who don't read spend scarce money on reading lamps?" I don't know the answer to that question. I only know it's my biggest surprise as I go from house to house, and the one I have most trouble explaining to myself comfortably.

Mary Ann re-enters the room, steaming mug in each hand. She settles herself in the chair opposite me, points to the tape recorder, and asks hesitantly, "Are you going to turn that on? I'm afraid I'll feel so funny I won't be able to talk." I reply, "If you don't mind, I'd like to try it. Most people forget it pretty quickly; but if it continues to bother you, I'll turn it off. Okay?" She shifts slightly in her chair, still uncomfortable, but nods assent. We begin the interview.

A week later, I'm back on the same street, this time to meet Jim Corbett. It's early evening—six-thirty; dinner is over, and the street is alive with activity. The sounds of children playing mix with the swish of water from a dozen houses. Here and there, women stand in twos and threes, chatting; several men are bent over the engines of their cars or trucks.

Once again, I climb out of my car and gather my equipment together. Only this time several people stop what they are doing and watch curiously. Some children come up to stand closer. "Who 'dja come to see?" asks one. "What's that?" calls out another, pointing to my recorder. We banter for the few moments it takes to collect myself. Then I head across the street. On my way, I see a man standing before a boat with a wrench in hand, puzzled. Two neighbors saunter over and offer advice.

Before I reach the front door, it is thrown open by eight-year-old Joanne. "C'mon in," she says in a rush. "We're getting ready to go to Grandma's, but my brother's a slow poke so he's not ready yet. And Mommy's mad at him. She said we were supposed to be gone before you came." Mary Ann hurries into the living room. "Hush, Joanne. Where are your manners? What kind of way is that to greet company?" And to me, "I'm sorry we're late getting out, but she's right, little Jimmy is such a slow poke, and the baby's been fussy. Jim's out in the backyard. I'll go get him, and then we'll be just about ready to leave so you two can talk privately."

Despite the pressures on her, Mary Ann's greeting is cordial, her smile genuinely friendly and welcoming. The eight hours we've spent together in the last week have created a bond between us. She has never before talked to anyone about such personal things; never before been able to express her conflicts about her life; indeed, never before even acknowledged them to herself so directly. It isn't that she doesn't have friends and family to talk to. She does. Both her mother and sister live nearby, and she sees them often. Some of her old high-school friends are now neighbors, and they retain close and warm relationships. But certain subjects—sex, for example—are too private to talk about. And others—her restless discontent, for example—are too frightening to talk about. Besides, she keeps telling herself, "What do I have to complain about? Jim's a steady worker; he doesn't drink; he doesn't hit me. That's a lot more than my mother had, and she's not complaining." Or else, "My friends, they all seem to like it okay, so there must be something the matter with me."

Such turning inward with self-blame is common among the women and men I met—a product, in part, of the individualist ethic in the American society which fixes responsibility for any failure to achieve the American dream in individual inadequacy. That same ethic—emphasizing as it does the isolated individual or, at most, the family unit—breeds a kind of isolation in American life that is common in all classes but more profoundly experienced in the working class, partly, at least, because they have fewer outside resources. It is, I suspect, the main reason why people agree to talk to me, and why they find the hours we spend together relieving. For one thing, the very fact that someone asks certain questions, raises certain issues, gives them a kind of universality and legitimacy. It means that other people must feel these feelings, too, so it's all right to talk about them—at least to this stranger who comes with the credentials of an expert. Like the rest of us, the Corbetts and their friends and neighbors feel the need for expert counsel once in a while. But if you're working class, even were it culturally acceptable to acknowledge the need, who can afford the cost? So talking to me offers the possibility for getting some advice and reassurance without even the requirement of admitting the need.

Mary Ann and Jim, the two older children trailing behind, come into the room. As the children dance around restlessly, Jim and I are introduced. He is a medium-tall, lean, sandy-haired man with long sideburns and a ruddy complexion. The lines of fatigue on his face coupled with the wrinkles around his eyes and mouth make him look older than his thirty years. His cordial words, when they come, belie his tight, anxious smile. "Mary Ann's talked a lot about you. I must say, life has been different since you've been coming around, and I'm glad to get a chance to see what you look like."

There's a small flurry as Mary Ann and the children leave, she calling out to Jim, "Call us when you're through. I won't come back until I hear from you." I object, "But it may be quite late; what about the children?" "Don't worry about that. I can put them down at Mama's; they're used to it." As they leave, Jim goes out to the kitchen to get a cold drink. I'm eager to get started. Almost half an hour has gone by since I arrived, and I know from past experience that these evenings can run very late.

I had been warned that I might be able to reach the women, but never the men. "What working-class guy will talk to a middle-class professional woman?" friends and colleagues wanted to know. Now, I knew the answer: the husbands of the women I met and talked to first. For those women became my most powerful allies in enlisting the cooperation of their men. Having found the experience pleasurable and useful, they were eager to expose their husbands to it as well, partly, no doubt, in the hope that some painful problem would be dealt with in the process. Sometimes it required a struggle—the wife pleading, cajoling, threatening. But more often, by the time I had finished visiting the wife, I had become a family "event," and the husbands were sufficiently curious and feeling sufficiently excluded that they participated willingly.

Still, I was surprised by the openness with which most of the men tried to talk about difficult and delicate subjects. So much so that I asked several about it. "Would it have been easier to talk about these personal issues with a man rather than a woman?" The answer required little thought: "No." And it was best explained by a thirty-one-year-old heavy-equipment mechanic as he walked me to my car very late one night:

> Guys don't talk about things like that to each other. Me, I'm used to talking to women. I talked to my mother when I was a kid, not my father. When I got older, I talked to girls, not to guys. And now I have my wife to talk to.

Of course, it makes sense, doesn't it? It is women, not men, who nurture, who comfort, who teach young boys. It is to women they run with their earliest pains and triumphs; it is to women they first confide their fears and fantasies. And to the degree that the American culture approves male expression of closeness or intimacy, it is between a man and a woman, not between two men.

From talking to Mary Ann, I already know a great deal about Jim. Like so many men of all classes in our culture, he's a quiet, controlled man—no big mood swings for him. She's the one in the family with the ups and downs. For Jim, there are no expressions of deep sadness or despair, no unreasoning flashes of anger; but there are none of ecstasy either.

Jim is a lonely man, although he doesn't often acknowledge it. He has no close friends, no close ties with his family. There are some guys at work with whom he goes drinking once in a while, a guy with whom he goes fishing sometimes. But nobody important, nobody he can talk to, nobody he can count on for anything.

He's done a variety of different kinds of work, including a stint on the assembly line—years he recalls with distaste. For the last three years he has been employed as an ironworker in heavy construction. He likes the work because he can move around and because it keeps him outdoors. The pay is great—$9.00 an hour—and when he works regularly, the weekly pay checks are large, indeed. But he doesn't work regularly. There are lay-offs because of weather, lay-offs because of industry slow-downs, lay-offs because of accidents on the job. Two years ago, a heavy beam caught him in the foot; he didn't walk again for three months. Even so, last year he earned close to $12,000, more than ever before, but still not enough to make a dent in the debts he has accumulated over the years— loans for the house, the car, to help pay for his mother's illness, to keep them going when he was hurt. Those debts ride always on his shoulders— sometimes he carries them easily, sometimes they drag him down. At those moments, he wonders wearily, "Is this really what life's all about? How did I get to this place anyway?"

Right at the moment, as he stands before the refrigerator, he's concerned with more immediate things. Mary Ann has talked a lot about how good it made her feel to have someone to talk to. He doesn't quite understand what she means, but things have certainly been different these last few days. She's been less edgy; she hasn't hollered at the kids so much; and last night she even seemed to enjoy making love. So if talking can do that, he's willing to let her talk as much as she wants, maybe even give it a try himself. Besides, it feels kind of good to think about telling *his* side of the story of their lives. Mary Ann at least has her girlfriends and her sister to talk to; he doesn't have anybody.

With that, he straightens and heads back into the living room. He seats himself in the chair across from me and, his face smiling, his voice serious, says, "I sure hope you got those tapes locked up good." I look at him, puzzled, about to reassure him about the confidentiality of our talk. Before I speak, he explains, "Well, I figure if they could steal those tapes from—what's his name? oh yeah—from Ellsberg's psychiatrist's office, then you better take care of your stuff. It's not that I have anything to be afraid of, but after all, I agreed to talk to you, not the whole world." I smile and assure him that the tape will be destroyed as soon as the interview is transcribed, that the interview will remain in a locked file to be seen by no eyes other than mine, and that his anonymity will be fully protected. The atmosphere in the room relaxes perceptibly. We begin the interview.

QUESTIONS FOR READING, RESPONDING, AND WRITING

Summarizing Main Points

1. Why does Rubin find "self-blame" important? How does it surface in the interviews? How does self-blame affect the people she is interviewing?

2. What does Rubin discover about working-class men and women that she didn't expect to find? What do the interviewees discover about themselves?

Analyzing Methods of Discourse

1. How does Rubin use specific details from her personal observations to describe working-class life? Why, for example, does she begin with a description of the streets? What does starting in that manner help her to achieve?
2. Can you point to any differences between Rubin's speech and that of the families she interviews? Does she speak to them for the most part professionally or personally? Does she address her readers differently from the way she addresses the families? Explain.

Focusing on the Field

1. In what ways does Rubin try to establish her close connection to working-class family life? What differences does she perceive between herself and the families?
2. How does Rubin allow her readers to see her subjects both as individuals and as representatives of a social class? Does this dual perception present any personal or professional complications?

Writing Assignments

1. Using the opening of the selection as a model, select a neighborhood (it need not be your own) and describe it in a way that clearly reveals its social class. Be sure you base your details on careful observation.
2. Imagine that you are one of Rubin's subjects. Write an essay in which you describe your impressions of the interviewer and differences between the way you perceive yourself and the way you think you are being perceived.

Mary McCarthy

CATHOLIC EDUCATION

Mary McCarthy was "born and brought up a Catholic" in Seattle, Washington. Orphaned in 1918 at the age of 6, McCarthy attended Forest Ridge Convent. Her further education at Vassar formed the basis for her most famous novel, *The Group* (1963), which was later produced as a film.

While at Vassar, McCarthy studied English literature and, in an effort to protest the policies of *The Vassar Review,* she helped form, along with Elizabeth Bishop and others, a competing magazine. In 1933, she moved to New York City, where she worked as a book reviewer for *The Nation, The New Republic,* and *The Partisan Review.* Her criticism and her novels are known for their acerbic and compelling wit. Her ability to make sex an issue without making it *the* issue stems from her provocative use of comedy and humor. Her numerous and wide-ranging books include her novels, *The Company She Keeps* (1957) and the award-winning *The Oasis* (1949), a collection of stories, *Cast a Cold Eye* (1950), a collection of reviews, *Sights and Spectacles, 1937–1956* (1956), two nonfiction books, *Vietnam* (1967) and *Hanoi* (1968), and an autobiography, *Memories of a Catholic Girlhood* (1957), from which the following selection is taken.

If you are born and brought up a Catholic, you have absorbed a good deal of world history and the history of ideas before you are twelve, and it is like learning a language early; the effect is indelible. Nobody else in America, no other group, is in this fortunate position. Granted that Catholic history is biased, it is not dry or dead; its virtue for the student, indeed, is that it has been made to come alive by the violent partisanship which inflames it. This partisanship, moreover, acts as a magnet to attract stray pieces of information not ordinarily taught in American schools. While children in public schools were studying American history, we in the convent in the eighth grade were studying English history down to the time of Lord Palmerston; the reason for this was, of course, that English history, up to Henry VIII, was Catholic history, and, after that, with one or two interludes, it became anti-Catholic history. Naturally, we were taught to sympathize with Bloody Mary (never called that in the convent), Mary Queen of Scots, Philip of Spain, the martyr Jesuits, Charles I (married to a Catholic princess), James II (married first to a Protestant and then to Mary of Modena), the Old Pretender, Bonnie Prince Charlie; interest petered out with Peel and Catholic Emancipation. To me, it does not matter that this history was one-sided (this can always be remedied later); the important thing is to have learned the battles and the sovereigns, their consorts, mistresses, and prime ministers, to know the past of a foreign country in such detail that it becomes one's own. Had I stayed in the convent, we would have gone on to French history, and today I would know the list of French kings and their wives and ministers, because French history, up to the Revolution, was Catholic history, and Charlemagne, Joan of Arc, and Napoleon were all prominent Catholics.

Nor is it only a matter of knowing more, at an earlier age, so that it becomes a part of oneself; it is also a matter of feeling. To care for the quarrels of the past, to identify oneself passionately with a cause that became, politically speaking, a losing cause with the birth of the modern world, is to experience a kind of straining against reality, a rebellious nonconformity that, again, is rare in America, where children are instructed in the virtues of the system they live under, as though history had achieved a happy ending in American civics.

So much for the practical side. But it might be pointed out that to an American educator, my Catholic training would appear to have no utility whatever. What is the good, he would say, of hearing the drone of a dead language every day or of knowing that Saint Ursula, a Breton princess, was martyred at Cologne, together with ten thousand virgins? I have shown that such things proved to have a certain usefulness in later life—a usefulness that was not, however, intended at the time, for we did not study the lives of the saints in order to look at Italian painting or recite our catechism in order to read John Donne. Such an idea would be atrocious blasphemy. We learned those things for the glory of God, and the rest, so to speak, was added to us. Nor would it have made us study any harder if we had been assured that what we were learning was going to come in handy in later life, any more than children study arithmetic harder if they are promised it will help them later on in business. Nothing is more boring to a child than the principle of utility. The final usefulness of my Catholic training was to teach me, together with much that proved to be practical, a conception of something prior to and beyond utility ("Consider the lilies of the field; they toil not, neither do they spin"), an idea of sheer wastefulness that is always shocking to non-Catholics, who cannot bear, for example, the contrast between the rich churches and the poor people of southern Europe. Those churches, agreed, are a folly; so is the life of a dirty anchorite or of a cloistered, non-teaching nun—unprofitable for society and bad for the person concerned. But I prefer to think of them that way than to imagine them as an investment, shares bought in future salvation. I never really liked the doctrine of Indulgences—the notion that you could say five Hail Marys and knock off a year in Purgatory. This seemed to me to belong to my grandmother McCarthy's kind of Catholicism. What I liked in the Church, and what I recall with gratitude, was the sense of mystery and wonder, ashes put on one's forehead on Ash Wednesday, the blessing of the throat with candles on St. Blaise's Day, the purple palls put on the statues after Passion Sunday, which meant they were hiding their faces in mourning because Christ was going to be crucified, the ringing of the bell at the Sanctus, the burst of lilies at Easter—all this ritual, seeming slightly strange and having no purpose (except the throat-blessing), beyond commemoration of a Person Who had died a long time ago. In these exalted moments of altruism the soul was fired with reverence.

QUESTIONS FOR READING, RESPONDING, AND WRITING

Summarizing Main Points

1. Contrast the "practical side" of McCarthy's education with that side she defines as "prior to and beyond utility." What did McCarthy learn? Why did she learn it? Which is more important to her?
2. What is the "final usefulness" that the "conception of something prior to and beyond utility" provides for McCarthy?

Analyzing Methods of Discourse

1. McCarthy begins her third paragraph, "So much for the practical side." Reread the first two paragraphs. Had you thought of the material in those paragraphs as "practical"? What do you think McCarthy means by the term? How does she use it to make the transition into her third paragraph?
2. McCarthy divides her essay into discussions of what she learned and why she learned it. How does the arrangement of these discussions—what she learned, first; why she learned it, second—help her to make her point about the "final usefulness" of her Catholic education? Would it have affected her argument had she reversed the order of her discussions? Why or why not?

Focusing on the Field

1. What does McCarthy assume about the "American educator" to whom her "Catholic training would appear to have no utility whatever"? Try to describe McCarthy's "American educator" from the information she provides and the implications of that information. Given your own experience with American education and educators, do you think McCarthy is being fair to them here?
2. Who do you suppose McCarthy is writing for here? What do you suppose the goal or goals behind this personal reminiscence might be?

Writing Assignments

1. Write a brief essay about your own education in which you describe its value for you and any drawbacks you might feel it presented.
2. Read Richard Rodriguez's "Memories of a Bilingual Childhood." Both Rodriguez's and McCarthy's essays are personal reminiscences from autobiographies. Compare and contrast these authors' views of their respective educational experiences and the lasting effects produced on them by those experiences.

Bruno Bettelheim

FAIRY TALE VERSUS MYTH
Optimism Versus Pessimism

Bruno Bettelheim writes on many subjects, but his main concern has always been children. Though a genuine heir of Freud, Bettelheim, who was born in 1903 in Vienna, Austria, where he received a doctorate in 1938, does not limit his thinking to strict Freudian theory. Instead, such theory becomes only a starting point for wider, less clinical, and more human insights.

His own experiences—his psychoanalysis during adolescence, his arrest by Nazis and subsequent two years in concentration camps as a young adult, and his many years of work with emotionally disturbed children at the Sonia Shankman Orthogenic School of the University of Chicago—have enriched Bettelheim's writings with a warmth and dignity and hope that make them more than psychological texts, though they are well respected as such. Some of their titles alone suggest Bettelheim's compassion: *Love Is Not Enough: The Treatment of Emotionally Disturbed Children* (1950), *The Informed Heart: Autonomy in a Mass Age* (1960), *The Children of the Dream: Communal Childbearing and American Education* (1970), *A Home for the Heart* (1974), which details the design and organization of a mental hospital, and *The Uses of Enchantment: The Meaning and Importance of Fairy Tales* (1976), from which the following selection is taken. In this essay, Bettelheim argues that fairy tales provide necessary models that enable the child to handle the difficult, emotionally painful process of growing up.

Plato—who may have understood better what forms the mind of man than do some of our contemporaries who want their children exposed only to "real" people and everyday events—knew what intellectual experiences make for true humanity. He suggested that the future citizens of his ideal republic begin their literary education with the telling of myths, rather than with mere facts or so-called rational teachings. Even Aristotle, master of pure reason, said: "The friend of wisdom is also a friend of myth."

Modern thinkers who have studied myths and fairy tales from a philosophical or psychological viewpoint arrive at the same conclusion, regardless of their original persuasion. Mircea Eliade, for one, describes these stories as "models for human behavior [that,] by that very fact, give meaning and value to life." Drawing on anthropological parallels, he and others suggest that myths and fairy tales were derived from, or give symbolic expression to, initiation rites or other *rites de passage*—such as metaphoric death of an old, inadequate self in order to be reborn on a higher plane of existence. He feels that this is why these tales meet a strongly felt need and are carriers of such deep meaning.

Other investigators with a depth-psychological orientation emphasize the similarities between the fantastic events in myths and fairy tales and those in adult dreams and daydreams—the fulfillment of wishes, the winning out over all competitors, the destruction of enemies—and conclude that one attraction of this literature is its expression of that which is normally prevented from coming to awareness.

There are, of course, very significant differences between fairy tales and dreams. For example, in dreams more often than not the wish fulfillment is disguised, while in fairy tales much of it is openly expressed. To a considerable degree, dreams are the result of inner pressures which have found no relief, of problems which beset a person to which he knows no solution and to which the dream finds none. The fairy tale does the opposite: it projects the relief of all pressures and not only offers ways to solve problems but promises that a "happy" solution will be found.

We cannot control what goes on in our dreams. Although our inner censorship influences what we may dream, such control occurs on an unconscious level. The fairy tale, on the other hand, is very much the result of common conscious and unconscious content having been shaped by the conscious mind, not of one particular person, but the consensus of many in regard to what they view as universal human problems and what they accept as desirable solutions. If all these elements were not present in a fairy tale, it would not be retold by generation after generation. Only if a fairy tale met the conscious and unconscious requirements of many people was it repeatedly retold, and listened to with great interest. No dream of a person could arouse such persistent interest unless it was worked into a myth, as was the story of the pharaoh's dreams as interpreted by Joseph in the Bible.

There is general agreement that myths and fairy tales speak to us in the language of symbols representing unconscious content. Their appeal is simultaneously to our conscious and unconscious mind, to all three of its aspects—id, ego, and superego—and to our need for ego-ideals as well. This makes it very effective; and in the tales' content, inner psychological phenomena are given body in symbolic form.

Freudian psychoanalysts concern themselves with showing what kind of repressed or otherwise unconscious material underlies myths and fairy tales, and how these relate to dreams and daydreams.

Jungian psychoanalysts stress in addition that the figures and events of these stories conform to and hence represent archetypical psychological phenomena, and symbolically suggest the need for gaining a higher state of selfhood—an inner renewal which is achieved as personal and racial unconscious forces become available to the person.

There are not only essential similarities between myths and fairy tales; there are also inherent differences. Although the same exemplary figures and situations are found in both and equally miraculous events occur in both, there is a crucial difference in the way these are communicated. Put simply, the dominant feeling a myth conveys is: this is absolutely unique; it could not have happened to any other person or in any other setting; such events are grandiose, awe-inspiring, and could not possibly happen to an ordinary mortal like you or me. The reason is not so much that what takes place is miraculous, but that it is described as such. By contrast, although the events which occur in fairy tales are often unusual and most improbable, they are always presented as ordinary, something that could happen to you or me or the person next door when out on a walk in the woods. Even the most remarkable encounters are related in casual, everyday ways in fairy tales.

An even more significant difference between these two kinds of story is the ending, which in myths is nearly always tragic, while always happy in fairy tales. For this reason, some of the best-known stories found in collections of fairy tales don't really belong in this category. For example, Hans Christian Andersen's "The Little Match Girl" and "The Steadfast Tin Soldier" are beautiful but extremely sad; they do not convey the feeling of consolation characteristic of fairy tales at the end. Andersen's "The Snow Queen," on the other hand, comes quite close to being a true fairy tale.

The myth is pessimistic, while the fairy story is optimistic, no matter how terrifyingly serious some features of the story may be. It is this decisive difference which sets the fairy tale apart from other stories in which equally fantastic events occur, whether the happy outcome is due to the virtues of the hero, chance, or the interference of supernatural figures.

Myths typically involve superego demands in conflict with id-motivated action, and with the self-preserving desires of the ego. A mere mortal is too frail to meet the challenges of the gods. Paris, who does the bidding of Zeus as conveyed to him by Hermes, and obeys the demand of the three goddesses in choosing which shall have the apple, is destroyed for having followed these commands, as are untold other mortals in the wake of this fateful choice.

Try as hard as we may, we can never live up fully to what the superego, as represented in myths by the gods, seems to require of us. The more we try to please it, the more implacable its demands. Even when the hero does not know that he gave in to the proddings of his id, he is still made to suffer horribly for it. When a mortal incurs the displeasure of a god without having done anything wrong, he is destroyed by these supreme superego representations. The pessimism of myths is superbly exemplified in the paradigmatic myth of psychoanalysis, the tragedy of Oedipus.

The myth of Oedipus, particularly when well performed on the stage, arouses powerful intellectual and emotional reactions in the adult—so much so, that it may provide a cathartic experience, as Aristotle taught all tragedy does. After watching Oedipus, a viewer may wonder why he is so deeply moved; and in responding to what he observes as his emotional reaction, ruminating about the mythical events and what these mean to him, a person may come to clarify his thoughts and feelings. With this, certain inner tensions which are the consequence of events long past may be relieved; previously unconscious material can then enter one's awareness and become accessible for conscious working through. This can happen if the observer is deeply moved emotionally by the myth, and at the same time strongly motivated intellectually to understand it.

Vicariously experiencing what happened to Oedipus, what he did and what he suffered, may permit the adult to bring his mature understanding to what until then had remained childish anxieties, preserved intact in infantile form in the unconscious mind. But this possibility exists only because the myth refers to events which happened in the most distant times, as the adult's oedipal longings and anxieties belong to the dimmest past of his life. If the underlying meaning of a myth were spelled out and presented as an event that could have happened in the person's adult conscious lifetime, then this would vastly increase old anxieties, and result in deeper repression.

A myth is not a cautionary tale like a fable which, by arousing anxiety, prevents us from acting in ways which are described as damaging to us. The myth of Oedipus can never be experienced as warning us not to get caught in an oedipal constellation. If one is born and raised as a child of two parents, oedipal conflicts are inescapable.

The oedipus complex is the crucial problem of childhood—unless a child remains fixated at an even earlier stage of development, such as the oral stage. A young child is completely caught up in oedipal conflicts as the inescapable reality of his life. The older child, from about age five on, is struggling to extricate himself by partly repressing the conflict, partly solving it by forming emotional attachments to others besides his parents, and partly sublimating it. What such a child needs least of all is to have his oedipal conflicts activated by such a myth. Suppose that the child still actively wishes, or has barely repressed the desire, to rid himself of one parent in order to have the other exclusively; if he is exposed—even though only in symbolic form—to the idea that by chance, unknowingly, one may murder a parent and marry the other, then what the child has played with only in fantasy suddenly assumes gruesome reality. The consequence of this exposure can only be increased anxiety about himself and the world.

A child not only dreams about marrying his parent of the other sex, but actively spins fantasies around it. The myth of Oedipus tells what happens if that dream becomes reality—and still the child cannot yet give up the wishful fantasies of marrying the parent at some future time. After hearing the myth of Oedipus, the conclusion in the child's mind could only be that similar horrible things—the death of a parent and mutilation of himself—will happen to him.

At this age, from four until puberty, what the child needs most is to be presented with symbolic images which reassure him that there is a happy solution to his oedipal problems—though he may find this difficult to believe—provided that he slowly works himself out of them. But reassurance about a happy outcome has to come first, because only then will the child have the courage to labor confidently to extricate himself from his oedipal predicament.

In childhood, more than in any other age, all is becoming. As long as we have not yet achieved considerable security within ourselves, we cannot engage in difficult psychological struggles unless a positive outcome seems certain to us, whatever the chances for this may be in reality. The fairy tale offers fantasy materials which suggest to the child in symbolic form what the battle to achieve self-realization is all about, and it guarantees a happy ending.

Mythical heroes offer excellent images for the development of the superego, but the demands they embody are so rigorous as to discourage the child in his fledgling strivings to achieve personality integration. While the mythical hero experiences a transfiguration into eternal life in heaven, the central figure of the fairy tale lives happily ever after on earth, right among the rest of us. Some fairy tales conclude with the information that if perchance he has not yet died, the hero may be still alive. Thus, a happy though ordinary existence is projected by fairy tales as the outcome of the trials and tribulations involved in the normal growing-up process.

True, these psychosocial crises of growing up are imaginatively embroidered and symbolically represented in fairy tales as encounters with fairies, witches, ferocious animals, or figures of superhuman intelligence or cunning—but the essential humanity of the hero, despite his strange experiences, is affirmed by the reminder that he will have to die like the rest of us. Whatever strange events the fairy-tale hero experiences, they do not make him superhuman, as is true for the mythical hero. This real humanity suggests to the child that, whatever the content of the fairy tale, it is but fanciful elaborations and exaggerations of the tasks he has to meet, and of his hopes and fears.

Though the fairy tale offers fantastic symbolic images for the solution of problems, the problems presented in them are ordinary ones: a child's suffering from the jealousy and discrimination of his siblings, as is true for Cinderella; a child being thought incompetent by his parent, as happens in many fairy tales—for example, in the Brothers Grimm's story "The Spirit in the Bottle." Further, the fairy-tale hero wins out over these problems right here on earth, not by some reward reaped in heaven.

The psychological wisdom of the ages accounts for the fact that every myth is the story of a particular hero: Theseus, Hercules, Beowulf, Brunhild. Not only do these mythical characters have names, but we are also told the names of their parents, and of the other major figures in a myth. It just wouldn't do to name the myth of Theseus "The Man Who Slew the Bull," or that of Niobe "The Mother Who Had Seven Daughters and Seven Sons."

The fairy tale, by contrast, makes clear that it tells about everyman, people very much like us. Typical titles are "Beauty and the Beast," "The Fairy Tale of One Who Went Forth to Learn Fear." Even recently invented stories follow this pattern—for example, "The Little Prince," "The Ugly Duckling," "The Steadfast Tin Soldier." The protagonists of fairy tales are referred to as "a girl," for instance, or "the youngest brother." If names appear, it is quite clear that these are not proper names, but general or descriptive ones. We are told that "Because she always looked dusty and dirty, they called her Cinderella," or: "A little red cap suited her so well that she was always called 'Little Red Cap.' " Even when the hero is given a name, as in the Jack stories, or in "Hansel and Gretel," the use of very common names makes them generic terms, standing for any boy or girl.

This is further stressed by the fact that in fairy stories nobody else has a name; the parents of the main figures in fairy tales remain nameless. They are referred to as "father," "mother," "stepmother," though they may be described as "a poor fisherman" or "a poor woodcutter." If they are "a king" and "a queen," these are thin disguises for father and mother, as are "prince" and "princess" for boy and girl. Fairies and witches, giants and godmothers remain equally unnamed, thus facilitating projections and identifications.

Mythical heroes are of obviously superhuman dimensions, an aspect which helps to make these stories acceptable to the child. Otherwise the child would be overpowered by the implied demand that he emulate the hero in his own life. Myths are useful in forming not the total personality, but only the superego. The child knows that he cannot possibly live up to the hero's virtue, or parallel his deeds; all he can be expected to do is emulate the hero to some small degree; so the child is not defeated by the discrepancy between this ideal and his own smallness.

The real heroes of history, however, having been people like the rest of us, impress the child with his own insignificance when compared with them. Trying to be guided and inspired by an ideal that no human can fully reach is at least not defeating—but striving to duplicate the deeds of actual great persons seems hopeless to the child and creates feelings of inferiority: first, because one knows one cannot do so, and second, because one fears others might.

Myths project an ideal personality acting on the basis of superego demands, while fairy tales depict an ego integration which allows for appropriate satisfaction of id desires. This difference accounts for the contrast between the pervasive pessimism of myths and the essential optimism of fairy tales.

QUESTIONS FOR READING, RESPONDING, AND WRITING

Summarizing Main Points

1. List the similarities between dreams, fairy tales, and myths. List the differences between fairy tales and myths in the order of importance Bettelheim gives them.
2. Why, according to Bettelheim, do dreams, myths, and fairy tales exist? Are they entirely controllable? According to Bettelheim, would a radical change in the way we live change those myths and fairy tales?

Analyzing Methods of Discourse

1. Bettelheim begins his essay with a short discussion of Plato and Aristotle. He quotes Aristotle: "The friend of wisdom is also a friend of myth." Explain this statement. Reread Bettelheim's first paragraph. Does it or does it not work as a sufficient introduction to Bettelheim's main point?
2. Bettelheim uses several technical terms from the field of psychology, such as "initiation rites," "id, ego, and superego," "cathartic experience," and "oedipus

complex." Find these terms and the other technical terms Bettelheim uses. Read the sentences that surround these terms carefully. How does Bettelheim redefine these terms for the reader who may not be familiar with them?

Focusing on the Field

1. Bettelheim refers often to psychoanalysis and to its prominent figures. List those references. How are these references to psychoanalysis crucial to one of Bettelheim's main points? Is it important to that point that the reader recognize *exactly* who these figures are? Why or why not?
2. Why does Bettelheim include dreams in his analysis of myths and fairy tales? Why does he choose to drop the discussion of dreams as he proceeds in his essay?

Writing Assignments

1. Following Bettelheim's guidelines, choose a myth or a fairy tale and rewrite one in the form of the other. In a short essay, defend your original choice and the manner in which you reworked it.
2. Read Margaret Mead's "New Superstitions for Old." Compare and contrast her analysis of superstitions with Bettelheim's analysis of fairy tales and myths. Consider, in particular, how each author describes the functions of his or her respective subject.

Margaret Mead

NEW SUPERSTITIONS FOR OLD

Margaret Mead's fame as an anthropologist is richly deserved, although perhaps not so much for any lasting theoretical contributions to anthropology as for her sensible and sensitive insights into the human condition as a whole. Mead (1901–1978) began her distinguished—and very public—career by doing field work in Samoa (1925–1926) which resulted in what is easily one of the most popular pieces of social science ever written, *Coming of Age in Samoa* (1923, 1971). She is almost single-handedly responsible for broadening the base of the then fledgling science of anthropology from the rigorous yet narrow analysis of statistics to a wider consideration that includes economic, ecological, and psychological factors.

Mead, whose myriad of awards and honors include twelve honorary degrees, attended DePauw University (M.A., 1924; Ph.D., 1929). Mead studied with Franz Boas and was for many years curator of ethnology at the American Museum of

Natural History. She was one of the first anthropologists to record the customs and habits of primitive cultures with still and motion pictures as well as one of the first to study semiotics—how people communicate by gesture. (See Desmond Morris's "Understanding Gestures: The Thumb Up.") Later in her career, Mead applied her understanding of culture in small primitive societies to several broader studies of contemporary culture, including her famous book *Male and Female: A Study of the Sexes in a Changing World* (1949). The following essay from *A Way of Seeing* (1970), coauthored with Rhoda Metraux, a French anthropologist, demonstrates Mead's characteristic style as she defines superstition in such a way as to make clear its very real bearing on contemporary culture.

Once in a while there is a day when everything seems to run smoothly and even the riskiest venture comes out exactly right. You exclaim, "This is my lucky day!" Then as an afterthought you say, "Knock on wood!" Of course, you do not really believe that knocking on wood will ward off danger. Still, boasting about your own good luck gives you a slightly uneasy feeling—and you carry out the little protective ritual. If someone challenged you at that moment, you would probably say, "Oh, that's nothing. Just an old superstition."

But when you come to think about it, what is a superstition?

In the contemporary world most people treat old folk beliefs as superstitions—the belief, for instance, that there are lucky and unlucky days or numbers, that future events can be read from omens, that there are protective charms or that what happens can be influenced by casting spells. We have excluded magic from our current world view, for we know that natural events have natural causes.

In a religious context, where truths cannot be demonstrated, we accept them as a matter of faith. Superstitions, however, belong to the category of beliefs, practices and ways of thinking that have been discarded because they are inconsistent with scientific knowledge. It is easy to say that other people are superstitious because they believe what we regard to be untrue. "Superstition" used in that sense is a derogatory term for the beliefs of other people that we do not share. But there is more to it than that. For superstitions lead a kind of half life in a twilight world where, sometimes, we partly suspend our disbelief and act as if magic worked.

Actually, almost every day, even in the most sophisticated home, something is likely to happen that evokes the memory of some old folk belief. The salt spills. A knife falls to the floor. Your nose tickles. Then perhaps, with a slightly embarrassed smile, the person who spilled the salt tosses a pinch over his left shoulder. Or someone recites the old rhyme, "Knife falls, gentleman calls." Or as you rub your nose you think, That means a letter. I wonder who's writing? No one takes these small responses very seriously or gives them more than a passing thought. Some-times people will preface one of these ritual acts—walking around instead of under a ladder or hastily closing an umbrella that has been opened inside a house—with such a remark as "I remember my great-aunt used to . . ." or "Germans used to say you ought not . . ." And then, having placed the belief at some distance away in time or space, they carry out the ritual.

Everyone also remembers a few of the observances of childhood—wishing on the first star; looking at the new moon over the right shoulder; avoiding the cracks in the sidewalk on the way to school while chanting, "Step on a crack, break your mother's back"; wishing on white horses, on loads of hay, on covered bridges, on red cars; saying quickly, "Bread-and-butter" when a post or a tree separated you from the friend you were walking with. The adult may not actually recite the formula "Star light, star bright . . ." and may not quite turn to look at the new moon, but his mood is tempered by a little of the old thrill that came when the obser-vance was still freighted with magic.

Superstition can also be used with another meaning. When I discuss the religious beliefs of other peoples, especially primitive peoples, I am often asked, "Do they really have a religion, or is it all just superstition?" The point of contrast here is not between a scientific and a magical view of the world but between the clear, theologically defensible religious beliefs of members of civilized societies and what we regard as the false and childish views of the heathen who "bow down to wood and stone." Within the civilized religions, however, where membership includes be-lievers who are educated and urbane and others who are ignorant and simple, one always finds traditions and practices that the more sophisti-cated will dismiss offhand as "just superstition" but that guide the steps of those who live by older ways. Mostly these are very ancient beliefs, some handed on from one religion to another and carried from country to country around the world.

Very commonly, people associate superstition with the past, with very old ways of thinking that have been supplanted by modern knowl-edge. But new superstitions are continually coming into being and flour-ishing in our society. Listening to mothers in the park in the 1930's, one heard them say, "Now, don't you run out into the sun, or Polio will get you." In the 1940's elderly people explained to one another in tones of resignation, "It was the Virus that got him down." And every year the cosmetics industry offers us new magic—cures for baldness, lotions that will give every woman radiant skin, hair coloring that will restore to the middle-aged the charm and romance of youth—results that are promised if we will just follow the simple directions. Families and individuals also have their cherished, private superstitions. You must leave by the back door when you are going on a journey, or you must wear a green dress when you are taking an examination. It is a kind of joke, or course, but it makes you feel safe.

These old half-beliefs and new half-beliefs reflect the keenness of our wish to have something come true or to prevent something bad from happening. We do not always recognize new superstitions for what they are, and we will follow the old ones because someone's faith long ago matches our contemporary hopes and fears. In the past people "knew" that a black cat crossing one's path was a bad omen, and they turned back home. Today we are fearful of taking a journey and would give anything to turn back—and then we notice a black cat running across the road in front of us.

Child psychologists recognize the value of the toy a child holds in his hand at bedtime. It is different from his thumb, with which he can close himself in from the rest of the world, and it is different from the real world, to which he is learning to relate himself. Psychologists call these toys—these furry animals and old, cozy baby blankets—"transitional objects"; that is, objects that help the child move back and forth between the exactions of everyday life and the world of wish and dream.

Superstitions have some of the qualities of these transitional objects. They help people pass between the areas of life where what happens has to be accepted without proof and the areas where sequences of events are explicable in terms of cause and effect, based on knowledge. Bacteria and viruses that cause sickness have been identified; the cause of symptoms can be diagnosed and a rational course of treatment prescribed. Magical charms no longer are needed to treat the sick; modern medicine has brought the whole sequence of events into the secular world. But people often act as if this change had not taken place. Laymen still treat germs as if they were invisible, malign spirits, and physicians sometimes prescribe antibiotics as if they were magic substances.

Over time, more and more of life has become subject to the controls of knowledge. However, this is never a one-way process. Scientific investigation is continually increasing our knowledge. But if we are to make good use of this knowledge, we must not only rid our minds of old, superseded beliefs and fragments of magical practice, but also recognize new superstitions for what they are. Both are generated by our wishes, our fears and our feeling of helplessness in difficult situations.

Civilized peoples are not alone in having grasped the idea of superstitions—beliefs and practices that are superseded but that still may evoke compliance. The idea is one that is familiar to every people, however primitive, that I have ever known. Every society has a core of transcendent beliefs—beliefs about the nature of the universe, the world and man—that no one doubts or questions. Every society also has a fund of knowledge related to practical life—about the succession of day and night and of the seasons; about correct ways of planting seeds so that they will germinate and grow; about the processes involved in making dyes or the steps necessary to remove the deadly poison from manioc roots so they become edible. Island peoples know how the winds shift and they know the star toward which they must point the prow of the canoe exactly so that as the sun rises they will see the first fringing palms on the shore toward which they are sailing.

This knowledge, based on repeated observations of reliable sequences, leads to ideas and hypotheses of the kind that underlie scientific thinking. And gradually as scientific knowledge, once developed without conscious plan, has become a great self-corrective system and the foundation for rational planning and action, old magical beliefs and observances have had to be discarded.

But it takes time for new ways of thinking to take hold, and often the transition is only partial. Older, more direct beliefs live on in the hearts and minds of elderly people. And they are learned by children who, generation after generation, start out life as hopefully and fearfully as their forebears did. Taking their first steps away from home, children use the old rituals and invent new ones to protect themselves against the strangeness of the world into which they are venturing.

So whatever has been rejected as no longer true, as limited, provincial and idolatrous, still leads a half life. People may say, "It's just a superstition," but they continue to invoke the ritual's protection or potency. In this transitional, twilight state such beliefs come to resemble dreaming. In the dream world a thing can be either good or bad; a cause can be an effect and an effect can be a cause. Do warts come from touching toads, or does touching a toad cure the wart? Is sneezing a good omen or a bad omen? You can have it either way—or both ways at once. In the same sense, the half-acceptance and half-denial accorded superstitions give us the best of both worlds.

Superstitions are sometimes smiled at and sometimes frowned upon as observances characteristic of the old-fashioned, the unenlightened, children, peasants, servants, immigrants, foreigners or backwoods people. Nevertheless, they give all of us ways of moving back and forth among the different worlds in which we live—the sacred, the secular and the scientific. They allow us to keep a private world also, where, smiling a little, we can banish danger with a gesture and summon luck with a rhyme, make the sun shine in spite of storm clouds, force the stranger to do our bidding, keep an enemy at bay and straighten the paths of those we love.

QUESTIONS FOR READING, RESPONDING, AND WRITING

Summarizing Main Points

1. What, according to Mead, is the primary motivation behind superstitions? According to Mead, are superstitions valuable or useless? Good or bad? Do you agree with her assessment?

2. List the differences between old superstitions and the reasons Mead gives for their existence and new superstitions and the reasons behind them.

Analyzing Methods of Discourse

1. After finishing the essay, reread Mead's first paragraph. How has your attitude changed toward Mead's introductory illustration and the "slightly uneasy feeling" Mead describes there?

2. Mead compares superstitions that have been partially rejected to dreams. Find this comparison and list the parallels between superstitions and dreams. Can you discover more points of comparison than Mead includes?

Focusing on the Field

1. Mead was a renowned anthropologist and known as such to the general public. Study the headnote that precedes this essay. Considering the headnote and using the essay presented here for evidence, suggest why you feel that Mead might have been so popular a social scientist.

2. Mead compares religious, scientific, and secular superstitions. How does her wide-ranging approach make her analysis of superstitions more convincing? In which area do you find her most convincing? Why?

Writing Assignments

1. Consider the world of the soap opera as a "culture" worthy of anthropological study. List the "rituals" or "superstitions" (e.g., amnesia) at work in this world. Then, using Mead's essay as a model, choose one of these rituals or superstitions and, in a short essay of your own, explain how it works.

2. As Mead points out, almost everyone follows certain superstitions, even the most hardheaded among us. (The example that Mead supplies about wearing a green dress to take an examination is typical.) In a short essay, describe a superstition that you follow. In the essay, try to discover the origin of that superstition. Also, consider the ways in which Mead's essay relates to your own superstition.

Anne Hollander

DRESSED TO THRILL

Anne Hollander was born in Cleveland, Ohio in 1930 and studied at Barnard College in New York City. In the following essay, which first appeared in *New Republic* in 1985, Hollander examines the "cool and casual style of the new American androgyny" and links it to the contemporary redefinitions of sexual roles in society.

As an art historian particularly interested in costume history and design, Hollander is well qualified for such an assessment. In her recent book, *Seeing Through Clothes,* Hollander demonstrates not that "clothes make the man," but that "clothes make the image of the man." Clothes "stand for knowledge and language, art and love, time and death."

Hollander, who is a frequent contributor to the *Times Literary Supplement,* the *New Republic, Commentary,* and the *New York Times Magazine,* lives in New York City.

When Quentin Bell applied Veblen's principles of Conspicuous Consumption and Conspicuous Waste to fashion, he added another—Conspicuous Outrage. This one now clearly leads the other two. In this decade we want the latest trends in appearance to strain our sense of the suitable and give us a real jolt. The old social systems that generated a need for conspicuous display have modified enough to dull the chic of straight extravagance: the chic of shock has continuous vitality. Dramatically perverse sexual signals are always powerful elements in the modern fashionable vocabulary; and the most sensational component among present trends is something referred to as androgyny. Many modish women's clothes imitate what Robert Taylor wore in 1940 publicity stills, and Michael Jackson's startling feminine beauty challenges public responses from every store window, as well as in many living replicas.

The mode in appearance mirrors collective fantasy, not fundamental aims and beliefs. We are not all really longing for two sexes in a single body, and the true hermaphrodite still counts as a monster. We are not seeing a complete and free interchange of physical characteristics across the sexual divide. There are no silky false moustaches or dashing fake goatees finely crafted of imported sable for the discriminating woman, or luxuriant jaw-length sideburns of the softest bristle sold with moisturizing glue and a designer applicator. Although the new ideal feminine torso has strong square shoulders, flat hips, and no belly at all, the corresponding ideal male body is certainly not displaying the beauties of a soft round stomach, flaring hips, full thighs, and delicately sloping shoulders. On the new woman's ideally athletic shape, breasts may be large or not—a flat chest is not required; and below the belt in back, the buttocks may sharply protrude. But no space remains in front to house a safely cushioned uterus and ovaries, or even well-upholstered labia: under the lower half of the new, high-cut minimal swimsuits, there is room only for a clitoris. Meanwhile the thrilling style of male beauty embodied by Michael Jackson runs chiefly to unprecedented surface adornment— cosmetics and sequins, jewels and elaborate hair, all the old privileges once granted to women, to give them every erotic advantage in the sex wars of the past.

The point about all this is clearly not androgyny at all, but the idea of detachable pleasure. Each sex is not trying to take up the fundamental qualities of the other sex, but rather of the other sexuality—the erotic dimension, which can transcend biology and its attendant social assumptions and institutions. Eroticism is being shown to float free of sexual function. Virility is displayed as a capacity for feeling and generating excitement, not for felling trees or enemies and generating children. Femininity has abandoned the old gestures of passivity to take on main force: ravishing female models now stare purposefully into the viewer's eyes instead of flashing provocative glances or gazing remotely away. Erotic attractiveness appears ready to exert its strength in unforseeable and formerly forbidden ways and places. Recognition is now being given to sexual desire for objects of all kinds once considered unsuitable—some of them inanimate, judging from the seductiveness of most advertising photography.

Homosexual desire is now an acknowledged aspect of common life, deserving of truthful representation in popular culture, not just in coterie vehicles of expression. The aging parents of youthful characters in movie and television dramas are no longer rendered as mentally stuffy and physically withered, but as stunningly attractive sexual beings—legitimate and non-ridiculous rivals for the lustful attentions of the young. The curved flanks of travel-irons and food processors in the Bloomingdale's catalogue make as strong an appeal to erotic desire as the satiny behinds and moist lips of the makeup and underwear models. So do the unfolding petals of lettuces and the rosy flesh of cut tomatoes on TV food commercials. In this general eroticization of the material world, visual culture is openly acknowledging that lust is by nature wayward.

To register as attractive under current assumptions, a female body may now show its affinities not only with delicious objects but with attractive male bodies, without having to relinquish any feminine erotic resources. Male beauty may be enhanced by feminine usages that increase rather than diminish its masculine effect. Men and women may both wear clothes loosely fashioned by designers like Gianni Versace or

Issey Miyake to render all bodies attractive whatever their structure, like the drapery of antiquity. In such clothes, sexuality is expressed obliquely in a fluid fabric envelope that follows bodily movement and also forms a graceful counterpoint to the nonchalant postures of modern repose. The aim of such dress is to emphasize the sexiness of a rather generalized sensuality, not of male or female characteristics; and our present sense of personal appearance, like our sense of all material display, shows that we are more interested in generalized sensuality than in anything else. In our multiform culture, it seems to serve as an equalizer.

In fashion, however, pervasive eroticism is still frequently being represented as the perpetual overthrow of all the restrictive categories left over from the last century, a sort of ongoing revolution. We are still pretending to congratulate ourselves on what a long way we have come. The lush men and strong girls now on view in the media may be continuing a long-range trend that began between the World Wars; but there have been significant interruptions and an important shift of tone. Then, too, men had smooth faces, thick, wavy hair and full, pouting lips, and women often wore pants, had shingled hair, and athletic torsos. But the important point in those days was to be as anti-Victorian as possible. The rigid and bearded Victorian male was being eased out of his tight carapace and distancing whiskers; the whole ladylike panoply was being simplified so that the actual woman became apparent to the eye and touch. Much of our present female mannishness and feminized manhood is a nostalgic reference to the effects fashionable for men and women in those pioneering days, rather than a new revolutionary expression of the same authentic kind.

There is obviously more to it all now than there was between the wars. We have already gone through some fake Victorian revivals, both unself-conscious in the 1950s and self-conscious in the '60s and '70s, and lately our sense of all style has become slightly corrupt. Apart from the sexiness of sex, we have discovered the stylishness of style and the fashionableness of fashion. Evolving conventions of dress and sudden revolts from them have both become stylistically forced; there have been heavy quotation marks around almost all conspicuous modes of clothing in the last fifteen or twenty years, as there were not in more hopeful days. Life is now recognized to have a grotesque and inflated media dimension by which ordinary experience is measured, and all fashion has taken to looking over its own shoulder. Our contemporary revolutionary modes are mostly theatrical costumes, since we have now learned to assume that appearances are detachable and interchangeable and only have provisional meanings.

Many of the more extreme new sartorial phenomena display such uncooked incoherence that they fail to represent any main trend in twentieth-century taste except a certain perverse taste for garbage—which is similarly fragmented and inexpressive, even though it can always be sifted and categorized. We have become obsessed with picking over the past instead of plowing it under, where it can do some good. Perversity has moreover been fostered in fashion by its relentless presentation as a form of ongoing public entertainment. The need for constant impact naturally causes originality to get confused with the capacity to cause a sensation; and sensations can always be created, just as in all show business, by the crudest of allusions.

In the '20s, the revolutionary new fashions were much more important but much less brutally intrusive. Photos from the '20s, '30s, and even the very early '40s, show the young Tyrone Power and Robert Taylor smiling with scintillating confidence, caressed by soft focus and glittering highlights, and wearing the full-cut casual topcoats with the collar up that we see in today's ads for women, then as now opened to show the fully-draped trousers, loose sweaters and long, broad jackets of that time. Then it was an alluring modern and feminized version of male beauty, freshly suggesting pleasure without violence or loss of decorum, a high level of civilization without any forbidding and tyrannical stiffness or antiquated formality. At the same time, women's fashions were stressing an articulated female shape that sought to be perceived as clearly as the male. Both were the first modern styles to take up the flavor of general physical ease, in timely and pertinent defiance of the social restrictions and symbolic sexual distinctions made by dress in the preceding time. Now, however, those same easy men's clothes are being worn by women; and the honest old figure of freedom seems to be dressed up in the spirit of pastiche. We did come a long way for a while, but then we stopped and went on the stage.

Strong and separate sexual definition in the old Victorian manner tried to forbid the generally erotic and foster the romantic. Against such a background even slightly blurring the definition automatically did the opposite; and so when Victorian women dared adopt any partial assortment of male dress they were always extremely disturbing. They called attention to those aspects of female sexuality that develop in sharp contrast to both female biology and romantic rhetoric. Consequently, when female fashion underwent its great changes early in this century, such aspects were deliberately and vehemently emphasized by a new mobility and quasi-masculine leanness. Women with no plump extensions at all but with obvious and movable legs suddenly made their appearance, occasionally even in trousers. They indicated a mettlesome eagerness for action, even unencumbered amorous action, and great lack of interest in sitting still receiving homage or rocking the cradle. Meanwhile when men adopted the casual suits of modern leisure, they began to suggest a certain new readiness to sit and talk, to listen and laugh at themselves, to dally and tarry rather than couple briskly and straightway depart for work or battle. Men and women visibly desired to rewrite the rules about how the two sexes should express their interest in sex; and the liberated modern ideal was crystallized.

But a sexual ideal of maturity and enlightened savoir faire also informed that period of our imaginative history. In the fantasy of the '30s, manifested in the films of Claudette Colbert, for example, or Gable and Lombard, adult men and women ideally pursued pleasure without sacrificing reason, humor, or courtesy—even in those dramas devoted to the ridiculous. The sexes were still regarded as fundamentally different kinds of being, although the style of their sexuality was reconceived. The aim of amorous life was still to take on the challenging dialectic of the sexes, which alone could yield the fullest kind of sexual pleasure. Erotic feeling was inseparable from dramatic situation.

By those same '30s, modern adult clothing was also a fully developed stylistic achievement. It duly continued to refine, until it finally became unbearably mannered in the first half of the '60s. The famous ensuing sartorial revolution, though perfectly authentic, was also the first to occur in front of the camera—always in the mirror, as it were. And somehow the subsequent two decades have seen a great fragmentation both of fashion and of sexuality.

Extreme imagery, much of it androgynous like Boy George's looks, or the many punk styles and all the raunchier fashion photos, has become quite commonplace; but it has also become progressively remote from most common practice. It offers appearances that we may label "fashion," but that we really know to be media inventions created especially to stun, provoke, and dismay us. At the same time, some very conventional outrageous effects have been revived in the realm of accessible fashion, where there is always room for them. Ordinary outrageousness and perverse daring in dress are the signs of licensed play, never the signal of serious action. They are licitly engaged in by the basically powerless, including clowns and children and other innocuous performers, who are always allowed to make extreme emotional claims that may stir up strong personal responses but have no serious public importance. Women's fashion constantly made use of outrage in this way during the centuries of female powerlessness, and selective borrowing from men was one of its most effective motifs.

After the '60s and before the present menswear mode, the masculine components in women's fashions still made girls look either excitingly shocking or touchingly pathetic. The various neat tuxedos made famous by Yves St. Laurent, for example, were intended to give a woman the look of a depraved youth, a sort of tempting Dorian Gray. The "Annie

Hall" clothes swamped the woman in oversized male garments, so that she looked at first like a small child being funny in adult gear, and then like a fragile girl wrapped in a strong man's coat, a combined emblem of bruised innocence and clownishness. These are both familiar "outrageous" devices culled particularly from the theatrical past.

Long before modern fashion took it up, the conventionally outrageous theme of an attractive feminine woman in breeches proved an invariably stimulating refinement in the long history of racy popular art, both for the stage and in print. The most important erotic aim of this theme was never to make a woman actually seem to be a man—looking butch has never been generally attractive—but to make a girl assume the unsettling beauty that dwells in the sexual uncertainty of an adolescent boy. It is an obvious clever move for modern fashionable women to combine the old show-business-like excitement of the suggestive trousered female with the cultivated self-possession of early twentieth-century menswear—itself already a feminized male style. It suits, especially in the present disintegrated erotic climate that has rendered the purer forms of outrageousness somewhat passé.

Such uses of men's clothes have nothing to do with an impulse toward androgyny. They instead invoke all the old tension between the sexes; and complete drag, whichever sex wears it, also insists on sexual polarity. Most drag for men veers toward the exaggerated accoutrements of the standard siren; and on the current screen, *Tootsie* and *Yentl* are both demonstrating how different and how divided the sexes are.

While the extreme phenomena are getting all the attention, however, we are acting out quite another forbidden fantasy in our ordinary lives. The really androgynous realm in personal appearance is that of active sports clothing. The unprecedented appeal of running gear and gym clothes and all the other garb associated with strenuous physical effort seems to be offering an alternative in sexual expression. Beyond the simple pleasures of physical fitness, and the right-minded satisfactions of banishing class difference that were first expressed in the blue-jeans revolution of the '60s, this version of pastoral suggests a new erotic appeal in the perceived androgyny of childhood. The short shorts and other ingenuous bright play clothes in primary colors that now clothe bodies of all sizes and sexes are giving a startling kindergarten cast to everybody's public looks, especially in summer.

The real excitement of androgynous appearance is again revealed as associated only with extreme youth—apparently the more extreme the better. The natural androgyny of old age has acquired no appeal. The tendency of male and female bodies to resemble each other in late maturity is still conventionally ridiculous and deplorable; sportswear on old women looks crisp and convenient, not sexually attractive. But the fresh, unfinished androgyny of the nursery is evidently a newly expanded arena for sexual fantasy.

In the unisex look of the ordinary clothing that has become increasingly common in the past two decades, there has been a submerged but unmistakable element of child-worship. This note has been struck at a great distance from the slick and expensive ambiguities of high fashion that include couture children's clothes aping the vagaries of current adult chic. It resonates instead in the everyday sexual ambiguity of rough duck or corduroy pants, flannel shirts, T-shirts, sweaters, and sneakers. Any subway car or supermarket is full of people dressed this way. The guises for this fantasy have extended past play clothes to children's underwear, the little knitted skirts and briefs that everyone wears at the age of 5. One ubiquitous ad for these even showed a shirtee sliding up to expose an adult breast, to emphasize the sexiness of the fashion; but the breast has been prudently canceled in publicly displayed versions.

Our erotic obsession with children has overt and easily deplored expressions in the media, where steamy 12-year-old fashion models star in ads and 12-year-old prostitutes figure in dramas and news stories. The high-fashion modes for children also have the flavor of forced eroticism. Child abuse and kiddy porn are now publicly discussed concerns, ventilated in the righteous spirit of reform; and yet unconscious custom reflects the same preoccupations with the sexual condition of childhood. The androgynous sportswear that was formerly the acceptable everyday dress only of children is now everyone's leisure clothing: its new currency must have more than one meaning.

On the surface, of course, it invokes the straight appeal of the physical life, the rural life, and perhaps even especially the taxing life of the dedicated athlete, which used to include sexual abstinence along with the chance of glory. The world may wish to look as if it were constantly in training to win, or equipped to explore; but there is another condition it is also less obviously longing for—freedom from the strain of fully adult sexuality. These styles of clothing signal a retreat into the unfinished, undefined sexuality of childhood that we are now finding so erotic, and that carries no difficult social or personal responsibilities.

From 1925 to 1965, 4-year-old girls and boys could tumble in the sandbox in identical cotton overalls or knitted suits, innocently aping the clothes of skiers, railroadmen, or miners, while their mom wore a dress, hat, and stockings, and their dad a suit, hat, and tie—the modern dress of sexual maturity, also worn by Gable, Lombard, and all the young and glittering Hollywood company. Now the whole family wears sweat suits and overalls and goes bareheaded. Such gear is also designed to encourage the game of dressing up like all the non-amorous and ultraphysical heroes of modern folklore—forest rangers and cowboys, spacemen and frogmen, pilots and motorcyclists, migrant workers and terrorists—that is constantly urged on children. The great masquerade party of the late '60s ostensibly came to an end; but it had irreversibly given to ordinary grownups the right to wear fancy costumes for fun that was formerly a child's privilege. The traditional dress of the separate adult sexes is reserved for public appearances, and in general it is now socially correct to express impatience with it. "Informal" is the only proper style in middle-class social life; and for private leisure, when impulse governs choices, kids' clothes are the leading one. Apparently the erotic androgynous child is the new forbidden creature of unconscious fantasy, not only the infantile fashion model or rock star but the ordinary kid, who has exciting sexual potential hidden under its unsexed dress-up play clothes.

Fashions of the remote past dealt straightforwardly with the sexuality of children by dressing them just like ordinary adults, suitably different according to sex. But in Romantic times, children were perceived to exist in a special condition much purer and closer to beneficent nature than their elders, requiring clothes that kept them visibly separate from the complex corruptions of adult society, including full-scale erotic awareness. The habit of putting children in fancy dress began then, too, especially boys. They were dressed as wee, chubby, and harmless soldiers and sailors, or Turks and Romans, to emphasize their innocence by contrast. Children's clothes still differed according to sex—girls had sweet little chemises and sashes instead of fancy costumes—but their overriding common flavor was one of artlessness.

Later on the Victorians overdid it, and loaded their children with clothing, but it was still two-sexed and distinctively designed for them. Finally the enlightened twentieth century invented the use of mock sportswear for the wiggly little bodies of both boys and girls. Nevertheless, the costumes now suitable for children on display still tend toward the Victorian, with a good deal of nostalgic velvet and lace. In line with Romantic views of women, some feminine styles also used to feature infantine suggestions drawn from little girls' costumes: the last was the tiny baby dress worn with big shoes and big hair in the later '60s, just before the eruption of the women's movement. But only since then has a whole generation of adults felt like dressing up in mock rough gear, like androgynous children at play, to form a race of apparently presexual but unmistakably erotic beings.

Once again, very pointedly, the clothes for the role are male. Our modern sense of artlessness seems to prefer the masculine brand; and when we dress our little boys and girls alike to blur their sexuality—or ourselves in imitation of them—that means we dress the girls like the boys, in the manifold costumes celebrating nonsexual physical prowess. At leisure, both men and women prefer to suggest versions of Adam alone in Eden before he knew he had a sex, innocently wearing his primal sweat suit made only of native worth and honor.

The Romantic sense of the child as naturally privileged and instinctively good like Adam seems to stay with us. But we have lately added the belief in a child's potential depravity, which may go unpaid for and unpunished just because of all children's categorical innocence. Perhaps this society abuses its children, and also aggressively dresses them in lipstick and sequins, for the same reason it imitates them—from a helpless envy of what they get away with. The everyday androgynous costume is the suit of diminished erotic responsibility and exemption from adult sexual risk. What it clothes is the child's license to make demands and receive gratification with no risk of dishonor—to be erotic, but to pose as unsexual and therefore unaccountable.

Even more forbidden and outrageous than the sexual child is its near relation, the erotic angel. While the ordinary world is routinely dressing itself and its kids in unisex jeans, it is simultaneously conjuring up mercurial apparitions who offer an enchanting counterpoint to life's mundane transactions. In the rock star form, they embody the opposing fantasy face of the troublesome domestic child or adolescent: the angelic visitor who needs to obey no earthly rules. Funny little E.T. was only one version. The type includes all those who may shine while they stomp and whirl and scream and hum and never suffer the slightest humiliation.

A child, however ideologized, is always real and problematic, but an angel has a fine mythic remoteness however palpable he seems. The opposing kind of androgyny invests him: he exists not before but beyond human sexual life, and he comes as a powerful messenger from spheres where there is no taking or giving in marriage, but where extreme kinds of joy are said to be infinite. Our rock-video beings cultivate the unhuman look of ultimate synthesis: they aim to transcend sexual conflict by becoming fearsome angels, universally stimulating creatures fit for real existence only out of this world. Like all angels, they profoundly excite; but they don't excite desire, even though they do make the air crackle with promise and menace. Their job is to bring the message and then leave, having somehow transformed the world. Michael Jackson reportedly leads a life both angelic and artificially childlike, and he makes his appearances in epiphanic style. David Bowie still appears to be the man who fell to earth, not someone born here. Grace Jones also seems to come from altogether elsewhere. Such idols only function in the sphere of unattainability. While they flourish they remain sojourners, leading lives of vivid otherness in what seems to be a sexual no-man's-land.

Angels were in fact once firmly male and uncompromisingly austere. The disturbing sensuality they acquired in the art of later centuries, like that of the luscious angel in Leonardo's *Virgin of the Rocks*, always reads as a feminization—and from this one must conclude that adding feminine elements to the male is what produces androgyny's most intense effects. Almost all our androgynous stars are in fact males in feminized trim; their muscular and crop-haired female counterparts, such as Annie Lennox, are less numerous and have a more limited appeal. The meaning in all our androgyny, both modish and ordinary, still seems to be the same: the male is the primary sex, straightforward, simple, and active. He can be improved and embellished, however, and have and give a better time if he allows himself to be modified by the complexities of female influence.

The process does not work the other way. Elegant women in fashionable menswear expound the same thought, not its opposite: traditional jackets and trousers are austerely beautiful, but they are patently enhanced by high heels, flowing scarves, cosmetics, and earrings. Lisa Lyon, the body builder, has been photographed by Robert Mapplethorpe to show that her excessively developed muscles do not make her mannish but instead have been feminized to go with, not against, her flowered hats and lipstick. Ordinary women wearing men's active gear while wheeling strollers on the street or carrying bags across the parking lot are subduing and adapting harsh male dress to flexible female life and giving it some new scope. Common androgynous costume is always some kind of suit or jumpsuit, or pants, shirt and jacket, not some kind of dress, bodice and skirt, or gown. A hat may go with it, or perhaps a hood or scarf, but not a coif or veil. A few real female skirts (not kilts or Greek evzone skirts) are now being very occasionally and sensationally tried out by some highly visible men—daring designers, media performers and their imitators, fashion models and theirs—but all kinds of pants are being worn by all kinds of women all the time. We can read the message: the male is the first sex, now at last prepared to consider the other one anew, with much fanfare. It is still a case of female sexuality enlightening the straight male world—still the arrival of Eve and all her subsequent business in and beyond the garden—that is being celebrated. The "androgynous" mode for both sexes suggests that the female has come on the scene to educate the male about the imaginative pleasures of sex, signified chiefly by the pleasures of adornment. About its difficulties, summed up by that glaringly absent round belly, she is naturally keeping quiet.

Meanwhile the more glittering versions of modish androgyny continue to reflect what we adore in fantasy. Many of us seem to feel that the most erotic condition of all could not be that of any man or woman, or of any child, or of a human being with two sexes, but that of a very young and effeminate male angel—a new version of art history's lascivious *putto*. Such a being may give and take a guiltless delight, wield limitless sexual power without sexual politics, feel all the pleasures of sex with none of the personal risks, can never grow up, never get wise, and never be old. It is a futureless vision, undoubtedly appropriate to a nuclear age; but if any of us manages to survive, the soft round belly will surely again have its day.

In the meantime, as we approach the end of the century and the millennium, the impulse toward a certain fusion in the habits of the sexes may have a more hopeful meaning. After a hundred years of underground struggle, trousers are no longer male dress sometimes worn by women. They have been successfully feminized so as to become authentic costume for both sexes, and to regain the authoritative bisexual status the gown once had in the early Middle Ages. This development is clearly not a quick trend but a true change, generations in the making. Male skirts have yet to prove themselves; but men have in fact succeeded in making long-term capital out of the short-lived and not forgotten Peacock Revolution of the late sixties. Whole new ranges of rich color, interesting pattern, texture and unusual cut have become generally acceptable in male dress since then, and so has a variety of jewelry. The sort of fashionable experiment once associated only with women has become a standard male option. Some new agreement between the sexes may actually be forming, signaled by all these persistent visual projections; but just what that accord will turn out to be it is not safe to predict, nor whether it will continue to civilize us further or only perplex us more.

QUESTIONS FOR READING, RESPONDING, AND WRITING

Summarizing Main Points

1. List the differences, according to Hollander, between fashions of the twenties and thirties and fashions today. Now list the differences in the attitudes people had toward their clothes in the twenties and thirties and the attitudes they have toward their clothes today.

2. Hollander says that conventionally outrageous "uses of men's clothes . . . involve all the old tension between the sexes." List the other different ways that Hollander says clothes and fashion reflect the changing—or stagnant—relation between the sexes. List the ways Hollander says fashion reflects "our erotic obsession with children."

Analyzing Methods of Discourse

1. Hollander's essay is ostensibly about fashion. How does she make it clear throughout the essay that fashion is merely a "persistent visual projection" of sexual standards and desires?

2. Hollander says that revolutions in clothes today have "become stylistically forced; there have been heavy quotation marks around almost all conspicuous modes of clothing in the last fifteen or twenty years." Explain this statement. Locate Hollander's own use of quotation marks in the essay and explain them. Are there any aspects of Hollander's essay that seem "stylistically forced"?

Focusing on the Field

1. Hollander refers often to film stars of the forties. She also refers to the revolution of the sixties as "the first to occur in front of the camera—always in the mirror, as it were." Compare her treatment of the technologies of the two decades. How does each provide Hollander with a research tool?
2. At several points, Hollander provides historical details about pre-twentieth-century fashion. Find them and explain their relation to her essay. Does Hollander's knowledge of the history of fashion make her essay more convincing?

Writing Assignments

1. Consider the fashions of your fellow students. Write an essay which argues that those fashions either support or deny Hollander's contentions.
2. Using Hollander's essay as a guide, write a brief essay predicting the fashions of the next decade. Describe how each sex may dress and reflect on the meaning of clothing in the 1990s.

Robert Coles

CHILDREN OF AFFLUENCE

A researcher, scholar, and professor of psychiatry at Harvard Medical School, Robert Coles is something of a maverick in his field, if only for his intensely personal commitment to those he cares for. Such commitment, along with his untraditional methods—Coles prefers to keep psychotherapy attached to the actual words of his patients, as the piece that follows demonstrates—allows Coles to turn the abstraction typical of professional or academic study into more concrete descriptions of real people and their problems. Thus, too, his conclusions, as he has pointed out, "are not sweeping, categorical, or easily translated into one or another program." Yet those conclusions have earned him multiple awards and numerous honors, including a Pulitzer Prize in 1973 for volumes two and three of his five-volume study, *Children of Crisis* (1967–1978), a compassionate investigation into the effects of poverty, discrimination, and stress on children.

Also renowned for his literary studies of southern American writers, including *Walker Percy: An American Search* and *Flannery O'Connor's South,* Coles contributes regularly to a wide range of periodicals: *Atlantic Monthly, The New Yorker, Book Week, Partisan Review, American Journal of Psychiatry, Appalachian Review,* and *Contemporary Psychoanalysis.* Born in Boston in 1929, Coles studied at Harvard and received his medical degree from Columbia in 1954. Coles is currently studying the "political-socialization" of Northern Ireland and South Africa.

It won't do to talk of *the* affluent in America. It won't do to say that in our upper-middle-class suburbs, or among our wealthy, one observes clear-cut, consistent psychological or cultural characteristics. Even in relatively homogeneous places there are substantial differences in homelife, in values taught, hobbies encouraged, beliefs advocated or sometimes virtually instilled. But it is the obligation of a psychological observer like me, who wants to know how children make sense of a certain kind of life, to document as faithfully as possible the way a common heritage of money and power affects the assumptions of particular boys and girls.

I started my work with affluent children by seeing troubled boys and girls; they were the ones I saw as a child psychiatrist *before* I began my years of "field work" in the South, then Appalachia, then the North, then the West. There are only a few hundred child psychiatrists in the United States, and often their time is claimed by those who have money. After a while, if one is not careful, the well-off and the rich come to be seen exclusively through a clinician's eye: homes full of bitterness, deceit, snobbishness, neuroses, psychoses; homes with young children in mental pain, and with older children, adolescents and young adults, who use drugs, drink, run away, rebel constantly and disruptively, become truants, delinquents, addicts, alcoholics, become compulsively promiscuous, go crazy, go wild, go to ruin.

We blame the alcoholism, insanity, meanness, apathy, drug usage, despondency, and, not least, cruelty to children we see or are told exists in the ghetto or among the rural poor upon various "socioeconomic factors." All of those signs of psychological deterioration can be found among quite privileged families, too—and so we remind ourselves, perhaps, that wealth corrupts.

No—it is not that simple. Wealth does not corrupt nor does it ennoble. But wealth does govern the minds of privileged children, gives them a peculiar kind of identity which they never lose, whether they grow up to be stockbrokers or communards, and whether they lead healthy or unstable lives. There is, I think, a message that virtually all quite well-off American families transmit to their children—an emotional expression of those familiar, classbound prerogatives, money and power. I use the word "entitlement" to describe that message.

The word was given to me by the rather rich parents of a child I began to talk with almost two decades ago, in 1959. I have watched those parents become grandparents, and have seen what they described as "the responsibilities of entitlement" handed down to a new generation. When the father, a lawyer and stockbroker from a prominent and quietly influential family, referred to the "entitlement" his children were growing up to know, he had in mind a social rather than a psychological phenomenon: the various juries or committees that select the Mardi Gras participants in New Orleans's annual parade and celebration. He knew that his daughter was "entitled" to be invited.

He wanted, however, to go beyond that social fact. He talked about what he had received from his parents and what he would give to his children, "automatically, without any thought," and what they too would pass on. The father was careful to distinguish between the social entitlement and "something else," a "something else" he couldn't quite define but knew he had to try to evoke if he was to be psychologically candid: "I mean they should be responsible, and try to live up to their ideals, and not just sit around wondering which island in the Caribbean to visit this year, and where to go next summer to get away from the heat and humidity here in New Orleans."

He was worried about what a lot of money can do to a personality. When his young daughter, during a Mardi Gras season, kept *assuming* she would one day become a Mardi Gras queen, he realized that his notion of "entitlement" was not quite hers. Noblesse oblige requires a gesture toward others.

He was not the only parent to express such a concern to me in the course of my work. In homes where mothers and fathers profess no explicit reformist persuasions, they nevertheless worry about what happens to children who grow up surrounded by just about everything they want, virtually on demand. "When they're like that, they've gone from spoiled to spoiled rotten—and beyond, to some state I don't know how to describe."

Obviously, it is possible for parents to have a lot of money yet avoid bringing up their children in such a way that they feel like members of a royal family. But even parents determined not to spoil their children often recognize what might be called the existential (as opposed to strictly psychological) aspects of their situation. A father may begin rather early on lecturing his children about the meaning of money; a mother may do her share by saying no, even when yes is so easy to say. And a child, by the age of five or six, has very definite notions of what is possible, even if it is not always permitted. That child, in conversation, and without embarrassment or the kind of reticence and secretiveness that come later, may reveal a substantial knowledge of economic affairs. A six-year-old girl I spoke to knew that she would, at twenty-one, inherit half a million dollars. She also knew that her father "only" gave her twenty-five cents a week, whereas some friends of hers received as much as a dollar. She was vexed; she asked her parents why they were so "strict." One friend had even used the word "stingy" for the parents. The father, in a matter-of-fact way, pointed out to the daughter that she did, after all, get "anything she really wants." Why, then, the need for an extravagant allowance? The girl was won over. But admonitions don't always modify the quite realistic appraisal children make of what they are heir to; and they don't diminish their sense of entitlement—a state of mind that pervades their view of the world.

In an Appalachian home, for instance, a boy of seven made the following comment in 1963, after a mine his father owned had suffered an explosion, killing two men and injuring seriously nine others: "I heard my mother saying she felt sorry for the families of the miners. I feel sorry for them, too. I hope the men who got hurt get better. I'm sure they will. My father has called in doctors from Lexington. He wants the best doctors in all Kentucky for those miners. Daddy says it was the miners' fault; they get careless, and the next thing you know, there's an explosion. It's too bad. I guess there are a lot of kids who are praying hard for their fathers. I wish God was nice to everyone. He's been very good to us. My daddy says it's been hard work, running the mine, and another one he has. It's just as hard to run a mine as it is to go down and dig the coal! I'm glad my father is the owner, though. I wouldn't want him to get killed or hurt bad down there, way underground. Daddy has given us a good life. We have a lot of fun coming up, he says, in the next few years. We're going on some trips. Daddy deserves his vacations. He says he's happy because he can keep us happy, and he does."

Abundance is this boy's destiny, he has every reason to believe, abundance and limitless possibility. He may even land on the stars. Certainly he has traveled widely in this country. He associates the seasons with travel. In winter, there is a trip south, to one or another Caribbean island. He worries, on these trips, about his two dogs, and the other animals—the guinea pigs, hamsters, rabbits, chickens. There is always someone in the house, a maid, a handyman. Still it is sad to say good-bye. Now if the family owned a plane, the animals could come along on those trips!

The boy doesn't really believe that his father will ever own a Lear jet; yet he can construct a fantasy: "I had this dream. In it I was walking through the woods with Daddy, and all of a sudden there was an open field, and I looked, and I saw a hawk, and it was circling and circling. I like going hunting with Daddy, and I thought we were hunting. But when

I looked at him, he didn't have his gun. Then he pointed at the hawk, and it was coming down. It landed ahead of us, and it was real strange—because the hawk turned into an airplane! I couldn't believe it. We went toward the plane, and Daddy said we could get a ride anytime we wanted, because it was ours; he'd just bought it. That's when I woke up, I think."

Four years after the boy dreamed that his father owned a plane, the father got one. The boom of the 1970s in the coal fields made his father even richer. The boy was, of course, eager to go on flying trips; eager, also, to learn to fly. At thirteen, he dreamed (by day) of becoming an astronaut, or of going to the Air Force Academy and afterwards becoming a "supersonic pilot."

He would never become a commercial pilot, however; and his reasons were interesting. "I've gone on a lot of commercial flights, and there are a lot of people on board, and the pilot has to be nice to everyone, and he makes all these announcements about the seat belts, and stuff like that. My dad's pilot was in the Air Force, and then he flew commercial. He was glad to get out, though. He says you have to be like a waiter; you have to answer complaints from the customers, and apologize to them, just because the ride gets bumpy. It's best to work for yourself, or work for another person, if you trust him and like him. If you go commercial, like our pilot says, you're a servant."

Many of the children I have worked with are similarly disposed; they do not like large groups of people in public places—in fact, have been taught the value not only of privacy but of the quiet that goes with being relatively alone. Some of the children are afraid of those crowds, can't imagine how it would be possible to survive them. Of course, what is strange, unknown, or portrayed as unattractive, uncomfortable, or just to be avoided as a nuisance can for a given child become a source of curiosity, like an event to be experienced at all costs. An eight-year-old girl who lived on a farm well outside Boston wanted desperately to go to the city and see Santa Claus—not because she believed in him, but because she wanted to see "those crowds" she had seen on television. She got her wish, was excited at first, then became quite disappointed, and ultimately uncomfortable. She didn't like being jostled, shoved, and ignored when she protested.

A week after the girl had gone through her Boston "adventure" (as she had called the trip *before* she embarked upon it), each student in her third-grade class was asked to draw a picture in some way connected to the Christmas season, and the girl obliged eagerly. She drew Santa Claus standing beside a pile of packages, presents for the many children who stood near him. They blended into one another—a mob scene. Watching them but removed from them was one child, bigger and on a higher level—suspended in space, it seemed, and partially surrounded by a thin but visible line. The girl wrote on the bottom of the drawing, "I saw Santa Claus." She made it quite clear what she had intended to portray. "He was standing there, handing out these gifts. They were all the same, I think, and they were plastic squirt guns for the boys and little dolls for the girls. I felt sorry for the kids. I asked my mother why kids wanted to push each other, just to get that junk. My mother said a lot of people just don't know any better. I was going to force my way up to Santa Claus and tell him to stop being so dumb! My mother said he was probably a drunk, trying to make a few dollars so he could spend it in a bar that evening! I don't want to be in a store like that again. We went up to a balcony and watched, and then we got out of the place and came home. I told my mother that I didn't care if I ever went to Boston again. I have two friends, and they've never been to Boston, and they don't want to go there, except to ride through on the way to the airport."

She sounded at that moment more aloof, condescending, and snobbish than she ordinarily is. She spends her time with two or three girls who live on nearby estates. Those girls don't see each other regularly, and each of them is quite able to be alone—in fact, rather anxious for those times of solitude. Sometimes a day or two goes by with no formal arrangement to play. They meet in school, and that seems to be enough. Each girl has obligations—a horse to groom, a stall to work on. They are quite "self-sufficient," a word they have heard used repeatedly by their parents. Even with one's own social circle there is no point surrendering to excessive gregariousness!

Once up on her own horse, she is (by her own description) in her "own world." She has heard her mother use that expression. The mother is not boasting, or dismissing others who live in other worlds. The mother is describing, as does the child, a state of progressive withdrawal from people, and the familiar routines or objects of the environment, in favor of a mixture of reverie and disciplined activity.

Nothing seems impossible, burdensome, difficult. There are no distractions, petty or boring details to attend to. And one is closer to one's "self." The mother talks about the "self," and the child does, too. "It is strange," the girl comments, "because you forget yourself riding or skiing, but you also remember yourself the way you don't when you're just sitting around watching television or reading or playing in your room."

None of the other American children I have worked with have placed such a continuous and strong emphasis on the "self"—its display, its possibilities, its cultivation and development, even the repeated use of the word *self*. A ten-year-old boy who lived in Westchester County made this very clear. I met him originally because his parents were lawyers, and active in the civil rights movement. His father, a patrician Yankee, very much endorsed the students who went south in the early 1960s, and worked on behalf of integrated schools up north. The boy, however, attended private schools—a source of anguish to both father and son, who do not lend themselves to a description that suggests hypocrisy.

The boy knew that he, also, *would* be (as opposed to *wanted* to be) a lawyer. He was quick to perceive and acknowledge his situation, and as he did so, he brought his "self" right into the discussion: "I don't want to tell other kids what to do. I told my father I should be going to the public schools myself. Then I could say anything. Then I could ask why we don't have black kids with us in school. But you have to try to do what's best for your own life, even if you can't speak up for the black people. When I'm grown up I'll be like my father; I'll help the black people all I can. It's this way: first you build *yourself* up. You learn all you can. Later, you can *give of yourself*. That's what Dad says: you can't help others until you've learned to help yourself. It's not that you're being selfish, if you're going to a private school and your parents have a lot of money. We had a maid here, and she wasn't right in the head. She lost her temper and told Daddy that he's a phony, and he's out for himself and no one else, and the same goes for my sister and me. Then she quit. Daddy tried to get her to talk with us, but she wouldn't. She said that's all we ever do—talk, talk. I told Daddy she was contradicting herself, because she told me a few weeks ago that I'm always doing something, and I should sit down and talk with her. But I don't know what to say to her! I think she got angry with me, because I was putting on my skis, for cross-country skiing, and she said I had too much, that was my problem. I asked her where the regular skis were, and she said she wouldn't tell me, even if she knew! It's too bad, what happened to her.

"I feel sorry for her, though. It's not fun to be a maid. The poor woman doesn't look very good. She weighs too much. She's only forty, my mother thinks, but she looks as if she's sixty, and is sick. She should take better care of herself. Now she's thrown away this job, and she told my mother last year that it was the best one she'd ever had, so she's her own worst enemy. I wonder what she'll think when she looks at herself in the mirror."

This boy was no budding egotist. If anything, he was less self-centered at ten than many other children of his community and others like it. He was willing to think about those less fortunate than himself—the maid, and black people in general. True, he would often repeat uncritically his father's words, or a version of them. But he was trying to respond to his father's wishes and beliefs as well as his words. It was impossible for him, no matter how compassionate his nature, to conceive of life as others live it—the maid and, yes, millions of children his age, who don't look in the mirror very often, and may not even own one; who don't worry about how one looks, and what is said, and how one sounds, and how one smells.

It is important that a child's sense of entitlement be distinguished not only from the psychiatric dangers of narcissism but from the less pathological and not all that uncommon phenomenon known as being "spoiled." It is a matter of degree; "spoiled" children are self-centered all right, petulant and demanding—but not as grandiose or, alas, saddled with illusions (or delusions) as the children clinicians have in mind when using the phrase "narcissistic entitlement." The rich or quite well-to-do are all too commonly charged with producing spoiled children. Yet one sees spoiled children everywhere, among the very poor as well as the inordinately rich.

In one of the first wealthy families I came to know there was a girl who was described by both parents as "spoiled." At the time, I fear, I was ready to pronounce every child in New Orleans's Garden District spoiled. Were they not all living comfortable, indeed luxurious, lives, as compared to the lives of the black or working-class white children I was getting to know in other sections of that city?

Nevertheless, I soon began to realize that it wouldn't do to characterize without qualification one set of children as spoiled, by virtue of their social and economic background, as against another set of children who were obviously less fortunate in many respects. One meets, among the rich, restrained, disciplined, and by no means indulged children; sometimes, even, boys and girls who have learned to be remarkably self-critical, even ascetic—anything but "spoiled" in the conventional sense of the word. True, one can find a touch and more of arrogance, or at least sustained self-assurance, in those apparently spartan boys and girls who seem quite anxious to deny themselves all sorts of presumably accessible privileges if not luxuries. But one also finds in these children a consistent willingness to place serious and not always pleasant burdens on themselves—to the point where they often struck me, when I came to their homes fresh from visits with much poorer age-mates, as remarkably *less* spoiled: not so much whining or crying; fewer demands for candy or other sweets; even, sometimes, a relative indifference to toys, however near at hand and expensive they may have been; a disregard of television—so often demanded by the children that I was seeing.

A New Orleans black woman said to me in 1961: "I don't know how to figure out these rich white kids. They're something! I used to think, before I took a job with this family, that the only difference between a rich kid and a poor kid is that the rich kid knows he has a lot of money and he grows up and becomes spoiled rotten. That's what my mother told me;

she took care of a white girl, and the girl was an only child, and her father owned a department store in McComb, Mississippi, and that girl thought she was God's special creature. My mother used to come home and tell us about the 'little princess'; but she turned out to be no good. She was so pampered, she couldn't do a thing for herself. All she knew how to do was order people around.

"It's different with these two children. I've never seen such a boy and such a girl. They think they're the best ones who ever lived—like that girl in McComb—but they don't behave like her. They're never asking me to do much of anything. They even ask if they can help me! They tell me that they want to know how to do everything. The girl says she wants to learn how to run the washing machine and the dishwasher. She says she wants to learn all my secret recipes. She says she'd like to give the best parties in the Garden District when she grows up, and she'd like to be able to give them without anyone's help. She says I could serve the food, but she would like to make it. The boy says he's going to be a lawyer and a banker, so he wants to know how much everything costs. He doesn't want to waste anything. He'll see me throw something away, and he wants to know why. I only wish that my own kids were like him!

"But these children here are special, and don't they know it! That's what being rich is: you know you're different from most people. These two kids act as if they're going to be tops in everything, and they're pleased as can be with themselves, because there is nothing they can't do, and there's nothing they can't get, and there's nothing they can't win, and they're always showing off what they can do, and then before you can tell them how good they are, they're telling the same thing to themselves. It's confusing! They're not spoiled one bit, but oh, they have a high opinion of themselves!"

Actually, children like the ones she speaks of don't allow themselves quite the unqualified confidence she describes, though she certainly has correctly conveyed the appearance they give. Boys and girls may seem without anxiety or self-doubt; they have been brought up, as the maid suggests, to feel important, superior, destined for a satisfying, rewarding life—and at, say, eight or nine they already appear to know all that. Yet there are moments of hesitation, if not apprehension. An eleven-year-old boy from a prominent and quite brilliant Massachusetts family told his teachers, in an autobiographical composition about the vicissitudes of "entitlement": "I don't always do everything right. I'd like to be able to say I don't make any mistakes, but I do, and when I do, I feel bad. My father and mother say that if you train yourself, you can be right *almost* 100 percent of the time. Even they make mistakes, though. I like to be first in sports. I like to beat my brothers at skiing. But I don't always go down the slopes as fast as I could and I sometimes fall down. Last year I broke my leg. When I get a bad cold, I feel disappointed in myself. I don't think it's right to be easy on yourself. If you are, then you slip back, and you don't get a lot of the rewards in life. If you really work for the rewards, you'll get them."

A platitude—the kind of assurance his teachers, as a matter of fact, have rather often given him. In the fourth grade, for instance, the teacher had this written on the blackboard (and kept it there for weeks): "Those who want something badly enough get it, provided they are willing to wait and work." The boy considers that assertion neither banal nor unrealistic. He has been brought up to believe that such is and will be (for him) the case. He knows that others are not so lucky, but he hasn't really met those "others," and they don't cross his mind at all. What does occur to him sometimes is the need for constant exertion, lest he fail to "measure up." One "measures up" when one tries hard and succeeds. If one slackens or stumbles, one ought to be firm with oneself—but not in any self-pitying or self-excusing or self-paralyzing way. The emphasis is on a quick and efficient moment of scrutiny followed by "a fast pick-up."

Such counsel is not as callous as it may sound—or, ironically, as it may well have been intended to sound. The child who hears it gets, briefly, upset; but unless he or she stops heeding what has been said, quite often "a fast pick-up" does indeed take place—an effort to redeem what has been missed or lost, or only somewhat accomplished. Again, it is a matter of feeling entitled. A child who has been told repeatedly that all he or she needs to do is try hard does not feel inclined to allow himself or herself long stretches of time for skeptical self-examination. The point is to feel *entitled*—then act upon that feeling. The boy whose composition was just quoted from used the word "entitled" in another essay he wrote, this one meant to be a description of his younger (age 5) brother. The writing was not, however, without an autobiographical strain to it: "I was watching my brother from my bedroom window. He was climbing up the fence we built for our corral. He got to the top, and then he just stood there and waved and shouted. No one was there. He was talking to himself. He was very happy. Then he would fall. He would be upset for a few seconds but he would climb right back up again. Then he would be happier! He was entitled to be happy. It is his fence, and he has learned to climb it, and stay up, and balance himself."

QUESTIONS FOR READING, RESPONDING, AND WRITING

Summarizing Main Points

1. List the differences and similarities between "narcissism," a "sense of entitlement," and "being spoiled." According to Coles, is it possible to be "entitled" without being "spoiled"? "Spoiled" without being "entitled"?

2. Why does Coles prefer the term "entitlement" to describe the children of the affluent? What do you think Coles means by the statement: "Noblesse oblige requires a gesture toward others"? How are the two terms "entitlement" and "noblesse oblige" related?

Analyzing Methods of Discourse

1. List the different children that Coles refers to. Are they all "entitled"? Does Coles's final description of the boy on the fence work as a summary? Why or why not?
2. The New Orleans black woman that Coles refers to recognizes that the two children in the house where she serves as a maid and cook are "special." Why do you suppose Coles includes this woman's description of these children?

Focusing on the Field

1. Why does Coles enclose the words "field work" in quotation marks? How do you suppose his "field work" is different from that of other social scientists? Coles also encloses several other words in quotation marks. List them and explain why each deserves quotation marks.
2. Coles confesses to being fearful of pronouncing "every child in New Orleans's Garden District spoiled." Does that confession modify your attitude toward his ability to remain objective?

Writing Assignments

1. Imagine and construct a response to Coles's essay by either one of the children he examines or one of their parents.
2. Read Richard Rodriguez's "Memories of a Bilingual Childhood," Langston Hughes's "Salvation," or Maya Angelou's "Champion of the World." In a short essay, compare their childhood experiences with the experiences of the children whom Coles interviews. Consider in particular their differing attitudes toward public versus private life, their "self-sufficiency," and their attitudes toward other socioeconomic classes.

Jay Haley

THE ART OF PSYCHOANALYSIS

Born in Midwest, Wyoming in 1923, Jay Haley studied at the University of California at Berkeley and then at Stanford, where he earned an M.A. in 1953. Haley's first important paper, "Toward a Theory of Schizophrenia," coauthored with Gregory Bateson in 1956 for *Behavioral Science,* remains a distinguished piece of psychological theory. Haley worked as a communications analyst for Stanford and has never lost his interest in communications and language, particularly the language of psychotherapy.

In the essay that follows, Haley identifies in a humorous way the games people play in psychotherapy. His comic touch in this essay, however, takes away nothing from his respect for the profession. In "The Art of Psychotherapy," Haley makes it clear that psychotherapy is indeed an art, and, for this reason, the profession needs to steer clear of the rigid hierarchies and methods of the harder sciences. Haley's research at Palo Alto and later at the Philadelphia Child Guidance Clinic, and his work as director of the Family Therapy Institute at Chevy Chase, Maryland, as well as his many respected texts, including *Strategies of Psychotherapy* (1963), *Techniques of Family Therapy* (1967), *Uncommon Therapy* (1972), and *Reflections on Therapy* (1982), make his remarks in "The Art of Psychotherapy" all the more clearly valuable, despite their satirical nature.

Enough research has been done by social scientists to corroborate many of Freud's ideas about unconscious processes. Yet there has been surprisingly little scientific investigation of what actually occurs during psychoanalytic treatment. Fortunately this situation has been remedied by a scholar on the faculty of Potter College in Yeovil, England. Assigned a field trip in America, this anonymous student spent several years here studying the art of psychoanalysis both as a patient and a practitioner. His investigation culminated in a three-volume work entitled *The Art of Psychoanalysis, or Some Aspects of a Structured Situation Consisting of Two-Group Interaction Which Embodies Certain of the Most Basic Principles of One-upmanship.* Like most studies written for Potter College the work was unpublished and accessible only to a few favored members of the clinical staff. However, a copy was briefly in this writer's hands and he offers here a summary of the research findings for those who wish to foster the dynamic growth of Freudian theory and sharpen the techniques of a difficult art.

Unfamiliar terms will be translated into psychoanalytic terminology throughout this summary, but a few general definitions are necessary at once. First of all, a complete definition of the technical term "one-upmanship" would fill, and in fact has filled, a rather large encyclopedia. It can be defined briefly here as the art of putting a person "one-down." The term "one-down" is technically defined as that psychological state which exists in an individual who is not "one-up" on another person. To be "one-up" is technically defined as that psychological state of an individual who is not "one-down." To phrase these terms in popular language, at the risk of losing scientific rigor, it can be said that in any human relationship (and indeed among other mammals) one person is constantly maneuvering to imply that he is in a "superior position" to the other person in the relationship. This "superior position" does not necessarily mean superior in social status or economic position; many servants are masters at putting their employers one-down. Nor does it imply intellectual superiority as any intellectual knows who has been put "one-down" by a muscular garbage collector in a bout of Indian wrestling. "Superior position" is a relative term which is continually being defined and redefined by the ongoing relationship. Maneuvers to achieve superior position may be crude or they may be infinitely subtle. For example, one is not usually in a superior position if he must ask another person for something. Yet he can ask for it in such a way that he is implying, "This is, of course, what I deserve." Since the number of ways of maneuvering oneself into a superior position are infinite, let us proceed at once to summarize the psychoanalytic techniques as described in the three-volume study.

Psychoanalysis, according to the Potter study, is a dynamic psychological process involving two people, a patient and a psychoanalyst, during which the patient insists that the analyst be one-up while desperately trying to put him one-down, and the analyst insists that the patient remain one-down in order to help him learn to become one-up. The goal of the relationship is the amicable separation of analyst and patient.

Carefully designed, the psychoanalytic setting makes the superior position of the analyst almost invincible. First of all, the patient must voluntarily come to the analyst for help, thus conceding his inferior position at the beginning of the relationship. In addition, the patient accentuates his one-down position by paying the analyst money. Occasionally analysts have recklessly broken this structured situation by treating patients free of charge. Their position was difficult because the patient was not regularly reminded (on payday) that he must make a sacrifice to support the analyst, thus acknowledging the analyst's superior position before a word was said. It is really a wonder that any patient starting from his weak position could ever become one-up on an analyst, but in private discussions analysts will admit, and in fact tear at their hair while admitting, that patients can be extremely adroit and use such a variety of clever ploys that an analyst must be nimble to maintain his superior position.

Space does not permit a review of the history of psychoanalysis here, but it should be noted that early in its development it became obvious that the analyst needed reinforcement of the setting if he was to remain one-up on patients more clever than he. An early reinforcement was the use of couch for the patient to lie down upon. (This is often called "Freud's ploy," as are most ploys in psychoanalysis.) By placing the patient on a couch, the analyst gives the patient the feeling of having his feet up in the air and the knowledge that the analyst has both feet on the ground. Not only is the patient disconcerted by having to lie down while talking, but he finds himself literally below the analyst and so his one-down position is geographically emphasized. In addition, the analyst seats himself behind the couch where he can watch the patient but the patient cannot watch him. This gives the patient the sort of disconcerted feeling a person has when sparring with an opponent while blindfolded. Unable to see what response his ploys provoke, he is unsure when he is one-up and when one-down. Some patients try to solve this problem by saying something like, "I slept with my sister last night," and then whirling around to see how the analyst is responding. These "shocker" ploys usually fail in their effect. The analyst may twitch, but he has time to recover before the patient can whirl fully around and see him. Most analysts have developed ways of handling the whirling patient. As the patient turns, they are staring off into space, or doodling with a pencil, or braiding belts, or staring at tropical fish. It is essential that the rare patient who gets an opportunity to observe the analyst see only an impassive demeanor.

Another purpose is served by the position behind the couch. Inevitably what the analyst says becomes exaggerated in importance since the patient lacks any other means of determining his effect on the analyst. The patient finds himself hanging on the analyst's every word, and by definition he who hangs on another's words is one-down.

Perhaps the most powerful weapon in the analyst's arsenal is the use of silence. This falls in the category of "helpless" or "refusal to battle" ploys. It is impossible to win a contest with a helpless opponent since if you win you have won nothing. Each blow you strike is unreturned so that all you can feel is guilt for having struck while at the same time experiencing the uneasy suspicion that the helplessness is calculated. The result is suppressed fury and desperation—two emotions characterizing the one-down position. The problem posed for the patient is this: how can I get one-up on a man who won't respond and compete with me for the superior position in fair and open encounter? Patients find solutions, of course, but it takes months, usually years, of intensive analysis before a patient finds ways to force a response from his analyst. Ordinarily the patient begins rather crudely by saying something like, "Sometimes I think you're an idiot." He waits for the analyst to react defensively, thus stepping one-down. Instead the analyst replies with the silence ploy. The patient goes further and says, "I'm *sure* you're an idiot." Still silence in reply. Desperately the patient says, "I said you were an idiot, damn you, and you are!" Again only silence. What can the patient do but apologize, thus stepping voluntarily into a one-down position? Often a patient discovers how effective the silence ploy is and attempts to use it himself. This ends in disaster when he realizes that he is paying twenty dollars an hour to lie silent on a couch. The psychoanalytic setting is calculatedly designed to prevent patients using the ploys of analysts to attain equal footing (although as an important part of the cure the patient learns to use them effectively with other people).

Few improvements have been made on Freud's original brilliant design. As the basic plan for the hammer could not be improved upon by carpenters, so the use of the voluntary patient, hourly pay, the position behind the couch, and silence are devices which have not been improved upon by the practitioners of psychoanalysis.

Although the many ways of handling patients learned by the analyst cannot be listed here, a few general principles can be mentioned. Inevitably a patient entering analysis begins to use ploys which have put him one-up in previous relationships (this is called a "neurotic pattern"). The analyst learns to devastate these maneuvers of the patient. A simple way, for example, is to respond inappropriately to what the patient says. This puts the patient in doubt about everything he has learned in relationships with other people. The patient may say, "Everyone should be truthful," hoping to get the analyst to agree with him and thereby follow his lead. He who follows another's lead is one-down. The analyst may reply with silence, a rather weak ploy in this circumstance, or he may say, "Oh?" The "Oh?" is given just the proper inflection to imply, "How on earth could you have ever conceived such an idea?" This not only puts the patient in doubt about his statement, but in doubt about what the analyst means by "Oh?" Doubt is, of course, the first step toward one-downness. When in doubt the patient tends to lean on the analyst to resolve the doubt, and we lean on those who are superior to us. Analytic maneuvers designed to arouse doubt in a patient are instituted early in analysis. For example, the analyst may say, "I wonder if that's *really* what you're feeling." The use of "really" is standard in analytic practice. It implies the patient has motivations of which he is not aware. Anyone feels shaken, and therefore one-down, when this suspicion is put in his mind.

Doubt is related to the "unconscious ploy," an early development in psychoanalysis. This ploy is often considered the heart of analysis since it is the most effective way of making the patient unsure of himself. Early in an analysis the skilled analyst points out to the patient that he (the patient) has unconscious processes operating and is deluding himself if he thinks he really knows what he is saying. When the patient accepts this idea he can only rely on the analyst to tell him (or, as it is phrased, "to help him discover") what he really means. Thus he burrows himself deeper into the one-down position, making it easy for the analyst to top almost any ploy he devises. For example, the patient may cheerfully describe what a fine time he had with his girl friend, hoping to arouse some jealousy (a one-down emotion) in the analyst. The appropriate reply for the analyst is, "I wonder what that girl *really* means to you." This raises a doubt in the patient whether he is having intercourse with a girl named Susy or an unconscious symbol. Inevitably he turns to the analyst to help him discover what the girl really means to him.

Occasionally in the course of an analysis, particularly if the patient becomes obstreperous (uses resistance ploys), the analyst makes an issue of free association and dreams. Now a person must feel he knows what he is talking about to feel in a superior position. No one can maneuver to become one-up while free associating or narrating his dreams. The most absurd statements inevitably will be uttered. At the same time the analyst hints that there are meaningful ideas in this absurdity. This not only makes the patient feel that he is saying ridiculous things, but that he is saying things which the analyst sees meaning in and he doesn't. Such an experience would shake anyone, and inevitably drives the patient into a one-down position. Of course if the patient refuses to free-associate or tell his dreams, the analyst reminds him that he is defeating himself by being resistant.

A resistance interpretation falls in the general class of "turning it back on the patient" ploys. All attempts, particularly successful ones, to put the analyst one-down can be interpreted as resistance to treatment. The patient is made to feel that it is *his* fault that therapy is going badly. Carefully preparing in advance, the skillful analyst informs the patient in the first interview that the path to happiness is difficult and he will at times resist getting well and indeed may even resent the analyst for helping him. With this background even a refusal to pay the fee or a threat to end the analysis can be turned into apologies with an impersonal attitude by the analyst (the "not taking it personally" ploy) and an inter-pretation about resistance. At times the analyst may let the patient re-enter the one-down position gently by pointing out that his resistance is a sign of progress and change taking place in him.

The main difficulty with most patients is their insistence on dealing directly with the analyst once they begin to feel some confidence. When the patient begins to look critically at the analyst and threaten an open encounter, several "distraction" ploys are brought into play. The most common is the "concentrate on the past" ploy. Should the patient discuss the peculiar way the analyst refuses to respond to him, the analyst will inquire, "I wonder if you've had this feeling before. Perhaps your parents weren't very responsive." Soon they are busy discussing the patient's childhood without the patient ever discovering that the subject has been changed. Such a ploy is particularly effective when the patient begins to use what he has learned in analysis to make comments about the analyst.

In his training the young analyst learns the few rather simple rules that he must follow. The first is that it is essential to keep the patient feeling one-down while stirring him to struggle gamely in the hope that he can get one-up (this is called "transference"). Secondly the analyst must never feel one-down (this is called "countertransference"). The training analysis is designed to help the young analyst learn what it is like to experience a one-down position. By acting like a patient he learns what it feels like to conceive a clever ploy, deliver it expertly, and find himself thoroughly put one-down.

Even after two or three years in a training analysis seeing his weak ploys devastated, an analyst will occasionally use one with a patient and find himself forced into a one-down position. Despite the brilliant structure of the analytic fortress, and the arsenal of ploys learned in training, all men are human and to be human is to be occasionally one-down. The training emphasizes how to get out of the one-down position quickly when in it. The general ploy is to accept the one-down position "voluntarily" when it is inescapable. Finding the patient one-up, the analyst may say, "You have a point there," or "I must admit I made a mistake." The more daring analyst will say, "I wonder why I became a little anxious when you said that." Note that all these statements *seem* to show the analyst to be one-down and the patient one-up, but one-downness requires defensive behavior. By deliberately acknowledging his inferior position the analyst is actually maintaining his superior position, and the patient finds that once again a clever ploy has been topped by a helpless, or refusal to do battle, ploy. At times the "acceptance" technique cannot be used because the analyst is too sensitive in that area. Should a patient discover that this analyst gets embarrassed when homosexual ideas are discussed, he may rapidly exploit this. The analyst who takes such comments personally is lost. His only chance for survival is to anticipate in his diagnostic interviews those patients capable of discovering and exploiting this weakness and refer them to analysts with different weaknesses.

The most desperate ploys by patients are also anticipated in analytic training. A patient will at times be so determined to get one-up on his analyst that he will adopt the "suicide" ploy. Many analysts immediately suffer a one-down feeling when a patient threatens suicide. They hallucinate newspaper headlines and hear their colleagues chuckling as they whisper the total number of patients who got one-up on them by jumping off the bridge. The common way to prevent the use of this ploy is to take it impersonally. The analyst says something like, "Well, I'd be sorry if you blew your brains out, but I would carry on with my work." The patient abandons his plans as he realizes that even killing himself will not put him one-up on this man.

Orthodox psychoanalytic ploys can be highlighted by contrasting them with the more unorthodox maneuvers. There is, for example, the Rogerian system of ploys where the therapist merely repeats back what the patient says. This is an inevitable winning system. No one can top a person who merely repeats his ideas after him. When the patient accuses the therapist of being no use to him, the therapist replies, "You feel I'm no use to you." The patient says, "That's right, you're not worth a damn." The therapist says, "You feel I'm not worth a damn." This ploy, even more than the orthodox silence ploy, eliminates any triumphant feeling in the patient and makes him feel a little silly after a while (a one-down feeling). Most orthodox analysts look upon the Rogerian ploys as not only weak but not quite respectable. They don't give the patient a fair chance.

The ethics of psychoanalysis require the patient be given at least a reasonably fair chance. Ploys which simply devastate the patient are looked down on. Analysts who use them are thought to need more analysis themselves to give them a range of more legitimate ploys and confidence in using them. For instance, it isn't considered proper to encourage a patient to discuss a subject and then lose interest when he does. This puts the patient one-down, but it is a wasted ploy since he wasn't trying to become one-up. If the patient makes such an attempt then of course losing interest may be a necessary gambit.

Another variation on orthodox psychoanalytic ploys demonstrates a few of their limitations. The psychotic continually demonstrates that he is superior to orthodox ploys. He refuses to "volunteer" for analysis. He won't take a sensible interest in money. He won't lie quietly on the couch and talk while the analyst listens out of sight behind him. The structure of the analytic situation seems to irritate the psychotic. In fact when orthodox ploys are used against him, the psychotic is likely to tear up the office and kick the analyst in the genitals (this is called an inability to establish a transference). The average analyst is made uncomfortable by psychotic ploys and therefore avoids such patients. Recently some daring therapists have found they can get one-up on a psychotic patient if they work in pairs. This is now called the "it takes two to put one down" therapy, or "multiple therapy." For example, if a psychotic talks compulsively and won't even pause to listen, two therapists enter the room and begin to converse with each other. Unable to restrain his curiosity (a one-down emotion) the psychotic will stop talking and listen, thus leaving himself open to be put one-down.

The master one-upman with psychotics is a controversial psychiatrist known affectionately in the profession as "The Bull." When a compulsive talker won't listen to him, the Bull pulls a knife on the fellow and attracts his attention. No other therapist is so adroit at topping even the most determined patient. Other therapists require hospitals, attendants, shock treatments, lobotomies, drugs, restraints, and tubs to place the patient in a sufficiently one-down position. The Bull, with mere words and the occasional flash of a pocket knife, manages to make the most difficult psychotic feel one-down.

An interesting contrast to the Bull is a woman known in the Profession as "The Lovely Lady of the Lodge." Leading the league in subtle one-upmanship with psychotics, she avoids the Bull's ploys which are often considered rather crude and not always in the best of taste. If a patient insists he is God, the Bull will insist that *he* is God and force the patient to his knees, thus getting one-up in a rather straightforward way. To handle a similar claim by a patient, the Lady of the Lodge will smile and say, "All right, if you wish to be God, I'll let you." The patient is gently put one-down as he realizes that no one but God can *let* anyone else be God.

Although orthodox psychoanalytic ploys may be limited to work with neurotics no one can deny their success. The experienced analyst can put a patient one-down while planning where to have dinner at the same time. Of course this skill in one-upmanship has raised extraordinary problems when analysts compete with one another at meetings of the psychoanalytic associations. No other gathering of people exhibits so many complicated ways of gaining the upper hand. Most of the struggle at an analytic meeting takes place at a rather personal level, but the manifest content involves attempts to (1) demonstrate who was closest to Freud or can quote him most voluminously, and (2) who can confuse the most people by his daring extension of Freud's terminology. The man who can achieve both these goals best is generally elected president of the association.

The manipulation of language is the most startling phenomenon at an analytic meeting. Obscure terms are defined and redefined by even more obscure terms as analysts engage in furious theoretical discussions. This is particularly true when the point at issue is whether a certain treatment of a patient was *really* psychoanalysis or not. Such a point is inevitably raised when a particularly brilliant case history is presented.

What happens between analyst and patient, or the art of one-up-manship, is rarely discussed at the meetings (apparently the techniques are too secret for public discussion). This means the area for debate becomes the processes within the dark and dank interior of the patient. Attempting to outdo one another in explanations of the bizarre insides of patients, each speaker is constantly interrupted by shouts from the back of the hall such as, "Not at all! You're confusing an id impulse with a weak ego boundary!" or "Heaven help your patients if you call *that* cathexis!" Even the most alert analyst soon develops an oceanic feeling as he gets lost in flurries of energy theories, libidinal drives, instinctual forces, and superego barriers. The analyst who can most thoroughly confuse the group leaves his colleagues feeling frustrated and envious (one-down emotions). The losers return to their studies to search their minds, dictionaries, science fiction journals, and Freud for even more elaborate metaphorical flights in preparation for the next meeting.

The ploys of analyst and patient can be summarized briefly as they occur during a typical course of treatment. Individual cases will vary depending on what maneuvers the individual patient uses (called "symptoms" by the analyst when they are ploys no sensible person would use), but a general trend is easy to follow. The patient enters analysis in the one-down posture by asking for help and promptly tries to put the therapist one-down by building him up. This is called the honeymoon of the analysis. The patient begins to compliment the therapist on how wonderful he is and how quickly he (the patient) expects to get well. The skilled analyst is not taken in by these maneuvers (known as the "Reichian resistance" ploys). When the patient finds himself continually put one-down, he changes tactics. He becomes mean, insulting, threatens to quit analysis, and casts doubt upon the sanity of the analyst. These are the "attempts to get a human response" ploys. They meet an impassive, impersonal wall as the analyst remains silent or handles the insults with a simple statement like, "Have you noticed this is the second Tuesday afternoon you've made such a comment? I wonder what there is about Tuesday," or "You seem to be reacting to me as if I'm someone else." Frustrated in his aggressive behavior (resistance ploy), the patient capitulates and ostensibly hands control of the situation back to the analyst. Again building the analyst up, he leans on him, hangs on his every word, insists how helpless he is and how strong the analyst, and waits for the moment when he will lead the analyst along far enough to devastate him with a clever ploy. The skilled analyst handles this nicely with a series of "condescending" ploys, pointing out that the patient must help himself and not expect anyone to solve everything for him. Furious, the patient again switches from subservient ploys to defiant ploys. By this time he has learned techniques from the analyst and is getting better. He uses what insight (ploys unknown to laymen) he has gained to try in every way to define the relationship as one in which the analyst is one-down. This is the difficult period of the analysis. However, having carefully prepared the ground by a thorough diagnosis (listing weak points) and having instilled a succession of doubts in the patient about himself, the analyst succeeds in topping the patient again and again as the years pass. Ultimately a remarkable thing happens. The patient rather casually tries to get one-up, the analyst puts him one-down, and the patient does not become disturbed by this. He has reached a point where he doesn't *really* care whether the analyst is in control of the relationship or whether he is in control. In other words, he is cured. The analyst then dismisses him, timing this maneuver just before the patient is ready to announce that he is leaving. Turning to his waiting list, the analyst invites in another patient who, by definition, is someone compelled to struggle to be one-up and disturbed if he is put one-down. And so goes the day's work in the difficult art of psychoanalysis.

QUESTIONS FOR READING, RESPONDING, AND WRITING

Summarizing Main Points

1. Haley uses a humorous method to address a serious topic in his essay. How far in the essay do you have to read before you notice Haley's humor? How much farther must you read before you recognize that the essay is doing more than merely poking fun?
2. List the distinctions Haley makes between "legitimate" ploys and the "unorthodox" ploys used on "psychotics." What separates "neurotics," "psychotics," and "sensible" people, according to Haley?

Analyzing Methods of Discourse

1. Why is Haley's comparison of "Freud's original, brilliant design" with "the basic plan for the hammer" particularly appropriate? How is that comparison similar to Haley's choice of words in describing the psychoanalytic situation as the "analytic fortress" with an "arsenal of ploys"? List other examples of particularly appropriate figures of speech.
2. Early in his essay, Haley says that "unfamiliar terms will be translated into psychoanalytic terminology throughout the essay." How does this statement make it clear that the language of psychotherapy may be part of the difficulty that Haley sees in the profession? What other examples of this sort of reversal of technical terminology do you see, and how does each example point out a particular problem in the profession, according to Haley?

Focusing on the Field

1. How closely do you suppose Haley's descriptions of psychoanalytic sessions—ignoring his terminology—come to actually (or "really") describing those sessions? What exactly do you believe Haley would change in the profession of psychology?
2. Who do you suppose Haley intends his audience to be? Why is his humorous method particularly important?

Writing Assignments

1. Most people have found themselves in the sort of "no-win" situation that Haley describes. Consider a situation of this sort that you have encountered and, in a short essay, analyze it. You need not be humorous.
2. Study Robert Coles's "The Children of Affluence." Coles often relies heavily on transcription of his patients' own words, and he avoids overusing professional or technical terminology. Write an essay supporting the assertion that Coles and Haley agree about what is wrong with the psychological profession. Support your claim with evidence from both essays.

Dorothy Wickenden

BOWDLERIZING THE BARD
How to Protect Your Kids from Shakespeare

Dorothy Wickenden was born in 1954 in Norwalk, Connecticut. A magna cum laude graduate of William Smith College (B.A., 1976), she received high honors in English. Best known for her political commentary and book reviews in the *New Republic* and *Saturday Review,* she is currently a managing editor of the *New Republic.* Earlier in her career, Wickenden worked for the Folger Shakespeare Library and for *Shakespeare Quarterly* as editor and production manager. Such experience, as well as her educational reporting for the *Washington Post* and *Book World's* Education Issue, lends much credence to her analysis of the age-old problem of censoring Shakespeare's works for young students.

As Wickenden points out, the problem is so old and so ubiquitous that it is too often forgotten or ignored. The publishers of student textbooks, in their effort to make Shakespeare and other works acceptable to a wide variety of "special interest" groups, become the accidental arbiters of moral and literary values. Faced with the bard's undoubted bawdiness and "no comfortable consensus" as to its appropriateness for different age levels, publishers have expunged and abridged without regard for the integrity of the work itself, the teachers who must teach it, or the students who will read it.

It was a studious ninth grader, not an anti-censorship brigade, who set off the most recent flurry about what kids ought to be reading in school. The culprits were not fervid fundamentalists but staid corporate publishers. And the object of censorship was not a science or history text or an obscene novel, but the work of the most revered playwright in the world.

Daniel Blum, a student at Madison High School in Vienna, Virginia, had seen a Folger Theatre production of *Romeo and Juliet*, and when he sat down with his Scott, Foresman *America Reads* textbook to write a paper about Mercutio's Queen Mab speech, he noticed that some of the lines were missing. For example, the "fairies' midwife" who "gallops night by night/Through lovers' brains" is no longer characterized as the hag who "when maids lie on their backs,/ . . . presses them and learns them first to bear,/Making them women of good carriage."

Around the time the story broke in Virginia, a parent in Minneapolis discovered that the same anthology had been altered as well as abridged. Romeo's line in Act V, "Well, Juliet, I will lie with thee tonight," was changed to read, "Well, Juliet, I will *be* with thee tonight." Investigations by a Fairfax County textbook advisory committee, school boards, columnists, and People For The American Way revealed not only that more than 300 lines had been eliminated from Scott, Foresman's *Romeo and Juliet*—most of them sexual allusions—but that high school textbook publishers routinely expurgate Shakespeare. Some, including Scott, Foresman, note in teachers' editions that "abridgments" have been made. Most do not.

The overwhelming reaction was one of astonished indignation. Scott, Foresman has received over 2,000 letters deploring the practice of "self-censorship." Yet there is nothing new or surprising about the bowdlerization of Shakespeare. On the contrary, the current batch of "censored" textbooks is resolutely faithful to the traditions of Dr. Bowdler and his sister Harriet, who published their first edition of *Family Shakespeare* in 1807. And publishers of literature anthologies for the public schools have always felt constrained to abridge and excerpt—keeping in mind both the sophistication of the students who will be reading them and the requirements of parents and school districts that will be buying them.

Marlene Blum, a member of the Fairfax County textbook advisory committee and the mother of Daniel, complained to Sandra Sugawara of *The Washington Post*, "It's as if [the publishers] have become the arbiter of what children are to read and not read." Yet if anything, textbook publishers have become more fearful over the years about making their own determinations of what children are to read and not read. They have found that they cannot afford to dismiss the bedrock fundamentalism of people like Mel and Norma Gabler, Texas's notorious textbook scourges, any more than they can the clamoring of countless other political, religious, and ethnic groups to cleanse their books of sexual and racial stereotyping. Jane Bachman, an editorial vice president at Scott, Foresman, guardedly told me, "Textbook publishers anticipate what may be a troublesome matter. We might be a little paranoid when we put a book together."

Clearly some things have changed since the heyday of bowdlerism. There is no comfortable consensus, as there was in the Victorian era, about matters of propriety, church, and state. In its absence, the public schools have become a stage for various special interest groups to perform their political dramas. As the requirements for textbooks have multiplied, publishers have honed their marketing skills, and the role of the editor has dwindled. No single sentinel trims the text and upholds moral and literary standards. Indeed, it is almost irrelevant what the editor believes. Before a textbook comes into being, surveys are conducted, focus groups are convened, and outside consultants are hired. As the book is prepared, armies of reading specialists, instructional designers, teachers, and computers zealously watch over it. They guard against unattractive book covers and ethnic slurs; they monitor "curricular congruence" (text, workbook, and teachers' guide must complement each other) and "readability" levels (vocabulary words and number of syllables per sentence are tabulated according to grade). When the book is finally published, it is subject to review and complaint by concerned citizens and put up for "adoption" by state and local textbook advisory committees equipped with complicated checklists of requirements.

In this Byzantine method of patching together textbooks, the integrity of any single story or play—not to mention the needs of students—often gets lost. Certain particularly troublesome items have been virtually abandoned—among them Shirley Jackson's famous short story, "The Lottery" (too violent), and *The Merchant of Venice* (anti-Semitic). Publishers have gone to absurd lengths to accommodate disparate interest groups and varying state guidelines. Elsa Walsh reported in *The Washington Post* that in a chapter from *Tom Sawyer*, which appears in Ginn and Company's sixth-grade reader *Flights of Color*, the colloquialisms have vanished, the grammar has been cleaned up, Tom's oath of "honest Injun" has been removed, and most references to boys or men have been changed to children or people. A story called "A Perfect Day for Ice Cream" was included in Scott, Foresman's 1985 eighth-grade anthology only after the words "ice cream" had been deleted from the title and a scene about a trip to the ice-cream parlor had been eliminated. The reason, apparently, was California's "social content guidelines" for textbooks, which warn against references to junk food. McGraw Hill's seventh-grade *Focus* anthology has expunged from "Rip Van Winkle" not only difficult vocabulary words here and there such as "dismembered," but the reference to "obsequious and conciliatory" men who go home to "shrews" and "termagant" wives.

And yet, this is an old story. As Jane Bachman of Scott, Foresman aptly, if perhaps inadvertently, punned in a letter to a man who had written to express dismay at the censoring of the Bard, "Stage and film directors have had their way with Shakespeare since his plays were first performed." One of those they have taken particular liberties with is *Romeo and Juliet*. In *Dr. Bowdler's Legacy* Noel Perrin describes David Garrick in 1750 preparing an acting version of the play in which he decided to dampen Juliet's ardent soliloquy in Act II. "He wasn't trying to spare the audience, though; he just thought it out of character for such a nice girl to speak of maidenheads, much less to wish openly that Romeo would hurry up and take hers." In the 1818 edition of *Family Shakespeare*, Dr. Bowdler removed almost exactly the same lines. Today's textbook publishers too have banished the stuff about maidenheads, both in the banter between Capulet's servants Samson and Gregory in Act I and in Juliet's soliloquy. Harcourt Brace Jovanovich; Scott, Foresman;

Macmillan; Ginn; McDougal, Littell and Company; and McGraw-Hill have all eliminated the lines:

> *Lovers can see to do their amorous rites*
> *By their own beauties, or, if love be blind,*
> *It best agrees with night. Come, civil night,*
> *Thou sober-suited matron all in black*
> *And learn me how to lose a winning match,*
> *Play'd for a pair of stainless maidenhoods.*
> *Hood my unmann'd blood, bating in my cheeks,*
> *With thy black mantle, till strange love grow bold,*
> *Think true love acted simple modesty . . .*

as well as,

> *O, I have bought the mansion of a love,*
> *But not possess'd it, and though I am sold,*
> *Not yet enjoy'd. . . .*

Bowdlerizers have long recognized that *Romeo and Juliet*, with its arousing themes of young love, sex, drugs, and death, is particularly appealing to adolescents, and thus a perfect candidate for the curriculum—and for excisions. In editions for the tender reader, it isn't just the impassioned words of a young girl that are generally deemed unprintable, but references to the body (notably nipples and genitals) and its natural functions (particularly childbearing and sexual desire or activity).

One of the salacious lines that has been consistently singled out over the years is Mercutio's remark in Act II, in which he teasingly replies to the Nurse's question about the time: " 'Tis no less, I tell you, for the bawdy hand of the dial is now upon the prick of noon." The first great American expurgation of Shakespeare, published in 1872 by Ginn ("selected and prepared for use in Schools, Clubs, Classes, and Families"), scrupulously retained the word "prick," but omitted "bawdy." Perrin surmises that the book's editor—a Shakespearean scholar—hoped that without the clue his readers wouldn't catch the double entendre. A century later no major textbook publisher is so daring. All have removed the entire line from their ninth-grade anthologies.

Macbeth and *Hamlet* have fared somewhat better. Among the 12th-grade anthologies that include *Macbeth* as their Shakespeare selection, five of the big publishers, like a number of their 19th-century predecessors, have left the play virtually intact—except for the Porter's second speech, where he expounds upon drunken lechery, which "provokes the desire," but "takes away the performance." Scott, Foresman restored the speech in 1979, but continues to do some damage (100 lines' worth) to

Hamlet. The scene in Act III where he viciously berates his mother for wallowing in incest has been robbed of some of the lines that would doubtless most appeal to teenagers, including: "Nay, but to live/In the rank sweat of an enseamed bed,/Stewed in corruption, honeying and making love/Over the nasty sty!"

As Perrin points out, the Victorians bowdlerized openly, secure in the belief that they were serving the cause of Christianity and assisting in society's moral progress. Today's textbook editors, by contrast, do it shamefully, defensively, on behalf of a cause that most of them don't fully believe in. Responding to the initial complaints about Scott, Foresman's fiddling with Shakespeare, Richard T. Morgan, the president, emphatically stated that "no language has been changed." That proved to be incorrect. It also skirts the tougher question about the line between abridgment and selective expurgation, and about the publisher's responsibility to state clearly what kinds of changes have been made. Jane Bachman insisted, "In no way has the basic nature of 'Romeo and Juliet' been altered." Ginn, which eliminated about 400 lines from *Romeo and Juliet* in its ninth-grade anthology, *Understanding Literature*, brazenly states in its teachers' edition, "The Tragedy of Romeo and Juliet' is presented here as Shakespeare wrote it."

Edmund Farrell, a professor of English education at the University of Texas at Austin who has been an author and outside editor for Scott, Foresman since 1958, says frankly: "We are putting out books for ninth graders, not for college students. Schools act in loco parentis. There is no way I know of that a publisher can print 'the bawdy hand of the dial is now upon the prick of noon.' The choice is between abridging the play or not including it at all." That may be understandable. What is not understandable, or acceptable, regardless of the book's market, is to purge and then insist that the basic nature of the play is unchanged. If certain passages must be trimmed, why not indicate with ellipses, as Scott, Foresman does in its 12th-grade *Hamlet?* Why not also point out in both the teachers' guide and the students' introduction that the play has been expurgated?

Textbook publishers and school boards have become so accustomed to covert bowdlerization that they apparently came to forget that it was even going on. The Virginia state board of education, for one, had been happily buying the disputed Scott, Foresman textbook series for years until a ninth grader and his mother objected to its cavalier treatment of Shakespeare. As for teachers, the good ones have always had more faith in their own judgment about what is suitable for their students than they have in the prepackaged selections of mass-market textbook publishers. Some have even taken advantage of their books' flaws. After Daniel Blum's discovery, his teacher supplied the students with the full text of

Romeo and Juliet, and discussed the anthology's cuts in class. Covert or open, censorship is a doomed enterprise, for it stimulates precisely that dangerous urge it set out to crush: curiosity.

QUESTIONS FOR READING, RESPONDING, AND WRITING

Summarizing Main Points

1. What, according to Wickenden, is the difference between Victorian bowdlerizing and current bowdlerizing?
2. What case do textbook publishers make for abridging and expurgating texts? How does Wickenden refute them?

Analyzing Methods of Discourse

1. Wickenden begins her essay with examples of student and parental dismay at finding a text of *Romeo and Juliet* bowdlerized. How does this beginning reinforce the case Wickenden proceeds to make against textbook publishers? Why do you suppose she returns to the example of Daniel Blum at the essay's end?
2. Wickenden uses military terminology throughout her essay. Locate examples, noting the subject under discussion when such language occurs and the people with whom the language is connected. What point do you suppose Wickenden might be trying to make through the use of this sort of language?

Focusing on the Field

1. In paragraph six, Wickenden traces the route a textbook takes on its way to publication. Make a list of all those to whom Wickenden assigns a role in this process and describe those roles as well. Then, consider what point Wickenden might be trying to make by charting this process.
2. Who is Wickenden's audience here? What do you suppose her goal in writing this essay might be?

Writing Assignments

1. Locate two textbooks aimed at different age groups, both of which contain the same Shakespearean play. Also, locate a copy of the complete text of that same play. Compare a likely scene from the full play to the two textbook versions and the two textbook versions to each other. Are there cuts in either or both of the textbooks? If so, do you consider the particular audience at which each textbook is aimed to be a factor in these cuts? Do the publishers acknowledge the cuts? Write an essay on your findings.
2. Read Flannery O'Connor's "The Teaching of Literature." Then, write an essay in which you argue that Wickenden's account of what happens in textbook publishing does or does not contribute to producing the sort of literary education that O'Connor complains about.

David Weinberger

COMPUTER LITERACY IS NOT LITERACY

David Weinberger, born in 1950 on Long Island, New York, received a B.A. from Bucknell University in 1972 and a Ph.D. in philosophy from the University of Toronto in 1979. He has taught for six years, most recently at Stockton State College in New Jersey in the philosophy-religion program. Weinberger often writes free-lance for popular publications like *MacLean's,* a Canadian newsweekly, *Profiles,* a magazine devoted to KayPro computing where he has a regular column, "Popular Computing," *TV Guide,* and the *New York Times Educational Supplement,* where the following essay appeared in 1983. Weinberger also writes for academic publications like the philosophical journal *Idealistic Studies.* For one such issue, in an essay entitled "Plato's Cave," Weinberger argued that one reason artificial intelligence seems so plausible today stems from our Greek philosophical heritage and the conception of thinking the Greeks held. He also writes often on the philosophical and ethical aspects of the arms race. The breadth of Weinberger's talents is perhaps best exemplified by his seven years as a gag writer for various well-known comedians. Weinberger is currently expanding his expertise to include technical writing for the computer industry.

In the following essay, Weinberger questions the role of computers in education: How much do students need to know about computers, and how can computers best help students to learn?

I was the last person on my block to own a digital watch. In a typical liberal-arts way, I suppose, I resisted and resented everything about computers. Yet now I own a computer, have taught myself BASIC, am learning assembly-language programming, subscribe to computer magazines and find myself discussing baud rates more often than epistemology. I have, in short, become computer literate.

Having done so, I now see that despite the clamor for computer literacy from educators afraid their schools will be left behind in today's demanding educational marketplace, we certainly should not require our students to spend much more than, say, 45 minutes on it.

There is no denying that students should learn something about how computers work, just as we expect them at least to understand that the internal-combustion engine has something to do with burning fuel, expanding gases and pistons being driven. For people should have some basic idea of how the things that they use do what they do. Further, students might be helped by a course that considers the computer's impact on society. But that is not what is meant by computer literacy. For computer literacy is not a form of literacy; it is a trade skill that should not be taught as a liberal art.

Learning how to use a computer and learning how to program one are two distinct activities. A case might be made that the competent citizens of tomorrow should untether themselves from their fear of computers. But this is quite different from saying that all ought to know how to program one. Leave that to people who have chosen programming as a career. While programming can be lots of fun (I enjoy it immensely), and while our society needs some people who are experts at it, the same is true of auto repair and violin-making.

Learning how to use a computer is not that difficult, and it gets easier all the time as programs become more "user-friendly." I am composing this article on my Kaypro II using a word-processing program called WordStar, produced by MicroPro International. WordStar is not considered to be particularly easy to learn, yet with half an hour of instruction, one can be writing letters with it.

To learn all the complexities of WordStar might take another hour, and then it's just a matter of practicing until use of it becomes automatic. The newer word-processing programs, particularly on machines designed for them (such as the Epson QX-10) are even easier to learn. Learning to use WordStar, in other words, is a skill considerably easier to acquire than learning to drive with a stick shift.

Now, let us assume that in the future everyone is going to have to know how to use a computer to be a competent citizen. What does the phrase "learning to use a computer" mean? It sounds like "learning to drive a car"; that is, it sounds as if there is some set of definite skills that, once acquired, enable one to use a computer.

In fact, "learning to use a computer" is much more like "learning to play a game," but learning the rules of one game may not help you play a second game. So, when I first got my computer, before I knew anything about programming, I learned how to use it by learning the rules of WordStar. But those rules (e.g., type control-T to have it delete a word, control-QF to have it look for a word) are not transferrable. They will not work with ValDocs, or Perfect Writer, much less with a filing program, or a spreadsheet program.

There is no such thing as teaching someone how to use a computer. One can only teach people to use this or that program, and generally that is easily accomplished.

And we need not worry about helping our children over their fear of computers. What fear of computers? If they aren't using one at home, then they are at the corner arcade computing hostile aliens into glowing smithereens. This is a generation of Pactots and Intellivisinfants. Entire adolescences are being spent courting green-screened consoles. The last child who was afraid to use a computer is today Ricky Nelson's age.

Programming is a different matter. It cannot be taught in half an hour. Indeed, it is an open-ended, creative skill that many students will find enjoyable. But so is chess; it is not a liberal art we should be teaching in our schools.

Learning programming may have beneficial effects. To program, one must be able to analyze a problem into small steps. It requires a sort of analytic thinking, and students ought to be trained in analytic thinking. Unfortunately, the nature of the steps is dictated by the programming language the student is learning.

For example, you want your programs to run as quickly as possible. This means they should have as few steps as possible. In S-BASIC (the version of BASIC I use, which is close to Pascal), there are various sorts of commands (FOR . . . NEXT, REPEAT . . . UNTIL, WHILE . . . UNTIL) one could use. You will decide which one to use by analyzing your program in light of the options S-BASIC offers.

While this requires a desirable rigor of thought, it would be more useful for students to learn to analyze problems into terms other than those set by their programs. If we want students to learn analytic thinking, logic would be a better course to require than computer programming, for in logic they will discover the distinctions drawn by careful thought uninfluenced by the practical demand of having a machine respond properly.

Let them take philosophy where they will learn how to think in ways that respond to the needs of the time and of the subject matter, rather than learning how to analyze all problems into a series of computer commands.

A programming language in some ways is truly a language. I find myself at times thinking in S-BASIC. Perhaps it will be argued that it is beneficial for students to learn a new language. I agree. Let it be Latin. Let it be one that makes them more literate. That, after all, is the true goal of a liberal education.

QUESTIONS FOR READING, RESPONDING, AND WRITING

Summarizing Main Points

1. List Weinberger's alternatives to teaching "computer literacy." Explain what Weinberger feels is the advantage of each alternative.
2. Weinberger's argument for not teaching computer languages or programming is based on a single assumption. What is it? From what Weinberger says about the many different kinds of computer programs, do you feel he would advocate computer literacy as a "trade skill"? Why or why not?

Analyzing Methods of Discourse

1. Weinberger compares learning to use a computer to several other kinds of learning. List them. Which, according to Weinberger, is the most successful comparison, the one with the most similarities? Why do you suppose Weinberger includes unsuccessful comparisons?
2. Weinberger uses his own computer education as an example more than once. List those examples and explain how each does or does not work to maintain Weinberger's objectivity.

Focusing on the Field

1. Weinberger's last paragraph defines the goal of a liberal education as making students more "literate." Why do you suppose Weinberger waits until his last paragraph to define that goal? What is Weinberger's own attitude toward a liberal arts education?
2. Weinberger suggests that "students might be helped by a course that considers the computer's impact on society." How could his own essay be used as an example in such a course? Are there ways in which the computer has already affected your own life?

Writing Assignments

1. Weinberger claims that "people should have some basic idea of how the things that they use do what they do." In a short paper based on your own experience either defend Weinberger's claim or object to it. Either way, be sure to provide evidence to support your argument.
2. Compare and contrast Weinberger's essay with John Anderson's "The Heartbreak of Cyberphobia." Do they agree about what should be taught about computers? Support your answer with evidence from both essays.

Thomas Sowell

PINK AND BROWN PEOPLE

Thomas Sowell was born in Gastonia, North Carolina on June 30, 1930. A magna cum laude graduate of Harvard University, Sowell also studied at Columbia University (A.M., 1959) and the University of Chicago (Ph.D., 1968). Once project director of the Urban Institute in Washington, D.C., Sowell began his career working as an economic analyst for the U.S. Department of Labor. He later joined American Telephone and Telegraph Company, where he contributed to *Bell Telephone Magazine*. From AT&T, Sowell went on to teach full-time at Cornell University and later became an associate professor at the University of California at Los Angeles, where he began to publish books and texts on economic and social history, including *Economics: Analysis and Issues* (1971), *Black Education: Myths and Tragedies* (1972), *Say's Law: An Historical Analysis* (1972), and *Affirmative Action Reconsidered: Was It Necessary in Academia?* (1975), and many, many books since. Sowell has also contributed essays to such periodicals as *Education Digest*, *Black Political Economy*, *Ethics*, and *Administrative Science Quarterly*.

The essay presented below is taken from *Pink and Brown People and Other Controversial Essays* (1981). In it, Sowell puts a historical perspective on the paranoia and "reckless rhetoric" that surrounds discussion of race in the United States today.

A man who says we should really "tell it like it is" refers to whites and blacks as "pink people" and "brown people." These jarring phrases are of course more accurate, but that may be why they are jarring. Race is not an area especially noted for accuracy—or for rationality or candor. More often it is an area of symbolism, stereotype, and euphemism. The plain truth sounds off-key and even suspicious. Gross exaggerations like *white* and *black* are more like the kind of polarization we are used to. Racial classifications have always been a problem, but in the United States such attempts at neat pigeonholing become a farce, in view of the facts of history.

Less than a fourth of the "black" population of the United States is of unmixed African ancestry. And a noted social historian estimates that tens of millions of whites have at least one black ancestor somewhere in generations past. Even in the old South, where "one drop of Negro blood" was supposed to make you socially black, the actual laws required some stated fraction of black ancestry, to avoid "embarrassing" some of the "best" white families.

What all this boils down to is a wide spectrum of racial mixtures with an arbitrary dividing line and boldly contrasting labels applied to people on either side of the line. The human desire for classification is not going to be defeated by any biological facts. Those who cannot swallow pseudobiology can turn to pseudohistory as the basis for classification. Unique cultural characteristics are now supposed to neatly divide the population.

In this more modern version, the ghetto today is a unique social phenomenon—a unique problem calling for a unique solution. Many of those who talk this way just happen to have this solution with them and will make it available for a suitable combination of money and power.

Ghettos today certainly differ from white middle-class neighborhoods. But past ghettos always differed from past middle-class neighborhoods, even when both were white. Indeed, the very word *ghetto* came historically from a white minority community of people, classified by the fact that they held religious services one day earlier than others. People will classify on any basis. With today's recreation-oriented weekends, religious classifications are often based on what service you *would have* attended.

American ghettos have always had crime, violence, overcrowding, filth, drunkenness, bad school teaching, and worse learning. Nor are blacks historically unique even in the degree of these things. Crime and violence were much worse in the nineteenth-century slums, which were almost all white. The murder rate in Boston in the middle of the nineteenth century was about three times what it was in the middle of the twentieth century. All the black riots of the 1960s put together did not kill half as many people as were killed in one white riot in 1863.

The meaning of the term *race riot* has been watered down in recent times to include general hell raising (and posing for television) in the hell-raisers' own neighborhood. In the nineteenth century it was much uglier. Thousands of members of one "race" invaded the neighborhood of another "race"—both, typically, European—to maim, murder, and burn. Today's disorders are not in the same league, whether measured in blood or buildings.

Squalor, dirt, disease? Historically, blacks are neither first nor last in any of these categories. There were far more immigrants packed into the slums (per room or per square mile) than is the case with blacks today—not to mention the ten thousand to thirty thousand children with no home at all in nineteenth-century New York. They slept under bridges, huddled against buildings or wherever they could find some semblance of shelter from the elements.

Even in the area where many people get most emotional—educational and I.Q. test results—blacks are doing nothing that various European minorities did not do before them. As of about 1920, any number of European ethnic groups had I.Q.'s the same as or lower than the I.Q.'s of blacks today. As recently as the 1940s, there were schools on the Lower East Side of New York with academic performances lower than those of schools in Harlem.

Much of the paranoia that we talk ourselves into about race (and other things) is a result of provincialism about our own time as compared to other periods of history. Violence, poverty, and destroyed lives should never be accepted. But there is little chance of solving any problem unless we see it for what it is, not what it appears to be in the framework of reckless rhetoric.

QUESTIONS FOR READING, RESPONDING, AND WRITING

Summarizing Main Points

1. What point is Sowell trying to make about the "unique cultural characteristics that divide the population"?
2. How does the title of Sowell's essay reinforce his main point?

Analyzing Methods of Discourse

1. Sowell spends three paragraphs on "the ghetto." In the first paragraph, he describes current attitudes toward it as a "unique social phenomenon;" in the second, he presents the history of its use as a divider; in the third paragraph, he suggests the ways in which its history identifies it as a social phenomenon shared by both blacks and whites. Examine the paragraphs which follow this discussion and note that Sowell develops each of his topics in approximately the same way. Do you note any differences? How do you account for those differences?
2. List the topics that Sowell treats in the order in which he discusses them. What kind of a progression do you see in the "unique social phenomena" he chooses to debunk? Why do you suppose he chose to arrange these topics in the order in which he did?

Focusing on the Field

1. Given the point Sowell is trying to make, can you determine the appropriate audience for his piece? Do you think he is successful in reaching that audience?
2. In his final paragraph, Sowell states: "Much of the paranoia that we talk ourselves into about race is a result of provincialism about our own time as compared to other periods of history." What do you think Sowell means by this statement? How does he attempt to combat such "provincialism" in his essay?

Writing Assignments

1. Read Robert Coles's "The Children of Affluence." Write an essay in which you compare Sowell's methods of arguing the meaning of economic status at a point in society's history to Coles's.
2. Choose a stereotype with which you are familiar (e.g., "jock," "egghead," "town boy," "preppie," "nerd," "frat-boy") and write a short essay in which you explain the ways the terms that describe these stereotypes are unrealistic or gross exaggerations.

Irving R. Kaufman

THE INSANITY PLEA ON TRIAL

Born in 1910 in New York City, Irving R. Kaufman attended Fordham Law School, where he earned his LL.B. in 1931. In 1935, he was appointed as a special assistant to the U.S. attorney for the southern district of New York. He acted as assistant U.S. attorney from 1936 to 1940 and as special assistant to the U.S. attorney general from 1947 to 1948. In 1949, Kaufman was appointed a U.S. district judge and became a judge for the U.S. Court of Appeals for the Second Circuit in 1961, serving as its chief judge from 1973 to 1980.

In the course of a distinguished legal career, Kaufman has received numerous awards, including the American Bar Association Special Citation for Extraordinary Service, the American Judicature Society's Herbert Harley Award, the Federal Bar Council's Learned Hand Medal for Excellence in Federal Jurisprudence, and several honorary degrees. He has also been a past president of the Institute of Judicial Administration and served from 1966 to 1973 as chairman of the Committee on the Operation of the Jury System. He is currently the chairman for the President's Commission on Organized Crime.

In the following essay, first published in the *New York Times Magazine* in August, 1982, in the wake of John Hinckley, Jr.'s acquittal by reason of insanity in the assassination attempt on President Ronald Reagan, Kaufman addresses the "public outrage" over the verdict, while explaining the complicated evolution of the "insanity defense."

On March 30, 1981, I was asking to be loved. I was asking my family to take me back and I was asking Jodie Foster to hold me in her heart. My assassination attempt was an act of love. I'm sorry love has to be so painful.

Sitting alone in his prison cell awaiting what he thought would be the inevitable verdict, John W. Hinckley Jr. penned these words as part of his "sentencing speech." Hinckley was so convinced he would be found guilty of the attempted assassination of the President and the shooting of James S. Brady, Timothy J. McCarthy and Thomas K. Delahanty that he titled his speech "The Conviction."

The paunchy young drifter was not alone in his expectations. Most Americans thought Hinckley would be found guilty of each of the charges in the 13-count indictment. The jury, however, had other ideas. On June 21, 1982, after an eight-week trial replete with conflicting psychiatric testimony and capped by complex legal instructions, 12 citizens selected at random in the District of Columbia decided that Hinckley had lacked the mental capacity necessary to be held responsible for his crimes. As Judge Barrington D. Parker successively read the verdict on each charge to a stunned and silent courtroom, the result for each count was the same: not guilty by reason of insanity.

A hearing was scheduled for tomorrow to determine Hinckley's immediate future. Unless Hinckley can show at that time that he has recovered his sanity and is no longer a danger to himself or the community, he will be committed to a mental hospital whcre he will remain indefinitely. If committed, Hinckley would have the option, at six-month intervals, to petition the court for a hearing in which he could again attempt to show that he is sane and not dangerous. Should he ever succeed in doing so, he would be released.

Outrage over the verdict was immediate and intense. Numerous Government officials called for changes in the laws concerning the insanity defense. A United States Senate subcommittee conducted hearings to consider amending the relevant Federal statutes, summoning five of the jurors in the Hinckley case to testify. Countless commentators attacked the verdict and suggested their own reforms. And among the general populace there was widespread anger and resentment.

As the hue and cry rose, some experts responded by pointing out that the insanity defense is rarely successful. In New York, for example, it is estimated that the insanity defense is invoked in no more than 1.5 percent of all felony indictments, and that it fails approximately 75 percent of the time. Yet that sort of statistic belies the true impact the insanity defense has upon our criminal-justice system.

The problem is that acquittals by reason of insanity in highly publicized cases such as the Hinckley affair tend to undermine the public's faith in the court's ability to respond to crime in a rational fashion. And there is no denying that there have been mistaken applications of the insanity defense, instances in which individuals have been erroneously relieved of criminal responsibility by reason of insanity and all too quickly released from custody to engage again in criminal conduct. At the same time, it needs to be emphasized that no criminal-justice system that finds a defendant guilty while ignoring his mental inability to control his actions can be viewed as fair and just.

The Hinckley verdict and the public reaction to it clearly indicate that there are a number of problems with our judicial approaches to the insanity plea, problems that have deeply disturbed those of us who have worked on shaping the rules relating to the insanity defense. (My own views on the subject can be traced back to 1966, when I authored the opinion in *United States v. Freeman* for the United States Court of Appeals for the Second Circuit, which established the standards for insanity pleas in the district courts of New York, Connecticut and Vermont. I will return to the substance of that standard later.) But as we look for reforms, a healthy skepticism should inform our search.

The currently fashionable proposal to create a "guilty but mentally ill" verdict, for example, is beset with practical and constitutional impediments that, as we shall see, require careful consideration. Problems also arise from laws aimed at requiring the defendant to prove his insanity before being relieved of criminal responsibility. Yet these options—as well as others designed to ease the obvious burdens a lay jury faces in assessing the highly technical, often contradictory testimony of prosecution and defense psychiatrists—are clearly worth further examination.

Underlying the entire issue is a basic conflict between the legal and psychiatric understandings of insanity. Essentially, the law is concerned with establishing fault; it focuses on individual responsibility as a way of controlling behavior and articulating public morality. Psychiatry, by contrast, is interested in identifying, diagnosing and treating mental disorders and in understanding the attitudes, actions and environmental causes behind such disorders.

The current debate over the insanity defense will not be settled quickly or easily. It touches on deeply felt American attitudes toward crime, punishment and personal responsibility, and raises some of the most complex questions in criminal jurisprudence. But whatever changes are made should not be the result of an urge to punish a particular man. The principle behind the insanity defense—that individuals may take actions for which they cannot justly be held criminally responsible— should not be abandoned thoughtlessly.

The first point that needs to be understood is why an insanity defense is necessary at all. A time-honored idea in Anglo-American jurisprudence is that conduct should be punished only when it is blameworthy. Accordingly, a generally overriding condition of criminal liability has been the presence of a criminal "state of mind," which lawyers call *mens rea*. The essence of the *mens rea* requirement is the conscious choice to commit an act warranting moral blame and deserving of punishment.

Although there is more than one legal category of *mens rea*, the one that applies in the context of the current controversy simply seeks to absolve from criminal responsibility certain individuals who—as a result of mental defect, lack of maturity, or other reasons—differ substantially from the rest of us. Why should mental infirmity be a ground for absolution? The explanation lies in an understanding of the purposes our society seeks to achieve through the enactment of penal laws. Criminal law is an expression of the community's belief that certain acts committed by individuals under certain conditions are blameworthy and deserving of punishment. The purposes to be served by the imposition of criminal sanctions have been grist for the mills of legal philosophers for centuries.

But from this age-old debate, four accepted objectives of criminal law have been distilled: rehabilitation, deterrence, protection of the public from dangerous individuals, and retribution (which I prefer to call *just punishment*).

An insanity defense, legal scholars have argued, is justified because none of these purposes is fulfilled when one who is truly irresponsible, and lacks substantial capacity to control his actions or comply with the law, is punished as a criminal. No rehabilitative function is served when the mentally incompetent are placed in prisons rather than in institutions specifically designed to treat them. No deterrence is achieved, since those who cannot restrain their conduct are, by definition, "undeterrable," and their imprisonment cannot serve as an example to other individuals who may contemplate committing a crime. Therefore, the only benefit that derives from placing a mentally incompetent individual in a prison, rather than in a hospital, is a punishment that seems not at all just. While society may need some form of punishment in the case of crimes committed by those who are able to control themselves, imprisonment of the truly incompetent, scholars maintain, is nothing more than sadistic revenge. And "revenge," in the words of Francis Bacon, "is a kind of wild justice which the more man's nature runs to, the more ought law to weed it out."

Even more vexing has been the attempt to determine what kinds and degrees of mental disorders should absolve an individual defendant of criminal responsibility. In short, what should be the standard governing the determination of legal insanity? From the layman's point of view, at least, that question contains a disconcerting Catch-22. After all, can anyone who commits a horrible crime really be in his right mind?

To understand how the American judicial system currently grapples with this question requires some knowledge of the history of the insanity defense. Revisions of the legal test for insanity over the centuries reflect concurrent developments in the fields of both psychiatry and the law. In 1582, William Lambard of Lincoln's Inn—one of England's several Inns of Court—articulated the test in a primitive fashion by asking whether "a man or a natural fool or a lunatic in the time of his lunacy, or a child who apparently has no knowledge of good or evil," committed the offending act. Lambard argued that an act committed by such a person could not be considered felonious because the offender "cannot be said to have any understanding will." Over the next 150 years, emphasis shifted from this quasi-religious concept of good and evil to the more modern concept of knowledge of right and wrong. In 1724, a test was devised in England which provided for exculpation where the defendant "doth not know what he is doing no more than . . . a wild beast."

In the 17th and early 18th centuries, belief in the practice of witch-craft was widespread and this, unfortunately, influenced popular legal conceptions of the sources of mental disorders. Beginning in the 18th century, other approaches to the problem of mental illness began to develop. Phrenologists, for example, asserted that the human brain was divided into 37 separate regions, each with a unique mental function. One of these areas, they maintained, was responsible for "destruc-tiveness" because it was located above the ear, believed to be the widest section of the skull of carnivorous animals. Other experts of that era advanced a concept known as monomania. Their belief was that mental disorder occurred when one insane idea predominated while the rest of the cognitive processes remained normal. The science of the mind, at this point, was clearly not in a position to offer the legal world adequate conceptual tools for a sound and workable insanity defense.

The showcase for 19th-century ideas on insanity as a defense for criminal liability was the celebrated case of Daniel M'Naghten, decided in England in 1843. The parallels between M'Naghten's story and the Hinckley case are striking. Like Hinckley, M'Naghten attempted to as-sassinate his nation's leader, in this case Prime Minister Robert Peel. M'Naghten also failed in his attempt. Peel happened to be riding in Queen Victoria's carriage during her absence from London, and M'Naghten mistakenly shot and killed the Prime Minister's secretary, who was riding in Peel's carriage.

M'Naghten was found not guilty by reason of insanity following a lengthy trial, at which evidence was presented to show M'Naghten suf-fered from the delusion he was being persecuted by many people, includ-ing the Prime Minister. The trial was significant because defense counsel relied heavily on quotations from Dr. Isaac Ray's historic work, "Medical Jurisprudence of Insanity," which had been published in 1838. That book severely criticized phrenology, monomania and the early definitions of mental incompetency based solely on whether the defendant could dis-tinguish right from wrong. The court was so impressed with the defense's reasoning, including the argument that a defect in one aspect of the personality could spill over and affect other areas, that Lord Chief Justice Tindal practically directed the jury to bring in a verdict for the defense.

Many in England were not pleased with this development in the law. With a perspective much like that following the Hinckley verdict, the Lord Chancellor addressed the House of Lords and condemned M'Naghten's acquittal. Having survived several attempts on her life, and concerned that the growing social upheaval in England at that time could lead to more violence, the Queen herself addressed the House of Lords and asked them to gather the judges of the common-law courts to have them give their opinion on the rationale behind the verdict. In this highly charged atmosphere, 14 of the 15 common-law judges, including Lord Chief Justice Tindal, repudiated the approach that led to M'Naghten's acquittal and announced what has since been known, ironically, as the M'Naghten Rule. Reaffirming the restricted right-wrong test—which was deeply rooted in earlier concepts of mental illness and the erroneous theories of phrenology and monomania—this rule focuses exclusively on whether "at the time of the committing of the act, the party accused was laboring under such a defect of reason from disease of the mind as not to know the nature and quality of the act he was doing, or if he did know it, that he did not know he was doing what was wrong."

The British continue to follow the M'Naghten Rule today. And approximately 20 states in our country also continue to use this standard to determine criminal responsibility. But in many ways, developments in modern psychiatry have rendered the M'Naghten Rule obsolete. This standard focuses only on the cognitive elements of the human psyche: the ability to know right from wrong. It prevents testimony relating to other mental disorders that may have produced the defendant's conduct.

Dr. Lawrence C. Kolb, Professor Emeritus of Psychiatry at Columbia University College of Physicians and Surgeons and former director of the New York Psychiatric Institute, has stated that psychiatric participation at trials using the M'Naghten test amounts to nothing less than professional perjury. In excluding all but the single cognitive aspect, the test recognizes no other type of incompetency. Yet our mental institutions undoubtedly contain many inmates who can distinguish right from wrong to some extent but who have no control over their wrongful actions. The problem with the M'Naghten Rule then, is that it results in the punishment of individuals who are not mentally responsible for their actions, individuals who require treatment in mental hospitals, but who instead are placed in prisons where they receive no meaningful psychiatric care and who may later be released as potential recidivists.

Many courts have attempted to improve upon the M'Naghten definition of mental incompetency. One early approach was the adoption of an exemption from criminal liability for those defendants driven by "irresistible impulses." As that requirement was interpreted, however, it focused exclusively on spur-of-the-moment reactions and excluded any crimes committed after prolonged contemplation. This distinction between actions resulting from a sudden and explosive fit and those produced by other kinds of mental disorders was arbitrary and unreasoned.

It was not until 1954 that most American courts or legislatures began to recognize that a wide variety of diseases or defects may impair the mind. In that year, in *Durham v. United States*, Judge David Bazelon, of the United States Court of Appeals for the District of Columbia, authored an opinion setting forth the rule that a defendant is not criminally responsible "if his unlawful act was the product of a mental disease or defect." While this rule remedied many of the difficulties of the over-simplified M'Naghten test, it proved too general and too difficult to guide juries in their legal responsibilities.

The standard set forth in the opinion I wrote in *United States v. Freeman*, 1966, was originally formulated by the American Law Institute after consultation with distinguished lawyers, psychiatrists and penologists. It provides that "a person is not responsible for criminal conduct if at the time of such conduct as a result of mental disease or defect he lacks substantial capacity either to appreciate the wrongfulness of his conduct or to conform his conduct to the requirements of law." With slight alterations, this formulation is now the law in a majority of states and Federal circuits. It has been endorsed by the American Bar Association House of Delegates, and its continued use was recommended in the Provisional Criminal Justice Mental Health Standards recently drafted by a group of leading lawyers, psychiatrists and professors under the aegis of Prof. B. James George Jr. of the New York Law School. As is apparent from its language, this test focuses not only on the defendant's understanding of his conduct, which remains a key element in any inquiry into mental capacity, but also on the defendant's ability to control his actions. It would absolve from criminal punishment an individual who knows what he is doing yet is driven to crime by delusions, fears or compulsions. This result conforms to the modern view of the mind as a unified entity whose functioning may be impaired in numerous ways.

Formulating an appropriate standard, of course, represents only the beginning, and not the end, of the complexities of the insanity defense. As the Hinckley trial reveals, the real difficulties commence when any definition of insufficient mental capacity must be applied in the courtroom. The Hinckley jury's obvious confusion after hearing seven psychiatrists tell as many different stories represents a serious problem. Indeed, Dr. Alan Stone, psychiatrist and professor of law at Harvard Law School, has described the typical trial involving the insanity defense as a three-ring circus where the lawyers are the ringmasters and the psychiatrists the clowns. Dr. Lee Stewart Coleman, a psychiatrist in Berkeley, Calif., has stated that psychiatrists are "widely unreliable" as witnesses, capable of recording only subjective impressions. He maintains that "the courts would be better off" without psychiatric testimony. In light of all this, it is not surprising that many excellent psychiatrists now refuse to testify at trials. At the same time, there are always going to be a few psychiatrists willing to tailor their opinions to the needs of the side paying the bill.

Other critics have blamed the jury system itself, arguing that lay jurors are simply not qualified to interpret the abstruse information that psychiatrists provide. These detractors go too far, however, by failing to recognize the important functions juries serve in cases where legal standards seem incompatible with responsible lay judgments. Indeed, in evaluating conflicting descriptions of a set of events, the jury has been known to rely upon its own experience to fashion a more appropriate decision than would be suggested by a dry and formal review of the evidence.

The task assigned to the jury in the Hinckley trial, however, namely that of determining mental competency, differs significantly from the jury's role in the typical criminal or civil case, where the jury is called upon only to weigh factual evidence. In the Hinckley case, the basic facts—that he shot President Reagan and three other victims—were uncontested, in this regard there was nothing for the jury to decide. In addition, psychiatrists are not typical witnesses: When attempting to evaluate the psychiatrists' testimony, the jury was not assessing who was telling the truth and who was not. Unlike average witnesses, psychiatrists and other experts are permitted to give opinion testimony. The jury's job is essentially to determine which psychiatrists are stating the correct medical opinion. And in this case, because the burden of proof was placed squarely on the Government, the jurors were instructed that if they had a reasonable doubt concerning the testimony of the prosecution psychiatrists on Hinckley's mental condition, they should return a verdict of not guilty.

It is not entirely unusual, of course, to require juries to evaluate conflicting-opinion testimony. Medical malpractice cases, for example, often call upon jurors to determine which doctor is presenting a more accurate interpretation of the medical evidence. In such cases, however, doctors frequently base their testimony on objective evidence. Little disagreement will exist on the issue of whether a biopsy reveals a malignant or a benign tumor. By contrast, the ambiguities in current psychiatric learning make it likely that psychiatrists hired by the adversaries will adopt diametrically opposed positions in their trial testimony. In addition, this uncertain quality of psychiatric judgments increases the difficulty judges face in instructing the jury on its function as the ultimate arbiter of the defendant's criminal responsibility. Caught in the crosscurrents of esoteric professional jargon, jurors may forget that they and not the experts are charged with the responsibility to decide whether a defendant should be held morally and legally accountable for his acts. At the same time, we cannot ignore the increased knowledge of the workings of the mind that psychiatry now provides.

Faced with this dilemma, there are at least two avenues to pursue. Steps can be taken to assist the jury in its difficult deliberations. And ways of removing from the jury those questions that are more properly left solely for judicial and expert consideration can be explored.

The task of assisting a jury is a delicate one. There is always the danger that any participation by the court will be viewed not as guidance but as interference with the jury's deliberations. Certain measures, however, can be adopted relatively safely. Judges, through case-by-case experience, can develop instructions that will more precisely explain to the jury how to appraise psychiatric testimony. The jury can be told that psychiatrists are only giving opinions which the jury is at all times free to ignore. The jury should also be instructed on the precise judgment that the court expects concerning the defendant's mental capacity.

One means of improving the guidance provided juries is to ask them, in addition to returning a general verdict of guilty or not guilty, to answer questions concerning the defendant's competency. (It should be noted that juries may be instructed to do this pursuant to the Federal Rules of Criminal Procedure, but that such instructions are not given often enough.) For example, juries might be asked whether the defendant intended his action, whether he understood that his action was wrongful, and whether he had the capacity to comply with the law. By examining the consistency of the jury's answers, the court may determine whether the jurors carefully considered and understood the evidence of insanity.

In suggesting that more effort should be devoted to jury instructions, let me hasten to add that I in no way wish to be understood as criticizing the fine instructions delivered by Judge Parker in the Hinckley trial. Rather, it is my objective to suggest possible paths to travel in the search for improvement of the system in which Judge Parker was required to operate. At the same time, it is clear that there are no magic words or special incantations that will make the complexities disappear altogether.

Another reform would be the creation of panels of independent psychiatrists and psychologists who would be appointed by the judge and appear at trial to testify as the court's experts. At the beginning of the trial, such professionals could assist judges by preparing memorandums, which would be made available to all parties, concerning the difficult psychological concepts involved in the case. They could also help the jury to evaluate the partisan testimony of expert witnesses called by either the prosecution or the defense. Of course, any such expert would also be subject to cross-examination by either. (Rule 706 of the Federal Rules of Evidence now authorizes the Federal courts to appoint expert witnesses of their own selection, and such procedures could be used more frequently in the context of trials involving the insanity defense.) The use of panels might reduce the reluctance of many professionals to become involved in litigation. And perhaps it would also discourage the use of those few individuals whose opinions are flexible and available to the highest bidder.

The use of a panel of court-appointed experts is not without dangers, however. The independence of the board from any influence by the prosecuting arm of Government would be essential to safeguard the impartiality of the trial. Moreover, the trial judge needs to take care that the court-appointed experts do not acquire an aura of infallibility in the jury's eyes. There is also a possibility that the introduction of more psychiatrists into the courtroom will only result in further confusion for the jury.

Legislatures in eight states have taken another approach to the problem of crime and insanity by experimenting with a new verdict: guilty but mentally ill. Basically, the jurors may render a verdict of guilty but mentally ill if they are convinced that the defendant is mentally ill but that his mental illness does not negate his ability to understand the unlawful nature of his conduct or his ability to conform his actions to the requirements of the law. Upon pronouncement of such a verdict, the defendant is sentenced as a criminal, but undergoes psychiatric evaluation prior to actual imprisonment. If the psychiatrists find that he is indeed mentally ill, the defendant is transferred to the state mental-health department for treatment. If at any time prior to the completion of his sentence, he is found to have recovered his mental health, he is taken from the mental institution and returned to the state's department of corrections to complete his prison term. Questioned after their controversial decision, several jurors in the Hinckley case reported that they would have preferred such a verdict. The Attorney General's Task Force on Violent Crime, in a report released one year ago, recommended that this new verdict be enacted into Federal law.

The old adage that hard cases make bad law should deter us from adopting such innovations without considered analysis. A careful look at this new verdict indicates that it may in some instances increase rather than reduce jury confusion. Juries faced with an insanity plea have three possible verdicts to choose from: guilty, guilty but mentally ill, and not guilty by reason of insanity. The danger is that they may often choose the middle option as a form of compromise verdict rather than as a carefully reasoned decision. (So far, however, this does not appear to be the case. Studies indicate that in Michigan, for example, where the guilty but mentally ill verdict was passed into law seven years ago, there has been no appreciable change in the number of defendants found not guilty by reason of insanity since the introduction of the new verdict.)

Experiments with a guilty but mentally ill verdict must also respond to a set of practical concerns. Psychiatric evaluations of convicted defendants are routinely included in presentencing reports delivered to judges prior to the imposition of sentences. Procedures must be established to insure that such psychiatric evaluations are thorough and not simply a meaningless ritual in cases in which judges have an option (but no compulsion) to transfer defendants found guilty but mentally ill to the custody of the state mental-health department. If such guidelines are not well drafted, there is a possibility that defendants found guilty under the new verdict will be treated little differently from convicted defendants under previous law. Moreover, proper application of a guilty but mentally ill verdict requires that states commit the necessary resources to house and treat those recommended for psychiatric supervision. If we are serious about treating the ills of the insanity laws, we must be willing to pay the medical bills for the cures.

Despite these practical difficulties, important and justifiable motives underlie efforts to give juries the option of recognizing that some defendants may be criminally responsible for their actions but nonetheless have a need for psychiatric treatment. As the post-verdict doubts of the Hinckley jurors have revealed, members of the community often have legitimate disagreements concerning wrongdoers who have mental or emotional problems. On the one hand, we desire to express our most profound disapproval of violent and reprehensible acts so that other potential offenders do not gain the impression that we condone their actions. On the other hand, we wish to show mercy to those whose diminished mental capacities render them unable to control themselves. A verdict of guilty but mentally ill would provide society with an opportunity to express both these conflicting desires.

The task ahead, then, lies in the direction of testing and experimenting with different versions of the new verdict that will come to grips with these practical problems. One possible amendment to procedures governing the guilty but mentally ill verdict would be to require that whenever this verdict is rendered, the defendant, after being sentenced to a term of incarceration appropriate to a guilty verdict, would be placed for some minimum period of time (for example, one year) in a hospital rather than a penal institution. After that time, the state could be required to prove that the defendant had sufficiently recovered from his mental illness to warrant transfer to conventional prison. The defendant would not, however, be eligible to be released from institutional custody before serving the balance of his sentence.

A second suggestion worthy of exploration is the proposal to combine the verdict of guilty but mentally ill with measures to relieve juries of responsibility for deciphering psychiatric testimony. This could be accomplished through the bifurcation of criminal trials in which the insanity defense is raised. During the first stage, the jury would consider whether the defendant is guilty of each element of the crime charged. During the second, the judge would decide whether the defendant possessed the mental capacity necessary to be punished as a criminal. This approach would place in the judge's hands the responsibility for evaluating much of the complex psychiatric testimony. Such innovations, however, put forth in an effort to lift from the shoulders of lay jurors the heavy burden of interpreting conflicting psychiatric testimony, must respond to important constitutional considerations based on the Sixth Amendment to the United States Constitution, which guarantees a criminal defendant's right to a trial by jury.

As I described earlier, one of the basic principles of the Anglo-American criminal-justice system has been that no one can be found guilty of a crime without the requisite criminal intent, or in legal terms, *mens rea*. This concept is so deeply embedded in our law that virtually every statute concerning violent crime includes intent as an element of the crime charged. Accordingly, pursuant to due-process principles, the jury, in the first stage of this revised system, would still have to determine that the defendant intended to commit his crime.

This constitutional requirement does not preclude further experimentation. Initially, the determination of intent differs significantly from the inquiry into a defendant's sanity as defined by modern standards. Under one possible approach, the jury would need only find that the defendant understood the nature of his actions when he pulled the trigger and acted with the purpose of achieving the proscribed result.

The judge would then be required to apply the more modern insanity standard, which focuses on whether the defendant is mentally capable of conforming his conduct to the requirements of law. One measure the trial judge could take to avoid a constitutional challenge would be to urge both the prosecution and defense to waive the right to a jury determination on the issue of insanity. Since it is clear that psychiatric testimony is often too technical for a lay jury to understand, enlightened lawyers would welcome a court rather than a jury determination of the issue in many cases. Such a technique is often employed in complicated antitrust and patent cases.

Giving the judge added responsibilities may increase the likelihood that the insanity standard will be more uniformly applied and that defendants who do not meet this standard will be convicted and not be prematurely released. One serious shortcoming of this approach, however, would be a partial loss of the jury's constitutional function as the sole evaluator of the defendant's moral responsibility.

In addition, some modification of the rules concerning the burden of proof might be considered. The burden of proof determines which side should be required to convince the jury of its claims concerning the defendant's sanity. Under the standard applied in the Hinckley trial, for example (a Federal standard since Congress has made attempted assassination of the President a Federal crime), the Government was required to prove to the jury's satisfaction that he was sane beyond any reasonable doubt when he shot President Reagan and the three other men. A moment's reflection reveals the extreme difficulty of this task. It is hard to imagine trying to prove to anyone beyond a reasonable doubt that a particular person is sane. What evidence would you produce? Considering that sanity is defined by the law and not medicine, even the testimony of psychiatrists would hardly prove sufficient.

It is thus not surprising that quite a few states and the District of Columbia now shift the burden of proof to the defendant and require him to show by a preponderance of evidence that, at the time of his crime, he lacked the requisite mental capacity to be held responsible. The British also place the burden of proof on the defendant. Given the difficulty in proving an individual sane beyond a reasonable doubt, especially when that person has committed a heinous offense, a rule placing the burden of proof on the defendant seems preferable.

This rule, however, may also be subject to constitutional challenges. Although the Supreme Court has held, as long ago as 1952 in *Leland v. Oregon*, that the burden of proof on the issue of insanity may be shifted to the defendant, the Court has also held more recently in *In re Winship*, 1970, that the Government must prove every element of the crime beyond a reasonable doubt. As I explained above, one of the elements of almost every crime is that the defendant must have intended his actions. Accordingly, where the defendant claims that mental incapacity interfered with his ability to form a criminal intent, an ambiguity exists concerning the constitutionality of shifting the burden of proof to the defense. Recent Supreme Court cases have not eliminated this ambiguity, and this complex subject must await further judicial resolution.

One of the problems created by current rules relating to the burden of proof, however, calls for more immediate action. In many states, after the jury has found a defendant not guilty by reason of insanity, it becomes the obligation of the *prosecution* to prove to the satisfaction of the court that the defendant does, indeed, have a dangerous mental disorder or is mentally ill before he may be committed to a psychiatric hospital. This seemingly benign procedural requirement can result in the bizarre possibility that the state will fail in its attempt to prove the defendant sane at the criminal trial and then, at the post-acquittal hearing, fail to prove the defendant sufficiently mentally ill to require commitment. In addition, many experts argue that the procedures for release of an individual committed to an institution after being found not guilty by reason of insanity are often not sufficiently stringent. As a result, it too frequently occurs that an individual is prematurely released from a hospital only to engage again in violent acts.

In the final analysis, the key question facing society is this: What should be done with mentally disturbed offenders. As psychiatrists struggle to improve their treatment methods, judges and legislators must continue to seek procedures that will not only keep dangerous persons off the streets, but also avoid the revenge syndrome of penalizing as criminals those who are truly unable to conform their conduct to the requirements of the law.

At the same time, we must endeavor to fashion fair and workable rules governing the insanity defense, for the criminal-justice system will fail if the public loses respect for society's ability to apply the criminal law in a rational fashion. If we are serious in our efforts to remedy the shortcomings of the present approaches to the insanity defense, we must be open to experimentation. Yet momentary outrage in response to a particular verdict should not lead to incautious response. As Justice Brandeis once wrote: "We must be ever on our guard, lest we erect our prejudices into legal principles. If we would guide by the light of reason, we must let our minds be cold."

QUESTIONS FOR READING, RESPONDING, AND WRITING

Summarizing Main Points

1. Near the beginning of his essay, Kaufman states that the "insanity defense is rarely used and even more rarely successful," and provides statistical evidence to support this statement. However, he goes on to state that statistical evidence "belies the true impact of the insanity defense upon our criminal justice system." What is that "true impact," according to Kaufman?
2. Why, according to Kaufman, is an insanity defense necessary? List the four reasons he gives. What does he mean when he says that the mentally ill are, "by definition, 'undeterrable' "? What, according to Kaufman, is the difference between the verdicts "not guilty by reason of insanity" and "guilty, but mentally ill"?

Analyzing Methods of Discourse

1. Kaufman traces the history of the insanity defense. Try to summarize the changes it has gone through and the reasons for those changes. How does Kaufman's presentation of the history of the insanity plea relate to the "case" he presents on the current problem with the insanity defense?
2. Why do you suppose Kaufman begins his essay with a quotation from John Hinckley, Jr.'s "sentencing speech"? What relation does it bear to the argument that follows it?

Focusing on the Field

1. List the "avenues" that need to be pursued, the "tasks" that need to be performed, and the problems attendant on both, as Kaufman describes them. What do you make of his "case"? Do you find his proposed "solutions" acceptable? As an average reader, how do you react to Kaufman's proposal to give the judge in an insanity trial added responsibility so as to relieve the jury of dealing with often highly technical psychiatric testimony?
2. Early in the essay, Kaufman tells the reader: "My own views on the subject can be traced back to 1966, when I authored the opinion in *United States v. Freeman* for the United States Court of Appeals for the Second Circuit, which established the standard for insanity pleas in the district courts of New York, Connecticut, and Vermont." What bearing does this information have on the reader's attitude toward Kaufman and the positions he advocates later?

Writing Assignments

1. Taking note of Kaufman's argument, write a short essay in which you give reasons for your agreement or disagreement with his position.
2. In "The Art of Psychoanalysis," Jay Haley argues in a satirical fashion that an individual's ability or inability to use "Freud's ploys" marks him as neurotic, psychotic, or "sensible." Study Haley's essay and in a short essay of your own apply his analysis to Kaufman's argument on the insanity plea. Do you feel that Haley would support Kaufman's position? Support your conclusions with evidence from both essays.

George F. Kennan

CEASE THIS MADNESS
The Nuclear Arms Race

Born in Milwaukee, Wisconsin in 1904, George Frost Kennan graduated from Princeton University, where he is now associated with the Institute of Advanced Study. According to one critic, his writings provide "a wealth of information, a bedrock of integrity, and a fountainhead of thorough understanding of world politics." *Russia Leaves the War*, the first part of Kennan's three-part study, *Soviet-American Relations, 1917–1920*, was awarded the 1957 Pulitzer Prize in history as well as a National Book Award, a Francis Parkman Prize, and a Bancroft Prize. Kennan won a second Pulitzer and a National Book Award for his *Memoirs, 1925–1950*, and among his other numerous awards, Kennan has received over a dozen honorary doctorates. He has served as president of both the National Institute of Arts and Letters and the American Academy of Arts and Letters.

Kennan writes so knowledgeably on foreign relations in part because he has lived them. Between 1927 and 1952, Kennan served the State Department as consul of Vienna and Prague, held posts in Hamburg, Lisbon, and Berlin, and was ambassador to Moscow. For several years, he was chief long-range advisor to the secretary of state, helping to fashion American foreign policy in the 1950s. Kennan has lectured at Harvard, Princeton, Oxford, and the University of Chicago, and among his many books, *American Democracy, 1900–1950* and *Realities of American Foreign Policy* are still used as textbooks in the history of American foreign policy.

When I glance back over the past fifty years, it seems evident that the East–West relationship has been burdened by certain unique factors that lie in the very nature of the respective societies. When it comes to describing these factors, permit me—so far as the Western side is concerned—to confine myself to my own society.

I have no doubt that there are a number of habits, customs, and uniformities of behavior, all deeply ingrained in the American tradition, that complicate for others the conduct of relations with the American government. There is, for example, the extensive fragmentation of authority throughout our government—a fragmentation that often makes it hard for a foreign representative to know who speaks for the American government as a whole. There is the absence of any collective Cabinet responsibility, or indeed of any system of mutual responsibility between the executive and legislative branches of government. There are the large powers exercised, even in matters that affect foreign relations, by state, local, or private authorities with which the foreign representative cannot normally deal. There is the susceptibility of the political establishment to the emotions and vagaries of public opinion, particularly in this day of confusing interaction between the public and the various commercialized mass media. There is the inordinate influence exercised over American foreign policy by individual lobbies and other organized minorities. And there is the extraordinary difficulty a democratic society experiences in taking a balanced view of any other country that has acquired the image of a military and political enemy—the tendency, that is, to dehumanize that image, to oversimplify it, to ignore its complexities. Democratic societies do very poorly in coping, philosophically, with the phenomenon of serious challenge and hostility to their values.

In the light of these conditions, I can well understand that dealing with our government can be a frustrating experience at times for any foreign representative. I regret these circumstances, as do some other Americans. They constitute one of the reasons I personally advocate a more modest, less ambitious American foreign policy than do many of my compatriots. But these conditions flow from the very nature of our society, and they are not likely to be significantly changed at any early date.

When we look at the Soviet regime, we also encounter a series of customs and habits, equally deeply rooted in history and weighing heavily on the external relationships of that regime. These, strangely enough, seem to have been inherited much less from the models of the recent Petersburg epoch than from those of the earlier Grand Duchy of Muscovy. And they have found a remarkable reinforcement in some of the established traditions of Leninist Marxism itself: in its high sense of orthodoxy, its intolerance for contrary opinion, its tendency to identify ideological dissent with moral perversity, its ingrained distrust of the heretical outsider.

One example is the extraordinary passion for secrecy in all governmental affairs—a passion that prevents the Soviet authorities from revealing to outsiders even those aspects of their own motivation that, if revealed, would be reassuring to others. Excessive secrecy tends, after all, to invite excessive curiosity, and thus serves to provoke the very impulses against which it professes to guard.

Along with this passion for secrecy goes a certain conspiratorial style and tradition of decision-making, particularly within the Party—a practice that may have its internal uses but often inspires distrust. And there is the extraordinary espionomania that appears to pervade so much of Soviet thinking. Espionage is a minor nuisance, I suppose, to most governments. But nowhere, unless it be in Albania, is the preoccupation with it so intense as it appears to be in the Soviet Union. This is surprising, for one would expect to encounter it, if anywhere, in a weak and precariously situated state, not in one of the world's greatest and most secure military powers.

The foreigner who has to deal with the Soviet government often has the impression of being confronted, in rapid succession, with two quite disparate, and not easily reconcilable, Soviet personalities: one, a correct and reasonably friendly personality, which would like to see the relationship assume a normal, relaxed, and agreeable form; the other, a personality marked by a suspiciousness so dark and morbid, so sinister in its implications, as to constitute in itself a form of hostility. I sometimes wonder whether the Soviet leaders ever realize how much they damage their own interests by their cultivation of it.

Finally, there is the habit of polemic exaggeration and distortion, carried often to the point of denial of the obvious and solemn assertion of the absurd—a habit that has offended and antagonized a host of foreigners, and to which even some of the old-timers find it hard to accustom themselves.

These, then, are what I might call the permanent complications of the East–West relationship. There have been others, less permanent but even more serious.

The first, and the one that marked the relationship throughout much of the 1920s and 1930s, was the world-revolutionary commitment of the early Leninist regime, with its accompanying expression in rhetoric and activity. It is true that the period of the intensive pursuit of world revolution was brief. As early as 1921, aims of this nature were already ceasing to enjoy the highest priority in the policies of the Kremlin. Their place was being taken by concern with the preservation of the regime and the agricultural and industrial development of the country. But world-revolutionary rhetoric remained substantially unchanged throughout the twenties and much of the thirties; and Moscow continued to maintain in the various Western countries small factions of local Communist followers over whom it exerted the strictest discipline, whom it endeavored to use as instruments for the pursuit of its policies, and whose unquestioning loyalty it demanded even when this conflicted with loyalty to their own governments. So unusual were these practices, and so disturbing to Western governments and publics, that they formed the main cause for the high degree of tension between Russia and the West.

With the triumph of Hitler in Germany, however, an important change occurred. Beginning about 1935, the menace of Hitler began to loom larger in Western eyes than did the ideological differences with Soviet communism or the resentment of world-revolutionary activities. The result was that the Soviet Union came to be viewed in the West no longer primarily from the standpoint of its hostility to Western capitalism but rather from the standpoint of its relationship to Nazi Germany.

And this had several confusing consequences. For one thing, it tended to obscure from the attention of the Western public the full savagery of the Stalinist purges of the late 1930s. But then, after 1941 the common association of the Western powers with the Soviet Union in the war against Germany gave rise to sentimental enthusiasms in the West and to unreal hopes of a happy and constructive postwar collaboration with Soviet Russia. It was this factor, as the war came to an end, that brought the various Western statesmen to accept without serious remonstrance not only the recovery by the Soviet Union of those border areas of the former Russian empire that had been lost at the time of the Revolution but also the establishment of a virtual Soviet military-political hegemony over the remainder of the eastern half of the European continent; in other words, a geopolitical change of historic dimensions, bound to complicate the restoration, in the postwar years, of anything resembling a really stable balance of power.

It was not surprising that when the war came to an end, and people in the West turned to the construction of a new world order, a reaction set in. There was a sudden realization that the destruction of Germany's armed power and the effective cession to the Soviet Union of a vast area of military deployment in the very heart of the continent had left Western Europe highly vulnerable to a Soviet military attack, or at least to heavy military-political pressures from the Soviet side. Added to this was the growing realization that with the establishment of Communist regimes, subservient to Moscow, in the various Eastern European countries, the relations of those countries with the West had become subject to the same limiting factors that already operated in relations with the Soviet Union. Then came the Korean War—a conflict in which, though Soviet forces were not actually involved, people in the West soon came to see a further manifestation of Soviet aggressiveness. And it was just at this time that the nuclear weapon began to cast its baleful shadow over the entire world, stirring up the fear, confusion, and defensive panic that were bound to surround a weapon of such apocalyptic—indeed, suicidal— implications.

The death of Stalin, the establishment of the dominant position of Khrushchev, and the accompanying relaxations in Soviet policy gave rise to new hopes for the peaceful resolution of East–West differences. Although Khrushchev was crude, he wanted no war; and he believed in human communication. But he overplayed his hand. And such favorable prospects as his influence presented went largely without response in the West. The compulsions of military competition and military thinking were already too powerful.

For, during this entire period, Soviet leaders persisted in the traditional Russian tendency to go too far in the cultivation of military strength, particularly conventional strength. They continued to maintain along their western borders, as their czarist predecessors had done before them, forces numerically greater than anyone else could see the need for. And the situation was not made better by the tendency of Western strategists and military leaders to exaggerate the strength of these forces, with a view to wheedling larger military appropriations out of their own reluctant parliaments, or by the tendency of the Western media to dramatize these exaggerations as a means of capturing public attention.

The Americans, meanwhile, unable to accommodate to the recognition that the long-range nuclear missile had rendered their country no longer defensible, threw themselves headlong into the nuclear arms race, followed at every turn by the Russians. In the U-2 episode and the Cuban missile crisis, the two great nuclear powers traded fateful mistakes, further confirming each other's conviction that armed force, and armed force alone, would eventually determine the outcome of their differences. Out of all these ingredients was brewed the immensely disturbing and tragic situation in which we find ourselves today: anxious competition in the development of new armaments; blind dehumanization of the prospective adversary; systematic distortion of that adversary's motivation and intentions; steady displacement of political considerations by military ones in the calculations of statesmanship; in short, a dreadful militarization of the entire East–West relationship.

This moral and political cul-de-sac represents a basic change, as compared with the first two decades of Soviet power, in the source of East–West tensions. It is not the capacity of the Kremlin for promoting social revolution in other countries that is feared and resented. Rather, the Soviet Union is seen primarily as an aggressive military menace.

But there is no rational reason for the militarization of the Cold War. Neither side wants a third world war. Neither side sees in such a war a promising means of advancing its interests. The West has no intention of attacking the Soviet Union. The Soviet leadership, I am satisfied, has no intention of attacking Western Europe. The interests of the two sides conflict, to be sure, at a number of points. Experience has proven, most unfortunately, that in smaller and more remote conflicts, where the stakes are less than total, armed force on a limited scale might still continue to play a certain role, whether we like it or not. The United States has used its armed forces in this manner three times since World War II: in Lebanon, in the Dominican Republic, and in Vietnam. The Soviet Union now does likewise in Afghanistan. I am not entertaining, by these remarks, the chimera of a total world disarmament. But for the maintenance of armed forces on a scale that envisages the total destruction of an entire people there is no rational justification. Such a practice can flow only from fear, and irrational fear at that. It can reflect no positive aspirations, and it is dangerous.

No one will understand the danger we are all in today unless he recognizes that governments in this modern world have not yet learned how to create and cultivate great military establishments, particularly those that include the weapons of mass destruction, without becoming the servants rather than the masters of what they have created. Modern history offers no example of the cultivation by rival powers of armed force on a huge scale that did not in the end lead to an outbreak of hostilities. And there is no reason to believe that we are greater, or wiser, than our ancestors. It would take a very strong voice, indeed a powerful chorus of voices, from the outside, to say to the decision-makers of the two superpowers what should be said to them.

"For the love of God, of your children, and of the civilization to which you belong, cease this madness. You have a duty not just to the generation of the present; you have a duty to civilization's past, which you threaten to render meaningless, and to its future, which you threaten to render nonexistent. You are mortal men. You are capable of error. You have no right to hold in your hands—there is no one wise enough and strong enough to hold in his hands—destructive powers sufficient to put an end to civilized life on a great portion of our planet. No one should wish to hold such powers. Thrust them from you. The risks you might thereby assume are not greater—could not be greater—than those which you are now incurring for us all."

But where is the voice powerful enough to say it?

There is a very special tragedy in this weapons race. It is tragic because it creates the illusion of a total conflict of interest between the two societies. It tends to conceal the fact that both of these societies are today confronted with internal problems never envisaged in the ideologies that originally divided them. In part, I am referring to environmental problems: the question whether great industrial societies can learn to exist without polluting, exhausting, and thus destroying the natural resources essential to their very existence. These are not only problems common to the two ideological worlds; they are ones the solution of which requires each other's collaboration, not each other's enmity.

But there are deeper problems—social, and even moral and spiritual—that increasingly affect all the highly industrialized, urbanized, and technologically advanced societies. What is involved here is essentially the question of how life is to be given an adequate meaning, how the quality of life and experience is to be assured for the individual citizen in the highly artificial and overcomplicated social environment that modern technology has created. Neither we in the West nor they in the East are doing well in the solution of these problems. We are both failing—each in our own way. If one wants an example of this, one has to look only at our respective failures in our approach to teenage youth. The Russians demoralize their young people by giving them too little freedom. We demoralize ours by giving them too much. Neither system finds itself able to provide them with the leadership and inspiration and guidance needed to realize their potential as individuals and to meet the responsibilities the future is inevitably going to place upon them.

And this is only one point at which we are failing. Neither here nor there is the direction of society really under control. We are all being swept along, in our fatuous pride, by currents we do not understand and over which we have no command. And we will not protect ourselves from the resulting dangers by continuing to pour great portions of our substance, year after year, into the instruments of military destruction. On the contrary, we will only be depriving ourselves, by this prodigality, of the resources essential for any hopeful attack on these profound emerging problems.

The present moment is in many respects a crucial one. Not for thirty years has political tension reached so dangerous a point as it has attained today. Not in all this time has there been so high a degree of misunderstanding, of suspicion, of bewilderment, and of sheer military fear.

The United States and possibly the Soviet Union will see extensive changes in governmental leadership this year. Will the new leaders be able to reverse these trends?

Two things, as I see it, would be necessary to make possible this transition.

First, statesmen on both sides should take their military establishments in hand and insist that these become the servants, not the masters and determinants, of political action. Both sides must learn to accept the fact that only in the reduction, not in the multiplication, of existing monstrous arsenals can the true security of any nation be found.

But beyond this, we must learn to recognize the gravity of the social, environmental, and even spiritual problems that assail us all in this unreal world of the machine, the television screen, and the computer. We and our Marxist friends must work together in finding hopeful responses to these insidious and ultimately highly dangerous problems.

QUESTIONS FOR READING, RESPONDING, AND WRITING

Summarizing Main Points

1. What is Kennan's main goal in this essay? List the similarities and differences he points out between Russia and the United States early in his essay. Do the differences seem so great? Are they more or less than you would have thought before reading the essay?
2. Kennan traces the comparison between Russia and the United States from World War I until the present. List the ways Kennan says that the relation between Russia and the United States has changed. List the ways it has remained the same.

Analyzing Methods of Discourse

1. In the latter part of his essay, Kennan quotes what he imagines "a chorus of voices, from the outside" might say "to the decision-makers of the two superpowers." Reread that paragraph. How does it compare in tone—in sentence length and structure, in word choice and length, in its point of view—with what precedes it and follows it? Why do you suppose Kennan changes his tone here?
2. Reread Kennan's last sentence. What words here make Kennan's solutions

seem more easily achievable than they have seemed elsewhere in the essay? Where else in the essay does Kennan's attitude toward the possibility of solving the problems he outlines seem to change? How does the reader recognize these changes?

Focusing on the Field

1. Kennan tries to prove that "there is no rational reason for the militarization of the Cold War." How does his history of the Cold—and Hot—Wars of the past support his claim?
2. Kennan talks often about the "dehumanization" of both governments. Why do you suppose that Kennan is so concerned with dehumanization? He also speaks early on about the "susceptibility of the political establishment to the emotions and vagaries of public opinion." What bearing does he think public opinion should have on the problems he is discussing?

Writing Assignments

1. In a short essay that considers the problems Kennan outlines, discuss your own view of disarmament. Do you feel the solution that Kennan offers is practical or possible? Why or why not?
2. Read Bruno Bettelheim's "Fairy Tale versus Myth." Following Bettelheim's guidelines, write a short political fairy tale of your own that illustrates the problematic escalation of armaments that Kennan outlines.

Malcolm Cowley

SOCIOLOGICAL HABIT PATTERNS IN LINGUISTIC TRANSMOGRIFICATION

"The writer's trade is a laborious, tedious, but lovely occupation of putting words into patterns. I love that trade, profession, vocation." Malcolm Cowley knows of what he speaks. In the selection that follows, Cowley wryly demonstrates not the tedious labor but the love of writing, as he chastens those social scientists who rely on the "new grammar and syntax" of a professional slang, a language "much inferior to English grammar in force and precision."

Always a student of language, Cowley first achieved acclaim as a literary historian with his intimate, autobiographical study of literary life in the 1920s, *Exile's Return* (1934). About the same time, Cowley helped organize the first American Writer's Congress, proving himself to be not only a fine critic, but an active reformer as well. Cowley, a cum laude graduate of Harvard University, was born in 1898 in Belsano, Pennsylvania. An award-winning critic and poet, Cowley has been a visiting professor at many colleges and universities around the country, and since 1948 has been literary advisor for the Viking Press. His studies of Hemingway, Whitman, Fitzgerald, Hawthorne, and, particularly, Faulkner have helped establish Cowley as among the finest literary historians and critics in America.

I have a friend who started as a poet and then decided to take a postgraduate degree in sociology. For his doctoral dissertation he combined his two interests by writing on the social psychology of poets. He had visited poets by the dozen, asking each of them a graded series of questions, and his conclusions from the interviews were modest and useful, though reported in what seemed to me a barbarous jargon. After reading the dissertation I wrote and scolded him. "You have such a fine sense of the poet's craft," I said, "that you shouldn't have allowed the sociologists to seduce you into writing their professional slang—or at least that's my judgmental response to your role selection."

My friend didn't write to defend himself; he waited until we met again. Then, dropping his voice, he said: "I knew my dissertation was badly written, but I had to get my degree. If I had written it in English, Professor Blank"—he mentioned a rather distinguished name—"would have rejected it. He would have said it was merely belletristic."

From that time I began to study the verbal folkways of the sociologists. I read what they call "the literature." A few sociologists write the best English they are capable of writing, and I suspect that they are the best men in the field. There is no mystery about them. If they go wrong, their mistakes can be seen and corrected. Others, however—and a vast majority—write in a language that has to be learned almost like Esperanto. It has a private vocabulary which, in addition to strictly sociological terms, includes new words for the commonest actions, feelings, and circumstances. It has the beginnings of a new grammar and syntax, much inferior to English grammar in force and precision. So far as it has an effect on standard English, the effect is largely pernicious.

Sometimes it misleads the sociologists themselves, by making them think they are profoundly scientific at points where they are merely being verbose. I can illustrate by trying a simple exercise in translation, that is, by expressing an idea first in English and then seeing what it looks like in the language of sociology.

An example that comes to hand is the central idea of an article by Norman E. Green, printed in the February, 1956, issue of the *American Sociological Review*. In English his argument might read as follows:

"Rich people live in big houses set farther apart than those of poor people. By looking at an aerial photograph of any American city, we can distinguish the richer from the poorer neighborhoods."

I won't have to labor over a sociological expression of the same idea, because Mr. Green has saved me the trouble. Here is part of his contribution to comparative linguistics. "In effect, it was hypothesized," he says— a sociologist must never say "I assumed," much less "I guessed"—"that certain physical data categories including housing types and densities, land use characteristics, and ecological location"—not just "location," mind you, but "ecological location," which is almost equivalent to locational location—"constitute a scalable content area. This could be called a continuum of residential desirability. Likewise, it was hypothesized that several social data categories, describing the same census tracts, and referring generally to the social stratification system of the city, would also be scalable. This scale could be called a continuum of socio-economic status. Thirdly, it was hypothesized that there would be a high positive correlation between the scale types on each continuum."

Here, after ninety-four words, Mr. Green is stating, or concealing, an assumption with which most laymen would have started, that rich people live in good neighborhoods. He is now almost ready for his deduction, or snapper:

"This relationship would define certain linkages between the social and physical structure of the city. It would also provide a precise definition of the commonalities among several spatial distributions. By the same token, the correlation between the residential desirability scale and the continuum of socio-economic status would provide an estimate of the predictive value of aerial photographic data relative to the social ecology of the city."

Mr. Green has used 160 words—counting "socio-economic" as only one—to express an idea that a layman would have stated in thirty-three. As a matter of fact, he has used many more than 160 words, since the whole article is an elaboration of this one thesis. Whatever may be the virtues of the sociological style—or Socspeak, as George Orwell might have called it—it is not specifically designed to save ink and paper. Let us briefly examine some of its other characteristics.

A layman's first impression of sociological prose, as compared with English prose, is that it contains a very large proportion of abstract words, most of them built on Greek or Latin roots. Often—as in the example just quoted—they are used to inflate or transmogrify a meaning that could be clearly expressed in shorter words surviving from King Alfred's time.

These Old English or Anglo-Saxon words are in number less than one-tenth of the entries in the largest dictionaries. But they are the names of everyday objects, attributes, and actions, and they are also the pronouns, the auxiliary verbs, and most of the prepositions and conjunctions, so that they form the grammatical structure of the language. The result is that most novelists use six Anglo-Saxon words for every one derived from French, Latin, or Greek, and that is probably close to the percentage that would be found in spoken English.

For comparison or contrast, I counted derivations in the passage quoted from the *American Sociological Review*, which is a typical example of "the literature." No less than 49 percent of Mr. Green's prose consists of words from foreign or classical languages. By this standard of measurement, his article is more abstruse than most textbooks of advanced chemistry and higher mathematics, which are said to contain only 40 percent of such words.

In addition to being abstruse, the language of the sociologists is also rich in neologisms. Apparently they like nothing better than inventing a word, deforming a word, or using a technical word in a strange context. Among their favorite nouns are "ambit," "extensity" (for "extent"), "scapegoating," "socializee," "ethnicity," "directionality," "cathexis," "affect" (for "feeling"), "maturation" (for both "maturing" and "maturity"), and "commonalities" (for "points in common"). Among their favorite adjectives are "processual," "prestigeful," and "insightful"—which last is insightful to murder—and perhaps their favorite adverb is "minimally," which seems to mean "in some measure." Their maximal pleasure seems to lie in making new combinations of nouns and adjectives and nouns used as adjectives, until the reader feels that he is picking his way through a field of huge boulders, lost among "universalistic-specific achievement patterns" and "complementary role-expectation-sanction systems," as he struggles vainly toward "ego-integrative action orientation," guided only by "orientation to improvement of the gratification-deprivation balance of the actor"—which last is Professor Talcott Parsons's rather involved way of saying "the pleasure principle."

But Professor Parsons, head of the Sociology Department at Harvard, is not the only delinquent recidivist, convicted time and again of corrupting the language. Among sociologists in general there is a criminal fondness for using complicated terms when there are simple ones available. A child says "Do it again," a teacher says "Repeat the exercise," but the sociologist says "It was determined to replicate the investigation." Instead of saying two things are alike or similar, as a layman would do, the sociologist describes them in being either isomorphic or homologous. Instead of saying that they are different, he calls them allotropic. Every form of leadership or influence is called a hegemony.

A sociologist never cuts anything in half or divides it in two like a layman. Instead he dichotomizes it, bifurcates it, subjects it to a process of binary fission, or restructures it in a dyadic conformation—around polar foci.

So far I have been dealing with the vocabulary of sociologists, but their private language has a grammar too, and one that should be the subject of intensive research by the staff of a very well-endowed foundation. I have space to mention only a few of its more striking features.

The first of these is the preponderance of nouns over all the other parts of speech. Nouns are used in hyphenated pairs of dyads, and sometimes in triads, tetrads, and pentads. Nouns are used as adjectives without change of form, and they are often used as verbs, with or without the suffix "ize." The sociological language is gritty with nouns, like sanded sugar.

On the other hand, it is poor in pronouns. The singular pronoun of the first person has entirely disappeared, except in case histories, for the sociologist never comes forward as "I." Sometimes he refers to himself as "the author" or "the investigator," or as "many sociologists," or even as "the best sociologists," when he is advancing a debatable opinion. On rare occasions he calls himself "we," like Queen Elizabeth speaking from the throne, but he usually avoids any personal form and writes as if he were a force of nature.

The second-personal pronoun has also disappeared, for the sociologist pretends to be speaking not to living persons but merely for the record. Masculine and feminine pronouns of the third person are used with parsimony, and most sociologists prefer to say "the subject," or "X——," or "the interviewee," where a layman would use the simple "he" or "she." As for the neuter pronoun of the third person, it survives chiefly as the impersonal subject of a passive verb. "It was hypothesized," we read, or "It was found to be the case." Found by *whom?*

The neglect and debasement of the verb is another striking feature of "the literature." The sociologist likes to reduce a transitive verb to an intransitive, so that he speaks of people's adapting, adjusting, transferring, relating, and identifying, with no more of a grammatical object than if they were coming or going. He seldom uses transitive verbs of action, like "break," "injure," "help," and "adore." Instead he uses verbs of relation, verbs which imply that one series of nouns and adjectives, used as the compound subject of a sentence, is larger or smaller than, dominant over, subordinate to, causative of, or resultant from another series of nouns and adjectives.

Considering this degradation of the verb, I have wondered how one of Julius Caesar's boasts could be translated into Socspeak. What Caesar wrote was "*Veni, vidi, vici*"—only three words, all of them verbs. The English translation is in six words: "I came, I saw, I conquered," and three of the words are first-personal pronouns, which the sociologist is taught to avoid. I suspect that he would have to write: "Upon the advent of the investigator, his hegemony became minimally coextensive with the areal unit rendered visible by his successive displacements in space."

The whole sad situation leads me to dream of a vast allegorical painting called "The Triumph of the Nouns." It would depict a chariot of victory drawn by the other conquered parts of speech—the adverbs and adjectives still robust, if yoked and harnessed; the prepositions bloated and pale; the conjunctions tortured; the pronouns reduced to sexless skeletons; the verbs dichotomized and feebly tottering—while behind them, arrogant, overfed, roseate, spilling over the triumphal car, would be the company of nouns in Roman togas and Greek chitons, adorned with laurel branches and flowering hegemonies.

QUESTIONS FOR READING, RESPONDING, AND WRITING

Summarizing Main Points

1. What are the linguistic characteristics of "Socspeak," according to Cowley?
2. What, according to Cowley, are the problems created by Socspeak? Do you think his attack on the language constitutes a more subtle attack on the profession of sociology as well? Why or why not?

Analyzing Methods of Discourse

1. Cowley does his own objective analysis of "Socspeak" by cataloging the use and transformation of various parts of speech, providing percentages, and translating from English into "Socspeak." How does this objective analysis differ from the sort of objective analysis done by some sociologists? What point is he trying to make through his own method of analysis?
2. Reread the first two paragraphs and the last paragraph of Cowley's essay. Do you see any relation between his account of his friend's dissertation problems and his dreams of the painting "The Triumph of the Nouns"? In the first two paragraphs, Cowley's friend *must* translate his ideas into "barbarous jargon" in order to have it accepted. In the last paragraph, what does Cowley do to that "barbarous jargon"?

Focusing on the Field

1. What do you suppose Cowley's goal might be here? Who is his audience? Did his title suggest a different audience from those he turned out to address? How does that title work in relation to the essay?
2. Cowley's essay is humorous. How do the jokes work here? List examples and explain them, starting with the essay's title. How does Cowley's use of humor help him to make his points?

Writing Assignments

1. Find examples of obfuscatory language in areas other than sociology and apply Cowley's method of analysis to them. Write an essay on your findings.
2. In a short essay, apply Cowley's analysis of "Socspeak" to Willis, Gier, and Smith's "Stepping Aside: Correlates of Displacements in Pedestrians." Do they avoid "Socspeak" in your opinion? Give evidence to support your claim.

Ernest Hartmann

WHAT IS A NIGHTMARE?

Ernest Hartmann was born in Vienna, Austria in 1934. After graduating from the University of Chicago in 1952, he studied medicine at Yale. Hartmann was awarded an American Cancer Society fellowship, which enabled him to spend a year at research before his psychiatric residency at Massachusetts Mental Health Center in Boston in 1960. From 1964 through 1969, Hartmann taught at Tufts University, where he is currently professor of psychiatry at Boston State Hospital and director of its sleep and dream laboratory.

Hartmann is a member of many medical organizations, including the Society for Neuroscience, the Association for the Psychophysiological Study of Sleep and the American Psychiatric Association. He has contributed over 130 articles to professional journals. While at Yale, Hartmann was awarded the Holt Book Prize for his writing, and since then he has published several important texts on sleep and dreaming, among them *The Biology of Dreaming* (1967), *Sleep and Dreaming* (1970), *The Function of Sleep* (1973), and *The Nightmare: The Psychology and Biology of Terrifying Dreams* (1982), which includes "What Is a Nightmare?," the essay reprinted below. When not writing on the subject of dreams, Hartmann addresses himself to the waking equivalent—composing fables and poetry in his spare time.

A generally accepted definition of nightmare is *waking up from sleep terrified* (without an external cause) or *something from inside that awakens a person with a scared feeling.* We can accept this as a broad definition of all nightmarelike phenomena, but we will see that it includes several very different conditions.

A nightmare is a very well-defined psychological and biological phenomenon. In order to discuss it clearly, we must first distinguish it from other closely related phenomena with which it is often confused. Specifically, it is necessary to make a distinction between two quite different biopsychological phenomena—the night terror and the nightmare. The sleep laboratory has helped us make this conceptual distinction. Here is an example of a classical night terror, as described in the laboratory studies of Charles Fisher, who has done much of the original work on this condition:

> Fifty minutes after sleep onset during stage 4 sleep, a body movement occurs, HS [the subject] rolls over screaming repeatedly, "Help, help." He mutters about swallowing something and choking. His pulse rate has increased from 60 to 90 per minute during the 15 seconds it takes him to awaken. He quickly falls asleep again, and later has no recall for the event (Fisher et al. 1974).

The most common vocalization is simply a scream. The sleeper does not remember a dream but sometimes remembers feeling crushed or suffocated. A mother will typically report, "My five-year-old screams and screams a half hour or so after falling asleep. I go in and he's sort of half awake, standing up. It takes five minutes for him to come out of it. Then he just falls back asleep peacefully." The child says, "I don't remember anything. I sleep okay, but Mommy says I scream a lot in my sleep."

Here, on the other hand, is a nightmare from my laboratory. Ellen, a twenty-four-year-old woman, sleeping in the lab as part of a study, awoke at 7:50 A.M. after a nineteen-minute REM-period (Rapid Eye Movement or dreaming sleep).

TECHNICIAN: Anything going on?
ELLEN: I know I dreamt something. Oh, yeah. I was at this man's house. . . . I can't remember who it was. And um, the first part of the dream there was a trial in his house. And the last part of the dream there was a big storm . . . an awful rainstorm. It poured like I've never seen it pour before and there was all these frogs all over the street outside. . . . I don't know if it was this dream or the dream before. . . . I had a really awful dream. . . . I was at my parents' house and they had gone out to some party . . . or something like that and I was home alone. Suddenly, this guy from next door came over and he just kind of walked through the house. And I asked him what he needed and he told me he was having trouble moving his house. And it turned out that he was having some kind of legal trouble so that he had to move his house a certain number of feet. And in the dream I went out into the yard and he had moved his whole house and it crashed into my parents' house. . . . All this stuff just started happening. His house slipped and it started crashing and then there was these two trucks that just kind of came flying down towards me. It was just like a disaster. Everything that possibly could have gone wrong did. . . . Then something else hap-

pened. . . . I don't remember . . . and I really got scared and I started to run. And this other guy ran after me and caught me . . . and I kept struggling. I remember struggling. While we were struggling, I thought how much stronger he was than me, but I knew that I could hurt him . . . but I didn't want to hurt him. I don't remember what happened after that. I woke up.

TECHNICIAN: Would you call this a nightmare?

ELLEN: Yeah.

More commonly, someone will report a long dream ending something like, "Then this huge man, or maybe some kind of monster, started after me; I tried to run but I couldn't get away. He caught up to me and just then I woke up terrified."

Some differences between night terrors and nightmares are obvious from these accounts. We can learn more about the distinctions—and about dreaming in general—if we review the characteristics of a typical night of sleep, as we have learned about it in the last thirty years of sleep laboratory research.

As a person falls asleep, his brain waves go through certain characteristic changes, classified as stages 1, 2, 3, and 4. The waking EEG (data from an electroencephalograph) is characterized by alpha waves (brain waves of eight to twelve cycles per second) and low-voltage activity of mixed frequency. As the person falls asleep, he enters stage 1, considered the lightest stage of sleep, and begins to show a reduction of alpha-activity. This stage is characterized by low-voltage desynchronized activity and sometimes by low-voltage, regular activity at four to six cycles per second. After a few seconds or minutes, this stage gives way to stage 2, a pattern showing frequent spindle-shaped tracings at thirteen to fifteen cycles per second (sleep spindles) and certain high-voltage spikes known as K-complexes. Soon thereafter, in stage 3, delta waves—high-voltage activity at 0.5 to 2.5 cycles per second—make their appearance. Eventually, in stage 4, the delta waves occupy the major part of the record.

The division of sleep into stages 1 through 4 is an arbitrary demarcation of a continuous process. In fact, sleep is a cyclical process, with four or five periods of emergence from stages 2, 3, and 4 to a stage similar to stage 1 (figure 2-1). The periods of emergence are characterized not only by stage 1 EEG patterns and by rapid conjugate eye movements (REM's) but by a host of other distinguishing factors, including irregularity in pulse rate, respiratory rate, and blood pressure; the presence of full or partial penile erections; and generalized muscular atony (absent muscle tone) interrupted by sporadic movements in small muscle groups. These periods differ from typical stage 1 sleep (although they exhibit the same EEG pattern) as well as from the other three stages. Persons awakened

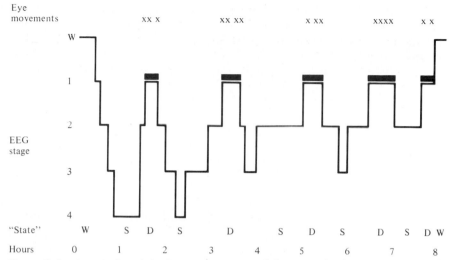

Eye
movements

Figure 2-1 A typical night's sleep in a young adult. *Note:* The four EEG "stages of sleep" are described in the text. The "states" are W—Waking; S—Synchronized sleep, also referred to as NREM (nonrapid eye movement) sleep; D—Desynchronized or Dreaming sleep, also referred to as REM (rapid eye movement) sleep.

during periods of emergence frequently—60 to 90 percent of the time— report that they have been dreaming, while persons awakened from stages 2, 3, or 4 sleep very seldom report dreams. Because of their distinctive traits and specific neurophysiological and chemical character, these periods are now almost universally seen as constituting a separate state of sleep, referred to as D-sleep (desynchronized or dreaming sleep). This view is reinforced by the fact that similar periods of sleep are experienced by nearly all mammals and birds studied. The remainder of the sleep period is referred to as S-sleep (synchronized sleep). These two states of sleep are also known as REM-sleep (rapid eye movement sleep) and NREM-sleep (nonrapid eye movement sleep), as paradoxical sleep and orthodox sleep, and as active sleep and quiet sleep.

There are several other important characteristics of the typical night's sleep. First, there are four or five D-periods (REM or dreaming sleep) during the night, and the total time taken up by them is about one and a half hours, a little more than 20 percent of the total sleep time. There is some variation, of course, but all the many hundreds of people studied have such D-periods, and in young adults these periods almost always take up 20 to 25 percent of the total night's sleep. The first D-period occurs about seventy to one hundred twenty minutes after the onset of sleep; the interval may be longer in some normal persons, but it is significantly shorter only in a few unusual clinical conditions including the disease known as narcolepsy. Narcolepsy is a condition characterized by sudden irresistible attacks of sleep in the daytime as well as other related symptoms.

The cyclical nature of sleep is quite regular and reliable; a D-period occurs about every ninety to one hundred minutes during the night. The first D-period tends to be the shortest, usually lasting less than ten minutes; the later D-periods may last fifteen to forty minutes each. Most D-time occurs in the last third of the night, whereas most stage 4 sleep occurs in the first third of the night (see figure 2-1). S-sleep (synchronized or non-REM sleep) can be neatly organized according to depth; stage 1 is the lightest stage, and stage 4 is the deepest stage, as measured by arousal threshold and by the appearance of the EEG. D-sleep (desynchronized, dreaming, or REM-sleep), however, does not fit into that continuum. Human EEG data alone might indicate that D-sleep is a light sleep. But the arousal threshold (difficulty of arousal) in animals is higher in D-sleep than in S-sleep, and resting muscle potential is lowest during D-sleep. Thus, D-sleep is neither truly light sleep nor deep sleep but a qualitatively different kind of sleep.

Now that we have examined the general characteristics of sleep, we can look more closely at the chief differences between nightmares and night terrors: the night terror occurs early during the sleep period, usually within two hours of sleep onset. It consists of a simple awakening in terror, most often accompanied by a scream, by sweating, by body movements, and sometimes by sleepwalking. Studies in a sleep laboratory show that the night terror occurs usually in sleep stage 3 or 4 (see figure 2-2)—deep or slow-wave sleep—most commonly during the first hours of sleep. During the fifteen to sixty seconds of awakening, tremendous autonomic nervous system changes can be recorded: pulse and respiratory rates sometimes double. Sleepers do not remember the night terror as they might a dream. Either they recall nothing at all and are only aware of the episode because they are told of it, or they are aware of a single frightening image—"something is sitting on me," "I am choking," "something is closing in on me" (Fisher et al. 1973b, 1974; Broughton 1968).

The typical nightmare is a very different experience. It usually occurs later during the night, or the second half of the sleep period. Sleep laboratory studies show it arises during a period of D-sleep (figure 2-2). There may be some increase in autonomic measures—pulse, respiration, and so on—but not to the extent found during a night terror. Finally, the nightmare is definitely a dream—a long, frightening dream which awakens the sleeper. It is clearly remembered as a very detailed, vivid, and intense dream experience (Fisher, Byrne, and Edwards 1968).

Another way to emphasize the difference is to be aware that a nightmare is a dream, and like other dreams, occurs over a period of five

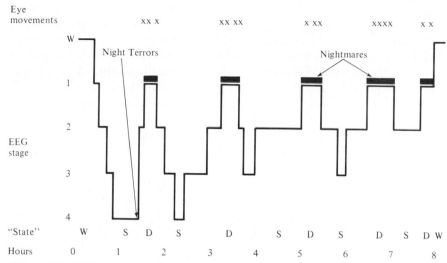

Figure 2-2 Night terrors and nightmares in the sleep laboratory. *Note:* Night terrors occur early (often within an hour of falling asleep), during stage 3 or 4 of sleep. Nightmares occur toward morning, during REM or dreaming sleep.

to thirty minutes; one awakes from it, perhaps quickly, and may recall a long, detailed, frightening dream; the awakening itself is not remarkable. A night terror is not a dream, but the unusual awakening itself; it has been called a "disorder of arousal" (Broughton 1968). Something internal or external (it can even be an experimenter) arouses the sleeper, and the arousal itself is unusual, characterized by rapid changes in the nervous system. The arousal may include motor activity and sleep walking. This arousal itself *is* the night terror. One study showed that a night terror episode could be induced, in a child prone to night terrors, by pulling the child upright, producing a partial arousal (Kales and Jacobson 1968). This indicates that night terror is not a long, ongoing process from which the sleeper awakens, but rather is something involved in the arousal itself.

A sleep laboratory can confirm the diagnosis of nightmare or night terror, but this is usually not necessary. Even without the use of sleep laboratory data, I can almost always find out clinically whether a patient has nightmares or night terrors (although he or she may refer to either one as a "nightmare") by asking, "Are your nightmares dreams?" The question seems simplistic both to people who suffer from nightmares and to those who experience night terrors. Those with nightmares answer, "Of course." They have no doubt that their nightmares are very frightening dreams. They cannot imagine a nightmare that is not a dream, and after waking from one, they nearly always remember having had a long dream that they can recount in vivid detail. Usually the dream is complicated, with elements that become more and more frightening as the dream lengthens: ". . . and then the monster was chasing me and I couldn't get away"; "the people I had been talking with now had evil looks on their faces; after a while they pulled out knives; somebody slashed my arm." Night terror victims find my question equally absurd. Asked if their nightmares are dreams, they reply, "No, of course not." They sometimes remember dreams, like anyone else, but they know that their episodes of terror are quite different from their dreams.

I have emphasized these differences at length to help us make sense of past and present work on nightmares. I hope it is clear that the person in the classical descriptions of "nightmares" who sits upright in bed, or gets out of bed, screaming, with a glazed expression on his face, is a person having a night terror, not a nightmare. Nightmares and night terrors are indeed quite different phenomena psychologically, physiologically, and occur in quite different persons, as we shall see.

However, life is never quite this simple. Unfortunately, there are cases in which the type of experience is not entirely clear, even when one asks all the right questions. This can be due to poor memory, or poor descriptive abilities on the part of the patient or subject. Or it can be the fact that the person actually has both nightmares and night terrors concurrently—I have seen six or seven such cases—that makes description of and delineation between them difficult. But there are also cases that cannot be explained in these ways. There may be other rarer phenomena falling within the general term nightmare. For instance, Fisher in his original laboratory studies found what he called a "stage 2 nightmare." These were much more like night terrors than nightmares, as we have described them. They seemed to represent mild or less prominent forms of night terrors and, indeed, stage 2 sleep is in most ways a milder, less prominent form of stage 4 sleep. Some cases of post-traumatic nightmares in soldiers sound quite similar. They were described as starting out with feelings of terror and a great deal of movement, vocalization, and so on, and they were indeed found in laboratory studies to occur during stage 2 sleep (Schlosberg and Benjamin 1978). These could be considered a subgroup of the night terror phenomenon. However, we have seen a case in which the same "dream"—an almost exact replay of the wartime trauma—occurred at very different times of night and from different stages of sleep, including D-sleep as well as stage 2.[1] I believe they represent something different from either classical nightmares or night terrors.

Just to complicate matters further, nightmarelike phenomena have also occasionally been described as occurring at sleep onset (Gastaut and

---

[1]Similar cases have been reported to me by other sleep researchers, including Peretz Lavie and Milton Kramer.

Broughton 1964). These seem to occur out of stage 1 sleep—a time often characterized by somewhat dreamlike "hypnagogic" imagery, hypnagogic referring to a state between wakefulness and sleep. These sleep onset "nightmares" consist of frightening hypnagogic imagery leading to an awakening, or rather a pulling back from a not-quite-asleep state. These may be considered an intense form of an experience most of us have at times, called the "hypnagogic jerk" in which we are suddenly jerked back awake while falling asleep. "Nightmares" of sleep onset can also be episodes of sleep paralysis—inability to move while apparently awake—and of hypnagogic hallucinations, both of which are common in narcoleptic patients and occasionally occur in others. These episodes are not usually experienced as nightmares but as an especially intense hypnagogic hallucination, or a hallucination combined with the experience of paralysis, sometimes assuming a nightmarelike quality. All these phenomena of falling asleep can also occur, though more rarely, while waking up at the end of sleep.

Despite these exceptions, we will not go far astray by concentrating primarily on two basic forms of "nightmares"—the nightmare proper and the often misidentified night terror. Current evidence strongly suggests that psychological or personality characteristics of persons who experience nightmares are different from those who suffer night terrors. For instance, I recently analyzed information from thirty adults with severe night terrors, but no nightmares (Hartmann, Greenwald, and Brune 1982). These persons turned out not to resemble in the least the nightmare sufferers we studied in detail. The nightmare sufferers had some features of schizophrenia or a vulnerability to schizophrenia; they had artistic tendencies and a kind of openness and sensitivity.

The night terror sufferers could not be characterized in this way. They included all kinds of people with no specific psychopathology and no particular artistic tendencies; their psychological tests did not show the unusual characteristics found in the tests of the nightmare sufferers. Many were psychologically quite average; some had psychopathology, but not of any single type; a subgroup seemed unusually tightly controlled, but the relationship of this characteristic to night terrors (were they "holding in" or "holding down" angry impulses excessively?) was not clear.[2]

---

[2]Material collected by other authors is consistent with this distinction. Dr. Charles Fisher, who performed some of the first laboratory studies of nightmares and night terrors fifteen years ago, made available to me detailed notes on nightmare content and his interviews with his subjects who had frequent nightmares as well as those who had frequent night terrors. I carefully reviewed his notes, and indeed his group with frequent nightmares had many schizophrenic and borderline features. This was not the case with the subjects who had night terrors, even though these were especially severe cases who experienced night terrors repeatedly in the laboratory. These results are entirely compatible with my data.

QUESTIONS FOR READING, RESPONDING, AND WRITING

Summarizing Main Points

1. Chart the typical night of sleep, according to Hartmann. Then, define the two categories of sleep of which it is composed, listing the characteristics of each type. Also, list the variety of names Hartmann provides for each category. Why do you suppose he lists so many names for each category?
2. What, according to Hartmann, distinguishes "night terrors" from "nightmares"? How do their respective sufferers differ psychologically, according to Hartmann?

Analyzing Methods of Discourse

1. Hartmann makes the initial distinction between night terrors and nightmares by providing an account of each. Was the distinction Hartmann was trying to make apparent to you? Why do you suppose Hartmann chose to begin his essay in this way? Did you find it effective? Why or why not?
2. Hartmann goes on to describe a typical night of sleep, first defining the two types of sleep and their respective characteristics before moving chronologically through that typical night. How does this arrangement help the reader understand the typical night of sleep more fully? Do you think it would have been more or less effective if Hartmann had gone through the typical night and incorporated the explanatory material for the first time as he went? Why or why not?

Focusing on the Field

1. Hartmann uses two graphs to illustrate his argument. Note their relation to the rest of the essay. Would you have been able to understand the graphs without the preceding written accounts? Once you have read those accounts, consider the ways in which the graphs help you to *see* more clearly what the writing describes.
2. In addition to his use of graphs, Hartmann cites a number of supporting studies by other sleep researchers and often uses a scientific vocabulary in discussing his findings. Yet these characteristics do not seem to limit Hartmann's audience as much as one might think. List some of the ways in which Hartmann makes his essay available to the average reader.

Writing Assignments

1. After studying the psychological traits Hartmann assigns the sufferers of night terrors and nightmares, write a short essay in which you use your own experience (your perception of your own psychology and your experience with nightmares or night terrors) to support or refute Hartmann's findings.
2. Read Margaret Mead's "New Superstitions for Old." In that essay, Mead claims that superstitions "give us all ways of moving back and forth among the different worlds in which we live—the sacred, the secular, and the scientific." Write an essay in which you argue for the value of nightmares in the same way that Mead argues for the value of superstitions.

Frank N. Willis, Jr.
Joseph A. Gier
David E. Smith

STEPPING ASIDE: CORRELATES OF DISPLACEMENT IN PEDESTRIANS

As is the case with many professional and academic studies, the following essay, first published in the *Journal of Communication* (August 1979), was written and researched by a team of social scientists: Frank N. Willis, Jr., Joseph A. Gier, and David E. Smith. As Frank Willis has pointed out, such studies require no elaborate equipment for research as they are based on the systematic and unobtrusive observation of people in field studies much like those that record the behavior patterns of animals. The report here represents the distillation of pages of notes into the statistics that support the major contention: that "gallantry" may be as important as power in determining who steps aside for whom.

Willis, the "first author" in the language of professional journals, was born in 1930. He earned both a B.A. (1956) and an M.A. (1957) from the University of Kansas City and a Ph.D. (1961) from the University of Missouri at Columbia. Long interested in "interpersonal touch," he is currently working on a study of personality types in relation to patterns of touch. Willis has published several studies in professional journals such as the *Journal of Personality and Social Psychology,* the *Journal of Basic and Applied Social Psychology,* and *Psychological Reports.* Gier, who is currently a candidate for a Ph.D. at the University of Nebraska, works for a corporation in Omaha. Smith, who also works for a business concern in St. Louis, recently received his Ph.D. in community psychology.

COMPLEX PATTERNS OF BOTH POWER AND GALLANTRY
MAY DETERMINE WHO YIELDS TO AND DEFERS TO WHOM.

When people meet head-on, who steps aside for whom and what is the reason they do so? Among animals (see 10, 12), this question has commonly been used as a measure of dominance, and recent research has argued that a similar principle applies in human interaction. Henley (6) argues that spatial displacement reflects human power relationships, with males being dominant over females and older persons being dominant over younger ones. Silveria (9) observed people passing on a sidewalk and noted that in 19 mixed-sex encounters, women moved 12 times. Dabbs and Stokes (2) observed that pedestrians more often changed their paths to avoid a male standing beside a sidewalk than a female, and changed more often for two persons than for one, and more for an attractive female than for an unattractive one. Knowles (8) also reported that passersby were more likely to change their paths for four persons than for two, and to do so for higher status people more than for lower status ones; however, in this case, sex was not related to the probability of being displaced.

Sex and status differences were also found in people's use of the space around them. When forced to intrude upon the space of either a male or a female in an elevator, males more often intruded upon the females' space, found Buchanan, Juhnke, and Goldman (1). Similar findings were obtained in Dabbs's study of men and women waiting for a traffic light. In related finding, Evans and Howard (4) concluded from a review of research that females have smaller personal space zones. Males pass each other at a closer distance than that at which they pass females or females pass each other, according to Ing (7). Dean, Willis, and Hewitt (3) observed that subordinates tend to stand back from superiors as they initiate conversation, while superiors are free to approach their subordinates more closely when initiating conversation.

Are all these findings solely attributable to power relationships and dominance? Goffman (5) provides an explanation for certain types of spatial displacement in human interaction. Often a spatial displacement between unlike individuals or groups results in giving priority to physical weakness attributable to age, sex, or medical condition. This concept of "gallantry" seemed to us an important one in balancing the notion of power as the sole determinant of displacements.

SPATIAL DISPLACEMENT IN HUMAN ENCOUNTERS IS A COMPLEX PHENOMENON RELATED TO MANY CHARACTERISTICS OF THE PARTICIPANTS.

Our study was designed to provide a relatively large number of observations of spatial displacement in a general population, in order to examine the effects of gender, age, race, group size, and other characteristics. We hoped to derive clearer statements about the relative contributions of power, gallantry, and other attributes.

We observed 1038 displacements involving 3141 persons—173 black females, 101 black males, 1761 white females, 1062 white males, 24 Chicano or Oriental females, and 20 Chicano or Oriental males. Of these, 539 persons were observed in 226 displacements in an aisle 2 meters wide in a university restaurant, and 2602 pedestrians were observed in 812 displacements in aisles approximately 4 meters wide in four enclosed shopping center malls in the greater Kansas City area. The university observations were made during lunch periods from Monday through

Friday. The shopping center observations were made on Saturdays between 11:00 a.m. and 4:00 p.m.

A displacement was recorded when individuals or groups of pedestrians approached one another and one or more was judged to change his/her path or body angle. If any doubt was present as to whether a displacement occurred, no displacement was recorded. As a result, many subtle movements, which might also affect the interaction, were not coded.

We recorded the gender, ethnic group, and age (in decades) of the pedestrians for all encounters. We also recorded the type of movement (path change or body turn), the presence of vehicles (wheelchairs or baby strollers), the carrying of infants, the carrying of burdens requiring both hands, and the wearing of uniforms indicating employment within the setting (janitor, waitress, policeman, etc.). In the university restaurant, we sat at tables with a view of a section of the aisle approximately 10 meters in length. We found that observations had to be made in line with the traffic rather than from the side in order to avoid missing movements. In the shopping center malls we sat on benches in the center of the mall permitting a view of a section of approximately 15 meters of the aisle. Again, we chose positions that allowed an in-line view. In no instance did a person being observed notice our recording, although we were frequently questioned by others seated near us.

For our study we did not record the displacements involving

—persons crossing the stream of traffic. Unlike vehicular traffic, pedestrians crossing traffic were almost always avoided; see (5).

—stationary people. In these encounters, pedestrians always moved for stationary persons.

—pedestrians moving so slowly that they were being passed consistently. Others almost always moved for these slow moving persons.

—pedestrians moving so swiftly that they were passing most others. These persons almost always moved for others.

—persons whose heads were turned to view shops, crossing aisles, etc. Those who do not "look where they are going" were expected to be involved in collisions; we observed two collisions during the study.

Since we observed only predetermined sections of the aisles, adjustments made prior to entry into our viewing area were not seen. According to Goffman (5), pedestrians scan an area three or four sidewalk squares in front of them, so some adjustments probably took place before we had an opportunity to make observations. On numerous occasions a person or group first appeared to change their path to avoid other people, only to continue their movement along a second path; these people were not recorded as having been displaced.

A sub-sample of two hours of displacement encounters was made in order to evaluate the effects of moving with or against the flow of pedestrian traffic. We made no attempt to evaluate the relative status of pedestrians, even though previous research had shown this to be related to displacement. Nor did we attempt to discover whether pedestrians knew each other, particularly likely in the university setting. Both kinds of information would have been difficult to estimate in public settings.

In pretesting for reliability with regard to movement, body turns, and age, agreement among two or three observers was over 95 percent for all three variables after practice. Subsequent observations were made by single observers.

Because of the large number of characteristics being observed, we examined effects of single characteristics on displacement, rather than using a multiple classification design. Such a design would have resulted in large numbers in some cells and few or none in others, making it difficult to assess the effects of possible interactions between variables. Most of the data were analyzed with a one-by-two chi square test of "goodness of fit," with a theoretical frequency of 50 percent for each cell.

Data were combined for the university and shopping center settings because relationships between characteristics of those observed and their probability of being displaced did not differ in the two settings. The university did include more pedestrians alone or in pairs and had a much more restricted age range.

IN SAME-GENDER GROUPS OF EQUAL SIZE (ONE, TWO, OR THREE MEMBERS), MALES WERE MORE OFTEN DISPLACED BY FEMALES THAN FEMALES WERE BY MALES.

In 79 instances, males were displaced by females; females were displaced by males 39 times ($X^2 = 23.14(1)$, $p \leq .001$). When one member of a mixed-gender pair was displaced by another person or group of any size, the males were displaced 78 times as compared to 54 times for females ($X^2 = 4.36(1)$, $p \leq .05$). We had speculated that mixed-gender pairs would be displaced more often than they displaced others, as compared to same-gender pairs, since the former were often holding hands or otherwise touching. The difference was not significant, however, with 58 same-gender pairs being displaced, compared to 47 mixed-gender pairs ($X^2 = 1.14$). Single pedestrians were more likely to be displaced by mixed-gender pairs (N = 109) than they were to displace mixed-gender pairs (N = 31). On the other hand, mixed-gender pairs were more likely to be displaced by larger groups (N = 19) than they were to displace them (N =

7). There were also gender differences with regard to the type of displacement. Males moved 408 times and turned their bodies 63 times, while females moved 531 times and turned their bodies 36 times ($X^2 = 14.59(1)$, $p \leq .01$). It appeared that males were more likely to turn their bodies at the last moment to avoid a collision.

Whites were more likely to be displaced by blacks ($N = 125$) than blacks were to be displaced by whites ($N = 85$) ($X^2 = 7.62$, $p \leq .01$). These totals include groups of all sizes, since whites were more likely to be displaced by blacks in smaller, same size, and larger groups. There were too few members of other racial groups to permit a reliable comparison between whites and those groups.

Group size proved to be the most reliable predictor of displacement. There were 424 instances in which smaller groups were displaced by larger ones, and only 132 instances in which larger groups were displaced by smaller ones ($X^2 = 153.35(1)$, $p \leq .001$).

In encounters involving lone pedestrians, younger pedestrians were displaced by older ones 61 times, and older pedestrians were displaced by younger ones 51 times ($X^2 = .94$). For groups of individuals of different ages, comparisons on the basis of average age in the group would not be meaningful. We did, however, compare groups where all members of one group were judged to be older than all members of the other group. In these encounters younger groups were more likely to be displaced ($N = 57$) than they were to displace older groups ($N = 24$) ($X^2 = 13.44(1)$, $p \leq .01$).

We also observed 25 interactions in which one person was carrying an infant. This person or the group including such a person was displaced on only six occasions, compared to 19 occasions in which the other person or group was displaced ($X^2 = 6.76$, $p \leq .01$). Interactions between persons carrying burdens requiring both hands yielded similar, although non-significant, results. Persons with burdens were displaced 17 times, compared to 27 times for the other persons or groups ($X^2 = 2.28$). Pedestrians with vehicles (wheelchairs or baby strollers) were less likely to be displaced by persons or groups without such a vehicle ($N = 7$) than vice versa ($N = 47$) ($X^2 = 29.6(1)$, $p \leq .001$).

We observed 11 interactions involving a person with an obvious handicap (cane, limp, etc.) and on all of these occasions the other person or group was displaced ($X^2 = 10.8(1)$, $p \leq .01$). On the 13 occasions in which one person or group had a uniform indicating employment in the setting (janitor, waitress, policeman, etc.), that group was displaced 4 times as compared to 9 times for the other person or group. This difference was not significant ($X^2 = 1.76$). Finally, we recorded displacements as related to the flow of traffic for a one-hour period. Those moving in the direction of the majority of pedestrians were displaced 32 times as compared to 30 displacements for those moving in the direction opposite to the majority ($X^2 = .06$).

HENLEY'S ARGUMENT (6) THAT DISPLACEMENTS IN PEDESTRIAN MOVEMENT REFLECT DIFFERENCE IN STATUS AND POWER RECEIVED ONLY PARTIAL SUPPORT FROM THESE RESULTS.

Persons or groups moved for larger groups and younger groups tended to move for older groups, but women did not tend to move for men nor did blacks tend to move for whites. Goffman's conclusion that some kind of "gallantry" exists in which priority is given to physical weakness attributable to age, sex, or medical condition receives more support. The notion of maneuverability also is important here. It is easier for smaller groups to move for larger ones, as it is easier to move for those who are not carrying an infant, not handicapped, and not maneuvering a wheelchair or stroller.

The finding that whites are more likely to be displaced by blacks is not easily explained within this framework. It may be related to previous observations that whites tend to stand back from blacks (11). Or it may be related to other factors involved in the sociopolitical environment.

If dominance is involved in the displacement of pedestrians, then the "intention displays" mentioned by Goffman (5) indicating resoluteness should be observable prior to displacement. To determine this would require overhead video or movie cameras for recording.

The most important implication of these findings is that "gallantry" may be as important as power in determining displacements. Yielding to someone stronger in physical or status attributes is a very different act from that of deferring to someone deemed weaker by the conventions attached to age, sex, and health. That the two kinds of acts look the same does not mean that their ramifications are equivalent, or that they serve the same functions in regulating the physical and social traffic that governs day-to-day life.

REFERENCES

1. Buchanan, D. R., R. Juhnke, and M. Goldman. "Violation of Personal Space as a Function of Sex." *Journal of Social Psychology* 99, 1976, pp. 187–192.
2. Dabbs, J. M. and N. A. Stokes. "Beauty is Power: The Use of Space on the Sidewalk." *Sociometry* 38, 1975, pp. 551–557.
3. Dean, L. M., F. N. Willis, and J. Hewitt. "Initial Interaction Distance Among Individuals Equal and Unequal in Military Rank." *Journal of Personality and Social Psychology* 32, 1975, pp. 294–299.

4. Evans, G. W. and R. B. Howard. "Personal Space." *Psychological Bulletin* 80, 1973, pp. 334–344.
5. Goffman, E. *Relations in Public.* New York: Harper and Row, 1971.
6. Henley, N. M. *Body Politics.* Englewood Cliffs, N.J.: Prentice-Hall, 1977.
7. Ing, D. C. "Sex Differences and Street Proxemics." Paper presented at the Annual Meeting of the Western Speech Association, November 1974.
8. Knowles, E. S. "Boundaries Around Group Interaction." *Journal of Personality and Social Psychology* 26, 1973, pp. 37–331.
9. Silveria, J. "Thoughts on the Politics of Touch." *Women's Press* 1, Feb. 1972, p. 13.
10. Washborn, S. L. and I. Devore. "The Social Life of Baboons." *Scientific American* 204(6), 1961, pp. 62–71.
11. Willis, F. N. "Initial Speaking Distance as a Function of the Speaker's Relationship." *Psychonomic Science* 5, 1966, pp. 221–222.
12. Willis, F. N. and W. B. Ghiselli. "Spatial Dominance and Food Success in Cichlid and Centrarchid Fishes." *Psychological Record* 26, 1976, pp. 523–528.

QUESTIONS FOR READING, RESPONDING, AND WRITING

Summarizing Main Points

1. Willis, Gier, and Smith cite a number of studies on pedestrian displacement. List the findings in those studies. What overall reasons for displacement do they give?
2. What reasons for displacement does the authors' study give? How does it compare to the findings the authors cite in the beginning? What do you suppose they mean when they say that the "ramifications are [not] equivalent" or that "they [do not] serve the same functions in regulating the physical and social traffic that governs day-to-day life"? Can you suggest some possible ramifications of their findings?

Analyzing Methods of Discourse

1. Willis, Gier, and Smith provide brief summary headings for each section of their essay. Reread all those headings, but don't reread the rest of the essay. Do you feel that when taken all together, these headings provide a reliable summary of the essay? How do they help you to understand it more completely? Compare the style of the headings to the style of the title and the rest of the essay.
2. Willis, Gier, and Smith arrange their argument by presenting current views on pedestrian displacement, then setting up and conducting their study, and, finally, presenting their views. How does this arrangement help them to get their points across? Explain.

Focusing on the Field

1. The language and arrangement of this essay reflect the authors' efforts to make their study as scientific as possible. List the ways in which the authors create

that scientific effect. Why do you suppose it is important that they construct their essay in this way?

2. In their study, Willis, Gier, and Smith not only record their observations but also record the position of the observer or observers in relation to those observations. Why is this information important? How might it affect their findings?

Writing Assignments

1. Read Annie Dillard's "Lenses." Then write an essay in which you compare and contrast the type of observations and the methods of observation that both essays describe. What are the similarities? What are the differences?
2. Both this essay and Desmond Morris's "Understanding Gestures: The Thumb Up" are about "body language." Write an essay of your own in which you account for the similarities and differences in the authors' respective methodologies.

T·H·R·E·E

SCIENCE AND TECHNOLOGY
Physical Sciences/Life Sciences/ Technology/Computer Science/ Medicine/Agriculture

Reading maketh a full man; conference a ready man; and writing an exact man.

Francis Bacon, "Of Studies"

In Science the credit goes to the man who convinces the world, not to the man to whom the idea first occurs.

Sir William Osler

I have as much difficulty as ever in expressing myself clearly and concisely; and this difficulty has caused me a very great loss of time; but it has the compensating advantage of forcing me to think long and intently about every sentence, and thus I have been often led to see errors in reasoning and in my own observations or those of others.

Charles Darwin, *Autobiography*

The influence of writing on science and policy deserves more attention than it gets. The history of ideas is filled with wide turns caused by "mere" lucidity and elegance of expression. Galileo's *Dialogo* succeeded not because it was a Copernican tract (there were others) or because it contained much new evidence (it did not) but because it was a masterpiece of Italian prose. Poincaré's French and Einstein's German were no trivial elements in their influence.

Donald McCloskey

What we observe is not nature in itself but nature exposed to our method of questioning.

Werner Heisenberg

Technical words in the sciences are like adzes, planes, gimlets, or razors. A word like "experience," or "feeling," or "true" is like a pocket-knife. In good hands it will do most things—not very well. In general we will find that the more important a word is, and the more central and necessary its meanings are in our pictures of ourselves and the world, the more ambiguous and possibly deceiving the word will be. Naturally these words are also those which have been most used in philosophy. But it is not the philosophers who have made them ambiguous; it is the position of their ideas, as the very hinges of all thought.

I. A. Richards

I have great love and respect for my native tongue, and take great pains to use it properly. Sometimes I write essays half a dozen times before I get them into the proper shape; and I believe I become more fastidious as I grow older.

T. H. Huxley: *Letter to H. de Varigny,* May 17, 1891

Lest it seem that the modes of connecting in art and science are separated by an unbridgeable gap, that in all ways they are different modes of knowing, one primitive similarity should be mentioned—one that partakes of the nature of metaphor. It is the manner in which the scientist gets his hypothesis.

Jerome S. Bruner, *On Knowing*

We must be wary, as Moliere taught us, of explanations couched in fancy language. It is a basic maxim for serious thought that whatever there is to be said can, through perseverence, be said clearly. Something that persistently resists clear expression, far from meriting reverence for its profundity, merits suspicion. Pressing the question "What does this really say?" can reveal that the fancy language masked a featureless face.

W. V. Quine and J. S. Ullian, from *The Web of Belief*

The technician's background allows him to compare good syntax with a valid equation. If the sentence balances, ambiguity has vanished: *it* refers to what it should, and the dangling modifiers are gone; the sentence is lean and direct, with its verb doing the right thing even if subject and object aren't clearly labeled; transitions are clean, sentence to sentence, paragraph to paragraph. Common-sense logic has organized a mass of words; the writer is learning to treat language with the respect he shows science.

William Gilman, *The Language of Science*

Seeing is of course very much a matter of verbalization. Unless I call my attention to what passes before my eyes, I simply won't see it. It is, as Ruskin says, "not merely unnoticed, but in the full, clear sense of the word, unseen." My eyes alone can't solve analogy tests using figures, the ones which show, with increasing elaborations, a big square, then a small square in a big square, then a big triangle, and expect me to find a small triangle in a big triangle. I have to say the words describe what I'm seeing. If Tinker Mountain erupted, I'd be likely to notice. But if I want to notice the lesser cataclysms of valley life, I have to maintain in my head a running description of the present. It's not that I'm observant; it's just that I talk too much. Otherwise, especially in a strange place, I'll never know what's happening. Like a blind man at the ball game, I need a radio.

Annie Dillard, "Seeing"

Engineers and scientists from the earliest days of recorded history have written reports, proposals, and other documents about their work. Much of the world's best-known technical writing has been done by outstanding engineers and scientists, such as Vitruvius, Agricola, Smeaton, Rankine, Parsons, Taylor, Hoover, Perry, Marks, Kent, and Rutherford. Studies show that, in general, the greater a man's engineering or scientific achievements, the larger the number of his published works of all kinds.

Tyler G. Hicks, *Writing for Engineering and Science*

Annie Dillard

LENSES

In the following essay, Annie Dillard describes looking at the world through different kinds of lenses. In the process, she describes what it is like to be looked at herself, to live "in that circle of light." With the publication of her first book, *Pilgrim at Tinker Creek* (1974), and her subsequent garnering of a Pulitzer Prize for general literature, Dillard certainly found herself in the limelight. Critically, her first book received more than praise. It was favorably compared with Henry David Thoreau's *Walden*, from which Dillard found thematic inspiration: She described *Pilgrim at Tinker Creek* as "a meteorological journal of the mind." According to one critic, Dillard's writing belongs "squarely in the American tradition of essayistic narratives in which one person . . . tries to 'front the essential facts,' to make sense of the universe starting at degree zero." Dillard would be proud of such a description. She has said herself that writing "is all hard, conscious, terribly-frustrating work! But this never occurs to people. They think it happens in a dream, that you just sit on a tree stump and take dictation from some little chipmunk!" Dillard's writing regimen—when she writes—stretches seven days a week, fifteen to sixteen hours a day. And though it produces results, it takes its toll as well. "I rarely write," says Dillard, "I hate to write!"

Born in Pittsburgh, Pennsylvania in 1945, Dillard graduated from Hollins College with both a bachelor's and master's degree in art in 1968. She has spent some time teaching her skills to others as a teacher of poetry and creative writing at Western Washington State University and as a distinguished visiting professor at Wesleyan University. Her other writings include *Tickets for a Prayer Wheel* (poems, 1974), *Holy the Firm* (1978), and *Teaching a Stone to Talk* (1982), from which the essay below is taken.

You get used to looking through lenses; it is an acquired skill. When you first look through binoculars, for instance, you can't see a thing. You look at the inside of the barrel; you blink and watch your eyelashes; you play with the focus knob till one eye is purblind.

The microscope is even worse. You are supposed to keep both eyes open as you look through its single eyepiece. I spent my childhood in Pittsburgh trying to master this trick: seeing through one eye, with both eyes open. The microscope also teaches you to move your hands wrong, to shove the glass slide to the right if you are following a creature who is swimming off to the left—as if you were operating a tiller, or backing a trailer, or performing any other of those paradoxical maneuvers which require either sure instincts or a grasp of elementary physics, neither of which I possess.

A child's microscope set comes with a little five-watt lamp. You place this dim light in front of the microscope's mirror; the mirror bounces the light up through the slide, through the magnifying lenses, and into your eye. The only reason you do not see everything in silhouette is that microscopic things are so small they are translucent. The animals and plants in a drop of pond water pass light like pale stained glass; they seem so soaked in water and light that their opacity has leached away.

The translucent strands of algae you see under a microscope— Spirogyra, Oscillatoria, Cladophora—move of their own accord, no one knows how or why. You watch these swaying yellow, green, and brown strands of algae half mesmerized; you sink into the microscope's field forgetful, oblivious, as if it were all a dream of your deepest brain. Occasionally a zippy rotifer comes barreling through, black and white, and in a tremendous hurry.

My rotifers and daphniae and amoebae were in an especially tremendous hurry because they were drying up. I burnt out or broke my little five-watt bulb right away. To replace it, I rigged an old table lamp laid on its side; the table lamp carried a seventy-five-watt bulb. I was about twelve, immortal and invulnerable, and did not know what I was doing; neither did anyone else. My parents let me set up my laboratory in the basement, where they wouldn't have to smell the urine I collected in test tubes and kept in the vain hope it would grow something horrible. So in full, solitary ignorance I spent evenings in the basement staring into a seventy-five-watt bulb magnified three hundred times and focused into my eye. It is a wonder I can see at all. My eyeball itself would start drying up; I blinked and blinked.

But the pond water creatures fared worse. I dropped them on a slide, floated a cover slip over them, and laid the slide on the microscope's stage, which the seventy-five-watt bulb had heated like a grill. At once the drop of pond water started to evaporate. Its edges shrank. The creatures swam among algae in a diminishing pool. I liked this part. The heat worked for me as a centrifuge, to concentrate the biomass. I had about five minutes to watch the members of a very dense population, excited by the heat, go about their business until—as I fancied sadly—they all caught on to their situation and started making out wills.

I was, then, not only watching the much-vaunted wonders in a drop of pond water; I was also, with mingled sadism and sympathy, setting up a limitless series of apocalypses. I set up and staged hundreds of ends-of-the-world and watched, enthralled, as they played themselves out. Over and over again, the last trump sounded, the final scroll unrolled, and the known world drained, dried, and vanished. When all the creatures lay motionless, boiled and fried in the positions they had when the last of their water dried completely, I washed the slide in the sink and started over with a fresh drop. How I loved that deep, wet world where the colored algae waved in the water and the rotifers swam!

But oddly, this is a story about swans. It is not even a story; it is a description of swans. This description of swans includes the sky over a pond, a pair of binoculars, and a mortal adult who had long since moved out of the Pittsburgh basement.

In the Roanoke valley of Virginia, rimmed by the Blue Ridge Mountains to the east and the Allegheny Mountains to the west, is a little semi-agricultural area called Daleville. In Daleville, set among fallow fields and wooded ridges, is Daleville Pond. It is a big pond, maybe ten acres; it holds a lot of sky. I used to haunt the place because I loved it; I still do. In winter it had that airy scruffiness of deciduous lands; you greet the daylight and the open space, and spend the evening picking burrs out of your pants.

One Valentine's Day, in the afternoon, I was crouched among dried reeds at the edge of Daleville Pond. Across the pond from where I crouched was a low forested mountain ridge. In every other direction I saw only sky, sky crossed by the reeds which blew before my face whichever way I turned.

I was looking through binoculars at a pair of whistling swans. Whistling swans! It is impossible to say how excited I was to see whistling swans in Daleville, Virginia. The two were a pair, mated for life, migrating north and west from the Atlantic coast to the high arctic. They had paused to feed at Daleville Pond. I had flushed them, and now they were flying and circling the pond. I crouched in the reeds so they would not be afraid to come back to the water.

Through binoculars I followed the swans, swinging where they flew. All their feathers were white; their eyes were black. Their wingspan was six feet; they were bigger than I was. They flew in unison, one behind the other; they made pass after pass at the pond. I watched them change from white swans in front of the mountain to black swans in front of the sky. In clockwise ellipses they flew, necks long and relaxed, alternately beating their wide wings and gliding.

As I rotated on my heels to keep the black frame of the lenses around them, I lost all sense of space. If I lowered the binoculars I was always amazed to learn in which direction I faced—dazed, the way you emerge awed from a movie and try to reconstruct, bit by bit, a real world, in order to discover where in it you might have parked the car.

I lived in that circle of light, in great speed and utter silence. When the swans passed before the sun they were distant—two black threads, two live stitches. But they kept coming, smoothly, and the sky deepened to blue behind them and they took on light. They gathered dimension as they neared, and I could see their ardent, straining eyes. Then I could hear the brittle blur of their wings, the blur which faded as they circled on, and the sky brightened to yellow behind them and the swans flattened and darkened and diminished as they flew. Once I lost them behind the mountain ridge; when they emerged they were flying suddenly very high, and it was like music changing key.

I was lost. The reeds in front of me, swaying and out of focus in the binoculars' circular field, were translucent. The reeds were strands of color passing light like cells in water. They were those yellow and green and brown strands of pond algae I had watched so long in a light-soaked field. My eyes burned; I was watching algae wave in a shrinking drop; they crossed each other and parted wetly. And suddenly into the field swam two whistling swans, two tiny whistling swans, infinitesimal, beating their tiny wet wings, perfectly formed.

QUESTIONS FOR READING, RESPONDING, AND WRITING

Summarizing Main Points

1. Dillard observes life both through a microscope and through binoculars. Compare and contrast what she sees through each. Compare the actual process of observing through the different lenses as well—that is, describe the steps Dillard must perform in order to use each lens.

2. List the ways the process of observing life through each lens affects Dillard herself, both her physical state and her emotional state. How does her description of her physical state reflect on her emotional state?

Analyzing Methods of Discourse

1. Dillard says that her essay "is a story about swans." She then qualifies that statement by going on to say, "it is not even a story; it is a description of swans" that includes "a mortal adult who had long since moved out of the Pittsburgh

basement." Do you feel that the essay is more than a description? What elements of a story line or plot development can there be with only one character?
2. How does Dillard's description of the "dense population" under the microscope and the "mated swans" help create other "characters" to interact with each other and with Dillard? What elements of Dillard's description of each seem similar?

Focusing on the Field

1. About the writing process Dillard has said: "The truth of your life is literature! You're writing consciously, off hundreds of index cards, often distorting the literal truth to achieve an artistic one." List any "distortions" you see in this essay.
2. Compare the process of looking through "lenses" as Dillard describes it with the action of writing about science. How is writing about science "an acquired skill"? What things, besides "eyelashes," can also hinder objective scientific observation?

Writing Assignments

1. In a short essay, record your own description of the process of scientific observation. You need not use any scientific apparatus, though you should include not only a description of physical details you observe but also a description of the circumstances surrounding those observations that might affect them, your own attitude, and any ways that the observational environment has been altered by the process of observation.
2. Choose one essay from this section on "Science and Technology" (e.g., John McPhee's "Ice Pond," Steven Levy's "My Search for Einstein's Brain") and one from "Social Sciences" (e.g., Bruno Bettelheim's "Fairy Tale versus Myth," Robert Coles's "Children of Affluence"), and, in a short essay of your own, compare the process of observation in each. Do both authors take into account their own attitudes and preconceptions? Do they both discuss changes in the observed due to the observer?

Richard Selzer

THE ART OF SURGERY

Richard Selzer is a self-avowed doctor of two sorts, both a poet and a surgeon. As he puts it, each "gazes, records, diagnoses, and prophesies." Selzer's lyrical yet vivid writing most often takes the form of the essay, yet his narrative autobiographical techniques approach the style of fiction and poetry. Like other scientist-essayists collected in this section, Selzer finds a language that bridges the gap between science and art.

Selzer, the son of a physician, was born in Troy, New York in 1928 and studied locally at both Union College (B.S., 1948) and Albany Medical College (M.D., 1953). Since then he has settled in New Haven, Connecticut, where, after postdoctoral work at Yale, he began a private practice in general surgery. His first book, a collection of short stories, *Rituals of Surgery*, was followed by mostly nonfiction work, including *Mortal Lessons, Confessions of a Knife,* and *Letters to a Young Doctor,* a book which offers personal advice on Selzer's demanding profession to those considering medicine as a career. As their titles suggest, all his books concern the medical profession, yet all are especially engaging to general readers.

Someone asked me why a surgeon would write. Why, when the shelves are already too full? They sag under the deadweight of books. To add a single adverb is to risk exceeding the strength of the boards. A surgeon should abstain. A surgeon, whose fingers are more at home in the steamy gulleys of the body than they are tapping the dry keys of a typewriter. A surgeon, who feels the slow slide of intestines against the back of his hand and is no more alarmed than were a family of snakes taking their comfort from such an indolent rubbing. A surgeon, who palms the human heart as though it were some captured bird.

Why should he write? Is it vanity that urges him? There is glory enough in the knife. Is it for money? One can make too much money. No. It is to search for some meaning in the ritual of surgery, which is at once murderous, painful, healing, and full of love. It is a devilish hard thing to transmit—to find, even. Perhaps if one were to cut out a heart, a lobe of the liver, a single convolution of the brain, and paste it to a page, it would speak with more eloquence than all the words of Balzac. Such a piece would need no literary style, no mass of erudition or history, but in its very shape and feel would tell all the frailty and strength, the despair and nobility of man. What? Publish a heart? A little piece of bone? Preposterous. Still I fear that is what it may require to reveal the truth that lies hidden in the body. Not all the undressings of Rabelais, Chekhov, or even William Carlos Williams have wrested it free, although God knows each one of those doctors made a heroic assault upon it.

I have come to believe that it is the flesh alone that counts. The rest is that with which we distract ourselves when we are not hungry or cold, in pain or ecstasy. In the recesses of the body I search for the philosophers' stone. I know it is there, hidden in the deepest, dampest cul-de-sac. It awaits discovery. To find it would be like the harnessing of fire. It would illuminate the world. Such a quest is not without pain. Who can gaze on so much misery and feel no hurt? Emerson has written that the poet is the only true doctor. I believe him, for the poet, lacking the impediment of speech with which the rest of us are afflicted, gazes, records, diagnoses, and prophesies.

I invited a young diabetic woman to the operating room to amputate her leg. She could not see the great shaggy black ulcer upon her foot and ankle that threatened to encroach upon the rest of her body, for she was blind as well. There upon her foot was a Mississippi Delta brimming with corruption, sending its raw tributaries down between her toes. Gone were all the little web spaces that when fresh and whole are such a delight to loving men. She could not see her wound, but she could feel it. There is no pain like that of the bloodless limb turned rotten and festering. There is neither unguent nor anodyne to kill such a pain yet leave intact the body.

For over a year I trimmed away the putrid flesh, cleansed, anointed, and dressed the foot, staving off, delaying. Three times each week, in her darkness, she sat upon my table, rocking back and forth, holding her extended leg by the thigh, gripping it as though it were a rocket that must be steadied lest it explode and scatter her toes about the room. And I would cut away a bit here, a bit there, of the swollen blue leather that was her tissue.

At last we gave up, she and I. We could no longer run ahead of the gangrene. We had not the legs for it. There must be an amputation in order that she might live—and I as well. It was to heal us both that I must take up knife and saw, and cut it off. And when I could feel it drop from her body to the table, see the blessed *space* appear between her and that leg, I too would be well.

Now it is the day of the operation. I stand by while the anesthetist administers the drugs, watch as the tense familiar body relaxes into narcosis. I turn then to uncover the leg. There, upon her kneecap, she has drawn, blindly, upside down for me to see, a face; just a circle with two ears, two eyes, a nose, and a smiling upturned mouth. Under it she has printed SMILE, DOCTOR. Minutes later I listen to the sound of the saw, until a little crack at the end tells me it is done.

So. I have learned that man is not ugly, but that he is Beauty itself. There is no other his equal. Are we not all dying, none faster or more slowly than any other? I have become receptive to the possibilities of love (for it is love, this thing that happens in the operating room), and each day I wait, trembling in the busy air. Perhaps today it will come. Perhaps today I will find it, take part in it, this love that blooms in the stoniest desert.

All through literature the doctor is portrayed as a figure of fun. Shaw was splenetic about him; Molière delighted in pricking his pompous medicine men, and well they deserved it. The doctor is ripe for caricature. But I believe that the truly great writing about doctors has not yet been done. I think it must be done *by* a doctor, one who is through with the love affair with his technique, who recognizes that he has played Narcissus, raining kisses on a mirror, and who now, out of the impacted masses of his guilt, has expanded into self-doubt, and finally into the high state of wonderment. Perhaps he will be a nonbeliever who, after a lifetime of grand gestures and mighty deeds, comes upon the knowledge that he has done no more than meddle in the lives of his fellows, and that he has done at least as much harm as good. Yet he may continue to pretend, at least, that there is nothing to fear, that death will not come, so long as people ask it of him. Later, after his patients have left, he may closet himself in his darkened office, sweating and afraid.

A writing doctor would treat men and women with equal reverence. For what is the "liberation" of either sex to him who knows the diagrams, the inner geographies of each? I love the solid heft of men as much as I adore the heated capaciousness of women—women in whose penetralia is found the repository of existence. I would have them glory in that. Women are physics and chemistry. They are matter. It is their bodies that inform of the frailty of men. We have not their cellular, enzymatic wisdom. Man is albuminoid, proteinaceous, laked pearl; woman is yolky, ovoid, rich. Both are exuberant bloody growths. I would use the defects and deformities of each for my sacred purpose of writing, for I know that it is the marred and scarred and faulty that are subject to grace. I would seek the soul in the facts of animal economy and profligacy. Yes, it is the exact location of the soul that I am after. The smell of it is in my nostrils. I have caught glimpses of it in the body diseased. If only I could tell it. Is there no mathematical equation that can guide me? So much pain and pus equals so much truth? It is elusive as the whippoorwill that one hears calling incessantly from out the night window, but which, nesting as it does low in the brush, no one sees. No one but the poet, for he sees what no one else can. He was born with the eye for it.

Once I thought I had it: Ten o'clock, one night; the end room off a long corridor in a college infirmary; my last patient of the day; degree of exhaustion suitable for the appearance of a vision, some manifestation. The patient is a young man recently returned from Guatemala, from the excavation of Mayan ruins. His left upper arm wears a gauze dressing which, when removed, reveals a clean punched-out hole the size of a dime. The tissues about the opening are swollen and tense. A thin brownish fluid lips the edge, and now and then a lazy drop of the overflow spills down the arm. An abscess, inadequately drained. I will enlarge the opening to allow better egress of the pus. Nurse, will you get me a scalpel and some. . . .

What happens next is enough to lay Francis Drake avomit in his cabin. No explorer ever stared in wilder surmise than I into that crater from which there now emerges a narrow gray head whose sole distinguishing feature is a pair of black pincers. The head sits atop a longish flexible neck arching now this way, now that, testing the air. Alternately it folds back upon itself, then advances in new boldness. And all the while, with dreadful rhythmicity, the unspeakable pincers open and close. Abscess? Pus? Never. Here is the lair of a beast at whose malignant purpose I could but guess. A Mayan devil, I think, that would soon burst free to fly about the room, with horrid blanket-wings and iridescent scales, raking, pinching, injecting God knows what acid juice. And even now the irony does not escape me, the irony of my patient as excavator excavated.

With all the ritual deliberation of a high priest I advance a surgical clamp toward the hole. The surgeon's heart is become a bat hanging upside down from his rib cage. The rim achieved—now thrust—and the ratchets of the clamp close upon the empty air. The devil has retracted. Evil mocking laughter bangs back and forth in the brain. More stealth. Lying in wait. One must skulk. Minutes pass, perhaps an hour. . . . A faint disturbance in the lake, and once again the thing upraises, further and further, hovering. Acrouch, strung, the surgeon is one with his instrument; there is no longer any boundary between its metal and his flesh. They are joined in a single perfect tool of extirpation. It is just for this that he was born. Now—thrust—and clamp—and *yes*. Got him!

Transmitted to the fingers comes the wild thrashing of the creature. Pinned and wriggling, he is mine. I hear the dry brittle scream of the dragon, and a hatred seizes me, but such a detestation as would make of Iago a drooling sucktit. It is the demented hatred of the victor for the vanquished, the warden for his prisoner. It is the hatred of fear. Within the jaws of my hemostat is the whole of the evil of the world, the dark concentrate itself, and I shall kill it. For mankind. And, in so doing, will open the way into a thousand years of perfect peace. Here is Surgeon as Savior indeed.

Tight grip now . . . steady, relentless pull. How it scrabbles to keep its tentacle-hold. With an abrupt moist plop the extraction is complete. There, writhing in the teeth of the clamp, is a dirty gray body, the size and shape of an English walnut. He is hung everywhere with tiny black hooklets. Quickly . . . into the specimen jar of saline . . . the lid screwed tight. Crazily he swims round and round, wiping his slimy head against the glass, then slowly sinks to the bottom, the mass of hooks in frantic agonal wave.

"You are going to be all right," I say to my patient. "We are *all* going to be all right from now on."

The next day I take the jar to the medical school. "That's the larva of the warble fly," says a pathologist. "The fly usually bites a cow, and deposits its eggs beneath the skin. There, the egg develops into the larval form which, when ready, burrows its way to the outside through the hide, and falls to the ground. In time it matures into a full-grown warble fly. This one happened to bite a man. It was about to come out on its own, and, of course, it would have died."

The words *imposter, sorehead, servant of Satan* spring to my lips. But now he has been joined by other scientists. They nod in agreement. I gaze from one gray eminence to another, and know the mallet-blow of glory pulverized. I tried to save the world, but it didn't work out.

No, it is not the surgeon who is God's darling. He is the victim of vanity. It is the poet who heals with his words, stanches the flow of blood, stills the rattling breath, applies poultice to the scalded flesh.

Did you ask me why a surgeon writes? I think it is because I wish to be a doctor.

QUESTIONS FOR READING, RESPONDING, AND WRITING

Summarizing Main Points

1. According to Selzer, why must a surgeon write?
2. Early in the essay, Selzer tells the reader that he believes Emerson's statement that "the poet is the only true doctor." Explain what Selzer means by this. Do you believe Emerson's statement yourself?

Analyzing Methods of Discourse

1. At the end of his essay, Selzer calls the surgeon "the victim of vanity." How do the two anecdotes he tells illustrate this point?
2. Selzer makes a number of literary allusions throughout the essay to make two different, but related points. Write down all the sentences in which these allusions appear. Identify the points Selzer uses them to make and the ways in which their use helps to clarify his own aims.

Focusing on the Field

1. Selzer makes an implicit comparison between surgery and writing when he names the former an "art." What is it about his descriptions of surgery that encourage you to view it as you view writing or literature? Look specifically at his account of his removal of the warble fly from the young man's arm. Compare his account of the situation to the pathologist's account which follows.
2. In paragraph ten, Selzer describes the role of the "writing doctor." He employs both a medical and a spiritual vocabulary to imply that he would use a careful

study of the flesh to ascertain the "exact location of the soul." How does the conjunction of medical and spiritual language help Selzer make his point about the "writing doctor"? Can you find other examples of this strategy elsewhere in the essay?

Writing Assignments

1. In "The Chart of the Novel," Gerald Weissmann defines "a view of patient and disease based on the human, novelistic approach of the last century." In a short essay, discuss the ways in which Selzer's self-portrait works as an illustration of Weissmann's definition. Use material from both essays in your own essay.

2. Weissmann provides beginnings from three sets of hospital records in his essay. Using Selzer's stories of the young diabetic or the young excavator as models, turn one of Weissmann's openings into a story that ends on an optimistic note.

Steven Levy

MY SEARCH FOR EINSTEIN'S BRAIN

The following essay details Steven Levy's exhaustive search for "Einstein's brain." Einstein himself no doubt would have been puzzled by Levy's search but not by his conclusion: "Einstein's brain is physiologically no different from yours or mine."

Albert Einstein (1879–1955) was one of the greatest scientists of all time. In 1905, at the age of 26, Einstein contributed three papers to the German scientific periodical *Annals of Physics* that, of themselves, provided the basis for three entirely new branches of physics. At the time, Einstein was working as an examiner in a Swiss patent office, which allowed him the free time for his scientific investigations, though he had yet to hold an academic position. Only in 1909 did Einstein become a professor, teaching and studying first in Switzerland and later in Prague and Zurich.

In 1933, Einstein visited England and the United States, where, at Princeton, he accepted a lifetime position as director of the newly founded Institute for Advanced Study. There, Einstein spent the remaining years of his life, working to demonstrate a unified field theory that combined gravitational and electromagnetic equations. At the time of his death, Einstein had provided the impetus for others to pursue that demonstration. He had also become something of an international folk hero, a modest man whose life transcended the laws of physics, so that his death and the "gross material" of his brain would become, in the words of Roland Barthes in another essay included in this section, "a mythical object."

The mystery of the world is its comprehensibility.

Albert Einstein

Albert Einstein lived in Princeton. A small house, address 112 Mercer Street. He was a familiar figure in the town, usually walking around in a ragged sweater and tennis shoes, thin gray hair awry, thoughts entangled in a complex mathematical labyrinth. Children loved him; he would occasionally help them with their homework.

In 1955, he was working on a theory of gravitation that he would never perfect. He had turned down the presidency of Israel three years earlier, and was now involved in drafting a letter with Bertrand Russell imploring the nations of the world to abolish war. He was noted as the greatest thinker in the world. He had changed our conception of time and space. But at 76, his health was failing.

The doctors called it a hardened aorta. It leaked blood. He had known about the fault in his heart for several years. When first hearing that the artery might develop an aneurysm that could burst, he said, "Let it burst." On April 13, it looked as if it might.

His physician, Dr. Guy K. Dean, called in two consultants, and the three doctors concluded that unless surgery was attempted, the outlook was grim. The creator of the theory of relativity refused. On Friday, April 15, Einstein was persuaded to move his sickbed from Mercer Street to the Princeton Hospital.

During the weekend, things began to look better. Einstein's son, Hans Albert, flew in from California. His stepdaughter Margot was already in the hospital, being treated for a minor illness. On Sunday, it looked as if the aneurysm might heal temporarily. Dr. Dean took a look at his patient at eleven P.M. He was sleeping peacefully.

The nurse assigned to Einstein was named Alberta Roszel. After midnight, she noticed some troubled breathing in her patient. She went to get help. The bed was cranked up. Pale and emaciated, Albert Einstein was muttering something in German, a language Alberta Roszel did not understand. He took two deep breaths and died.

Princeton Hospital in 1955 was not the major facility it would become in later years. A major mobilization was needed to handle publicity on the occasion of the death of such a well-known international figure. Almost seven hours after the death, the hospital announced it and set up a news conference at 11:15. During the hours between the death and the release of details, the Einstein family, their friends, and the hospital officials worked in concert to deny the reporters then flooding to Princeton any scenes to witness, any physical evidence to describe to the millions who craved more than cold facts. Einstein had specifically asked that he not become the subject of a "personality cult." He did not want 112 Mercer Street to become a museum. He did not want his remains available to admirers making pilgrimages. His family shared his zeal for privacy. By the time the news conference began, an autopsy had been performed. The hospital pathologist, Dr. Thomas S. Harvey, had presided. He worked alone, under the eyes of Dr. Otto Nathan, a friend and colleague of the deceased who was the designated executor of the Einstein literary estate. For a period of time, Dr. Dean was also in the autopsy room. It was Dr. Dean who signed the death certificate. Official Cause: rupture of the arteriosclerotic. Birthplace: Ulm, Germany. Citizen of: U.S.A. Occupation: scientist.

If the assembled reporters hoped for any details of the autopsy, they were disappointed; they learned only the cause of Einstein's death. The body was not available for viewing. It was taken to the Mather Funeral Home in Princeton, where it sat for an hour and a half, until it was driven to the Ewing Crematory in Trenton. At four-thirty in the afternoon, the body was cremated. Later, Dr. Nathan took the ashes and dispersed them in a river, presumably the Delaware.

But part of the remains was spared. Einstein had requested his brain be removed for posthumous study, and his family bid it be done at the autopsy. It was placed in a jar. A *New York Times* reporter on April 20 wrote an article headlined "KEY SOUGHT IN EINSTEIN BRAIN." It talked of a study to be performed on the brain and the possible implications. The study, said the story, "may shed light on one of nature's greatest mysteries—the secret of genius." More details were to be released on how the study would be performed. Another press conference was scheduled for the following week.

The Einstein family was upset by the article and told the doctors entrusted with the brain that there was to be no publicity whatsoever concerning the study. The press conference never took place. Einstein's brain had gone into hiding.

"I want you to find Einstein's brain."

Of course I knew who Albert Einstein was. I knew, like most people, about the theory of relativity, but could provide little detail. Something about e equaling mc², and something about atomic energy, and something about how time and space differed depending on your point of view. I knew it changed the world, and I knew that although it was responsible for nuclear weapons, the theory itself was a step forward, and Einstein was recognized as a humanitarian as well as a genius. I didn't know that his brain was still around.

Neither, really, did my editor. He had done some work on the subject of the brain and had wondered what had happened to this brain of brains, this organic masterpiece of gray matter and cerebral cortex. He had read the last pages of Ronald Clark's *Einstein: The Life and Times*, where the author says of Einstein, "He had insisted his brain be used for research . . ." and then drops the subject. And my editor had heard all sorts of rumors. Einstein's brain was lost. Einstein's brain was examined and found to be normal. Einstein's brain was examined and found to be extraordinary. Einstein's brain was hidden in a vault, frozen for cloning. And so on.

So the editor had written to Clark, asking him what happened to the brain. The author of Einstein's standard biography wrote back saying, "I'm afraid I don't know the answer, but have a recollection that it *was* preserved somewhere." He suggested contacting Otto Nathan, the executor of the Einstein estate. Nathan replied promptly. His one-paragraph letter confirmed that the brain had been removed before cremation, and stated that the pathologist in charge had been a Dr. Thomas Harvey. "As far as I know," Nathan concluded, "he is no longer with the hospital."

The letter was a year old. Now my editor wanted to know where the brain was. And he wanted me to find it.

"Sure," I said.

I had to wait a long time. Then a voice came over the phone. "Mr. Seligman will be right with you," it said. While someone in the hospital paged him, I read some more of a book explaining relativity. My reading habits had changed drastically. This was the third "layman's" book on Einstein's theories I had been through. In each book I did fine until the mathematical formulas, "easily handled by the average high school graduate," began a relentless progression of incremental obliqueness. I would plod onward, and though I didn't grasp the intricacies of relativity, I now at least misunderstood it clearly. I could see how Einstein convinced the scientific community that neither time nor space was absolute. According to my books, this applied chiefly to someone walking to the bathroom on a moving train while simultaneously comparing fixed points with a friend on a moving supersonic transport. Or, failing that, it would become obvious at speeds approaching the speed of light (the famous *c*), the velocity of some subatomic particles. It is only at these speeds that we can perceive that the universe is not as it seemed to Isaac Newton. It all sounds quite irrelevant until you consider that applications of the theory of relativity have given us everything from nuclear energy to laser beams and have helped explain many major astronomical discoveries in the past few decades. The brain I was looking for had changed our perception of the universe, and since Walter Seligman was a vice-president of the

Princeton Medical Center, where the brain had been removed from the highly recognizable head of Albert Einstein, I hoped for a clue.

Finally, he reached a phone. "Yes, the operation took place here," he conceded. "But there are no records." He paused. "The only person who would know anything about it would be the pathologist who performed the operation. Doctor Thomas Harvey."

Where would Dr. Harvey be found?

"I'm afraid I don't know. He left here years ago."

Would your personnel department have any records?

"No. He moved several times since, I've heard. He's out of the state, I'm sure."

What about records of the autopsy itself? Exact time? Who worked there with Harvey? Which operating room? Anyone who might know if. . . .

"No. He was the only one working on it and he took all records with him. We have nothing on file here. All this, of course, was before my time."

It was before many of our times—it was twenty-three years ago. The world was gloomy, worried about a cold war that threatened to heat into a nuclear disaster. No one was more concerned than Albert Einstein. All his life he had tried to nudge mankind toward a pacifist ideal. His efforts were inconstant because his pacifism was always subordinated to his physics; he knew it was by his mental labors that he could make his greatest contributions. So while he worked for peace, he worked harder at his formulas, even as his heart leaked blood and a blister on his aorta verged on a fatal rupture. During his short final stay in Princeton Hospital, he had requested pencil and paper to continue his calculations. With these he could work—"My brain is my laboratory," he once said.

And the whereabouts of his brain? God knows where. I had spent hours of library work and found items of negative value. The brain, it seemed, had been sectioned soon after his death (this I learned from the article that led Einstein's family to impose secrecy on the project), and would never be able to regain its original form. Pieces had still been under study as late as 1963 (this from a minor biography of Einstein). And, according to all available indices of scientific research, *nothing had been published concerning studies of Einstein's brain.* Nothing.

Reading about Einstein, and about the workings of the human brain, I began thinking about the subject more than was reasonable. I would create uneasy silences in editorial lunches by remarking how the timing of the Michelson-Morley experiments paved the way for Einstein's work on relativity. I carried on barroom seminars on the relation between brain size and human intelligence (little—scientists have found that a moron's brain can be larger than a genius's). I learned that current theories postulate that intelligence is probably a function of the speed with which electrical impulses jump through the synapses between the billions of cells in the brain, and that these impulses are triggered by enzymes in a process still not totally understood. I had no idea how quickly impulses had jumped through the gray matter of Albert Einstein. I wanted to know. Above all, I wanted my eyes to allow light to trigger off impulses in my optic nerve that would excite sensations in my own brain, and that through some magical process I hope we will never understand, these sensations would thrill me and edify me, seeing the brain that all brains aspire to.

My growing obsession distracted me. One night I drove to a friend's house in Princeton. The hour was late and I was two drinks silly. I missed a turn off Hodge Road, and somewhere along the line made a left, thinking it the right direction. It wasn't, so I made a U-turn. I felt an itchy discomfort as I veered toward town; checking a road sign I saw I was traveling on Mercer Street. In half a block, I saw it, a common white frame house, no different than any other of the common single houses on Mercer Street. Lights were on. I could see plants in the window. Einstein had lived here.

"You're looking for Einstein's brain?" said a coworker. "I have a friend who saw a picture of it."

What?

"She's a medical student in California. Her teacher had slides of it. Here's her number."

I called. The woman, it seemed, had not seen the slide, but had once been invited to by her instructor, a Dr. Moore. Supposedly he had in his possession slides that pictured Einstein's brain. She wasn't sure how he got them. She gave me his number.

Dr. Moore was willing to talk.

"I worked on the study of the brain," he said. "In Chicago. Sets of the section were sent to various experts for analysis. The man I was working for, Dr. Sidney Schulman, specialized in the thalamus, and we got portions of Einstein's thalamus, sectioned and stained for microscopic study."

The thalamus is a part of the brain which transmits impulses to the cerebral cortex.

"As far as the thalamus is concerned," said Dr. Moore, "Einstein's brain cells were like anyone else's at that age. If you showed the slides blind to someone, he would say that they came from any old man. Even so, I took Kodachromes of a couple slides to show to my students."

I wondered if Dr. Moore knew where the brain section came from and whether he knew of parts of the brain that might still be around.

"I'm not sure. I think the stuff we got was from some pathologist from Princeton."

Dr. Sidney Schulman seemed surprised that someone was calling him about Einstein's brain at this late date, and he told me to wait while he got his files. I hoped he wouldn't change his mind before he got back to the phone.

"I couldn't find the file," he said after a nearly interminable hiatus. "All it really would have for you is the name of the pathologist who was doing the study. He was the man who performed the autopsy on Einstein."

A Dr. Thomas Harvey?

"*That's* the name. He came to me soon after Einstein's death. He had heard about my interest in the thalamus and had sent me some microscopic slides with material from the brain. Later he visited me and took back the slides. I did keep a few for my own use."

What came of the studies?

"Well, Dr. Harvey was interested in finding out if the brain varied from the norm. Using the methods then available I found no variation. But the problem was that methods used today weren't available back then. And even if they were, they couldn't have been used in this case.

"You see, today studies like these are done with electron microscopes. But they can only be used with samples fixed directly after removal from a live body. In something like Einstein's case, the delay between death and fixation (the use of a substance like formaldehyde) causes post-mortem changes. Partially because of this, there *are* no established standards of normality in cells like these.

"Dr. Harvey wanted me to do a more intensive study, to count the cells and cell types, but I didn't think it would be worthwhile. I suggested another expert, a Dr. Kuhlenbeck of Philadelphia. I don't know whether he took my advice."

Have you heard anything from Doctor Harvey? Do you know where he is?

"No, I haven't heard from him since he took back the samples. And I have never seen anything published. Do *you* know where to reach him?"

No, I didn't know where to reach him. But I had one last idea. Since my man was a doctor, he must be a member of the American Medical Association. Surely they keep track of their members.

The AMA is headquartered in Chicago. They told me that they don't give out members' whereabouts over the phone. But I'm a reporter on a

deadline, I insisted. They transferred me to several people before someone, apparently exasperated enough to bend a regulation, asked me the
name of the person I sought.

I told her. A silence. Did I hear the rustling of pages while I waited?

"What's the middle initial? And how old would he be?" the woman
asked.

"S," I said. "And he'd be up in years by now."

"Well, there's a Thomas S. Harvey, born 1912, in Wichita, Kansas."

Wichita? So be it. But please, please, give me the number.

"We don't have a number," she said. "How about an address?"

Fine. As I wrote it down, I wondered—was this the address of Albert
Einstein's brain?

Since Dr. Harvey was the obvious key to my search, I was nervous
before calling him. If he hung up on me, I would never see the brain. On
the other hand, he might be very nice. We might have a pleasant conversation and he might tell me that he did study the brain, found nothing,
and tossed the pieces into a Jiffy Bag. Or, just as bad, the man I called
might not be the Dr. Harvey I sought. In the twenty-three years since
taking out Albert Einstein's brain, Dr. Thomas S. Harvey might well have
died and taken with him whatever secrets Einstein's brain held.

There was a tense pause when I asked the man who came to the
phone whether he was the same Dr. Harvey who had worked at Princeton
Hospital in the mid-1950s. Almost as if he had been considering a denial,
he slowly said yes. I told him I was interested in Einstein's brain and I was
willing to visit him to talk about it. I didn't mention the obsessive character my search had begun to take on.

He told me that there had been an agreement not to talk to anyone about the study of the brain. He was sorry, but. . . .

I was more than sorry. I persisted, telling him about the impeccable
reputation of my publication, and how the letter from Dr. Nathan giving
Harvey's name (though not where to find him) was an implicit go-ahead
from the Einstein estate. The doctor finally agreed to see me, on the
condition that he not be bound to tell me any scientific information that
might yet be published.

Throughout the conversation, Dr. Harvey had sounded very uncomfortable. I felt as if the wrong question would lead him to dismiss any idea
of dealing with me. So I hadn't asked him some obvious questions. Like
why nothing had been published. Like why the subject was still so
touchy. Like whether he still had any of the brain in his possession.

These questions I would ask in Wichita.

As far as I can ascertain, Albert Einstein never visited Wichita during his three-quarters century of life. I quickly saw why. Kansas is about as appealing as a day-old wheat pancake. The Kansas headquarters for my search was the Wichita Plaza Holiday Inn, at twenty-six stories the tallest building in the state.

The twenty-fifth story housed the Penthouse Club. The view at midnight is not breathtaking—many streetlights illuminating vacant sidewalks. I was visiting the Penthouse Club as a new member—signing up was the requirement for buying a drink in Kansas, a "dry" state. Albert Einstein would not have appreciated that. He enjoyed a good glass of wine. When his doctors eventually forbade him his drink, he would sniff at a full glass and remark, in a tone of mock tragedy, that the sniff was the extent of the pleasures the medical establishment allowed him. They probably would have made him join the Penthouse Club to sniff wine in Wichita.

My wakeup call came at seven, two hours before my appointment with Dr. Harvey. It was a miserable morning, blackened by rainclouds that looked intent on dropping great volumes of water on Wichita. The torrent began about the time I started looking for a taxi to the residential area of town where Dr. Harvey worked as a medical supervisor in a bio-testing lab. In no time, the streets were pocked with puddles the size of bomb craters. The cabdriver thought nothing of nosing the taxi into one of these instant lakes. All I was concerned about was making my appointment. Especially if it meant finding Einstein's brain.

Only a few minutes late, I was met by Dr. Harvey. To get to his corner office, he ushered me through a maze of noisy computers and silent medical technicians working on blood and urine samples. He seemed a gentle man. His hair was gray, but there was spunk in his blue eyes. He wore a pastel shirt and patterned tie. In his shirt pocket was the kind of pen capable of writing three different colors. He smiled as we shook hands. He seemed somewhat embarrassed at the situation.

Some small talk disposed of, we got down to the subject I was yearning to discuss—Albert Einstein.

Dr. Harvey had met Einstein several times. He had been to Einstein's house to take samples for lab tests. "He was very informal and cordial," Dr. Harvey recalled. "A very kind sort of man."

Then came Einstein's fatal illness. It changed the life of Thomas Harvey, who had come to Princeton by way of Yale Medical School, Philadelphia General Hospital, and Pepper Laboratories. By virtue of his job as hospital pathologist, it was up to him to conduct the autopsy on Einstein and to take the brain out. And somehow it fell to him to conduct the study on this exceptional brain.

It made sense to appoint a regular hospital pathologist to make sure the task of studying the brain would be done properly—Harvey apparently was eager to take on a large project that could be, as he put it, "one of my major professional contributions." Harvey confirmed that it was luck that led him to conduct the study. "By being there, I felt that I had a responsibility to do an adequate and complete examination," he said in a friendly but nervous tone. He was still talking as if he expected some buzzer to ring and a voice from the heavens to boom down and say, "That's quite enough." But as he told the story of Einstein's brain, his voice took on confidence. At times, it took on a tone of awe.

What the reporters weren't told in 1955 was that Dr. Harvey was enlisting some brain experts to assist him in studying the most significant chunk of "gross material," as Harvey put it, ever to become available to medical science. Dr. Harvey himself had a special interest in neuropathology (the study of disorders of the nervous system), but he realized that he needed specialists to help him in his marathon task of searching for the clues to genius. One of the initial specialists he contacted was Dr. Harry Zimmerman in New York, and eventually he lined up Percival Bailey of Chicago and Hartwig Kuhlenbeck of Philadelphia. There were others, but Dr. Harvey was reluctant to give their names.

The first step in the process was an exacting measurement and complete photographing of the whole brain. This was done at Princeton Hospital, which had agreed to partially fund the study. From these measurements, there was apparently no difference between Einstein's brain and a "normal" one. Certainly it was no bigger, and at two and sixty-four hundredths pounds, it was no heavier. This was no surprise; the real work would take place in microscopic studies of the dissected brain.

So sometime in the early fall of 1955, Dr. Harvey packed up the brain of Albert Einstein, made sure it was well cushioned in its formaldehyde-filled jar, and drove—very, very carefully—from Princeton to Philadelphia, where the brain would be sectioned in a laboratory at the University of Pennsylvania.

"They had a big lab there," Dr. Harvey recalled. "They had equipment for sectioning whole brains, including a microtome used only for brain work. Those particular microtomes are very scarce, and special technicians are needed to operate them. Dr. Erich, who ran the laboratory, had such a technician, and though it took six months to do, we did a beautiful job of sectioning the brain."

From there, the sections of the brain, some in small chunks preserved in celloidin (a gelatinous material), some on microscopic slides, went off to various parts of the country to be studied by specialists. "I usually delivered the pieces myself," said Harvey. "It could have been handled by mail, I guess, but I wanted to meet these men."

The idea was that the specialists would eventually publish papers on the brain parts they studied. Meanwhile, Harvey would perform his own tests, some paralleling the other work and some that no one was duplicating.

"In order to do a study like this," said Dr. Harvey, "you have to have seen enough of the normal brain to have a pretty good idea what would be extraordinary. Unfortunately, not a lot of brains have been studied completely. Less than a dozen. Of course, when it comes to genius . . . not even that many. It really is a mammoth task. There's a tremendous number of cells in the brain. You don't examine every one of them in detail, but you look at an awful lot of sections. Almost all the brain now is in sections. There's a little left as brain tissue, but very little."

How little, I wondered to myself. And where was it? All this history had been fascinating, but I wanted to *view* the damn thing. Of course, you couldn't just bust in on a guy and demand to see a brain. Somehow I had to steer things toward the "gross material" itself. I asked Dr. Harvey if it might be possible to see . . . a slide, perhaps.

"I don't really have any slides here in this office," he said. "So I can't do it here."

Where are the slides? At your home?

"No, they're not there. . . ." He was shifting uncomfortably in his chair. "I really don't think it'll be of much help to you to see one of the slides. I can show you a slide of something else, to show you what they're *like* . . . as I say, I don't have any of the brain here."

My heart sank. "Is any of it in Wichita?" I asked.

"Um, yes. But not in the office here. Aren't you familiar with microscopic slides?"

"Yes, but—"

"Well, I don't want to say any more about it," he said with an air of finality.

Perhaps I could have accepted not seeing the brain if I knew that it didn't exist, or that it existed only in an unreachable place—like the ocean bottom. But to leave Wichita knowing that there might well be some brain to see? Unthinkable. Dr. Harvey noted my obvious dismay, and almost as a consolation asked me if I had any more questions about the study.

Well, all right. Why had things been taking so long?

"We had no urgency to publish. And the actual examination didn't take this long, of course. Though there is some work still to be done. You see, my career since I did the autopsy has been sort of interrupted. I left Princeton Hospital in 1960 and moved to Freehold. And for the past few years, I've been here in Wichita. I don't work on it as much as I used to. But we're getting closer to publication. I'd say we're perhaps a year away."

Has the study found the brain to be . . . different?

Dr. Harvey thought a bit before answering. "So far it's fallen within normal limits for a man his age. There are changes that occur within the brain with age. And his brain showed these. No more so than the average man. The anatomical variations," he said, "are within normal limits."

Another uneasy silence followed. Dr. Harvey shifted in his seat. He seemed to have something he wanted to say, but was agonizing whether to voice it or not.

"Do you have a *photograph* of it here?" I blurted out.

"No, I don't," he said. "I don't have any material here." Then he paused. A shy grin came over his face. "I *do* have a little bit of the gross here," he said, almost apologetically.

Pardon?

"Gross material. Unsectioned. But that's all."

Here? *In this office we're sitting in?*

I looked around. Dr. Harvey was sitting across from me, behind a large desk piled with papers and magazines. On one side of the room was a bookshelf brimming with books and journals; on the other, a small clutter of cardboard boxes and a cooler one might take on a fishing trip. Certainly no temperature-controlled vaults such as I imagined would hold such a scientific treasure.

Without another word, Dr. Harvey rose from his seat and walked around the desk, crossing in front of me to get to the corner of the room. He bent down over the clutter on the floor, stopping at the red plastic cooler. He picked it up and put it on a chair next to me. It didn't fit between the arms of the chair. Moving slowly, he placed it on the floor.

Einstein's brain in a beer cooler?

No. He turned away from the cooler, going back to the corner. Of the two cardboard boxes stacked there, he picked up the top one and moved it to the side. Then he bent down over the bottom box, which had a logo reading COSTA CIDER on the side. There was no top to the box, and it looked filled with crumpled newspapers. Harvey, still wearing a sheepish grin, thrust his hand into the newspapers and emerged with a large mason jar. Floating inside the jar, in a clear liquid solution, were several pieces of matter. A conch shell–shaped mass of wrinkly material the color of clay after kiln firing. A fist-sized chunk of grayish, lined substance, the apparent consistency of sponge. And in a separate pouch, a mass of pinkish-white strings resembling bloated dental floss. All the material was recognizably brain matter.

Dr. Harvey pointed out that the conch-shaped mass was Einstein's cerebellum, the gray blob a chunk of cerebral cortex, and the stringy stuff a group of aortic vessels.

"It's all in sections, except for this," he said. I had risen up to look into the jar, but now I was sunk in my chair, speechless. My eyes were fixed upon that jar as I tried to comprehend that these pieces of gunk bobbing up and down had caused a revolution in physics and quite possibly changed the course of civilization. *There it was!* Before I could regain my wits, Dr. Harvey had reached back into the box for another jar. This one was larger, and since it was not a mason jar, the top had been fixed in place by yellowed masking tape. Inside it were dozens of rectangular translucent blocks, the size of Goldenberg's Peanut Chews, each with a little sticker reading CEREBRAL CORTEX and bearing a number. Encased in every block was a shriveled blob of gray matter.

Dr. Harvey explained the fixative process, and told me what part of the brain the chunks were from. Not a word penetrated my own gray cells. I made no objection as he placed the jars back in the newspaper-filled cider box and moved the cooler back to its original position. Doctor Harvey didn't know it, but I had accomplished my mission. I was too stunned, though, for self-congratulation. We made some more perfunctory conversation, he said he was sorry he couldn't show me his laboratory or give me scientific data, and he offered to write to Dr. Nathan of Einstein's estate to see if I could be authorized to receive some more information. I nodded, but my heart was not in it. Having seen the object of my search, the scientific details seemed superfluous.

A few weeks later, writing this, the scientific details do not seem so superfluous. It would be nice to know all the scientists who worked with Dr. Harvey. It would be nice to know the exact nature of the tests performed on the brain. It would be nice to know if there were any technical qualifiers to Dr. Harvey's generalization that, as of now, it looks as if Einstein's brain is essentially no different than that of a nongenius. But for that, we'll have to wait the year or so that Dr. Harvey said remains between now and the publication of the study that's been twenty-three years in the making. When Dr. Harvey contacted Otto Nathan about giving me the scientific information, Nathan apparently became upset that Harvey had talked to me at all—I had penetrated a secret that the Einstein trust wished preserved.

All along, I had feared that if I ever did get to see Einstein's brain, the experience would be a terrific letdown. I had suspected that the inevitable lifelessness of the material would make looking at the brain matter as interesting as viewing a dead jellyfish. My fears were unjustified. For a moment, with the brain before me, I had been granted a rare peek into an organic crystal ball. Swirling in formaldehyde was the power of the smashed atom, the mystery of the universe's black holes, the utter miracle of human achievement.

I could see why the efforts of Einstein before his death, and of his family and estate afterwards, had been directed toward keeping the brain out of the limelight. It was powerful, capable of refocusing attention on the mystical aspects of Einstein that his family always tried to understate. But as much as a family has a right to privacy, I think a case can be made for discarding the shroud that surrounds this "gross material." Whether you see it or merely contemplate it, there is something very awesome in the post-mortem remains of Albert Einstein's brain. It is something of ourselves at our best, or something of what we humans can be—using our own awesome powers to work out the relation between ourselves and our surroundings. The fact that twenty-three years of study indicate that Einstein's brain is physiologically no different from yours or mine seems to bear this out. "God does not play dice with the Universe," Albert Einstein liked to say, and he spent the bulk of his life trying to prove it. I think that he would be happy to find that, with no better a roll than most of us, he managed to beat the house. What we do with our own dice rolls is up to us, and not chance. There are no better lessons to extract from Albert Einstein's brain.

QUESTIONS FOR READING, RESPONDING, AND WRITING

Summarizing Main Points

1. What does Levy expect to discover about Einstein's brain when he begins his search? Are his expectations fulfilled?
2. What bearing does the fact that studies have so far revealed no differences between Einstein's brain and "nongenius" brains have on Levy's conclusions? Does this fact suggest to you what it suggests to Levy?

Analyzing Methods of Discourse

1. Levy quotes Einstein at the beginning and end of his essay. How do these quotations support Levy's own argument?
2. Levy begins his essay with very specific details surrounding Einstein's life and death. What impression of Einstein does the reader get from the details Levy includes? Compare this initial description of Einstein to Levy's later description of the way in which Dr. Harvey has stored the remaining "gross matter" of his brain.

Focusing on the Field

1. At one point in his search for Einstein's brain, Levy states, "above all, I wanted my eyes to allow light to trigger off impulses in my optic nerve that would excite sensations in my own brain, and that through some magical process I hope we will never understand, these sensations would thrill me and edify me, seeing the brain that all brains aspire to." What is Levy's point here? How does his use of scientific language help make it clear? Locate other examples of this strategy in the essay.

2. Though he includes a fair amount of scientific information from medical experts, Levy is clearly writing for a nonscientific audience. List a few ways in which he makes this point clear. Why is audience an important consideration in this essay?

Writing Assignments

1. Choose a person, place, or thing that holds the same fascination for you that Einstein's brain came to hold for Levy (e.g., Plymouth Rock, the Lincoln Memorial, New York City). Write an essay in which you record a portion of its history and both your reflections and reactions on your first contact with that person, place, or thing.
2. Read Joyce Maynard's "Europe for the First Time." Both Maynard's and Levy's essays are public explorations that lead to personal revelations. Write an essay in which you compare both the public and private aspects of each essay.

Roland Barthes

THE BRAIN OF EINSTEIN

Roland Barthes, born in Cherbourg, France in 1915, figured among the finest thinkers of the twentieth century until his tragic death in 1980. His criticism, at once literary and social, investigated signs and symbols and their relation to human understanding. In *Mythologies* (1957), where the following essay appeared, Barthes frequently took seemingly unusual, yet often mundane objects—plastic, soap detergents, wrestling matches, Greta Garbo's face, toys—and analyzed them in such a way that their more mysterious or mystical functions in society became clear. Though Barthes wrote in French, nearly all his books have been translated into English, including his most popular works, *Writing Degree Zero, A Lover's Discourse, Image/Music/Text,* and *Camera Lucida.*

Barthes began his studies with French literature and classics at the University of Paris and later became involved in sociology and lexicology. He taught and studied at institutions in France, Egypt, Rumania, and the United States, specifically at Johns Hopkins University. Edward Said, himself a renowned literary and social critic, paid Barthes perhaps the ultimate compliment when he said that Barthes had "never written a bad or uninteresting page."

Einstein's brain is a mythical object: paradoxically, the greatest intelligence of all provides an image of the most up-to-date machine, the man who is too powerful is removed from psychology, and introduced into a world of robots; as is well known, the supermen of science-fiction always have something reified about them. So has Einstein: he is commonly signified by his brain, which is like an object for anthologies, a true museum exhibit. Perhaps because of his mathematical specialization, superman is here divested of every magical character; no diffuse power in him, no mystery other than mechanical: he is a superior, a prodigious organ, but a real, even a physiological one. Mythologically, Einstein is matter, his power does not spontaneously draw one towards the spiritual, it needs the help of an independent morality, a reminder about the scientist's 'conscience' (*Science without conscience*, they said . . .).

Einstein himself has to some extent been a party to the legend by bequeathing his brain, for the possession of which two hospitals are still fighting as if it were an unusual piece of machinery which it will at last be possible to dismantle. A photograph shows him lying down, his head bristling with electric wires: the waves of his brain are being recorded, while he is requested to 'think of relativity'. (But for that matter, what does 'to think of' mean, exactly?) What this is meant to convey is probably that the seismograms will be all the more violent since 'relativity' is an arduous subject. Thought itself is thus represented as an energetic material, the measurable product of a complex (quasi-electrical) apparatus which transforms cerebral substance into power. The mythology of Einstein shows him as a genius so lacking in magic that one speaks about his thought as of a functional labour analogous to the mechanical making of sausages, the grinding of corn or the crushing of ore: he used to produce thought, continuously, as a mill makes flour, and death was above all, for him, the cessation of a localized function: '*the most powerful brain of all has stopped thinking*'.

What this machine of genius was supposed to produce was equations. Through the mythology of Einstein, the world blissfully regained the image of knowledge reduced to a formula. Paradoxically, the more the genius of the man was materialized under the guise of his brain, the more the product of his inventiveness came to acquire a magical dimension, and gave a new incarnation to the old esoteric image of a science entirely contained in a few letters. There is a single secret to the world, and this secret is held in one word; the universe is a safe of which humanity seeks the combination: Einstein almost found it, this is the myth of Einstein. In it, we find all the Gnostic themes: the unity of nature, the ideal possibility of a fundamental reduction of the world, the unfastening power of the word, the age-old struggle between a secret and an utterance, the idea that total knowledge can only be discovered all at once, like a lock which suddenly opens after a thousand unsuccessful attempts. The historic equation $E = mc^2$, by its unexpected simplicity, $E = mc^2$ almost embodies the pure idea of the key, bare, linear, made of one metal, opening with a wholly magical ease a door which had resisted the desperate efforts of centuries. Popular imagery faithfully expresses this: *photographs* of Einstein show him standing next to a blackboard covered with mathematical signs of obvious complexity; but *cartoons* of Einstein (the sign that he has become a legend) show him chalk still in hand, and having just written on an empty blackboard, as if without preparation, the magic formula of the world. In this way mythology shows an awareness of the nature of the various tasks: research proper brings into play clockwork-like mechanisms and has its seat in a wholly material organ which is monstrous only by its cybernetic complication; discovery, on the contrary, has a magical essence, it is simple like a basic clement, a principial substance, like the philosophers' stone of hermetists, tar-water for Berkeley, or oxygen for Schelling.

But since the world is still going on, since research is proliferating, and on the other hand since God's share must be preserved, some failure on the part of Einstein is necessary: Einstein died, it is said, without having been able to verify '*the equation in which the secret of the world was enclosed*'. So in the end the world resisted; hardly opened, the secret closed again, the code was incomplete. In this way Einstein fulfils all the conditions of myth, which could not care less about contradictions so long as it establishes a euphoric security: at once magician and machine, eternal researcher and unfulfilled discoverer, unleashing the best and the worst, brain and conscience, Einstein embodies the most contradictory dreams, and mythically reconciles the infinite power of man over nature with the 'fatality' of the sacrosanct, which man cannot yet do without.

QUESTIONS FOR READING, RESPONDING, AND WRITING

Summarizing Main Points

1. According to Barthes, what are the contradictions that Einstein embodies? List them.
2. Barthes begins the last paragraph of his essay with the following statement: "But since the world is still going on, since research is proliferating, and on the other hand since God's share must be preserved, some failure on the part of Einstein is necessary. . . ." What do you think each part of this sentence means? What do you think is Barthes's overall point here?

Analyzing Methods of Discourse

1. Barthes organizes his essay into a series of reductions on the order of $E = mc^2$ (e.g., Einstein = brain, greatest intelligence = machine, formula = magic, etc.). List as many of these reductions as you can find in the order in which they appear in the text. How do these reductions and their arrangement help the reader to understand the "myth of Einstein"?
2. Barthes's essay is built on the principle of contradiction and paradox, such as that contained in the last sentence: "Einstein . . . mythically reconciles the infinite power of man over nature with the 'fatality' of the sacrosanct, which man cannot yet do without." Find examples of other paradoxical statements in this essay. How are they "reconciled"? How does Barthes's paragraph arrangement reflect this same strategy of paradox? What relation does the last paragraph bear to the others in the essay?

Focusing on the Field

1. In this essay, Barthes uses both a vocabulary usually associated with science and one usually associated with magic or story-telling. After identifying examples of both sorts of language, consider the ways in which Barthes uses these two different vocabularies to make his points about "the conditions of myth" and the nature of its "euphoric security."
2. Barthes suggests in this essay that the passage of time ("since the world is still going on") and the resulting discoveries ("since research is proliferating") have not only had an effect on our view of Einstein's discoveries, but have gone so far as to help turn him into a myth. Consider whether or not the additional passage of time and additional research discoveries since Barthes wrote this essay in the late fifties may have had any effect on the myth of Einstein.

Writing Assignments

1. Read Bruno Bettelheim's "Myth versus Fairy Tale." Write an essay in which you argue that Barthes's presentation of Einstein does or does not fulfill Bettelheim's definition of myth.
2. Read Steven Levy's "My Search for Einstein's Brain." Compare and contrast Barthes's essay to Levy's, looking at their respective modes of presentation and their respective conclusions.

Horace Freeland Judson

SCIENTIFIC INVESTIGATION:
The Rage to Know

Horace Freeland Judson was born in 1931 in New York City. The son of an economic statistician, Judson opted to study in the liberal arts, receiving his B.A. from the University of Chicago in 1948 and studying further at both Chicago and Columbia Universities. Working as a journalist and editor in New York City and overseas, Judson wrote a prize-winning article, "The British and Heroin" (1974), which, as he puts it, led to work "in the history of science and along that contentious border where science marches with public policy."

Judson's method—intensive interviewing and study of the written record in correspondence, papers, and notes—is by his own account not especially original, "and yet, in an era when more than half the scientists who have ever lived are still alive, I am repeatedly surprised to find that historians of science are reluctant to attempt interviews or rely on them. I'm forced to suppose that I pursue the materials . . . more intensively than most." Pursue them, he does. For his study of molecular biology, *The Eighth Day of Creation,* Judson interviewed scores of scientists, most of them Nobel Prize winners, and worked with well over a million words of research. _The Search for Solutions_ likewise relies on interviews with Nobel Prize-winning scientists, as the following selection shows. Judson has called _The Search for Solutions_ "a set of short, interlocking essays on the various ways that scientists approach the doing of science."

Certain moments of the mind have a special quality of well-being. A mathematician friend of mine remarked the other day that his daughter, aged eight, had just stumbled without his teaching onto the fact that some numbers are prime numbers—those, like 11 or 19 or 83 or 1,023, that cannot be divided by any other integer (except, trivially, by 1). "She called them 'unfair' numbers," he said. "And when I asked her why they were unfair, she told me, 'Because there's no way to share them out evenly.'" What delighted him most was not her charming turn of phrase nor her equitable turn of mind (17 peppermints to give to her friends?) but—as a mathematician—the knowledge that the child had experienced a moment of pure scientific perception. She had discovered for herself something of the way things are.

The satisfaction of such a moment at its most intense—and this is what ought to be meant, after all, by the tarnished phrase "the moment of truth"—is not easy to describe. It partakes at once of exhilaration and tranquillity. It is luminously clear. It is beautiful. The clarity of the moment of discovery, the beauty of what in that moment is seen to be true about the world, is the most fundamental attraction that draws scientists on.

Science is enormously disparate—easily the most varied and diverse of human pursuits. The scientific endeavor ranges from the study of animal behavior all the way to particle physics, and from the purest of mathematics back again to the most practical problems of shelter and hunger, sickness and war. Nobody has succeeded in catching all this in one net. And yet the conviction persists—scientists themselves believe, at heart—that behind the diversity lies a unity. In those luminous moments of discovery, in the various approaches and the painful tension required to arrive at them, and then in the community of science, organized worldwide to doubt and criticize, test and exploit discoveries—somewhere in that constellation there are surely constants, to begin with. Deeper is the lure that in the bewildering variety of the world as it is there may be found some astonishing simplicities.

Philosophers, and some of the greatest among them, have offered descriptions of what they claim is the method of science. These make most scientists acutely uncomfortable. The descriptions don't seem to fit what goes on in the doing of science. They seem at once too abstract and too limited. Scientists don't believe that they think in ways that are wildly different from the way most people think at least in some areas of their lives. "We'd be in real trouble—we could get nowhere—if ordinary methods of inference did not apply," Philip Morrison said in a conversation a while ago. (Morrison is a theoretical physicist at the Massachusetts Institute of Technology.) The wild difference, he went on to say, is that scientists apply these everyday methods to areas that most people never think about seriously and carefully. The philosophers' descriptions don't prepare one for either this ordinariness or this extreme diversity of the scientific enterprise—the variety of things to think about, the variety of obstacles and traps to understanding, the variety of approaches to solutions. They hardly acknowledge the fact that a scientist ought often to find himself stretching to the tiptoe of available technique and apparatus, out beyond the frontier of the art, attempting to do something whose difficulty is measured most significantly by the fact that it has never been done before. Science is carried on—this, too, is obvious—in the field, in the observatory, in the laboratory. But historians leave out the arts of the chef and the watchmaker, the development at the bench of a new procedure or a new instrument. "And *making it work*," Morrison said. "This is terribly important." Indeed, biochemists talk about "the cookbook." Many a Nobel Prize has been awarded not for a discovery, as such, but for a new technique or a new tool that opened up a whole field of discovery. "I am a theoretician," Morrison said. "And yet the most important problem for me is to be in touch with the people who are making new instruments or finding new ways of observing, and to try to get them to do the right experiments." And then, in a burst of annoyance, "I feel very reluctant to give any support to descriptions of 'scientific method.' The scientific enterprise is very difficult to model. You have to look at what scientists of all kinds *actually do*."

It's true that by contrast philosophers and historians seem bookbound—or, rather, paper-blindered, depending chiefly on what has been published as scientific research for their understanding of the process of discovery. In this century, anyway, published papers are no guide at all to how scientists get the results they report. We have testimony of the highest authenticity for that. Sir Peter Medawar is one who has both done fine science and written well about how it is done: he won his Nobel Prize for investigations of immunological tolerance, which explained, among other things, why foreign tissue, like a kidney or a heart, is rejected by the body into which it is transplanted, and he has described the real methods of science in essays of grace and distinction. A while ago, Medawar wrote, "What scientists *do* has never been the subject of a scientific . . . inquiry. It is no use looking to scientific 'papers', for they not merely conceal but actively misrepresent the reasoning that goes into the work they describe." The observation has become famous, its truth acknowledged by other scientists. Medawar wrote further, "Scientists are building explanatory structures, *telling stories* which are scrupulously tested to see if they are stories about real life."

Scientists do science for a variety of reasons, of course, and most of them are familiar to the sculptor, say, or to the surgeon or the athlete or the builder of bridges: the professional's pride in skill; the swelling gratification that comes with recognition accorded by colleagues and peers; perhaps the competitor's fierce appetite; perhaps ambition for a kind of fame more durable than most. At the beginning is curiosity, and with curiosity the delight in mastery—the joy of figuring it out that is the birthright of every child. I once asked Murray Gell-Mann, a theoretical physicist, how he got started in science. His answer was to point to the summer sky: "When I was a boy, I used to ask all sorts of simple questions—like, 'What holds the clouds up?'" Rosalind Franklin, the crystallographer whose early death deprived her of a share in the Nobel Prize that was given for the discovery of the structure of DNA (the stuff that genes are made of), one day was helping a young collaborator draft an application for research money, when she looked up at him and said, "What we can't tell them is that it's so much *fun!*" He still remembers her glint of mischief. The play of the mind, in an almost childlike innocence, is a pleasure that appears again and again in scientists' reflections on their work. The geneticist Barbara McClintock, as a woman in American science in the 1930s, had no chance at the academic posts open to her male colleagues, but that hardly mattered to her. "I did it because it was *fun!*" she said forty years later. "I couldn't wait to get up in the morning! I never thought of it as 'science.'"

The exuberant innocence can be poignant. Francois Jacob, who won his share of a Nobel Prize as one of the small group of molecular biologists in the fifties who brought sense and order into the interactions by which bacteria regulate their life processes, recently read an account I had written of that work, and said to me with surprise and an evident pang of regret, "We were like children playing!" He meant the fun of it— but also the simplicity of the problems they had encountered and the innocence of mind they had brought to them. Two hundred and fifty years before—although Jacob did not consciously intend the parallel— Isaac Newton, shortly before his death, said:

> I do not know what I may appear to the world, but to myself I seem to have been only like a boy playing on the sea shore, and diverting myself in now and then finding a smoother pebble or a prettier shell than ordinary, whilst the great ocean of truth lay all undiscovered before me.

For some, curiosity and the delight of putting the world together deepen into a life's passion. Sheldon Glashow, a fundamental-particle physicist at Harvard, also got started in science by asking simple questions. "In eighth grade, we were learning about how the earth goes around the sun, and the moon around the earth, and so on," he said. "And I thought about that, and realized that the Man in the Moon is always looking at us"—that the moon as it circles always turns the same face to the earth. "And I asked the teacher, 'Why is the Man in the Moon always looking at us?' She was pleased with the question—but said it was hard. And it turns out that it's not until you're in college-level physics courses that one really learns the answers," Glashow said. "But the *difference* is, that most people would look at the moon and wonder for a moment, and say, 'That's interesting'—and then forget it. But some people can't let go."

Curiosity is not enough. The word is too mild by far, a word for infants. Passion is indispensable for creation, no less in the sciences than in the arts. Medawar once described it in a talk addressed to young scientists. "You must feel in yourself an exploratory impulsion—an *acute discomfort* at incomprehension." This is the rage to know. The other side of the fun of science, as of art, is pain. A problem worth solving will surely require weeks and months of lack of progress, whipsawn between hope and the blackest sense of despair. The marathon runner or the young swimmer who would be a champion knows at least that the pain may be a symptom of progress. But here the artist and the scientist part company with the athlete—to join the mystic for a while. The pain of creation, though not of the body, is in one way worse. It must not only be endured but reflected back on itself to increase the agility, variety, inventiveness of the play of the mind. Some problems in science have demanded such devotion, such willingness to bear repeated rebuffs, not just for years but for decades. There are times in the practice of the arts, we're told, of abysmal self-doubt. There are like passages in the doing of science. Albert Einstein took eleven years of unremitting concentration to produce the general theory of relativity; long afterward, he wrote, "In the light of knowledge attained, the happy achievement seems almost a matter of course, and any intelligent student can grasp it without too much trouble. But the years of anxious searching in the dark, with their intense longing, their alternations of confidence and exhaustion, and the final emergence into the light—only those who have experienced it can understand it." Einstein confronting Einstein's problems: the achievement, to be sure, is matched only by Newton's and perhaps Darwin's—but the experience is not rare. It is all but inseparable from high accomplishment. In the black cave of unknowing, when one is groping for the contours of the rock and the slope of the floor, tossing a pebble and listening for its fall, brushing away false clues as insistent as cobwebs, a touch of fresh air on the cheek can make hope leap up, an unexpected scurrying whisper can induce the mood of the brink of terror. "Afterwards it can be told—trivialized—like a *roman policier*, a detective story," François Jacob once said. "While you're there, it is the sound and the fury." But it was the poet and adept of mysticism St. John of the Cross who gave to this passionate wrestling with bafflement the name by which, ever since, it has been known: *the dark night of the soul*.

Enlightenment may not appear, or not in time; the mystic at least need not fear forestalling. Enlightenment may dawn in ways as varied as the individual approaches of scientists at work—and, in defiance of stereotypes, the sciences far outrun the arts in variety of personal styles and in the crucial influence of style on the creative process. During a conversation with a co-worker—and he just as baffled—a fact quietly shifts from the insignificant background to the foreground; a trivial anomaly becomes a central piece of evidence, the entire pattern swims into focus, and at last one sees. "How obvious! We knew it all along!" Or a rival may publish first but yet be wrong—and in the crashing wave of fear that he's got it right, followed and engulfed by the wave of realization that it must be wrong, the whole view of the problem skews, the tension of one's concentration twists abruptly higher, and at last one sees. "Not that way, *this* way!"

One path to enlightenment, though, has been reported so widely, by writers and artists, by scientists, and especially by mathematicians, that it has become established as a discipline for courting inspiration. The first stage, the reports agree, is prolonged contemplation of the problem, days of saturation in the data, weeks of incessant struggle—the torment of the unknown. The aim is to set in motion the unconscious processes of the mind, to prepare the intuitive leap. William Lipscomb, a physical chemist at Harvard who won a Nobel Prize for finding the unexpected structures of some unusual molecules, the boranes, said recently that, for him, "The unconscious mind pieces together random impressions into a continuous story. If I really want to work on a problem, I do a good deal of the work at night—because then I worry about it as I go to sleep." The worry must be about the problem intensely and exclusively. Thought must be free of distraction or competing anxieties. Identification with the problem grows so intimate that the scientist has the experience of the detective who begins to think like the terrorist, of the hunter who feels, as though directly, the silken ripple of the tiger's instincts. One great physical chemist was credited by his peers, who watched him awestruck, with the ability to think about chemical structures directly in quantum terms—so that if a proposed molecular model was too tightly packed he felt uncomfortable, as though his shoes pinched. Joshua Lederberg, president of the Rockefeller University, who won his Nobel for discoveries that established the genetics of microorganisms, said recently, "One needs the ability to strip to the essential attributes of some actor in a process, the ability to imagine oneself *inside* a biological situation; I literally had to be able to think, for example, 'What would it be like if I were one of the chemical pieces in a bacterial chromosome?'—and to try to understand what my environment was, try to know *where* I was, try to know when I was supposed to function in a certain way, and so forth." Total preoccupation to the point of absentmindedness is no eccentricity—just as the monstrous egoism and contentiousness of some scientists, like some artists, are the overflow of the strength and reserves of sureness they must find how they can.

Sometimes out of that saturation the answer arises, spontaneous and entire, as though of its own volition. In a famous story, Friedrich Kekulé, who was a German chemist of the mid-nineteenth century, described how a series of discoveries came to him in the course of hypnagogic reveries—waking dreams. His account, though far from typical, is supremely charming. Kekulé was immersed in one of the most perplexing problems of his day: to find the structural basis of organic chemistry— that is, of the chemistry of compounds that contain carbon atoms. Enormous numbers of such compounds were coming to be known, but their makeup—from atoms of carbon, hydrogen, oxygen, and a few other elements—seemed to follow no rules. Kekulé had dwelt on the compounds' behavior so intensely that the atoms themselves on occasion seemed to appear to him and dance. In the dusk of a summer evening, he was going home by horse-drawn omnibus, sitting outside and alone. "I fell into a reverie, and lo! The atoms were gamboling before my eyes," he later wrote. "I saw how, frequently, two smaller atoms united to form a pair; how a larger one embraced two smaller ones; how still larger ones kept hold of three or even four of the smaller; whilst the whole kept whirling in a giddy dance. I saw how the larger ones formed a chain." He spent hours that night sketching the forms he had envisioned. Another time, when Kekulé was nodding in his chair before the fire, the atoms danced for him again—but only the larger ones, this time, in long rows, "all twining and twisting in snakelike motion. But look! What was that? One of the snakes had seized hold of its own tail, and the form whirled mockingly before my eyes." The chains and rings that carbon atoms form with each other are indeed the fundamental structures of organic chemistry.

Although without Kekulé's vivid details, several scientists have told me that the fringes of sleep set the problem-sodden mind free to make uninhibited, bizarre, even random connections that may throw up the unexpected answer. One said that the technical trick that led to one of his most admired discoveries—it was about the fundamental, molecular nature of genetic mutations—had sprung to mind while he was lying insomniac at three in the morning. Another said he was startled from a deep sleep one night by the fully worked-out answer to a puzzle that had blocked him for weeks—except that at breakfast he was no longer able to remember any detail except the jubilant certainty. So the next night he went to sleep with paper and pencil on the bedside table; and when, once again, he awoke with the answer he was able to seize it.

More usually, though, in the classic strategy for achieving enlightenment the weeks of saturation must be followed by a second stage that begins when the problem is deliberately set aside—put out of the active mind, the ceaseless pondering switched off. After several days of silence, the solution wells up. The mathematician Henri Poincaré was unusually introspective about the process of discovery. (He also came nearer than anyone else to beating Einstein to the theory of relativity, except that in that case, though he had the pieces of the problem, inspiration did not strike.) In 1908, Poincaré gave a lecture, before the Psychological Society of Paris, about the psychology of mathematical invention, and there he described how he made some of his youthful discoveries. He reassured his audience, few of them mathematical: "I will tell you that I found the proof of a certain theorem in certain circumstances. The theorem will have a barbarous name, which many of you will never have heard of. But that's of no importance, for what is interesting to the psychologist is not the theorem—it's the circumstances." The youthful discovery was about a class of mathematical functions which he named in honor of another mathematician, Lazarus Fuchs—but, as he said, the mathematical content is not important here. The young Poincaré believed, and for fifteen days he strove to prove, that no functions of the type he was pondering could exist in mathematics. He struggled with the disproof for hours every day. One evening, he happened to drink some black coffee, and couldn't sleep. Like Kekulé with his carbon atoms, Poincaré found mathematical expressions arising before him in crowds, combining and recombining. By the next morning, he had established a class of the functions that he had begun by denying. Then, a short time later, he left town to go on a geological excursion for several days. "The changes of travel made me forget my mathematical work." One day during the excursion, though, he was carrying on a conversation as he was about to board a bus. "At the moment when I put my foot on the step, the idea came to me, without anything in my former thoughts seeming to have paved the way for it, that the transformations I had used to define the Fuchsian functions were identical with those of non-Euclidian geometry." He did not try to prove the idea, but went right on with his conversation. "But I felt a perfect certainty," he wrote. When he got home, "for conscience's sake I verified the result at my leisure."

The quality of such moments of the mind has not often been described successfully; Charles P. Snow was a scientist and a novelist as well, and when his experience of science came together with his writer's imagination his witness is assured and authentic. In *The Search*, a novel about scientists at work, the protagonist makes a discovery for which he had long been striving.

> Then I was carried beyond pleasure. . . . My own triumph and delight and success were there, but they seemed insignificant beside this tranquil ec-stasy. It was as though I had looked for a truth outside myself, and finding it had become for a moment a part of the truth I sought; as though all the world, the atoms and the stars, were wonderfully clear and close to me, and I to them, so that we were part of a lucidity more tremendous than any mystery.
>
> I had never known that such a moment could exist. . . . Since then I have never quite regained it. But one effect will stay with me as long as I live; once, when I was young, I used to sneer at the mystics who have described the experience of being at one with God and part of the unity of things. After that afternoon, I did not want to laugh again; for though I should have interpreted the experience differently, I thought I knew what they meant.

This experience beyond pleasure, like the dark night of the soul, has a name: the novelist Romain Rolland, in a letter to Sigmund Freud, called it "the oceanic sense of well-being."

Science is our century's art. Nearly four hundred years ago, when modern science was just beginning, Francis Bacon wrote that *knowledge is power.* Yet Bacon was not a scientist. He wrote as a bureaucrat in retirement. His slogan was actually the first clear statement of the prom-ise by which, ever since, bureaucrats justify to each other and to king or taxpayer the spending of money on science. Knowledge is power; today we would say, less grandly, that science is essential to technology. Bacon's promise has been fulfilled abundantly, magnificently. The rage to know has been matched by the rage to make. Therefore—with the proviso, abundantly demonstrated, that it's rarely possible to predict which program of fundamental research will produce just what tech-nology and when—the promise has brought scientists in the Western world unprecedented freedom of inquiry. Nonetheless, Bacon's promise hardly penetrates to the thing that moves most scientists. Science has several rewards, but the greatest is that it is the most interesting, difficult, pitiless, exciting, and beautiful pursuit that we have yet found. Science is our century's art.

The takeover can be dated more precisely than the beginning of most eras: Friday, June 30, 1905, will do, when Albert Einstein, a clerk in the Swiss patent office in Bern, submitted a thirty-one-page paper, "On the Electrodynamics of Moving Bodies," to the journal *Annalen der Physik*.

No poem, no play, no piece of music written since then comes near the theory of relativity in its power, as one strains to apprehend it, to make the mind tremble with delight. Whereas fifty years ago it was often said that hardly twoscore people understood the theory of relativity, today its essential vision, as Einstein himself said, is within reach of any reasonably bright high school student—and that, too, is characteristic of the speed of assimilation of the new in the arts.

Consider also the molecular structure of that stuff of the gene, the celebrated double helix of deoxyribonucleic acid. This is two repetitive strands, one winding up, the other down, but hooked together, across the tube of space between them, by a sequence of pairs of chemical entities—just four sorts of these entities, making just two kinds of pairs, with exactly ten pairs to a full turn of the helix. It's a piece of sculpture. But observe how form and function are one. That sequence possesses a unique duality: one way, it allows the strands to part and each to assemble on itself, by the pairing rules, a duplicate of the complementary strand; the other way, the sequence enciphers, in a four-letter alphabet, the entire specification for the substance of the organism. The structure thus encompasses both heredity and embryological growth, the passing-on of potential and its expression. The structure's elucidation, in March of 1953, was an event of such surpassing explanatory power that it will reverberate through whatever time mankind has remaining. The structure is also perfectly economical and splendidly elegant. There is no sculpture made in this century that is so entrancing.

If to compare science to art seems—in the last quarter of this century—to undervalue what science does, that must be, at least partly, because we now expect art to do so little. Before our century, everyone of course supposed that the artist imitates nature. Aristotle had said so; the idea was obvious, it had flourished and evolved for two thousand years; those who thought about it added that the artist imitated not just nature as it accidentally happens, but by penetrating to nature as it has to be. Yet today that describes the scientist. "Scientific reasoning," Medawar also said, "is a constant interplay or interaction between hypotheses and the logical expectations they give rise to: there is a restless to-and-fro motion of thought, the formulation and reformulation of hypotheses, until we arrive at a hypothesis which, to the best of our prevailing knowledge, will satisfactorily meet the case." Thus far, change only the term "hypothesis" and Medawar described well the experience the painter or the poet has of his own work. "Scientific reasoning is a kind of dialogue between the possible and the actual, between what might be and what is in fact the case," he went on—and there the difference lies. The scientist enjoys the harsher discipline of what is and is not the case. It is he, rather than the painter or the poet in this century, who pursues in its stringent form the imitation of nature.

Many scientists—mathematicians and physicists especially—hold that beauty in a theory is itself almost a form of proof. They speak, for example, of "elegance." Paul Dirac predicted the existence of antimatter (what would science fiction be without him?) several years before any form of it was observed. He won a share in the Nobel Prize in physics in 1933 for the work that included that prediction. "It is more important to have beauty in one's equations than to have them fit experiment," Dirac wrote many years later. "It seems that if one is working from the point of view of getting beauty in one's equations, and if one has really a sound insight, one is on a sure line of progress."

Here the scientist parts company with the artist. The insight must be sound. The dialogue is between what might be and what is in fact the case. The scientist is trying to get the thing right. The world is there.

And so are other scientists. The social system of science begins with the apprenticeship of the graduate student with a group of his peers and elders in the laboratory of a senior scientist; it continues to collaboration at the bench or the blackboard, and on to formal publication—which is a formal invitation to criticism. The most fundamental function of the social system of science is to enlarge the interplay between imagination and judgment from a private into a public activity. The oceanic feeling of well-being, the true touchstone of the artist, is for the scientist, even the most fortunate and gifted, only the midpoint of the process of doing science.

QUESTIONS FOR READING, RESPONDING, AND WRITING

Summarizing Main Points

1. List the reasons that Judson gives as to why certain people become scientists. What personality traits do you feel separate scientists from other people?
2. Describe the typical methods of scientific investigation as prescribed by Judson. Describe those Judson considers atypical. Are they related at all?

Analyzing Methods of Discourse

1. Reread Judson's description of Henri Poincaré's lecture before the Psychological Society of Paris. Describe how Poincaré's remarks might serve as a paradigm, or model, for Judson's own analysis.
2. Judson begins and ends the paragraph that opens the final section of his essay with the sentence: "Science is our century's art." Reread that paragraph. In what ways is Judson's repetition effective? Would you have believed his statement without the paragraph that follows its first appearance?

Focusing on the Field

1. Judson quotes Francis Bacon's statement that "knowledge is power." He suggests that "today we would say, less grandly, that science is essential to technology." Describe the connection that Judson makes between the two

statements. You might wish to compare Judson's analysis to Isaac Asimov's in "Pure and Impure: The Interplay of Science and Technology."
2. Describe what Judson calls the "social system of science." How does Judson suggest that this system separates the scientist from the artist? Do you agree or disagree with his position?

Writing Assignments

1. Judson quotes Sir Peter Medawar: "It is no use looking to scientific 'papers,' for they not merely conceal but actively misrepresent the reasoning that goes into the work they describe. . . . Scientists are building explanatory structures, *telling stories* which are scrupulously tested to see if they are stories about real life." Read Annie Dillard's "Lenses." In a short essay that provides supporting evidence from both Judson's and Dillard's essays, prove that Dillard either is or is not writing a "scientific paper."
2. Richard Selzer in "The Art of Surgery" likens a doctor's duties to a poet's: each "gazes, records, diagnoses, and prophesies." After reading Selzer's essay, compare and contrast Selzer's description of a doctor with Judson's analysis of a scientist's procedures.

Robert Jastrow

THE LAW OF THE EXPANDING UNIVERSE

Robert Jastrow, science editor and author, was born in 1925 in New York City. He studied at Columbia University, earning a doctorate in physics in 1948, and is at present director of the Goddard Institute for Space Studies in New York City. Internationally renowned for his theory and research, Jastrow has lectured, studied, and taught at prestigious institutions around the country, including Columbia University, where he was awarded both a University Medal for Excellence in 1962 and a Graduate Faculties Alumni Award in 1967; the Institute for Advanced Study in Princeton, New Jersey; Yale University in New Haven, Connecticut; the U.S. Naval Research Laboratory in Washington, D.C., where he was a consultant in nuclear physics; and the National Aeronautics and Space Administration, where he was chief of the theoretical division.

His stellar career as a physicist has been complemented since 1960 by a burgeoning writing career. Serving first as editor for two academic publications, *Exploration in Space* and *Origin of the Solar System* (1963), Jastrow turned his talents to benefit the general reader with the publication of *Red Giants and White Dwarfs: The Evolution of the Stars, Planets, and Life* in 1967 (rev. 1971). Since then, Jastrow has published several other academic works and another general book on science, *God and the Astronauts* (1978), from which the following selection is taken.

Edwin Powell Hubble was an exceptional man among scientists—athlete, scholar, soldier, lawyer and astronomer. Hubble was born in Marshfield, Missouri, November 20, 1889, one of seven children. He won a scholarship to the University of Chicago, studied physics there, was very active in college athletics, and played with the champion basketball team of the West. At one point he boxed the French champion, Carpentier.

In 1910 he graduated from the University of Chicago, and was awarded a Rhodes scholarship. On returning to the United States, he practiced law in Louisville, Kentucky. He "chucked the law for astronomy" and returned to Chicago for graduate work in 1914.

Hubble enlisted in the Army at the start of World War I, was commissioned a Captain, and later became a Major. He was wounded in November, 1918, returned to the United States the following year, and went to Pasadena to begin his study of the galaxies.

In 1924, Hubble married Grace Burke in Pasadena. One of Hubble's colleagues at Mount Wilson, W. W. Wright, gave Mrs. Hubble a character sketch of her husband before their marriage: "He is a hard worker. He wants to find out about the Universe; that shows how young he is."

Hubble worked without interruption at Mount Wilson and later at Palomar Mountain, with the exception of a tour of duty at Aberdeen Proving Grounds during World War II. His great achievements with the 100-inch telescope, pushing this instrument to the limit of its range, proved the potential value of still larger telescopes. He worked on the design of the 200-inch telescope and used it from its completion in 1948 until his death in 1953.

Hubble was always sensitive to the larger implications in his results, and their relation to the theories of de Sitter and others, but in his system of values what could be seen through a telescope ranked well above a theoretical idea. The concluding sentence of *The Realm of Nebula*, Hubble's classic account of the galaxies, expresses his working philosophy: "Not until the empirical resources are exhausted, need we pass on to the dreamy realms of speculation."

The Hubble Law is one of the great discoveries in science: it is the foundation of the scientific story of Genesis. Yet it is a mysterious law. Why should a galaxy recede from us at a higher speed simply because it is farther away?

An analogy will help to make the meaning of the law clear. Consider a lecture hall whose seats are spaced uniformly, so that everyone is separated from his neighbors in front, in back, and to either side by a distance of, say, three feet. Now suppose the hall expands rapidly, doubling its size in a short time. If you are seated in the middle of the hall, you will find that your immediate neighbors have moved away from you and are now at a distance of six feet. However, a person on the other side of the hall, who was originally at a distance from you of, say, 300 feet, is now 600 feet away. In the interval of time in which your close neighbors moved three feet farther away, the person on the other side of the hall increased his distance from you by 300 feet. Clearly, he is receding at a faster speed.

This is the Hubble Law, or the Law of the Expanding Universe. It applies not only to the Cosmos, but also to inflating balloons and loaves of bread rising in the oven. All uniformly expanding objects are governed by this law; if the seats in the lecture hall moved apart in any other way, they would pile up in one part of the hall or another; similarly, if galaxies moved outward in accordance with any law other than Hubble's law, they would pile up in one part of the Universe or another.

One point remains to be explained. How did Slipher and Humason measure the speeds of distant galaxies? It is impossible to make such measurements directly by tracking a galaxy across the sky, because the great distances to these objects render their motions imperceptible when they are observed from night to night, or even from year to year. The closest spiral galaxy to us, Andromeda, would have to be observed for 500 years before it moved a measurable distance across the sky.

The method used by astronomers is indirect, and depends on the fact that when a galaxy moves away from the earth, its color becomes redder than normal.[1] The degree of the color change is proportional to the speed of the galaxy. This effect is called the red shift. All distant galaxies show a distinct red shift in their color. The red shift, which betrays the retreating movements of the galaxies, is the basis for the picture of the expanding Universe.

How is the red shift itself measured? First, a prism or similar device is attached to a telescope. The prism spreads out the light from the moving galaxy into a band of colors like a rainbow. This band of colors is called a spectrum. In the next step, the spectrum is recorded on a photographic plate. Finally, the spectrum of the galaxy is lined up alongside the spectrum of a nonmoving source of light. The comparison of the two spectra determines the red shift.

The illustration on the facing page shows how the method works. The photographic images of the several galaxies are shown at left, while

---

[1]The effect occurs because light is a train of waves in space. When the source of the light moves away from the observer, the waves are stretched or lengthened by the receding motion. The length of a light wave is perceived by the eye as its color; short waves create the sensation that we call "blue," while long waves create the sensation of "red." Thus, the increase in the length of the light waves coming from a receding object is perceived as a reddening effect.

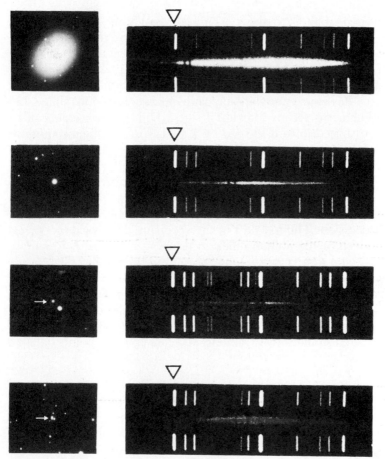

The diffuse spots of light in the photographs above are galaxies. The galaxies in the lower photographs, indicated by arrows, are barely visible because they are several billion light years away. The spectrum for each galaxy is the tapering band of light on the right. For each spectrum, the position of the encircled pair of dark lines indicates the amount of the red shifts.

the spectra of the same galaxies, recorded photographically, appear at right as tapering bands of light. The short, vertical lines above and below each tapering band are the spectrum of a nonmoving source of light, which is placed directly on the photograph for comparison.

The spectra of the galaxies are rather indistinct because the galaxies are faint and far away. However, each spectrum contains one important feature. This is the pair of dark lines circled in white. The lines are colors created by atoms of calcium in the galaxy, which make useful markers for determining the amount of the red shift in a galaxy's spectrum.

The triangle points to the position the calcium colors normally would have in the galaxy's spectrum, if this galaxy were not moving away from us. The distance between this pointer and the white circle is the amount of the red shift.

The topmost photograph shows a galaxy that is about 70 million light years from us. It is close enough to appear as a large, luminous shape, but too distant for us to see its individual stars. The calcium colors in its spectrum are shifted toward the red by a small but significant amount. The speed of this retreating galaxy, calculated from its red shift, turns out to be three million miles an hour.

The next galaxy is over one billion light years away, and correspondingly smaller and fainter. The position of the calcium colors in its spectrum reveals a much greater shift toward the red, indicating a greater velocity of recession. The red shift in the spectrum of this galaxy corresponds to a speed of 126 million miles an hour.

The third and fourth galaxies are more than three billion light years away. Because of their great distances, they appear as exceedingly small and faint objects. The red shifts in their spectra are very great, and correspond to speeds of recession of more than 200 million miles an hour.

If the speeds and distances of the four galaxies are plotted on a graph, as Hubble plotted similar measurements 40 years ago, the points fall on a straight line *below*.

Distance in light years.

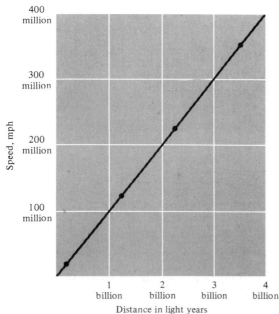

The line indicates a simple proportion between speed and distance; that is, if one galaxy is twice as far away from us as another, it will be moving away twice as fast; if it is three times as far, it will be moving away three times as fast, and so on. This proportion is the mathematical statement of the Hubble Law.

The steepness of the line in the graph indicates how fast the Universe is expanding; a steep line means that the galaxies are moving away at very high speeds; that is, the Universe is expanding rapidly. A line with a gentle slope means that the galaxies are retreating at relatively modest speeds, hence the Universe is expanding slowly.

These remarks about the steepness of the line in the Hubble graph suggest an important check on the theory of the expanding Universe. According to the picture of the explosive birth of the Cosmos, the Universe was expanding much more rapidly immediately after the explosion than it is today. If someone were around to measure the speeds and distances of the galaxies many billions of years ago, and he plotted the same graph, a straight line would still appear, but it would be much steeper than it is today. A copy of that ancient graph, compared with a similar graph today, would test the concept of a Universe that had exploded outward and then slowed down under the pull of gravity.

Can the test be performed? That would seem to be an impossible task, since astronomical records do not go back several billion years. But consider the following facts: the light that reaches the earth from the Andromeda galaxy left that galaxy two million years ago; when an astronomer photographs Andromeda through a telescope, he sees that galaxy as it was two million years earlier, and not as it is today. Similarly, the light that reaches the earth today from the Virgo galaxy left the galaxy 70 million years ago. A photograph of the galaxy shows it as it was 70 million years in the past, and not as it is today.[2]

Now we see how to obtain a picture of the Universe as it was billions of years ago. First, photograph galaxies that are within a distance of 100 million light years. These galaxies will yield a picture of the expanding Universe as it has been during the last 100 million years. Since 100 million years is a relatively short time on a cosmic time scale, we can consider this picture to represent the Universe as it is today. If the speeds and distances of these relatively nearby galaxies are plotted on a graph, they should form a straight line. The steepness of the line will tell us how fast the Universe is expanding at the present time.

Next, extend the measurements farther out into space, to galaxies whose distances from us are about 500 million light years. The speeds and

---

[2]This is true is terrestrial affairs also, but the effect is too small to be important. When you see a friend across the room you see him as he was in the past. How far in the past? About one hundred-millionth of a second.

distances of these galaxies will give us another graph, and another line, whose steepness represents the rate of expansion of the Universe approximately 500 million years ago. If the accuracy of our measurements permits us to go still farther out into space, we can measure galaxies at a distance of one billion light years, and then two billion light years, and so on. The farther out we look in space, the farther back we see in time. In this way, using a giant telescope as a time machine, we can discover the conditions in the expanding Universe billions of years ago.

The idea behind the measurement is very simple, but the measurement is hard to carry out in practice because it is difficult to measure the distances to remote galaxies with the necessary accuracy. The most complete study made thus far has been carried out on the 200-inch telescope by Allan Sandage. He compiled information on 42 galaxies, ranging out in space as far as six billion light years from us. His measurements indicate that the Universe was expanding more rapidly in the past than it is today.[3] This result lends further support to the belief that the Universe exploded into being.

QUESTIONS FOR READING, RESPONDING, AND WRITING

Summarizing Main Points

1. Jastrow explains the scientific phenomenon known as the "red shift." Describe why this phenomenon is essential to measuring the speed at which far distant galaxies move. In what ways is it essential in proving Hubble's "Law of the Expanding Universe"?
2. Explain Hubble's "Law of the Expanding Universe." What significance does this law hold for theories about the origin of the universe? Given the "Law of the Expanding Universe," can one predict what the end of the universe will be like?

Analyzing Methods of Discourse

1. Jastrow begins his essay by providing an analogy or extended comparison between the expanding universe and a lecture hall. Describe the ways this analogy helps the reader. Could you imagine galaxies if they were to "pile up in one part of the Universe or another"?
2. Jastrow provides three kinds of information in his essay: biographical, theoretical, and technical. He separates the biographical information physically, that is, he boxes it separately from the major part of his essay. He relies on analogies to explain the theoretical and charts and graphs to analyze the technical. Describe how all three methods are helpful to the reader. Is each method well suited to its subject matter?

---

[3]Sandage's work provides additional evidence against the Steady State theory. If that theory were correct, the rate of expansion would never change.

Focusing on the Field

1. Jastrow relies on a chart and graph to help explain his points. Do you find them useful? Reread Jastrow's analysis of the differing speeds at which the universe expands. Do you feel you would have been able to comprehend the relative speeds or different galaxies without a graph? Reread the analogy that Jastrow creates early on concerning the seats in a lecture hall. Can you plot their movement on a graph? What would the graph look like?
2. Jastrow's essay demonstrates the validity of Hubble's "Law of the Expanding Universe." In order to do so, Jastrow must acquaint his readers with several technologies and theoretical advances in science. What are those advances? Can you find examples of this sort of reliance on background information in other essays?

Writing Assignments

1. In a short essay, describe a process with which you are familiar, but which others may not have the technical expertise to appreciate fully (e.g., preparing a special dish that requires knowledge of special foods or equipment, automotive repair that requires special tools or methods, specific training for a particular sport). Make your explanation as accessible to the layman as Jastrow makes his.
2. Read Horace Freeland Judson's "Scientific Investigation: The Rage to Know." In a short essay, describe the ways that Jastrow's analysis of Hubble's Law demonstrates the scientist's "rage to know."

John McPhee

ICE POND

John McPhee was born in Princeton, New Jersey in 1931, gained his degree at the university there, lives and teaches writing there, and wrote his first book, *A Sense of Where You Are* (1965), about Princeton University basketball star Bill Bradley. McPhee's book uniquely foreshadowed Bradley's future accomplishments—he would later become a Rhodes scholar at Oxford, play for the New York Knickerbockers, and serve as a U.S. senator—while it also demonstrated McPhee's own successful style of nonfiction. McPhee describes his subjects, whatever they may be, such that we see not only the superficial details of the subject, but also its place within a larger world. Thus McPhee's books on such diverse and unusual topics as oranges (*Oranges*, 1967), tennis (*Levels of the Game*, 1970), experimental aircraft (*The Deltoid Pumpkin Seed*, 1973), birch-bark canoes (*The Survival of the Birch-Bark Canoe*, 1975), and Alaska

(*Coming into the Country,* 1977) are remarkable, not for their subject matters but for the substance his precise style lends them.

McPhee has written for television, worked for *Time* magazine, and is now a staff writer for *The New Yorker.* He has been nominated twice for National Book Awards for science writing, once for *Encounters with the Arch Druid* (1972), and once for *The Curve of Binding Energy* (1974), which describes the problem of safeguarding the world's nuclear materials. McPhee has also published geographical, ecological, and geological studies, including *The Pine Barrens* (1968), *Basin and Range* (1981), and *In Suspect Terrain* (1982), as well as several collections of miscellaneous pieces drawn from his contributions to *The New Yorker* and other popular magazines, such as *Holiday, National Geographic, Playboy,* and *Atlantic.* The essay that follows is from his most recent collection, *Table of Contents* (1985).

Summer, 1981

At Princeton University, off and on since winter, I have observed the physicist Theodore B. Taylor standing like a mountaineer on the summit of what appears to be a five-hundred-ton Sno-Kone. Taylor now calls himself a "nuclear dropout." His has been, at any rate, a semicircular career, beginning at Los Alamos Scientific Laboratory, where, as an imaginative youth in his twenties, he not only miniaturized the atomic bomb but also designed the largest-yield fission bomb that had ever been exploded anywhere. In his thirties, he moved on to General Atomic, in La Jolla, to lead a project called Orion, his purpose being to construct a spaceship sixteen stories high and as voluminous as a college dormitory, in which he personally meant to take off from a Nevada basin and set a course for Pluto, with intermediate stops on Ganymede, Rhea, and Dione—ice-covered satellites of Jupiter and Saturn. The spaceship Orion, with its wide flat base, would resemble the nose of a bullet, the head of a rocket, the ogival hat of a bishop. It would travel at a hundred thousand miles an hour and be driven by two thousand fission bombs. Taylor's colleague Freeman Dyson meant to go along, too, extending spectacularly a leave of absence from the Institute for Advanced Study, in Princeton. The project was developing splendidly when the nuclear treaty of 1963 banned explosions in space and the atmosphere. Taylor quelled his dreams, and turned to a sombre subject. Long worried about the possibility of clandestine manufacture of nuclear bombs by individuals or small groups of terrorists, he spent his forties enhancing the protection of weapons-grade uranium and plutonium where it exists in private industries throughout the world. And now, in his fifties—and with the exception of his service as a member of the President's Commission on the Accident at Three Mile Island—he has gone flat-out full-time in pursuit of sources of energy that avoid the use of fission and of fossil fuel, one example of which is the globe of ice he has caused to be made in Princeton. "This isn't Ganymede," he informs me, scuffing big crystals under his feet. "But it's almost as exciting."

Taylor's hair is salt-and-peppery now but still stands in a thick youthful wave above his dark eyebrows and luminous brown eyes. He is tall, and he remains slim. What he has set out to do is to air-condition large buildings or whole suburban neighborhoods using less than ten per cent of the electricity required to cool them by conventional means, thereby saving more than ninety per cent of the oil that might be used to make the electricity. This way and that, he wants to take the "E" out of OPEC. The ice concept is simple. He grins and calls it "simple-minded— putting old and new ideas together in a technology appropriate to our time." You scoop out a depression in the ground, he explains—say, fifteen feet deep and sixty feet across—and line it with plastic. In winter, you fill it with a ball of ice. In summer, you suck ice water from the bottom and pump it indoors to an exchanger that looks something like an automobile radiator and cools air that is flowing through ducts. The water, having picked up some heat from the building, is about forty-five degrees as it goes back outside, where it emerges through shower heads and rains on the porous ice. Percolating to the bottom, the water is cooled as it descends, back to thirty-two degrees. Taylor calls this an ice pond. A modest number of ice ponds could cool, for example, the District of Columbia, saving the energy equivalent of one and a half million barrels of oil each summer.

The initial problem was how to make the ice. Taylor first brooded about this some years ago when he was researching the theoretical possibilities of constructing greenhouses that would aggregately cover tens of millions of acres and solve the pollution problems of modern agriculture. The greenhouses had to be cooled. He thought of making ice in winter and using it in summer. For various regions, he calculated how much ice you would have to make in order to have something left on Labor Day. How much with insulation? How much without insulation? The volumes were small enough to be appealing. How to make the ice? If you were to create a pond of water and merely let it freeze, all you would get, of course, would be a veneer that would break up with the arrival of spring. Ice could be compiled by freezing layer upon layer, but in most places in the United States six or eight feet would be the maximum thickness attainable in an average winter, and that would not be enough. Eventually, he thought of artificial snow. Ski trails were covered with it not only in Vermont and New Hampshire but also in New Jersey and Pennsylvania, and even in North Carolina, Georgia, and Alabama. To make ice, Taylor imagined, one might increase the amount of water moving through a ski-resort snow machine. The product would be slush.

In a pondlike receptacle, water would drain away from the slush. It could be pumped out and put back through the machine. What remained in the end would be a ball of ice.

Taylor had meanwhile become a part-time professor at Princeton, and on one of his frequent visits to the university from his home in Maryland he showed his paper ice ponds to colleagues at the university's Center for Energy and Environmental Studies. The Center spent a couple of years seeking funds from the federal government for an ice-pond experiment, but the government was not interested. In 1979, the Prudential Insurance Company of America asked the university to help design a pair of office buildings—to be built just outside Princeton—that would be energy-efficient and innovative in as many ways as possible. Robert Socolow, a physicist who is the Center's director, brought Taylor into the Prudential project, and Taylor soon had funds for his snow machine, his submersible pumps, his hole in the ground.

At Los Alamos, when Taylor got together on paper the components of a novel bomb he turned over his numbers and his ideas to other people, who actually made the device. Had such a job been his to do, there would have been no bombs at all. His mind is replete with technology but innocent of technique. He cannot competently change a tire. He has difficulty opening doors. The university hired Don Kirkpatrick, a consulting solar engineer, to assemble and operate appropriate hardware, while unskilled laborers such as Taylor and Freeman Dyson would spread insulating materials over the ice or just stand by to comment.

"The first rule of technology is that no one can tell in advance whether a piece of technology is any good," Dyson said one day. "It will hang on things that are unforeseeable. In groping around, one wants to try things out that are quick and cheap and find out what doesn't work. The Department of Energy has many programs and projects—solar-energy towers and other grandiose schemes—with a common characteristic: no one can tell whether they're any good or not, and they're so big it will take at least five years and probably ten to find out. This ice pond is something you can do cheaply and quickly, and see whether it works."

A prototype pond was tried in the summer of 1980. It was dug beside a decrepit university storage building, leaky with respect to air and water, that had cinder-block walls and a flat roof. Size of an average house, there were twenty-four hundred square feet of space inside. Summer temperatures in the nineties are commonplace in New Jersey, and in musty rooms under that flat roof temperatures before the ice pond were sometimes close to a hundred and thirty. The 1980 pond was square— seventy-five feet across and fifteen feet deep. It contained a thousand tons of ice for a while, but more than half of that melted before insulation was applied: six inches of dry straw between sheets of polyethylene, weighed down with bald tires. Even so, the old building was filled most of the time from June to September with crisp October air. Something under seven tons of ice would melt away on a hot day. Nonetheless, at the end of summer a hundred tons remained. "It's a nice alternative to fossil fuels," Robert Socolow commented. "It has worked too well to be forgotten."

The concept having been successfully tested, the next imperative was to refine the art—technically, economically, and aesthetically. "The point is to make it elegant this time," said Freeman Dyson, and, from its hexagonal concrete skirt to its pure-white reflective cover, "elegant" is the word for the 1981 pond. Concealing the ice is a tentlike Dacron-covered free-span steel structure with six ogival sides—a cryodesic dome—which seems to emerge from the earth like the nose of a bullet, the head of a rocket, the hat of a bishop. Lift a flap and step inside. Look up at the summit of a white tower under insulation. Five hundred tons of ice— fifty-eight feet across the middle—rise to a conical peak, under layers of polyethylene foam, sewn into fabric like enormous quilts. It is as if the tip of the Finsteraarhorn had been wrapped by Christo.

Taylor, up on the foam, completes his inspection of the ice within, whose crystals are jagged when they first fall from the snow machine, and later, like glacier ice, recrystallize more than once into spheres of increasing diameter until the ultimate substance is very hard and resembles a conglomerate of stream gravel. The U.S. Army's Cold Regions Research and Engineering Laboratory has cored it with instruments of the type used on glaciers in Alaska. Suspended from a girder high above Taylor's head and pointing at the summit of the ice is something that appears to be a small naval cannon with a big daisy stuck in its muzzle. This is SMI SnowStream 320, the machine that made the ice. In its days of winter operation, particles plumed away from it like clouds of falling smoke. Unlike many such machines, it does not require compressed air but depends solely on its daisy-petalled propeller blades of varying length for maximum effectiveness in disassembling water. "We are harvesting the cold of winter for use in the summer," Taylor says. "This is natural solar refrigeration, powered by the wind. Wind brings cold air to us, freezes the falling water, and takes the heat away. We are rolling with nature—trying to make use of nature instead of fighting it. That machine cost seven thousand dollars. It can make about eight thousand tons of ice in an average winter here in Princeton—for thirty-five dollars a hundred tons. A hundred tons is enough to air-condition almost any house, spring to fall. In the course of a winter, that machine could make ten thousand tons of ice in Boston, seven thousand in Washington, D.C., fifteen thousand in Chicago, thirty thousand in Casper, Wyoming, fifty thousand in Minneapolis, and, if anybody cares, a hundred thousand tons of ice in Fairbanks. The lower the temperature, the more water you can move through the machine. We don't want dry snow, of course. Snow is too fluffy. We want slop. We want wet sherbet. At twenty degrees Fahrenheit, we can move fifty gallons a minute through the machine. The electricity that drives the snow machine amounts to a very small fraction of the electricity that is saved by the cooling capacity of the ice. In summer, electrical pumps circulate the ice water from the bottom of the pond for a few tenths of a cent a ton. The cost of moving air in ducts through the building is the same as in a conventional system and is negligible in comparison with the electrical cost of cooling air. We're substituting ice water made with winter winds for the cold fluid in a refrigerated-air-conditioner, using less than a tenth as much electrical energy as a conventional air-conditioning system. Our goal is to make the over-all cost lower than the cost of a conventional system and use less than one-tenth of the energy. We're just about there."

The Prudential's new buildings—a hundred and thirty thousand square feet each, by Princeton's School of Architecture and Skidmore, Owings & Merrill—will be started this summer on a site a mile away. They are low, discretionary structures, provident in use of resources, durable, sensible, actuarial—with windows shaded just enough for summer but not too much for winter, with heat developing in a passive solar manner and brought in as well by heat pumps using water from the ground—and incorporating so many other features thrifty with energy that God will probably owe something to the insurance company after the account is totted up. An ice pond occupying less than half an acre can be expected to compound His debt.

A man who could devise atomic bombs and then plan to use them to drive himself to Pluto might be expected to expand his thinking if he were to create a little hill of ice. Taylor has lately been mulling the potentialities of abandoned rock quarries. You could fill an old rock quarry a quarter of a mile wide with several million tons of ice and then pile up more ice above ground as high as the Washington Monument. One of those could air-condition a hundred thousand homes. With all that volume, there would be no need for insulation. You would build pipelines at least ten feet in diameter and aim them at sweltering cities, where heat waves and crime waves would flatten in the water-cooled air. You could make ice reservoirs comparable in size to New York's water reservoirs and pipe ice water to the city from a hundred miles away. After the water had served as a coolant, it would be fed into the city's water supply.

"You could store grain at fifty degrees in India," Taylor goes on. "We're exploring that. The idea is to build an aqueduct to carry an ice slurry from the foothills of the Himalayas down to the Gangetic plain. With an insulated cover over the aqueduct, the amount of ice lost in, say, two hundred miles would be trivial—if the aqueduct is more than ten feet across. In place of electric refrigeration, dairies could use ice ponds to cool milk. Most cheese factories could use at least fifty thousand tons of ice a year. If all the cheese factories in the United States were to do that, they alone would save, annually, about six million barrels of oil. When natural gas comes out of the earth, it often contains too much water vapor to be suitable for distribution. One way to get rid of most of the water is to cool the gas to forty degrees. If ice ponds were used to cool, say, half the natural gas that is produced in this country, they would save the equivalent of ten million barrels of oil each year. Massive construction projects, such as dams, use amazing amounts of electricity to cool concrete while it hardens, sometimes for as much as three years. Ice ponds could replace the electricity. Ice ponds could cool power plants more effectively than environmental water does, and therefore make the power plants more efficient. Ice would also get rid of the waste heat in a manner more acceptable than heating up a river. In places like North Dakota, you can make ice with one of these machines for a few cents a ton—and the coolant would be economically advantageous in all sorts of industrial processing."

Taylor shivers a little, standing on the ice, and, to warm himself, he lights a cigarette. "You could also use snow machines to freeze seawater," he continues. "As seawater freezes, impurities migrate away from it, and you are left with a concentrated brine rich in minerals, and with frozen water that is almost pure—containing so little salt you can't taste it. As seawater comes out of the snow machine and the spray is freezing in the air, the brine separates from the pure frozen water as it falls. To use conventional refrigeration—to use an electric motor to run a compressor to circulate Freon to freeze seawater—is basically too costly. The cost of freezing seawater with a ski-slope machine is less than a hundredth the cost of freezing seawater by the conventional system. There are sixty-six pounds of table salt in a ton of seawater, almost three pounds of magnesium, a couple of pounds of sulphur, nearly a pound of calcium, lesser amounts of potassium, bromine, boron, and so forth. Suppose you had a ship making ice from seawater with snow machines that had been enlarged and adapted for the purpose. You would produce a brine about ten times as concentrated with useful compounds as the original seawater. It would be a multifarious ore. Subsequent extraction of table salt, magnesium, fertilizers, and other useful material from the brine would make all these products cheaper than they would be if they were extracted from unconcentrated seawater by other methods. The table salt alone would pay for the ship. You could separate it out for a dollar a ton. A ship as large as a supertanker could operate most of the year, shuttling back and forth from the Arctic to the Antarctic. At latitudes like that, you can make twenty times as much ice as you can in Princeton."

"What do you do with the ice?"

"Your options are to return it to the sea or to put it in a skirt and haul it as an iceberg to a place where they need fresh water. The Saudis and the French have been looking into harvesting icebergs in Antarctica and towing them to the Red Sea. Someone has described this as bringing the mountain to Muhammad. I would add that if you happen to live in a place like New York the mountain is right at your doorstep—all you have to do is make it. The cost of making fresh water for New York City with snow machines and seawater would be less than the cost of delivered water there now. Boston looks awfully good—twice as good as Princeton. Boston could make fresh water, become a major producer of table salt and magnesium and sulphur, and air-condition itself—in one operation. All they have to do is make ice. It would renew Boston. More than a hundred years ago, people cut ice out of ponds there and shipped it around Cape Horn to San Francisco. When this country was getting going, one of Boston's main exports was ice."

QUESTIONS FOR READING, RESPONDING, AND WRITING

Summarizing Main Points

1. Where and how does McPhee establish the credibility of Taylor as a thinker?
2. List the potential uses for ice ponds, according to Taylor. Do you notice any sort of progression in this list?

Analyzing Methods of Discourse

1. Trace Taylor's career. What do you make of McPhee's statement that a "man who could devise atomic bombs and then plan to use them to drive himself to Pluto might be expected to expand his thinking if he were to create a little hill of ice"? Consider this statement in light of Taylor's own statement that the ice concept is "simple-minded—putting old and new ideas together in a technology appropriate to our time." Also compare McPhee's opening account of Taylor's plans for the spaceship Orion to Taylor's comments on Boston at the essay's end.
2. Toward the middle of the essay, McPhee tells the reader that Taylor "showed his paper ice ponds to colleagues." In the next paragraph, he tells the reader that Taylor "got together on paper the components of a novel bomb." His repetition of the word "paper" helps us to see the similarity of Taylor's actions in very different situations. Locate other examples of this strategy and explain the way in which McPhee uses this strategy to link Taylor's two careers.

Focusing on the Field

1. In commenting on the success of the ice pond in Princeton, McPhee quotes the Institute for Advanced Study's Robert Socolow, who says that the ice pond "is a nice alternative to fossil fuels," and that "it has worked too well to be forgotten." What do you make of Socolow's second statement? Why would ice ponds "be forgotten"? Locate other comments or phrases in the essay that suggest a similar consequence. Do you see any connection between this idea and Freeman Dyson's comment on the next "imperative" for the ice pond— "to make it elegant this time"?

2. McPhee never directly states his attitude toward the ice pond concept, letting Taylor, Dyson, and others do all the talking on the subject. What do you think McPhee's attitude is toward Taylor and his project? How do you think he makes it known?

Writing Assignments

1. McPhee quotes Taylor's colleague, Freeman Dyson, as saying "the first rule of technology is that no one can tell in advance whether a piece of technology is any good. . . . It will hang on things that are unforeseeable." Read Isaac Asimov's "Pure and Impure: The Interplay of Science and Technology" and, using one of the technologies Asimov mentions, write an essay in which you show how that technology's invention or development illustrates Dyson's claim.

2. Choose one of the essays from the business section that charts the development of a business or product (e.g., Louise Bernikow's "Trivia, Inc.," Calvin Trillin's "The Great Ice Cream War," Stan Luxenberg's "McDonald's: The Franchise Factory") and write an essay that compares its development to Taylor's development of the ice pond, noting both the circumstances and ultimate goals behind each.

Gerald Weissmann

THE CHART OF THE NOVEL
Medical Records and Fiction

Professor of medicine at New York University Medical Center, Gerald Weissmann spends most of his year teaching internal medicine to students and researching inflammation at Bellevue Hospital. His summers, however, are spent at the Marine Biological Laboratory at Woods Hole, Massachusetts, where he works on "marine creatures who, by virtue of simpler cellular arrangements, display in convenient form the origins of human pathology." His ability to recognize similarities between such diverse organisms as human beings and sea urchin eggs helps account, perhaps, for Weissmann's ability to find the common language that unites scientist and layman.

In the following piece, taken from *The Woods Hole Cantata: Essays on Science and Society* (1985), Weissmann exploits the doctor's medical chart as a record of societal change. Weissmann analyzes here, as well as elsewhere, "anomie" or the alienation of the individual from an increasingly disorganized or unfit social structure. He has said, "It is difficult to say whether it is good news that we are about to be the first generation to enter, consciously, the Age of Ignorance," but the evidence of Weissmann's own personal optimism and commitment to "care" in his writing eloquently and clearly states that even "ignorance" can be regarded as good news. According to Weissmann, "admission of ignorance is . . . rarely a refusal to get involved in controversy."

Like other professionals—football scouts, diplomats, and underwriters come to mind—doctors write many words, under pressure of time and for a limited audience. I refer, of course, to the medical charts of our patients. Most of these manuscripts (for even now this material is written almost entirely by hand) are rarely consulted by anyone other than doctors, nurses, or (Heaven forbid!) lawyers. I have always found the libraries of this literature, the record rooms of hospitals, to contain a repository of human, as well as clinical, observations. On their tacky shelves, bound in buff cardboard and sometimes only partially decipherable, are stories of pluck and disaster, muddle and death. If well compressed and described, these *Brief Lives* are more chiseled than Aubrey's. Best of all, I love the conventional paragraph by which the story is introduced. Our tales invariably begin with the chief complaint that brought the patient to the hospital. Consider this sampling from three local hospitals:

> This is the third MSH admission of a chronically wasted 64-year-old, 98-pound male Hungarian refugee composer, admitted from an unheated residential hotel with the chief complaint of progressive weakness (1945).

> This is the second SVH admission of a 39-year-old, obese Welsh male poet, admitted in acute coma after vomiting blood (1953).

> This is the first BH admission of a 22-year-old black, female activist transferred from the Women's House of Detention with chief complaints of sharp abdominal pains and an acutely inflamed knee (1968).

How evocative of time, place, and person—and how different in tone and feeling from other sorts of opening lines! They certainly owe little to the news story: "Secretary of State Schultz appeared today before the Foreign Relations Committee of the Senate to urge ratification of . . ." Nor does the description of a chief complaint owe its punch to any derivation from formal scientific prose: "Although the metabolism of arachidonic acid has been less studied in neutrophils than . . ."

The opening sequence of a medical record is unique, and when well written, there's nothing quite like it. These lines localize a human being of defined sex, age, race, occupation, and physical appearance to a moment of extreme crisis: He or she has been "admitted." Attention must therefore be paid, and everything recorded on that chart after the admitting note is a narrative account of that attention, of medical "care."

But this enthusiasm for the products of clinical prose may be unwarranted. There may be other forms which, by their nature, tug at the reader with such firm hands: I have not found them. Now, my search has not been exhaustive—indeed, my inquiries are based on a sort of hunt-and-peck excursion amongst the yellowing survivors of my dated library. I must report, however, that no similar jabs of evocative prose hit me from the opening lines of biographer, of critic, of historian—not at all the kind of impact I was looking for. No, the real revelation came from the nineteenth-century novelist. I should not have been surprised:

> Emma Woodhouse, handsome, clever and rich, with a comfortable home and happy disposition, seemed to unite some of the best blessings of existence; and had lived nearly twenty-one years in the world with very little to distress or vex her.
>
> —*Emma*
> Jane Austen

> Madame Vauquer (nee Deconflans) is an elderly person who for the past forty years has kept a lodging house in the Rue Neuve-Sainte-Genevieve, in the district that lies between the Latin Quarter and the Faubourg Saint-Marcel. Her house receives men and women and no word has ever been breathed against her respectable establishment.
>
> —*Le Père Goriot*
> Honoré de Balzac

> Fyodor Pavlovitch Karamazov, a landowner well known in our district in his own day, and still remembered among us owing to his mysterious and tragic death, was a strange type, despicable and vicious, and at the same time absurd.
>
> —*The Brothers Karamazov*
> Fyodor Dostoyevsky

Now, that sort of beginning is a little more like the opening paragraphs of our charts. Does this mean that we've been writing nineteenth-century novels all our professional lives, but without knowing it? Do the white, pink, and blue sheets which describe the events between admission and discharge—between beginning and end—constitute a multi-authored *roman à clef?* If we go on to the rest of the record, it is more likely than not that other sources can be identified. The "History of Present Illness," with its chronological listings of coughs, grippes, and disability, owes much to the novelist, but more to the diarist. But the "Past Medical History," drawn to the broader scale of social interactions, returns us again to the world of the novel, and the more detailed "Family and Social History," which describes the ailments of aunts and of nephews, which lists not only military service but the patient's choice of addiction, puts us into the very middle of the realistic novel of 1860.

Now comes the "Physical Examination." Here the world of the clinic or the laboratory intrudes: numbers, descriptions, and measurements. Indeed, from this point on, the record is written in recognition of the debt medicine owes to formal scientific exposition. In this portion of the chart, after all the histories are taken, after the chest has been thumped and the spleen has been fingered, after the white cells have been counted and the potassium surveyed, the doctor can be seen to abandon the position of recorder and to assume that of the natural scientist. He arrives at a "Tentative Diagnosis," a hypothesis, so to speak, to be tested, as time, laboratory procedures, or responses to treatment confirm or deny the initial impression. The revisions of this hypothesis, together with accounts of how doctors and patient learn more about what is *really* wrong, constitute the bulk of our manuscript.

So we can argue that our records are an amalgam between the observational norms of the nineteenth-century novelist and the causal descriptions of the physiologist. There is, perhaps, a connection between the two. If we agree that a novelist not only tells a story but weaves a plot, we imply by this the concept of causality. E. M. Forster, in *Aspects of the Novel*, draws the distinction nicely. He suggests that when a writer tells us, "The King dies, and then the Queen died," we are being told a story. When, however, the sentence is altered to read, "The King dies, and therefore the Queen died of grief," we are offered a plot—the notion of causality has been introduced. In much of our medical record keeping we are busy spinning a series of clinical plots: the temperature went down *because* antibiotics were given, etc.

Pick up a chart at random, and you will see what I mean. The sixty-year-old taxi driver has been treated for eight days with antibiotics for his pneumonia. "Intern's Note: Fever down, sputum clearing, will obtain follow-up X-ray." A few days later: "X-ray shows round nodule near segment with resolving infiltrate. Have obtained permission for bronchoscopy and biopsy." Then, "JAR Note: Results of biopsy discussed with patient and family." Months intervene, and at the end of the readmission chart we find the dreary "Intern's Note: 4:00 A.M. Called to see patient . . ." Infection and tumor, hypothesis and test, beginning and end. And so we read these mixtures of story and plot, learning as much along the way about the sensibilities of the doctor as we do of the patient and his disease. The physician-narrator becomes as important to the tale as the unseen Balzac lurking in the boarding house of Madame Vauquer.

An optimistic attempt to reconcile both sources of our clinical narratives, the novel and the scientist's notebook, was made by that great naturalist—and optimist—Emile Zola. After an exhilarating dip into the work of Claude Bernard, Zola decided that the new modes of scientific description and their causal analyses might yield a *method* which would apply to the novel as well. Basing his argument on Bernard's *An Introduction to the Study of Experimental Medicine* (1865), Zola wrote an essay entitled *The Experimental Novel*. Zola explained that the novelist customarily begins with an experimental fact: He has observed—so to speak—the behavior of a fictional protagonist. Then, using the inference of character as a sort of hypothesis, the novelist invents a series of lifelike situations which test, as it were, whether the observations of behavior are concordant with the inference. The unfolding of the narrative, interpreted causally as plot, will then naturally, and inevitably, verify the hypothesis. How neat—and how reductionist!

But however simplified this scheme of Zola may appear to us today, it has the merit of suggesting how strong, indeed, is the base in scientific optimism upon which traditional clinical description rests. Our descriptions imply our confidence that detailed observation of individual responses to common disease have a permanent value, which can be used predictively. They reveal an upbeat conviction that causal relations, when appreciated, lead to therapeutic (or narrative) success. Recent views of medicine and the novel seem to challenge these assumptions.

If we look at the ways in which we have changed our records in the last decade to the "Problem-Oriented Patient Record," to the "Defined Data Base," we appear to have shifted from a view of patient and disease based on the human, novelistic approach of the last century to one based on the flow sheet of the electronic engineer or the punch card of the computer. No longer do our early narratives end in a tentative diagnosis, a testable hypothesis: we are left with a series of unconnected "problems." The stories dissolve into a sort of diagnostic litany—e.g., anemia, weight loss, fever, skin spots—without the unifying plot that ties these up with the causal thread of leukemia. Worse yet, these records are now frequently transformed into a series of checks scrawled over preprinted sheets which carry in tedious detail a computer-generated laundry list of signs and symptoms. The anomie of impersonal, corporate personnel forms has crept into these records. Added to these forces, which have turned the doctor's prose into institutional slang, is the movement to eliminate reflections on sex preference, race, and social background. In the name of convenience and egalitarianism, we seem to have exchanged the story of the single sick human at a moment of crisis for an impersonal checklist which describes a "case" with "problems." When we fail at words, we fail to understand, we fail to feel.

But, I'm afraid that the new novelists have anticipated us here, too. As the naturalistic novel has yielded to the stream of consciousness, to existential angst, and to flat introspection, the anomie of the clinic has been foreshadowed by that of the artist. The opening lines of our major modern novels sound the tones of disengagement as clearly as our clinical records:

> Today, mother is dead. Or perhaps yesterday. I don't know. I received a telegram from the Home. "Mother dead. Funeral tomorrow. Best Wishes." It means nothing. Perhaps it was yesterday.
>
> —*The Stranger*
> Albert Camus (1942)

> If only I could explain to you how changed I am since those days! Changed yet still the same, but now I can view my old preoccupation with a calm eye.
>
> —*The Benefactor*
> Susan Sontag (1963)

> What makes Iago evil? Some people ask. I never ask.
>
> —*Play It As It Lays*
> Joan Didion (1970)

Perhaps as doctors we are now committed to acting as a group of "benefactors" ministering to the sick "strangers"—we cannot, or will not, be involved in the lives of those who have come to us for care; we will now simply describe and solve the problems of the case. We will play it as it lays.

QUESTIONS FOR READING, RESPONDING, AND WRITING

Summarizing Main Points

1. According to Weissmann, what part of the patient's chart is the "story"? Which part is the "plot"? What is revealed in their combination?
2. What are the two views of medicine and the novel that Weissmann presents? Which does he prefer? Why?

Analyzing Methods of Discourse

1. Compare (1) the openings from the three hospital records to the openings from the three nineteenth-century novels (Austin, Balzac, Dostoevsky) and (2) the

nineteenth-century novel openings to the modern novel openings (Camus, Sontag, Didion). Explain the ways in which they illustrate the steps in Weissmann's argument.

2. In his opening paragraph, Weissmann states, "Best of all, I love the conventional paragraph by which the story is introduced." Reread Weissmann's opening paragraph. How does it compare to the openings he talks about? Does it contain elements of "plot" and "story"? What does it tell you about Weissmann? About the "tale" his essay tells?

Focusing on the Field

1. In paragraph eight, Weissmann describes the chart of a 60-year-old taxi driver. At the end of the chart, Weissmann provides the "dreary Intern's Note: 4:00 A.M. Called to see patient . . ." Weissmann obviously breaks off the description before the end of the intern's note. Why do you think he leaves it out? What does this omission tell you about Weissmann? Why is such an omission appropriate at this point in the essay?

2. Throughout the first part of his essay, Weissmann explains the medical chart in literary or novelistic terms. With the introduction of Emile Zola and "The Experimental Novel," he reverses this procedure, describing the ways one novelist applies medical or scientific terms and methods to fiction. Look at the scientific language he uses to describe Zola's application. Why may Zola's method of description be called "reductionist"? How does this "reduction" foreshadow the "reduction" in the last part of Weissmann's argument? Why do you think Weissmann thinks Zola's method is "optimistic"?

Writing Assignments

1. Read Flannery O'Connor's "The Teaching of Literature." Comment on the similarities and differences between O'Connor's and Weissmann's views of literature. Can one be considered "humanistic" and the other "scientific"? Explain.

2. Read Richard Selzer's "The Art of Surgery." Using Weissmann's models, write hospital record openings for the two patients Selzer treats.

Sheila Tobias

WHO'S AFRAID OF MATH, AND WHY?

Sheila Tobias has herself felt the "sudden death" of math anxiety. In an effort to help others overcome such fears, she cofounded a "math clinic" at Wesleyan University where she was working as an associate provost. Her experiences there helped initiate her seminal study, *Overcoming Math Anxiety*, from which the following essay is taken. Tobias dispels the popular myth that a woman could genetically or biologically lack a "mathematical mind." Instead, Tobias shows how parental expectations and cultural ideologies may prevent women from succeeding in quantitative areas.

Tobias gained an A.B. from Radcliffe College (1957) and advanced degrees in history from Columbia University. She has worked as a journalist, both for network television and for *American Weekend,* a periodical based in Frankfurt, West Germany. She lives with her husband, Carlos Stein, an environmentalist, in Washington, D.C. A founding member of the National Organization for Women (NOW), Tobias has also worked for *Female Studies I* (1970). She is the author of more than 100 articles, on both math anxiety and women's studies. "Mathphobic" individuals will be happy to know that she is continuing her research into math anxiety.

The first thing people remember about failing at math is that it felt like sudden death. Whether the incident occurred while learning "word problems" in sixth grade, coping with equations in high school, or first confronting calculus and statistics in college, failure came suddenly and in a very frightening way. An idea or a new operation was not just difficult, it was impossible! And, instead of asking questions or taking the lesson slowly, most people remember having had the feeling that they would never go any further in mathematics. If we assume that the curriculum was reasonable, and that the new idea was but the next in a series of learnable concepts, the feeling of utter defeat was simply not rational; yet "math anxious" college students and adults have revealed that no matter how much the teacher reassured them, they could not overcome that feeling.

A common myth about the nature of mathematical ability holds that one either has or does not have a mathematical mind. Mathematical imagination and an intuitive grasp of mathematical principles may well be needed to do advanced research, but why should people who can do college-level work in other subjects not be able to do college-level math as well? Rates of learning may vary. Competency under time pressure may differ. Certainly low self-esteem will get in the way. But where is the evidence that a student needs a "mathematical mind" in order to succeed at learning math?

Consider the effects of this mythology. Since only a few people are supposed to have this mathematical mind, part of what makes us so passive in the face of our difficulties in learning mathematics is that we suspect all the while we may not be one of "them," and we spend our time waiting to find out when our nonmathematical minds will be exposed. Since our limit will eventually be reached, we see no point in being methodical or in attending to detail. We are grateful when we survive fractions, word problems, or geometry. If that certain moment of failure hasn't struck yet, it is only temporarily postponed.

Parents, especially parents of girls, often expect their children to be nonmathematical. Parents are either poor at math and had their own sudden-death experiences, or, if math came easily for them, they do not know how it feels to be slow. In either case, they unwittingly foster the idea that a mathematical mind is something one either has or does not have.

MATHEMATICS AND SEX

Although fear of math is not a purely female phenomenon, girls tend to drop out of math sooner than boys, and adult women experience an aversion to math and math-related activities that is akin to anxiety. A 1972 survey of the amount of high school mathematics taken by incoming freshmen at Berkeley revealed that while 57 percent of the boys had taken four years of high school math, only 8 percent of the girls had had the same amount of preparation. Without four years of high school math, students at Berkeley, and at most other colleges and universities, are ineligible for the calculus sequence, unlikely to attempt chemistry or physics, and inadequately prepared for statistics and economics.

Unable to elect these entry-level courses, the remaining 92 percent of the girls will be limited, presumably, to the career choices that are considered feminine: the humanities, guidance and counseling, elementary school teaching, foreign languages, and the fine arts.

Boys and girls may be born alike with respect to math, but certain sex differences in performance emerge early according to several respected studies, and these differences remain through adulthood. They are:

1. Girls compute better than boys (elementary school and on).
2. Boys solve word problems better than girls (from age thirteen on).
3. Boys take more math than girls (from age sixteen on).
4. Girls learn to hate math sooner and possibly for different reasons.

Why the differences in performance? One reason is the amount of math learned and used at play. Another may be the difference in male-female maturation. If girls do better than boys at all elementary school tasks, then they may compute better for no other reason than that arithmetic is part of the elementary school curriculum. As boys and girls grow older, girls become, under pressure, academically less competitive. Thus, the falling off of girls' math performance between ages ten and fifteen may be because:

1. Math gets harder in each successive year and requires more work and commitment.

2. Both boys and girls are pressured, beginning at age ten, not to excel in areas designated by society to be outside their sex-role domains.
3. Thus girls have a good excuse to avoid the painful struggle with math; boys don't.

Such a model may explain girls' lower achievement in math overall, but why should girls even younger than ten have difficulty in problem-solving? In her review of the research on sex differences, psychologist Eleanor Maccoby noted that girls are generally more conforming, more suggestible, and more dependent upon the opinion of others than boys (all learned, not innate, behaviors). Being so, they may not be as willing to take risks or to think for themselves, two behaviors that are necessary in solving problems. Indeed, in one test of third-graders, girls were found to be not nearly as willing to estimate, to make judgments about "possible right answers," or to work with systems they had never seen before. Their very success at doing what is expected of them up to that time seems to get in the way of their doing something new.

If readiness to do word problems, to take one example, is as much a function of readiness to take risks as it is of "reasoning ability," then mathematics performance certainly requires more than memory, computation, and reasoning. The differences in math performance between boys and girls—no matter how consistently those differences show up—cannot be attributed simply to differences in innate ability.

Still, if one were to ask the victims themselves, they would probably disagree: they would say their problems with math have to do with the way they are "wired." They feel they are somehow missing something—one ability or several—that other people have. Although women want to believe they are not mentally inferior to men, many fear that, where math is concerned, they really are. Thus, we have to consider seriously whether mathematical ability has a biological basis, not only because a number of researchers believe this to be so, but because a number of victims agree with them.

THE ARGUMENTS FROM BIOLOGY

The search for some biological basis for math ability or disability is fraught with logical and experimental difficulties. Since not all math underachievers are women, and not all women are mathematics-avoidant, poor performance in math is unlikely to be due to some genetic or hormonal difference between the sexes. Moreover, no amount of research so far has unearthed a "mathematical competency" in some tangible, measurable substance in the body. Since "masculinity" cannot be injected into women to test whether or not it improves their mathematics, the theories that attribute such ability to genes or hormones must depend for their proof on circumstantial evidence. So long as about 7 percent of the Ph.D.'s in mathematics are earned by women, we have to conclude either that these women have genes, hormones, and brain organization different from those of the rest of us, or that certain positive experiences in their lives have largely undone the negative fact that they are female, or both.

Genetically, the only difference between males and females (albeit a significant and pervasive one) is the presence of two chromosomes designated X in every female cell. Normal males exhibit an X-Y combination. Because some kinds of mental retardation are associated with sex-chromosomal anomalies, a number of researchers have sought a converse linkage between specific abilities and the presence or absence of the second X. But the linkage between genetics and mathematics is not supported by conclusive evidence.

Since intensified hormonal activity commences at adolescence, a time during which girls seem to lose interest in mathematics, much more has been made of the unequal amounts in females and males of the sex-linked hormones androgen and estrogen. Biological researchers have linked estrogen—the female hormone—with "simple repetitive tasks," and androgen—the male hormone—with "complex restructuring tasks." The assumption here is not only that such specific talents are biologically based (probably undemonstrable) but also that one cannot be good at *both* repetitive and restructuring kinds of assignments.

SEX ROLES AND MATHEMATICS COMPETENCE

The fact that many girls tend to lose interest in math at the age they reach puberty (junior high school) suggests that puberty might in some sense cause girls to fall behind in math. Several explanations come to mind: the influence of hormones, more intensified sex-role socialization, or some extracurricular learning experience exclusive to boys of that age.

One group of seventh-graders in a private school in New England gave a clue as to what children themselves think about all of this. When asked why girls do as well as boys in math until the sixth grade, while sixth-grade boys do better from that point on, the girls responded: "Oh, that's easy. After sixth grade, we have to do real math." The answer to why "real math" should be considered to be "for boys" and not "for girls" can be found not in the realm of biology but only in the realm of ideology of sex differences.

Parents, peers, and teachers forgive a girl when she does badly in math at school, encouraging her to do well in other subjects instead.

"'There, there,' my mother used to say when I failed at math," one woman says. "But I got a talking-to when I did badly in French." Lynn Fox, who directs a program for mathematically gifted junior high boys and girls on the campus of Johns Hopkins University, has trouble recruiting girls and keeping them in her program. Some parents prevent their daughters from participating altogether for fear that excellence in math will make them too different. The girls themselves are often reluctant to continue with mathematics, Fox reports, because they fear social ostracism.

Where do these associations come from?

The association of masculinity with mathematics sometimes extends from the discipline to those who practice it. Students, asked on a questionnaire what characteristics they associate with a mathematician (as contrasted with a "writer"), selected terms such as rational, cautious, wise, and responsible. The writer, on the other hand, in addition to being seen as individualistic and independent, was also described as warm, interested in people, and altogether more compatible with a feminine ideal.

As a result of this psychological conditioning, a young woman may consider math and math-related fields to be inimical to femininity. In an interesting study of West German teenagers, Erika Schildkamp-Kuendiger found that girls who identified themselves with the feminine ideal underachieved in mathematics, that is, did less well than would have been expected of them based on general intelligence and performance in other subjects.

STREET MATHEMATICS: THINGS, MOTION, SCORES

Not all the skills that are necessary for learning mathematics are learned in school. Measuring, computing, and manipulating objects that have dimensions and dynamic properties of their own are part of the everyday life of children. Children who miss out on these experiences may not be well primed for math in school.

Feminists have complained for a long time that playing with dolls is one way of convincing impressionable little girls that they may only be mothers or housewives—or, as in the case of the Barbie doll, "pinup girls"—when they grow up. But doll-playing may have even more serious consequences for little girls than that. Do girls find out about gravity and distance and shapes and sizes playing with dolls? Probably not.

A curious boy, if his parents are tolerant, will have taken apart a number of household and play objects by the time he is ten, and, if his parents are lucky, he may even have put them back together again. In all of this he is learning things that will be useful in physics and math.

Taking parts out that have to go back in requires some examination of form. Building something that stays up or at least stays put for some time involves working with structure.

Sports is another source of math-related concepts for children which tends to favor boys. Getting to first base on a not very well hit grounder is a lesson in time, speed, and distance. Intercepting a football thrown through the air requires some rapid intuitive eye calculations based on the ball's direction, speed, and trajectory. Since physics is partly concerned with velocities, trajectories, and collisions of objects, much of the math taught to prepare a student for physics deals with relationships and formulas that can be used to express motion and acceleration.

What, then, can we conclude about mathematics and sex? If math anxiety is in part the result of math avoidance, why not require girls to take as much math as they can possibly master? If being the only girl in "trig" is the reason so many women drop math at the end of high school, why not provide psychological counseling and support for those young women who wish to go on? Since ability in mathematics is considered by many to be unfeminine, perhaps fear of success, more than any bodily or mental dysfunction, may interfere with girls' ability to learn math.

QUESTIONS FOR READING, RESPONDING, AND WRITING

Summarizing Main Points

1. What is the major reason that girls are afraid of math, according to Tobias? Is math anxiety a genetically or environmentally triggered difficulty? Do you agree or disagree with Tobias's main point?
2. List the major reasons why, according to Tobias, researchers have difficulty ascribing genetic or biological reasons for sex-based differences in math performance.

Analyzing Methods of Discourse

1. Tobias devotes most of her essay to a discussion of the problems in researching math anxiety, reserving her last paragraph only for advocating solutions. Why do you suppose she chooses this tactic?
2. Early in her essay, Tobias charts the differences between boys' and girls' performances in math. Later, she provides the arguments that typically support that chart, that is, provide the causes for those differences. How does this technique give the reader a clearer picture of the difficulties in proving these cause-effect relations?

Focusing on the Field

1. According to Tobias, who is most likely to be able to change sex-based differences in math performance: educators, parents, or the children themselves? Do you feel her solutions are realistic? Will they be easy to carry out?
2. In this essay, Tobias provides no researched statistics on environmental causes

for sex-based differences in math performance. Where would she have to go for such statistics? What difficulties would she encounter in providing or validating such statistics?

Writing Assignments

1. After informally interviewing students at your school about their own math anxieties, report on your results. Be sure to include your own conclusions about the validity of your poll.
2. Read Margaret Henning's and Anne Jardim's essay, "The Managerial Woman: The Middle Management Career Path." In a short essay, demonstrate how Tobias's essay supports the conclusions that Henning and Jardim make about women in middle management.

John J. Anderson

THE HEARTBREAK OF CYBERPHOBIA

John J. Anderson considers himself "a word-oriented person, disenfranchised in large part from the world of mathematics." Yet he works as a computer-science journalist, contributing essays on computers to such magazines as *Psychology Today, The Economist,* and *Games Magazine,* as well as contributing to and editing *Creative Computing.* His dual interests began during his college career. At first a linguist, Anderson became interested in computer models of language, which, in turn, eventually led him to graduate study at New York University in computational linguistics. Riding the crest of the computer wave, Anderson introduced the first microcomputer courses at New York University, running microcomputer seminars for several years there.

In addition to more than 100 articles on computers written for both the general reader and the specialist, Anderson has published *Commodore G-4 Sight and Sound* and *Computers for Kids.* In the essay that follows, which first appeared in *Creative Computing,* Anderson demonstrates his ability to make the too-often forbidding world of computers intellectually accessible, and even entertaining.

"What—me a cyberphobe?" You may scoff at the accusation. I realize you are reading a computer periodical, one, in fact, which usually makes the assumption that its audience feels quite comfortable around small computers. Yet a good deal of the material we present assumes advanced knowledge on the part of our readers.

In actuality many of our readers are in a more or less fledgling state when it comes to computers. They want to know more—they want to be comfortable with the material, but are finding it to be tough going. There is so much to learn, to begin. I remember how I felt the first time I ever leafed through the pages of *Creative Computing*; it was like nothing I had ever seen before. Although the words looked a lot like English, I was able to understand very little.

The people I wish to address here are in that beginner category. They may or may not own microcomputers. They are making an effort to educate themselves, but are intimidated, whether or not they openly admit it. Intimidation, with its longtime partner, fear, are extremely effective blockers of learning. My goal here is to loosen their hold. Even if you are on intimate terms with one or more CPUs, you may find the following to be of interest.

OF MAINFRAMES AND MYTHS

Let's step back a little, and attempt to gain a long-range view.

Way back in April 1969, *Psychology Today* addressed the question of the impending "computer revolution." It took stock of tools versus toils in the ascendency of the computer. We are still asking, and will be for some time, what price will be exacted from humanity, relying increasingly on computer guidance, as it courses headlong into the twenty-first century.

The prospects offered then were tinged with warnings, but rather cautiously cheerful overall. In the pages of that issue, B. F. Skinner and Dean Wooldridge unabashedly argued for the point of view that man is a machine.

Marvin Minsky tackled optimistically some of the philosophical and engineering problems in the modeling of intelligence. Isaac Asimov went so far as to say that "the human brain is made up of a finite number of cells of finite complexity, arranged in a pattern of finite complexity. When a computer is built of an equal number of equally complex cells in an equally complex arrangement, we will have something that can do just as much as a human brain can do to its uttermost genius."

Those are the kinds of assertions that evoke, unknowingly and unintentionally, grave consternation among the cyberphobic.

Asimov, in a follow-up piece, spoke of the "Frankenstein Complex," which he coined as the generally accepted and deeply internalized notion that, as put forth in an occasional Late Show, some things were simply never meant for man to tamper with. He attempted to puncture the myth, but I got the strange feeling he had strengthened it with his earlier prediction concerning intelligent machines.

I have great respect and admiration for each of these authors and, in fact, share their hopes for the future. But, with their unbridled predictions, they were certainly fueling the pyre at the time.

They can hardly be blamed for it—in 1969, there was a different perspective. One facet of this perspective was that computers were huge, unwieldy, unreliable nests of multimillion-dollar spaghetti. It is not inconsistent that informed opinion, then, had grown so dramatically imposing as to nurture Promethean visions.

Today computers fit on the head of a pin, and while they still sometimes evoke images from Orwell, they are at least physically less forbidding. They are also encroaching upon us irrevocably, inexorably, and unceasingly. They sneak up on us in various forms we may not immediately recognize: they are in our toys, our tools, our timepieces. And today $125 will buy the computer power that cost $125,000 in April of 1969.

Doubtless, we must overcome our inhibitions concerning computers before we can effectively direct their proliferation. This is a lasting challenge to educators.

It is nonetheless clear now that educators themselves have done more to foster fear and trembling about computers than any group of axe-wielding Neo-Luddities. Even sane people (I include myself) have spent weak moments pondering whether and when the microwave oven was going to begin barking orders.

APPERCEPTION WITHOUT APPREHENSION

"Cyberphobia" is a term of growing usage, import, and incidence. Courses across the country now attract members, young and old, of a new and needful group: those willing but unable to understand much about computers, owing to a chronic anxiety concerning them. The term is no passing bit of Valspeak or computer jargon. It describes a tangible and often socioeconomically debilitating malady. I, along with many others in the field of computers and education, have worked to create programs that help cyberphobes break the grip of fear and gain some insight into a remarkable direction upon which the human race has lately embarked.

HIS CRT HAS WIPERS

When dealing with cyberphobia, a favorite analogy of mine concerns computers and cars; I have heard much criticism of the comparisons, but indulge them for a moment. The car is a lever of physical mobility. The computer is a lever of mental mobility.

The advent of the automobile radically altered our perspectives. The scope of our daily environment, as well as our grasp within that environment, was entirely redrawn. As its popularity grew and costs dropped, the alterations wrought by the car became permanent and unilateral. The changes have been changes for good and ill. The benefits are obvious, and, undeniably, the gains have been strewn with lamentable compromise.

So it is with computers. They are swiftly changing the fabric of society as informational, educational, and recreational tools. These innovations will serve not only a technocratic elite, as has been suggested by some; they will be so cheap as to be readily available to all who desire them. They will become easier and easier to use. There exist already serious potentials for misuse; these are numerous and ominous. Yet the side effects of computers are arguably less lethal, polluting, and energy-dependent than those of the automobile.

The driver of a car need not understand much about how an automobile works to use it. In fact a thorough understanding is rarely possessed by the driver. Though the automakers have done their best to obscure the fact, a car is less an end in itself than it is a means; it is used to reach some desired destination.

This is also true of the computer. The user can decide how much or how little to become involved with its internal workings. He may choose to learn little about the machine and still gain a great deal from its use.

Some people become disoriented when they think about computers because they make the mistake of asking what computers do, expecting a single answer. Computers are multipurpose machines. In contrast to the cotton gin, butter churn, and safety pin, computers are designed with no sole, dedicated purpose in mind. Only upon execution of some certain and specific program will any "destination" be reached. The universality of the computer is in itself threatening—perhaps to some as threatening as being run over by a car, only more insidious. There are many different and subtle ways to be squashed, you see.

During those first experiences behind the wheel of a car, a learner experiences fear. This is natural, even necessary, to learn control and proper operation of a machine as powerful (and potentially dangerous) as an automobile.

Most important, there is but one way to overcome this fear: to drive. After many hours on the road, a modicum of confidence is obtained.

The only way to conquer fear of computers is to get to know them. My advice to the timid: sit in front of one as soon as possible. Remember, it is much more difficult to kill yourself or others staring at a video screen than peering out of a windshield, even in your first minutes at the console.

To judge computers without having touched one is like learning to drive by studying geography. And yet many people, especially and unfortunately otherwise intelligent people, have done just that. Until you sit down and start interacting with a computer, you have not even turned on the ignition, so to speak.

And knowing how to use computers is already as necessary a skill for many as knowing how to drive.

BELLETRISTIC COMPUTING

Some people have accused me of being obsessed with computers—of being in the worst case "cyberphenic" in my attitude. I deny this. My penchant for computers grows not from any compulsion to program or natural affinity for number crunching. On the contrary, I am a word-oriented person, disenfranchised in large part from the world of mathematics (as were many of my kind at an early age, no doubt as a result of archaic teaching methods). I am "right-brained," to further abuse a much-celebrated thesis.

No, I have no programmable calculator dangling from my belt, and the word "calculus" still induces weakness in my knees. I have always had trouble with long division, and though I greatly admire the unshakable foundations of the hard sciences, I will usually skip the math, taking the theorist's word that the results invariably fit the facts. And that is one reason I love computers. They do my math for me.

The microcomputer, for me and a growing number like me, is not an end in itself. It is a means to an end. The creative potential of the micro is in a sense limitless and certainly goes far beyond balancing checkbooks or processing words. Among my own interests are computer graphics and sound, and their use in education.

Okay. You might now have a better idea of what a microcomputer should be. I've gassed you up, and you're ready to "get behind the wheel." Next question: where to?

Let's do exactly what I cautioned against above, namely, summarily survey some geography; in order to carve a foothold we shall take a guided tour of some major software destinations in an effort to underscore three promising directions. The inclusions and omissions of course reflect my own biases, and what follows should not be construed as definitive in any way. What I wish to provide is a group of starting points. As more and more "right-brained" types invade the field, the scope and quality of this software will continue to soar. I enjoy imagining that some of the minds that will take part in the process are reading this now.

ENRICHING EDUCATION

Remember Rubik's Cube? I spent a dozen hours or so learning to solve it, as have a few million other people around the world. Mathematicians were simply tickled pink with the physical embodiment of mathematical set theory the cube presented. In fact, Professor Rubik originally designed the cube as a tool to teach the concept to his own students.

The thing that excites math teachers about the cube is the way it can impart an intrinsic sense of how it works to its users. What is to be stressed is that no kind of learning is more effective than "hands-on" experience: in learning to solve the cube, the user gets a "feeling" for set theory.

Now imagine the graphic potential of the microcomputer to embody mathematical concepts. Several microcomputer programs, for instance, simulate a Rubik's Cube, with one slight improvement—the user can see all the faces of the cube simultaneously. This provides a more complete idea of what is happening as the faces spin. The microcomputer is unparalleled at providing this kind of tutorial power. Software developers who tap this potential are making the best use of the micro as an educational tool.

One name should spring to mind during any explanation of educational software for the microcomputer: Seymour Papert. If you are interested in the topic of microcomputers and have not read his book *Mindstorms*, you are ill-prepared for this decade. Papert is a long-time crony of Minsky at MIT, as well as one of the venerated group of geniuses who spent the late sixties making optimistic predictions for the field they called AI, for artificial intelligence. I'll be addressing the question of AI a little farther on.

Things didn't turn out quite as dramatically as the MIT boys predicted in 1969, nor on the predicted timetable. However, in the interim, Papert took a language of his inner circle, Lisp, which is a powerful structure of lists built upon lists, and whipped it into Logo, a language that is now revolutionizing the elementary school classroom.

For years now, some educators have had the extremely unfortunate notion that computers are tools for only drill and practice—and so developed a field they called CAI, for computer-assisted instruction. Papert refers to this as the computer programming the learner. A computer is tirelessly terrific at administering drill and practice, and I believe there is a place for drill and practice in learning. But care should be taken that drill and practice never become the only purposes for which microcomputers are touched by students. The misuse of CAI has surely in some cases exacerbated latent cyberphobia.

A much preferable situation, states Papert, is one in which the student tells the computer what to do. That is a goal of Logo—to provide a language whereby the user "teaches" the computer how to complete a certain task. Turtle graphics, as an example, use this approach to help young children develop an intrinsic sense of geometry. The user does a great deal of learning in the process, of course. Learning about solving big problems by breaking them into groups of smaller problems; learning about logical thinking; learning to express solutions; learning that computers are tools to be manipulated by the user, not vice versa. These are indispensable lessons.

How soon should these types of interactions be introduced to the student? Some evidence indicates that kindergarten may well be too late, but I would confidently state that a first-grade class will benefit greatly from access to a machine that runs Logo or another language with simple but pretty graphics and sound capabilities. Motivation of children will quite often be unnecessary—a teacher needs simply to work with them at their pace to achieve the results the children desire. Piaget would have been proud.

Another important group of educational programs (though they are often not viewed as such) are simulations. Rubik's Cube programs are simulations of an actual cube. In other simulations, the user sits in the cockpit of a 747 or on the throne of a medieval city-state; at the helm of a supertanker, perhaps, or even at the controls of a nuclear reactor. In situations otherwise dangerous, costly, or impossible to recreate, the computer can simulate the major factors that obtain, giving the students valuable first-person experience. I have been heartened by the joy of a group of fourth graders who have just avoided a meltdown. An experience of this kind does much more for a child than merely hearing or reading about it. It becomes a self-motivated, reinforced, and above all exciting learning experience.

ENRICHING ENTERTAINMENT

There is much controversy today concerning the dangers of the video game. Even the surgeon general of our nation has expressed serious concern (while admitting a lack of hard evidence) that the games are "hazardous to your health." While some seek legislation to stop their proliferation, others seek to harness the power of the video game to constructive ends.

Some of the dangers associated with arcades (such as the availability of drugs and pilfering of quarters) can be rightfully ascribed not to the games themselves, but to the environment in which they appear. I think that some regulation of arcades is a prudent course. The best place to play video games is obviously within the home. The atmosphere is healthier there, games do not require coins, and supervision can be much more effective.

I do not think the right kinds of games are harmful in the short or long run. As a member of the first TV generation that sat passively in front of the set, I find it refreshing to see kids who take it for granted that video screens are a two-way street. At the least, the video world is not a show. It is an interaction. The key is moderation; obsession with anything is not a good idea.

Unfortunately, a very few home video games on the market today have attempted to base sales on sexism, murder, rape, arson, and other crimes (as humorously kinky, I suspect their hype would assert). Parents must now add video play to their vigilance concerning what their kids watch, read, eat, and so on. It is only to be expected in the final score of our fast-moving century.

Likewise, I don't believe that space "shoot-'em-ups" or games such as Pac-Man are harmful. Though they may at times seem to induce frustration or violent urges, they serve much more frequently to release those feelings—something of which passive video is incapable. I reject arguments that condemn the games on the basis of eventual and inevitable loss. Those arguments are raised by folks who have no idea why anybody plays the games at all.

The video game poses a world—a much simpler world than our own, wherein success is very clearly defined and, for a time, clearly attainable. Through practice, a player can control this world for a while. He can escape from the anxieties of real life into a place where his own actions always count, where he can be a hero. When the game is over, he hasn't lost or been beaten. Is a surfer beaten when he flies from a wave?

Most video games call for some semblance of hand-eye coordination, and some hospitals are now using them in rehabilitation programs for brain-damaged patients. It has been found that some patients who were otherwise thought to be unreachable have been "brought out" through their use. Moreover, experimental research is now being conducted regarding the feasibility of video games as a test for drunken driving. Intoxicants act to slow reaction time and impair coordination—and nowhere is this kind of impairment more measurable than on the video game playfield. Some day a poor showing at "Six-Pack Man" may cost you your license.

Video games for the microcomputer are not restricted to mere "twitch" games, however. Strategy games are at least as popular, and among these are the so-called "fantasy role-playing" adventures. These games allow the player to construct a whole new personality, choosing strengths and weaknesses from a list of possible character traits.

One might choose, for instance, a character who is extremely dexterous and swift, but these positive traits must be traded off against others, such as strength and endurance. Players have a tendency to become extremely attached to their characters. My preference runs toward brawn as opposed to brain, which probably reflects some compromise between reality and my own desires. I'm also attached to extrasensory powers, which are likewise denied to me in the real world.

After characters are created, they enter and interact within entire fantasy worlds: worlds wherein they can exercise a kind of free will, choose their fates, even experience their own deaths. These fantasy games are being used experimentally now with autistic and severely withdrawn adolescents. Though results are preliminary, they seem quite positive. To the threatened personality, interaction in an environment where even death isn't fatal can have real therapeutic value.

Even the group we typically dismiss as "normal" can derive release through adventure games. I have predicted they will become, before long, as popular a fictional form as the novel or film. A portentous prediction, but one which I assert is utterly credible.

ENRICHING DEMOCRACY

As I hope we begin to see, the microcomputer can do quite a great deal on its own, sitting on a desktop, coffee table, or TV cart. But hook it up to the phone lines, and you have established a new medium of expression: the telecommunications network.

Telecommunications through a home computer present a great deal of potential. The growing possibilities of travel reservations, ticket purchases, shop-at-home services, a broad range of databases at your fingertips, are worthy and practical. They herald a truly useful place for the microcomputer in the home.

I do not believe, however, that any of these practical notions constitutes the real basis for the mushrooming popularity of modern communications. Rather, the reason many people have discovered is the possibility of establishing a dialogue. They are less interested in using a modem to pay their gas and phone bills than to state their opinions, to have their voices heard, and to respond to the voices of others.

Networks and bulletin-board services are blossoming nationwide and worldwide. These are phone lines tied to computers, big or small, running programs that accept and display information sent from other computers. The concept is powerful and limitlessly extensible. It creates a new kind of forum—a medium of communication—through which ideas can be expressed, shot down, modified, and spread. The importance of this kind of interaction, and its potential, is now being discovered. It will be some time before it emerges as a medium of major influence, but it is going to happen; it is happening now.

Why should my computer communicate with your computer, you

may ask, when we could just as easily converse by voice? I assert that if we were strangers, it would not be nearly so easy. Modem communication transmits information purely—untainted by ego, personality, idiolect, affect, or mannerism. Only the ideas are transmitted. It is, therefore, truly an equal-opportunity medium.

Further, through the use of unlocked electronic mail, I may with my data establish a sort of long-term party line—I may pose questions to be answered by many over a period of months. I may respond to queries put forth six weeks ago and discussed by dozens of others before me. I may even enter into a "real-time" conversation with someone a thousand miles distant at 3:00 A.M. without feeling that my privacy is in any way compromised.

For the lonely, the bedridden, the handicapped, the advent of the telecommunications network will be an important psychological boost. Special-interest boards have already made an appearance, the emphasis of which is on a single topic, such as science fiction or philosophy. This trend toward specialization is bound to continue.

STILL WARY, HUH?

I'm aware that none of what I have stated so far will help you make better sense of the more esoteric components of *Creative Computing*. What I have tried to do, by way of demystification, coaxing, and a bit of hard sell, is instill in you the will to plow through the learning process—to help you understand why and how it would be worthwhile to tame your cyberphobic tendencies. And still, you are not convinced. Implicitly, I have been asking you all along to trust the power of computers: perhaps that is something you are still far from ready to do.

Well, I can relate to that.

It could be that you have fallen into the same hole as many other folks: you wonder if the machines will beat us at our own game; you are hung up on the question of whether computers can think. You are in some impeccable company, believe me. Many smart people have spent many anxious hours worrying about this very concept. Their assumptions differ antithetically, but they are united in that they never get very far in their reasoning.

One problem that crops up immediately concerns the definition of the word "intelligence." A person's definition of the term will certainly dictate, in large part, his views on the subject. We have a hard enough time agreeing on criteria by which to measure natural intelligence, let alone any synthetic varieties.

The definition of artificial intelligence I have heard most often is something like "that which would be ascribed to intelligence if it were done by a human." This approach, of course, can get us into heaps of trouble. The chess-playing computer, for example, has forced a wide-ranging reappraisal of just what does and does not imply "intelligence" in a given context.

As is often my style, I will now casually sidestep the question to approach it from a different angle. Don't panic.

SOFTWARE CELEBRITIES

In 1966, Joseph Weizenbaum, another AI mogul from MIT, demonstrated a program he called Eliza. This program acted as a rudimentary psychiatrist, incorporating simple grammatical rules to hold limited "conversations" with its users. Though Weizenbaum has gone to great lengths to debunk the notion that anything about Eliza was in any way intelligent (he has written a very readable book, *Computer Power and Human Reason*, which makes the point), some people actually claimed to have benefited from Eliza's brand of nondirective therapy. This horrified Weizenbaum, whose strong humanist feelings helped temper the AI bluster coming out of MIT in the early seventies. To him the idea of Rogerian sessions conducted by an unthinking computer was ludicrous.

He missed an important point, however. In a sense, the fact that Eliza employed "tricks" in order to converse, turning user's statements around and shooting them right back, was less important than what some found to be the quality of "her" conversation. Eliza-like programs are now available for microcomputers, and though their capabilities remain quite limited, technology is providing new and inexpensive means for the simulation of human qualities, undreamed of in 1966.

Computers with increasing powers of speech and, more important, powers to listen to commands, are decreasing in price. I fully expect "personality programs" to make an appearance within the next two years. They will speak, accept voice commands, undoubtedly be endowed with the ability to answer the telephone, asking whether the caller wants a voice or data connection. They will in addition provide entertaining, though limited, conversation. Talk about a user-friendly operating system!

Additional pioneers in intelligence simulation are already coming to us from the field of robotics. The first true robot stars, real-life R2-D2s and C3-POs, of which, rest assured, there will be an unending lineage, have begun to appear. Whether these machines are truly "intelligent" or "conscious" will be much less important than the fact that they are fun to use and interact with.

THINKING ABOUT THINKING

I believe, as did the estimable mathematician Alan Turing, that the question of machine intelligence will die a quiet and very natural death by the early part of the next century. It will be resolved not by some sage, or by any sort of scientific proof, but as a practicality of language. Humanity will soon speak of machines thinking without a flinch. And yet, they will realize that machines will never think—at least not in exactly the way that human beings do.

Allow me to put forward another and much used metaphor. I attribute it to Donald Michie, though I have heard it in many forms.

When humanity first learned how to fly, the study of aerodynamics was coupled with, and in large part stemmed from, the study of the flight of birds. From the time of da Vinci, human attempts at flight often mimicked the real and supposed mechanics of bird physiology. These attempts were linked by a single thread—failure. No one today would argue that airplanes fly in exactly the same way as do birds. And yet both do fly.

We could, if we so desired, introduce the term "artificial flight" to describe the flight of the airplane. But there seems no need for this. The airplane does not mimic the bird; both call upon the rules of aerodynamics to leave the ground. We know these rules apply to both, that the study of these rules has enhanced our knowledge of animal flight, while the study of animal flight has advanced the cause of mechanical flight.

When thinking machines were first discussed, the term "artificial intelligence" was introduced. It may take humanity a while to realize that the term is superfluous. Machines do not think in the same sense that humans do, nor do computers mimic human thinkers. Both follow the rules of cybernetics.

Here is a suggestion: if the idea of an intelligent machine really bothers you to the point of distraction, try using the term "syntelligence" to describe these growing capabilities. That way our friend the computer can garner some of the credit it deserves, and at the same time that nasty word "artificial" has been eliminated. Feel a little better? C'mon now. Even the tiniest bit?

THANKS FOR NOTHING

Well, where are we left? Cyberphobes of the world, I don't know how much better off you are for this little excursion. It is as if I had sat you down and explained every reason why you shouldn't be afraid of confined spaces, somehow expecting to cure your claustrophobia. The best approach, of course, would be to put you in a small closet: first with the door open, then with it half closed, three-quarters closed, closed for a second, closed for two seconds, and so on, until you were able to extinguish your fear. I would also provide an opportunity for you to meet others with the same malady.

And so the question with which we are left is the following: where can you go to receive that kind of gradual treatment for your cyberphobia?

Contact the school of continuing education at your local university, community college, or high school, and find out what "hands-on" micro courses are available. Although educators can be slow to catch on, many have by now realized that microcomputers are something worth teaching people about, and that a sizable part of this process is helping them overcome cyberphobic trepidation.

Visit your local computer store and ask if they offer seminars. If they don't, ask why not. Then, after you have determined your needs, get yourself a microcomputer and sit down at the keyboard. You'll be cruising in no time.

THE PUNCHLINE

And by all means, keep wading through *Creative:* you'll catch a little more each time. I nearly understand it now myself!

QUESTIONS FOR READING, RESPONDING, AND WRITING

Summarizing Main Points

1. What is "cyberphobia," according to Anderson? How has it come about? List the ways that Anderson suggests individuals can combat "cyberphobia."
2. List the many uses for the computer that Anderson analyzes. Were you aware of them all? Does your awareness—or lack of it—make you "cyberphobic"?

Analyzing Methods of Discourse

1. List all the ways that Anderson suggests a computer is like a car. List the ways that Anderson says that a computer is not like a car. Can you think of any comparisons Anderson has left out? Do you think Anderson's analogy, that is, his extended comparison, is helpful?
2. Anderson compares computers to many things other than cars, often calling computers by unusual names. List those comparisons and names. How is each helpful in making the reader more comfortable with computers?

Focusing on the Field

1. Aside from the unusual comparisons and figures of speech, Anderson's choice of words is also often surprising. For example, he often addresses his readers

directly and in a very informal manner, as in his subtitle, "Still Wary, Huh?" What effect does that informality and directness have on his readers? How does it help Anderson to achieve his purpose? How is his word choice appropriate for computer beginners?

2. How does Anderson's defense of video games widen his audience? Does Anderson consider all the arguments against video games? How does Anderson make comparisons between playing video games and using computers for more serious purposes?

Writing Assignments

1. In Anderson's section on "Apperception without Apprehension," he suggests that many people have a "chronic anxiety" about computers. Sheila Tobias in "Who's Afraid of Math, and Why?" describes a similar anxiety toward math. In a short essay, describe how the two points are similar and how they are different.

2. Anderson cites many authorities on computers and "artificial intelligence." After listing these authorities and their theories, write an essay that analyzes Anderson's own opinion of "artificial intelligence," or "syntelligence," as he prefers to call it. In your essay, compare and contrast Anderson's theories to at least two of the other theories.

Isaac Asimov

PURE AND IMPURE
The Interplay of Science and Technology

Isaac Asimov was born in Russia in 1920 and emigrated with his parents to Brooklyn, New York at the age of 3. He earned a Ph.D. in biochemistry from Columbia in 1948 and taught for a while at Boston University School of Medicine, but he eventually gave in completely to his obsessive writing habit—as he puts it, writing is his "only interest"—and quit teaching to write full-time. Yet many of his over 200 books of fiction and nonfiction suggest that Asimov has not left teaching, but merely left the classroom. Aided by a photographic memory and an incredibly multifarious range of expertise, he has rewarded an international reading public with a clearer understanding of such diverse subjects as the Bible, ancient history, Shakespeare, and the slide rule. Many of his popular books on science, *The Chemicals of Life* (1954), *Inside the Atom* (1956; 1966), *The Realm of Numbers* (1959), and *The Intelligent Man's Guide to Science* (1960), allow the layman to come to grips with an increasingly complex scientific revolution and the ethical difficulties that surround it. Asimov has also explored science in his many entertaining—and challenging— science-fiction novels, including the award-winning classics *I, Robot* (1950) and *The Foundation Trilogy* (1974).

In the following essay, Asimov turns his attention to the division between science and technology. He helps the reader discover that this conventional distinction obscures the "fundamental truth" that "there is only one scientific endeavor on earth—the pursuit of knowledge and understanding."

It is easy to divide a human being into mind and body and to attach far greater importance and reverence to the mind. Similarly, the products of the human mind can be divided into two classes: those that serve to elevate the mind and those that serve to comfort the body. The former are the "liberal arts," the latter, the "mechanical arts."

The liberal arts are those suitable for free men who are in a position to profit from the labors of others in such a way that they are not compelled to work themselves. The liberal arts deal with "pure knowledge" and are highly thought of, as all things pure must be.

The mechanical arts, which serve agriculture, commerce, and industry, are necessary, too; but as long as slaves, serfs, peasants, and others of low degree know such things, educated gentlemen of leisure can do without them.

Among the liberal arts are some aspects of science. Surely the kinds of studies that have always characterized science—the complex influences that govern the motions of the heavenly bodies, for instance, and that control the properties of mathematical figures and even of the universe itself—are pure enough. As history progressed, though, science developed a low habit of becoming applicable to the work of the world and, as a result, those whose field of mental endeavor lies in the liberal arts (minus science) tend to look down on scientists today as being in altogether too great a danger of dirtying their hands.

Scientists, in response, tend to ape this Greek-inherited snobbishness. They divide science into two parts; one deals only with the difficult, the abstruse, the elegant, the fundamental—in other words, "pure science," a truly liberal art. The other type of science is any branch that goes slumming and becomes associated with such mechanical arts as medicine, agriculture, and industry—clearly a form of impure science. "Impure" is a rather pejorative adjective. It is more common to talk of "basic science" and "applied science." On the other hand, differentiation by adjective alone may not seem enough. The same noun applied to both makes the higher suspect and lends the lower too much credit. There has thus been a tendency to call applied science "technology."

We can therefore speak of "science" and "technology" and we know very well which is the loftier, nobler, more aristocratic, and (in a whisper) the purer of the two. Yet the division is man-made and arbitrary and has no meaning in reality. The advance of knowledge of the physical universe rests on science *and* technology; neither can flourish without the other.

Technology is, indeed, the older of the two. Long before any human being could possibly have become interested in vague speculations about the universe, the hominid precursors of modern human beings were chipping rocks in order to get a sharp edge, and technology was born. Further advances, by hit and miss, trial and error, and even by hard thought, were slow, of course, in the absence of some understanding of basic principles that would guide the technologists in the direction of the possible and inspire them with a grasp of the potential.

Science, as distinct from technology, can be traced back as far as the ancient Greeks who advanced beautiful and intricate speculations. The speculations perhaps tended to become more beautiful, certainly more intricate, but there was no way in which they could have become more in accord with reality. The Greeks, alas, spun their speculations out of deductions based on what they guessed to be principles, and they sharply limited any temptation to indulge in a comparison of their conclusions with the world about them.

It was only when scientists began to observe the real world and to manipulate it that "experimental science" arose. This was in the 16th century, and the most able practitioner was the Italian scientist, Galileo Galilei, who began work toward the end of that century. Thus began the Scientific Revolution.

In the 18th century, when enough scientists recognized their responsibility toward the mechanical arts, we had the Industrial Revolution; it reshaped human life.

Such is the psychological set of our minds toward a separation of science into pure and impure, basic and applied, useless and useful, intellectual and industrial, that even today it is difficult for people to grasp the frequent and necessary interplay between them.

Consider the first great technologist of the modern era, the Scottish engineer, James Watt. Though he did not invent the steam engine, he developed the first one with a condensing chamber and was the first to devise attachments that converted the back-and-forth motion of a piston into the turning of a wheel. He also invented the first automatic feedback devices that controlled the engine's output of steam. In short, beginning in 1769, he developed the first truly practical and versatile mechanism for turning inanimate heat into work and thus started the Industrial Revolution. But was Watt a mere tinkerer? Was he a technologist and nothing more?

At the time there lived a Scottish chemist, Joseph Black, who, in his scientific studies of heat in 1764, measured the quantity of heat it takes to boil water. As heat energy pours into water, he found, its temperature goes up rapidly. As water begins to boil, however, vast quantities of heat are absorbed without further rise in temperature. The heat goes entirely into the conversion of liquid to vapor, a phenomenon known as "the latent heat of evaporation." The result is that steam contains far more energy than does hot water at exactly the same temperature.

Watt, who knew Black, learned of this latent heat and familiarized himself with the principle involved. That principle guided him in his improvements of the already existing steam engines. Black, in turn, impressed with the exciting application of his discovery, lent Watt a large sum of money to support him in his work. The Industrial Revolution, then, was the product of a fusion of science and technology.

Nor is the flow of knowledge entirely in the direction from science toward technology. While many people (even nonscientists) can now recognize that scientific research and discovery, however pure and abstract they may seem, may turn out to have some impure and practical application, few (even among scientists) seem to recognize that, if anything, the flow is stronger in the other direction. Science would stop dead without an input from technology.

In 1581, Galileo, then 17 years old, discovered the principle of the pendulum. In the 1590s, he went on to study the behavior of falling bodies and was greatly hampered by his lack of any device to measure small intervals of time accurately. The first good timepiece was not developed until 1656, when the Dutch scientist, Christiaan Huygens, applied Galileo's principle of the pendulum to construct what we would today call a "grandfather's clock." The principle of the pendulum, by itself, would have done little to advance science. The application of the pendulum principle and the technological development of timepieces made it possible for scientists to make the kind of observations they could never have made before.

In similar fashion, astronomy could not possibly have progressed much past Copernicus without technology. The crucial key to astronomical advance began with spectacle-makers, mere artisans who ground lenses, and with an idle apprentice boy, who, in 1608, played with those lenses—and discovered the principle of the telescope. Galileo built such a telescope and turned it on the heavens. No greater revolution in knowledge has ever occurred in so short a time as the second it took him to turn his telescope on the moon and discover mountains there. In brief, the history of modern science is the history of the development, through technology, of the instruments that are its tools.

Yet tools do not represent the only influence of technology. The products of technology offer a field for renewed speculation. For instance, although Watt had greatly increased the efficiency of the steam engine, it still remained very inefficient. Up to 95 percent of the heat energy of the burning fuel was wasted and was not converted into useful work. A French physicist, Nicolas Carnot, applied himself to this problem. Involving himself with something as technological as the steam engine, he began to consider the flow of heat from a hot body to a cold body and ended up founding the science of thermodynamics (from the Greek for "heat-movement").

Nor is it true that science and technology interacted only in the past. The year 1979 is, by coincidence, a significant year for two great men who seem to typify the very epitome of the purest of science on the one hand and the most practical of technology on the other—Albert Einstein, the greatest scientist since Newton, and Thomas Alva Edison, the greatest inventor since anybody. This year marks the centennial of Einstein's birth. It is also the centennial of Edison's greatest invention, the electric light. How did the work of each man invade the field of the other?

Surely, the theory of relativity, which Einstein originated, is as pure an example of science as one can imagine. The very word "practical" seems a blasphemy when applied to it. Yet the theory of relativity describes the behavior of objects moving at sizable fractions of the speed of light as nothing else can. Subatomic particles move at such speeds, and they cannot be studied properly without a consideration of their "relativistic motions." This means that modern particle accelerators can't exist without taking into account Einstein's theory, and all our present uses of the products of these accelerators would go by the board. We would not have radioisotopes, for instance, for use in medicine, in industry, in chemical analysis—and, of course, we would not have them as tools in advancing research into pure science, either.

Out of the theory of relativity, moreover, came deductions that interrelated matter and energy in a definite way (the famous $E = mc^2$). Until Einstein gave us this equation, matter and energy had been thought to be independent and unconnected entities. Guided by the theory, we came to see more meaning in energy aspects of research in subatomic particles, and in the end, the nuclear bomb was invented and nuclear-power stations were made possible.

Einstein worked outside the field of relativity, too. In 1917, he pointed out that if a molecule is at a high-energy level (a concept made possible by the purely scientific quantum theory, which had its origin in 1900) and if it is struck by a photon (a unit of radiation energy) of just the proper frequency, the molecule drops to lower energy. It does this because it gives up some of its energy in the form of a photon of the precise frequency and moving in the precise direction as the original photon.

Thirty-six years later, in 1953, Charles Hard Townes made use of Einstein's theoretical reasoning to invent the "maser" that could amplify a short-wave radio ("micro-wave") beam of photons into a much stronger beam. In 1960, Theodore Harold Maiman extended the principle to the still shorter-wave photons of visible light and devised the first "laser." The laser has infinite applications, from eye surgery to possible use as a war weapon.

And Edison?

The net result of his inventions was to spread the use of electricity the world over; to increase greatly the facilities for the generation and transmission of electricity; to make more important any device that would make that generation and transmission more efficient and economical. In short, Edison made the pure-science study of the flow and behavior of the electric current an important field of study.

Charles Proteus Steinmetz was certainly a technologist. He worked for General Electric and had two hundred patents in his name. Yet he also worked out, in complete mathematical detail, the intricacies of alternating-current circuitry, a towering achievement in pure science. Similar work was done by Oliver Heaviside.

As for Edison himself, his own work on the electric light unwittingly led him in the direction of purity. After he had developed the electric light, he labored for years to improve its efficiency and, in particular, to make the glowing filament last longer before breaking. As was usual for him, he tried everything he could think of. One of his hit-and-miss efforts was to seal a metal wire into the evacuated electric light bulb near, but not touching, the filament. The two were separated by a small gap of vacuum.

Edison then turned on the electric current to see if the presence of the metal wire would somehow preserve the life of the glowing filament. It didn't, and Edison abandoned the approach. However, he noticed that an electric current flowed from the filament to the wire across that vacuum gap. Nothing in Edison's vast practical knowledge of electricity explained this flow of current, but he observed it, wrote it up in his notebooks, and patented it. The phenomenon was called the "Edison effect," and it was Edison's only discovery in pure science—but it arose directly out of his technology.

Did this seemingly casual observation lead to anything? Well, it indicated that an electric current has, associated with it, a flow of matter of a particularly subtle sort—matter that was eventually shown to be electrons, the first subatomic particles to be recognized. Once this was discovered, methods were found to modify and amplify the electron flow in vacuum and, in this way, to control the behavior of an electric current with far greater delicacy than the flipping of switches could. Out of the Edison effect came the huge field of electronics.

There are other examples. A technological search for methods to eliminate static in radiotelephony served as the basis for the development of radio astronomy and the discovery of such phenomena as quasars, pulsars, and the big bang.

The technological development of the transistor brought on an improved way of manipulating and controlling electric currents, and has led to the computerization and automation of society. Computers have become essential tools in both technology and science. A computer was even necessary for the solution of one of the most famous problems in pure mathematics—the four-color problem.

The technological development of a liquid-fuel rocket has led to something as purely astronomical as the mapping, in detail, of Mars and of experiments with its soil.

The fact is that science and technology are one.

Just as there is only one species of human being on earth, and all divisions into races, cultures, and nations are but man-made ways of obscuring that fundamental truth, so there is only one scientific endeavor on earth—the pursuit of knowledge and understanding—and all divisions into disciplines and levels of purity are but man-made ways of obscuring *that* fundamental truth.

QUESTIONS FOR READING, RESPONDING, AND WRITING

Summarizing Main Points

1. Make a list of those men and discoveries that, according to Asimov, fall into the category of technology. Make another list of those men and discoveries that, according to Asimov, fall into the category of science. Do you find any overlap, that is, men and discoveries that seem to belong in both categories for some reason? What might be some reasons for this overlap?
2. What is the initial separation Asimov presents? Make a list of the separations which follow it. Do you see a pattern, a relation, or logic that informs the list? What is the connection between this initial separation and the "psychological set of our minds" as Asimov defines it? What is the connection between this initial separation and the "fundamental truth" he advocates at the essay's end?

Analyzing Methods of Discourse

1. Asimov not only notes a historical division between science and technology, but states that the division operates vertically, separating the two endeavors by levels—high and low. The vocabulary Asimov develops plays on the notion of levels in a variety of ways. Locate examples. Then identify the ways in which Asimov's final sentence plays off this structure in order to upset it.
2. Why do you think the sentence, "the fact is that science and technology are one" exists as its own paragraph?

Focusing on the Field

1. Though this essay describes a number of scientific discoveries, procedures, and theories, it may be easily understood by those outside the profession. Do you see any relationship between this fact and Asimov's argument? Pay particular attention to Asimov's last sentence in this regard.
2. Late in the essay, Asimov states, "A computer was even necessary for the solution of one of the most famous problems in pure mathematics—the four-color problem." Though Asimov defines the problem in terms of mathematics, most people associate "four-color" with printing and graphics. Why do you think Asimov shifts the terms of definition? Do you find any other examples of this strategy in the essay?

Writing Assignments

1. Choose a product in which you are interested (e.g., microwave oven, compact disc player, video recorder) and research the parts pure science and technology played in its development. Write an essay based on your research.

2. Read Steven Levy's "My Search for Einstein's Brain," Roland Barthes's "The Brain of Einstein," and Asimov's own discussion of Einstein. Using material from all three essays, write an essay of your own in which you look at Einstein's life and discoveries to explain his own statement that "the mystery of the world is its comprehensibility."

Lewis Thomas

NURSES

Lewis Thomas was born in Flushing, New York in 1913. Studying medicine has been his lifelong vocation; making those years of study available to the general public in popular essays is a more recent avocation. Currently the head of the prestigious Memorial Sloan-Kettering Cancer Center in New York City, Thomas, in his long career as medical researcher and teacher at Harvard (where he received his M.D. in 1937), Johns Hopkins, Tulane, Minnesota, New York University, and Yale, has written hundreds of professional articles for medical and scientific journals where "absolute unambiguity in every word" is the rule. Though he claims that his popular essays are the exception to that rule and that he "decided to give up being orderly" and "changed his method to no method at all," his easy-to-understand explanations of complex scientific issues suggest a more rigorous writing process than he allows.

Thomas's first collection of essays, *The Lives of a Cell: Notes of a Biology Watcher* (1974), won him not only recognition as a superior prose stylist but also the National Book Award. Since then, he has published several other collections of essays, including *The Medusa and the Snail* (1979), *Late Night Thoughts on Listening to Mahler's Ninth Symphony* (1984), and *The Youngest Science: Notes of a Medicine Watcher* (1983), which, as the following essay from it demonstrates, combines autobiography with perceptive commentary on current medical issues.

When my mother became a registered nurse at Roosevelt Hospital, in 1903, there was no question in anyone's mind about what nurses did as professionals. They did what the doctors ordered. The attending physician would arrive for his ward rounds in the early morning, and when he arrived at the ward office the head nurse would be waiting for him, ready to take his hat and coat, and his cane, and she would stand while he had his cup of tea before starting. Entering the ward, she would hold the door for him to go first, then his entourage of interns and medical students, then she followed. At each bedside, after he had conducted his examination and reviewed the patient's progress, he would tell the nurse what needed doing that day, and she would write it down on the part of the chart reserved for nursing notes. An hour or two later he would be gone from the ward, and the work of the rest of the day and the night to follow was the nurse's frenetic occupation. In addition to the stipulated orders, she had an endless list of routine things to do, all learned in her two years of nursing school: the beds had to be changed and made up with fresh sheets by an exact geometric design of folding and tucking impossible for anyone but a trained nurse; the patients had to be washed head to foot; bedpans had to be brought, used, emptied, and washed; temperatures had to be taken every four hours and meticulously recorded on the chart; enemas were to be given; urine and stool samples collected, labeled, and sent off to the laboratory; throughout the day and night, medications of all sorts, usually pills and various vegetable extracts and tinctures, had to be carried on trays from bed to bed. At most times of the year about half of the forty or so patients on the ward had typhoid fever, which meant that the nurse couldn't simply move from bed to bed in the performance of her duties; each typhoid case was screened from the other patients, and the nurse was required to put on a new gown and wash her hands in disinfectant before approaching the bedside. Patients with high fevers were sponged with cold alcohol at frequent intervals. The late-evening back rub was the rite of passage into sleep.

In addition to the routine, workaday schedule, the nurse was responsible for responding to all calls from the patients, and it was expected that she would do so on the run. Her rounds, scheduled as methodical progressions around the ward, were continually interrupted by these calls. It was up to her to evaluate each situation quickly: a sudden abdominal pain in a typhoid patient might signify intestinal perforation; the abrupt onset of weakness, thirst, and pallor meant intestinal hemorrhage; the coughing up of gross blood by a tuberculous patient was an emergency. Some of the calls came from neighboring patients on the way to recovery; patients on open wards always kept a close eye on each other: the man in the next bed might slip into coma or seem to be dying, or be indeed dead. For such emergencies the nurse had to get word immediately to the doctor on call, usually the intern assigned to the ward, who might be off in the outpatient department or working in the diagnostic laboratory (interns of that day did all the laboratory work themselves; technicians had not yet been invented) or in his room. Nurses were not allowed to give injections or to do such emergency procedures as spinal punctures or chest taps, but they were expected to know when such maneuvers were indicated and to be ready with appropriate trays of instruments when the intern arrived on the ward.

It was an exhausting business, but by my mother's accounts it was the most satisfying and rewarding kind of work. As a nurse she was a low person in the professional hierarchy, always running from place to place on orders from the doctors, subject as well to strict discipline from her own administrative superiors on the nursing staff, but none of this came through in her recollections. What she remembered was her usefulness.

Whenever my father talked to me about nurses and their work, he spoke with high regard for them as professionals. Although it was clear in his view that the task of the nurses was to do what the doctor told them to, it was also clear that he admired them for being able to do a lot of things he couldn't possibly do, had never been trained to do. On his own rounds later on, when he became an attending physician himself, he consulted the ward nurse for her opinion about problem cases and paid careful attention to her observations and chart notes. In his own days of intern training (perhaps partly under my mother's strong influence, I don't know) he developed a deep and lasting respect for the whole nursing profession.

I have spent all of my professional career in close association with, and close dependency on, nurses, and like many of my faculty colleagues, I've done a lot of worrying about the relationship between medicine and nursing. During most of this century the nursing profession has been having a hard time of it. It has been largely, although not entirely, an occupation for women, and sensitive issues of professional status, complicated by the special issue of the changing role of women in modern society, have led to a standoffish, often adversarial relationship between nurses and doctors. Already swamped by an increasing load of routine duties, nurses have been obliged to take on more and more purely administrative tasks: keeping the records in order; making sure the supplies are on hand for every sort of ward emergency; supervising the activities of the new paraprofessional group called LPNs (licensed practical nurses), who now perform much of the bedside work once done by RNs (registered nurses); overseeing ward maids, porters, and cleaners; seeing to it that patients scheduled for X rays are on their way to the X-ray department on time. Therefore, they have to spend more of their time at desks in the ward office and less time at the bedsides. Too late maybe, the nurses have begun to realize that they are gradually being excluded from the one duty which had previously been their most important reward but which had been so taken for granted that nobody mentioned it in listing the duties of a nurse: close personal contact with patients. Along with everything else nurses did in the long day's work, making up for all the tough and sometimes demeaning jobs assigned to them, they had the matchless opportunity to be useful friends to great numbers of human beings in trouble. They listened to their patients all day long and through the night, they gave comfort and reassurance to the patients and their families, they got to know them as friends, they were depended on. To contemplate the loss of this part of their work has been the deepest worry for nurses at large, and for the faculties responsible for the curricula of the nation's new and expanding nursing schools. The issue lies at the center of the running argument between medical school and nursing school administrators, but it is never clearly stated. Nursing education has been upgraded in recent years. Almost all the former hospital schools, which took in high-school graduates and provided an RN certificate after two or three years, have been replaced by schools attached to colleges and universities, with a four-year curriculum leading simultaneously to a bachelor's degree and an RN certificate.

The doctors worry that nurses are trying to move away from their historical responsibilities to medicine (meaning, really, to the doctors' orders). The nurses assert that they are their own profession, responsible for their own standards, coequal colleagues with physicians, and they do not wish to become mere ward administrators or technicians (although some of them, carrying the new and prestigious title of "nurse practitioner," are being trained within nursing schools to perform some of the most complex technological responsibilities in hospital emergency rooms and intensive care units). The doctors claim that what the nurses really want is to become substitute psychiatrists. The nurses reply that they have unavoidable responsibilities for the mental health and well-being of their patients, and that these are different from the doctors' tasks. Eventually the arguments will work themselves out, and some sort of agreement will be reached, but if it is to be settled intelligently, some way will have to be found to preserve and strengthen the traditional and highly personal nurse-patient relationship.

I have had a fair amount of firsthand experience with the issue, having been an apprehensive patient myself off and on over a three-year period on the wards of the hospital for which I work. I am one up on most of my physician friends because of this experience. I know some things they do not know about what nurses do.

One thing the nurses do is to hold the place together. It is an astonishment, which every patient feels from time to time, observing the affairs of a large, complex hospital from the vantage point of his bed, that the whole institution doesn't fly to pieces. A hospital operates by the constant interplay of powerful forces pulling away at each other in different directions, each force essential for getting necessary things done, but always at odds with each other. The intern staff is an almost irresistible force in itself, learning medicine by doing medicine, assuming all the responsibility within reach, pushing against an immovable attending and administrative staff, and frequently at odds with the nurses. The attending physicians are individual entrepreneurs trying to run small cottage industries at each bedside. The diagnostic laboratories are feudal fiefdoms, prospering from the insatiable demands for their services from the interns and residents. The medical students are all over the place, learning as best they can and complaining that they are not, as they believe they should be, at the epicenter of everyone's concern. Each individual worker in the place, from the chiefs of surgery to the dieticians to the ward maids, porters, and elevator operators, lives and works in the conviction that the whole apparatus would come to a standstill without his or her individual contribution, and in one sense or another each of them is right.

My discovery, as a patient first on the medical service and later in surgery, is that the institution is held together, *glued* together, enabled to function as an organism, by the nurses and by nobody else.

The nurses, the good ones anyway (and all the ones on my floor were good), make it their business to know everything that is going on. They spot errors before errors can be launched. They know everything written on the chart. Most important of all, they know their patients as unique human beings, and they soon get to know the close relatives and friends. Because of this knowledge, they are quick to sense apprehensions and act on them. The average sick person in a large hospital feels at risk of getting lost, with no identity left beyond a name and a string of numbers on a plastic wristband, in danger always of being whisked off on a litter to the wrong place to have the wrong procedure done, or worse still, *not* being whisked off at the right time. The attending physician or the house officer, on rounds and usually in a hurry, can murmur a few reassuring words on his way out the door, but it takes a confident, competent, and cheerful nurse, there all day long and in and out of the room on one chore or another through the night, to bolster one's confidence that the situation is indeed manageable and not about to get out of hand.

Knowing what I know, I am all for the nurses. If they are to continue their professional feud with the doctors, if they want their professional status enhanced and their pay increased, if they infuriate the doctors by their claims to be equal professionals, if they ask for the moon, I am on their side.

QUESTIONS FOR READING, RESPONDING, AND WRITING

Summarizing Main Points

1. Toward the end of the essay, Thomas states that a hospital "is held together, *glued* together, enabled to function as an organism, by the nurses and by nobody else." According to Thomas, what is it that nurses do that separates them from the rest of the medical team?
2. According to Thomas, what problems have changes in the nursing profession created for nurses? For doctors?

Analyzing Methods of Discourse

1. Identify the three points of view from which Thomas speaks. Which do you think is most important? Why?
2. The first paragraph, like others in the essay, is quite long. How might the length of the paragraph help Thomas make his point about the subject discussed in it? Does he repeat this strategy elsewhere in the essay?

Focusing on the Field

1. Thomas has written over 200 articles for medical journals. Why do you think he chose to write this essay for a wider audience? Why might it be more appropriate for this audience than for a professional medical audience?
2. What details of the essay reveal knowledge that would ordinarily be unavailable to someone not in the medical field? How does Thomas present these details so that the nonprofessional understands them?

Writing Assignments

1. Choose a subject with which you are familiar and write an essay in which your point of view on that subject goes through a change that allows you to understand the subject more fully.
2. Read Richard Selzer's "The Art of Surgery." Write an essay in which you discuss the ways in which Selzer's characterization of himself as a surgeon corresponds to, and deviates from, Thomas's more generalized portrait of doctors and their role in hospitals.

William Tucker

CONSERVATION IN DEED

Born in 1942, William Tucker graduated from Amherst College in 1964, and has since pursued a successful career as a free-lance journalist, writing on a wide variety of political, social, and economic subjects for numerous magazines and newspapers. He has published articles in the *American Spectator, New Republic, Atlantic Monthly, Reason,* the *New York Times,* the *Wall Street Journal,* the *Washington Post, Life,* and *Harper's,* where he is currently a contributing editor. In addition to his numerous articles, Tucker has also written two books, *Progress and Privilege* (1982) and *Vigilante: The Backlash against Crime in America* (1985). In his second book, which focuses on the New York subway shooting involving Bernhard Goetz, Tucker, in part, uses the theories of economist Thomas Sowell (see "Pink and Brown

People") to analyze what he feels are the current inefficient approaches to crime and criminal justice.

In the following essay, Tucker turns his attention to a less violent though equally explosive topic—environmental protection—and advocates a policy change that challenges not only the "conventional wisdom," but also the government's own fitness for its role as steward of the environment. Following the essay is an interview with Tucker on the process of writing this essay.

I would like to propose a redefinition of the problem of environmental degradation. It goes like this: Environmental damage occurs when someone is *losing* money. Or, alternately, losing money leads to environmental problems.

It's as simple as that. Operating an inefficient, money-losing enterprise causes persistent environmental damage. Making money, on the other hand, protects the environment and conserves resources for the future. A profit-making economy is the best system there is for protecting the natural environment.

Of course, this is directly contrary to the conventional wisdom. Environmental degradation, we have been told over the years, is caused by greedy business enterprises, driven by the "profit motive" in pursuit of the "almighty dollar." Pollution, the destruction of landscapes, and the squandering of resources are all the result of an unfettered business sector that recognizes no other value but dollars and cents. After all, wouldn't business, if left unfettered, be putting a hydroelectric dam in the Grand Canyon to make money?

The answer is no. It wasn't business that wanted to put a dam in the Grand Canyon in the 1960s. It was the *government*—the Bureau of Reclamation, to be exact. And the government wasn't going to make any money at it, either. It was going to *lose* money—which is the only way the project was feasible in the first place.

Losing money damages the environment, spoils nature, and exhausts resources. Making money preserves the environment, protects nature, and conserves resources. In this simple lesson lies the way toward renewing the battle for environmental improvement in the hard-pressed 1980s—and returning a sense of individual responsibility to the American people.

How can making money conserve and improve the environment? Why is it that environmental damage is a violation of sensible economics? Understanding the point requires breaking out of the contemporary prison wherein all economic activity is seen as a two-sided conflict between "business" and "the consumer," or "the big interests" and "the people."

If this simplistic formulation is accepted, there are only two possible explanations of environmental destruction. The first says that the people are innocent (a popular enough notion), and big business is at fault. This latter, malicious sector, so the story goes, pollutes and destroys nature as a result of its "relentless pursuit of profits." Thus, the only solution is to "countervail" the power of business with a big government that spins a web of regulation and blocks business owners from doing just about anything. After 15 years of environmental effort, this is approximately where we are: the battle between environmentalists and their adversaries has become nothing more than a tug-of-war over whether to tighten or relax regulatory snares.

The only other possible view—a bit more jaundiced, perhaps—is that *people themselves* are the problem. There are too many people, it is argued, and only draconian programs for population control or perpetual stagnation (more romantically advocated as "no-growth" or "zero-sum" societies) can save us. People are perceived as being unnatural, out of tune with the harmony of nature. Only by cultivating some kind of mystical oneness with nature or retreating toward a pastoral, preindustrial state can we avoid overrunning our fragile environment.

Neither of these explanations of environmental problems gets to the real heart of the matter. Both miss a third player in the economic game, one who has a specific, personal interest in preserving the environment and protecting its value into the future. This is the *landlord*, the person who *owns* the natural resources in question. The environmental crisis has essentially been a problem of the decline of landlords. We no longer have landlords—owners—in place to protect and preserve the resources we are busy degrading. No one has a *personal interest* in protecting the environment.

Why don't we have contemporary landlords? There are two reasons. First, many of the resources we have begun to abuse are so diffuse that it is difficult to bring them under private ownership. It is difficult to define ownership for the air we breathe, running streams, groundwater aquifers, or whales that roam the far corners of the world the way we do for, say, an acre of land or a steer on the hoof. In all these instances, establishing rules for ownership and enforcing them may require some creativity. European kings once claimed ownership of all the deer in the forest, for example, and labeled anyone who killed one without permission a poacher. Ownership of a resource is necessary in order to prevent it from being treated as a "common pool" and exploited by all.

Far more frequently, however, the situation has worked in the opposite direction. In a wide variety of instances, government itself has insisted on acting as the owner of resources that could just as well be held in private hands. In these instances—the national forests, grazing lands in the West, water supplies, for example—government has insisted on playing the role of the landlord, under the illusory idea that it is best suited both to protect *and* to develop these resources for the greatest good of all.

Yet government does not make a very good landlord. Its agents, with no personal stake in the matter, do not try to maximize the government's rents, or income, from the resources; they do not employ the resources so that they will have their highest value for both today and tomorrow. Instead, under its common mandate to make everyone happy, government generally *subsidizes* the use of resources and shovels them onto today's market at far *below* their potential future value. As a result, these natural resources are abused, overused, and generally treated at far less than their true worth. *This* is why we have an "environmental crisis."

How did it all begin? Interestingly enough, an overwhelming number of today's environmental problems can be traced back to the first effort to deal with them, during the great conservation era of the early 1900s. It was then that the fateful decision was made to keep the vast majority of the West's resources—two-thirds of the land, for example, west of the Rockies—in the hands of the federal government.

The original logic of the conservation movement, under Theodore Roosevelt's leadership, was perhaps justified. In 1900, there simply weren't enough landlords around to take responsibility for the vast resources available. The country didn't yet have enough people to own them all. It seemed likely that selling them on the market would have meant turning them over to the railroad companies and other corporate baronies, which were already the object of extreme public resentment.

But the mandate with which progressive conservationism took over control of these resources was at best obscure and confusing—political, in other words—and has long outlived its usefulness. The government, strangely enough, was both to *conserve* resources and to *develop* them "for the greatest good of the greatest number in the long run," as the prominent conservationist Gifford Pinchot put it. These were lofty terms, but devoid of much practical meaning. To one person, *conservation* might mean a magnificent new dam backing up miles of running water for irrigation of the desert, while to another person it means preserving the landscape the way it was before human beings ever laid eyes on it.

Most important, the government made no attempt to collect proper *rents* on these resources. Rents—the income from resources—are the measure of how well they are being employed. Most people, environmentalists included, often believe that the only way people make money on land, for example, is to exploit it as quickly as possible. But this common conception completely misinterprets the economic motivation of the landlord. For the permanent owner of a resource, the best way to maintain high rents on a property is to *conserve its value* as far into the future as possible.

Landlords are not business operators. Businesses make their money out of current production. But a landlord expects to own a resource far into the future (or to sell it based on its value far into the future). Therefore, he wants to make its value last as long as possible. With renewable resources, this means using them at a pace that gives them plenty of time to regenerate. For a nonrenewable resource, it may mean holding it off the market as long as possible, while similar resources are diminishing, in order to optimize its scarcity value.

Governments, however, do the opposite. Under constant political pressure to please voters and build satisfied constituencies, they throw resources onto the market much more quickly than do private owners, sometimes even subsidizing development out of "their own" pockets—that is, with taxpayers' money. They plunder their own, or "the people's," resources in a way that no private landlord ever would.

Thus, in the end, the old conservation agencies have ended up the biggest environmental offenders of all.

- The Bureau of Land Management's ranchlands in the West are constantly overgrazed, while private landlords have no trouble keeping their own lands in good shape.
- The Bureau of Reclamation, with the ever-ready assistance of the Army Corps of Engineers, regularly drowns huge areas of prime farmland in order to create barely equivalent amounts of marginal farmland through ridiculously subsidized irrigation projects.
- The development of remote, useless federal lands has been promoted to such a degree that environmentalists have been forced to invent the tortured concept of "wilderness" in order to keep these areas from being invaded. The US Forest Service, for example, continues to subsidize expensive logging in remote "roadless" areas, while letting more accessible forest lands go untouched. John Baden, director of the Center for Political Economy and Natural Resources at Montana State University, estimates that the Forest Service, with the richest timber holdings in the world, still manages to lose $500 million a year on its operations. They must be doing something wrong; indeed, they are undervaluing "their" resources.

All this is poignant verification of Garrett Hardin's principle of the "tragedy of the commons"—that when a resource is held in common by a group of people, say by the American people, no individual user bears the full cost of using the resource, which is consequently overexploited.

Is it any wonder, then, that when contemporary environmentalists entered the political fray in the 1960s and '70s, they aimed their first fire at the old conservation agencies themselves—the US Forest Service, the Army Corps of Engineers, the Bureau of Land Management, and the Reclamation Bureau?

Environmentalists are, in a sense, landlords without an estate. They have the "land ethic," as their early prophet Aldo Leopold defined it. They understand the value of natural resources, even if they don't own them outright. They see that we cannot forever pillage our natural inheritance in order to promote immediate consumption. They recognize that undervaluing natural resources leads us into vicious cycles of technological extravagance, where it soon seems that we cannot tolerate even the slightest increase in scarcity without worrying that we are "running out of everything."

What environmentalists have not understood so clearly, however, is that in almost every instance it is government ownership of resources— which is naturally accompanied by government subsidization of consumption through low or nonexistent prices, tax incentives, and other popular measures—that leads to this dilemma. Governments don't mind losing money on resources, since they can always carry the bill back to the taxpayers. In fact, it is often assumed that government is doing something *virtuous* by losing money in managing resources.

But private landlords know better. Without the opportunity to cover their losses through taxation, they realize that losing money simply means badly managing resources and squandering their value. In the hard-pressed 1980s, protecting the environment is going to mean getting resources *out* of government hands and into the private sector. Only then can the spontaneous corrections of the marketplace spur owners to maintain the value of resources far into the future.

The problem of government ownership of resources did not begin in our era, nor did the dilemmas of environmental depredation. With these things in mind, let us take a closer look at the idea of landlords as a third force in economic history and see how the present situation has evolved.

Through the long annals of civilization, government ownership and participation in enterprise has been much more the rule than the exception. This is often overlooked by environmentalist interpretations of history. Environmentalists, for example, often cite the denuded hills of Greece, the ruined "breadbasket" of North Africa, or the sheep-stripped countryside of rural Spain as proof that (to try a common paraphrase) "humanity has never learned to be very kind to our natural surroundings."

Yet, in how many of these instances has it been government-subsidized industry, rather than private effort, at work? The point is critical, since private enterprises are subject to the checks of profits and losses, while government enterprises are not.

The Spanish crown, for example, ruined many of Spain's rural areas by establishing a national woolens industry with the money brought back from the New World by the conquistadors. The government appropriated huge amounts of private farmland and set up enclosures for sheep pasturage. The market was soon flooded by wool, of course, but the royal government paid no mind, intensifying its efforts. Eventually, it squandered all the gold of El Dorado and beat to death much of its medieval farmlands at the same time.

This depredation of Spain's countryside, then, is hardly an example of "man's destructive instincts." It is much more an example of the ability of centralized governments to ignore the checks and balances of the market system. Had a variety of individual independent landlords been making decisions to convert Spanish countryside to sheep pasture, the consequences for the wool market would have halted the process, and the countryside would have been far less devastated than by the decision of a single, centralized government.

The free-enterprise system, as we know it, didn't really evolve until after the time of Adam Smith—who didn't win his place in history by describing some free-market Garden of Eden around him but by envisioning what *could* exist if governments would leave off their mercantile interference in the economy and allow the checks and balances of the market system to operate freely.

Smith argued that there are three players in the economic game—laborers, capitalists, and landlords. Labor contributes its sweat and skills and earns its money through wages. Capitalists own and manage the tools of production and collect their return through profits. Landlords own the *natural resources*—land, for the most part, in Smith's day—and make their returns through *rents*.

Smith is chiefly remembered as an apologist for business, even though *Wealth of Nations* is actually one long political treatise *against* businesses for getting government to restrict trade on their behalf. Yet in retrospect, it is easy to see why Smith is still considered the "philosopher of big business." He was at least willing to accept the *legitimacy* of both profits and rents in the economic system. By constantly seeking higher profits, he argued, capitalists ensure that their materials will be put to their highest-valued uses. At the same time, by constantly seeking to optimize their rents, landlords direct natural resources to their highest-valued uses—which includes the possibility of reserving them altogether from present consumption in order to save them for future use.

Later economists doubted the stability of the system. David Ricardo, the outstanding economist of the early 19th century, for example, argued that this model was irrevocably biased in favor of landlords. A successful banker himself, Ricardo said that because the amount of land is fixed, landlords would keep raising their rents, eventually accumulating most of the wealth in the economy.

Like Malthus, his contemporary, Ricardo did not see that the value of land is not economically immutable—that through additional infusions of both capital and labor, less land can produce more goods. Thus, US production has developed to the point where, presently, the contribution of labor is estimated at about 80 percent of the total value, capital at about 12 percent, and natural resources at only about 8 percent. In 1961, economist Robert Heilbroner could write that "the landlord's domination over the economy is a textbook curiosity" and that "the problem of rent has become almost an academic side issue in the modern world." This was before the environmental crisis began to emerge.

While Ricardo suggested that rents are illegitimate, Karl Marx went even further. He argued that both rents and profits—but particularly profits—represent "exploitation" and are actually "stolen" from their rightful owners, the workers. Moreover, he argued, these "excess profits" are so unbalancing that capitalists would end up with all the money. This, in turn, would lead workers to revolt, overthrow the system, and set up a utopian society.

Neither of these criticisms of Smith's basic model has proved very good at predicting history. Neither landlords nor capitalists have become all-powerful, while the lot of the average worker in capitalist countries has steadily improved. Smith's model holds up very well indeed for contemporary society.

Smith's model does suggest, however, where to start looking for consequences if one or more of the three groups succeeds in gaining, not enough wealth, but enough *political domination* to try to manipulate the system in its favor. If capitalists, for example, manage to artificially hold down wages through legal means—as they often did during the 19th century—then we can expect the lot of laborers to deteriorate, leading perhaps to the sort of consequences that Marx predicted of a pure free-market system. If, on the other hand, capitalists are politically prevented from collecting their profits, then we can expect an abatement of their enterprising efforts and perhaps the sort of "stagflation" that afflicts so many economies today.

And finally, if *landlords* are politically prevented from collecting their *rents*, then we can expect the *resource base* to deteriorate. Thus, the question of rents and landlords is not a "textbook curiosity." On the contrary, when landlords are gradually excluded from their role in the economy, an "environmental crisis" ensues.

What has clearly happened in contemporary economies is a distinct diminution in the ability of landlords to act as stewards of natural resources. This evolution is fairly easy to trace. Landlords have never been very popular in history—perhaps even less popular than business people. Gradually, political pressures have constricted their latitude in exercising control over their own resources. Or, alternately, these same pressures have pushed resources completely out of private hands and into the arms of government. There they become "the people's" resources, "free" for exploitation.

This pattern of pressure against landlords inevitably leads to overexploitation of resources and environmental damage. The "common ruin of all," as Garrett Hardin described it, is the unavoidable consequence. Without landlords, there can be no environmental protection.

Let me illustrate all this with a homely, and perhaps a bit oblique, example—rent control in New York City. Apartment buildings are not a "natural" resource, but as a standing resource they operate very much like one in the market. As with land itself, they are continuously renewable if used properly. The builders of apartments are capitalists, but their long-term owners can be properly called landlords.

These resource-owners have two basic impulses—to collect optimal rents today, given the market supply of and demand for apartments, and to go on collecting them into the future. The owner will one day die, of course, but he can always sell the building first or pass it on to his heirs. *At no point does it ever pay a landlord to allow the value of his property to deteriorate.* All the damage would be absorbed by the landlord himself, with no compensating benefit. Landlords have a built-in "conservation ethic" that comes with the job.

The politics of New York City, however, does not allow landlords to collect market rents on their apartments. This is accomplished under a variety of political flim-flams, dating back to a "temporary" measure imposed during World War II that has never been removed. Despite all the demagoguery about "greedy landlords" that continually rationalizes rent control, most people recognize that, at bottom, rent control is nothing but an immensely popular political device that allows the city's huge tenant population to exploit a small minority of landlords. (The proof of this is that nothing upsets "tenants' rights" groups so much as the suggestion that they themselves take on the responsibilities of being landlords. Condominium and cooperative conversions are fought with even greater fury than the occasional fuel pass-along or rent increase. Without a captive landlord population, tenants would have no one left to exploit.)

Is it only landlords that are exploited, however? The answer is no.

Unable to collect market rents, the landlords begin to lose money. They can no longer afford to make repairs on their buildings. The apartments begin to deteriorate, which drives down rents (both economically and legally), which in turn makes it even harder to pay for repairs. Landlords then are even more greatly condemned, and rents are pushed down even further. Eventually, many owners simply abandon buildings, even though they may represent a lifetime investment. Without proper rents, no one can play the role of landlord forever.

The deterioration and destruction of New York City's rental housing market is there for all to see. Despite population growth and a continuously high demand for housing, the city now has fewer available rental units than it did in 1942, when rent controls were originally imposed. Whole blocks of apartment buildings now stand in ruins, while privately owned houses only a few blocks away remain in perfect condition.

Obviously, it is not only landlords who suffer when they are not allowed to collect market rents. Sooner or later, the exploiting population will have eaten its way through all the landlords' wealth. People then begin to devour the *resource itself* that landlords, in their own private interest, originally had set out to protect.

New York City's tenants are a population in the process of destroying its environment. Though it is not a natural environment, the economic principles are the same. When popular pressures prevent landlords from collecting proper rents and playing their legitimate role as conservors and protectors of resources, it is only a matter of time before the *resources themselves* will be degraded and eventually destroyed.

The contemporary economist who has perceived this dilemma most clearly is, not surprisingly, also generally regarded as the leading theorist of the environmental movement. He is Herman Daly, professor of resource economics at Louisiana State University.

In his 1977 book, *Steady-State Economics*, Daly identified the economic root of the contemporary environmental crisis as the success of both contemporary labor (which I take to be interchangeable with "consumers") and business in politically exploiting a much-reduced "landlord class."

> Landlords were the most powerful social class in feudal times, but in modern capitalism they are the least powerful class, and whatever power they might exert toward raising resource prices is undercut by the government, which is the largest resource owner and which follows a policy of cheap resources in order to benefit and ease the conflict between the two dominant classes, labor and capital. . . .
>   Capital and labor are the two social classes that produce and divide up the firm's product. They are in basic conflict but must live together. They minimize conflict by growth and by throwing the growth-induced burden of

diminishing returns onto resource productivity. How do they get away with it? In earlier times it might not have worked; a strong landlord class would have had an interest in keeping resource prices from falling too low. But today we have no such class to exert countervailing upward pressure on resource prices. . . .

Should we, by a kind of reverse land reform, reinstate a landlord class? Landlord rent is unearned income, and we find income based on ownership of that which no one produced to be ethically distasteful. No one loves a landlord . . . and not many lament the historical demise of the landowning aristocracy. But not all the long-run consequences of this demise are favorable. Rent may be an illegitimate source of income, but it is a totally legitimate and necessary price, without which efficient allocation of scarce resources would be impossible.

Although Daly was writing for the environmental movement, few environmentalists have taken his points to heart. In particular, many still seem fixed on the idea that making money is the root of all environmental problems. This is because they confuse business people with landlords. Businesses do indeed make money by using resources for current production. But landlords make money by *limiting* the use of scarce resources, by conserving and protecting them for future availability. This is why the profit motive—or, more correctly, the "rent motive"—is the most important tool we have for protecting the environment.

The model of missing landlords makes understandable a whole range of environmental difficulties. Take the following examples:

Question: Why did the Bureau of Reclamation want to build a dam in the Grand Canyon? Answer: Because it is in the business of subsidizing the use of the resources it controls. The underpricing of its land and water leads to an ever-increasing demand for both, which can only be met by building more and bigger projects. If the government charged people market prices—collected proper rents and profits, in other words—then conservation would become economical and the accelerating demand for these resources would quickly vanish.

Question: Why did we develop such an oil-dependent economy before the 1970s? Answer: Because, right from the beginning, the government subsidized oil development, at the behest of both industry and consumers. As early as 1920, oil-depletion allowances reversed the ordinary economics of a finite resource and artificially accelerated its development. Only when US oil resources had been prematurely drawn down by the early 1970s were US suppliers forced to go abroad. Even then, nothing happened until the landlords of world oil supplies—the OPEC nations—began to collect market rents. When these economic realities finally sank in (delayed somewhat by our decade-long romance with oil price controls), technology and consumption habits quickly shifted to a more efficient basis. As a result, the "oil crisis" of the last decade has quickly disappeared.

Question: Why is it necessary to create designated wildernesses to preserve even the most marginal federal lands from development? Answer: Because the development of the lands is being subsidized. Without the government accepting losses on the use of these lands, they would remain just what they are today—wildernesses.

Question: Why is the Army Corps of Engineers such an environmental disaster? Answer: Because it never has to make money.

Question: Why are groundwater supplies in many parts of the nation being rapidly exhausted? Answer: Because forms of ownership of these natural "common pools" have not been defined. Instead, people can draw on them for free. A sensible landlord would charge people for drilling wells into these underground reservoirs. And once market rents were collected on these resources, pricing mechanisms would stimulate the proper conservation practices, and the "groundwater crisis" would disappear.

Question: Why don't we see the development of clean, efficient "alternative" energy technologies? Answer: Because governments everywhere subsidize centralized electricity. Researchers John Baden and Richard Stroup, of Montana State University, have discovered that a private utility, the Jacobs Wind Electric Company, was successfully selling windmill-generated electricity to midwestern farmers in the 1920s—a promising start on the technology. The business was wiped out, however, by the Rural Electrification Administration, which brought in subsidized coal power in the 1930s. Early solar water-heating efforts in southern California suffered a similar fate. Even today, the major obstacle to solar systems is the constant subsidized overconsumption of electricity encouraged by state utility commissions, plus federal price controls on natural gas.

And so on and so forth. In each of these instances, it is government intervention in the economy, not the working of the marketplace itself, that leads to the short-changing of environmental values.

Some environmental problems are far more tricky, of course. For instance, it is difficult to define property rights for the air around us. It cannot be parceled out in one-acre lots (although it can be defined in terms of "airsheds"). To prevent pollution, however, there must be some kind of ownership, and people must be charged for using the air as a dumping ground. (We have, instead, clumsy regulations that tell industries where and when to install antipollution equipment, and even what kind of equipment to install. The result is a ham-handed bureaucracy and endless lawsuits, rather than an efficient clean-up.) Problems like toxic chemicals and pesticides, with their long-delayed after-effects, pose unique problems of liability and long-term responsibility that may require new inventions in risk insurance.

But there is not an environmental problem anywhere that cannot be reduced to the fundamental paradigm of resource ownership and the failure to allow landlords to take care of their property. This is because (1) ownership structures, where they are difficult to define, have not been set up; (2) governments, under popular pressures, have prevented private landlords from exercising their rights of ownership; or (3) the government itself has taken control of a resource and makes it available to the public on a subsidized or common-pool basis, without charging adequate rents to optimize its value. In all three cases, the result is the same—degradation of the resource and erosion of the quality of the environment.

Does this mean, as Herman Daly suggests, that we have to "reinstate a landlord class" to solve environmental problems? Not, I believe, in the way Daly implies. (Daly himself shies away from the dilemma and, strangely and paradoxically, calls for *even more* government control over resources as a solution. He apparently does not recognize that in an industrial society capital and labor are a permanent majority and will always, if given the chance, use government to exploit landlords and natural resources.)

Instead, I would like to suggest a very American solution to the problem. "Reinstating a landlord class" does not have to mean a return to the landholding aristocracies of the Middle Ages. Rather, it should mean that we would all get a chance to become landlords. That would give everyone a piece of the "conservation ethic"—just as the diffusion of industrial wealth throughout the population has given everyone a stake in the economy.

Let us take, for example, the 170 million acres owned and managed "for the greatest good of the greatest number" by the Bureau of Land Management, a sprawling federal bureaucracy with 5,000 employees operating on an annual budget of well over $1 billion. Selling off whatever lands private owners would be willing to purchase (probably only about 10 percent)—and abolishing the federal mandate to develop the rest at any cost—would alleviate the problems of collective ownership and put resources in the hands of people who would conserve them because it would be in their *private interest* to do so. It would, incidentally, also pay off at least $200 billion of the national debt, which only illustrates how "land poor" the federal government and its bureaucracies have become. In the early 19th century, the federal government paid off its Revolutionary War debts in the same way. Such a land sale would represent a continuation of the principle of decentralized ownership on which the country was founded.

land Sale

Federal bureaucrats, of course, will oppose it. So will many environmentalists—who have, unfortunately, grown quite accustomed to exercising their power in the halls of Washington's bureaucracies. They and others will continue to confuse businesses with landlords and will argue that the desire of every private property owner will only be to develop and exploit his resources as fast as possible.

But a true understanding of the historic role of landlords should make us realize that it is the property owner's "land ethic" that ultimately keeps us from destroying our natural heritage. True stewardship and conservation are only nurtured by the experience of individual ownership—in a system where landlords are left free to preserve the value of their property and are protected from the universal political tendency to exploit someone else's resource without paying the costs. Until the impulse to protect the environment is harnessed to the private desires of landlords to care for their own property, environmental problems will never be solved. We are all going to have to learn to become landlords.

QUESTIONS FOR READING, RESPONDING, AND WRITING

Summarizing Main Points

1. According to Tucker, what is wrong with the way in which the government currently handles the environment? List examples of the resulting "environmental degradation."
2. According to Tucker, how do landlords differ from businessmen? Why does he think landlords should be the best stewards of our environment? Do you agree with him?

Analyzing Methods of Discourse

1. Trace Tucker's characterization of landlords, government, and "tenants." How do these characterizations aid Tucker in his argument? Do you find them accurate?
2. Tucker uses questions to develop the first and last parts of his argument. What purpose do these questions serve? How do they enhance the material which follows them? Would his argument be affected if he merely provided the information without the questions?

Focusing on the Field

1. Tucker admits right from the start that his "redefinition" of environmental problems into economic terms goes against "conventional wisdom." What is that "conventional wisdom"? Do you find Tucker's redefinition appropriate? Why or why not?
2. At one point in his essay, Tucker quotes resource economist Herman Daly, who, in *Steady-State Economics*, states, "landlord rent is unearned income, and we find income based on ownership of that which no one produced to be

ethically distasteful. No one loves a landlord." This statement addresses one underlying objection to Tucker's plan. Locate other places in the essay in which Tucker anticipates and deals with objections. Why do you think he incorporates these objections into his argument? Can you think of any he does not incorporate or address?

Writing Assignments

1. Tucker uses the predicament of New York City landlords as support for his argument. Do some research of your own on the issue of "rent control" and write an essay in which you argue for or against Tucker's position, using material from both his essay and your own research for support.
2. Read Dennis Avery's "U.S. Farm Dilemma: The Global Bad News Is Wrong." Write an essay in which you compare the positions that Tucker and Avery take on their respective issues. Compare, too, their methods of presentation.

William Tucker

ON WRITING "CONSERVATION IN DEED"

An old newspaper adage I heard once is this: "You're not a real writer until you can sell a story six times." There is an important truth in this. A writer must always judge his audience. The same material can often be written in many different ways for different audiences. The article, "Conservation in Deed," written for *Reason* magazine in 1983, is an example of an article whose ideas have been reworked several different times in this way, as I'll try to describe.

When I started "Conservation in Deed," I had already written a book criticizing the environmental movement. I had criticized environmentalists by arguing that they were really "preservationists," rather than "conservationists." The distinction was originally invented in the conservation era of the early twentieth century, when large tracts of western resources were put aside for future development under the leadership of President Theodore Roosevelt and Gifford Pinchot, his deputy secretary of agriculture. The federal conservation agencies, I noted, were originally designed to *develop* resources "for the greatest good of the greatest number." Recent environmentalists—although they called themselves "conservationists"—were really "preservationists" opposing all development.

On the whole, I was never very happy with this analysis. It revolved around word definitions, which are always indefinite and change over time. One person's "conservation" can be another person's "preservation," and a third person's "development." The semantics really didn't do much to solve the problem. Still, it was the best I could see into the problem at the time.

Shortly after finishing my book I ran into the words of John Baden and Richard Stroup, two resource economists at Montana State University, who had given the issue some truly original thought. Both owned land in Montana and both were amazed to see how the Bureau of Land Management could overgraze its own land without suffering any economic penalties. They finally realized it was the government ownership—which removed the necessity of making any money on the land—that made this resource degradation possible. Private landlords, they argued, couldn't overgraze their land because they would be ruining the value of their property. But the Bureau of Land Management, with the federal treasury to fall back on, had no incentive to economize. The bureau could push the use of its own resources far beyond what the marketplace would dictate.

I was quite bowled over by Baden and Stroup's writing. I could see right away that they penetrated to the heart of the matter in a much better way than I had ever done. I immediately set out to publicize their ideas—which had only appeared in obscure academic journals—and to present them as a replacement for my own earlier analysis. I had argued that environmentalism, although justified in many ways, had been taken to extremes. Baden and Stroup were justifying environmentalism, but in a way that environmentalists might not necessarily appreciate.

My first choice for an article was *Harper's* magazine. I had already written several stories for *Harper's* that were critical of environmentalism. Now I would be writing a sequel that took the edge off some of my earlier criticisms and proposed a middle ground. Since magazines like to work with established writers and breed a sense of continuity, it seemed like a good idea.

Unfortunately, *Harper's* was going through a financial crisis and had changed management. The new editor wanted a new tone for the magazine and wasn't receptive. So I had to start looking for another publication.

Most magazines work out of a fairly narrow perspective. Although they will all tell you they are "neutral" and "tolerant of all ideas," every publication has pretty clear prejudices. If your story doesn't match their ideas, they will send you a little note saying it is "not quite right for us." It isn't anything to be too discouraged about. Most successful writers can paper their walls with their rejection slips.

As it happened, events were moving in a way that favored my story. By 1982, the Reagan Revolution was having an enormous impact, and environmental groups were very much on the defensive. While environmentalists were having some luck in personally attacking Secretary of Interior James Watt and EPA Administrator Ann Gorsuch, it seemed obvious that their political heyday had passed.

In this situation, a conservative free-market redefinition of environmentalism seemed to be just what both sides needed. It would tone down the liberal vs. conservative aspect of the issue and perhaps offer an approach that both sides could tolerate.

Sensing that environmental groups might themselves be rethinking the issues, I began a series of interviews. Sure enough, there was lots of brainstorming going on behind the scenes. I went to Washington to visit with six environmental groups, and found that three of them had put economists on their staff for the first time in history *within the past three months.* Many environmentalists were claiming they had been "in favor of the free market all along," and that it was only the belligerence of the Reagan administration that was clouding the issue.

By this time I had that exhilarating newspaper reporter's feeling of sitting on top of a breaking news story. Every night on television environmentalists were portrayed pillorying James Watt and Ann Gorsuch and shouting, "They shall not pass." Yet behind the scenes both sides were rethinking the issues in a way the reporters and newscasters were completely missing. It seemed as if any magazine would be happy to jump on the story.

My first drafts concentrated mainly on the environmentalists themselves. I titled the piece, "Meet the Free-market Environmentalists," and sent it off to *Atlantic Monthly* and the *New York Times Sunday Magazine.* Unfortunately, no one shared my enthusiasm.

Both these publications are more liberal than conservative and apparently their editors felt very gingerly about introducing an idea that might appear to give some ground to the Reagan administration. They all turned it down. As frequently happens, they told me that this was a "conservative" story and therefore should be written for a conservative magazine—*National Review* or *Commentary.* I was reluctant to do this. The idea seemed at least as liberal as conservative, and putting it in a stereotypically conservative publication would immediately label it as unacceptable to one side.

I tried several other middle-of-the-road publications, but finally settled for *Reason* magazine. *Reason* is an obscure publication headquartered in Santa Barbara, California. They are "libertarians," which involves an unusual combination of being "right-wing" on economic issues and "left-wing" on civil libertarian issues. ("Free minds, free markets" is their slogan.) They are almost completely unknown.

Once again, then, it was a matter of preaching to the converted. Few *Reason* readers would find my ideas radically objectionable, and many were probably already familiar with them. Still, it would give me a chance to explore the ideas in depth. *Atlantic Monthly* readers would be unlikely to sit still for a long excursion through the economics of David Ricardo and Karl Marx, but *Reason* readers might. In addition, I could speak with a more authoritative tone. Editors in general-interest magazines usually prefer to deal with experts, while I am only a journalist. Thus, their first question is often: "Who are you to say all this?" In the end, it is sometimes necessary to find a lot of experts who will say things that are really your ideas. *Reason*'s editors and readers, on the other hand, would be more willing to accept my opinions.

The essay as it appears before you, then, was written for a very specific audience. *Reason* is one of those small, clubby publications in which most readers share the same general assumptions. In these circumstances, it is often difficult to avoid falling into an insider's jargonistic tone.

Looking back at this essay, I can see that I only half-avoided the problem. The title itself (which was provided by the editors) is a little obscure. A "deed," of course, is a title to private ownership, and the phrase "Conservation in Deed" thus conveys the idea of market environmentalism, but in a way that is not likely to be immediately apparent to a general reader. In reading it over, it seems that the word "resources" occurs about twice as often as it should. There are also several slangy episodes. In one paragraph I say that bureaucrats "sometimes even subsidize development out of 'their own' pockets—that is, with taxpayers' money." Four paragraphs later I repeat the same inside joke. Bureaucrats "must be doing something wrong—indeed they are undervaluing 'their' resources." Using the cutesy quotation marks to characterize other people's arguments is generally considered a poor device. When done twice in a row with the same phrase it becomes obnoxious.

All these are the little fine details—the "sanding and finishing"—that often make the difference in whether an essay will be readable or not. There are a few basic rules to remember.

First, you don't have to tell the reader *everything*. You must assume some intelligence. This is what we usually do in conversations. A printed transcript of a conversation often seems sparse and uninformative. This is because much communication is done through intonations of voice, facial expressions, and body gestures plus all the other little cues of everyday talk. Writing can't be carried by these, of course, which is why writing always *reads* so much better than a speech transcript or an actual record of everyday conversation. Whatever is conveyed must be done through the words on the page.

Second, you shouldn't be repetitive. Some of the most awkward results in writing come from the repetition of the same words over and over again. You shouldn't litter your writing with obscure or unusual words, but you should avoid the deadening sound of repetition. I often use a thesaurus to create variety.

Finally, your sentences should be relatively simple and comprehensible. A sentence is supposed to represent a complete thought. If it runs so long that you have forgotten what it was about by the time you have gotten to the end of it, then it is too long.

Most intelligent readers anticipate the completion of sentences as they move along. When I am proofreading my own work I usually end up waiting for certain words and phrases. If they don't turn up, I go back and put them in. (The exception is when you are trying to surprise the reader.) Also, if I read a sentence through once and can't understand it, then I rewrite it. Something is almost always out of place.

This is where all your old grammatical rules—"misplaced modifiers," "pronoun antecedents," and so forth—come into play. They all probably seemed maddeningly unimportant when you were diagraming sentences on the blackboard in eighth grade. But when you are trying to make a sentence understandable, you soon realize why they are so important. Nothing slows a reader down more than a poorly constructed sentence. If things aren't in the right place, you almost have to go back and rewrite the sentence yourself to figure out what it meant. Just who does "he" refer to in the sentence, "George went to Bob's house before he went out"? What has been "found" in the sentence, "Mary found her purse sitting in the chair that she lost"? After awhile your readers won't even try to figure it out.

Ideally, a reader should experience good writing as if it were a "mirror of his own mind." When writing moves well, you don't have to think about the author or his prejudices. You can just move along with the underlying rhythms. What you discover on the page is what is already forming in your own mind.

It sounds easy, of course, but it is very hard work. You have to read a sentence over and over again, ruthlessly knocking out unnecessary words, eliminating repetitions, and tightening the logic. Sentence structure and paragraphing are one of the keys. Where two possible constructions present themselves, the simplest is probably the best. "When in doubt, leave it out," is another adage among professional writers. In fact, good writing is often just as much a matter of eliminating things as it is of filling up the page.

These remarks, of course, have mainly to do with writing on the sentence level and apply to writing for everyone in all businesses and professions. But I'd like to add some of the things I learned in my own trade as a journalist, in the hope they might be of interest or of help to those of you who might be thinking of taking up writing as a full-time occupation.

Writing for me is a business. I do it to make a living. I have been a free-lance writer for more than ten years. Every penny I make comes out of my typewriter.

This has advantages and disadvantages, but for me they seem mostly advantages. Every professional writer is somewhat at the mercy of the market. Think about it like this. Every magazine and newspaper makes most of its money on revenues from advertising. The amount of ads it can sell determines the size of a publication's "news hole." Material that writers like myself contribute is made to fill that hole. Journalism is basically what comes between the ads.

This is a harsh reality, but there is an important lesson to be learned. The amount of writing space available is limited. First, newspapers, magazines, and book publishers can only print so much. Second, people only have a limited amount of time to read. When you write for a living, you are competing on both levels. The lesson to be learned is this— writing should be clear, short, precise, and comprehensible.

The average person does not always seem to be aware of just how little space is available in newspapers. I remember noticing this in my early days in journalism. People would often respond to a story with a three-page, typewritten letter that was four times as long as the original article itself. They would expect the whole thing to be printed. (The letters you read in the newspaper are usually chopped down to one or two short paragraphs.) The average person does not always seem to recognize how important it is to write economically—and how difficult it is to do.

On the other hand, as far as "writer's block" is concerned, once you have written for deadlines on a newspaper you will probably never have to worry about it again. Imagine having to write a term paper in a single afternoon. That's what it often feels like to write a newspaper story. It seems impossible, but once you have done it a few times you begin to work out a method. Of course, much newspaper writing is sloppy and superficial. ("They didn't even spell my name right!" people will say.) But there is an art to doing things quickly. Mostly it involves learning to ask the right questions and preparing the story in your mind as you go along.

On the whole, most writers wouldn't want to be trapped in the deadline syndrome for very long. It's just good training—like running 45 miles a week in order to prepare for a two-mile race. The thing that began to frighten me after a few years was how quickly things went in and out of my head. I would come across a story I had written only a few weeks before and find I couldn't remember a single detail of the story. They were written fine—it's just that I couldn't remember writing them. After awhile you begin to feel like a fireman, racing from blaze to blaze until the whole thing becomes a blur.

Newspaper writing often serves as an apprenticeship for other things, just as journal-writing, working on term papers, or even writing long, thoughtful letters to friends can get you interested in writing for its own sake. Doing lots of reading is also important. Reading familiarizes you with words and styles, and can introduce you to the world's great literature. But you can't do it all just by knowing what other people have written. At some point you have to take up pen or pencil, screw the paper into the typewriter or turn on the word processor, and write.

I have known editors who could run over the range of the world's great literature with you, but who said they felt a sense of panic whenever they confronted a blank page in the typewriter. I think that comes from the sense of thinking you have to write a perfect masterpiece on the first draft. If people could only see the writing and rewriting that goes into a completed work—all the scratchings over and crossings out—they wouldn't feel half so intimidated.

My newspaper experience taught me a few basic things, but fortunately they were the right things. Actually, when I first became a reporter I expected I would be sitting at the feet of cigar-chomping editors, gruffly but affectionately spouting newspaper lore. ("Son, we spell 'cemetery' here all e's," was the first thing I heard after writing my first obituary.) As it turned out the paper on which I started was an expanding suburban chain where the whole staff was as young as I was. We all pretty much taught ourselves.

Then on the day I was finally moving to a more established paper, I came across my long-lost mentor, an old grizzled reporter who had retreated to the sales department. I asked him quickly to tell me all he knew about newspapers. He thought a minute and said, "The whole thing is in that lead. Your lead paragraph should never be more than three lines. If you can get that lead right, then you've got your whole story."

That is the best advice I have ever had. I have only refined it into a more general principle that says this: *"If you can't convey the point of your whole story or essay in your opening paragraph, then you probably haven't really understood your story."*

This means, of course, that your reader won't understand it either. An editor of a major publishing house once gave me another nice piece of advice. "I spend all day reading books, and I have to understand things real fast," she said. "Often when I get to the end of a paragraph I realize I don't know what the writer is talking about. Inevitably, when I read back through the passage, I find that the writer doesn't really know what he is talking about either."

Thus, a second important point is to take as much time as possible in thinking things through when you are writing. You have to handle a story in your mind for awhile, judging its size and shape. After all, when you write you are doing people's thinking for them. If you don't take the time to think things through, then who will?

With newspaper stories there is a standard style of writing called the "inverted pyramid." The most important information should come in the first paragraph. Each succeeding paragraph then contains progressively less important information. There is a simple reason for this. Stories are often shortened significantly because of lack of space. The editor hunts through your story to find out what's important. He will simply "cut from the bottom," lopping off enough material until it fits the page. If your best phrases or information are near the bottom, you are out of luck.

With longer newspaper or magazine stories—or with student essays—you have a little more leeway. You do not have to present information in strict descending order. You can lead the reader through various twists and turns of logic or metaphor. Often it is a good practice to save one striking phrase or idea for the very end.

The important thing, though, is to *keep the reader's attention.* Useless repetitions, ideas that are out of place or go nowhere, run-on sentences—all these wear the reader out and make him or her lose interest. After all, few people are ever absolutely required to read anything. (One exception, of course, is English teachers, who must read student essays. This accounts for their often cranky nature after correcting a pile of papers.)

Basically, anything that catches the reader's attention and holds it is worthwhile. For example, I once introduced a story about suburban zoning with a long metaphor that compared town planners looking for taxpaying industries to the New Guinea "cargo tribes" who clear small airports in the jungle, hoping airplanes will land on them to bring them riches. It was a roundabout introduction that might have lost the reader's interest. So I started the story with the word "anthropologists." I figured that anyone finding such an unexpected word at the beginning of the story would be intrigued enough to read on.

In fact, one thing that I finally realized in newspaper work is that there is only one thing that has basically motivated all writers, from Shakespeare to Hemingway to the grubbiest little pamphleteer. That is that somebody will *read what they have written.* In order to attract readers you have to be comprehensible and concise, and hold the reader's interest.

In writing a longer essay, I often think of it in terms of painting. An artist doesn't paint *September Morn* by starting in one corner and working straight across the canvas. He begins by blocking out where the major figures are going to go, getting the general shape of the picture. Then he starts to fill in details. Only when the painting is almost complete does he zero in on those precisions that mark a professional effort.

Using a phrase from painting, I often think of myself as "blocking out" a story, sometimes even before I have any clear idea of what I am going to say. The material is often nothing but an elusive jumble in my head, filled with only fleeting ideas or phrases. Sometimes the best thing to do is just start writing and see what happens.

Often I have written a draft of fifteen pages, only to discover on the last page what I really wanted to say. But that is important. I have gotten from point A to point B. I may have taken the most circuitous route. But now I know where I am going. Now I can go back and draw a straight line.

Blocking out a piece usually reveals the information you lack, and suggests where to go to find it. Stories are often filled with notes like: "[Insert quote from oil company executive here]." (Standard journalistic jargon would be "Oil company exec quote tk," meaning "to come.") Your first draft will be filled with incomplete thoughts. Sometimes it is good to work it through right then and there. But where I need more information, I find it best to push on to the end so that at least I know the shape of the story. Then I can fill in the details. (Of course, once you get all the details, the shape of your story may change as well.)

Writing is a process of trial and error. One reporter I once worked with used to clown around by telling people, "I know exactly what I want to say in the story, but I just can't put it into words." The joke, of course, is that as far as writing is concerned, you don't know anything until you have put it into words. Frequently, in fact, you may think you know something *until* you try to put it into words. Then you discover your ideas were really quite vague, incomplete, and amorphous.

So there you have some of the things I know about writing. I hope you have found it helpful. Ultimately, writing is a lot of fun. I'm sure you'll enjoy it if you stick to it. And now if you'll excuse me, I'm going to have to go back and tighten up this essay a bit to make it just a little more readable.

Stephen Jay Gould

A BIOLOGICAL HOMAGE
TO MICKEY MOUSE

Stephen Jay Gould, born in 1941, has gone on record as saying, "Science is not a heartless pursuit of objective information. It is a creative human activity." Gould's many essays for *Natural History* substantiate not only his claim but his own heart. Those essays and others, collected for the most part in *The Panda's Thumb, Ever Since Darwin,* and *Hen's Teeth and Horse's Toes,* reflect Gould's ability to make complex scientific theory accessible to the nonscientist. As a contributor of more than 100 articles to scientific journals, the general editor of the *History of Paleontology* in twenty volumes, and the author of several specialized science texts, including *Ontogeny and Phylogeny,* Gould also demonstrates his extensive and respected knowledge of the sciences.

Trained as a paleontologist, Gould holds degrees from Antioch College and Columbia University. For his essays, which, according to Gould, "range broadly from planetary and geological to social and political history" but are united "by the common thread of evolutionary theory—Darwin's version," he has received numerous honors, including a National Book Award and a MacArthur Prize fellowship. Gould vowed early to "depart from a long tradition of popular writing in natural history. I would not tell the fascinating tales of nature for their own sake. I would tie my particular story to a general principle of evolutionary theory." The essays below substantiate that claim by providing fascinating displays of the principles of evolutionary theory. Gould has speculated that "new species usually arise, not by the slow and steady transformation of entire ancestral populations, but by the splitting off of small isolates from an unaltered parent stock." Mickey Mouse, of course, has yet to transform into a species, yet "since Mickey's chronological age never altered," his change in appearance at a constant age is a true evolutionary transformation." Mickey's "parent stock" remains perhaps unaltered, but he has become, according to Gould, a far more likable mouse by small leaps and isolated bounds.

Age often turns fire to placidity. Lytton Strachey, in his incisive portrait of Florence Nightingale, writes of her declining years:

> Destiny, having waited very patiently, played a queer trick on Miss Nightingale. The benevolence and public spirit of that long life had only been equalled by its acerbity. Her virtue had dwelt in hardness. . . . And now the sarcastic years brought the proud woman her punishment. She was not to die as she had lived. The sting was to be taken out of her; she was to be made soft; she was to be reduced to compliance and complacency.

Mickey's evolution during 50 years (left to right). As Mickey became increasingly well behaved over the years, his appearance became more youthful. Measurements of

I was therefore not surprised—although the analogy may strike some people as sacrilegious—to discover that the creature who gave his name as a synonym for insipidity had a gutsier youth. Mickey Mouse turned a respectable fifty last year. To mark the occasion, many theaters replayed his debut performance in *Steamboat Willie* (1928). The original Mickey was a rambunctious, even slightly sadistic fellow. In a remarkable sequence, exploiting the exciting new development of sound, Mickey and Minnie pummel, squeeze, and twist the animals on board to produce a rousing chorus of "Turkey in the Straw." They honk a duck with a tight embrace, crank a goat's tail, tweak a pig's nipples, bang a cow's teeth as a stand-in xylophone, and play bagpipe on her udder.

Christopher Finch, in his semiofficial pictorial history of Disney's work, comments: "The Mickey Mouse who hit the movie houses in the late twenties was not quite the well-behaved character most of us are familiar with today. He was mischievous, to say the least, and even displayed a streak of cruelty." But Mickey soon cleaned up his act, leaving to gossip and speculation only his unresolved relationship with Minnie and the status of Morty and Ferdie. Finch continues: "Mickey . . . had become virtually a national symbol, and as such he was expected to behave properly at all times. If he occasionally stepped out of line, any number of letters would arrive at the Studio from citizens and organizations who felt that the nation's moral well-being was in their hands. . . . Eventually he would be pressured into the role of straight man."

As Mickey's personality softened, his appearance changed. Many Disney fans are aware of this transformation through time, but few (I suspect) have recognized the coordinating theme behind all the altera-

three stages in his development revealed a larger relative head size, larger eyes, and an enlarged cranium—all traits of juvenility. © Walt Disney Productions

tions—in fact, I am not sure that the Disney artists themselves explicitly realized what they were doing, since the changes appeared in such a halting and piecemeal fashion. In short, the blander and inoffensive Mickey became progressively more juvenile in appearance. (Since Mickey's chronological age never altered—like most cartoon characters he stands impervious to the ravages of time—this change in appearance at a constant age is a true evolutionary transformation. Progressive juvenilization as an evolutionary phenomenon is called neoteny. More on this later.)

The characteristic changes of form during human growth have inspired a substantial biological literature. Since the head-end of an embryo differentiates first and grows more rapidly in utero than the foot-end (an antero-posterior gradient, in technical language), a newborn child possesses a relatively large head attached to a medium-sized body with diminutive legs and feet. This gradient is reversed through growth as legs and feet overtake the front end. Heads continue to grow but so much more slowly than the rest of the body that relative head size decreases.

In addition, a suite of changes pervades the head itself during human growth. The brain grows very slowly after age three, and the bulbous cranium of a young child gives way to the more slanted, lower-browed configuration of childhood. The eyes scarcely grow at all and relative eye size declines precipitously. But the jaw gets bigger and bigger. Children, compared with adults, have larger heads and eyes, smaller jaws, a more prominent, bulging cranium, and smaller, pudgier legs and feet. Adult heads are altogether more apish, I'm sorry to say.

Mickey, however, has traveled this ontogenetic pathway in reverse during his fifty years among us. He has assumed an ever more childlike appearance as the ratty character of *Steamboat Willie* became the cute and inoffensive host to a magic kingdom. By 1940, the former tweaker of pig's nipples gets a kick in the ass for insubordination (as the *Sorcerer's Apprentice* in *Fantasia*). By 1953, his last cartoon, he has gone fishing and cannot even subdue a squirting clam.

The Disney artists transformed Mickey in clever silence, often using suggestive devices that mimic nature's own changes by different routes. To give him the shorter and pudgier legs of youth, they lowered his pants line and covered his spindly legs with a baggy outfit. (His arms and legs also thickened substantially—and acquired joints for a floppier appearance.) His head grew relatively larger and its features more youthful. The length of Mickey's snout has not altered, but decreasing protrusion is more subtly suggested by a pronounced thickening. Mickey's eye has grown in two modes: first, by a major, discontinuous evolutionary shift as the entire eye of ancestral Mickey became the pupil of his descendants, and second, by gradual increase thereafter.

Mickey's improvement in cranial bulging followed an interesting path since his evolution has always been constrained by the unaltered convention of representing his head as a circle with appended ears and an oblong snout. The circle's form could not be altered to provide a bulging cranium directly. Instead, Mickey's ears moved back, increasing the distance between nose and ears, and giving him a rounded, rather than a sloping, forehead.

To give these observations the cachet of quantitative science, I applied my best pair of dial calipers to three stages of the official phylogeny—the thin-nosed, ears-forward figure of the early 1930s (stage 1), the latter-day Jack of Mickey and the Beanstalk (1947, stage 2), and the modern mouse (stage 3). I measured three signs of Mickey's creeping juvenility: increasing eye size (maximum height) as a percentage of head length (base of the nose to top of rear ear); increasing head length as a percentage of body length; and increasing cranial vault size measured by rearward displacement of the front ear (base of the nose to top of front ear as a percentage of base of the nose to top of rear ear).

All three percentages increased steadily—eye size from 27 to 42 percent of head length; head length from 42.7 to 48.1 percent of body length; and nose to front ear from 71.7 to a whopping 95.6 percent of nose to rear ear. For comparison, I measured Mickey's young "nephew" Morty Mouse. In each case, Mickey has clearly been evolving toward youthful stages of his stock, although he still has a way to go for head length.

You may, indeed, now ask what an at least marginally respectable scientist has been doing with a mouse like that. In part, fiddling around and having fun, of course. (I still prefer *Pinocchio* to *Citizen Kane*.) But I

At an early stage in his evolution, Mickey had a smaller head, cranial vault, and eyes. He evolved toward the characteristics of his young nephew Morty (connected to Mickey by a dotted line).

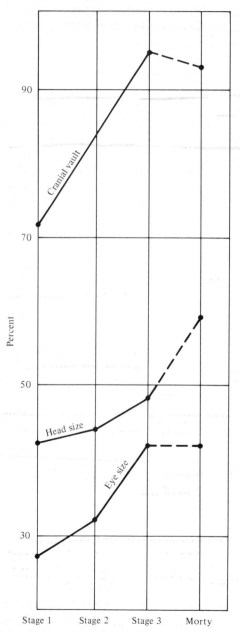

do have a serious point—two, in fact—to make. We must first ask why Disney chose to change his most famous character so gradually and persistently in the same direction? National symbols are not altered capriciously and market researchers (for the doll industry in particular) have spent a good deal of time and practical effort learning what features appeal to people as cute and friendly. Biologists also have spent a great deal of time studying a similar subject in a wide range of animals.

In one of his most famous articles, Konrad Lorenz argues that humans use the characteristic differences in form between babies and adults as important behavioral cues. He believes that features of juvenility trigger "innate releasing mechanisms" for affection and nurturing in adult humans. When we see a living creature with babyish features, we feel an automatic surge of disarming tenderness. The adaptive value of this response can scarcely be questioned, for we must nurture our babies. Lorenz, by the way, lists among his releasers the very features of babyhood that Disney affixed progressively to Mickey: "a relatively large head, predominance of the brain capsule, large and low-lying eyes, bulging cheek region, short and thick extremities, a springy elastic consistency, and clumsy movements." (I propose to leave aside for this article the contentious issue of whether or not our affectionate response to babyish features is truly innate and inherited directly from ancestral primates—as Lorenz argues—or whether it is simply learned from our immediate experience with babies and grafted upon an evolutionary predisposition for attaching ties of affection to certain learned signals. My argument works equally well in either case for I only claim that babyish features tend to elicit strong feelings of affection in adult humans, whether the biological basis be direct programming or the capacity to learn and fix upon signals. I also treat as collateral to my point the major thesis of Lorenz's article—that we respond not to the totality or *Gestalt*, but to a set of specific features acting as releasers. This argument is important to Lorenz because he wants to argue for evolutionary identity in modes of behavior between other vertebrates and humans, and we know that many birds, for example, often respond to abstract features rather than *Gestalten*. Lorenz's article, published in 1950, bears the title *Ganzheit und Teil in der tierischen und menschlichen Gemeinschaft*— "Entirety and part in animal and human society." Disney's piecemeal change of Mickey's appearance does make sense in this context—he operated in sequential fashion upon Lorenz's primary releasers.)

Lorenz emphasized the power that juvenile features hold over us, and the abstract quality of their influence, by pointing out that we judge other animals by the same criteria—although the judgment may be utterly inappropriate in an evolutionary context. We are, in short, fooled

Humans feel affection for animals with juvenile features: large eyes, bulging craniums, retreating chins (left column). Small-eyed, long-snouted animals (right column) do not elicit the same response. From *Studies in Animal and Human Behavior*, Vol. II, by Konrad Lorenz, 1971. Methuen and Co. Ltd.

by an evolved response to our own babies, and we transfer our reaction to the same set of features in other animals.

Many animals, for reasons having nothing to do with the inspiration of affection in humans, possess some features also shared by human babies but not by human adults—large eyes and a bulging forehead with retreating chin, in particular. We are drawn to them, we cultivate them as pets, we stop and admire them in the wild—while we reject their small-eyed, long-snouted relatives who might make more affectionate companions or objects of admiration. Lorenz points out that the German names of many animals with features mimicking human babies end in the diminutive suffix *chen*, even though the animals are often larger than close relatives without such features—*Rotkehlchen* (robin), *Eichhornchen* (squirrel), and *Kaninchen* (rabbit), for example.

In a fascinating section, Lorenz then enlarges upon our capacity for biologically inappropriate response to other animals, or even to inanimate objects that mimic human features. "The most amazing objects can acquire remarkable highly specific emotional values by 'experiential attachment' of human properties. . . . Steeply rising, somewhat overhanging cliff faces or dark stormclouds piling up have the same, immediate display value as a human being who is standing at full height and leaning slightly forwards"—that is, threatening.

We cannot help regarding a camel as aloof and unfriendly because it mimics, quite unwittingly and for other reasons, the "gesture of haughty rejection" common to so many human cultures. In this gesture, we raise our heads, placing our nose above our eyes. We then half-close our eyes and blow out through our nose—the "harumph" of the stereotyped upperclass Englishman or his well-trained servant. "All this," Lorenz argues quite cogently, "symbolizes resistance against all sensory modalities emanating from the disdained counterpart." But the poor camel cannot help carrying its nose above its elongate eyes, with mouth drawn down. As Lorenz reminds us, if you wish to know whether a camel will eat out of your hand or spit, look at his ears, not the rest of his face.

In his important book *Expression of the Emotions in Man and Animals*, published in 1872, Charles Darwin traced the evolutionary basis of many common gestures to originally adaptive actions in animals later internalized as symbols in humans. Thus, he argued for evolutionary continuity of emotion, not only of form. We snarl and raise our upper lip in fierce anger—to expose our nonexistent fighting canine tooth. Our gesture of disgust repeats the facial actions associated with the highly adaptive act of vomiting in necessary circumstances. Darwin concluded, much to the distress of many Victorian contemporaries: "With mankind some expressions, such as the bristling of the hair under the influence of extreme terror, or the uncovering of the teeth under that of furious rage, can hardly be understood, except on the belief that man once existed in a much lower and animal-like condition."

In any case, the abstract features of human childhood elicit powerful emotional responses in us, even when they occur in other animals. I submit that Mickey Mouse's evolutionary road down the course of his own growth in reverse reflects the unconscious discovery of this biological principle by Disney and his artists. In fact, the emotional status of most Disney characters rests on the same set of distinctions. To this extent, the magic kingdom trades on a biological illusion—our ability to abstract and our propensity to transfer inappropriately to other animals the fitting responses we make to changing form in the growth of our own bodies.

Donald Duck also adopts more juvenile features through time. His elongated beak recedes and his eyes enlarge; he converges on Huey, Louie, and Dewey as surely as Mickey approaches Morty. But Donald, having inherited the mantle of Mickey's original misbehavior, remains more adult in form with his projecting beak and more sloping forehead.

Dandified, disreputable Mortimer (here stealing Minnie's affections) has strikingly more adult features than Mickey. His head is smaller in proportion to body length; his nose is a full 80 percent of head length. ©Walt Disney Productions

Mouse villains or sharpies, contrasted with Mickey, are always more adult in appearance, although they often share Mickey's chronological age. In 1936, for example, Disney made a short entitled *Mickey's Rival*. Mortimer, a dandy in a yellow sports car, intrudes upon Mickey and Minnie's quiet country picnic. The thoroughly disreputable Mortimer has a head only 29 percent of body length, to Mickey's 45, and a snout 80 percent of head length, compared with Mickey's 49. (Nonetheless, and was it ever different, Minnie transfers her affection until an obliging bull from a neighboring field dispatches Mickey's rival.) Consider also the exaggerated adult features of other Disney characters—the swaggering bully Peg-leg Pete or the simple if lovable, dolt Goofy.

As a second, serious biological comment on Mickey's odyssey in form, I note that his path to eternal youth repeats, in epitome, our own evolutionary story. For humans are neotenic. We have evolved by retaining to adulthood the originally juvenile features of our ancestors. Our australopithecine forebears, like Mickey in *Steamboat Willie*, had projecting jaws and low vaulted craniums.

Our embryonic skulls scarcely differ from those of chimpanzees.

Cartoon villains are not the only Disney characters with exaggerated adult features. Goofy, like Mortimer, has a small head relative to body length and a prominent snout. © Walt Disney Productions

And we follow the same path of changing form through growth: relative decrease of the cranial vault since brains grow so much more slowly than bodies after birth, and continuous relative increase of the jaw. But while chimps accentuate these changes, producing an adult strikingly different in form from a baby, we proceed much more slowly down the same path and never get nearly so far. Thus, as adults, we retain juvenile features. To be sure, we change enough to produce a notable difference between baby and adult, but our alteration is far smaller than that experienced by chimps and other primates.

A marked slowdown of development rates has triggered our neoteny. Primates are slow developers among mammals, but we have accentuated the trend to a degree matched by no other mammal. We have very long periods of gestation, markedly extended childhoods, and the longest life span of any mammal. The morphological features of eternal youth have served us well. Our enlarged brain is, at least in part, a result of extending rapid prenatal growth rates to later ages. (In all mammals, the brain grows rapidly in utero but often very little after birth. We have extended this fetal phase into postnatal life.)

But the changes in timing themselves have been just as important. We are preeminently learning animals, and our extended childhood permits the transference of culture by education. Many animals display flexibility and play in childhood but follow rigidly programmed patterns as adults. Lorenz writes, in the same article cited above: "The characteristic which is so vital for the human peculiarity of the true man—that of always remaining in a state of development—is quite certainly a gift which we owe to the neotenous nature of mankind."

In short, we, like Mickey, never grow up although we, alas, do grow old. Best wishes to you, Mickey, for your next half-century. May we stay as young as you, but grow a bit wiser.

QUESTIONS FOR READING, RESPONDING, AND WRITING

Summarizing Main Points

1. Summarize Gould's account of individual human growth. Then, summarize his account of Mickey Mouse's evolution. According to Gould, why did the Disney artists, knowingly or unknowingly, change Mickey's appearance?
2. What are the two "serious" points Gould is trying to make through his discussion of Mickey's evolution?

Analyzing Methods of Discourse

1. Chart the development of Gould's essay. How does Gould's arrangement of the material help him make his "serious" points? Would his essay be as

effective had he started with those serious points and then gone on to illustrate them? Why or why not?

2. When Gould gets to his first difficult scientific word, "neotony," he defines it for the reader. Yet as he proceeds, he uses a number of other difficult scientific words: Ontogenic, australopithecine, and morphological are among the most difficult that he does not directly define. List some of the ways in which Gould makes it possible for the reader to discover, without resorting to a dictionary, either the specific meaning or at least an approximate meaning of those words. Do the charts and illustrations help? Why do you think Gould provides them? Could you understand the essay without them?

Focusing on the Field

1. At what point in the essay did you first become aware of Gould's fondness for Mickey Mouse? Do you think his affection for his subject makes his argument more or less persuasive? Why or why not?
2. After tracing his own argument on Mickey's evolution in both scientific and unscientific terms, Gould enlists the support of Konrad Lorenz and Charles Darwin. Study his discussion of both Lorenz's and Darwin's theories. How does he make those theories accessible to the average reader? Do you think his efforts to make them accessible might constitute another "serious" point?

Writing Assignments

1. Research another cartoon character (e.g., Bugs Bunny, Fred Flintstone, Snoopy) and write an essay in which you apply Gould's scientific analysis to its development. If your character does not follow the same juvenilization process that Mickey Mouse does, suggest theories of your own for the course of development it does take. Make sure you provide sufficient explanation and evidence for your findings.
2. "Evolution" is a term used to describe changes in many fields. Using Gould's essay as a model and employing similar research and writing techniques, do an analysis of another aspect of popular culture (e.g., the "evolution" of popular rock-and-roll music from the 1950s to the present).

Stephen Jay Gould

DARWINISM AND THE EXPANSION
OF EVOLUTIONARY THEORY

A sketch of Stephen Jay Gould's life and career appears as an introduction to "A Biological Homage to Mickey Mouse." In the following essay, written mainly for a professional rather than a general audience, Gould argues for a "kind of higher Darwinism"—a hierarchical theory of "directed speciation." This theory challenges the "reductionist assertion" that natural selection takes place only at the level of the individual organism, making it the "locus of evolutionary change." Gould captures "in abstract form the essence of Darwin's vision" in his theory, while asserting that natural selection directs evolution at each level in a *species*. His theory itself—which starts with and builds upon Darwin—not only demonstrates a form of "directed speciation," but, according to Gould, "may impose a literal wisdom upon that famous last line of *Origin of Species,* 'There is grandeur in this view of life.'"

Summary. The essence of Darwinism lies in the claim that natural selection is a creative force, and in the reductionist assertion that selection upon individual organisms is the focus of evolutionary change. Critiques of adaptationism and gradualism call into doubt the traditional consequences of the argument for creativity, while a concept of hierarchy, with selection acting upon such higher-level "individuals" as demes and species, challenges the reductionist claim. An expanded hierarchical theory would not be Darwinism, as strictly defined, but it would capture, in abstract form, the fundamental feature of Darwin's vision—direction of evolution by selection at each level.

Ben Sira, author of the apocryphal book of Ecclesiasticus, paid homage to the heroes of Israel in a noted passage beginning, "let us now praise

Teachers

famous men." He glorified great teachers above all others, for their fame shall eclipse the immediate triumphs of kings and conquerors. And he argued that the corporeal death of teachers counts for nothing—indeed, it should be celebrated—since great ideas must live forever: "His name will be more glorious than a thousand others, and if he dies, that will satisfy him just as well." These sentiments express the compulsion we feel to commemorate the deaths of great thinkers; for their ideas still direct us today. Charles Darwin died 100 years ago, on 19 April 1882, but his name still causes fundamentalists to shudder and scientists to draw battle lines amidst their accolades.

WHAT IS DARWINISM?

Darwin often stated that his biological work had embodied two different goals (1): to establish the fact of evolution, and to propose natural selection as its primary mechanism. "I had," he wrote, "two distinct objects in view; firstly to show that species had not been separately created, and secondly, that natural selection had been the chief agent of changes" (2).

Although "Darwinism" has often been equated with evolution itself in popular literature, the term should be restricted to the body of thought allied with Darwin's own theory of mechanism, his second goal. This decision does not provide an unambiguous definition, if only because Darwin himself was a pluralist who granted pride of place to natural selection, but also advocated an important role for Lamarckian and other nonselectionist factors. Thus, as the 19th century drew to a close, G. J. Romanes and A. Weismann squared off in a terminological battle for rights to the name "Darwinian"—Romanes claiming it for his eclectic pluralism, Weismann for his strict selectionism (3).

If we agree, as our century generally has, that "Darwinism" should be restricted to the world view encompassed by the theory of natural selection itself, the problem of definition is still not easily resolved. Darwinism must be more than the bare bones of the mechanics: the principles of superfecundity and inherited variation, and the deduction of natural selection therefrom. It must, fundamentally, make a claim for wide scope and dominant frequency; natural selection must represent the primary directing force of evolutionary change.

I believe that Darwinism, under these guidelines, can best be defined as embodying two central claims and a variety of peripheral and supporting statements more or less strongly tied to the central postulates: Darwinism is not a mathematical formula or a set of statements, deductively arranged.

(1) The creativity of natural selection. Darwinians cannot simply claim that natural selection operates since everyone, including Paley and

the natural theologians, advocated selection as a device for removing unfit individuals at both extremes and preserving, intact and forever, the created type (4). The essence of Darwinism lies in a claim that natural selection is the primary directing force of evolution, in that it creates fitter phenotypes by differentially preserving, generation by generation, the best adapted organisms from a pool of random variants that supply raw material only, not direction itself (5). Natural selection is a creator; it builds adaptation step by step.

Darwin's contemporaries understood that natural selection hinged on the argument for creativity. Natural selection can only eliminate the unfit, his opponents proclaimed: something else must create the fit. Thus, the American Neo-Lamarckian E. D. Cope wrote a book with the sardonic title *The Origin of the Fittest* (6), and Charles Lyell complained to Darwin that he could understand how selection might operate like two members of the "Hindoo triad"—Vishnu the preserver and Siva the destroyer—but not like Brahma the creator (7).

The claim for creativity has important consequences and prerequisites that also become part of the Darwinian corpus. Most prominently, three constraints are imposed on the nature of genetic variation (or at least the evolutionarily significant portion of it). (i) It must be copious since selection makes nothing directly and requires a large pool of raw material. (ii) It must be small in scope. If new species characteristically arise all at once, then the fit are formed by the process of variation itself, and natural selection only plays the negative role of executioner for the unfit. True saltationist theories have always been considered anti-Darwinian on this basis. (iii) It must be undirected. If new environments can elicit heritable, adaptive variation, then creativity lies in the process of variation, and selection only eliminates the unfit. Lamarckism is an anti-Darwinian theory because it advocates directed variation; organisms perceive felt needs, adapt their bodies acccordingly, and pass these modifications directly to offspring.

Two additional postulates, generally considered part and parcel of the Darwinian world view, are intimately related to the claim for creativity, but are not absolute prerequisites or necessary deductive consequences: (i) *Gradualism.* If creativity resides in a step-by-step process of selection from a pool of random variants, then evolutionary change must be dominantly continuous and descendants must be linked to ancestors by a long chain of smoothly intermediate phenotypes. Darwin's own gradualism precedes his belief in natural selection and has deeper roots (8); it dominated his world view and provided a central focus for most other theories that he proposed, including the origin of coral atolls by subsidence of central islands, and formation of vegetable mold by earthworms (9, 10). (ii) *The adaptationist program.* If selection becomes creative by superintending, generation by generation, the continuous incorporation of favorable variation into altered forms, then evolutionary change must be fundamentally adaptive. If evolution were saltational, or driven by internally generated biases in the direction of variation, adaptation would not be a necessary attribute of evolutionary change.

The argument for creativity rests on relative frequency, not exclusivity. Other factors must regulate some cases of evolutionary change—randomness as a direct source of modification, not only of raw material, for example. The Darwinian strategy does not deny other factors, but attempts to circumscribe their domain to few and unimportant cases.

(2) Selection operates through the differential reproductive success of individual organisms (the "struggle for existence" in Darwin's terminology). Selection is an interaction among individuals; there are no higher-order laws in nature, no statement about the "good" of species or ecosystems. If species survive longer, or if ecosystems appear to display harmony and balance, these features arise as a by-product of selection among individuals for reproductive success.

Although evolutionists, including many who call themselves Darwinians, have often muddled this point (11), it is a central feature of Darwin's logic (12). It underlies all his colorful visual imagery including the metaphor of the wedge (13, p. 67), or the true struggle that underlies an appearance of harmony: "we behold the face of nature bright with gladness," but . . . (13, p. 62). Darwin developed his theory of natural selection by transferring the basic argument of Adam Smith's economics into nature: an ordered economy can best be achieved by letting individuals struggle for personal profits, thereby permitting a natural sifting of the most competitive (laissez-faire); an ordered ecology is a transient balance established by successful competitors pursuing their own Darwinian edge (14).

As a primary consequence, this focus upon individual organisms leads to reductionism, not to ultimate atoms and molecules of course, but of higher-order, or macroevolutionary, processes to the accumulated struggles of individuals. Extrapolationism is the other side of the same coin—the claim that natural selection within local populations is the source of all important evolutionary change.

DARWINISM AND THE MODERN SYNTHESIS

Although Darwin succeeded in his first goal, and lies in Westminster Abbey for his success in establishing the fact of evolution, his theory of natural selection did not triumph as an orthodoxy until long after his death. The Mendelian component to the modern, or Neo-Darwinian, theory only developed in our century. Moreover, and ironically, the first

Mendelians emphasized macromutations and were non-Darwinians on the issue of creativity as discussed above.

The Darwinian resurgence began in earnest in the 1930's, but did not crystallize until the 1950's. At the last Darwinian centennial, in 1959 (both the 100th anniversary of the *Origin of Species* and the 150th of Darwin's birth), celebrations throughout the world lauded the "modern synthesis" as Darwinism finally triumphant (*15*).

Julian Huxley, who coined the term (*16*), defined the "modern synthesis" as an integration of the disparate parts of biology about a Darwinian core (*17*). Synthesis occurred at two levels: (i) The Mendelian research program merged with Darwinian traditions of natural history, as Mendelians recognized the importance of micromutations and their correspondence with Darwinian variation, and as population genetics supplied a quantitative mechanics for evolutionary change. (ii) The traditional disciplines of natural history, systematics, paleontology, morphology, and classical botany, for example (*18*), were integrated within the Darwinian core, or at least rendered consistent with it.

The initial works of the synthesis, particularly Dobzhansky's first (1937) edition of *Genetics and the Origin of Species*, were not firmly Darwinian (as defined above), and did not assert a dominant frequency for natural selection. They were more concerned with demonstrating that large-scale phenomena of evolution are consistent with the principles of genetics, whether Darwinian or not; and they therefore, for example, granted greater prominence to genetic drift than later editions of the same works would allow.

Throughout the late 1940's and 1950's, however, the synthesis hardened about its Darwinian core. Analysis of textbooks and, particularly, the comparison of first with later editions of the founding documents, demonstrates the emergence of natural selection and adaptation as preeminent factors of evolution. Thus, for example, G. G. Simpson redefined "quantum evolution" in 1953 as a limiting rate for adaptive phyletic transformation, not, as he had in 1944, as a higher-order analog of genetic drift, with a truly inadaptive phase between stabilized end points (*19*). Dobzhansky removed chapters and reduced emphasis upon rapid modification and random components to evolutionary change (*20*). David Lack reassessed his work on Darwin's finches and decided that minor differences among species are adaptive after all (*21*). His preface to the 1960 reissue of his monograph features the following statements (*22*):

> This text was completed in 1944 and . . . views on species-formation have advanced. In particular, it was generally believed when I wrote the book that, in animals, nearly all of the differences between subspecies of the same species, and between closely related species in the same genus, were without adaptive significance. . . . Sixteen years later, it is generally believed that all,

or almost all, subspecific and specific differences are adaptive. . . . Hence it now seems probable that at least most of the seemingly nonadaptive differences in Darwin's finches would, if more were known, prove to be adaptive.

Mayr's definition of the synthesis, offered without rebuttal at a conference of historians and architects of the theory, reflects this crystallized version:

> The term "evolutionary synthesis" was introduced by Julian Huxley . . . to designate the general acceptance of two conclusions: gradual evolution can be explained in terms of small genetic changes ("mutations") and recombination, and the ordering of this genetic variation by natural selection; and the observed evolutionary phenomena, particularly macroevolutionary processes and speciation, can be explained in a manner that is consistent with the known genetic mechanisms (23).

This definition restates the two central claims of Darwinism discussed in the last section: Mayr's first conclusion, with its emphasis on gradualism, small genetic change, and natural selection, represents the argument for creativity; while the second embodies the claim for reduction. I have been challenged for erecting a straw man in citing this definition of the synthesis, but it was framed by a man who is both an architect and the leading historian of the theory, and it is surely an accurate statement of what I was taught as a graduate student in the mid-1960's (24). Moreover, these very words have been identified as the "broad version" of the synthesis (as opposed to a more partisan and restrictive stance) by White (25), a leading evolutionist and scholar who lived through it all.

The modern synthesis has sometimes been so broadly construed, usually by defenders who wish to see it as fully adequate to meet and encompass current critiques, that it loses all meaning by including everything. If, as Stebbins and Ayala claim, " 'selectionist' and 'neutralist' views of molecular evolution are competing hypotheses within the framework of the synthetic theory of evolution" (26), then what serious views are excluded? King and Jukes, authors of the neutralist theory, named it "non-Darwinian evolution" in the title of their famous paper (27). Stebbins and Ayala have tried to win an argument by redefinition. The essence of the modern synthesis must be its Darwinian core. If most evolutionary change is neutral, the synthesis is severely compromised.

WHAT IS HAPPENING TO DARWINISM

Current critics of Darwinism and the modern synthesis are proposing a good deal more than a comfortable extension of the theory, but much less than a revolution. In my partisan view, neither of Darwinism's two central themes will survive in their strict formulation; in that sense, "the modern synthesis, as an exclusive proposition, has broken down on both of its fundamental claims" (28). However, I believe that a restructured evolutionary theory will embody the essence of the Darwinian argument in a more abstract, and hierarchically extended form. The modern synthesis is incomplete, not incorrect.

CRITIQUE OF CREATIVITY: GRADUALISM

At issue is not the general idea that natural selection can act as a creative force; the basic argument, in principle, is a sound one. Primary doubts center on the subsidiary claims—gradualism and the adaptationist program. If most evolutionary changes, particularly large-scale trends, include major nonadaptive components as primary directing or channeling features, and if they proceed more in an episodic than a smoothly continuous fashion, then we inhabit a different world from the one Darwin envisaged.

Critiques of gradualist thought proceed on different levels and have different import, but none are fundamentally opposed to natural selection. They are therefore not directed against the heart of Darwinian theory, but against a fundamental subsidiary aspect of Darwin's own world view—one that he consistently conflated with natural selection, as in the following famous passage: "If it could be demonstrated that any complex organ existed, which could not possibly have been formed by numerous, successive, slight modifications, my theory would absolutely break down" (29).

At the levels of microevolution and speciation, the extreme saltationist claim that new species arise all at once, fully formed, by a fortunate macromutation would be anti-Darwinian, but no serious thinker now advances such a view, and neither did Richard Goldschmidt (30), the last major scholar to whom such an opinion is often attributed. Legitimate claims range from the saltational origin of key features by developmental shifts of dissociable segments of ontogeny (31) to the origin of reproductive isolation (speciation) by major and rapidly incorporated genetic changes that precede the acquisition of adaptive, phenotype differences (32).

Are such styles of evolution anti-Darwinian? What can one say except "yes and no." They do not deny a creative role to natural selection, but neither do they embody the constant superintending of each event, or the step-by-step construction of each major feature, that traditional views about natural selection have advocated. If new *Baupläne* often arise in an adaptive cascade following the saltational origin of a key feature, then part of the process is sequential and adaptive, and therefore Darwinian; but the initial step is not, since selection does not play a creative role in building the key feature. If reproductive isolation often precedes adaptation, then a major aspect of speciation is Darwinian (for the new species will not prosper unless it builds distinctive adaptations in the sequential model), but its initiation, including the defining feature of reproductive isolation, is not.

At the macroevolutionary level of trends, the theory of punctuated equilibrium (33) proposes that established species generally do not change substantially in phenotype over a lifetime that may encompass many million years (stasis), and that most evolutionary change is concentrated in geologically instantaneous events of branching speciation. These geological instants, resolvable (34) in favorable stratigraphic circumstances (so that the theory can be tested for its proposed punctuations as well as for its evident periods of stasis), represent amounts of microevolutionary time fully consistent with orthodox views about speciation. Indeed, Eldredge and I originally proposed punctuated equilibrium as the expected geological consequence of Mayr's theory of peripatric speciation. The non-Darwinian implications of punctuated equilibrium lie in its suggestions for the explanation of evolutionary trends (see below), not in the tempo of individual speciation events. Although punctuated equilibrium is a theory for a higher level of evolutionary change, and must therefore be agnostic with respect to the role of natural selection in speciation, the world that it proposes is quite different from that traditionally viewed by paleontologists (and by Darwin himself) as the proper geological extension of Darwinism.

The "gradualist-punctuationalist debate," the general label often applied to this disparate series of claims, may not be directed at the heart of natural selection, but it remains an important critique of the Darwinian tradition. The world is not inhabited exclusively by fools, and when a subject arouses intense interest and debate, as this one has, something other than semantics is usually at stake. In the largest sense, this debate is but one small aspect of a broader discussion about the nature of change: Is our world (to construct a ridiculously oversimplified dichotomy) primarily one of constant change (with structure as a mere incarnation of the moment), or is structure primary and constraining, with change as a "difficult" phenomenon, usually accomplished rapidly when a stable structure is stressed beyond its buffering capacity to resist and absorb. It would be hard to deny that the Darwinian tradition, including the modern synthesis, favored the first view while "punctuationalist" thought in general, including such aspects of classical morphology as D'Arcy Thompson's theory of form (35), prefers the second.

CRITIQUE OF CREATIVITY: ADAPTATION

The primary critiques of adaptation have arisen from molecular data, particularly from the approximately even ticking of the molecular clock, and the argument that natural populations generally maintain too much genetic variation to explain by natural selection, even when selection acts to preserve variation as in, for example, heterozygote advantage and frequency-dependent selection. To these phenomena, Darwinians have a response that is, in one sense, fully justified: Neutral genetic changes without phenotypic consequences are invisible to Darwinian processes of selection upon organisms and therefore represent a legitimate process separate from the subjects that Darwinism can treat. Still, since issues in natural history are generally resolved by appeals to relative frequency, the domain of Darwinism is restricted by these arguments.

But another general critique of the adaptationist program has been reasserted within the Darwinian domain of phenotypes (36). The theme is an old one, and not unfamiliar to Darwinians. Darwin himself took it seriously, as did the early, pluralistic accounts of the modern synthesis. The later, "hard" version of the synthesis relegated it to unimportance or lip service. The theme is two-pronged, both arguments asserting that the current utility of a structure permits no assumption that selection shaped it. First, the constraints of inherited form and developmental pathways may so channel any change that even though selection induces motion down permitted paths, the channel itself represents the primary determinant of evolutionary direction. Second, current utility permits no necessary conclusion about historical origin. Structures now indispensable for survival may have arisen for other reasons and been "coopted" by functional shift for their new role.

Both arguments have their Darwinian versions. First, if the channels are set by past adaptations, then selection remains preeminent, for all major structures are either expressions of immediate selection, or channeled by a phylogenetic heritage of previous selection. Darwin struggled mightily with this problem. Ultimately, in a neglected passage that I regard as one of the most crucial paragraphs in the *Origin of Species* (37), he resolved his doubts, and used this argument to uphold the great British tradition of adaptationism. Second, if coopted structures initially arose as adaptations for another function, then they too are products of selection, albeit in a regime not recorded by their current usage. We call this phenomenon preadaptation; as the primary solution to Mivart's taunt (38) about "the incipient stages of useful structures," it is a central theme of orthodox Darwinism.

But both arguments also have non-Darwinian versions, not widely appreciated but potentially fundamental. First, many features of organic architecture and developmental pathways have never been adaptations to anything, but arose as by-products or incidental consequences of changes with a basis in selection. Seilacher has suggested, for example, that the divaricate pattern of molluscan ornamentation may be nonadaptive in its essential design. In any case, it is certainly a channel for some fascinating subsidiary adaptations (39). Second, many structures available for cooptation did not arise as adaptations for something else (as the principle of preadaptation assumes) but were nonadaptive in their original construction. Evolutionary morphology now lacks a term for these coopted structures, and unnamed phenomena are not easily conceptualized. Vrba and I suggest that they be called exaptations (40), and present a range of potential examples from the genitalia of hyenas to redundant DNA.

Evolutionists admit, of course, that all selection yields by-products and incidental consequences, but we tend to think of these nonadaptations as a sort of evolutionary frill, a set of small and incidental modifications with no major consequences. I dispute this assessment and claim that the pool of nonadaptations must be far greater in extent than the direct adaptations that engender them. This pool must act as a higher-level analog of genetic variation, as a phenotypic source of raw material for further evolution. Nonadaptations are not just incidental allometric and pleiotropic effects on other parts of the body, but multifarious expressions potentially within any adapted structure. No one doubts, for example, that the human brain became large for a set of complex reasons related to selection. But, having reached its unprecedented bulk, it could, as a computer of some sophistication, perform in an unimagined range of ways bearing no relation to the selective reasons for initial enlargement. Most of human society may rest on these nonadaptive consequences. How many human institutions, for example, owe their shape to that most terrible datum that intelligence permitted us to grasp—the fact of our personal mortality.

I do not claim that a new force of evolutionary change has been discovered. Selection may supply all immediate direction, but if highly constraining channels are built of nonadaptations, and if evolutionary versatility resides primarily in the nature and extent of nonadaptive pools, then "internal" factors of organic design are an equal partner with selection. We say that mutation is the ultimate source of variation, yet we grant a fundamental role to recombination and the evolution of sexuality—often as a prerequisite to multicellularity, the Cambrian explosion and, ultimately, us. Likewise, selection may be the ultimate source of evolutionary change, but most actual events may owe more of their shape to its nonadaptive sequelae.

IS EVOLUTION A PRODUCT OF SELECTION AMONG INDIVIDUALS?

Although arguments for a multiplicity of units of selection have been advanced and widely discussed (41), evolutionists have generally held fast to the overwhelming predominance, if not exclusivity, of organisms as the objects sorted by selection—Dawkins' (42) attempt at further reduction to the gene itself notwithstanding. How else can we explain the vehement reaction of many evolutionists to Wynne-Edwards' theory of group selection for the maintenance of altruistic traits (43), or the delight felt by so many when the same phenomena were explained, under the theory of kin selection, as a result of individuals pursuing their traditional Darwinian edge. I am not a supporter of Wynne-Edwards' particular hypothesis, nor do I doubt the validity and importance of kin selection; I merely point out that the vehemence and delight convey deeper messages about general attitudes.

Nonetheless, I believe that the traditional Darwinian focus on individual bodies, and the attendant reductionist account of macroevolution, will be supplanted by a hierarchical approach recognizing legitimate Darwinian individuals at several levels of a structural hierarchy, including genes, bodies, demes, species, and clades.

The argument may begin with a claim that first appears to be merely semantic, yet contains great utility and richness in implication, namely the conclusion advanced by Ghiselin and later supported by Hull that species should be treated as individuals, not as classes (44). Most species function as entities in nature, with coherence and stability. And they display the primary characteristics of a Darwinian actor; they vary within their population (clade in this case), and they exhibit differential rates of birth (speciation) and death (extinction).

Our language and culture include a prejudice for applying the concept of individual only to bodies, but any coherent entity that has a unique origin, sufficient temporal stability, and a capacity for reproduction with change can serve as an evolutionary agent. The actual hierarchy of our world is a contingent fact of history, not a heuristic device or a logical necessity. One can easily imagine a world devoid of such hierarchy, and conferring the status of evolutionary individual upon bodies alone. If genes could not duplicate themselves and disperse among chromosomes, we might lack the legitimately independent level that the "selfish DNA" hypothesis establishes for some genes (45). If new species usually arose by the smooth transformation of an entire ancestral species, and then changed continuously toward a descendant form, they would lack the stability and coherence required for defining evolutionary individuals. The theory of punctuated equilibrium allows us to individuate species to both time and space; this property (rather than the debate about evolutionary tempo) may emerge as its primary contribution to evolutionary theory.

In itself, individuation does not guarantee the strong claim for evolutionary agency: that the higher-level individual acts as a unit of selection in its own right. Species might be individuals, but their differential evolutionary success might still arise entirely from natural selection acting upon their parts, that is, upon phenotypes of organisms. A trend toward increasing brain size, for example, might result from the greater longevity of big-brained species. But big-brained species might prosper only because the organisms within them tend to prevail in traditional competition.

But individuation of higher-level units is enough to invalidate the reductionism of traditional Darwinism—for pattern and style of evolution depend critically on the disposition of higher-level individuals, even when all selection occurs at the traditional level of organisms. Sewall Wright, for example, has often spoken of "interdemic selection" in his shifting balance theory (46), but he apparently uses this phrase in a descriptive sense and believes that the mechanism for change usually resides in selection among individual organisms, as when, for example, migrants from one deme swamp another. Still, the fact of deme structure itself—that is, the individuation of higher-level units within a species—is crucial to the operation of shifting balance. Without division into demes, and under panmixia, genetic drift could not operate as the major source of variation required by the theory.

We need not, however, confine ourselves to the simple fact of individuation as an argument against Darwinian reductionism. For the strong claim that higher-level individuals act as units of selection in their own right can often be made. Many evolutionary trends, for example, are driven by differential frequency of speciation (the analog of birth) rather than by differential extinction (the more usual style of selection by death). Features that enhance the frequency of speciation are often properties of populations, not of individual organisms, for example, dependence of dispersal (and resultant possibilities for isolation and speciation) on size and density of populations.

Unfortunately, the terminology of this area is plagued with a central confusion (some, I regret to say, abetted by my own previous writings). Terms like "interdemic selection" or "species selection" (47) have been used in the purely descriptive sense, when the sorting out among higher-level individuals may arise solely from natural selection operating upon organisms. Such cases are explained by Darwinian selection, although they are irreducible to organisms alone. The same terms have been restricted to cases of higher-level individuals acting as units of selection. Such situations are non-Darwinian, and irreducible on this strong criterion. Since issues involving the locus of selection are so crucial in evolutionary theory, I suggest that these terms only be used in the strong and restricted sense. Species selection, for example, should connote an irreducibility to individual organisms (because populations are acting as units of selection); it should not merely offer a convenient alternative description for the effect of traditional selection upon organisms.

The logic of species selection is sound, and few evolutionists would now doubt that it can occur in principle. The issue, again and as always in natural history, is one of relative frequency: how often does species selection occur, and how important is it in the panoply of evolutionary events. Fisher himself dismissed species selection because, relative to organisms, species are so few in number (within a clade) and so long in duration (48):

> The relative unimportance of this as an evolutionary factor would seem to follow decisively from the small number of closely related species which in fact do come into competition, as compared to the number of individuals in the same species; and from the vastly greater duration of the species compared to the individual.

But Fisher's argument rests on two hidden and questionable assumptions. (i) Mass selection can almost always be effective in transforming entire populations substantially in phenotype. The sheer number of organisms participating in this efficient process would then swamp any effect of selection among species. But if stasis be prevalent within established species, as the theory of punctuated equilibrium asserts and as paleontological experience affirms (overwhelmingly for marine invertebrates, at least), then the mere existence of billions of individuals and millions of generations guarantees no substantial role for directional selection upon organisms. (ii) Species selection depends on direct competition among species. Fisher argues for differential death (extinction) as the mechanism of species selection. I suspect, however, that differential frequency of speciation (selection by birth) is a far more common and effective mode of species selection. It may occur without direct competition between species, and can rapidly shift the average phenotype within a clade in regimes of random extinction.

J. Maynard Smith (49) has raised another objection against species selection: simply, that most features of organisms represent "things individual creatures do." How, he asks, could one attribute the secondary palate of mammals to species selection? But the origin of a feature is one thing (and I would not dispute traditional selection among organisms as the probable mechanism for evolving a secondary palate), and the spread of features through larger clades is another. Macroevolution is fundamentally about the combination of features and their differential spread. These phenomena lie comfortably within the domain of effective species selection. Many features must come to prominence primarily through their fortuitous phyletic link with high speciation rates. Mammals represent a lineage of therapsids that may have survived (while all others died) as a result of small body size and nocturnal habits. Was the secondary palate a key to their success or did it piggyback on the high speciation rates often noted (for other reasons) in small-bodied forms. Did mammals survive the Cretaceous extinction, thereby inheriting the world from dinosaurs, as a result of their secondary palate, or did their small size again preserve them during an event that differentially wiped out large creatures.

EVOLUTIONARY PATTERN BY INTERACTION BETWEEN LEVELS

The hierarchical model, with its assertion that selection works simultaneously and differently upon individuals at a variety of levels, suggests a revised interpretation for many phenomena that have puzzled people where they implicitly assumed causation by selection upon organisms. In particular, it suggests that negative interactions between levels might be an important principle in maintaining stability or holding rates of change within reasonable bounds.

The "selfish DNA" hypothesis, for example, proposes that much middle-repetitive DNA exists within genomes not because it provides Darwinian benefits to phenotypes, but because genes can (in certain circumstances) act as units of selection. Genes that can duplicate themselves and move among chromosomes will therefore accumulate copies of themselves for their own Darwinian reasons. But why does the process ever stop? The authors of the hypothesis (45) suggest that phenotypes will eventually "notice" the redundant copies when the energetic cost of producing them becomes high enough to entail negative selection at the level of organism. Stability may represent a balance between positive selection at the gene level and the negative selection it eventually elicits at the organism level.

All evolutionary textbooks grant a paragraph or two to a phenomenon called "overspecialization," usually dismissing it as a peculiar and peripheral phenomenon. It records the irony that many creatures, by evolving highly complex and ecologically constraining features for their immediate Darwinian advantage, virtually guarantee the short duration of their species by restricting its capacity for subsequent adaptation. Will a peacock or an Irish elk survive when the environment alters radically? Yet fancy tails and big antlers do lead to more copulations in the short run of a lifetime. Overspecialization is, I believe, a central evolutionary phenomenon that has failed to gain the attention it deserves because we have lacked a vocabulary to express what is really happening: the negative interaction of species-level disadvantage and individual-level advantage. How else can morphological specialization be kept within bounds, leaving a place for drab and persistent creatures of the world. The general phenomenon must also regulate much of human society, with many higher-level institutions compromised or destroyed by the legitimate demands of individuals (high salaries of baseball stars, perhaps).

Some features may be enhanced by positive interaction between levels. Stenotopy in marine invertebrates, for example, seems to offer advantages at both the individual level (when environments are stable) and at the species level (boosting rates of speciation by brooding larvae and enhancing possibilities for isolation relative to eurytopic species with planktonic larvae). Why then do eurytopic species still inhabit our oceans? Suppression probably occurs at the still higher level of clades, by the differential removal of stenotopic branches in major environmental upheavals that accompany frequent mass extinctions in the geological record.

If no negative effect from a higher level suppressed an advantageous lower-level phenomenon, then it might sweep through life. Sex in eukaryotic organisms may owe its prominence to unsuppressed positive interaction between levels. The advantages of sex have inspired a major debate among evolutionists during the past decade. Most authors seek traditional explanation in terms of benefit to organisms (50), for example, better chance for survival of some offspring if all are not Xeroxed copies of an asexual parent, but the genetically variable products of two individuals. Some, however, propose a spread by species selection, for example, by vastly higher speciation rates in sexual creatures (51).

The debate has often proceeded by mutual dismissal, each side proclaiming its own answers correct. Perhaps both are right, and sex predominates because two levels interact positively and are not suppressed at any higher level. No statement is usually more dull and unenlightening than the mediator's claim, "you're both right." In this case, however, we must adopt a different view of biological organization itself to grasp the mediator's wisdom—and the old solution, for once, becomes interesting in its larger implication. We live in a world with reductionist traditions, and do not react comfortably to notions of hierarchy. Hierarchical theories permit us to retain the value of traditional ideas, while adding substantially to them. They traffic in accretion, not substitution. If we abandoned the "either-or" mentality that has characterized arguments about units of selection, we would not only reduce fruitless and often acrimonious debate, but we would also gain a deeper understanding of nature's complexity through the concept of hierarchy.

A HIGHER DARWINISM?

What would a fully elaborated, hierarchically based evolutionary theory be called? It would neither be Darwinism, as usually understood, nor a smoothly continuous extension of Darwinism, for it violates directly the fundamental reductionist tradition embodied in Darwin's focus on organisms as units of selection.

Still, the hierarchical model does propose that selection operates on appropriate individuals at each level. Should the term "natural selection" be extended to all levels above and below organisms; there is certainly nothing unnatural about species selection. Some authors have extended the terms (48), while others, Slatkin for example (52), restrict natural selection to its usual focus upon individual organisms: "Species selection is analogous to natural selection acting on an asexual population" (52).

Terminological issues aside, the hierarchically based theory would not be Darwinism as traditionally conceived; it would be both a richer and a different theory. But it would embody, in abstract form, the essence of Darwin's argument expanded to work at each level. Each level generates variation among its individuals; evolution occurs at each level by a sorting out among individuals, with differential success of some and their progeny. The hierarchical theory would therefore represent a kind of "higher Darwinism," with the substance of a claim for reduction to organisms lost, but the domain of the abstract "selectionist" style of argument extended.

Moreover, selection will work differently on the objects of diverse levels. The phenomena of one level have analogs on others, but not identical operation. For example, we usually deny the effectiveness of mutation pressure at the level of organisms. Populations contain so many individuals that small biases in mutation rate can rarely establish a feature if it is under selection at all. But the analog of mutation pressure at the species level, directed speciation (directional bias toward certain phenotypes in derived species), may be a powerful agent of evolutionary trends (as a macroevolutionary alternative to species selection). Directed speciation can be effective (where mutation pressure is not) for two reasons: first, because its effects are not so easily swamped (given the restricted number of species within a clade) by differential extinction; second, because such phenomena as ontogenetic channeling in phyletic size increase suggest that biases in the production of species may be more prevalent than biases in the genesis of mutations.

Each level must be approached on its own, and appreciated for the special emphasis it places upon common phenomena, but the selectionist style of argument regulates all levels and the Darwinian vision is extended and generalized, not defeated, even though Darwinism, strictly constructed, may be superseded. This expansion may impose a literal wisdom upon that famous last line of *Origin of Species*, "There is grandeur in this view of life."

Darwin, at the centenary of his death, is more alive than ever. Let us continue to praise famous men.

REFERENCES

1. I have argued [*Nat. Hist.* **91**, 16 (April 1982)] that a third and larger theme captures the profound importance and intellectual power of Darwin's work in a more comprehensive way: his successful attempts to establish principles of reasoning for historical science. Each of his so-called "minor" works (treatises on orchids, worms, climbing plants, coral reefs, barnacles, for example) exhibits both an explicit and a covert theme—and the covert theme is a principle of reasoning for the reconstruction of history. The principles can be arranged in order of decreasing availability of information, but each addresses the fundamental issue: how can history be scientific if we cannot directly observe a past process: (i) If we can observe present processes at work, then we should accumulate and extrapolate their results to render the past. Darwin's last book, on the formation of vegetable mold by earthworms (1881), is also a treatise on this aspect of uniformitarianism. (ii) If rates are too slow or scales too broad for direct observation, then try to render the range of present results as stages of a single historical process. Darwin's first book on a specific subject, the subsidence theory of coral atolls (1842), is (in its covert theme) a disquisition on this principle. (iii) When single objects must be analyzed, search for imperfections that record constraints of inheritance. Darwin's orchid book (1862), explicitly about fertilization by insects, argues that orchids are jury-rigged, rather than well built from scratch, because structures that attract insects and stick pollen to them had to be built from ordinary parts of ancestral flowers. Darwin used all three principles to establish evolution as well: (i) observed rates of change in artificial selection, (ii) stages in the process of speciation displayed by modern populations, and (iii) analysis of vestigial structures in various organisms. Thus we should not claim that all Darwin's books are about evolution. Rather, they are all about the methodology of historical science. The establishment of evolution represents the greatest triumph of the method.
2. C. Darwin, *The Descent of Man* (Murray, London, ed. 2, 1889), p. 61.
3. G. J. Romanes, *Darwin, and After Darwin* (Longmans, Green, London, 1900), pp. 1–36.
4. Failure to recognize that all creationists accepted selection in this negative role let Eiseley to conclude falsely that Darwin had "borrowed" the principle of natural selection from his predecessor E. Blyth [L. Eiseley, *Darwin and the Mysterious Mr. X* (Dutton, New York, 1979)]. The Reverend William Paley's classical work *Natural Theology*, published in 1803, also contains many references to selective elimination.
5. By "random" in this context, evolutionists mean only that variation is not inherently directed towards adaptation, not that all mutational changes are equally likely. The word is unfortunate, but the historical tradition too deep to avoid.

6. E. D. Cope, *The Origin of the Fittest* (Appleton, New York, 1887).
7. L. G. Wilson, Ed., *Sir Charles Lyell's Scientific Journals on the Species Question* (Yale Univ. Press, New Haven, Conn., 1970), p. 369.
8. Darwin was convinced, for example, in part by reading a theological work arguing that extreme rapidity (as in the initial spread of Christianity) indicated a divine hand, that gradual and continuous change was the mark of a natural process [H. Gruber, *Darwin on Man* (Dutton, New York, 1974)].
9. C. Darwin, *The Structure and Distribution of Coral Reefs* (Smith, Elder, London, 1842).
10. ———, *The Formation of Vegetable Mould, Through the Action of Worms* (Murray, London, 1881).
11. The following works have done great service in identifying and correcting this confusion: G. C. Williams, *Adaptation and Natural Selection* (Princeton Univ. Press, Princeton, N.J., 1966); J. Maynard Smith, *The Evolution of Sex* (Cambridge Univ. Press, New York, 1978).
12. A persuasive case for Darwin's active interest in this subject and for his commitment to individual selection has been recently made by M. Ruse, *Ann. Sci.* **37**, 615 (1980).
13. C. Darwin, *On the Origin of Species* (Murray, London, 1859).
14. S. S. Schweber, *J. Hist. Biol.* **10**, 229 (1977).
15. S. Tax, Ed., *Evolution After Darwin* (Univ. of Chicago Press, Chicago, 1960), vols. 1–3.
16. J. Huxley, *Evolution, the Modern Synthesis* (Allen & Unwin, London, 1942).
17. For example: "The opposing factions became reconciled as the younger branches of biology achieved a synthesis with each other and with the classical disciplines: and the reconciliation converged upon a Darwinian center" (16, p. 25).
18. E. Mayr, *Systematics and the Origin of Species* (Columbia Univ. Press, New York, 1942); G. G. Simpson, *Tempo and Mode in Evolution* (Columbia Univ. Press, New York, 1944); B. Rensch, *Neuere Probleme der Abstammungslehre* (Enke, Stuttgart, 1947); G. L. Stebbins, *Variation and Evolution in Plants* (Columbia Univ. Press, New York, 1950).
19. S. J. Gould, in *The Evolutionary Synthesis*, E. Mayr and W. B. Provine, Eds. (Harvard Univ. Press, Cambridge, Mass., 1980), p. 153.
20. S. J. Gould, *Dobzhansky and the Modern Synthesis*, introduction to reprint of first (1937) edition of Th. Dobzhansky, *Genetics and the Origin of Species* (Columbia Univ. Press, New York, 1982).
21. D. Lack, *Darwin's Finches* (Harper Torchbook Edition, New York, 1960).
22. This statement appears as the first paragraph in the preface to (21).
23. E. Mayr, in *The Evolutionary Synthesis*, E. Mayr and W. B. Provine, Eds. (Harvard Univ. Press, Cambridge, Mass, 1980), p. 1.
24. S. Orzack, *Paleobiology* **7**, 128 (1981).
25. M. J. D. White, *ibid.*, p. 287.
26. G. L. Stebbins and F. J. Ayala, *Science* **213**, 967 (1981).
27. J. L. King and T. H. Jukes, *ibid.*, **164**, 788 (1969).

28. S. J. Gould, *Paleobiology* **6**, 119 (1980).
29. C. Darwin (*13*, p. 189). On the day before publication of the *Origin of Species*, T. H. Huxley wrote to Darwin (letter of 23 November 1859): "You load yourself with an unnecessary difficulty in adopting *Natura non facit saltum* so unreservedly."
30. S. J. Gould, *The Uses of Heresy*, introduction to the republication of the 1940 edition of R. Goldschmidt, *The Material Basis of Evolution* (Yale Univ. Press, New Haven, Conn., 1982).
31. P. Alberch, *Am. Zool.* **20**, 653 (1980).
32. M. J. D. White, *Modes of Speciation* (Freeman, San Francisco, 1978); G. L. Bush, S. M. Case, A. C. Wilson, J. L. Patton, *Proc. Natl. Acad. Sci. U.S.A.* **74**, 3942 (1977).
33. N. Eldredge and S. J. Gould, in *Models in Paleobiology*, T. J. M. Schopf, Ed. (Freeman, Cooper, San Francisco, 1972), p. 82; S. J. Gould and N. Eldredge, *Paleobiology* **3**, 115 (1977).
34. P. Williams, *Nature (London)* **293**, 437 (1981).
35. D'Arcy W. Thompson, *On Growth and Form* (Cambridge Univ. Press, New York, 1942).
36. S. J. Gould and R. C. Lewontin, *Proc. R. Soc. London Ser. B.* **205**, 581 (1979); G. V. Lauder, *Paleobiology* **7**, 430 (1981).
37. It is the concluding comment of chapter 6, and reads, in part: "It is generally acknowledged that all organic beings have been formed on two great laws—Unity of Type, and the Conditions of Existence. . . . Natural selection acts by either now adapting the varying parts of each being to its organic and inorganic conditions of life, or by having adapted them during long-past periods of time. . . . Hence, in fact, the law of the Conditions of Existence is the higher law; as it includes, through the inheritance of former adaptations, that of Unity of Type."
38. St. G. Mivart, *On the Genesis of Species* (Macmillan, London, 1871).
39. A. Seilacher, *Lethaio* **5**, 325 (1972).
40. S. J. Gould and E. S. Vrba, *Paleobiology*, in press.
41. R. C. Lewontin, *Annu. Rev. Ecol. Syst.* **1**, 1 (1970).
42. R. Dawkins, *The Selfish Gene* (Oxford Univ. Press, New York, 1976).
43. V. C. Wynne-Edwards, *Animal Dispersion in Relation to Social Behavior* (Oliver & Boyd, Edinburgh, 1962).
44. M. Ghiselin, *Syst. Zool.* **23**, 536 (1974); D. L. Hull, *Annu. Rev. Ecol. Syst.* **11**, 311 (1980).
45. W. F. Doolittle and C. Sapienza, *Nature (London)* **284**, 601 (1980); L. E. Orgel and F. H. C. Crick, *ibid.*, p. 604.
46. S. Wright, *Evolution and the Genetics of Population* (Univ. of Chicago Press, Chicago, 1968–1978), vols. 1–4.
47. S. M. Stanley, *Macroevolution* (Freeman, San Francisco, 1979); *Proc. Natl. Acad. Sci. U.S.A.* **72**, 646 (1975); also references in (*33*).
48. R. A. Fisher, *The Genetical Theory of Natural Selection* (Dover, ed. 2, New York, 1958), p. 50.
49. J. Maynard Smith, personal communication.

50. G. C. Williams, *Sex and Evolution* (Monographs in Population Biology, No. 8, Princeton Univ. Press, Princeton, N.J., 1975).
51. S. M. Stanley, *Science* **190**, 382 (1975).
52. M. Slatkin, *Paleobiology* 7, 421 (1981).
53. I thank Ernst Mayr, Philip Kitcher, Montgomery Slatkin, and Steven Stanley for their most helpful comments. Malcolm Kottler kindly pointed out to me the passage from David Lack quoted in (*21, 22*).

QUESTIONS FOR READING, RESPONDING, AND WRITING

Summarizing Main Points

1. Describe the differences between "directed speciation" and Darwin's original theory of "natural selection." List the difficulties in cause and effect recognized by modern biologists that beset "natural selection" that "direct speciation" solves, according to Gould.
2. Gould's essay argues that "we live in a world with reductionist traditions, and do not react comfortably to notions of hierarchy. Hierarchical theories permit us to retain the value of traditional ideas, while adding substantially to them. They traffic in accretion, not substitution." Explain Gould's statement in your own words. How does it enable Gould to include Darwin's theory of evolution within his own more sophisticated theory?

Analyzing Methods of Discourse

1. Gould claims that in "my partisan view, neither of Darwin's claims will survive in their strict formulation," but that "a restructured evolutionary theory will embody the essence of the Darwinian argument." Explain this statement in your own words. How does Gould's claim itself embody a "hierarchically extended" form of natural selection?
2. Gould chooses his examples very carefully. How does Gould's use of the human brain as an example of "nonadaptive consequences" reflect on his claim in question two above about reductionist versus hierarchical thinking? Why is it important that Gould introduces a comparison between the human brain and a computer in his example?

Focusing on the Field

1. Reread Gould's first and last paragraphs. Describe the relation between the two. How does Gould's statement that "the corporeal death of teachers counts for nothing—indeed, it should be celebrated" reflect on what he proposes about Darwin's theory? How does Gould's work here with Darwin and other individuals mirror his proposed theory of "directed speciation"?
2. Reread Gould's essay, taking special note of his references to textbooks. What is Gould's attitude toward textbooks? Does he consider them as examples of evolutionary change? At one point, Gould regrets a confusion of terminology "abetted by my own previous writings." Explain that confusion. How does Gould's own redefinition of many terms in this essay reflect both "differential death" and "differential frequency of speciation (selection by birth)"?

Writing Assignments

1. In a short paper that considers some of the questions above, argue that Gould's topic itself describes either a kind of "natural selection" or a "directed speciation" of scientific theories. In your essay, make sure you include a discussion of the reductionist versus hierarchical concepts.
2. In a short paper, compare this essay with Gould's "A Biological Homage to Mickey Mouse." How is each an essay on "evolutionary change"? Be sure to include a discussion of how Gould changes his writing techniques for his two separate audiences, popular for the Mickey Mouse essay and specialized for the Darwin.

Dennis Avery

U.S. FARM DILEMMA: THE GLOBAL BAD NEWS IS WRONG

Dennis Avery works as a senior agricultural analyst for the Bureau of Intelligence and Research in Washington, D.C. Avery has called his job—"keeping track of changing world agriculture in over 150 countries in the world"—one of the best in the world. According to Avery, "the pace of change and ferocity of competition in the agricultural world today are both greater than ever before." The essay reprinted below from *Science* reflects the challenge of Avery's job, while it also sounds a note of optimism in that ferociously competitive world. The essay appears in an expanded version in a U.S. Department of State publication, *Potential for Expanding World Food Production* (1985). Avery has also recently published *Rising World Food Self-Sufficiency: Temporary or Long Term?* (1985) for the State Department.

Born in Lansing, Michigan on October 24, 1936, Avery gained a B.A. with honors from Michigan State University and an M.S. from the University of Wisconsin. In 1966, he worked for the National Advisory Commission on Food and Fiber and he also spent five years on the Commodity Futures Trading Commission.

Summary. World agricultural production is at an all-time high and is climbing fast, especially in the developing countries. Even Africa has ample land and technology to feed its population, given more effective national policies. Higher agricultural output has been stimulated primarily by new technology, but also by investments and improved government policies. Constraints such as cropland shortage, soil erosion, and higher oil prices have been readily surmounted. High-technology agriculture has even overcome some major "systems breaks." Thus U.S. farmers will continue to face commercial surpluses of farm products in world markets in the years ahead.

America's farmers entered the 1980's feeling more prosperous and secure than at any time in modern history. They had just survived a furious onslaught of new farm technology, which helped to cut the proportion of farmers in the U.S. population to less than 4 percent. Overseas demand for food was being stimulated by economic growth. World trade in agricultural commodities had increased by some 10 million metric tons per year through the 1970's, and the United States had received most of the new business. Land values rose 50 percent in real terms during the decade.

If any farmers still had doubts about their future, the *Global 2000 Report (1)*, which was presented to President Carter in 1980 and which was based on the best projections of the U.S. government, predicted that world demand for food would increase vastly in the next 20 years, that real food prices would double, and that developed countries would have to supply most of the increase (1). Conservationists immediately expressed concern about the tremendous pressure this food demand would put on the world's cropland. Some even suggested that resulting deforestation and erosion might alter world climate. Improved farm technology looked like a slender hope; yield increases were tapering off and higher oil prices threatened to expose our dependence on petrochemical-based fertilizers and pesticides.

Today, just 5 years later, the world of the American farmer lies in disarray, with mounting surpluses, heavy farm debt, and massive farm subsidy costs. Demand for U.S. farm products is weak, land values are down, and farm policy seems to be at a dead end.

Yet the long-term need for food is as critical as ever. The population continues to increase. Erosion and deforestation are still being reported. The worst famine in Africa's history has caused thousands of deaths and has malnourished millions.

THE BAD NEWS IS WRONG

The bad news for the American farmer is that the global bad news is wrong. The world is not on the brink of famine or ecological disaster brought on by desperate food needs. According to the Food and Agricultural Organization, world agricultural output rose 25 percent between 1972 and 1982 to reach an all-time high. Farm output in less-developed countries (LDC's) rose 33 percent. Compared to an increase of only 18 percent in developed countries (DC's), where markets were already saturated. Per capita food production rose 16 percent in South America and 10 percent in Asia. Equally important, the annual rate of growth in farm output in LDC's has been rising—from 2.7 percent in the early 1970's to 3.3 percent in 1977–1982. (The *Global 2000 Report* projected an overall farm production growth of 2.2 percent, with most of it in the developed countries.) The growth rate in the LDC's would have been even higher if the averages had not been skewed by some dismal farm policy failures in countries with good agricultural resources, especially in sub-Saharan Africa.

The improved performance by farmers in LDC's is basically due to improved technology and stronger incentives to use it. The wheat and rice varieties of the Green Revolution are legend; genetics has gone on to produce the world's first hybrid wheat, cotton, rice, and rapeseed (2). Triticale, a hybrid of wheat and rye, outyields other cereals by 250 percent under certain unfavorable conditions. There are new sorghums for Africa that may have Green Revolution potential (3). Farmers in LDC's are also benefiting from better pest control technology, such as new low-volume pesticides and small electrostatic sprayers (4). Fertilizer use in LDC's has doubled and fertilizer production has tripled (5). LDC's tripled their real spending for farm research in the 1970's (6), and a global network of internationally funded farm research centers has been established with promising results.

Even Africa has the technology to double its crop yields and drought-proof its food supplies. The fact that this technology has not been more widely applied represents both a tragedy and an indictment of the farm and food policies followed by the African nations themselves.

The farm and food policies of the Third World are improving, however, prodded by population growth and, ironically, by the sharp declines in external financing for Third World governments. For the first time, the Third World is focusing on productivity rather than spending. The LDC's are also learning from the successful experiences of such nations as China and Malaysia. All of this is good news for the hungry of the world, but it will not ease the pressure on U.S. farmers.

CONSTRAINTS LESS SEVERE THAN EXPECTED

The constraints that were expected to limit food production during the 1980's and 1990's have been far less severe than almost anyone foresaw.

Cropland

One of the most obvious constraints is cropland. Most of the world's best and most accessible cropland is already in use. [Some nations, such as the Sudan, Zimbabwe, and Thailand, still have large areas of uncropped arable land, but much of it is far from consumer markets and lacks a transportation infrastructure (8).] Man still cannot create new land. However, many developments now under way have the same effect:

- New corn varieties are ready to double yields for small farmers in Central America and West Africa (7). New high-yielding varieties are raising the output of wheat, sorghum, cassava, peanuts, and most other crops.
- Irrigation has been expanding. Most of this is in the form of highly efficient, small-scale wells. Turkey, however, is building dams to irrigate 7 million hectares in the upper Euphrates Valley—an area equal to all the cropland in Nebraska.
- Wet areas are being drained. West Africa may become self-sufficient in rice production by shifting from upland to swamp rice production (this will require ditches, dikes, and disease control efforts) (9).
- Brazil is opening up 50 million hectares of acid soils on the Cerrado plateau; lime and phosphate make the area productive and competitive (10).
- New ways are being found to farm the world's 300 million hectares of black, sticky vertisol soils, which occur principally in India, Australia, and the Sudan (11). Much of this land was not cropped at all in the past; some is now being triple-cropped.
- Australia has developed the "ley" system for farming its semiarid land. An annual legume crop is substituted for the normal fallow year, sharply increasing the forage supply and fixing enough nitrogen to raise cereal yields in the ensuing year 15 to 30 percent. Overall, the ley system increases the productivity of dry lands 30 to 40 percent. Spain, Portugal, and the North African countries are trying to adapt similar farming systems to their millions of semiarid hectares. The systems require sophisticated management, but the long-term prospects are good.
- Argentina, which has huge tracts of prime land oriented to pasturing beef cattle, is gradually shifting to more intensive cropping of grains and oilseeds. The government last year abolished a 25 percent tax on nitrogen imports, and nitrogen use jumped 54 percent. Since 1980 the grain exports of Argentina have been increasing by about 1 million tons per year (12), and average yields of hybrid sunflower varieties have recently increased 25 percent (13).
- Peru has raised its rice production by 40 percent in each of the past 2 years with a new upland variety that tolerates the aluminum toxicity of the soils in the western Amazon Basin (14).
- Even the United States has been draining, terracing, and irrigating land and making other investments that add to our cropland base.

Erosion

Soil erosion has been both less severe and less detrimental to the world's crop yields than many expected. Conservation tillage and minimum tillage techniques have spread rapidly in many countries. Perhaps one-third of the Corn Belt is currently farmed with some form of conservation tillage (15), probably including most of the land at serious risk. The University of Minnesota Soil Science Department recently concluded that current rates of soil erosion, extended over the next 100 years, would cause irreplaceable losses in Corn Belt yields of less than 8 percent. Such losses would not be negligible, but seem certain to be dwarfed as we find even better conservation methods and improved production technologies over the next century.

Much of the world's cropland has a more serious erosion problem than the Corn Belt, of course. But raising the productivity of the best land relieves the pressure on fragile land. Steep and rocky land in New England and West Virginia has been relegated to pastures and forestry. Investments in drainage, land leveling, contour cultivation, and tree planting have made cropping safer on other land. The moldboard plow is disappearing from many farming regions.

In the developing world the productive potential of the best land has not been fully realized. Africa has the worst erosion problem in the world, yet plants a relatively small fraction of its arable land to crops in any given year. Traditional bush fallow periods range from 6 to 20 years. Population growth is now forcing shorter fallow periods, sharply increasing erosion rates. Most of Africa's food production takes place on millions of tiny subsistence farms with no fertilizer and seeds that are the horticultural equivalent of Indian corn. Overgrazing has been encouraged by communal landholding and by traditions that give status to owners of larger herds of undernourished animals. A new sorghum hybrid has been developed in the Sudan that triples the yields of traditional varieties in much of East Africa and that is much more drought-resistant (16). A new sorghum for the drier conditions of the Sahel apparently can double cereal yields there (3). The International Potato Research Center has achieved test yields as high as 50 metric tons per hectare in Ethiopia—but few people in that poor country know what a potato is.

Oil prices

Oil prices are constraining agriculture much less severely than was expected as recently as 1981. Real oil prices have already dropped one-third from their peak and may well decline further. More efficient techniques are being developed for such energy needs as crop drying. Low-volume pesticides are effective in applications of less than 100 grams per hectare. The prices of petrochemical-based fertilizers never rose as much as oil prices because of relatively cheap natural gas produced in association with oil. Fertilizer is often the most attractive market outlet for such gas. Indonesia has increased its annual production of fertilizer from a few

Fuel Cell tractor _ _ _ _ . .

thousand tons to 1.2 million tons in the past decade, and is using most of it on its own crops. Such major oil producers as Iran and Nigeria are still flaring off large quantities of gas (although Nigeria is now building one medium-sized plant).

RUNNING OUT OF FARM SCIENCE?

The pessimists assumed that the major discoveries which could sharply increase world agricultural output had already been made. Superficially, there was some justification for accepting this premise. Productivity gains in the United States and other developed countries had slowed in the late 1970's. However, progress in agricultural science has always been somewhat erratic. Over the longer term agricultural science has always moved forward in tandem with other areas of research.

Ongoing research throughout the world has produced a host of new developments that raise agricultural potential:

- The first genetically engineered vaccines. One prevents a major form of malaria, the other is the first fully safe weapon against foot-and-mouth disease (17). Both vaccines are made from the protein coatings of the disease organism, which triggers the immune reaction without risk of infection.
- The first viral insecticide, which attacks only the *Heliothis* genus of insects (corn earworm, tomato hornworm, tobacco budworm, soybean podworm) (18). The spores of the virus remain in the field after the worms have been killed, and attack any succeeding generations.
- A weed, *Stylosanthes capitata*, turned into a high-yielding forage legume for the huge acid savannas of Latin America (19). The plant outyields the best previous forage crops in the region by 25 percent.
- Isoacids, a new class of feed additives for dairy cows. They increase bacterial action and protein synthesis in bovine stomachs, raising milk production or reducing feed requirements. The product is already being test-marketed.
- Embryo transplant operations to boost the genetic impact of top-quality dairy cows. The cows are given fertility drugs to induce multiple ovulation, and the fertilized eggs are then transplanted into the ovaries of average cows for gestation. The supercow can thus produce dozens of calves per year instead of just one. Thousands of such operations are now being performed each year.
- Short-season hybrids that have extended corn production 250 miles nearer to the earth's poles in the past decade (20). The grain is now being grown as far north as central Manitoba. East Germany has developed a corn hybrid and plans to shift its hog feed from imported shelled corn to a domestically produced mix of corn and cobs (21).
- The first practical hybrids for wheat, rice, and cotton. Hybrid alfalfa

and rapeseed are at the field test stage. Triticale has recently outyielded the best wheats under difficult conditions, such as cool temperatures and acid soils (22).

- A system of agricultural research institutions for the Third World. The Consultative Group on International Agricultural Research (CGIAR) now has 14 research centers attacking farm production constraints. These centers produced the original dwarf wheat and rice varieties that launched the Green Revolution. The International Crops Research Institute for the Semi-Arid Tropics (ICRISAT), in Hyderabad, India, produced the potential breakthrough varieties of sorghum for Africa. The International Institute for Tropical Agriculture (IITA), at Ibadan, Nigeria, has produced a cassava that resists several endemic diseases, and thus outyields current varieties by three to five times. New peanut varieties from ICRISAT under test in India and Africa show yields several times greater than those of current varieties. The International Laboratory for Research on Animal Diseases (ILRAD), in Nairobi, Kenya, plans to launch a new vaccination program against Africa's tick-borne East Coast cattle fever within the next year. The International Center for Tropical Agriculture (CIAT), in Cali, Columbia, has produced varieties that double bean yields in Latin America. The International Maize and Wheat Center (CIMMYT), in Mexico City, has new white corn varieties that could nearly double yields in Central America and West Africa. The International Board for Plant Genetic Resources (IBPGR), in Rome, is preserving species. IITA is experimenting with alley cropping for African food production. The International Livestock Center for Africa (ILCA), in Ethiopia, is designing new farming systems that could sharply increase food production in Ethiopia's famine-wracked highlands. The latest miracle rice from the International Rice Research Institute (IRRI), in the Philippines, needs only two-thirds as much nitrogen and one-tenth as much pest protection as previous high-yielding varieties.
- Biotechnology, which may ultimately add more to farm productivity than any other development. Biotechnology has already produced the foot-and-mouth disease vaccine and high-fructose corn syrup. In the offing are such possibilities as ammonia-producing soil bacteria that farmers can plant to fertilize their crops, the first plant protein that is nutritionally complete for humans, crops with more built-in drought and pest resistance, and animals with better fat-to-lean ratios.

A SYSTEMS BREAK?

With productivity trends now so strongly positive, pessimistic arguments center on the possibility of "systems breaks"—sudden, sharp changes in external variables that affect agricultural success. In fact, however, high-technology farming has demonstrated tremendous capacity to adjust to sharp economic and environmental changes. It successfully overcame the oil crisis and its attendant escalation in fertilizer prices. It has surmounted the banning of the early persistent pesticides and their broad side-effects, such as the buildup of insect resistance.

Irrigation helps to drought-proof India and Bangladesh. Sudan's new sorghum seeds, in a year so dry that local varieties failed completely, yielded more than the local varieties do in a good year. Dams and drainage cut flood risks and convert swamps to cropland where necessary.

Technology can also broaden the range of production possibilities: Florida's most frost-prone citrus groves are going out of production; imports of frozen juice from Brazil now fill the gap when Florida's crop is hit, and the high prices that used to make the frost risk worthwhile no longer occur.

Neither drought in the Corn Belt nor massive crop failure in the Soviet Union nor the most severe drought in Africa's modern history have produced actual shortages of food in the world (although there have been regional shortages, complicated by transportation difficulties). Most significant, high-technology agriculture is producing more food per capita nearly everywhere in the world, despite the most rapid rates of growth in population and food demand in history.

High-technology agriculture could probably even take a significant degree of change in global climate in stride. Farmers already successfully cope with annual and seasonal weather variability that has far more impact on crop production than would even a major global cooling or warming trend. Any climatic change in the foreseeable future is likely to have only a moderate net effect on world cereal production, with some countries being helped and others hurt, but with the world retaining ample productive capability (23). Moreover, past changes in world climate have come over periods of centuries—ample time for breeding programs to adapt plants and animals to the new conditions. (There is no solid evidence that a global climatic change is taking place. Meteorologists say that, while overgrazing and deforestation play a part in the drought cycle of the Sahel, the broader African drought of 1983 and 1984 was too large to have been produced by human activities on the continent; rather, the drought was caused by a severe Southern Oscillation, a periodic global weather phenomenon that has often produced African droughts in the past.)

FAMINE IN THE MIDST OF PLENTY

Africa's famine proves only that population growth has pushed traditional African agriculture to the limits of its productivity, even in good years. Any drought there now means hunger. The inevitable next drought will mean more deaths unless African agriculture can be modernized.

Fortunately for Africa, much of the technology for modernization is already available. New varieties of corn, sorghum, peanuts, and cassava are raising yield potentials from the Sahel to Zimbabwe. New farming systems promise help for Ethiopia and Nigeria. Improved pest control and new varieties are raising West African yields of cowpeas tenfold (7). A leguminous tree native to Central America (*Leucaena leucocephala*) is well adapted to many arid parts of Africa; it can be planted for timber and erosion control and is very effective in alley cropping, in which the roots of these trees planted in rows fix nitrogen for food crops planted between them (24).

Improved seeds are relatively cheap, and so are moderate levels of fertilization and pest protection for most farmers getting efficient off-farm support. Farmers increasingly use them because they cut per-unit production costs and raise the productivity of land and labor. Tree planting and improved crop rotations may cost nothing except some family labor. Desperately poor farmers become less desperately poor by using such improved methods.

The most serious constraints on African agriculture are those imposed by the national policies of African nations. Most of these nations achieved independence in the 1960's, when the popular development model argued that LDC's could skip agricultural development and move straight into modern industrialism. Even the countries that were able to export industrial products, however, were soon spending most of their new earnings to import food for growing urban populations. Ghana nearly destroyed one of the continent's most productive export agricultures with low prices and state-run farms. Tanzania forcibly gathered its small family farmers into collectivized villages, where their productivity sagged. Ethiopia's tiny agricultural research station 10 years ago produced improved varieties of wheat and sorghum; with a little fertilizer, they were capable of doubling yields on the small highland farms. The Mengistu government sent the seeds and fertilizer to its new state farms, where yields with the new inputs were lower than those at the peasant farms without them.

Only recently have African governments begun to recognize the need for agricultural research and farmer incentives. African agriculture is likely to make significant strides in the next decade, partly because Africans are learning from past mistakes and partly because they no longer have the financial backing to continue making them.

DECLINING ADVANTAGE OF U.S. CROPLAND

American farmers have long believed that an important part of their competitive advantage lay in the nation's superior cropland and climate. Those factors now mean less because technology and investment are rapidly diminishing production constraints on other land in other countries.

Because of the advent of short-season corn, corn-growing potential can be expanded in Asia, Europe, and Latin America; even the Soviet Union is trying again to expand its corn production. The European Economic Community has greatly increased its output of rapeseed, sunflower seed, and field peas and other legume crops in order to displace soybean meal in its livestock feeds. Saudi Arabia produced 130,000 metric tons of wheat in 1975, and in 1985 is expected to produce 2.3 million metric tons. High wheat prices have turned the Saudi desert green. Palm oil production is rapidly expanding in the Pacific Rim to compete with soybean oil. Cassava from Asia competes with corn for the feed market. Sweden has a new seed treatment that makes wheat more winter-hardy, and already has its own grain surplus.

Agricultural output is becoming less a function of natural factors and more a function of the degree to which cost-effective technology is utilized. High land values today no longer mean farm prosperity; rather, like expensive machinery or chemicals, they just mean high production costs.

The real competitive advantages of U.S. farmers today lie in their high output per farmer and in the scientific and industrial infrastructure that supports them. The United States has the best-trained farm managers in the world—vitally important when a modern commercial farmer has to master a broad range of scientific, engineering, and business skills.

U.S. farmers also get exceptional support from off the farm. When export markets for feedstuffs expanded rapidly in the 1970's, the United States already had farm-to-market roads, railroads, farm equipment manufacturers, and food processors able to handle large volumes efficiently. The government had grain inspection and grading services with worldwide reputations. Agribusiness radically increased investment in unit trains, barges, and export elevators. (Canada and Argentina are still trying to get their export-handling capacity up to their farming potential—a decade after the opportunity appeared.) The United States also has outstanding research institutions, both government and private, to produce new technology.

These advantages will continue to be critically important, because world farm export markets will be fiercely competitive in the next decade. Production in LDC's is increasing rapidly because of technology, experience, and the need to feed populations and to service debts. This output is not only displacing imports but is producing some export competition as well. China, for example, is suddenly exporting cotton and corn.

Some middle-income countries, like Brazil and Argentina, are also under strong debt pressures to maximize their export potential. Others are doing it just to achieve economic growth for their swelling populations.

Finally, most of the DC's still maintain farm subsidy programs that stimulate additional farm output. The most significant of these is in the European Economic Community, which has increased the tax base for its farm subsidies by 40 percent in the last year and which will take Spain and Portugal into membership in 1986. Wheat yields in the community increased 23 percent in 1984, field pea harvests in France have jumped 50 percent in 2 years, and farm productivity in Spain could readily increase by one-third in the next few years.

OUTLOOK FOR THE U.S. FARMER

In the longer term, population increases and economic growth will increase the overall market for farm products. Protein foods will continue to increase their importance in international trade. New products will emerge—just as the soybean emerged to profitably occupy 50 million hectares of cropland. The agricultures that meet these emerging demands are headed for higher productivity, increasing affluence, and broader opportunity, but they are also headed for more competition.

The U.S. farmer is in an awkward position to compete for this long-term market growth. The strength of the dollar has raised U.S. farm price supports in recent years by perhaps 35 percent above the levels Congress thought it was establishing. This has provided a profit umbrella for competing farmers all over the world. (It may be technically impossible to effectively administer dollar-denominated price supports in today's world of volatile exchange rates.)

The U.S. share of world farm export markets has dropped significantly, in part because of our long-term policy of storing surpluses rather than selling them. In the past several years, the payment-in-kind (PIK) program cut U.S. production, further encouraging competitors. Grain can now be imported into the United States more cheaply than it can be bought here, while the annual cost of U.S. farm programs has soared from less than $1 billion to about $15 billion per year.

The current mechanisms of the General Agreement on Tariffs and Trade are weak, and ill-suited to defending free trade for farmers. Renouncing farm exports, however, would mean renouncing export earnings—recently about 25 percent of U.S. farm income. This would cost hundreds of thousands of jobs on U.S. farms and in farm-related industries, while worsening the U.S. balance of trade and weakening economic growth.

The U.S. farm policy of the future must be geared to competing for buyers who have more alternative sources of supply than ever—their own agricultures, competing agricultures all over the globe, and more synthetics and substitutes. This means that our policies must be designed to reduce costs per unit and to provide farmers with the latest technology. Strong efforts are also needed to lower trade barriers; this will not only be good for U.S. farmers but will help the world to benefit from fuller utilization of global comparative advantages. Researchers need to look at farmland not only in the traditional sense but also as a potential source of biomass and the various kinds of complex chemical feedstocks that could be produced from genetically engineered plant life.

One thing seems certain: the price supports, land diversion, and storage programs that have dominated U.S. farm policy for the past 50 years work against the U.S. farmer in a world of high technology and rising productivity.

REFERENCES AND NOTES

1. *The Global 2000 Report to the President* (Government Printing Office, Washington, D.C., 1980).
2. G. Sollenberger, *Furrow* **90** (No. 1), 10 (January–February 1985).
3. *At. ICRISAT* (December 1984), p. 1.
4. A. K. Stapleton, paper presented at the 1984 World Bank Agricultural Symposium, Washington, D.C.
5. *International Trade in the Fertilizer Sector* (United Nations Conference on Trade and Development, New York, 1984).
6. *IFPRI Rep.* **4** (No. 2), 1 (May 1982).
7. M. Read, personal communication.
8. "Sudan agricultural sector survey" (Report 1836a-SU, World Bank, Washington, D.C., 1979); "Zambia: Policy options and strategies for growth" (Report 4764-ZA, World Bank, Washington, D.C., 1984); T. Slayton, "Thailand annual agricultural situation revisited" (8 July 1985).
9. "Liberian agricultural sector review" (Report 4200-LBR, World Bank, Washington, D.C., 1984); "Guinea agricultural sector review" (Report GUI 4672, World Bank, Washington, D.C., 1984); "Sierra Leone agricultural sector review" (Report 4469-SL, World Bank, Washington, D.C., 1984).
10. W. J. Goedert, E. Lobato, E. Wagner, *Besq. Agropecu. Bras.* **15** (1980); P. Sanchez, personal communication.
11. *News from CGIAR* **1** (No. 2), 1 (September 1981).
12. "World grain situation and outlook" (Foreign Agriculture Circular FAS FG-7-85, Department of Agriculture, Washington, D.C., 1985).
13. J. D. Ahalt, "Argentina annual agricultural situation report" (9 March 1985).
14. E. Schumacher, *New York Times*, 11 August 1983, p. A-2; J. D. Flood, personal communication.
15. National Conservation Tillage Information Center, *1984 Conservation Tillage Survey* (Department of Agriculture, Washington, D.C., 1984).
16. *News from CGIAR* **2** (No. 4), 4 (December 1982); A. Bertrand, personal communication.

17. *U.S. Dept. Agric. Newsmakers* (September 1981), p. 2.
18. R. Enlow, *Agric. Res.* **32** (No. 5), 12 (January 1984).
19. *CIAT Int.* **3** (No. 1), 1 (June 1984).
20. J. L. Geadelman, personal communication.
21. W. P. Huth, *Grain Feed Annu. Rep. Ger. Democr. Rep.* (11 February 1985),
    p. 1.
22. "International Maize and Wheat Improvement Center Annual Report, 1984"
    (CIMMYT, Mexico City, 1985).
23. Research Directorate, "Crop yields and climate change to the year 2000"
    (National Defense University, Washington, D.C., 1980).
24. *News from CGIAR* **4** (No. 4), 5 (December 1984).

QUESTIONS FOR READING, RESPONDING, AND WRITING

Summarizing Main Points

1. According to Avery, what factors formerly gave Americans a competitive advantage in the world farm market? Why, according to Avery, have those factors become less important? What factors does Avery think might currently provide American farmers with a competitive advantage?
2. What goals does Avery set for future farm policy? What changes does he advocate in order to achieve those goals?

Analyzing Methods of Discourse

1. Though the title of his essay is "U.S. Farm Dilemma," Avery spends the first two-thirds of his essay amassing examples of technological advances that have increased productivity in less-developed countries before discussing U.S. farmers and farm policy. Why do you suppose Avery structures his argument in this way? Do you see any relationship between the arrangement of his essay and his position on future U.S. farm policy?
2. What do you suppose might be his purpose in the summary at the beginning of the essay? After reading the essay, look back at the summary. What information does it leave out and why?

Focusing on the Field

1. Though Avery uses a vocabulary that seems specifically to address an audience familiar with farm science, farm policy, and their histories, he does seem aware of the nonprofessional reader and is willing to be accommodating so that his terms become less of a mystery to that reader. Locate places in which Avery provides either definitions of difficult words or other clues to their approximate meanings.
2. Though Stephen Jay Gould's "Darwinism" and Avery's "U.S. Farm Dilemma" are on entirely different subjects, both essays were published in the same professional journal—*Science*. Given this fact, list any similarities you can find in the authors' respective presentations, strategies of development, organization, or language.

Writing Assignments

1. Avery mentions the "Green Revolution" several times in his essay. Research this topic and write an essay in which you define the relationship between that revolution and Avery's presentation of the current world farm situation.

2. Read Michael Korda's "When Business Becomes Blood Sport." Write an essay in which you evaluate Avery's presentation of, and final position on, the U.S. farm dilemma in terms of the "survival strategies" Korda describes. According to Korda's criteria, do you think U.S. farmers will survive the eighties?

F·O·U·R

BUSINESS AND ECONOMICS
Careers/Finance/Corporate Management/ Retailing/ Marketing/Ethics

Much of his [the business executive's] writing presents judgments that require fine, subtle expression: an estimate of the value of a distinguished colleague, an analysis of a budget that may determine the success or failure of a project. . . .

Helen J. Tichy

Whatever your program in college, be sure to include courses in writing. . . . Managers must constantly write instructions, reports, and memos, letters, and survey conclusions.

James A. Newman and Ray Alexander, *Climbing the Corporate Matterhorn*

No man but a blockhead ever wrote for anything but money!

Samuel Johnson, from Boswell's *Life*

I use a simple black book with a tab for every executive who reports to me. They all file a written plan of what they intend to achieve in the next three months. I expect them to do the same with *their* people.

They all know they're going to report back at the end of the quarter and tell how they did. They'll be embarrassed if they have to say they didn't achieve a thing. The process forces performance. When I left Ford Motor Company, it was making $1.8 billion annual profit. That had something to do with the written quarterly plans.

In a big company or a small one, goals must be written down clearly and concisely.

Lee Iacocca

I could be the best buyer in the world and have the most magnificent merchandise coming in, but I'd be worthless if I couldn't excite the department managers and salespeople about it. My newsletters and memos have to be enthusiastic and appealing.

Laura Svatek, Neiman-Marcus

Every business article, report, or letter is directed to an individual or a well-defined group of individuals. The writer adjusts himself to the point of view of his audience. A technical article by a structural engineer to be published in an engineering journal would be out of place in *The Saturday Evening Post*. The same principle applies to individuals. A collection letter to a highly rated debtor differs from a letter to a poor risk. A sales letter to a jobber differs from a letter presenting the same product to a female customer. The reader's age, sex, occupation, and environment must be considered in establishing the most appropriate point of view.

Charles Chandler Parkhurst, *Modern Executive's Guide to Effective Communication*

. . . a person who can write clearly and gracefully goes out into the world with an uncommon skill. One important reason working business people and professionals do not achieve what their potential might otherwise allow is their inability to communicate, to get their good ideas down on paper in a way that lets others understand those ideas quickly and easily. In every survey that asks business people what subjects they wish they had studied more carefully, their first or second answer is always communication.

Joseph Williams

Whatever a CPA may do in behalf of his clients, the end result must always be communicated, usually in writing, sometimes orally. However communicated, it is essential that there be clarity and specificity, unblemished by incoherence, disunity or ambiguity, untarnished by grammatical, syntactical, or rhetorical errors. We have sought to recognize this essential role of written and spoken English by declaring that those who cannot perform above a minimum threshold should be denied admission to the profession.

Robert H. Roy and James H. MacNeill

Let's go back to the subject of English a moment. Of all subjects none is potentially more useful—as Peter Drucker has remarked, the most vocational course a future businessman can take is one in the writing of poetry or short stories.

William H. Whyte, Jr., *The Organization Man*

Communication is the essence of managerial procedure. It is the focal point of executive action, is central to the control and survival of organizations, and is a requisite to effective management. If there were one activity which describes the function of a manager, it would be communication.

Philip V. Lewis, *Organizational Communications:*
The Essence of Effective Management

The biggest untapped source of net profits for American business lies in the sprawling, edgeless area of written communication where waste cries out for management action. Daily, this waste arises from the incredible amount of dull, difficult, obscure, and wordy writing that infests plants and offices. Such writing slows and complicates mass communication both in and out of the company.

Langley Carleton Keyes, *Harvard Business Review*

Some industrial corporations, in an effort to eliminate the losses caused by oral misunderstandings, maintain signs upon their walls that say: "Put it in writing." Such a sign refers partly to interdepartmental letters and memoranda, but it also refers to written as opposed to oral reports. It indicates the growing realization of the superiority of a permanent record suitable for filing away.

Philip B. McDonald, *English and Science*

Peter Cohen

WRITING COUNTS
The Gospel According to the Harvard
Business School

"**O**f all the instruments of fear and terror at the disposal of the Business School, none can match a WAC's effectiveness in reducing a healthy first-year body to a mess of gastric disorders, fluttering eyelids, and recurring nightmares. . . ." The "WAC" here is a "Written Analysis of Cases"; the "Business School" is Harvard's; and the "first-year body" is Peter Cohen's, the author of *The Gospel According to the Harvard Business School,* from which the following selection is taken.

Born in 1939 in Switzerland, where he now makes his home, Cohen earned a B.A. at Princeton University, before going on for an advanced business degree. In his book, which came out of a journal he kept while at Harvard, Cohen gives the reader a "tour" of an experience, the pressure of which meant for him not only business case analysis but a kind of self-analysis as well. He describes the stringent requirements of the WAC—from its final presentation on "special green paper on which it is almost impossible to erase" to its due date, "every other Saturday by 6 P.M.," at the stroke of which the university watchman closes the WAC box so that papers turned in even a minute late end up on top of it "at a full grade less." Such pressure takes its toll not only on Cohen's own body as the WAC becomes an obsession, but on the student body as well. The pressure of the WAC creates camaraderie but turns it to competition, for each student must ultimately struggle through the WAC alone. The reader may imagine that Cohen speaks for all his fellow students when he writes, "You truly want this Harvard degree, but it is getting a little costly." Apparently, for Cohen, the degree was worth the cost: He did receive his M.B.A. and lived to tell the tale.

WEEK OF DECEMBER 2

Monday: Of all the instruments of fear and terror at the disposal of the Business School, none can match a WAC's effectiveness in reducing a healthy first-year body to a mess of gastric disorders, fluttering eyelids, and recurring nightmares that make the poor bastard jump up in the middle of the night screaming for Mother.

A set of instructions told us at the beginning of the year:

> The substance of the WAC course is the process of analysis. It is useful to think of the evolution of a WAC report, the product of that process, as having three related but separate stages. The first stage or phase is the actual analysis of the assigned case, leading to the development of a plan of action. The second phase is the selection and organization of ideas that have been developed in the analysis in preparation for the third stage, which is the presentation of the analysis in written form.

In written form (typewritten) and on special green paper on which it is almost impossible to erase. Due: Every other Saturday, in a brown, clearly labeled envelope, at the West End of Baker Library by 6 P.M.

We picked up a twenty-page case at Baker 20 today, of which the cover sheet contained the following information:

Written Assignment #5
December 14,19—

HARVARD UNIVERSITY
GRADUATE SCHOOL OF BUSINESS
ADMINISTRATION
George F. Baker Foundation

WRITTEN ANALYSIS OF CASES
Written Assignment #5
The Petra Cement Company EA-G 265

Assignment: What should Petra Cement do? Why?
Word Limit: 1500 words, excluding exhibits if any
Due: West End of Baker Library by 6:00 P.M., on Saturday, December 14, 19—

Wednesday: As far as you understand it, a committee of executives recommends that Petra's new plant should be built at Kuta. Unless Petra's bid for the nearby river dam fails. Then the plant should be built at Pelam. Petra's economic department, on the other hand, recommends Verna as the plant site best suited—bid or no bid. As for the Kuta site—there are rumors that Petra's major competitor, the Davon Cement

Corporation, is going to build a plant at Belton. And Belton is only twelve miles from Kuta.

Six pages of exhibits and two appendixes provide the numbers.

Thursday: The first discussions are springing up. Quietly, in small groups of friends. Insights into a WAC are too valuable to be wasted on just anybody.

The consensus seems to be that Petra must do everything to win the bid for the river dam. Because whoever wins it will have to build so much cement production capacity that he will dominate the entire region. It's an all-or-nothing proposition. Compared to winning the bid, the problem of site selection seems of secondary importance. But what if they *do* win the bid?

Friday: The discussions are becoming more frequent, louder, more intense. People are hoping to get a lead they can follow over the weekend. Especially those who can't type and have to hand their drafts to the typists early.

Discussion is permitted but, at the same time, everybody is supposed to write the WAC on their own. So even among friends, the discussion always stays kind of cautious, general, almost superficial.

Maguire and Erwinger think that Pelam is out of the question because of a bad geological structure there. Maguire is going to try with a decision tree. He works extremely fast and probably will be done by the end of the weekend. But he is an exception.

Saturday and Sunday: You've been able to take the case apart all right but you can't, for all you try, put it back together. It's like sitting in the front row of a CinemaScope movie. Everything melts into one big blur.

You have spent Saturday and almost all of Sunday, but no progress, except a wad of yellow note paper filled with beginnings of beginnings and worthless diagrams.

Everything is related to everything else in this bloody case. By picking up one tiny piece you pick up the whole mess. A real merry-go-round. There is nothing so demoralizing as to try hard and get nowhere. The incredibly tight rules of a WAC strangle your thoughts. No leaps of faith allowed; no grandiose assumptions permitted. You've got to slug it out, covering all your bases.

THE WEEK FOLLOWING

Monday: In order to be done in time, you are forced to spend at least an hour a day on the WAC—in addition to the three daily cases. You are thinking Petra Cement as you brush your teeth. You think Petra Cement as you sip your coffee, as you walk to school. You think Petra Cement while you are supposed to listen to class discussion. You eat Petra Cement, you sleep Petra Cement, you've got Petra Cement oozing out of your ears.

Tuesday: WAC classes, like so many other aspects of our life as a Section, are caught in the conflicting demands of competition and co-operation. And while, earlier in the year, co-operation had seemed to win out, the growing familiarity with our surroundings is loosening the bond of fear, is tipping the scales in favor of competition. The anonymous mass that used to offer shelter from the school's pressures is breaking up into a federation of groups, an alliance of cliques—each with its distinct traits, each with its own ambitions.

Especially in WAC class—a regular class held about a week before each WAC is due—people no longer make a real effort. WAC classes have turned into a ritual in which everybody pays lip service to a goal that nobody is really interested in attaining. As a result, WAC classes move along slowly, haltingly, frequently retracing their steps, irresolutely searching for a promising direction.

Still, a good number of people do speak up. Some because called on by Mr. O'Neil, but most of them voluntarily. Their motives too diverse to allow for a clear explanation. For some it's the habit of impressing others. For others it's a securing of flanks by trying to assure themselves of the good will of Mr. O'Neil. (Although no grade is given in WAC for class participation.) For still others it's a genuine interest in the case or a true or naive generosity. Because of such people, even the slowest, most difficult WAC class is not without its meaning, its helpful bits and pieces of information.

Today's class on Petra Cement was no exception.

Wednesday: The way things are going, or rather the way they aren't going, you'll have to make some real wild assumptions. But that's taking your chances. Because No. 13 may not like it.

No. 13 is your WAC reader; the girl who has been assigned to read and grade your WACs. All you've seen and all you probably will ever see of her is the comments she makes in the margins. She writes neatly and straight up. The shapes of her letters are soft and round, and there is an elegant down swing to her "gs." Like somebody tall and cautious with a lovely, symmetrical face.

As it is, you're not exactly getting love letters from her. The first comments were devastating. But once you began to force your thoughts through the rigor of the WAC-type analysis—dressing each one of them up in a three-piece suit with tie—things began to look up. Up to about a P+ (Pass Plus). And that's the level on which No. 13 and you have continued to carry on your mute conversation. She, meticulous but fair. You, gnashing your teeth and trying harder.

Friday, morning: Time is running out. You can't afford to miss today's classes but you can't really afford to go, either. So you won't go. The WAC doesn't let you.

Midnight: It's no longer funny. You're getting clutched. You *must* begin to write if you want to have it done by tomorrow evening. Verna, Kuta, Pelam . . . if, if, if . . . a haze of ifs.

You truly want this Harvard degree, but it is getting a little costly.

Saturday, three in the morning: The stream of cars outside has slowed to a trickle. The late, late show must be over. There isn't a sound—except for your typewriter. You hope it won't wake up anybody.

Everything is kind of light and automatic now. The anger is giving way to detachment. A numbing indifference is setting in. Still, you have no beginning, but decide to go ahead and write anyway. You can't do better than your best and with a little bit of luck you'll come out in the right place.

Eight in the morning: Finally to bed a little after three. After you'd gone just far enough to make sure that you would have something to hand in.

Some people go straight through the whole night. But after a day and half a night of intense concentration you just couldn't go any further. These four and a half hours of sleep have somewhat refreshed. And now, on to finishing the rough draft.

Noon: You're getting there. But the finished draft is still three pages too long.

Five o'clock: Night is falling. You're done. Done and done for. It reads coherently, amazing considering the circumstances.

You proofread and staple it together. You slip it into the carefully labeled, heavy brown envelope. Outside it's cold—even through the coat—and the banks of the Charles lie totally deserted.

At the West End of Baker Library it's the big circus. People are popping out of the twilight, queueing up at the slot in the basement window. You hear the hissing sound as the envelopes go down the chute and the fat "plop" as they fall into the WAC box.

Five-thirty: There is a long line of headlights and idling motors. With people jumping out, dropping off their envelopes, jumping back in. People start arriving at a trot. Five more minutes.

Six: Rien ne va plus! The university watchman, down in the cellar, has closed the box. There is the sound of diminishing footsteps, and soon the street is restored to its desolate quiet, typical of late-winter evenings. Some people will undoubtedly be coming, but their papers will end up on top of the closed WAC box, at a full grade less.

Ten after six: It isn't easy to get your bearings in the dense smoke, the din of elated voices, the swirling crowd. What used to be the lounge of Gallatin Hall has been converted into a pub, has been divided into some six alcoves with a large round table in each, all the alcoves opening toward the center of the room where there is a bar. The alcoves make the large room quite cozy and especially after a WAC, the place is jam-packed.

McGrady's massive, balding head, set on an equally massive six-foot frame, like a bell tower, signals the location of Section B. Their table is loaded with brimful pitchers of beer and they are in the sorry sort of state to which only a WAC can reduce people. Torn and soiled slacks, the sort most suitable to spend a night in at the typewriter; shirts as crumpled as yesterday's newspaper; the faces marked by a day's growth of beard.

"Worst paper I ever wrote," Holton claims with a silly grin, to which O'Mara adds that "an outfit with that kind of an operation . . ." but somehow gets sidetracked. Somebody lets off a sharp burp and the only thing that gets finished in this conversation is the beer. McGrady feels an urge to play a game of darts but nobody can really warm up to the idea. Baxter, meanwhile, hangs slumped over in his chair and somebody, for about the sixth time, says he has to go, he really has to go home now . . .

And in a couple of weeks, usually at the end of an eleven-ten class, our two SA reps will walk in, each with an armful of brown envelopes, and the Section, like a flock of geese, will go: "WAC, WAC, WAC." The brown envelopes will fly through the air, landing amid a flurry of excited hands.

Petra Cement! You will look frantically for the little white slip, and you don't care what Petra Cement should or could have done, what your mistakes were, or the flaws in your argument, or whatever No. 13 has got you down for; all you want to know is that she put at least a P (for Pass) on the slip; that you have made it past yet another one, and that—thank God—five WACs down. Only six to go.

QUESTIONS FOR READING, RESPONDING, AND WRITING

Summarizing Main Points

1. Why do you suppose Cohen doesn't present his reader with his finished WAC analysis?
2. At what point in the essay does camaraderie among the students give way to competition? Why?

Analyzing Methods of Discourse

1. Cohen states his main point in the first sentence of the essay. What is the relationship between the rest of the essay and that first sentence?
2. Reread the set of instructions for the WAC and note its division into phases. Are there corresponding phases that Cohen goes through in suffering through the WAC? If so, describe them. If not, why not?

Focusing on the Field

1. Until the Friday morning before the due date, Cohen follows a fairly regular, but not rigid system of journal entries—usually, but not always, making one per day. Yet starting Friday morning, his entries become more and more frequent. What point is Cohen trying to make with this strategy? Now look at the sentence structure in Cohen's entries. Do you notice an equivalent change?
2. Why do you suppose Cohen's essay is presented as a series of journal entries? Consider the differences between the WAC guidelines and the "guidelines" a person uses when writing in a journal. Also, consider the audience for each type of "essay."

Writing Assignments

1. Using the stringent WAC guidelines, write an analysis of Cohen's process of writing the WAC. The question you will seek to answer is: Should Cohen stay in Harvard Business School? Why or why not? Your essay should be "1500 words, excluding exhibits, if any."
2. Read Michael Korda's "When Business Becomes Blood Sport." Write an essay in which you evaluate the Harvard Business School WAC course in terms of the qualities necessary for survival in the business world of the eighties that Korda describes. Does this course teach "survival"?

Joan Didion

ON THE MALL

Essayist, novelist, screenwriter, and editor, Joan Didion was born in Sacramento, California. Upon graduating from the University of California at Berkeley in 1956, Didion received *Vogue's Prix de Paris* award and moved to New York, where she spent the next seven years as an editor for *Vogue.* A frequent contributor to the *National Review* and *The Saturday Evening Post,* as well as *Vogue,* Didion still managed to write her first novel, for which she was awarded a Bread Loaf Fellowship in fiction. She has since returned to California, living now with her husband, writer John Gregory Dunne, in Los Angeles. Aside from her novels, *Run River* (1963), *Play It as It Lays* (1970), and *A Book of Common Prayer* (1978), and her essays, collected in *Slouching Towards Bethlehem* (1968) and *The White Album* (1979), from which "On the Mall" is taken, Didion has collaborated with her husband on screenplays, including the 1976 version of *A Star Is Born.* In all her work, Didion manages to blend the seemingly disparate forms of autobiography, fiction, journalism, and commentary into a style that, though it owes to "new journalism" (see the headnote for Tom Wolfe in "Humanities"), still remains uniquely her own. In the following selection, Didion combines personal reminiscence, facts, narrative, history, and "shopping-center theory" to make her essay, like the malls themselves, more than the sum of its parts.

They float on the landscape like pyramids to the boom years, all those Plazas and Malls and Esplanades. All those Squares and Fairs. All those Towns and Dales, all those Villages, all those Forests and Parks and Lands. Stonestown, Hillsdale, Valley Fair, Mayfair, Northgate, Southgate, Eastgate, Westgate, Gulfgate. They are toy garden cities in which no one lives but everyone consumes, profound equalizers, the perfect fusion of the profit motive and the egalitarian ideal, and to hear their names is to recall words and phrases no longer quite current. Baby Boom. Consumer Explosion. Leisure Revolution. Do-It-Yourself Revolution. Backyard Revolution. Suburbia. "The Shopping Center," the Urban Land Institute could pronounce in 1957, "is today's extraordinary retail business evolvement. . . . The automobile accounts for suburbia, and suburbia accounts for the shopping center."

It was a peculiar and visionary time, those years after World War II to which all the Malls and Towns and Dales stand as climate-controlled monuments. Even the word "automobile," as in "the automobile accounts for suburbia and suburbia accounts for the shopping center," no longer carries the particular freight it once did: as a child in the late Forties in California I recall reading and believing that the "freedom of movement" afforded by the automobile was "America's fifth freedom." The trend was up. The solution was in sight. The frontier had been reinvented, and its shape was the subdivision, that new free land on which all settlers could recast their lives *tabula rasa*. For one perishable moment there the American idea seemed about to achieve itself, via F.H.A. housing and the acquisition of major appliances, and a certain enigmatic glamour attached to the architects of this newfound land. They made something of nothing. They gambled and sometimes lost. They staked the past to seize the future. I have difficulty now imagining a childhood in which a man named Jere Strizek, the developer of Town and Country Village outside Sacramento (143,000 square feet gross floor area, 68 stores, 1000 parking spaces, the Urban Land Institute's "prototype for centers using heavy timber and tile construction for informality"), could materialize as a role model, but I had such a childhood, just after World War II, in Sacramento. I never met or even saw Jere Strizek, but at the age of 12 I imagined him a kind of frontiersman, a romantic and revolutionary spirit, and in the indigenous grain he was.

I suppose James B. Douglas and David D. Bohannon were too.

I first heard of James B. Douglas and David D. Bohannon not when I was 12 but a dozen years later, when I was living in New York, working for *Vogue*, and taking, by correspondence, a University of California Extension course in shopping-center theory. This did not seem to me eccentric at the time. I remember sitting on the cool floor in Irving Penn's studio and reading, in *The Community Builders Handbook*, advice from James B. Douglas on shopping-center financing. I recall staying late in my pale-blue office on the twentieth floor of the Graybar Building to memorize David D. Bohannon's parking ratios. My "real" life was to sit in this office and describe life as it was lived in Djakarta and Caneel Bay and in the great chateaux of the Loire Valley, but my dream life was to put together a Class-A regional shopping center with three full-line department stores as major tenants.

That I was perhaps the only person I knew in New York, let alone on the Condé Nast floors of the Graybar Building, to have memorized the distinctions among "A," "B," and "C" shopping centers did not occur to me (the defining distinction, as long as I have your attention, is that an "A," or "regional," center has as its major tenant a full-line department store which carries major appliances; a "B," or "community," center has as its major tenant a junior department store which does not carry major appliances; and a "C," or "neighborhood," center has as its major tenant only a supermarket): my interest in shopping centers was in no way casual. I did want to build them. I wanted to build them because I had fallen into the habit of writing fiction, and I had it in my head that a couple of good centers might support this habit less taxingly than a pale-blue office at *Vogue*. I had even devised an original scheme by which I planned to gain enough capital and credibility to enter the shopping-center game: I would lease warehouses in, say, Queens, and offer Manhattan delicatessens the opportunity to sell competitively by buying cooperatively, from my trucks. I see a few wrinkles in this scheme now (the words "concrete overcoat" come to mind), but I did not then. In fact I planned to run it out of the pale-blue office.

James B. Douglas and David D. Bohannon. In 1950 James B. Douglas had opened Northgate, in Seattle, the first regional center to combine a pedestrian mall with an underground truck tunnel. In 1954 David D. Bohannon had opened Hillsdale, a forty-acre regional center on the peninsula south of San Francisco. That is the only solid bio I have on James B. Douglas and David D. Bohannon to this day, but many of their opinions are engraved on my memory. David D. Bohannon believed in preserving the integrity of the shopping center by not cutting up the site with dedicated roads. David D. Bohannon believed that architectural setbacks in a center looked "pretty on paper" but caused "customer resistance." James B. Douglas advised that a small-loan office could prosper in a center only if it were placed away from foot traffic, since people who want small loans do not want to be observed getting them. I do not recall whether it was James B. Douglas or David D. Bohannon or someone else altogether who passed along this hint on how to paint the lines around the parking spaces (actually this is called "striping the lot," and the spaces are "stalls"): make each space a foot wider than it need be—ten feet, say, instead of nine—when the center first opens and business is slow. By this single stroke the developer achieves a couple of important objectives, the appearance of a popular center and the illusion of easy parking, and no one will really notice when business picks up and the spaces shrink.

Nor do I recall who first solved what was once a crucial center dilemma: the placement of the major tenant vis-à-vis the parking lot. The dilemma was that the major tenant—the draw, the raison d'être for the financing, the Sears, the Macy's, the May Company—wanted its customer to walk directly from car to store. The smaller tenants, on the other hand, wanted that same customer to *pass their stores* on the way from the car to, say, Macy's. The solution to this conflict of interests was actually very simple: *two major tenants*, one at each end of a mall. This is called "anchoring the mall," and represents seminal work in shopping-center theory. One thing you will note about shopping-center theory is that you could have thought of it yourself, and a course in it will go a long way toward dispelling the notion that business proceeds from mysteries too recondite for you and me.

A few aspects of shopping-center theory do in fact remain impenetrable to me. I have no idea why the Community Builders' Council ranks "Restaurant" as deserving a Number One (or "Hot Spot") location but exiles "Chinese Restaurant" to a Number Three, out there with "Power and Light Office" and "Christian Science Reading Room." Nor do I know why the Council approves of enlivening a mall with "small animals" but specifically, vehemently, and with no further explanation, excludes "monkeys." If I had a center I would have monkeys, and Chinese restaurants, and Mylar kites and bands of small girls playing tambourine.

A few years ago at a party I met a woman from Detroit who told me that the Joyce Carol Oates novel with which she identified most closely was *Wonderland*.

I asked her why.

"Because," she said, "my husband has a branch there."

I did not understand.

"In Wonderland the center," the woman said patiently. "My husband has a branch in Wonderland."

I have never visited Wonderland but imagine it to have bands of small girls playing tambourine.

A few facts about shopping centers.

The "biggest" center in the United States is generally agreed to be Woodfield, outside Chicago, a "super" regional or "leviathan" two-million-square-foot center with four major tenants.

The "first" shopping center in the United States is generally agreed to be Country Club Plaza in Kansas City, built in the twenties. There were some other early centers, notably Edward H. Bouton's 1907 Roland Park in Baltimore, Hugh Prather's 1931 Highland Park Shopping Village in Dallas, and Hugh Potter's 1937 River Oaks in Houston, but the developer of Country Club Plaza, the late J. C. Nichols, is referred to with ritual frequency in the literature of shopping centers, usually as "pioneering J. C. Nichols," "trailblazing J. C. Nichols," or "J. C. Nichols, father of the center as we know it."

Those are some facts I know about shopping centers because I still want to be Jere Strizek or James B. Douglas or David D. Bohannon. Here are some facts I know about shopping centers because I never will be Jere Strizek or James B. Douglas or David D. Bohannon: a good center in which to spend the day if you wake feeling low in Honolulu, Hawaii, is Ala Moana, major tenants Liberty House and Sears. A good center in which to spend the day if you wake feeling low in Oxnard, California, is The Esplanade, major tenants the May Company and Sears. A good center in which to spend the day if you wake feeling low in Biloxi,

Mississippi, is Edgewater Plaza, major tenant Godchaux's. Ala Moana in Honolulu is larger than The Esplanade in Oxnard, and The Esplanade in Oxnard is larger than Edgewater Plaza in Biloxi. Ala Moana has carp pools. The Esplanade and Edgewater Plaza do not.

 These marginal distinctions to one side, Ala Moana, The Esplanade, and Edgewater Plaza are the same place, which is precisely their role not only as equalizers but in the sedation of anxiety. In each of them one moves for a while in an aqueous suspension not only of light but of judgment, not only of judgment but of "personality." One meets no acquaintances at The Esplanade. One gets no telephone calls at Edgewater Plaza. "It's a hard place to run in to for a pair of stockings," a friend complained to me recently of Ala Moana, and I knew that she was not yet ready to surrender her ego to the idea of the center. The last time I went to Ala Moana it was to buy *The New York Times*. Because *The New York Times* was not in, I sat on the mall for a while and ate carmel corn. In the end I bought not *The New York Times* at all but two straw hats at Liberty House, four bottles of nail enamel at Woolworth's, and a toaster, on sale in Sears. In the literature of shopping centers these would be described as impulse purchases, but the impulse here was obscure. I do not wear hats, nor do I like carmel corn. I do not use nail enamel. Yet flying back across the Pacific I regretted only the toaster.

QUESTIONS FOR READING, RESPONDING, AND WRITING

Summarizing Main Points

1. Shopping malls are at least as much a part of the American landscape today as they were in the fifties. Yet Didion suggests that "for one perishable moment, there the American idea seemed about to achieve itself." Do you feel that moment has perished? Support your opinion with examples from contemporary life.
2. Didion provides many details of "shopping-center theory." List those details. Do you agree with her that most business theory is such "that you could have thought of it yourself"?

Analyzing Methods of Discourse

1. Didion moves back and forth, sometimes rather abruptly, between describing her own personal history and describing the history of shopping malls and shopping-mall theory. How does this technique reflect the nature of shopping malls? Later, Didion tells the reader that a friend of hers "was not yet ready to surrender her ego to the idea of the center." Do you think Didion is ready to surrender her ego completely?
2. In the first paragraph of her essay, Didion provides a rather extensive list of potential locales for shopping malls. How does this list suggest the pervasiveness of shopping malls?

Focusing on the Field

1. Through personal narration and observation, Didion makes it clear that shopping malls have had a profound influence on her life. Do you think that she extends that influence to include American culture? If so, how?
2. List the things that Joyce Maynard buys in "Europe for the First Time" as well as those that Didion buys in this essay. Compare and contrast the two lists. What aspects of American culture do these lists suggest to you?

Writing Assignments

1. Choose a popular American institution with which you are very familiar (e.g., video arcades, fast food restaurants, multiplex movie theaters, convenience stores) and research its history. Write an essay, like Didion's, that links personal observation and narration to researched material.
2. Compare and contrast Didion's writing style with Tracy Kidder's in "How to Make a Lot of Money." Both provide a wealth of facts and details about their respective subjects. From which do you feel you gain a more comprehensive picture of the relation of their particular interests to American culture as a whole? How do you account for your feeling?

Calvin Trillin

COMPETITORS: THE GREAT ICE CREAM WAR

Calvin Trillin now lives in New York City, where he has been writing for the *New Yorker* since 1963, but he has left his heart—or more accurately, his stomach—in Kansas City, Missouri, which he has dubbed the home of the world's best restaurants. Born in that culinary capital in 1935, Trillin attended Yale University, and went on to work for *Time* magazine from 1960 to 1963, when he joined the staff of the *New Yorker*.

Trillin is a versatile essayist and has over the years proved himself entertaining on virtually any topic. His *New Yorker* columns on his travels through America have been collected in *U.S. Journal,* and his more political columns for the *Nation* have been collected in *Uncivil Liberties.* But Trillin is perhaps most widely known as the man from Kansas City—an eater who writes, and writes best about eating. Hailed by Craig Claiborne, former food editor of the *New York Times,* as the "Homer, Dante, and Shakespeare of American food," Trillin has written numerous essays on this delicious pastime. Collected mostly from the *New Yorker,* they comprise three hearty and satisfying volumes: *American Fried: Adventures of a Happy Eater* (1974), *Alice, Let's Eat* (1978), and *Third Helpings* (1983).

In the following essay, Trillin whets the reader's appetite with the history of the superpremium ice cream wars. But his report from the front does not pronounce a champion. Trillin leaves it to his reader's own discriminating palate to discover both his or her champion and favorite flavor.

Reduced to its essentials, the dispute between Ben & Jerry's Homemade and Häagen-Dazs involved a simple case of what antitrust lawyers call market foreclosure, but nobody was ever tempted to reduce it to its essentials. The players were a lot more interesting than the game. The founder of Häagen-Dazs, Reuben Mattus, fits easily into the role of the prototypical immigrant entrepreneur—the plugger who overcomes his lack of education and connections and capital with tenacity and shrewdness and an enormous capacity for hard work and one simply brilliant idea. By just about any account, Reuben Mattus created the field that is now known by the appropriately excessive name of "superpremium ice cream," and he was appropriately rewarded: the Pillsbury Company bought his company for a price usually estimated at eighty million dollars. The president of Ben & Jerry's Homemade, Ben Cohen, makes a fine, shaggy-bearded prototype of what has come to be known lately as the hippie entrepreneur—one of the people who carried the style of the sixties into consumer businesses aimed at their contemporaries, and whose response to success is to express not gratitude for living in a land of opportunity but astonishment at a world so weird that people like themselves are considered respectable businessmen. When Ben Cohen and his partner, Jerry Greenfield, felt the need to complain that their ice cream was being denied access to the marketplace in violation of federal laws on fair competition, the forums they chose included not just federal district court but the classified-advertisement section of *Rolling Stone*. They took an ad under the "Bumperstickers" heading. The ad asked readers to "help two Vermont hippies fight the giant Pillsbury corporation" by buying a bumper sticker that carried the war cry "WHAT'S THE DOUGHBOY AFRAID OF?" Actually, it's closer to one Vermont hippie. Jerry Greenfield, at the age of thirty-four, has been spending most of his time in Arizona, in a condition somewhere between semi-retired and dropped out—although he did bestir himself last spring long enough to carry on a one-man picket line in front of Pillsbury headquarters, in Minneapolis. Semi-retirement at thirty-four and picketing a competitor's headquarters are both subjects that can cause Reuben Mattus to shake his head in wonderment at how times have changed. When he tries to be gracious toward Ben and Jerry—and graciousness toward competitors is not a hallmark of the sort of ice-cream business he has known for half a century—he will say, "They're very . . . unconventional."

There is no doubt that Ben and Jerry carry on in a way that nobody inside the corporate headquarters of Pillsbury would recognize as conventional behavior for executives. They must be, for instance, among the very few American executives who periodically perform an act in which one of them places a cinder block on his stomach and the other one shatters the cinder block with a sledgehammer. The act is a staple of an autumnal celebration—the Fall Down—that Ben & Jerry's has sometimes staged on the lawn of the First Congregational Church in Burlington, Vermont. Until recently, Burlington was the site of Ben & Jerry's corporate headquarters—if the phrase can be applied in this case. A typical Fall Down also includes an apple-peeling contest (longest unbroken peel), entertainment by Don Rose on his honky-tonk piano, a lip-sync contest, and a Ben & Jerry's look-alike contest. The highlight, though, is what Ben & Jerry's normally advertises as "the Dramatic Sledgehammer Smashing of a cinder block on the bare stomach of the noted Indian mystic Habeeni Ben Coheeni." Ben appears in a sort of bare-midriff swami costume and warms up with what he calls "some metabolic chants." Then he suspends himself between two chairs, and a cinder block is placed on his stomach. Because Ben is beginning to show the effect of steady product-sampling, he acknowledges, there has been a tendency in recent years for the cinder block to roll off his stomach unless volunteers stand by to hold it in place. Then Jerry Greenfield, wearing a pith helmet, is carried onto the scene by four bearers. The background music is "The Rubber-band Man" by the Spinners. Jerry approaches Ben with a perfectly conventional sledgehammer, takes a mighty swing, and pulverizes the cinder block without harming his partner.

When Ben Cohen is asked about the origin of the Dramatic Sledgehammer Smashing, he says that Jerry happened to learn the trick when he took a half-credit course called Carnival Techniques at Oberlin. Ben conveys that information matter-of-factly—the way some businessmen might explain a partner's concentration on long-range financial planning by saying that finance was his specialty at Wharton. In commenting on such matters, Ben speaks as someone whose own brush with higher education included a semester or two studying pottery- and jewelry-making in an open-university program at Skidmore. The other trick Jerry learned in Carnival Techniques was the Flaming Tongue Transfer. In the Flaming Tongue Transfer, the performer, working alone, ignites a fire on his tongue with a flaming torch and then uses the fire to ignite a second torch. Jerry Greenfield has sometimes done the Flaming Tongue Transfer as well as the Dramatic Sledgehammer Smashing at the Fall

Down, if the wind wasn't up. Reuben Mattus might well shake his head in wonderment at that. It is amazing enough that someone could study such subjects in a respectable American college. Who could have predicted that they would prove valuable in a business career?

Reuben Mattus—who is now in his early seventies, and still chairman of Häagen-Dazs—studied neither finance at Wharton nor carnival techniques at Oberlin. He had to drop out of high school to help support his family. "We all came up the hard way," he often says. "Just like all the other immigrants." When Mattus was brought to Brooklyn from Poland by his widowed mother, shortly after the First World War, one of his uncles was already in an early form of the ice-cream business. In partnership with an Italian, Uncle Nathan peddled Italian lemon ice from a horse cart, after taking the precaution of teaching the horse, a rusticated cavalry nag, to understand Yiddish. The rules concerning fair and unfair competition that Reuben Mattus learned as a child from his mother's family were pretty straightforward. Because his mother was a widow with a family to support, it was fair for her brother, Reuben's Uncle Nathan, to become partners with her in establishing a noncompeting ice-cream business in the Bronx. But another brother set up his ice-cream business right across the street from Uncle Nathan, and the two of them spent the rest of their lives trying to steal each other's customers.

When Reuben Mattus was growing up, Brooklyn and the Bronx had dozens of little ice-cream companies, most of them run by immigrants, who competed with the ferocity of people who know that they have no capital to fall back on. The product changed steadily over the years. Starting out with lemon ice, the Mattus family gradually changed over to ice-cream novelties like Popsicles and ice-cream sandwiches, then began making bulk ice cream, and eventually was producing something called Ciro's Ice Cream in pint and quart containers. The battlefields changed almost as often as the product. For a while, the ice-cream makers supplied mostly candy stores. Then it was grocery stores. Then it was supermarkets. After the advent of refrigeration, the independent companies that had fought for the New York-area business for years found themselves with more to fight than one another. Refrigeration transformed the ice-cream business from a seasonal local occupation into something that could be carried on year round by large companies distributing over vast areas. When the large companies first began providing grocery stores with refrigerated cabinets, Mattus recalled recently, small operators tossed their novelties into the same cabinets, whereupon the large companies used their political muscle to pass state legislation making that illegal. The history of the ice-cream business as Reuben Mattus tells it consists of one such crisis after another. There were times during the Second World

War when it seemed impossible to get ingredients. There was a time just after the war when the large corporations, armed with the capacity for paying supermarket chains thousands in what were euphemistically called advance rebates, seemed unstoppable in their efforts to purge the freezer case of independent local brands. Reuben Mattus fought on. He survived. When he talks about it, his survival seems almost miraculous. Mattus's tales of trying to make a living in the ice-cream business during all those years sound a bit like what Odysseus might say about what a person has to go through just to get home from Troy.

Recalling the early days, Mattus figures that he survived partly by brute application of labor. He worked all the time; his wife, Rose, worked all the time. But he also believes that he managed to stay one jump ahead of the competition through an ability to innovate. Almost from the start, he thought of himself as an inventor of techniques—color-coding pint containers, for instance, or devising a display case called the Happy Cabinet. That sort of thing can just bring along another crisis, of course, since imitators were never far behind. "All my life, people copied me," he said recently. "I would start something; they would copy it and undermine me." In the late fifties, when the business had become focussed on mass-marketing ice cream through supermarkets, there came a time when Mattus thought his inventiveness had run out. He feared that the big companies were about to drive him out of business—mostly by economic muscle but partly, in his view, by using some marketing techniques that he himself had helped develop. "My people said, 'You got to come up with something new,'" he said recently. "I said, 'Whaddya think I am—a magician? You don't come up with something new just like that.'" Then, in 1960, Reuben Mattus came up with something new just like that. He invented Häagen-Dazs.

Like a lot of people who have created entirely new ways of approaching something, Mattus had an idea that in retrospect seems simple, maybe even obvious. In the fifties, as supermarkets spread across the country and American housewives seemed to be judging foodstuffs purely on their cost and convenience, the entire ice-cream industry was competing to produce the cheapest possible ice cream in the largest possible containers. It was a competition that small, independent ice-cream companies were unlikely to survive. Reuben Mattus's idea was, in its simplest form, to produce the best possible ice cream instead of the cheapest possible ice cream. In that endeavor, he figured the size of his operation was actually an advantage: he could maintain quality control that would be impossible for huge corporations with plants spread across the country. Instead of mixing into his new product as much air as the law allowed—government regulations prohibit manufacturers from using the phrase "ice cream" to describe a product that is more than fifty per cent air—he would use very little air. Instead of skimping on butterfat, he would produce an ice cream with a butterfat content of sixteen per cent. Years before a significant number of Americans had demonstrated any interest in making a distinction between artificial and natural ingredients, he would use only natural ingredients. Years before a significant number of Americans had indicated any willingness to spend a lot of money for what came to be called gourmet foods, he would gamble on finding enough people who didn't mind spending half again as much as they had to on a pint of ice cream just because it happened to be superior ice cream. After years of being knocked about in the unruly procession of ice-cream makers, Reuben Mattus just turned around and marched smartly in the opposite direction.

Of course, Mattus had Simon Levowitz to help point the way. Mattus thought of Simon Levowitz as a sort of mentor—someone a person could turn to for advice, in the way people in the old country might have turned to a particularly wise rebbe. Levowitz had once been in the ice-cream business, but, unlike most Brooklyn practitioners of that trade, he was an educated man—so learned, Mattus says, that as a sideline he wrote sermons for rabbis and ministers, and even Catholic priests. Levowitz had travelled in Europe—not the way most ice-cream people had travelled in Europe, from the shtetl to the dock, but as a businessman. He was a man of wide business experience. He was a scholar. Most of all, he was a talker. "He used to exhaust me with all the words he'd throw at me," Mattus said long ago. "But sometimes a diamond would come out." Mattus says Levowitz talked constantly about the importance of quality and consistency. He often told the parable of the stale milk powder. During the war, when ingredients were hard to find, Levowitz had bought a large supply of milk powder that was usable but had a slightly stale taste. Once ingredients were available again, he replaced the milk powder, only to find himself beset by customers complaining that the taste of the ice cream had changed. Consistency!

Levowitz often spoke of the quality and consistency maintained by an ice-cream operation in Copenhagen called Premier Is. When Mattus was searching for a European name to add some Continental cachet to his new brand, he naturally thought of Denmark. Premier was in Denmark. Denmark was a dairy country. For someone who had grown up in the immigrant neighborhoods of Brooklyn, Denmark had another advantage. "I figured there were people who hated the Irish, there were people who hated the Italians, there were people who hated the Poles, there were people who hated the Jews," Mattus has said. "But nobody hated the Danes." Mattus put a map of Scandinavia on his pint containers, and settled on the ersatz Danish words "Häagen-Dazs" for a name. He figured that the strangeness of the phrase would be an advantage: slowing up shoppers for the split second required to register the words might be enough to cause some of them to take another look. At first, he was concerned that customers might feel awkward about trying to pronounce the words—words as foreign to a Dane as to anyone else—but then he realized that "the type of people we were looking for, if they mispronounced it they'd think they were right and any other way was wrong."

"The big companies could have crushed him in a minute," one of Reuben Mattus's competitors from Brooklyn has said. "They weren't paying any attention." Mattus had trouble getting distribution for Häagen-Dazs, not because the big companies were trying to shut him out of the market but because distributors didn't think anyone would buy astonishingly expensive ice cream. Mattus plugged away, though, and eventually American tastes caught up with his ice cream. The story of Mattus's invention of a product and his perhaps even more imaginative invention of a name became a sort of capitalist folktale, repeated in *Fortune* and *People*. During the strongest blast of publicity, four or five years ago, Mattus grew a beard: not a shaggy beard like Ben Cohen's but a neatly trimmed beard that made him look more—well, Continental. Even though the container with the map of Scandinavia on it had said from the start that Häagen-Dazs was made in the Bronx (or, in later years, in equally prosaic New Jersey), Mattus found in pre-beard days that people he met were disappointed to discover that the company had been created by "just an ordinary guy."

The other ordinary guys were right on his heels, of course. Sooner or later, a superpremium ice cream called Alpen Zauber appeared in the stores; sooner or later, a superpremium ice cream called Frusen Glädjé appeared in the stores. What was particularly irritating to Mattus was that the people copying Häagen-Dazs were his old competitors from Brooklyn. One of the principals in the company that produces Frusen Glädjé is Mattus's cousin, a son of one of the warring uncles. Gold Seal Riviera, the company that makes Alpen Zauber, is owned by the Kroll family, who were plumbers on Mattus's block in Brooklyn when he first arrived from Poland, but who went into the ice-cream business early enough to battle Mattus and his family for customers at every turn. Mattus's views on Alpen Zauber can be expressed succinctly: "The Krolls have been knocking me off forever."

At one point Mattus went to court in an attempt to stop the knock-offs. Häagen-Dazs tried, unsuccessfully, to stop the marketing of Frusen Glädjé on the ground that the packaging was a trademark infringement on Häagen-Dazs's "unique Scandinavian marketing theme"—a position that the unkind took as basically a matter of Mattus's accusing someone of stealing his scam. Häagen-Dazs also tried to protect its market by imposing exclusive contracts on distributors. In 1981, the national sales director of Häagen-Dazs sent a letter to distributors and subdistributors spelling out a policy toward ice creams like Alpen Zauber and Frusen Glädjé. "It would be potentially confusing to the public and inconsistent with the *proper* handling and marketing of Häagen-Dazs ice cream for a distributor or subdistributor to simultaneously sell Häagen-Dazs and the other ice-cream brands," the letter said. "If a distributor in the exercise of his best independent business judgment elects to handle one of these other brands, it is our intention . . . not to supply him with Häagen-Dazs ice cream." (A few years later, in an interview with *USA Today*, Mattus expressed the same thoughts in a different way: "If you want to have a wife and a mistress, I don't blame you, but it's no good for the wife.") Alpen Zauber went to court for a preliminary injunction. In granting it, the judge was inspired to quote Gilbert and Sullivan ("Things are seldom what they seem/ Skim milk masquerades as cream") as well as the phrase that Thomas Carlyle attributes to Charles V ("the iron hand in a velvet glove"). Then Reuben Mattus and Abe Kroll, of Gold Seal Riviera—two men who had known each other for sixty years or so—came to an out-of-court agreement. The lawyer for Alpen Zauber was Martin Kroll, a younger-generation member of the Gold Seal Riviera family. He said recently that he persuaded his Uncle Abe and Reuben Mattus to settle by reminding them how long they had known each other and by telling them the old shtetl tale about the two men who argued over the ownership of a cow—one pulling on the head, one pulling on the tail, and lawyers milking the beast the entire time. Alpen Zauber got access to the distributors. Reuben Mattus still had more than seventy per cent of the cow.

When Ben and Jerry's began, in 1978, there was no mistaking it for a knockoff of Häagen-Dazs; it seemed more like a knockoff of Steve's, a homemade-ice-cream parlor in Somerville, Massachusetts, on the edge of Cambridge. In fact, what Ben Cohen and Jerry Greenfield, high-school pals from Long Island, had in mind was to move to a relatively quiet college town and start some more or less entertaining business of the sort that had already proved itself in places like Cambridge and Berkeley and Ann Arbor. It didn't have to be ice cream. In fact, it is now an established part of the Ben & Jerry's startup story—a capitalist folktale that is rapidly becoming almost as well known as the one about Reuben Mattus—that Cohen and Greenfield were leaning toward a bagel operation before they discovered how much bagel-baking equipment cost. They simply figured that having a business together would be an improvement over what they had found themselves doing. Greenfield, who had not been able to get into medical school, was working as a lab technician in North Carolina. Cohen, whose academic aspirations had not extended much past the pottery-making and jewelry-making courses, was teaching pottery-making to emotionally disturbed children near Lake Champlain. Something like a homemade-ice-cream store, they thought, would be a way to have some independence and a way to live in a pleasant college town, and maybe even a way to have some fun. They raised eight thousand dollars for capital. They bought an old-fashioned rock-salt ice-cream maker. They rented an abandoned gas station in Burlington, half a mile or so from the campus of the University of Vermont, and began fixing it up themselves. They read several books about homemade ice cream. Then they capped off their preparations by sending away to Pennsylvania State University for a five-dollar correspondence course in ice-cream making—two-fifty apiece. Like a lot of people who were in college during the late sixties and early seventies, they had been educated to think small.

College-town ice-cream parlors like Steve's seemed to be founded on the principle that the atmosphere of a retail business—at least a retail business selling homemade ice cream to young people—could be more or less the atmosphere one might expect to find in an Ugliest Man on Campus contest. In the original Steve's store—which still exists in roughly its original form, even though the business has changed hands and has been expanded into a franchise operation—there was an old-fashioned homemade-ice-cream maker in the window producing the store's entire ice-cream supply. Steve's also provided a player piano, elaborate rules posted on the wall concerning which combinations of ice cream and toppings and mix-ins were allowed, a bulletin board for notices of yoga classes and rides to New York, and a trivia contest to pass the time spent standing in what always seemed to be a long line. That's the sort of operation Cohen and Greenfield opened in Burlington. Greenfield made the homemade ice cream, which was popular from the start, and Cohen handled the hot food, which wasn't. On summer evenings, they showed free movies on the wall of a building next door. On cold winter days, they instituted an ice-cream-cone discount scheme they still call POPCDBZWE, pronounced the way it's spelled, which stands for "Penny Off Per Celsius Degree Below Zero Winter Extravaganza." On just about any day, customers were likely to be entertained by Don Rose on his honky-tonk piano. Rose was a volunteer, and his service to the cause earned him the rare distinction of being named a "Ben & Jerry's lifer": he is entitled to free ice cream for the rest of his life.

Ben & Jerry's drifted into the wholesale-ice-cream business partly because some local restaurants began to ask about being supplied and partly, Cohen always says, because meeting the salesmen who called on the ice-cream parlor persuaded him that travelling around the state selling ice cream might be a pleasanter life than being stuck in front of a stove in a former filling station. Ben & Jerry's started to manufacture ice cream by the pint, with Jerry acting as production manager while Ben lived out his travelling-salesman dreams on the roads of Vermont. Their approach to presenting their wares did not have much in common with what Reuben Mattus had done at Häagen-Dazs. Instead of concocting an ersatz European name, they called their ice cream Ben & Jerry's Home-made—although Cohen likes to say that there was some consideration given to putting an umlaut over the "e" in Ben. The picture on top of their pint container was not a map of Scandinavia but a photograph of the two of them, looking pretty much like two Vermont hippies. The description of the ingredients on the container was done in the sort of hand printing often used on the sort of menu that lists a variety of herbal teas. The geographical connection Ben & Jerry's tried to project was not with the capitals of Europe but with rural Vermont. Times had changed. For the generation Ben and Jerry belonged to, the Continent had lost its cachet. Cachet had lost its cachet. Cohen and Greenfield were interested not simply in using natural ingredients but in being natural themselves.

They still speak of what they do as being "in our style." From the start, it was their style to be funky. It was their style to be slightly embarrassed at being in business at all. "We grew up in the sixties, when it wasn't cool to be businessmen," Greenfield said last year to a trade-magazine reporter while trying to explain why Ben & Jerry's has a policy of turning back part of its profits to the community. "Our whole motivation for doing business was never to get rich." It was their style to assume that part of the reason for going into business was to have fun. Their promotional style can be summed up by the fact that a trip to Florida offered as a prize in the Ben & Jerry's "Lick Winter" promotion a couple of years ago included not just airfare and hotels but dinner with Jerry's parents, who are retired down there, and a day at Walt Disney World with Ben's uncle.

The two Vermont hippies set out to produce the sort of high-butter-fat, low-air-content ice cream that Reuben Mattus had pioneered. Like Mattus, they used natural flavor, and they used plenty of it. (Jerry says that was because it took a strong dose of flavor to get any response from Ben, the sampler, who "doesn't have a real acute sense of taste.") When it came to marketing, though, Ben & Jerry's had practically nothing in common with Häagen-Dazs and Alpen Zauber and Frusen Glädjé. Even the flavors were different. When Reuben Mattus began marketing Häagen-Dazs, he carried only vanilla, chocolate, and coffee; Ben & Jerry's seemed to specialize right away in flavors like Chocolate Health Bar Crunch and White Russian and Dastardly Mash. (Even now, the two brands have only half a dozen flavor names in common.) When Cohen is asked to compare his ice cream with brands like Häagen-Dazs and Alpen

Zauber and Frusen Glädjé, he often says that Ben & Jerry's is "the only superpremium ice cream you can pronounce." In their strategy of positioning their ice cream in the market, Cohen and Greenfield had, in their own consciously small way, turned around and marched smartly in the opposite direction.

Their sixties sense of limitations was reflected in their motto, "Vermont's Finest All-Natural Ice Cream"—a motto that is, by the standards of ice-cream-business superlatives, almost pathologically modest. In the summer of 1981, a year after Ben & Jerry's started producing pints, *Time* ran a widely noticed cover story on the popularity of ice cream, and the writer, John Skow, commented on the inflation of ice-cream bragging by routinely referring to just about every brand mentioned as the best ice cream in the world. The irony in the way the phrase was being used became clear before the end of the first paragraph, but in the opening sentence of the story the superlative still carried an impact. That sentence said, "What you must understand at the outset is that Ben & Jerry's, in Burlington, Vt., makes the best ice cream in the world."

The recognition by *Time* added momentum to what had been a steady expansion of Ben & Jerry's wholesale operation. By 1983, Ben & Jerry's was selling well over a million dollars' worth of wholesale ice cream annually, even though the ice cream was being distributed almost entirely in Vermont and New Hampshire and Maine and upstate New York—states that are noted for per-capita ice-cream consumption but are not long on capita. (Cohen's explanation for the fact that New Englanders, who live in one of the coldest parts of the country, eat the most ice cream per capita rests on his theory that what makes people feel cold is not air temperature, as is commonly believed, but the difference between air temperature and body temperature—a difference that can be reduced by a steady intake of ice cream.) Some grownup business decisions had to be made. Should Ben & Jerry's reach toward the lucrative markets in lower New England? If so, how could enough ice cream be produced to meet a large market's demands? Ben & Jerry's manufacturing operation consisted of a tiny staff of young people in a tiny galvanized-tin building that a Ford dealer had formerly used to repair trucks—a production setup that a succinct visitor might have described as five dropouts in a garage.

Jerry Greenfield had already made a business decision on his own— to move to Arizona. He recently moved back to the East—but not to full-time participation in Ben & Jerry's. "It got to the point where it was too big for me," he said not long ago. "It wasn't as personally rewarding. I was more comfortable in the filling station." As the partner who spent a lot of his time presiding over production, Greenfield found that quality control had put forty or fifty pounds on him. The young woman he lived with wanted to go back to graduate school at Arizona State. The obvious move was semi-retirement. While he was in Arizona, he was asked what he did with his time, and he said, "I help out some at the public library." He also helped out some at Ben & Jerry's. He still owns ten per cent of the company. Ordinarily, he has returned in the summer to pitch in with high-season production and to lend his talents, as the leaves begin to fall, to the shattering of a cinder block on Ben's stomach. It's a corporate stint that is done in the spirit of an ex-counsellor coming back to camp at the end of the season to help put on the big show, and it makes Jerry neither uncomfortable nor fat.

What the remaining partner had decided was to test the Boston market and, if that augured well, to figure out how to finance a new plant. Once it was clear that Boston looked promising, the new plant was financed partly through a scheme that was well attuned to Ben & Jerry's style. An intrastate stock issue was floated; only bona-fide Vermont residents were eligible. The relevant executives—Cohen and Greenfield and the new general manager, a young man named Fred (Chico) Lager—travelled from town to town last summer talking to potential stockholders in informational meetings that included a sample of something like Chocolate Oreo Mint but stopped short of the Dramatic Sledgehammer Smashing. Three-quarters of a million dollars was raised in the stock offering, an urban-development grant and industrial revenue bonds were obtained, and last August ground was broken on a large plot along a country road that happens to run between two large ski areas. Chico Lager figured that the plant would sooner or later be the third-largest tourist attraction in Vermont, with a thriving company store, a guided tour, and a rustic atmosphere featuring his father-in-law's dairy cows grazing on the lawn.

Meanwhile, according to allegations made by Ben & Jerry's in a complaint filed in federal district court, the manufacturers of Häagen-Dazs had, in both Boston and Connecticut, "engaged in a pattern of conduct designed to coerce and require distributors who handle both Häagen-Dazs and Ben & Jerry's superpremium ice cream to cease dealing with Ben & Jerry's as a condition of such distributors continuing to function as distributors of Häagen-Dazs superpremium ice cream." All of which would, the complaint maintained, enable Häagen-Dazs to have "entrenched its dominant position in the marketplace, stifled competition, thwarted Ben & Jerry's entry into the Greater Boston and the Massachusetts and Connecticut geographic markets for superpremium ice cream, and illegally acquired and maintained a monopoly in such superpremium ice-cream markets." Or, as Chico Lager put it, "they were going for the throat."

Merely suing would not have been Ben & Jerry's style. It wouldn't have been much fun. It wouldn't have sold much ice cream. Also, Cohen says he feared that in the absence of some public pressure a corporation the size of Pillsbury could keep a corporation the size of Ben & Jerry's Homemade in court long enough to run it out of money. Cohen says that the possibility of being shut out of Boston and Connecticut was also a genuine threat to Ben & Jerry's survival. The company was already deeply involved in putting together the complicated package of financing for the large new plant, whose existence had been predicated on an expanded market. "We were really scared," Chico Lager has said. "This was not a joke to us. How we responded was a lot of fun, but the matter itself was very serious."

But what fun! It was a marketing opportunity made for Ben & Jerry's. Although the lawsuit was filed against Häagen-Dazs, the publicity barrage was directed against the parent company, Pillsbury—the sort of huge, faceless corporation that makes a perfect foil for a company whose founders have their faces right on the pint container. Ben & Jerry's could play the hit-and-run guerrillas against the cumbersome regiments of Pillsbury's conventional army. It took some effort to come up with a war cry that encompassed the accusations against Pillsbury and the unevenness of the contest. "We were hung up for a long time on the word 'strangle,'" Chico Lager has said. Finally, during a long meeting at which the strategists agreed that it might be worth trying to use Pillsbury's corporate symbol in some way, Lager blurted it out: "What's the Doughboy Afraid Of?" The slogan went up on bus signs in Boston. It was made into a bumper sticker. It got printed on T-shirts. A Doughboy Hot Line was set up, so that interested citizens could, by calling an 800 number, receive a Doughboy kit that explained the battle. The kit included two versions of a form letter that could be sent to W. H. Spoor, the chairman of Pillsbury, criticizing "the lack of ethics your company is showing in trying to keep Ben & Jerry's ice cream out of the market." One version began, "I've tasted Ben & Jerry's and I know what the Pillsbury Doughboy is afraid of." Both versions ended with "P.S. Why don't you pick on someone your own size?"

The campaign started slowly, but eventually thousands of people called the Doughboy Hot Line, and thousands of words appeared in the press about Ben & Jerry's. For Ben & Jerry's customers, it was almost as much fun as the Fall Down. Some of the letters people sent to Pillsbury or Häagen-Dazs were businesslike ("I would admonish you to adopt a policy of fair play"), but it was more typical for them to express outrage at "the desire to use the corporate heel to stamp out your competition" or to begin by saying "CORPORATIONS LIKE YOURS REALLY MAKE ME SICK!" A remarkable number of the letters of support received by

Ben & Jerry's mentioned the writer's favorite flavor; some of them even mentioned the writer's favorite flavor of Häagen-Dazs. One of them was signed "Helene 'Dastardly Mash' Jones." Some of them were from outraged schoolchildren, who offered to help by, say, forming gangs of Doughboy Busters. Chico Lager sent a copy of one of those letters to W. H. Spoor at Pillsbury, along with a note that ended "Why not think it over and repent?"

The lawyer hired by Cohen to handle the case that was going on at the same time is not a hippie. The Ben & Jerry's style doesn't go that far. After the Pillsbury legal department had more or less brushed aside a couple of letters from attorneys—one was from a lawyer who is on the board of Ben & Jerry's, the other was from a member of a Vermont firm—Cohen went to Ropes & Gray, a prominent Boston law firm whose reputation has been built partly on defending corporations like Pillsbury from anti-trust actions launched by irritants like Ben & Jerry's Homemade. The partner who handled the case for Ropes & Gray, Howard Fuguet, began in May of 1984 by writing Pillsbury a ten-page letter that went into precedents in some detail and suggested that the cause of action was a straightforward matter of the sort not requiring protracted and expensive litigation—what he has called on other occasions a "garden-variety violation" of the Clayton Act. "It would be wishful thinking on the part of your subsidiary's officers to imagine that it can bully Ben & Jerry's, stifle its growth, and cause it to roll over," Fuguet wrote toward the end of the letter. "Ben & Jerry's is a classic entrepreneurial success, and its owners are aggressive. They like the taste of success and will fight for it." The Ben & Jerry's crowd liked Fuguet's style, even though he had stopped short of naming his favorite flavor. They also liked his knowledge of the precedents. Chico Lager said the letter was "inspiring."

Pillsbury was also impressed. By the time Fuguet was ready to file for a temporary restraining order, the Pillsbury lawyers were ready to go along with its terms. After that, the two sides began negotiating, although without the benefit of any old shtetl stories. Fuguet was confident that he could win in court and that Pillsbury's lawyers knew it. Exclusive contracts with distributors are not inherently illegal, but they are illegal if they have the effect of substantially reducing competition in the marketplace—if, for instance, there is a limited number of distributors and the manufacturer imposing the exclusive contract on them already has a dominant share of the market. In the early exchanges, the Pillsbury lawyers claimed that Häagen-Dazs had only a tiny share of the overall ice-cream market. After nearly a year of negotiations, though, they agreed to an out-of-court settlement by which Häagen-Dazs promised to impose no exclusive contracts in the area for two years—presumably long enough for Ben & Jerry's to establish itself in the market. Fuguet, of course, had been prepared to demonstrate in court that Häagen-Dazs did have a dominant share because a special market exists in superpremium ice cream. Reuben Mattus had created it.

Mattus saw the entire episode as a publicity stunt. And it was a publicity stunt, although Ben Cohen says that he genuinely saw it as publicity to expose corporate bullying as well as publicity that might result in some ice-cream sales. ("If we were going to go down this way, I was going to at least make sure people knew what was happening.") Ben and Jerry are among those creatures who are good copy even when they behave the way they would normally behave—or the way they would normally behave except for a little stronger dose of flavor. Jerry Green-field thought picketing Pillsbury was fun; everybody at Ben & Jerry's thought that directing bales of letters in the direction of W. H. Spoor was fun. Mattus, a man who understands the value of publicity in marketing, couldn't help being impressed by the Doughboy campaign. ("These are sharp, creative guys—a little wild, but very sharp.") He was also irritated, however. He said that if Ben & Jerry's had really been interested in distribution rather than in publicity it would have simply found other distributors or distributed the product on its own—more or less what he had done in the early days of Häagen-Dazs. "They got P.R. and exposure they couldn't buy for millions," he has said. "What they did in a couple of years took me eighteen years to do. I did it the hard way."

Mattus says that sort of thing with a certain amount of pride in his voice. He speaks of Ben and Jerry as good promoters but not as "real ice-cream people." Real ice-cream people did it the hard way. It didn't have to be fun. Mattus sees Ben and Jerry as the sort of people who might make money in the ice-cream business and then sell out and go into something else. "There's a special kind of people dedicated to their business," he said not long ago. "Certain other people are like bees—first this flower, then the next flower. People like the Krolls and myself, we're horses."

QUESTIONS FOR READING, RESPONDING, AND WRITING

Summarizing Main Points

1. List the differences between Reuben Mattus and Ben and Jerry. List the similarities. What is Reuben Mattus's opinion of Ben and Jerry?
2. Trace the steps in Trillin's narrative. At what point does the confrontation between Häagen-Dazs and Ben & Jerry's take place? Who are "the players" at this point? Whose side is Trillin on? Why?

Analyzing Methods of Discourse

1. Though Trillin begins with an anecdote about Ben and Jerry, he tells Reuben Mattus's "capitalist folktale" before he tells Ben & Jerry's. Why? Why do you suppose he ends Reuben's story before the Pillsbury takeover?
2. At one point in the essay, Trillin states, "after years of being knocked about in the unruly procession of ice-cream makers, Reuben Mattus just turned around and marched smartly in the opposite direction." Later, Trillin uses the same language to describe actions taken by Ben and Jerry. How does this repetition help make Trillin's implied main point more obvious?

Focusing on the Field

1. Trillin tells the reader that "Ben and Jerry still speak of what they do as being 'in our style.'" How does Trillin characterize their style? Reuben Mattus's style? Pillsbury's style? Locate examples of each.
2. Trillin begins with a very "unbusinesslike" anecdote about Ben and Jerry. Yet even Ben and Jerry cannot remain completely unbusinesslike. Locate evidence of their increasing involvement in more standard business practices.

Writing Assignments

1. Read Michael Korda's "When Business Becomes Blood Sport." Then, write an essay in which you argue that Ben & Jerry's will or will not survive the eighties.
2. Read Stan Luxenberg's "McDonald's—The Franchise Factory." Compare Ray Kroc's personality and business techniques to either Ben and Jerry's or Reuben Mattus's.

Margaret Henning
Anne Jardim

THE MANAGERIAL WOMAN
The Middle Management Career Path

Why are only 2.5 percent of the 500,000 managers earning over $25,000 a year in the United States women? Margaret Henning and Anne Jardim attempted to answer this question and change that fact in their best-seller, *The Managerial Woman* (1977). As the following essay, which comprises Chapter 3 of that book, suggests, a woman who would become one of the well-paid few in management must change her attitude toward her work—and her coworkers. Team spirit and the avoidance of overspecialization are the themes here, though elsewhere in their book, Henning and Jardim explain how the corporations themselves might better accommodate the changing male and female roles in business. Critics have called this ground-breaking book "invaluable" and "required reading for future bosses, male and female, and for present feminists, male and female."

Some of the material for the book emerged from Margaret Henning's doctoral thesis for the Harvard Business School, where Henning received both a master's and a doctorate in business administration. Aside from her writing career, Henning has been a visiting professor at Harvard, where she cofounded and jointly directed a graduate program in management for women. She has also worked as a business consultant in general management and organizational behavior.

Middle management positions are often inaccurately defined on the basis of salary, fringe benefits or status—office size, a rug on the floor. They are almost never defined in terms of the actual on-the-job changes which accompany what is essentially a shift from supervisory management to broader, across-department responsibilities.

This shift is critical for both men and women and it needs to be looked at in two ways: from the standpoint of the "normal" career path leading up to it and from the point of view of a man and a woman moving toward it.

First the "normal" career path. The typical management career path moves individuals from an initial experience in a technical or specialist's role to the more general role of a middle manager. From that point career paths lead upward to new levels of specialization which demand a broader and more conceptual approach to decision-making and problem-solving.

In terms of progressive job functions, the specialist's job is essentially one of applying particular kinds of technical knowledge and experience to the solution of primarily routine problems so as to ensure the completion of assigned tasks. Supervisory responsibilities at this level are closely related to task completion and to the proper use of techniques and skills.

The middle manager's job in contrast is much more one of coordination with counterparts in other functional areas to see that the work of his or her own group or department is related as effectively as possible to the immediate objectives and operations of the enterprise; and it is primarily for this much broader task that he or she is held responsible.

At a higher level more senior managers are much less involved in seeing that work is actually done, or in meeting the day-to-day requirements of operational interdependence between and among functional areas. They are much more closely involved in setting long-term directions and developing policies for entire functional areas in order to give coherence to the operations of the enterprise as a whole.

Looked at in this way, career paths leading ultimately to the most senior levels of management inevitably and critically depend on that first important transition from technical or specialist supervision to the broader and much less precise role of a middle manager.

The transition itself demands an ability to deal competently with the following shifts in responsibility, which bear repeating, among others that are more specific to the new job function:

TRANSITION FROM SUPERVISION TO MIDDLE MANAGEMENT

TECHNICAL EXPERTISE:	Mastery of a specific function or area	Working knowledge of requirements of other functions/areas
GOAL SETTING:	Meeting goals set by superiors. Short-term	Breaking down broader and longer-term interdepartmental goals and setting subgoals for subordinates
PLANNING:	Carrying out plans already decided on	Developing plans for the achievement of objectives
PROBLEM-SOLVING:	Solving problems as they arise	Anticipating problems and preparing alternative solutions in advance
INTERDEPARTMENT LIAISON:	Usually not critical to job performance	Invariably of critical importance to job performance
LEARNING BASE:	Formal and technically oriented: classes, courses, manuals, texts	Informal and behaviorally oriented: learning from others—peers, superiors and subordinates
THE INFORMAL SYSTEM:	Incidental to getting the job done	Critical to getting the job done
SELF-RELIANCE VS. RELIANCE ON OTHERS:	Where necessary, performance requirements can be met by relying on one's own skills	Must depend increasingly on the ability to delegate task performance to others

This list is not meant to be exclusive but rather to highlight the critical changes which the transition to middle management demands. It is a transition which is difficult enough for men. For women it is even more difficult because the emphasis on formal ways of learning the job, doing the job and moving up in the job shifts to a much more informal base.

For the woman who enters an organization with aspirations that differ significantly from a man's aspirations, who finds it difficult to say with the same emphasis, "I'm going to work for the rest of my life and I want a career," who in fact concentrates on the acquisition of competence in whatever may be her current job, leaving career advancement largely to take care of itself, the transition is supremely difficult.

If we try to follow her from her first day of work to a position ten or twelve years into the future, she tends to share a number of the characteristics of the hypothetical woman we are about to describe. Typically this woman graduates with a liberal arts degree. She has done well in languages, literature, history, psychology or sociology, music or art. She leaves college not at all sure what a skill is, with a sinking feeling that whatever it is she hasn't got it. Many women like her go to a secretarial school to acquire something they can tell themselves *is* a skill because there is a demand for it, it is tangible, it can be used. She does so too but she is lucky enough to find a job as an administrative assistant in a staff department. She types for herself but not for others. Slowly she finds her feet and begins to realize that there *are* skills that she can learn, and she can learn them on the job. As she becomes more competent her sense of security increases. She *can* learn those skills, she *can* use them effectively. As time passes she finds that their effective use contributes to her sense of security in another way. The men with whom she works begin to see her as someone who, in spite of the fact that she's a woman, is extremely good at her job. In a real way she begins to develop a sense of legitimacy, of having a right to do the job she does, both in her own mind and, as she sees their reactions, in the minds of others.

Throughout this process she tends to have made no long-term career commitment. Her commitment has been to current performance and to on-the-job competence. She is not sure for how long she will work or whether she will work at all if she gets married. Given the lack of a longer-range objective, her concentration on the here and now is understandable. She wants to make the present as worthwhile as she can. She signs up for courses that add to her expertise. She reads manuals and professional journals.

Several years later her competence earns her a supervisory position. At this point she has invested a great deal in the skills she has acquired and they in turn have contributed heavily to her sense of who she is. It is difficult for her to accept that other people, those she now supervises, will make the same investment, and in reality a number of them don't. Her way of coping with this is to pick up the pieces for them, to do the extra work herself. She becomes a true working supervisor. She is responsible for all of her old assignments, the supervision of subordinates and the added work involved in ensuring that nothing leaves her small department unless it is perfect. To ensure this she often prefers to do the job herself. Her supervisory style is a close one, she is a scrupulous checker, a dotter of *i*'s and a crosser of *t*'s.

It is not a style which breeds initiative nor does it lend itself to delegating responsibility. She sends a very clear message—she trusts and relies on herself alone. Her friends tend to be from outside of the organization and her contacts within it tend to be formal and task-oriented. If she remains in this position until her early thirties the chances are that she will decide she has a career, or at the very least that she will continue to work over the long-term. The problem is that her style has now been formed. It is a close, non-delegative style, heavily dependent on self for performance and on formal structure and rules to define both job and performance.

This style was not formed consciously, she never thought about it in terms of whether it was helpful in advancing her position or not. Bosses came and went. Depending on how competent they were, she had often to do part of their job as well. They rated her an "outstanding supervisor," aware that if she left they would probably have had to replace her with at least two people. At the same time they rated her as "probably terminal in present position." The style she developed and never thought of changing stamped "lacking in management potential" all over her, and this at a point when possibly for the first time she began to think seriously of a long-term career. Yet why should she have thought of changing her behavior? For what reason? Superiors praised the scrupulous accuracy of the work she was responsible for. Raises were forthcoming. She wasn't looking ahead to anything specific. Getting the job done competently had often been more than enough to cope with.

For many, many women this is the extraordinarily painful dilemma of the transition to middle management. The style they develop in order to survive along the path to middle management, both psychologically and tactically, is a style that makes them the fabled outstanding supervisor. But it lacks a strategic dimension, a long-term objective. As a consequence they fail to build flexibility into it, they do not measure present cost against future benefit. They do not recognize the cues that signal a need for a change in style. They concentrate on task, skill and job performance and ignore the critically important behavioral variables.

Our hypothetical woman tends to arrive at the transition point to middle management an in-depth specialist and a close supervisor of other specialists. Yet she is a woman in her mid-thirties with another thirty years ahead of her. She is bright and she is competent.

For men behavior *is* a variable along the path to middle management, their own behavior and the behavior of others. However implicit, however unconscious, the assumption that they will have to work for most of their lives gives men an objective: to make the best of it that they can—which is widely interpreted as career advancement. Typically a man comes to his first management job not even conscious of the psychological preparation for it that he has undergone since he was a small boy. Typically too his high school and college years have given him mathematical skills or a background in economics or business, together with a clear recognition of competitive striving as an inherent factor in achievement.

To him, his first job is the beginning of an apprenticeship. His expectation that once he has mastered it he will move on is a comparatively modest expectation, for countless men have done it before him. Why not he? The central issue really lies in finding the most effective way, and while his judgment of what is effective may be good or poor, at a minimum he will try.

If he is a college graduate recruited into a fast track training program he is given considerable visibility as he moves about the company. If he enters a small department in finance or marketing, or if he is hired as an assistant foreman in a manufacturing plant, his environment is considerably more limited, but his assumption that he is not going to be there for the rest of his life determines his behavior.

Learn and move on. Act so that people will see you as having the ability to move on. Try to influence the people who can help you move on. Be needed by those people, become necessary to them. Try to identify what they want and don't want. Broaden your information base from what you need to do the job to include the people who can help you leave it. Who are they—good, bad, indifferent? On whom should you focus your efforts? Find out—and try to make sure you don't pick a loser. Do job changes make sense at this point—do they promise more, more quickly? Transfers, moves to other companies? Find out—and try to pick a winner whichever way you go, a winner who can become a godfather, a rabbi, a sponsor, a patron—who will invest in you, help you, teach you and speak up for you. If you're right you'll move with him. If you're wrong—disengage and try to leave him behind. But find another.

It would be fascinating to pursue the psychoanalytic implications of this pattern. It is a pattern which repeats the search for a father, ultimate revolt and then finally the drive to become a father oneself. It is a pattern drawn from a boy's earliest experience, with the father representing power, authority and freedom to take on the entire world. It is a pattern still basic to this society's definition of the male identity and it is the common heritage of men who manage. It is the way their world works.

It is against this background that our hypothetical young man reaches the middle management transition point. He reaches it more quickly and far more economically than the hypothetical young woman whose path we followed. When he gets there, what he did along the way tends to have given him a much broader knowledge and understanding of how the organization functions—of its purposes and its people, particularly those who matter to him. Like her he has more often than not had to master a particular technical area,* but his investment in it has not been as deep because the pressures on him were different. In her case overinvestment gave her legitimacy and thus security in her own eyes and in the eyes of others. In his case he brought legitimacy with him and saw his security as resting on quite different foundations: in being seen by men who mattered as a young man with "potential."

At the transition point her great fear is to be cut off from what she knows, from the comforting familiarity of an area she has mastered in depth, from the very basis of her sense of legitimacy and security, only to confront new and quite different problems, new and quite different people, in a setting where she may now be the *only* woman in such a position.

His great fear is that he may be entering a backwater, cut off from the people who helped him. Can he put a team together? Will he find capable subordinates? What will his peers be like? Will his new boss be a man from whom he can learn—who has influence enough to help him advance?

Her perception of the problems facing her is centered on herself, on her own capacity or lack of it. It is an inward preoccupation which dulls her ability to assess other people objectively. She tends to see them in terms of the impact they have on her own sense of adequacy.

His perception of the problems facing him is centered on the people around him, on *their* abilities. It is an outward preoccupation which sharpens his awareness of who those people are and what they want—and the one tends to condition whether he will give them the other.

Her problems feed upon each other. Where before, her expertise was proof of her right to be where she was, she feels she must prove that right all over again both to herself and to the men around her. And she must do it at a more complex level of responsibility, at a time when she is supremely conscious that she lacks mastery of the job she must do.

Driven by the old anxiety over legitimacy—the need to justify to herself and others that in spite of the fact she's a woman she knows the job and can handle it—and with few examples of other women who have

---

*However, we know of a number of cases, and there must be others, where men *began* their careers as assistants to the president, developed a basic knowledge of the function of a number of departments but no special expertise in any, came to be seen as true "generalists," stayed at the top with title changes designating more and more over-all responsibility and skipped the middle management bind completely.

ever done it to give her confidence, she retreats into herself. She avoids asking questions for fear they might indicate ignorance of the aspects of the job she feels she *should* know. This blocks her ability to learn. Anxiety invests every gap in knowledge and experience with the same importance and she drives herself to work on her own time at understanding every detail—relevant or not—while she copes, as she must, with the day-to-day pressures of the job. The apparent confidence and self-assuredness of the men around her, however unreal, make her situation seem even worse.

A third-level manager in a Bell System company gave us a description of this painful process a year after her promotion to district management.†

"I was promoted after the Consent Decree.‡ All of the companies had to promote a certain number of women and I guess I was one of them. I think I deserved the promotion but I sometimes wonder whether I would have gotten it without the decree.

"I came out of the Traffic Department. This is where all the operators are and it's really a women's department. Men used to come into it as management trainees. The women trained them. And then the men managed *us*—sometimes the very same men we'd trained.

"I came up the operators' route all the way to group chief and then chief operator. My promotion to district manager (third level) was one of the first for women.

"I'll never forget what those early months were like. I really had no management experience. I only knew vaguely what the other departments were responsible for and I didn't know whom to ask or what to ask. The worst thing was wondering whether my counterparts—who were all men—believed I'd got the job simply because of EEOC. I know some of them did, and at the beginning I couldn't even make myself ask a question in case it turned out to be a question I should have known the answer to. I was really afraid to have that happen. I could hear their minds clicking: 'Third level and doesn't even know the job.'

---

†In most Bell companies there are only seven levels of management, from first management job to president. Third or district level is the first true middle management level as we have defined it.

‡On January 18, 1973, American Telephone & Telegraph representing its twenty-two subsidiary companies entered into a landmark settlement with the Department of Labor and the Equal Employment Opportunity Commission. Under the terms of a Consent Decree, AT&T agreed to pay $15 million in restitution to an estimated fifteen thousand women and minorities who had allegedly been discriminated against in job assignments, pay and promotions; another $23 million a year in pay raises; and to establish goals and timetables for the hiring and promotion of women and minorities into its management ranks. In return, the EEOC and the Department of Labor agreed to withdraw the various charges leveled against the corporation. AT&T is the nation's largest private employer.

"My first district meeting was a total disaster. There I was, the only woman, a district manager, Traffic. There they were. They knew each other. Most of them had years of district experience. They came from the tough departments where there were *no* women—Plant, Network, Engineering, as well as the others.

"Most of the meeting went straight over my head. They got into a very technical discussion at one point. I didn't know what most of the equipment was or what it was supposed to do. I didn't know the technical systems definitions and they didn't bother to spell them out. They used letters. E.S.S. is a simple one—Electronic Switching Systems.

"By the end of the meeting I had a column of letters and I spent night after night with the manuals trying to figure them out. I didn't dare ask anyone. It sounds silly now—but it wasn't then. I nearly quit. If it hadn't been for my husband I *would* have quit. I remember one set of letters that nearly finished me. P.O.T.S. I looked it up in every manual. I went through literally hundreds of pages trying to find a reference. I finally got to know one of the district guys and a couple of months later I asked him. He laughed. He said it meant 'Plain Old Telephone Service.'"

It is difficult to forget that woman, the anxiety she felt and the obsessive way in which she tried to deal with it. Anxiety of the same kind drives the younger woman in search of psychological security and organizational legitimacy to overinvestment in specialization. When she finds it, the seal that reads "Yes, you belong. Yes, you have a right to be here. Yes, in spite of the fact that you're a woman, you *can* do this job" is a tough one to give up.

When it is given up at the middle management transition point the risks begin all over again and the psychological stakes are higher. The security of solid technical competence in a specific area is no longer enough. One can no longer rely on and trust oneself alone. The learning system changes, the system of implementation changes, and *in the nature of the relationships that men traditionally establish with each other lies the key to both.* Godfathers look after godsons.

For women who were daughters, not sons, such relationships are laden with difficulty. If they exist at all they are usually seen as heavily burdened with sexual overtones, or if not, as so asexual that the woman involved is described as "masculine," "a hard, tough bitch who's good at the job and nothing else."

Most women want neither and avoid both. Yet the trap is formidable; at one level, because you're a woman you feel you *must* know the job to justify even being there; at another level, because you're a woman there are far greater risks attached to developing the relationships which help you learn; and at still another deeper level, because you're a woman "femininity" and its relationship to your sense of who you are, are painfully manipulable variables.

The Bell System manager who said "If it hadn't been for my husband I would have quit" was almost certainly addressing this last issue. Whatever she faced as a woman on the job, her husband reinforced her as a person who was a woman and who could hold that job. Single women are far more vulnerable.

Given all of this, is there any answer? If there is, does it help women or does it merely certify that the difficulties are real?

We think that there is an answer, and that it does both. In acknowledging the difficulties, in explaining why they exist, it gives women a perspective of central importance. Women who thought that individually and alone they were the singular source of the problems they faced in "masculine" jobs, careers, roles and settings can see that to one degree or another all women share these problems because a common heritage of beliefs and assumptions shapes our concept of ourselves. If we are ever to change those that cripple our ability to achieve, then it is critically important to understand how and why they came to exist—beginning at the very beginning with the concept of femininity and the ways in which its formation differs from the psychological development of men.

QUESTIONS FOR READING, RESPONDING, AND WRITING

Summarizing Main Points

1. Point out the features of the "hypothetical" woman making the change from supervisor to middle management that, according to Henning and Jardim, make her ill-fitted to her new role. List those features in order, from most detrimental to least detrimental.
2. What, according to Henning and Jardim, is the *major* difference between men's and women's career attitudes? List the factors that lead to that major difference.

Analyzing Methods of Discourse

1. Henning and Jardim provide an illustration, that is, an extended example, of a woman's move from supervisor to middle management after they have provided considerable analysis of the difficulties of such a move. Why do you suppose the illustration comes after the analysis? Does the illustration change your understanding of the difficulties? Does it change your feelings about those difficulties?
2. Jardim and Henning describe the male career path in this way: "Learn and move on. Act so that people will see you as having the ability to move on. Try to influence the people who can help you move on," and so forth. What are the subjects for these sentences? Why do you suppose Henning and Jardim

abbreviate these sentences in this fashion? Compare the sentence structures and use of pronouns in these sentences with the structures and pronouns in other sentences that describe the "hypothetical" woman's career path.

Focusing on the Field

1. Read "Successful American Companies" by Thomas J. Peters and Robert H. Waterman, Jr. What solutions do you feel they might apply to the difficulties that Jardim and Henning outline?
2. Read Michael Korda's "When Business Becomes Blood Sport." What solutions do you feel he might apply to those difficulties? Do you think Jardim and Henning would find Korda's solutions appropriate or acceptable?

Writing Assignments

1. Write an essay that compares and contrasts two different kinds of students in college. You need not base your comparison on sex, but you should create clearly defined categories.
2. Write a short essay that analyzes a particular personality type that you feel succeeds in business. Provide an extended example to help illustrate your analysis.

Tracy Kidder

HOW TO MAKE A LOT OF MONEY

The following selection makes up the first chapter of Tracy Kidder's extremely successful and highly praised book, *The Soul of a New Machine* (1981). Kidder, who was born in New York City in 1945, graduated from Harvard University in 1967, after which he served in Vietnam as a lieutenant. On returning home, Kidder attended the University of Iowa, where he gained an M.F.A. in 1974. In the same year, Kidder published his first book, *The Road to Yuba City*. In a few years he was on a different road with *The Soul of a New Machine*, for which he received both a Pulitzer Prize and an American Book Award.

His research style unquestionably accounts for the unusual density of telling details in his nonfiction. For his latest book, *House* (1985), which describes every phase of the construction of a new building, Kidder spent the better part of a year, taking notes on the site of the new construction every day, keeping the same hours as the builders, while at the same time interviewing the future owners and the architects, as well as researching the history of building in America. From over 4,000 pages of notes—Kidder eschews the tape recorder—he compiled a book of intimate depth and remarkable precision.

Kidder, who is now at work on a study of business and finance, also contributes regularly to *Atlantic Monthly* and is currently a visiting lecturer at Smith College.

For a time after the first pieces of Route 495 were laid down across central Massachusetts, in the middle 1960s, the main hazard to drivers was deer. About fifteen years later, although traffic went by in processions, stretches on the highway's banks still looked lonesome. Driving down 495, you passed some modern buildings, but they quickly disappeared and then for a while there would be little to see except the odd farmhouse and acres of trees. The highway traverses some of the ghost country of rural Massachusetts. Like Troy, this region contains evidence of successive sackings: in the pine and hardwood forests, which now comprise two-thirds of the state, many cellar holes and overgrown stone walls that farmers left behind when they went west; riverside textile mills, still the largest buildings in many little towns, but their windows broken now, their machinery crumbling to rust and the business gone to Asia and down south. However, on many of the roads that lead back behind the highway's scenery stand not woods and relics, but brand-new neighborhoods, apartment houses, and shopping centers. The roads around them fill up with cars before nine and after five. They are going to and from commercial buildings that wear on their doors and walls descriptions of new enterprise. Digital Equipment, Data General—there on the edge of the woods, those names seemed like prophecies to me, before I realized that the new order they implied had arrived already.

A few miles north of the junction of Route 495 and the Massachusetts Turnpike, off an access road, sits a two-story brick building, surrounded by parking lots. A sign warns against leaving a car there without authority. The building itself looks like a fort. It has narrow windows, an American flag on a pole out front, a dish antenna on a latticed tower. Mounted on several corners of the roofs, and slowly turning, are little TV cameras.

This is Building 14A/B—14B was fastened seamlessly to 14A. Some employees call the place "Webo," but most refer to it as "Westborough," after the name of the town inside whose borders the building happens to exist. "Westborough" is worldwide headquarters of the Data General Corporation. Driving up to the building one day with one of the company's public relations men, I asked, "Who was the architect?"

"We didn't have one!" cried the beaming press agent.

Company engineers helped to design Westborough, and they made it functional and cheap. One contractor who did some work for Data

General was quoted in *Fortune* as saying, "What they call tough auditing, we call thievery." However they accomplished it, Westborough cost only about nineteen dollars a square foot at a time when the average commercial building in Massachusetts was going for something like thirty-four dollars a foot. But looks do matter here. The company designed Westborough not just for the sake of thriftiness, but also to make plain to investors and financial analysts that Data General really is a thrifty outfit. "There's no reason in our business to have an ostentatious display," a company analyst for investor relations explained. "In fact, it's detrimental."

The TV cameras on the roofs, the first defense against unscrupulous competitors and other sorts of spies and thieves, must comfort those who have a stake in what goes on inside. As for me, I imagined that somewhere in the building men in uniforms were watching me arrive, and I felt discouraged from walking on the grass.

The only door that opens for outsiders leads to the front lobby. A receptionist asks you to sign a logbook, which inquires if you are an American citizen, wants your license plate number, and so on. Still you cannot pass the desk and enter the hallways beyond—not until the employee you want to see comes out and gives you escort. When I inquired, the cheerful young receptionist said that once in a great while some outsider would *try* to break the rules and *try* to slip inside.

The lobby could belong to a motor inn. It has orange carpeting and some chairs and a sofa upholstered in vinyl, on which salesmen and would-be employees languish, awaiting appointments. Now and then, a visitor will stand and gaze into a plastic case. It contains the bare bones of a story that will feed the dreams of any ambitious businessman. THE FIRST NOVA, reads a legend on the case. Inside sits a small computer, about the size of a suitcase, with a cathode-ray tube—a thing like a television screen—beside it. A swatch of prose on the back wall, inside the case, explains that this was the first computer that Data General ever sold. But the animal in there isn't stuffed; the computer is functioning, lights on it softly blinking as it produces on the screen beside it a series of graphs—ten years' worth of annual reports, a précis of Data General Corporation's financial history.

Left to their own devices, the engineers who worked in the basement of Building 14A/B could surely have produced a flashier display, but a visitor from Wall Street who had never paid attention to this company before might have felt faint before the thing. The TV screen was blue. The graphs, etched in white, appeared in rotating sequence, and each one bore a name. "Cumulative Computers Shipped Since Our Founding" started with 100 in 1969 and went right up to 70,700 in 1979. The image vanished. "Net Sales" appeared, to show that revenues had ascended without a hitch from nothing in 1968 to $507.5 million in 1979. That graph went away and in its place came one describing profit margins. These hardly varied. The profits just rolled in, year after year, along a nearly straight line, at about 20 percent (before taxes) of those burgeoning net sales.

Someone unaccustomed to reading financial reports might have missed the full import of the numbers on the screen, the glee and madness in them. But anyone could see that they started small and got big fast. Mechanically, monotonously, the computer in the case was telling an old familiar story—the international, materialistic fairy tale come true.

The first modern computers arrived in the late 1940s, and although many more or less single-handed contributions fostered the technology, they did so mainly in the shade of a familiar association in America among the military, universities and corporations. On the commercial side, IBM quickly established worldwide hegemony; it brought to computers the world's best sales force, all dressed in white shirts and blue suits. For some years the computer industry consisted almost exclusively of IBM and several smaller companies—"IBM and the seven dwarfs," business writers liked to say. Then in the 1960s IBM produced a family of new computers, called the 360 line. It was a daring corporate undertaking. "We're betting the company," one IBM executive remarked. Indeed, the project cost somewhat more than the development of the atom bomb, but it paid off handsomely. It guaranteed for a long time to come IBM's continued preeminence in the making of computers for profit. Meanwhile, though, new parts of the business were growing up, and out from under IBM.

In the early days, computers inspired widespread awe and the popular press dubbed them giant brains. In fact, the computer's power resembled that of a bulldozer, it did not harness subtlety, though subtlety went into its design. It did mainly bookkeeping and math, by rote procedures, and it did them far more quickly than they had ever been done before. But computers were relatively scarce, and they were large and very expensive. Typically, one big machine served an entire organization. Often it lay behind a plate glass window, people in white gowns attending it, and those who wished to use it did so through intermediaries. Users were like supplicants. The process could be annoying.

Scientists and engineers, it seems, were the first to express a desire for a relatively inexpensive computer that they could operate themselves. The result was a machine called a minicomputer. In time, the demand for such a machine turned out to be enormous. Probably IBM could not have controlled this new market, the way it did the one for large computers. As it happened, IBM ignored it, and so the field was left open for aspiring entrepreneurs—often, in this case, young computer engineers who left corporate armies with dreams of building corporate armies of their own.

For many years sociologists and others have written of a computer revolution, impending or in progress. Some enthusiasts have declared that the small inexpensive computer inaugurated a new phase of this upheaval, which would make computers instruments of egalitarianism. By the late seventies, practically every organization in America had come to rely upon computers, and ordinary citizens were buying them for their homes. Within some organizations small bands of professionals had exercised absolute authority over computing, and the proliferation of small computers did weaken their positions. But in the main, computers altered techniques and not intentions and in many cases served to increase the power of executives on top and to prop up venerable institutions. A more likely place to look for radical change was inside the industry actually producing computers. Generally, that industry grew very big and lively, largely because of a single invention.

Shortly after World War II, decades of investigation into the internal workings of the solids yielded a new piece of electronic hardware called a transistor (for its actual invention, three scientists at Bell Laboratories won the Nobel Prize). Transistors, a family of devices, alter and control the flow of electricity in circuits; one standard rough analogy compares their action to that of faucets controlling the flow of water in pipes. Other devices then in existence could do the same work, but transistors are superior. They are solid. They have no cogs and wheels, no separate pieces to be soldered together; it is as if they are stones performing useful work. They are durable, take almost no time to start working, and don't consume much power. Moreover, as physicists and engineers discovered, they could be made very small, indeed microscopic, and they could be produced cheaply in large quantities.

The second crucial stage in the development of the new electronics came when techniques were developed to hook many transistors together into complicated circuits—into little packets called integrated circuits, or chips (imagine the wiring diagram of an office building, inscribed on the nail of your little toe). The semiconductor industry, which is named for the class of solids out of which transistors are made, grew up around these devices and began producing chips in huge quantities. Chips made spaceships and pocket calculators possible. They became the basic building blocks of TVs, radios, stereos, watches, and they made computers ubiquitous and varied. They did not eliminate the sizable, expensive computer; they made it possible for the likes of IBM to produce machines of increased speed and capability and still make handsome profits without raising prices much. At the same time, the development of chips fostered an immense and rapid growth of other kinds of computing machines.

After mainframes, as the big computers were known, came the cheaper and less powerful minicomputers. Then the semiconductor firms contributed the microprocessor, the central works of a computer executed on a chip. For a while, the three classifications really did describe a company's products and define its markets, but then main-framers and microcomputer companies started making minis and mini-computer companies added micros and things that looked like mainframes to their product lines. Meanwhile, a host of frankly imitative enterprises started making computers and gear for computers that could be plugged right into systems built around the wares of the big successful companies. These outfits went by the names of "plug compatibles" and "third-party peripheral manufacturers"; those who lost some business to them called them "knockoff companies." Probably they helped maintain competition in prices. Many "software" houses sprang up, to write pro-grams that would make all those computers actually do work. Many customers, such as the Department of Defense, wanted to buy complete systems, all put together and ready to run with the turn of a key; hence the rise of companies known as original equipment manufacturers, or OEMs—they'd buy the gear from various companies and put it together in packages. Some firms made computer systems for hospitals; some specialized in graphics—computers that draw pictures—and others worked on making robots. It became apparent that communications and computing served each other so intimately that they might actually become the same thing; IBM bought a share in a satellite, and that other nation-state, AT&T, the phone company, started making machines that looked suspiciously like computers. Conglomerates, of which Exxon was only the largest, seemed determined to buy up every small computer firm they could. As for those who observed the activity, they constituted an industry in themselves. Trade publications flourished; they bore names such as *Datamation, Electronic News, Byte, Computermania*. IBM, one executive of a mainframe company once said, represented not competi-tion but "the environment," and on Wall Street and elsewhere some people made a business solely out of attempting to predict what the environment would do next.

I once asked a press agent for a computer company what was the reason for all this enthusiasm. He held a hand before my face and rubbed his thumb across his fingers. "Money," he whispered solemnly. "There's so goddamn much money to be made." Examples of spectacular success abounded. The industry saw some classic dirty deals and some notable failures, too. RCA and Xerox lost about a billion dollars apiece and GE about half a billion making computers. It was a gold rush. IBM set up two main divisions, each one representing the other's main competition. Other companies did not have to invent competitors and did somewhat more of their contending externally. Some did sometimes use illicit tools. Currying favor, seeking big orders for chips, some salesmen of semiconductors, for instance, were known for whispering to one computer maker news about another computer maker's latest unannounced product. Firms fought over patents, marketing practices and employees, and once in a while someone would get caught stealing blueprints or other documents, and for these and other reasons computer companies often went to court. IBM virtually resided there. Everyone sued IBM, it seemed. The biggest suit, the *Jarndyce* v. *Jarndyce* of the industry, involved the Justice Department's attempt to break up IBM. Virtually an entire large law firm was created to defend IBM in this case, which by 1980 had run ten years and had been in continuous trial for several.

Data General took its place in this bellicose land of opportunity in 1968, as a "minicomputer company." By the end of 1978 this increasingly undescriptive term could in some senses be applied to about fifty companies. Their principal but by no means their only business, the manufacture and sale of small computers, had grown spectacularly—from about $150 million worth of shipments in 1968, to about $3.5 billion worth by 1978—and it would continue to grow, most interested parties believed, at the rate of about 30 percent a year. By 1978 Data General ranked third in sales of minicomputers and stood among the powers in this segment of the industry. The leader was Digital Equipment Corporation, or DEC, as it is usually called. DEC produced some of the first minicomputers, back in the early sixties. Data General was the son, emphatically the son, of DEC.

A chapter of DEC's official history, a technical work that the company published, describes the making of a computer called the PDP-8. DEC sent this machine to market in 1965. It was a hit. It made DEC's first fortune. The PDP-8, says the official history, "established the concept of minicomputers, leading the way to a multibillion dollar industry." But the book doesn't say that Edson de Castro, then an engineer in his twenties, led the team that designed the PDP-8. The technical history mentions de Castro only once, briefly, and in another context. They expunged de Castro.

In 1968 de Castro and two other young engineers seceded from DEC. Several completely different versions of their flight exist and have by now acquired the impenetrable quality of myth. Did they quit because, after long and heartfelt labor on a new design, they found that

DEC's management would not build their new machine? DEC's management did turn down a new design of de Castro's, and afterward, along with a man from another company named Herb Richman, de Castro and the two other engineers from Digital incorporated Data General and started building their own minicomputer. But did they design this new machine after they seceded, or had they done that job in secret, using DEC's facilities, while still on DEC's payroll? One version of the story suggested the latter. More than ten years later, DEC's founder and president would tell reporters from *Fortune*, "What they did was so bad we're still upset about it." But DEC never sued Data General's founders, and clearly there were other reasons why Digital might have become upset. For within a year, de Castro and company had set up shop in DEC's own territory and had started raking in the loot.

They rented space in what had been a beauty parlor, in the former mill town of Hudson, Massachusetts. Practically all that remains of that time is a black-and-white photograph of this first headquarters. In the foreground stand four young men with short hair, wearing white shirts and skinny ties and the sort of plain black shoes that J. Edgar Hoover's men favored. They are engaged in what is obviously meant to look like routine conversation. The linoleum floor, the metal furniture, evoke motor vehicle departments, and the youths in the picture could be members of some junior chamber of commerce, playing capitalists for a day. Not shown in this bemusing picture is the shrewd and somewhat older lawyer from a large New York firm who helped Data General's founders raise their capital and who became a crucial member of their team. What also doesn't show is the fact that some of these young men were already computer engineers of no mean repute—their age in this case was no impediment, for computer engineers like athletes often blossom early.

They started Data General at an auspicious time. In the late 1960s, the period memorialized in John Brooks's *The Go-Go Years*, venture capital (among other things) abounded, and although they started out with only $800,000, more lay in reserve. They also entered a good territory for fledglings. They could not have dreamed of moving in on IBM's markets without truly vast amounts of capital. But the people who bought minicomputers—engineers, scientists, and, mainly, purchasing agents of OEMs—understood the machines. A new manufacturer could reach them through relatively inexpensive ads in the trade journals, and didn't need to build a service organization right away, since these customers could take care of themselves. These were also the sorts of customers who could be expected to embrace a newcomer, if the price was right; they'd prefer a bargain to a brand name.

But around the time when Data General established itself in the beauty parlor, other entrepreneurs were starting up minicomputer companies at the rate of about one every three days. Only a few of those other new outfits survived the decade, whereas Data General, before it had exhausted its first and fairly modest dose of capital, achieved and never fell from that state of grace, a positive cash flow. Why?

The company's first machine, the NOVA, had a simple elegance about it that computer engineers I've talked to consider admirable, for its time. It had features that DEC's comparable offering didn't share, and it incorporated the latest, though not fully proven, advances in chips. Data General could build the NOVA very cheaply. Such an important advantage can depend, in computers, on small things. In the case of the NOVA, the especially large size of the printed-circuit boards—the plates on which the chips are laid down—made a crucial difference. For several reasons, large boards tend to reduce the amount of hardware in a computer. Data General used boards much larger than the ones that DEC was using. Speaking of this difference and other less important ones, one engineer remarked, "The NOVA was a triumph of packaging."

Good machines don't guarantee success, though, as RCA and Xerox and others had discovered. Herb Richman, who had helped to found Data General, said, "We did *everything* well." Obviously, they did not manage every side of their business better than everyone else, but these young men (all equipped with large egos, as one who was around them at this time remarked) somehow managed to realize that they had to attend with equal care to all sides of their operation—to the selling of their machine as well as to its design, for instance. That may seem an elementary rule for making money in a business, but it is one that is easier to state than to obey. Some notion of how shrewd they could be is perhaps revealed in the fact that they never tried to hoard a majority of the stock, but used it instead as a tool for growth. Many young entrepreneurs, confusing ownership with control, can't bring themselves to do this.

When they chose their lawyer, who would deal with the financial community for them, they insisted that he invest some of his own money in their company. "We don't want you running away if we get in trouble. We want you there protecting your own money," Richman remembered saying. Such an arrangement, though not illegal, might raise some eyebrows in some corners of the Bar Association. But the lawyer said, again according to Richman, "That's the first time anyone made an intelligent proposition to me." Richman also remembered that before they entered into negotiations over their second public offering of stock, after the company had been making money for a while and the stock they'd already issued had done very well indeed, their lawyer insisted that each of the founders sell some of their holdings in the company and each "take down a million bucks." This so that they could negotiate without the dread of losing everything ("Having to go back to your father's gas station," Richman called that nightmare). As for the name of the theory behind selling enough stock to become millionaires, Richman told me, "I don't know how you put it in the vernacular. We called it the Fuck You Theory."

In the computer business, your market can be your fate. Although by the late 1970s it was hard to define a company's place in the industry by the sorts of machines that it made, certain broad historic distinctions in ways of doing business still divided a large part of the industry into three segments. The differences showed up in the nature of a company's expenditures. IBM and other mainframe companies spent more money selling their products and serving their customers than they did actually building their machines. They sold their computers to people who were actually going to use them, not to middlemen, and this market required good manners. Microcomputer companies sold equipment as if it were corn, in large quantities; they spent most of their money making things and competed not by being polite but by being aggressive. Minicomputer companies split the differences more or less; they sold some machines and service to actual users, but spent most of their money on hardware and did a big business by selling machines in quantity to OEMs.

From these distinctions, others hung. A seasoned executive in marketing explained, "With micros it's even more competitive, but historically the world of minicomputers is very rough-and-tumble. IBM would say, 'You got a problem, Mr. Customer? A team of four will be there in an hour.' Implicitly a Data General would say to its customers, 'You have to look out for yourselves.' The sophisticated customer, particularly the OEM who buys a lot of computers and looks for discounts, not service, goes for minis. They're capable of living in a rough-and-tumble world. And I'm not sure that IBM, with its organization, can compete in the traditional minicomputer market. It's like putting a goldfish in a bowl with a piranha."

So you could say that Data General entered a territory that asked for a certain brashness. And you could also say that life in this territory became less decorous than it had been, when Data General came along. They set out to get noticed, first of all.

In the lobby at Westborough hangs a copy of the first advertisement that Data General ever ran. It consists of just one page. On one side of the page is a grainy photograph of a man's face. This person looks about to do something very mean. On the other side of the ad, he speaks: "I'm Ed de Castro, president of Data General Corporation. Seven months ago we started the richest small computer company in history. This month we're announcing our first product: the best small computer in the world." The message goes on for a while and winds up as follows:

> Because if you're going to make a small inexpensive computer you have to sell a lot of them to make a lot of money. And we intend to make a lot of money.

This ad's chief architect, a man named Allen Kluchman, who was the company's first director of marketing, told me with a smile, "That ad was independent of any aspect of Mr. de Castro's personality that I knew about at that time. He's the shyest guy I know. He's essentially a pretty humble, private guy."

The ad achieved a certain local fame. It said what many others presumably were thinking, but what none of them felt they should say publicly. For some years thereafter, most of Data General's advertisements contained something slightly brazen. One of the best-known ads wasn't published—some people in the company were by then apparently having second thoughts about the firm's image. But a copy of this unpublished ad hangs in de Castro's office. Over the Data General logo, on a field of white and blue, it reads:

> They Say IBM's Entry Into Minicomputers Will Legitimize The Market. The Bastards Say, Welcome.

Before Data General unveiled the NOVA in 1969—at the industry's yearly fair, the National Computer Conference—the marketeer Kluchman talked a trade magazine into putting a picture of the NOVA on its cover. They rented billboards on the road from the airport to the conference and put a picture of the NOVA on them; at the hotel where most of the people attending the conference stayed, they talked the management into having bellboys distribute free copies of the *Wall Street Journal* with Data General's advertising flyer inside; at the show itself, they raised the placard bearing their company's name higher than any other. When it came to pricing their machine, they announced extraordinary discounts for customers who bought machines in quantity. Never mind that customers had to buy a virtual warehouse of NOVAs to get the truly big discount. Data General had brought a new ferocity, a bit of Forty-second Street, to the pricing of minicomputers.

"DEC owned 85 percent of the business and there was no strong number two. We had to distinguish ourselves from DEC," Kluchman remembered. "DEC was known as a bland entity. Data General was gonna be unbland, aggressive, hustling, offering you more for your money. . . . We spread the idea that Data General's salesmen were more aggressive than DEC's, and they were, because ours worked on commissions and theirs worked on salaries. But I exaggerated the aggressiveness."

According to Kluchman, DEC actually gave them some help in setting up "the Hertz-Avis thing." DEC's management, he said, ordered their salesmen to warn their customers against Data General. "It was great! Because their customers hadn't heard about us." Kluchman imagined DEC's salesmen telling DEC's customers that a dangerous new company was on the prowl, and DEC's customers responding to this news by saying, "Where is this Data General, so we can be sure to avoid them? What's Data General's phone number, so we'll be sure not to call it?" Kluchman laughed. "The calls just *rolled* in. DEC's customers would say, 'We hear you're the bad guys. You must be doing something we oughta know about.'"

And thinking back to those first heady days, when nearly every little strategy seemed to pay off, and the first millions started coming in, Kluchman said, "It was probably more fun than I or anybody else has ever had in business. It was great ego satisfaction. It was just a *pure gas.*"

At the end of fiscal 1978, after just ten years of existence, Data General's name appeared on the list of the nation's five hundred largest industrial corporations—in that band of giants known as the Fortune 500. It stood in five-hundredth place in total revenues, but much higher in respect to the various indices of profit, and for a while climbed steadily higher on the list. Surely by 1980 such a record entitled Data General to respectability. But some trade journalists still looked askance at the company; one told me Data General was widely known among his colleagues as "the Darth Vader of the computer industry." Investors still seemed jittery about Data General's stock. An article published in *Fortune* in 1979 had labeled Data General "the upstarts," while calling DEC "the gentlemen." The memory of that article, particularly the part that made it sound as if Data General routinely cheated its customers, still rankled Herb Richman.

Building 14A/B is essentially divided into an upstairs and a downstairs, and in one corner of the upstairs the corporate officers reside. A wall of glass separates them from the rest of the company. There is no mahogany here. If there is ostentation in the bosses' quarters, it is ostentation in reverse. The table in their conference room, it was proudly said, was the same that they had used when the company was small. Richman's office was comparatively plush. But saying, "We consider ourselves the Robert Hall of the computer industry," Richman pointed out that he had paid for all his furnishings himself and that what looked like paneling on his walls was really just wallpaper.

Among the founders of the company, only de Castro—the much-talked-about president—and Richman remained engaged in daily operations. Richman had come up through the industry in sales—a super-salesman, some called him—and he had created and run Data General's sales force, which was known if not notorious for its aggressiveness. Curly-haired, trim and in his forties, Richman wore a nicely tailored denim jacket and no tie. "I'm one of the few guys that money made a nice guy out of," he said. "Before, I was just driven, clawing. . . . Success has made me more rational and introspective." He remarked that not long ago he had been playing tennis with a man who had seemed to him just an ordinary fellow, but then he had found out that the man was actually president of an oil company. "And it was one of the largest oil companies in the world, and I was just in awe of him," said Richman. He added, softly, "And yet I bet my net worth greatly exceeded his."

The stock that Richman himself owned in Data General was worth about $13 million then, but, he seemed to say, he was unhappy with the way certain organs of the press depicted his company's achievements. They were, Richman believed, too often depicted as "ruffians," not as merely rough, which they were proud to be. "We agree that a lot of things we've done around here are wild," he said. "But we can't understand why we're tabloid, instead of the *New York Times.*"

Some part of Data General's reputation was easy to explain. The company had promoted it themselves, and maybe it had gotten a little out of hand. Richman suggested, "We've done so much so well for so long that everyone seems to think we have to be doing something illegal." A good point, but not a full accounting.

Some years back, in the early seventies, a company called Keronix accused Data General's officers of arranging the burning of a factory. Keronix had been making computers that performed almost identically to Data General machines. The theory was that Data General had taken a shortcut in attempting to get rid of this competitor. In time, the courts found no basis for those charges and dismissed them. Indeed, it seemed preposterous to think that the suddenly wealthy executives of Data General would risk everything, including jail, and resort to arson, just to drive away what was, after all, a small competitor. But Wall Street didn't see it that way, apparently. When Keronix made its accusation, Data General's stock plummeted; there was such a rush to unload it that the New York Exchange had to suspend trading in it for a while. More peculiar was the fact that many years later, some veteran employees, fairly far down in the hierarchy, would say privately that they believed someone connected with the company had something to do with that fire. Not the officers, but some renegade within the organization. They had no basis for saying so, no piece of long-hidden evidence. It seemed to me that this was something that they wanted to believe.

I got this feeling more than once. Turning down the road to Building 14A/B one day, a veteran engineer pointed out the sign that warned against unauthorized parking. "The first sign you see says Don't," he remarked. He imagined another sign by the road; it would say: Use of Excessive Force Has Been Approved. The engineer laughed and laughed at the thought.

In a land of tough and ready companies, theirs, some of Data General's employees seemed to want to think, was the toughest and the readiest around.

Certainly Data General's reputation had other underpinnings besides advertisements and imagination. In an industry where sharp marketing practices were common, Data General's were as sharp as any, and by the late 1970s competitors were challenging some of them in federal court. To the contention, leveled in *Fortune,* that Data General played especially rough with its customers, it was only fair to add that many of Data General's customers knew very well what sort of market they were in, and moreover, it was clear that the company could not have survived if most of its customers had not felt at least fairly satisfied. But Data General was litigious, toward customers as well as others. "Sure," said Richman, "if people don't pay us or breach our contract, we litigate 'em." They did so at least in part to assure Wall Street that they weren't the sort of company that would accumulate a crippling number of bad debts.

The salient feature of Data General, however—what that sharp-eyed, astonished visitor from Wall Street would have pondered—was its growth. This was indeed the industry's salient characteristic. In the main, computer companies that were not dying were growing; they had to do so just to stay alive, it seemed. But no company whose primary business was making computers had grown more rapidly than Data General. Bursts of growth were not uncommon, but Data General had been bursting for a decade, and what's more, it had been maintaining the highest profit margins in the industry next to IBM's. All this would have impressed the analyst from Wall Street, of course, but would also have given him pause.

Building 14A/B and its sparse furnishings, the facts that Data General paid its stockholders no dividends and that its top managers dispensed to themselves and other officers exceptionally small salaries, meting out rewards in the form of stock instead—all were signs of a common purpose. The company had displayed extravagance when it came to financing its tendency to go to court. Otherwise, the management seemed bent on saving all their cash to feed the hungry beast of growth. And, of course, the more this beast gets fed, the bigger it becomes, the more it wants to eat. It is one thing for a company with revenues of a million dollars a year to grow 30 or 40 percent in a year and quite another for a half-a-billion-dollar company to pull off the same trick.

Analysts on Wall Street sometimes become boosters of the companies they follow. Looking for an opinion that was certain to be disinterested, I asked an old friend, a veteran analyst of securities, to take a look at Data General's numbers. He had the advantage of never having followed the company before, and in return for anonymity he agreed to my proposal. A couple of weeks later, he called me back. It seemed to him that Data General was bent on continuing to grow at 30 to 40 percent a year. He pointed out that this meant large growth in everything—in the need for capital, new buildings, new employees. Between 1974 and 1978, for instance, Data General had hired about 7,000 new employees, roughly tripling its numbers; in one year alone the company had increased its ranks by 71 percent. The analyst imagined the difficulties of finding that many qualified people so quickly. And what must it be like, he asked, to work at a place like that? You'd come to work some morning and suddenly find yourself in charge of a dozen people, or suddenly beneath a new boss to whom you would have to prove yourself all over again. "That sort of growth puts a strain on everything," the analyst concluded. "It's gonna be intriguing to see if they get caught." He thanked me for putting him onto such a marvelous entertainment.

Where did the risks lie? Where could a company go badly wrong? In many cases, a small and daily growing computer company did not fall on hard times because people suddenly stopped wanting to buy its products. On the contrary, a company was more likely to asphyxiate on its own success. Demand for its products would be soaring, and the owners would be drawing up optimistic five-year plans, when all of a sudden something would go wrong with their system of production. They wouldn't be able to produce the machines that they had promised to deliver. Lawsuits might follow. At the least, expensive parts would sit in inventory, revenues would fall, customers would go elsewhere or out of business themselves. Data General got one leg caught in this trap back around 1973. Six years later, a middle-level executive, sitting in an office upstairs at headquarters, remembered that time: "We were missing our commitments to customers. We just grossly fucked over our customers. We actually put some entrepreneurs out of business and I think some of them may have lost their houses. But we recovered from our shipment problems and never repeated them."

Another way of fouling up had less to do with a company's own growth than with the growth occurring all around it. From observers of the industry came such comments as: "Things change fast in the computer business. A year is a hell of a long time. It's like a year in a dog's life." In every segment of the industry, companies announced small new products for sale every day. Companies brought out new lines of computers, much more powerful than the ones they replaced, only every few years or so; but considering all the work that went into them and the fact that they required a redirection of effort throughout a company, the pace at which these major announcements came was very rapid too. Conventional wisdom held that if a company fell very far behind its competitors in producing the latest sorts of machines, it would have a hard time catching up. And failure to stay abreast could have serious consequences, because major new computers played crucial roles in the other business of the companies; they helped them sell all their little products and, often, their older types of machines.

At some companies the task of guarding against this sort of crisis fell mainly to engineers, working below decks, as it were. Executives might make the final decisions about what would be produced, but engineers would provide most of the ideas for new products. After all, engineers were the people who really knew the state of the art and who were therefore best equipped to prophesy changes in it. At Data General, an engineer could play such an important role. It was there for the taking. The president, de Castro, liked "self-starters," it was said. Initiative was welcomed at Data General, and in the late seventies it appeared that the company had need of some initiative from its engineers. For Data General was in a bind. The firm had fallen behind the competition: it hadn't yet produced the latest big thing in minicomputers.

Early in 1979 the businessman who told me about Data General's problems and recovery back in '73 hit upon a heroic metaphor for success in the computer business. "The major thing," he said, "is avoiding the big mistake. It's like downhill ski racing: Can you stay right on that edge beside disaster? At Data General we keep coming up with these things that are basically acts of recovery. What Tom West and his people are doing is a great act of recovery."

QUESTIONS FOR READING, RESPONDING, AND WRITING

Summarizing Main Points

1. What general impression do you get of Data General's business practices from Tracy Kidder's essay? Of DEC's? Of IBM's? Are those impressions the same as those the general public might hold? Which of the three companies would you most like to work for?

2. Look back at Kidder's first paragraph where he describes the countryside surrounding Data General. The area has gone through many changes. What evidence is there of those changes? What evidence is there of the most recent

change? How does the most recent change confuse Kidder? In what ways does that confusion and those changes affect your thinking about the rest of the essay? What do you feel this paragraph implies about the permanence of Data General?

Analyzing Methods of Discourse

1. In what ways do you feel that Kidder provides an objective analysis of Data General? In what ways is he subjective? After reading the entire essay, do you think that you find out how Kidder himself feels?
2. Kidder provides information about Data General from many points of view: the receptionist's, the engineers' and scientists', the sales representatives' and advertisers', a veteran analyst's, its competitors'. How are these points of view similar and how are they different?

Focusing on the Field

1. John Kouwenhoven, in "What's American about America," finds similarities in twelve apparently dissimilar things. How is his method similar to Kidder's?
2. This essay comprises the first chapter of a larger book, *The Soul of a New Machine*. Though Kidder leaves his reader with no factual questions unanswered, has he succeeded in arousing your interest enough to want to learn more about Data General?

Writing Assignments

1. Choose a topic of your own about which there are differing points of view (e.g., service at the college bookstore, usefulness of fraternities, usefulness of English composition classes). In one or two paragraphs, sketch those points of view so that your own point of view becomes clear.
2. Kidder suggests that the financial reports on Data General tell "an old familiar story—the international, materialistic fairy tale." Would the story of Data General fit the category of fairy tale as Bruno Bettelheim describes it in "Fairy Tale versus Myth"? Support your answer with evidence from both essays.

Louise Bernikow

TRIVIA INC.
A Simple Multimillion-Dollar
Board Game

Louise Bernikow—poet, journalist, scholar—is a graduate of Barnard College (B.A., 1961) and Columbia University (M.A., 1963; M.Phil., 1974). She also studied at Oxford and at the University of Madrid as a Fulbright scholar. She is a frequent lecturer on college campuses and has taught at Juilliard, City College of New York, and Queens College in New York City. A regular contributor to many magazines, including *Esquire,* where the following essay first appeared, as well as the *University Review,* the *Times of London, European Travel and Life, GQ,* and *Mademoiselle,* she has also served as a contributing editor for *Savvy.* In 1970, she published a historical profile of Soviet spy Rudolph Abel, *Abel.* She has edited a collection of poetry by women, *Among Women,* worked on several textbooks and anthologies, including *Basic English Reader* (1975), *Introduction to Sociology* (1973), and *Women and Sports* (1978). She is currently finishing a work entitled *Alone in America: The Search for Companionship.*

In *Trivia Inc.,* Bernikow follows the rags-to-riches success story of the creators of a board game that, for some people, has become more than a game and far more than a trivial pursuit.

The Woodbine Room at the Ascot Inn sounds wood-paneled and posh but is actually low-end Howard Johnson's. "Worse," Chris Haney says. It is the end of the road for Haney, his brother John, and Scott Abbott, the inventors of Trivial Pursuit, the board game whose retail sales in the United States approached $750 million in 1984. Ten minutes from Toronto's airport, this "seminar hotel" oozes Muzak, which they are unable to get turned off. Genus II, the latest of six editions of the game, is done. The room is lined with tables draped in food-stained indigo cloth and laden with encyclopedias, notebooks, a globe, beer cans, and overflowing ashtrays. The self-styled wackos chose to work in this godforsaken place, disdaining offices, secretaries, suits, or limos, because it is equidistant from their homes, remote from the hundreds of people who want access to them, and only twenty feet from a bar.

The story of Trivial Pursuit is a story about bars. In the Ascot's bar Chris Haney drops his six-foot-three hulk into a chair, smoothes his handlebar moustache, orders a light beer, lights a cigarette, and considers bangers and mash for lunch. Scott Abbott, Mutt to Haney's Jeff, smaller, fair-haired, precise, the "wordsmith" of the group, drops beside him, followed by John Haney, Chris's older brother, who looks younger, calmer, less worn out. They could be a rock band on a break, except they don't talk about licks or chord changes.

"What if we did a postnuclear edition of the game?" Chris says. "How about: 'What's the capital of the United States after the holocaust?'"

Abbott waits a beat. "'Air Force One,'" he answers.

"'And what are the first words of the President's first speech?'"

"'My fellow American. . . .'"

The journey ending at the Ascot Inn started in a similar merry mood at a kitchen table covered with beer bottles. It was Saturday afternoon, the middle of December 1979. Chris Haney, whose table it was, was a thirty-year-old photo editor at the Montreal *Gazette*. Scott Abbott was a thirty-year-old sportswriter for the Canadian Press. The two had been friends for four years. Abbott had moved in with Chris and his wife, Sarah, because the Haneys couldn't afford the house alone. They were not what you would call nose-to-the-grindstone guys. Haney dropped out of high school when he was seventeen. Vagabonding was in his blood. He had been to thirteen different schools and "every town we lived in, we were famous because our father read the news on the radio." His brother John, according to Sarah Haney, "is the serious, responsible one. He's the one who sends flowers to Mom on her birthday. Chris was always on a lark."

Scott Abbott was also a more settled and vaguely more respectable guy. He was a hockey player who had stayed in school and gone on to get a master's degree in communications at the University of Tennessee. In the American Tavern, across the street from the *Gazette*, where he and Chris spent a lot of pool-shooting, beer-drinking time, he was known for his unbelievable memory for sports trivia.

Haney and Abbott were playing Scrabble at the kitchen table that Saturday. They were also thinking about money. Think how many Scrabble games had been sold. Think how much you could make if you invented a game. This was not the first time the two had thought about money together. A year before, they'd organized a chain-letter scheme that brought in a couple of thousand dollars.

It took forty-five minutes to come up with the game. It would be an old-fashioned board game, the kind of game, Haney says, "everybody has stashed away in their closets." It would be a question-and-answer game, all about "the kind of things we knew from being in the news business, being attuned to small details." Trivia. Trivia Pursuit. Sarah Haney added an *l* to the name "because it sounded better."

Haney and Abbott turned out to be more serious about Trivial Pursuit than anyone would have thought. They went almost immediately to John Haney, who was then house manager of the Shaw Festival

Theatre in Niagara-on-the-Lake and trying to figure out what a hockey player past his prime might do with his life. Knowing they would need free legal advice, they added a lawyer to the group—Ed Werner, who had played hockey with John at Colgate University. In January of 1980 they formed a company called Horn Abbot Ltd., marrying Chris's nickname, said to be either Horn or Horny, with Abbott minus the final *t*. The *t* was dropped to allow them to create their logo: an abbot with a horn—a horny abbot. Horn Abbot would manufacture and sell the game. They'd copyright, trademark, and patent everything they could, including the design of the board. Chris Haney and Scott Abbott would each own 22 percent of the company; John Haney and Ed Werner would each have 18 percent. The remaining equity would be raised by selling shares at $200 apiece, with a minimum purchase of five shares. Since they knew the game could go stale, even with six categories of questions, one thousand questions per category, they committed themselves, right at the start, to creating two editions of the game a year for the next two years.

Their target audience was the baby-boom generation. Haney defined the market as "people like us," by which he meant something about sensibility as well as demographics. "The generation that made the Beatles rich would make us rich," he said. Scott Abbott was equally specific—they would aim at "the Howdy Doody to Gordon Liddy set." Whatever the inventors identified with and responded to would be the heart of the game. The "people like us" theme runs clear through the story of the game's creation, and the way Horn Abbot does business.

"People like us" were shaped by American culture. "Remember," Haney says, "I was born in 1950, and I lived on the U.S. border. I grew up on American television. Scott, John, and I all traveled a lot and did our own thing." So accustomed is Haney to dealing with "people like us" that he recently balked at a magazine reporter who kept asking why Trivial Pursuit had so many questions about President Kennedy's assassination. "The guy hadn't even been born then," Haney says, amazed that such people exist or that they could hope to understand. "I was thirteen. I'll never forget it." The young seem to exasperate him, particularly those with the sensibility of the Eighties. He had just talked with a twenty-one-year-old who was getting married and describing his career and financial plans. "For Chrissake," Haney said, "why don't you go to Morocco and beg for six months?"

"People like us" are sociable. They get by with a little help from their friends. They mistrust authority. They're still living in the Sixties. They don't like computers, and they're not big on video games, with their isolated pleasures. But Haney and Abbott understood that the next step was to acquire some expertise in the game business, which meant encountering people not exactly "like us." In February they went to the

Canadian Toy Fair in Montreal, the annual industry meeting at which manufacturers show their wares to potential buyers. Armed with a press pass and filmless camera, they "interviewed" toy company executives and retailers, saying afterward that they had gotten "a crash course in capitalism." Then they set out to find investors.

Mostly, they worked the bars. Hundreds of people turned them down. Derek Ramsey, a copyboy at the *Gazette*, coughed up $1,000, convinced he would never see it again but figuring it beat buying lottery tickets. By April Chris Haney had quit his job and perfected his pitch.

Thirty-four people were persuaded to invest a total of $40,000. Many of them had their hearts in their mouths as Chris, Sarah, and John sailed to Spain (Chris won't fly, although Sarah has a pilot's license) carrying duffel bags full of reference books. They made their way to Nerja, on the southern coast, a refuge for hippies, expatriates, and dropouts from around the world. They'd been to Nerja before—it was still full of "people like us." Daily, the brothers went down to the beach carrying beer bottles and a mock-up of the game. They made up questions and read them to "some Australian and English bums we'd picked up," Chris says.

What made for a good Trivial Pursuit question? Things that "got people going." All the questions were journalists' questions—who, what, when, where, and why? If people laughed at the answers or slapped their foreheads, realizing they had known all along, the questions were good. Scott Abbott, who kept his job and flew to Spain at vacation time, had a talent for phrasing. He wouldn't ask how many feet of wire a Slinky has, for example. That's too dry, too difficult. He'd ask, "What toy contains 66.6 feet of flattened wire?" Chris Haney had an instinct for the right kind of subject. The quintessential Trivial Pursuit question for Haney: "Where is the best place in Europe to buy a used Volkswagen van?" The answer— "American Express in Amsterdam"—would be known to players on the beach in Nerja, not from reference books, but from experience. People like us know things like that.

By the spring of 1981 everyone had reassembled in Canada; they holed up first in Ed Werner's house to edit the questions and then in an empty office next to T.J.'s bar to manufacture the game for test marketing. "We sat for days trying to figure out how to collate a thousand cards," Sarah Haney says. "The cards were about 80 percent of the cost of the game—getting the six colors printed right and then collating them. We thought maybe the post office had a machine, but we ended up at a bindery." Chris, the perfectionist, "really carried the ball," according to Sarah. "He'd be gone from 7:30 A.M. to 8:00 P.M." He was also drinking a good deal. The bartender "loved giving me triple Scotches at night."

In November 1,100 sets were ready to go. An eighteen-year-old out-of-work artist named Michael Wurstlin had designed the final board and been paid five shares in the company. Terry Mosher, a Canadian political cartoonist known as Aislin, had been recruited to draw posters that captured the game's irreverence, its politics, its fascination with touch-stones of American culture: Richard Nixon, nailed in a history book, with YOU LIVED THROUGH IT. NOW TRY AND REMEMBER IT written below. *The Last Supper* with everyone playing Trivial Pursuit. Sam and Rick from *Casablanca*. Mosher refused shares and took a $1,000 payment instead.

All the crucial decisions about Trivial Pursuit had been made by this point, and every one of them went against the grain of the game business. The questions were too sophisticated. The game was too expensive to make. Six companies were involved in production, and the finished games cost Horn Abbot sixty dollars apiece. They sold them for sixteen dollars wholesale, $29.95 retail—an exorbitant price for a board game. The package design was odd—a high, squarish box with no happy family, no descriptive material on the outside—a look that has since been de-scribed as a cross between a Brooks Brothers box and After Eight mints. The rationale behind it was to make the game upscale from the start and sell it in stores that didn't usually carry games. The $44,000 loss they would take on the trial run, Horn Abbot expected, would be offset by the credibility they would gain with banks when they sold out.

The partners flogged the game in Toronto, St. Catharines, and Vancouver. On one occasion, one partner placed two games in a store, another came in and bought one, the first returned and said, "You've sold 50 percent of your stock," and urged the retailer to "take a six-pack." They sold out. By the time the Toy Fair rolled around again, they sailed into Montreal with their hopes high. They expected several thousand orders to come from their descent first on Montreal, then on New York. In the end, they had orders for fewer than three hundred games. A Milton Bradley executive had turned them down; Parker Brothers had agreed to have a look but returned the game unopened.

Through February and March, Chris Haney says, "we were belly-up. We could have been had for a song." Chris suffered most. "I had done almost all the work," he says. "My heart and soul were in it. I drained my savings." He had been paying himself $150 a week. Sarah Haney returned beer and soda bottles and sewed lavender sachets for food money. She was pregnant with her second child and looking for a job. Chris was not eating, drinking heavily, and smoking five packs of Camels a day.

Canadian stores wanted more games, but Horn Abbot couldn't pro-duce them. Ed Werner finally turned up a savior. A St. Catharines bank manager came up with a $75,000 line of credit, but the partners had to sign for personal liability. Production was set for May 15. Then the "shit," as Chris Haney calls it, "hit."

He needs another beer before he will talk about it. His palms sweat. When he stumbles, John fills in. They were in a restaurant and Chris collapsed on the floor. John cradled his head in his arms. An ambulance sped them to the hospital, where Chris lay in intensive care for three days. It looked like a heart attack, but the eventual diagnosis was stress, compounded by the abuse he had been heaping upon his body. Released, he went right back to work. Two weeks later, Sarah got a phone call from John. "When I got there," she says, "Chris was a blithering idiot in a fetal position in the back of a car." Sarah decided against hospitalizing him and took him to her parents' farm. For weeks Chris chopped wood, cooked, and spoke to no one.

Twenty thousand games rolled into stores at the end of May. Scott Abbott left his job at last. He and John Haney closed ranks to cover Chris's absence. Then Tom Vernon, a former Parker Brothers executive who had become head of Chieftain Products, a Canadian game company, got interested. Chris came down from the farm to meet with Vernon and went right back. Negotiations began, and Vernon sent a game to Selchow & Righter, an American company whose games he distributed.

1982 was Pac-Man's big year. Retail sales of video games and software in the United States reached $2.1 billion. Board-game companies were in trouble. Selchow & Righter, the country's oldest game company, had made the decision early on to "stick to the knitting" and, except for a brief excursion, stayed out of the electronic game market. Scrabble and Parcheesi had been their bread and butter, reliable if unspectacular sellers for years. (The Scrabble connection makes skeptics wonder about the story of Trivial Pursuit's origins over a Scrabble board.) In 1981, according to Richard Selchow, who worked in the computer industry before taking over the presidency of his grandfather's company, "we had to take some write-offs." The next year was better, with revenues for Selchow & Righter around $20 million. In September 1982 a Trivial Pursuit game arrived in the company's Bay Shore, New York, headquarters.

Richard Selchow sat down in his office to play the game with his vice-president for marketing, John Nason, and his head of research and development, Ed Rivoir. They played it wrong, giving themselves tokens for every right answer. Nason couldn't think where the Wright Brothers had launched their first plane. Kitty Hawk never came to him. Nor did Nason know the name of Dagwood Bumstead's boss. Richard Selchow didn't know Marilyn Monroe's real name. He still doesn't.

The three men loved the game and decided to proceed, banking on a market they hoped was weary of the isolation of video games and ready for the "social interaction" they had just experienced. Ed Werner and

Scott Abbott arrived from Canada to negotiate. So the company that turned down Monopoly because it resembled gambling met the company made up of guys who loved the kinds of smart-aleck questions later excised from the first American edition of the game:

"How many months pregnant was Nancy Davis when she walked down the aisle with Ronald Reagan?" ("Two and a half.")

"What was Woody Allen's last line in *The Front?*" ("Go fuck yourselves.")

Haney calls the encounter "Ghostbusters meet Lawrence Welk." Selchow calls the Haneys and Abbott, collectively and affectionately, "a parent's nightmare." No matter. Selchow & Righter agreed to manufacture the game and distribute it in the United States, paying a 15-percent royalty and a $75,000 advance in an industry where royalties range from 5 to 7 percent and $5,000 advances are considered large.

On November 18 the Silver Screen edition of Trivial Pursuit was launched in Toronto. The next day Selchow and Ed Rivoir flew up for the official signing of their agreement. A television crew was at the Hampton Court Hotel to cover it. On Christmas Eve, Haney's bank took his Visa card away because he was late with a fifty-dollar payment.

It fell to John Nason to market Trivial Pursuit in the United States. Selchow & Righter couldn't afford to advertise, so Nason looked for a public relations firm instead.

At the suggestion of a college buddy, Nason called Linda Pezzano, who had been in business for a little more than two years. She had started out to be a folk singer in Greenwich Village, gone into the PR business instead, and done well enough to attract offers to buy her small agency. Pezzano occupied a cramped space on Fifty-seventh Street in Manhattan with the staff "sitting on each other's laps."

Nason said he was from Selchow & Righter.

"What's that?"

"We make Scrabble."

"Oh, I love Scrabble."

Between the call and the meeting Pezzano gave herself a weekend crash course in the game business like the one that the Haneys and Abbott had acquired at the start. By Monday morning she had a strategy ready. Nason liked the chemistry immediately. After their meeting he called Selchow to say the company should look no further. Nason offered Pezzano a six-month contract to introduce Trivial Pursuit. She would be paid $40,000, of which she said she'd take half in fees. Then he okayed the press release and told her to go ahead with the first promotional phase. The Toy Fair, scene of debacles for the game's inventors just a year before, was only eight weeks away. Could they intercept the buyers, get their attention?

"Usually," Pezzano says, "by the time a client responds to an idea, the window has closed. Nason doesn't wait around." Nor did Pezzano. She wanted to start with samples—the way soap companies hang sample products on your doorknob. She also loved teasers: "They address the crazy maniacs with piled-high desks and a three-second attention span." She'd do a teaser, but she knew no one read junk mail. So she found the smallest available envelope the U.S. mails would deliver and created a card in Trivial Pursuit blue, slipped it into the yellow envelope, had it handstamped, and left off the return address. Each folded card contained a sample question card from Trivial Pursuit. Outside, the first card said: TRIVIAL PURSUIT. A CANADIAN SUCCESS STORY. The second added the line OFFICIAL U.S. INTRODUCTION TOY FAIR '83. The third card ended with: NOW FROM SELCHOW & RIGHTER. For three weeks before the Toy Fair, 1,800 top buyers got a mailing a week. They started calling Selchow & Righter to complain if they missed one.

Later, Pezzano took the Trivial Pursuit cards that named living celebrities and sent them, along with letters and games, to eighty stars. Larry Hagman responded that he'd always known he was trivial, but not that he would become famous for it. James Mason sent a handwritten note from Switzerland. Gregory Peck said he played by his own rules. Both promotions, Pezzano says, were risky and went against traditional market wisdom: "How many clients would send something out that doesn't have marketing information—or their name? There was no way of measuring if these things were working. It was a leap of faith and they took it."

Pezzano and her client spurned the inventors' idea that Trivial Pursuit should be aimed at the baby-boom generation. They went for a larger audience—"high teens to sixty," Pezzano says, "upscale and educated. We never thought baby boom." Aislin's posters were never used in the United States.

For a long and frightening moment it looked as if nothing would happen. Pezzano sent John Haney and Scott Abbott on a promotional tour of New York, Chicago, and Los Angeles. They appeared mostly on radio programs aimed at trivia nuts. Chris Haney refused to come. Stores had the games, but the games weren't moving. Selchow & Righter rented warehouse space to store the surplus.

The Big Chill came as a big surprise. In Hollywood, unknown to Pezzano, the game had caught fire. People were giving Trivial Pursuit parties and using bootlegged copies of the Silver Screen edition, already on the market in Canada. The cast of the television show *St. Elsewhere* and the cast of *The Big Chill*, then being shot, were hooked. If ever there was a natural connection, it was the one between the game and the film about Sixties kids living in the Eighties. The connection was not immediately apparent to Pezzano, who was nonplussed when Columbia Pictures called. "I kept waiting for them to tell me that the game was in the movie," she says. It wasn't—Chris Haney said later a telegram from Columbia asking to use the game in the film had missed him—but Columbia wanted twenty games for a small promotion. Without dwelling on her mystification, Pezzano promised one hundred games and full cooperation. By the time she was done, she had arranged for every journalist who attended the film's New York screening to get a copy of the game, to have herself and Richard Selchow present at the Hollywood premiere of the film, and to say with ease, as though she had known it all along, that "the spirit of *The Big Chill* is the spirit of Trivial Pursuit."

In Canada, however, Scott Abbott was experiencing the spirit of burnout. He remembers the day: "On June 21, 1983, I was driving along a highway and I just stopped. My foot wouldn't work on the gas pedal. I pulled off the road. We were under the gun to get the sports edition ready. I had hangovers all the time and I was dreaming in Q and A. Thank God," he says, looking back, "we don't have to put ourselves through that anymore."

They don't. Abbott revived. Sales soared. In Canada the game sold 2.3 million copies in 1983. In the United States a million games had been sold by the fall, when game sales traditionally are just getting under way. Selchow & Righter was out of stock. A generation that had lived suspiciously through the oil shortage of the Seventies wondered whether the scarcity was on the up-and-up, but it was. Selchow & Righter began to subcontract the manufacturing to four new facilities. Retail sales for the year in the United States totaled about $40 million. Pezzano came in $2,000 over her initial budget. Her contract with Selchow & Righter was expanded. The Haneys went to Nerja to rest.

The year 1984 was the year of the empire. Trivial Pursuit became a cultural artifact. It was buried in a time capsule along with Michael Jackson's *Thriller* album. The inventors continued producing new editions—Baby Boomer and a Young Players edition in 1984, Genus II ready for introduction at the start of 1985.

To handle international licensing of the game, Horn Abbot recruited Blake LeBlanc from Ed Werner's law firm and set him up in Barbados. LeBlanc—whom Haney calls "another one of us; he's right out of a Jimmy Buffett song"—sold European and Australian distribution rights to General Mills and negotiated a $600,000 advance on the royalties. Adapting Trivial Pursuit in approximately sixteen countries is a network of journalists, some recruited, others old friends from Spain. The inventor of Rubik's Cube is working on the Hungarian version.

Now comes the merchandise. Licensing the Trivial Pursuit trademark for a range of products are Randy Gillen, a lawyer who took one of the last blocks of original shares in Horn Abbot because "I was impressed with the wackiness of these guys," and John Hozack, a former client of Gillen's, who has twenty years' experience in merchandising. At their first meeting Chris Haney told Gillen and Hozack to "get rid of those suits," but they still seem to find them useful. The strategy for licensing products follows standard Horn Abbot business practices. They deal only with manufacturers, are phobic about middlemen, and won't work with anyone they don't feel comfortable with. Gillen and Hozack receive royalties as high as the game brings, equally unheard of in the industry. They're starting with products aimed at an "upscale" market—a brass box to hold the game, gold electroplated playing pieces. The idea is to begin at the top and "trickle down" to the mass market. Although Gillen estimates the built-in aftermarket for products at "at least nine million units," they have no desire to go for a quick buck. No cheap promotions. No sleazy products. "Our livelihood," Gillen says, "depends on longevity."

At the end of the road lies a desire to leave town while everyone else thinks about longevity. Selchow & Righter has expanded its plant and launched new products. Linda Pezzano has moved to a posh office in lower Manhattan, where she has twenty employees and bills $500,000 a year in fees. But Horn Abbot has begun to entrust the empire to others—the staff of a Canadian children's magazine to do the Young Players edition, two music critics and a kid from Alabama to produce a game based on music history. Of the original trio, Scott Abbott is the only one with "a great concern about remaining occupied." John Haney seems content to be with the child he and his wife have just adopted. Chris Haney is sticking to light beer and ultralight cigarettes, that he might live to enjoy his success. All he wants to do now is "go to Dorset and watch the sheeps."

But first they have to think about money. A jarring note was struck last fall when free-lance writer Fred L. Worth filed a $300-million lawsuit in California claiming he'd been robbed. One third of the questions in the original Genus edition, and a good number of the Silver Screen questions, Worth says, were lifted, mistakes and all, from his *Complete Unabridged Super Trivia Encyclopedia*. Worth says he sued because he "felt like an unpaid partner" in Trivial Pursuit's success—he hasn't shared in the profits, the glory, or the credit. The case, which may take years to litigate, touches a fuzzy legal area—facts can't be copyrighted, but the *expression* of facts can be. How much borrowing from Worth's compilation can be considered "fair use"?

Lawyer Ed Werner won't comment except to say that "our noses are sufficiently out of joint about this suit," but that, on the other hand, "it's kind of neat to hang around the bar telling people you've been sued for $300 million."

Whether the suit is settled in or out of court, there is still a great deal of money at stake in Toronto. In 1984 Trivial Pursuit sold twenty-two million games in the U.S. alone, which means royalties of more than $50 million for Horn Abbot. By 1985, the company estimates, thirty-six million games will have been sold in North America and perhaps sixty million throughout the world. There hasn't been time to think about it yet, although the Haneys invested small amounts in the manufacture of a goalie stick and in a vineyard. Sarah Haney spent part of the first royalty check on eiderdowns for all her beds and on supporting a child in Bolivia. She wants to start a home for battered wives and children. "After the dust settles," she says, which will be when the year ends, "it's time we sit down and have a long talk about money. We can do anything we want to."

It's hard to imagine Chris Haney in Dorset forever. The pleasures of celebrity are fickle but immense. When the "couple of wackos" were given the Ontario Business Achievement Award in Toronto last fall, Chris was impressed by the Ontario Cabinet members present. "I respect businessmen now," he says. "They're in a tough world." In black tie, receiving the award, he felt like a movie star. Still, a habit of mind dies hard. Haney thinks he might write a cookbook. The title is a question— *Do Frozen Peas Float?*—and the answer is on the last page.

QUESTIONS FOR READING, RESPONDING, AND WRITING

Summarizing Main Points

1. List the positive and negative effects that the game has had on both Chris Haney and Scott Abbott. Do you think the positive effects outweigh the negative for either or both of them?
2. Bernikow tells the reader that the " 'people like us' theme runs clear through the story of the game's creation, and the way Horn Abbot does business." Define "people like us" and list examples of their business practice.

Analyzing Methods of Discourse

1. Bernikow begins and ends her essay with descriptions of what lies "at the end of the road" for the creators of Trivial Pursuit. What relation does the first description bear to what follows it? What relation does the last description bear to what precedes it? What relation do the two descriptions bear to each other?
2. Do you think Bernikow tries to influence the reader's opinion of Haney and Abbott or do you think she leaves the way open for the reader to make up his or her own mind about them? Cite examples in the essay to support your decision.

Focusing on the Field

1. What do the people Haney and Abbott do business with think of them professionally? What do you think of them as businessmen? Do you think the way "people like us" do business is unusual?

2. Does the introduction of a lawsuit late in the essay affect your view of Haney's and Abbott's business practices?

Writing Assignments

1. Read Calvin Trillin's "The Great Ice Cream War." Write an essay in which you compare Chris Haney and Scott Abbott to Ben and Jerry.
2. Thomas J. Peters and Robert H. Waterman, Jr., in "Successful American Companies," cite James March's business theory to support their argument. March attacks "the rational model [of doing business] with a vengeance." Would Abbott and Haney agree with March that "organizations learn and make decisions . . . almost randomly"? Support your assertions with evidence from "Trivia Inc."

Stan Luxenberg

McDONALD'S: THE FRANCHISE FACTORY

In *Roadside Empires: How the Chains Franchised America* (1985), the book from which the following essay is taken, Stan Luxenberg examines the distinctly American business phenomenon—the franchise—describing its history, its mode of operations, and its economic impact, with statistics like the following: "franchise companies now account for one-third of all retail sales in this country and 15 percent of our GNP. . . . Ninety percent of Americans over twelve eat fast food regularly, while 300,000 people a night sleep at Holiday Inns."

According to Luxenberg, through the power expressed by numbers like these, franchises have altered the face of America itself, just as surely as they have altered the face of American business. Yet in his book, Luxenberg argues convincingly that "franchises are simply inefficient and unproductive in comparison with traditional businesses," though they may not seem so at first. In "McDonald's: The Franchise Factory," Luxenberg traces the beginnings of the famous franchise, discovering its roots not only in Ray Kroc's inspired partnership with Maurice and Richard McDonald—the fictitious "Ronald" showed up much, much later—but in the assembly-line and mass-marketing techniques that make it work. Luxenberg, who is a graduate of the Columbia School of Journalism, lives in New York City and is a freelance business writer whose articles have been published in the *New Republic, Harper's, Inc.,* and other periodicals.

At first Ray Kroc was not impressed with the simple hamburger stand he had traveled halfway across the country to see. A small eight-sided building with high windows, it reminded some employees of a fishbowl. MCDONALD'S FAMOUS HAMBURGERS, a sign on the roof proclaimed. The drive-in located in San Bernardino, California, seemed little different from hundreds of establishments Kroc had seen in his thirty years as a salesman. As he sat in the parking lot one desert morning in 1954, Kroc wondered if the store could live up to its awesome reputation.

Shortly before the eleven a.m. opening time employees began pulling up, dressed in crisp white shirts, trousers, and hats. With carts they hauled potatoes and meat from a nearby shed into the store, bustling "like ants at a picnic," Kroc later wrote. Then the customers began to appear, lines of them filling the parking lot. They swarmed up to the drive-in, ordering hamburgers at the front windows and french fries at a side window. In a few minutes customers made purchases, then returned to their cars carrying bags of hamburgers. Kroc watched in disbelief. Curious to learn more about this ritual, Kroc stopped some customers and asked how often they visited the place. Every day, one workingman volunteered. A fashionably dressed young woman explained she stopped by as often as possible.

The customers came from miles away. What drew them was the best food at the lowest price in the area. The menu was fixed. Hamburgers cost fifteen cents, while a bag of fries was a dime. The sixteen-ounce milk shakes cost twenty cents. The plain fare never varied and neither did the quality. It was the most efficient money-making machine Kroc had ever seen. His excitement grew as he pondered the possibility of making this elegantly simple restaurant available to people around the country.

Most of his life Kroc had been on the prowl for ways to make a fortune. At fifty-two he was comfortably middle class, but the big success he had long sought eluded him. Short and cocky, the ebullient Kroc had pushed a variety of products, speaking in his flat Midwestern accent. For a time in the 1920s he worked as a paper-cup salesman for the Lily Tulip company in the Chicago area, selling to pushcart vendors and to concessions at the zoo and ballpark. One winter when business slowed Kroc decided to try his luck in Florida.

A skilled pianist, he landed a job playing with the Willard Robinson band at a swank speakeasy on Palm Island, called The Silent Night. Owned by a rum runner who brought illegal liquor from the Bahamas, the nightclub featured marble floors, Grecian pillars, and an unusual pricing policy. All drinks, whether champagne or whiskey, cost a dollar. There were only three choices on the menu—lobster, steak, and roast duckling. Years later Kroc recalled the stylish simplicity of the club and the efficiency achieved by serving only a few items.

After a brief career at the keyboard, Kroc returned to Chicago and selling cups. One of his customers was the young Walgreen Drug Company, which used pleated cups to serve sauces at its soda fountain counters. For drinks the drugstore used traditional glassware. Watching the lunch-hour crowds waiting for seats, Kroc developed a novel idea. With a new kind of Lily cup, Walgreen could sell milk shakes "to go." Instead of waiting, the overflow customers could take their drinks with them. Walgreen—and Kroc—would increase sales. The Walgreen executive Kroc approached thought the idea was ridiculous. The company was charging fifteen cents for each shake served in a glass. If the drugstore bought cups at one and a half cents apiece, profits would melt away.

Kroc suggested opening a special take-out counter. Walgreen resisted. Finally the salesman offered to *give* the store a supply of cups to try his idea for a week. From the first day the innovation succeeded. Kroc had won a big account, and each time Walgreen opened a new unit, cup sales increased. The big profits, Kroc had learned, came from the chains and large corporations. From then on he would spend less time chasing pushcart vendors and concentrate on a few big companies such as Swift and Armour, who ordered thousands of cups.

In 1938 Kroc began selling the Multimixer, a device that could produce five milk shakes at once. After the war, as the economy picked up, the salesman began doing business with a new breed of companies, franchised chains such as Dairy Queen and Tastee-Freeze. These growing operations provided steady demand for more milk shake makers. Even so, the profits of most soft-ice-cream stores were dwarfed by the earnings of a hamburger stand in San Bernardino that Kroc had heard about.

Kroc's curiosity was aroused when he learned that the drive-in had ordered eight Multimixers. How could one hamburger stand need to produce forty shakes at a time? The salesman flew to Southern California to find out.

The McDonald's outlet was one of dozens of drive-ins that had sprouted in Southern California, a growing region where cars had already assumed a special importance. In the early 1930s drive-in restaurants began appearing in city parking lots, then spread along the highways, most of them featuring chicken, barbecue beef, and pork. While the food in most places was similar, the restaurants competed by trying to come up with novel service ideas. Some hired aspiring Hollywood starlets as carhops, who dressed in outlandish costumes or worked on rollerskates.

Maurice and Richard McDonald took a different approach. The brothers came from New Hampshire to California in the late 1920s, hoping to find jobs in the movie industry. After handling props on Hollywood sets for a few years they bought a movie theater, then in 1940 turned to running a hamburger stand. The McDonalds knew little about the food business, but they learned quickly. By 1948, when they opened the San Bernardino restaurant, they had developed their powerfully streamlined operation.

From long experience on the road, Kroc appreciated how rare the McDonald's drive-in was. At most roadside stands the quality of the food might vary considerably from day to day. McDonald's provided a reliable meal. For the traveling salesman clean restrooms were an unexpected bonus. The McDonald brothers kept theirs immaculate.

Kroc eagerly introduced himself to the creators of this wondrous fast-food factory. The brothers were delighted to meet the salesman they called "Mr. Multimixer." The next day Kroc returned and again witnessed the long lines of customers. He envisioned hundreds of McDonald's restaurants around the country, each one using six of his Multimixers. "I've been in the kitchens of a lot of restaurants," he told the brothers, "and I have never seen anything to equal the potential of this place of yours."

But the brothers were not interested in expanding. They were already making $75,000 a year and owned three Cadillacs. Living in a big white house on a hill overlooking the restaurant, they enjoyed sitting on their porch watching the desert sunsets. They were not interested in a venture that would only create problems. The scrappy salesman was not easily discouraged. By franchising, he argued, the McDonalds could continue living their quiet lives while the royalty checks poured in. The brothers need only find someone to sell the franchise licenses. He, for example, would be willing to assume this headache.

Kroc returned to Chicago, having reached an agreement. He would sell franchises and split the proceeds with the McDonalds. In late middle-age the salesman threw himself into the project. Kroc's wife was furious at him for abandoning a secure business for this risky one. But Kroc had always hoped to become rich, and this seemed like his last chance.

The first step was to build a pilot unit in Des Plaines, Illinois. Franchise chains typically start with an experimental outlet where the business can be refined and new ideas can be tried. The pilot store can build a track record that will entice franchisees seeking a profitable business.

For a year Kroc and his staff worked on the Des Plaines store, making it into a smooth-running operation. Though the McDonald brothers' drive-in was an efficient model, Kroc saw areas where wastage could be reduced, pennies saved. He would no longer hand-dip ice cream for shakes as the McDonalds had done. The new store began using a soft product taken from a tank.

Kroc also began developing the uniform specifications that would serve as guides for franchises around the country trying to reproduce the McDonald's formula. The chain would offer a limited menu. This simplified purchasing, while quality could be controlled. By using assembly-line techniques and not offering any variety in hamburgers or condiments, the chain's labor costs could be kept to a minimum. McDonald's under Kroc could continue to sell hamburgers for fifteen cents, a price that seemed suspiciously low even in the 1950s.

Above all, the Kroc system aimed to achieve speed of service. The goal was to serve a hamburger, fries, and a shake in fifty seconds. After much discussion and experimentation Kroc settled on what he considered the ideal hamburger that would be simple to make yet appeal to the majority of palates. The patty weighed 1.6 ounces and measured 3.875 inches across before cooking. It was 19 percent fat and did not contain any lungs, hearts, or cereal. The bun was three and a half inches wide.

In the first years of operation Kroc and his staff refined their procedures. They determined how high to stack the patties so that the bottom ones would not be crushed out of shape. After considerable experimentation they settled on how much wax had to be in the wax paper, separating the patties so that the burgers could easily slip off the paper onto the grill.

In the 1950s french fries were an unimportant side dish that brought in little profit at most restaurants. The McDonald brothers, however, lavished considerable attention on their fries. Many customers were fiercely devoted to the product. Kroc believed the McDonald's fries were the best he had ever tasted. Convinced that they would be crucial for his chain he set out to master french fry production. "The french fry would become almost sacrosanct for me, its preparation a ritual to be followed religiously," he wrote in his autobiography, *Grinding It Out*.

Kroc cooked his first batch, carefully duplicating the brothers' method. He peeled the potatoes, leaving a bit of skin for flavor, then cut Idaho shoestring strips and soaked them in cold water. After the water was white with starch he rinsed off the potatoes and then fried them in fresh oil. Out of the grease the batch looked just right, golden brown. But something was amiss. The McDonald's fries were always crispy, but this batch was mushy. Kroc struggled to reproduce the perfect fries. After several phone calls to California he learned that the McDonald brothers stored their potatoes in bins where they naturally cured in the dry desert air. Kroc put an electric fan in the basement of his Illinois store, blowing on the potatoes to reproduce the desert drying effect. After three months of trying he achieved the correct formula.

Kroc insisted that his stores be clean and wholesome to appeal to the middle-class suburban families. All windows would be washed every day. Employees would be well-groomed. Kroc furnished the kitchens with gleaming stainless steel equipment that would flaunt the cleanliness of the operation. All the cooking was done in full view of customers. The

open work area enabled patrons to see that the cheap patties were prepared in a spotless environment. In addition, the employees laboring over
the grills provided diversion for customers standing in line.

Like the McDonald brothers Kroc wanted to keep away unsavory
teenagers, whose loud cars and reckless ways might scare away the family
trade. There would be no jukeboxes, cigarette machines, or pay phones
that would encourage loitering at the stand. While the carhop system
invited teenagers to linger in the parking lot, the McDonald's self-service
window insured that customers would eat their meals and quickly return
to the highway. For extra protection no young females would be hired,
since they might attract ill-mannered young men.

With the hamburger production system designed, Kroc set out to sell
franchises. By the end of 1957 there were thirty-seven McDonald's outlets
operating. By 1959 the total had reached one hundred. Each unit was
designed along the lines that Kroc had laid out. Operators who signed on
with the young chain were carefully indoctrinated in the McDonald's
system. They listened as Kroc hammered away at his theme of "QSC/
TLC" or "Quality Service Cleanliness/Tender Loving Care."

In the 1950s the new McDonald's outlets caused a sensation. People
traveled miles to witness the phenomenal stand dispensing cheap hamburgers. In later years Kroc would be compared to his hero, Henry Ford.
The praise was exaggerated but Kroc, like Ford, had extended the techniques of mass production into a new area. Before Ford's great Michigan
assembly lines screeched into production, cars had been individually
crafted conveniences for the rich. Relying on standardized parts and
economies of scale, the young company produced the Model T—a simple vehicle that came in one color, black. Selling at a price the masses
could afford, the Ford became wildly popular. By extending the mass-
production concept to hamburgers Kroc brought the ways of the factory
into a service industry. At McDonald's unskilled workers repeatedly performed specialized tasks. The hamburgers were identical units, like the
Model Ts. Thanks to Kroc's innovativeness, activities that had once been
conducted in the household or by small businesses could now be accomplished on a large scale. Giant corporations could be built to run restaurants, barbershops, and motels. With standardization, these businesses,
which had once been low-profit operations, could create fortunes for
distant central managements. Already accustomed to the use of factory-
produced goods, Americans accepted motels that looked alike and
muffler shops that promised uniform service.

Kroc's innovation came at a time when services were beginning to
dominate the economy. As Daniel Bell pointed out in *The Coming of
Post-Industrial Society*, at the turn of the century seven out of ten
American workers were engaged in production of goods, laboring in

fields, mines, and factories. The other 30 percent of workers were in the service sector, attending to goods produced by others. They labored as domestic servants or worked in businesses such as banking or insurance. After 1920 the number of jobs in industry increased, but the percentage of jobs claimed by the goods sector declined. Jobs in finance, real estate, and retailing were growing at a relatively faster rate. By 1950 employment was evenly divided between goods and services. As farms became mechanized, a lower proportion of national income was being spent on food. At first this additional money went to pay for durable goods, such as housing, automobiles, and clothing. Gradually people began spending on services that had once been luxuries—dry cleaning, restaurants, and travel. These were fields in which the Kroc methods could be applied.

Kroc inspired thousands of chain builders. Some attempted to duplicate every detail of the master's operation. One of the more successful imitators was Burger Queen, a company that began operating in Louisville, Kentucky, in 1961. (The chain later changed its name to Druther's.) George Clark, one of the founders, recognized that Kroc had developed a winning formula. "Most everybody copied McDonald's," he recalls, "either through observing or maybe they copied subconsciously. Our food was exactly the same as McDonald's. If I had looked at McDonald's and saw someone turning hamburgers while he was hanging by his feet I would have copied it. We were aware that they didn't have music or pinball machines, which every other drive-in had at that time. They didn't have a phone. So we followed them."

Kroc standardized all aspects of his business, not just the kitchen. Bookkeeping, personnel practices, and building construction were the same throughout the chain. Howard Johnson and other chains had been heading in the direction of standardization, but Kroc introduced an extreme regimentation that had never been attempted in a service business. McDonald's purchasing and quality-control procedures became a model for chains of all kinds. For the last three decades entrepreneurs have looked at McDonald's and said, "Well, if Kroc can make so much money selling hamburgers, why not apply his system to motels or real-estate offices?" What the imitators have particularly admired is the chain's unified image. This has come to be a hallmark of McDonald's and all the major franchise companies. Each outlet in a chain attempts to be like every other outlet. The service provided must be similar in all parts of the country. Kentucky Fried Chicken tastes the same in Vermont and New Mexico. Holiday Inns operates on a policy of "no surprises."

Following Ray Kroc's example, companies who decide to franchise begin by standardizing operations. The chef of the would-be franchise company can no longer cook by the seat of his pants. Recipes must be sharply defined and simplified so that others can reproduce them. Procedures for all phases of management must be carefully charted so that they may be taught to others. Product selection must be extremely limited. By establishing uniform standards companies can maintain control of costs. More important, standardization allows chains to project a brand image, advertising identical outlets over wide areas.

(Inevitably, local franchisees devise systems they believe are superior to the parent company's approaches. Anyone naturally welcomes profitable ideas, but in a franchise chain free-lance experiments are seriously discouraged. Deviations can destroy the company's standardized image. In addition, the parent companies provide what they believe are proven methods. An inexperienced franchisee who tampers with a recipe or architectural design may lower profits. Still, if a local operator does develop a profitable idea, it may be adopted by the parent and then introduced in all units of the chain.)

To ensure uniformity companies supply franchisees with a complete standardized package. The larger, more sophisticated companies supply precise specifications for equipment, food supplies, and signs. Minuteman Press, for example, details the type of printing press the franchisee should use and helps make the purchase. It provides a sign for the store and copy and design for Yellow Pages ads. The company explains how to hire a printer and solicit business by calling on potential customers.

The level of detail companies try to regulate varies. KOA [Kampgrounds of America] franchisees are free to sell any groceries they want as long as the camp stores provide customers with basic staples. Great Expectations insists that all its haircutting shops have bright orange-and-white fixtures. Some companies issue franchisee manuals containing hundreds of regulations. Dunhill Personnel System employment recruiters must make seventy phone calls a day in their efforts to match job vacancies with eligible executives. To use time effectively they are told not to open their mail until the end of the day. H & R Block tax returns must be checked twice for accuracy. A medium Pizza Hut pizza should measure thirteen inches across. Minuteman franchisees are supposed to join at least two service clubs in their communities, such as the Rotary and Kiwanis, so that they can meet influential businessmen who will provide customers.

Dunkin' Donuts offers detailed cooking instructions for each kind of its donuts. Honey-dip donuts, for example, should be fried at 375 degrees Fahrenheit. The donut company supplies a chart that shows symptoms of common problems. If the grid pattern in the cake donuts forms erratically, the dough may be too wet.

Some companies regularly send bulletins announcing new regulations. McDonald's franchisees complain that they receive so many volumes of materials they could spend all their time just trying to read and digest the information. The *H & R Block Tax News* bulletin of October

1981 informed franchisees about tax regulations covering the rental of a vacation home to relatives and surgical hair transplants for cosmetic purposes. An issue of *The Block Connection*, a newsletter, carried a word of caution under the headline WINDOW BANNERS FOR FARM RETURNS. "There are two different window banners for farm tax returns, one saying, 'We specialize in farm returns,' and 'Farm returns prepared here,'" the newsletter explained. "In using the window banners, be sure that if you use the 'specialize' banner someone in your office is very familiar with farm tax returns."

One issue of Dunkin' Donuts' *Journal of Quality* warned that the frozen wild blueberries used in the company's muffins should arrive at the store at a temperature no higher than zero degrees Fahrenheit. If the berries thaw and then refreeze they will bleed in the muffins. "You should not accept the delivery of blueberries that do not meet the criteria," the *Journal of Quality* cautioned.

Unfortunately, in a winter issue the donut journal editors could offer only a makeshift solution to the problem of "melting soup lids." "Now that you are, no doubt, in the midst of the peak soup season, you have probably had occasion when a customer may order more than one take-out soup. The end result many times may be the top container falling through into the bottom one. The most effective method found, to date, to inhibit the melting lid on multiple take-out soup orders is to have your hostesses place one or two napkins between the containers. The napkins seem to serve as a buffer and steam absorber between the lid and the container bottom.

"An industry check with all the prominent take-out container manufacturers tells us that the problem is a national one with no real answer to date. The usage of take-out containers for hot items probably does not warrant the mold and material investment necessary on the part of the manufacturers. Please contact us if you have any questions on this matter or other container problems you may have."

Fighting to survive in an increasingly franchised market, companies have come to regulate their operations even more tightly. All aspects of the business are examined to keep costs down. In the crowded restaurant industry, the quality of food may be sacrificed in the interest of maintaining profits.

Fast-food chains rely on portion control, calculating precisely the food supplies that will go on each sandwich. Prices are adjusted to ensure profits on each item. Arby's, a roast-beef-sandwich chain, carefully avoids waste. The Arby's meat is shipped to stores in "roasts" that weigh ten pounds each. A beef product minus the bones, the roasts are brown and gummy-looking masses covered with fat.

The meat is cooked slowly for about three and a half hours in an oven at 200 degrees Fahrenheit, until the internal temperature of the roast is 135 degrees as measured by a thermometer inserted into the beef. The beef is then removed from the oven and allowed to continue cooking in its own heat for about twenty minutes until the internal thermometer reads 140 degrees. The slow process is designed to keep shrinkage to a minimum. If cooked correctly the finished roast will weigh between nine pounds, four ounces, and nine pounds, seven ounces. The final figures are carefully recorded and sent to headquarters. Managers are held responsible for any inordinate weight loss. The ounces are closely watched because they quickly add up. Each Arby's beef sandwich contains three ounces of sliced meat. Managers are expected to produce around forty-seven sandwiches from each ten-pound roast. If the process is done improperly, each roast will yield fewer sandwiches and profit margins will be trimmed. In a business where thousands of roasts are sold each week, losses soon mount. McDonald's once attempted to sell roast beef sandwiches but soon abandoned the product. Profits were slim partly because the company could not control meat shrinkage.

In their efforts to achieve standardization and portion control most franchised restaurants have come to rely heavily on frozen and precooked food. As chains become larger, using fresh products becomes increasingly uneconomical. Ray Kroc managed to hold the price of McDonald's hamburgers to fifteen cents until 1967, when it rose to eighteen cents. To hold down prices the company soon resorted to frozen patties. Eventually McDonald's even abandoned the fresh potatoes Kroc cherished for his revered french fries. Franchises had long complained about the labor involved in peeling and slicing potatoes. The peels caused sewer backups. Since the stores constantly needed shipments of potatoes, many kept railroad cars full of them at all times. Bad weather could disrupt deliveries. As the demand from chains for fresh Idaho spuds increased, it became impossible to buy the highest grade at certain times of the year. Franchisees were forced to use inferior products.

Aficionados mourned the passing of McDonald's homemade fries, but franchisees watched their profits increase with the arrival of frozen precut potatoes. Today french fries are one of McDonald's most profitable items, accounting for $1 billion in sales annually.

QUESTIONS FOR READING, RESPONDING, AND WRITING

Summarizing Main Points

1. What does "standardization" allow chains and franchises to do that other businesses cannot?
2. According to Luxenberg, what other services have been standardized and made into franchises since McDonald's? Do you recognize any others that Luxenberg fails to mention? Are all kinds of franchises equally standardized?

Analyzing Methods of Discourse

1. Luxenberg begins his essay with a brief narrative: a scene at the "original" McDonald's that shows Ray Kroc amazed and delighted by "the most efficient money-making machine" he had ever seen. Why do you suppose Luxenberg begins his esssay in this way?
2. How does Luxenberg expand his essay to include other chains and franchises? How is McDonald's related to those other chains? Look back at the essay and find where Luxenberg restricts himself to commenting on only one kind of chain in a single paragraph and where he includes several kinds in a single paragraph. Why do you suppose Luxenberg organizes his paragraphs in this way?

Focusing on the Field

1. What business practices have changed at McDonald's since the fifties? What do you suppose accounts for these changes?
2. Stan Luxenberg is a free-lance writer specializing in business. What do you suppose first attracted him to writing about McDonald's? Can you tell where he gets his information?

Writing Assignments

1. Louise Bernikow, in "Trivia Inc.," analyzes the business attitudes of the inventors of the game Trivial Pursuit. Write an essay in which you compare and contrast those attitudes with Ray Kroc's attitude.
2. In a short essay, describe the ways in which colleges and universities might be considered "standardized." Is standardization necessarily bad? Explain.

Stanley Elkin

A LA RECHERCHE DU WHOOPEE CUSHION

Stanley Elkin was born in 1933 in New York City and went west for his education, receiving a B.A., an M.A., and in 1961, a Ph.D. from the University of Illinois. A year after finishing his Ph.D., Elkin became an associate professor at Washington University in St. Louis and two years later published his first novel, *Boswell: A Modern Comedy*. Elkin successfully manages his academic and artistic careers: Still a professor at Washington University, he has also been a visiting professor at Yale, Boston University, and the University of Iowa. He has also produced a steady stream of stories, novellas, and novels, among them *The Dick Gibson Show* (1971), *The Franchiser* (1976), *The Living End* (three contiguous novellas; 1979), and

George Mills (1982). His work has netted him numerous grants and awards: the *Paris Review* Humor Prize, a Guggenheim Fellowship, and both Rockefeller Foundation and National Endowment for the Arts and Humanities grants.

Elkin has been described as a "stand-up literary comedian," whose power is in the energy and flash of his rhetoric. A constant in his work is his use of "snowballing language" to invent characters who invent their own worlds as they talk, but who ultimately find themselves alone in their elaborate verbal constructions. Elkin's stylistic pyrotechnics have won him both praise and criticism, but they seem both to illustrate perfectly his love for the "excesses of America, the overstatement of the neon signs on our Broadways," and to suggest the loneliness and frustration that exist beyond the glow, and that are always the understatement of his work. In the following essay, first published in *Esquire* in 1974, Elkin satirically applies the high literary introspection of Marcel Proust's opus *A la recherche du temps perdu* (*In Search of Things Past*) to the mail-order gag trade to create a nostalgic but critical look at the company that sold America "those great old practical jokes."

Paul Smith owns that mail-order company we remember, the Johnson Smith Company, candy-butcher of Joy Buzzers and Whoopee Cushions to the world. There is nothing Phil Silvers about him, nothing top banana in the patter or handshake. If he hadn't been his father's son he would probably be doing something else now. He is an inheritor and has about him, even after all these years, the vague shuffling quality of the stand-in. When his brother Arthur retired in 1967—what can one say?—*all this became his*. And he can hardly wait to retire.

"Why?"

"Well, frankly, I have other interests."

"What?"

"Philosophy."

"Phi*lo*sophy?"

"To some extent I'm interested more or less in keeping up with various things that are going on." To some extent he is blowing smoke. He means it, but would not be saying it if he hadn't been asked. "I believe we're in an evolutionary culture. What interests me mostly is what you might call positive motivations of people. In other words, inspirational, creative aspects, if you want to call it that, and since I'm science oriented, my feeling is it's learning more about the unknown."

"The occult?"

"No, not the occult. For me the most interesting thing about living is solving problems. When the dynamics of a business is gone—I don't rate my ideas about life or about business very highly—I feel compelled to read and try to learn as much as I can."

"Who do you read? What philosophers?"

"Buber. Teilhard de Chardin. Proust. Proust isn't a philosopher, but I read him. Wodehouse is my favorite author. My eyes are—"

There is something wrong with his eyes. He blinks, rubs them. He carries two pairs of glasses and changes them frequently. Sometimes he wears neither pair, allows his eyes the air as one would walk barefoot. I like him.

"What will you do?" I know that he majored in math and physics at the University of Wisconsin. "Will you take up your physics again, your math?"

"It's all changed. I don't think I can even do calculus now." He pauses, brooding over his ruined calculus. "We'll travel. We'll travel a lot."

He looks a little like Dean Jagger, the actor of executives, and he wears the calm, off-dark handsome clothes of the conservatively dressed. He speaks quietly, in Jagger's sprung rhythms, a flat, faintly archaic American at distinct odds with the copy he has written all these years for the Johnson Smith Catalog. Great Lakes English. For some reason even his description of what Johnson Smith sells—"hobby merchandise, unusual rings, self-improvement books, electrical and scientific kits, fortune-telling, magic, novelty jokes and tricks, practical gadgets, time-savers"—sounds anachronistic, the dead diction of his father's faded spiel. What is there about the terms "hobby merchandise," "unusual rings" and "novelty jokes and tricks" that sounds, well, imported, faintly road show?

Alfred Johnson Smith founded the Johnson Smith Company in Australia in 1905. Following some homeopathic instinct, he brought it to Chicago in 1914. Chicago was the headquarters of Sears, Roebuck, another mail-order house. He published his first catalog there and stayed on until he moved the business to Racine, Wisconsin, in 1923, and then to Detroit in the late Thirties. Three years ago Paul Smith built a new office and warehouse in a small industrial park in Mt. Clemens, Michigan, so that everything could be on one floor. Always near the shore of one Great Lake or another, good, honest place, forth-, down- and up-right, football terms finally, Green Bay Packer country, locatable on maps, and not just this P.O. Box or that Drawer Something Something of ordinary mail-order arrangement. Smith has a theory that a mail-order business should have hub-ness. Trust and patience—it can take weeks to receive what you've sent away for—diminish exponentially with distance. Johnson Smith has always drawn most of its business from Chicago, Milwaukee, Cleveland, Toledo and Detroit—its freshwater-port nexus and the proximities of trust.

The items are a blur to him, he's seen so many, but he loves the catalog. A dozen exotic catalogs, opened and unopened, ride his desk like a convoy. Thousands, in love with their childhood, doing as adults that self-reflexive ancestor worship which is nostalgia, dote on their memories of the money they spent, the decisions made so carefully, the items chosen deliberately as first furniture. Smith loves the catalog and he can parse it like a scholar.

"Almost all Sears catalog illustrations were woodcuts. This was before photographs and halftones came in. I knew most of the fellas who made the woodcuts for us. We'd send the article to the woodcut maker and he'd reproduce it. You'd be surprised. It would have more detail than a photograph. Most of the great woodcuts came from Chicago. One fellow in Chicago and one in New York were the last fellas to do the woodcuts. I think they're still being made, but they're prohibitively expensive. They cost twenty-five to thirty dollars when we stopped having them made. The trend was toward photography and halftones. Now *this*, I think, is the perfect way to illustrate an item. You show the item and then you show what it does."

We are looking at #2753 in an old Johnson Smith Company catalog—the Rubber Coat Hanger. I think the man still in his coat and leaning forward on his cane is related to the man whose hat is falling. For one thing, their hats are alike, and they both have canes. They may have injured their legs on an earlier visit. I don't know who the fat man is.

I know *what* he is, however. Smith tells me.

"A lot of our practical jokes came from Germany. Before the war, our main source was Germany. The Rubber Coat Hanger is a German item. I would say all the items on this page are German."

"The Whoopee Cushion, was that a German item?"

"I would guess that the Germans had it. Whether they had it first I don't know."

Whether they had it first. One thinks of the Whoopee Cushion Race, of Whoopee Cushion Capabilities, Whoopee Cushion Gaps. Smith continues to point out page after page of German practical jokes. "There's an element," he says, "of sadism in almost any practical joke. A leveler. My way of bringing you down to my level, or at least pricking your bubble if you're too pompous. To an extent humor is retaliatory. A leveler. To my mind I guess I'm not a practical joker."

German. Germany. German. The funny little men whose rubber heads you pressed to make water squirt from their cigarettes—all Germans. All the fellows smiling benignly into trick kaleidoscopes which blackened their eyes as they ground their vision against the belly dancer. "Occasionally we'll get a letter from a parent who takes exception to an item. We've dropped itching powder and almost everything applied to the skin or taken internally. Five or six years ago the Food and Drug fellow came through. . . ." All the sneezers, their eyes squeezed tight as children's waiting to be shown a surprise, their faces distorted in the perfect way to illustrate an item, their mouths open in "AH!" and collapsed in

"CHOW!!" And Germans too the scratchers, fingers mining their itches, prospectors of their own persons in a desperate pantomime of greed and relief. As German as the nose holders—four out of five in the illustration oddly left-handed—pinching their schnozzes like men fixing the crease in fedoras, their jaws like clamps and the line of their mouths in puey's down-angled disdain.

I read the copy—"We also have PERFUME BOMBS. These are identical with the ANARCHIST STINK BOMBS excepting that the odor from the Perfume Bombs is more agreeable than that from the Stink Bombs. Perfume Bombs can be sent by parcel post. Stink bombs are not mailable and are shipped only by Express"—stare at the illustration, for despite the lockjaw, closed-for-the-duration position of their mouths, these men are speaking. Dialogue balloons from their heads as in any deodorized comic strip.

"WOW PU."

"-R-R."

"This way out. The street for mine."

"My. Oh my. What the————! Smells So Bad."

"SAY BOYS SOMEONE HAS A LIMBURGER HERE." (This remark unattributable, floating balloonless all over, the thrown voice perhaps of someone who has mastered the secrets of ventriloquism on another page.)

And from the sixth who walks among them, "That's an awful smell, boys." The speaker does not pinch his nostrils and he alone is smiling. I think he's the anarchist. Why doesn't he suffer? Has he been on the game so long? Has he realized that you can't make an omelet without breaking eggs? Does he *like* Limburger? Is the stink bomb an acquired taste? Whatever, there is a quality of "What's Wrong With This Picture?" throughout the Johnson Smith catalogs, particularly the older ones, as if the lacunae are planted, a necessary touch of the awry and askew to get you to look twice.

But all that was in the raw old days, times when Johnson Smith could call a spade a spade and worse. Since then the company has climbed down from true, gone soft on victims. Explosive matches and exploding cigars and auto scare bombs have given way to gift-wrapped pop boxes, and even the copy puts "explodes" in quotation marks. Illustrations make clear that all one is getting for one's $1.59 is a sort of modified jack-in-the-box. ("When the dynamics of a business is gone—") Nader's Raiders are abroad in the land, and ride childkind.

"There's been an increase in product-liability suits all over the country. Settlements are quite high. Until twenty years ago we didn't even carry product-liability insurance. Now our premiums compare to a doctor's. The company has become cautious. Our catalogs are submitted for inspection to the authorities. Fifteen or twenty years ago you could advertise indiscriminately. We subscribe to the Comic Code."

"The comic code?"

"Yes. Our advertising budget runs about one or two hundred thousand dollars a year. No, that's too high. Probably it's something under a hundred thousand. We do about a third of our advertising in hobby type books, *Popular Mechanics, Popular Science, Field and Stream*, and another third in miscellaneous places and, of course, comic books."

Oh, the *Comic* Code. I remember the Comic Code, the official-looking little cartoon seal like a stamp burning on a passport, remember the slick inside front cover of the comic book, the squeezed, tightly-printed brick ads like a high wall of the classified, the windows with their smear of illustration, the reduced crosshatch of woodcut like spoiled fingerprint or an imposition of fur, all the faces—who knew they were German?—bearing their stigmata of muddy track like galosh-marked rugs in the hall. Recall—but one was babied, only-childed, holier than thou—the sense one had that there was something not just illicit but perhaps actually illegal about the devices offered there, like flying soiled flags or photographing money. Maybe it had to do with state lines, maybe that's how they could do it. There was, when I was a boy in the Thirties, a teen-ager in the Forties, a mystique about state lines.

State lines were, for a few miles on this side and a few more on that, free ports of a kind, where ordinary ordinance and day-to-day due process could be fudged—law's and territory's olly olly okshen free, an odd three-mile limit where fireworks were openly sold, liquor and cigarettes at reduced rates, where kids could drive cars and people could get married without waiting for blood tests, where you could bet on horses or buy lottery tickets and the pinball machines paid off in cash, where whorehouses thrived and gambling in roadhouses, where soiled flags were flown and money photographed. West Memphis, Arkansas, and West Yellowstone, Montana, and Covington, Kentucky, and Calumet City, Illinois, and Crown Point, Indiana—American Ginzas. "Wide open," father said, but somehow working both ways and watch out for the speed traps. Everything up front, Wisconsin pushing its cheeses at you as soon as you left Illinois, Georgia its pecans. So maybe that's how they worked it, because it was all through the mails and they couldn't see you were a kid.

"The biggest problem of the mail-order business is finding an unusual item that's economical to ship and will get there without being broken. Another problem is handwriting. Sometimes I have to try to interpret what's wanted."

We are examining the 1974 catalog, the sixtieth-anniversary edition.

"It's only eighty pages."

"Oh yes. Our 1929 catalog was seven hundred sixty-eight pages. My father wrote virtually all the copy for that. I guess the last really hefty catalog we put out was in 1952. That was five hundred seventy-six pages. That catalog could be published for forty cents. We couldn't do that now."

As one goes through the 1974 edition, one notices certain things; it is changed yet unchanged. It's true that there is nowhere to be found among its sixteen hundred items—the 1929 edition must have had at least seven thousand—the "NIGGER MAKEUP WITHOUT BLACKING." ("Slipped on or off in a minute. No burnt cork or muss.") And I cannot find "THE JOLLY-NIGGER PUZZLE." ("The grinning nigger clings on to the brightly polished steel ball in his mouth. . . .") Or even "THE JEWISH NICKLE." ("A very clever pocket joke. Hand it to a friend, streetcar conductor, or a storekeeper and watch his face as he examines it." The illustration shows the pawnshop's odd testiculars on one side and on the obverse an anonymous, head-covered, pubic-bearded man with a great hooked nose.) But even in the current catalog there is #2870, a "BIG NOSE & GLASSES" set. The copy describes the nose as "realistically formed" and ambiguously advises the reader that he can "make fun of city slickers." City slickers? *City* slickers? Izzy, if the nose fits. . . .

And if there is a tendency in the new Johnson Smith to pull punches—#2092 is a "JAW HARP" and #1171, "1001 INSULTS," contains a section called Transylvania Jokes and Slams: "Sign on a Transylvania Garbage Truck: WE CATER WEDDINGS"; "Did you hear about the Transylvania beauty contest? Nobody won"—there is a strong, if deliberately vague, crime-in-the-streets orientation to the inventory. Along with the traditional five-foot shelf of body-building pamphlets and the more faddish how-to Kung Fu stuff, there is the "Pocket Shriek Alarm—You can Almost Knock 'em down with Sound"; a "Wide Angle Door Peek—See without being seen. Gives full view. No need to open door"; there is #1306, *Defense Tactics for Law Enforcement* ("Deal effectively with the most common assault situations without reliance on weapons. Covers the wide range of problems the policeman encounters on the job"). There are regulation police handcuffs, badges and badge cases, "official looking . . . realistic," the rubrics carefully imprecise: "Special Investigator," "Special Police," "Private Detective." The badge case is "perfect for use with all three badges" and comes with a "police identification card." And there are, if all else fails, weapons: an eight-inch "Zip Knife. Opens quickly and locks into position"; "Paratrooper" knives; knives for "emergencies"; ten-inch Bowie knives, designed by "Jim Bowie, great pioneer knife-fighter." (None of these may be sold in the Detroit area.) There are explosive pellets ("For use with slingshots") and shoulder holsters ("Conceal most any pistol under coat, shirt, jacket, etc. Similar holster often worn by special agents, commandos, detectives, etc. Takes most size handguns").

"I'll tell you the type of letter we get a lot of. It's kind of interesting. We get letters from a fella who will say, 'Gee, will you send this catalog to my son? I remember ordering from you in the Thirties and I had more fun. You got me into more trouble, but I want my son to have the experience, or to have the fun. They don't have the fun they used to.'"

Who *is* this man who floats above the levelers he flogs, this detached dealer who, trading in tricks, turns none? Who is he, this married-with-kids man—a son eleven, a daughter fifteen—this ecumenical Episcopalian who goes to church with his Catholic wife and drops in at the synagogue once in a while, who lives in Grosse Pointe Colonial and goes skiing in Colorado in the wintertime or down the man-made stuff in Michigan?

He writes the copy, plants subliminal and liminal suggestions. I mention a friend who once ordered a microphone from his company that was supposed to let him broadcast his voice through the family radio, but who could never get it to work, who'd have had to have been an engineer just to attach it. "Yes. We get enthusiastic in describing the ads. I think the children's imaginations carry them a little further. But there used to be more embellishing of the article. Basically, in our business we sell an item in its original development form. The ballpoint pen when it first came out was a good mail-order seller, but if anyone remembers, I'd say fifty to seventy-five percent of them didn't work for any length of time. And that's the type of state in which we usually get an item, when it's in the semi-developed form because it's a novelty and everyone wants to buy it. Sometimes it does what's promised but usually it's a little bit overstated." He fingers the novelties at the Leipzig Trade Fairs, rummages the gadgets at the Chicago and New York ones (though not so much anymore, not so much, only occasionally now). Who *is* he? An American. A-merican, like some ingrained quality of the privative as in *a*moral or *a*political, *a*symmetric, and maybe that's what America means finally, to be in but not of, some condition of dizzying *a*ssimilation, the state lines all erased and the country clean as a whistle.

And isn't my catalog of the catalog misleading? Hasn't Johnson Smith always given equal time? On page 369 of the big 1929 catalog, the company published a full-page advertisement for a volume called *Morgan's Exposure of Free Masonry*. On the next two pages it lists twenty-six "Books for Masons." Some are neutral, three or four hostile and the majority pro-Mason. On page 227 of the same catalog there is an ad for something called "The Alabama Coon Jigger," a mechanical black man standing on a platform of his own machinery. ("Perfect Time. Wonderful Agility. Marvelous Heel and Toe Work. You have only to wind up the very powerful spring mechanism, and the Coon will 'shake his legs' in the most amazing way.") On page 372 there is a full-page ad for a book called *Ku Klux Klan Exposed*, the copy for which rages against the practices of the Klan, particularly in its treatment of Negroes.

Johnson Smith still has it both ways. Crime stoppers, and a course on locksmithing and key-making—"How to pick locks . . . make master keys. . . . Many 'tricks of the trade.'" There is Houdini on escapes— **"Special emphasis on handcuff and jail escapes,"** bold-print Paul Smith's. A book on how to pick pockets without detection. "An invaluable guide to magicians," writes Smith in the copy. Marked cards and a two-headed coin. A cigarette maker. "Use any tobacco to suit your taste." (One is thinking now of Transylvania, of Transylvanian sausage and the Transylvania Corridor.) There is "phony money." ("With a bunch of these bills, it is easy for a person of limited means to appear prosperous by flashing a roll and peeling off a generous bill or two from the outside of the roll.") And electronic bugs. There is a secret money belt: "Wear under shirt. . . . Used in bandit country, smuggling. . . ."

"We're the biggest company in the world of this specialized type. Basically there's a limit to how big we can grow. First of all, our customers go into a phase where they're interested in practical jokes; and after a person has done a few, then he grows up and drifts away from these novelties. It's not a repeat business. The longevity of our customers is relatively short. So we have to keep getting the youngsters."

And "Life-Like Rubber Masks."

"The rubber masks have been used in holdups. As a matter of fact, that Brinks robbery in Boston—the F.B.I. came and went through our letters for a year back and tried to locate. . . . They took every order for rubber masks and checked it."

"Were they *your* rubber masks?"

"Oh no, but every once in a while I'll read where a gas station has been held up and the thieves were wearing rubber masks."

"Does that sort of thing happen often? I mean when your merchandise is used to . . .?"

"I don't think so. Not often. Some boy will steal some money or he'll forge a check and the police will go to his room and they'll find something that he's bought by mail, and they'll want to know if it was ordered from us, so we'll try to look up the order."

And if Johnson Smith sells marked cards, it sells marked men as well. Shoe lifts to make you taller, "bigger and stronger." Even "chest" hair: "Instant virility. If mother nature forgot you, simply press on this chest piece. So authentic that no one can tell the difference. On or off in seconds. Apply anywhere." The illustration depicts a three- or four-inch triangle of mat and, for my $1.95, it may be the most bizarre item in the catalog.

"Teen-age boys are our biggest market. Very few girls seem interested in our items."

So. A-merican. Privative. Something neutral in things, in *things* themselves, something both-sides-against-the-middle. Something guns-don't-kill-people, people-kill-people, and cigarettes-don't-cause-cancer, people-smoking-cigarettes-cause-cancer. In the Johnson Smith Catalog, the Peace patch lies down with the Swastika, the Love band with the Skull ring. Something neutral in things, on the fence, the democracy of matter. Something in things, perhaps, which does away with the fence entirely. And still I'm unfair to the catalog. I haven't talked about the engines and motors, the optics, computers, the coins and the stamps, the cameras, recorders, sporting goods, planes, the watches and rockets, art supplies, banks. (Catch the rhythm? There is rhythm in chaos.)

We are in the warehouse. Blue-jeaned women come down the aisles, order slips in their hands, bearing shallow tin trays. Abstracted, they fill the orders. They might be shoppers, housewives in some A&P of the odd, or browsers, perhaps, in the stacks of a wide Borgesian library of merchandise. They reach into bins consecutively numbered in shipping-clerk Dewey decimal, little Jacqueline Horners of the extraordinary, and pluck out the cloacal geegaws, a Noisy Nose Blower here, there some brown and yellow plastic upchuck like melted peanut brittle or cold pizza. Deadpan—Johnson Smith's on Automation Road—one girl lifts out a rubbery coil of dog poop like a shit rattlesnake and places it in her tray.

"We accept BankAmericard and Master Charge now. We fill two hundred fifty thousand orders a year, but I would say the average order doesn't run more than a dollar fifty or three dollars, so our sales are somewhere in the high six figures."

It is like strolling through some comic, transmogrified version of Victor Hugo's basement Paris, a sewery landscape of mucous membrane and intestine. Past the loaves of toilet paper—"Birthday Toilet Tissue" (*The only gift everyone can—and has to—use.* Comic birthday wishes printed on each section. 'Relax and do a good job on your birthday!'"), and toilet paper printed in the form of money, and "Used Toilet Tissue" ("Oops! Looks like someone forgot to throw this roll away. You can bet nobody is going to be anxious to use it!") Past the pay-toilet coin slots you attach to your bathroom door. Past the cigarette (spelled "cigaret" in the catalog) dispensers, the jackass that drives a cigarette at you out of his behind when you pull his ear, the elephant when you pull his tusk. (A-political.) Past life-size Peeping Tom torsos you put in the toilet bowl, and past the Whoopee Cushion ("When the victim unsuspectingly sits upon the cushion, it gives forth noises better imagined than described"), to the "Hilarious Talking Toilet" ("No more rest in your rest room! When victim sits down, 'someone down there' speaks out. Real surprise for party poopers!").

I ask Mr. Smith if I may listen to the talking toilet and he finds a battery somewhere and rigs it quickly. He presses the white rubber bulb that triggers the mechanism.

"HEY! CAN'T YOU SEE I'M WORKING DOWN HERE?"

And the feeling reinforced as we pass the last bins of the cloacal—the "Disgusting Mess" (fake dog mess and vomit), the "Oops! Somebody Missed!" contour turd you fix to the lid of your toilet like a bracelet. As we pass "GLOP," pass "Funny Phony Bird Mess" (two smeared yolks on a palette of fried eggs). "The S.S. Adams Company does those. Now to my mind the S.S. Adams Company of Neptune, New Jersey, is the most famous joke company in America. Mr. Adams, he was the one who had the best line of good quality jokes in the U.S. In fact, Mr. Adams invented and sold the Joy Buzzer, which I would think comes pretty close to being our all-time best seller and still is a good item. Now it's made in Japan but Mr. Adams held the patents on it."

And into another section—what? What can we call this? *Petit Guignol?* There are "Realistic Bloody Life-Sized Butchered" hands, realistic giant flies with "hairy legs, transparent wings," "real-looking fake blood . . . like the kind used in the movies, wrestling, roller derby, etc. Make cuts, bruises, gashes, scars. *Great way to get sympathy.*" There are plastic eyeballs that float in your drink ("weighted so pupil always looks up"), dummy nails and bandages, the bloody razor blade which "snaps on finger or toe."

"Shirley Temple used to be a customer in her heyday. Orson Bean, Johnny Carson. Rudy Vallee in the Thirties. We had an order from the King of Nepal two or three months ago. It was for two or three hundred dollars. He sent two or three orders before that."

There is the amputated bloody finger and the magic finger chopper and a skull "molded directly from a real human skull." (Real. Real. You could reel from real.) And I'm thinking of the voice of the toilet again, of the niche all men must have if there can *be* a talking toilet. *Molded directly* from a real human skull! Who knew him, Horatio? Who was he? Some silent toilet star who couldn't make it when the jakes went talkie? Who? *Who?* And one sees in this warehouse of toy pain and joke shit that there *are* more things in heaven and earth than are dreamt of in anyone's philosophy.

"Our all-time most popular item is the midget Bible. It's the size of a postage stamp"—things in Johnson Smith's Gulliver world are often the world's largest or smallest; I had already seen the world's largest bow tie, its longest necktie—"and we print it ourselves. In volume sales it's our biggest seller—two hundred thousand a year. We used to print a hundred different books. I wrote some of them myself."

"What books have you written?"

"Let's see, what books have I written? I wrote a book, one book on dance steps. I wrote most of my books before the Second World War."

"Were you in the war?"

"No. I was at the University of Chicago during the war."

"Inventing the atom bomb?"

"No. Working on it. I understood the science and I knew what was happening, but I was in administration, in purchasing."

Of course, he had decoded the catalog. No question. By dint of his legacy, his inheritance, middle child of the middleman. Middleman himself, from the exploding cigar to the atomic bomb, a purveyor of practical jokes, harmless and ultimate, to all the world.

And there is one last thing, *item*. One is rounding off the Borges image of the warehouse library. (The catalog holds a fun-house mirror up to men's desirings and imaginings, the hope of the heart writ small. Eschatological and scat—midget Bibles and counterfeit poop—the dream of power—the strongman's copper wristband—and treasure—metal detectors that may strike you rich in longshot's dirt landscape—all, all, everything, all, every last kick in the mind's cakewalk wardrobe.) Number 1929 in the new catalog is a reprint of the 768-page Johnson Smith catalog of 1929, #1169 a book on how mail-order fortunes are made. Paul Smith, who wants to retire, who has other interests, whose calculus is ruined and whose eyes bother him, who feels compelled to learn as much as he can, who no longer goes to the trade fairs and who never really cared much for practical jokes, wrote the copy himself. "Live," goes the last line, "like you've always wanted to live."

QUESTIONS FOR READING, RESPONDING, AND WRITING

Summarizing Main Points

1. Elkin makes several comparisons between the 1929 Johnson Smith catalog and the 1974 edition, noting that the latter "is changed, yet unchanged." What does Elkin mean by this statement? Find examples that illustrate both parts of it.

2. Elkin makes much of Johnson Smith's and Paul Smith's midwestern backgrounds. Why is the company's location important to Smith? Why is it important to Elkin?

Analyzing Methods of Discourse

1. Elkin's main strategy in this essay is paradox, such as that contained in his assertion that "in the Johnson Smith Catalog, the Peace patch lies down with the Swastika, the Love band with the Skull ring." Find other statements that work in this way and consider how the same strategy might also be at work in Elkin's larger organizational structure.

2. Elkin begins his essay with a profile of Smith's interests and plans before

starting to talk about his company. What is the impression of Smith conveyed in this profile? How does it affect your view of the analysis of the company which follows?

Focusing on the Field

1. At different points in the essay, Elkin states that both Paul Smith and the catalog's audience are "A-merican." Define his use of this term and consider the way in which it relates to other points he is trying to make about Johnson Smith. Do you see implications in this statement that go beyond the confines of this essay?
2. At one point in the essay, Elkin provides an exchange between himself and Smith on the subject of "Life-Like Rubber Masks" and their use in holdups. How would you characterize Smith's tone? Elkin's? What is Elkin's view of Smith and his company throughout the essay?

Writing Assignments

1. Elkin spends two paragraphs of this essay reminiscing about the Comic Code, its relation to state lines, and his feelings about them both. Following Elkin's model, construct a reminiscence of your own on some likewise trivial subject or object (e.g., a decoder ring, TV character, intriguing giveaway or advertisement) that held a certain mystique for you.
2. Read Calvin Trillin's "The Great Ice Cream War" and Louise Bernikow's "Trivia Inc." Then, write an essay that compares the business activities of Paul Smith to those of either Trillin's Reuben Mattus or Bernikow's Scott Abbott and Chris Haney.

James Atlas

BEYOND DEMOGRAPHICS
How Madison Avenue Knows Who You Are
and What You Want

Born in Chicago in 1949, James Atlas grew up in Evanston, Illinois. He studied at Harvard University (B.A., 1971), where he was president of *The Harvard Advocate* for a year. Atlas majored in English and studied under Robert Lowell, Elizabeth Bishop, and Robert Fitzgerald. He spent a summer during this time as an associate editor of *Poetry* in Chicago, living in a "begrimed apartment." He also published a poem in the *New Yorker* when he was only 20.

Yet, he eventually gave up poetry. As a Rhodes scholar at Oxford for two years, he "dabbled in various fields" before returning to America to become Philip Rahv's assistant on *Modern Occasions* for a brief period. He has published a biography, *Delmore Schwartz: The Life of an American Poet,* and his work has appeared in the *New York Times Book Review, Commentary,* the *Village Voice,* the *New Republic,* and *Partisan Review* as well as several other periodicals.

In the following essay, which first appeared in 1984 in the *Atlantic Monthly,* where he currently holds a position, Atlas looks at the Values and Lifestyles Program (VALS), a market research group, whose "bottom line," according to its own brochures, is "how to apply values and lifestyle information in marketing, planning, product development, and other areas of business," or, according to Atlas, "how to get across the message that it's okay to be a consumer again."

In the late 1960s the advertising firm of Ogilvy & Mather introduced a campaign for Merrill Lynch Pierce Fenner & Smith that featured a herd of bulls galloping across a plain; the slogan was "Bullish on America." By 1979 the herd was gone, replaced by a lone bull that wandered through the canyons of Wall Street or huddled in a cave (where it "found shelter"). One ad, which ran in fourteen large-circulation magazines, from *Forbes* and *Institutional Investor* to *Esquire* and *Scientific American,* showed the solitary bull silhouetted on a mountaintop beneath a sunset out of Tintoretto. Imagination, instinct, and versatility were the traits stressed in the text. Young & Rubicam, the largest ad agency in America, had taken over the Merrill Lynch account and come up with a new slogan: "A Breed Apart."

The campaign worked. A follow-up survey showed that within eighteen months the company's recall score—the percentage of people who noticed and remembered a Merrill Lynch ad—went from eight to 55; its share of the market on the New York Stock Exchange was up two points. "There's nothing wrong with being bullish on America," Jim Walsh, the advertising manager of Merrill Lynch, said when I spoke with him not long ago at the company's offices on Lower Broadway, in New York City, "but it didn't reflect who we were and what we were becoming"—less a giant investment house than an innovative firm dedicated to serving the private investor. "We'd conveyed an image of stability and reliability," Walsh said. "Now we were looking to capture the upwardly mobile, the self-motivated."

The lone-bull motif had actually been Ogilvy & Mather's invention. The problem for Young & Rubicam was the "Bullish on America" theme: an appeal to a clientele with the herd instinct instead of to entrepreneurial investors who saw themselves as visionary capitalists and self-made men. "We all love to see America grow, but the heavy investor wants an investment firm that's going to help *him* get a big share of that growth," Dr. Joseph Plummer, the executive vice-president for research at Young & Rubicam, told an audience of business and communications students at the University of Illinois last year. "Our strategy shift to 'A Breed Apart' was clearly emotionally on track with the Achievers target audience."

The Achievers target audience? Plummer was "talking VALS"—referring to one of the consumer types identified by the Values and Lifestyle Program of SRI International, formerly the Stanford Research Institute, in Menlo Park, California. Devised by a group of market-research analysts associated with the institute, the VALS typology divides Americans into nine life-styles or types, which are grouped in four categories, based on their self-images, their aspirations, and the products they use. Survivors and Sustainers are in the Need-Driven category, which accounts for 11 percent of the population; I-Am-Mes, Experientials, and the Societally Conscious are in the Inner-Directed category, 19 percent of the population; Belongers, Emulators, and Achievers (the ones Merrill Lynch was after) are in the Outer-Directed category, 68 percent of the population; and at the very top of the VALS hierarchy are the last type, the Integrateds, a mere two percent of the population. "VALS is a classic research model," Plummer said one afternoon in his airy corner office, high in the Young & Rubicam Building, on Madison Avenue. "It's a whole new dimension for us. Before VALS, we didn't really have a sense of who the consumer out there was. Now we know how they live and what they buy—and why they buy it."

Until the 1970s, market research was dominated by "demographic segmentation": the classification of consumers by age, income, level of education, and other quantitative variables ("two-point-one children, ninety percent married, with three-quarters of a dog," as Plummer puts it). The seventies were a difficult period for the advertising industry. "There were a lot of things going against it," says William Meyers, the author of *The Image-Makers*, a forthcoming book about Madison Avenue. "You had a baby-boom generation that was cynical about the American dream, at least the way Madison Avenue portrayed it; a stagnant economy; and more women entering the work force, which cut into the captive housewife audience."

Not that hard times in the advertising business are like hard times anywhere else. What had been a $19.6 billion industry in 1970 was a $54.6 billion industry in 1980. Total advertising expenditures increased faster than the GNP. "In a time of generally stuttering economic growth, advertising enjoyed remarkable, almost giddy leaps upward," Stephen Fox writes in *The Mirror Makers*, a newly published history of advertising. But the much-heralded "creative revolution" that had swept through advertising in the sixties—the vodka bottle in the Wolfschmidt ad propositioning a tomato ("We could make some beautiful Bloody Marys to-gether"); the Statue of Liberty modeling a Talon zipper; the Playtex commercial that featured a woman in a black evening gown walking a panther down the street ("Tames your figure like nothing else")—was over. "In less than a decade the creative revolution gathered, prospered, and then inevitably cycled away," Fox writes. "Nothing is more fragile than an advertising fashion."

In such a volatile climate VALS qualifies as a phenomenon with a long history. In six years it has grown from a modest in-house project at SRI to a two-million-dollar operation, billing each of its 151 clients up to $30,000 a year for access to its data. J. Walter Thompson and Doyle Dane Bernbach, *Newsweek* and *The New York Times*, Mitsubishi Motor Sales and Volvo of America, use it. Scarcely a week goes by without the unveiling of some new VALS-inspired campaign. A recent ad for *The National Geographic* that ran full-page in *The New York Times* carried the headline THE NATIONAL PSYCHOGRAPHIC above a text that declared: "According to VALS, 80% of our readers are in the three most desirable groups—Achievers, Societally Conscious, and Belongers." Potential advertisers knew what the terms meant. Dr. Pepper has based its latest campaign ("Hold Out for the Out of the Ordinary—Hold Out for Dr. Pepper") entirely on VALS. "As we see it, there is a new trend among the Inner-Directed, and a whole new realm opening up," David Millheiser, the brand manager for Dr. Pepper, recently told a reporter from the trade journal *Marketing & Media Decisions*. "We currently see 30% of the young population as being Inner-Directed; it's the most rapidly growing segment. Our projections indicate Inner-Directeds will make up 60% of that population by 1990." So convinced were Dr. Pepper's executives of this trend that they were willing to ignore ("turn off," in advertising parlance) the whole Outer-Directed market. "Those with an Inner-Directed interest will jump in," Millheiser predicted. "We must be differentiated from the mass-market products."

"People research," or "psychographics," as this kind of market research is known, has been around for a while. The Yankelovich Monitor, devised by Daniel Yankelovich, began measuring the effects of social trends on consumers in the early seventies, and a number of advertising firms have done elaborate surveys classifying consumers into categories and psychological types. In 1970 Benton & Bowles interviewed 2,000 housewives and came up with six categories (Outgoing Optimists, Conscientious Vigilants, and so on); in 1975 Needham, Harper & Steers identified five male and five female prototypes, among them the Self-Made Businessman, the Frustrated Factory-Worker, and the Militant Mother.

Plummer, who is probably the most vocal proponent of VALS on Madison Avenue, was a pioneer of psychographics. As early as 1969 he conducted what he calls "life-style analyses" for Schlitz. Heavy beer drinkers, he found, were "real macho people who lived life to the fullest and didn't take any crap from anybody"—a discovery that led to the famous "gusto world" commercials. Turning his attention to the development of a new laundry soap for Procter & Gamble, Plummer divided housewives into categories, or "attitude groups," based on what they were looking for in a detergent. There were Practical Women, Convenience-Oriented Women, the Economy-Minded, the Traditionals (known as "Mrs. Tide"), and the Experts—"people who, in effect, set up a laboratory in the basement," as Plummer describes them. "They had soaps, sprays, hot-water and cold-water detergents, and bleaches. You can just see them rolling up their sleeves and playing the mad-scientist role each washday." Plummer concluded that the heaviest users of detergent were young middle-class women with large families—women who cared about their families but didn't want to be chained to the laundry room. He recommended that Cheer, an established but poorly selling Procter & Gamble brand, be "repositioned" as an easy-to-use all-temperature product. A decade later Cheer had gone from seventh place to second among detergents.

While Plummer, then on the staff of the Leo Burnett Agency, in Chicago, was refining his method of life-style research, a marketing analyst named Arnold Mitchell, in Palo Alto, was producing reports on the business implications of social values for SRI's Long Range Planning Service. Mitchell, an Amherst alumnus who had done graduate work in English at Columbia during the 1940s ("I was a poet more than anything else"), joined SRI in 1948; twelve years later, in conjunction with two colleagues, he published a report called "Consumer Values and Demands." "In that first groping effort," Mitchell recalls in the preface to *The Nine American Lifestyles*, his 1983 book on VALS, "we tried to suggest that a neglected area of market research lay in how people's values influence their spending patterns." It wasn't a very influential paper, he concedes, "perhaps because it was ahead of its time but more likely because the arguments were ingenious rather than demonstrable."

The reports Mitchell produced during the late sixties and early seventies had a unifying aim: to predict how the children of the sixties would affect the consumer market. What would happen when a whole generation intent on rejecting the values of our capitalist society came of age? Business needed a strategy to deal with this troublesome generation, an early SRI report said. It was a generation that had "negative feelings toward money" and rejected the "traditional" consumer values: success in financial or power pursuits as a prime measure of an individual; conformity; functionalism at any cost; and materialism in its flamboyant forms." The report ended with a quote from F. Scott Fitzgerald's essay "My Generation": "A strongly individual generation sprouts most readily from a time of stress and emergency—tensity, communicated from parent to child, seems to leave a pattern on the heart." The challenge was to discern this pattern, anticipate the needs of the new generation—and know how to satisfy those needs.

America would be a more affluent society in 1990 than it was in the early seventies, Mitchell predicted in "Consumer Values," a 1974 report. It would be more diverse, offering greater opportunities for leisure and self-expression. Consumers in this progressive, "person-centered" epoch would be less receptive to mass-produced goods, "more aware of their values and increasingly able emotionally as well as financially to buy in accord with them." The old acquisitive, conformist values would give way to "individualism, experimentalism, direct experience, naturalism, appreciation of diversity, and taste." Marketers would face the paradox of an affluent society that was aware of ecological issues and disapproved of conspicuous consumption: "The central problem in advertising will be how to sell to values increasingly geared to processes, not things. Sales appeals directed toward the values of individualism, experimentalism, person-centeredness, direct experience, and some forms of pleasure and escape will need to tap intangibles—human relationships, feelings, dreams, and hopes—rather than tangible things or explicit actions."

How do you merchandise intangibles? "Messages will need to convey genuine warmth, emotional content, and a sense of reality," Mitchell suggested. They must be "value-sensitive"—that is, addressed to "the distinctive qualities of the individual consumer." The "old status-wealth focus" needed to be changed; advertisers would do well to keep in mind the new ecological consciousness, reflecting in their ads "a sense of the cosmic, of healthiness, simplicity, ruggedness, openness, and the interconnectedness of things."

In 1976 Mitchell and a colleague at SRI named Duane Elgin published a paper, "Voluntary Simplicity," that elaborated on the consumer profile that Mitchell had been developing in his papers for the Long Range Planning Service. It identified an emerging life-style that was "outwardly simple and inwardly rich." Encouraged by the response to their work, which achieved a wide circulation in the business community, Mitchell, Elgin, and Marie Spengler (a co-founder of VALS) presented "values seminars" to corporations and advertising agencies around the country, among them Leo Burnett. Plummer, who had known Mitchell's work since he was a graduate student in communications at Ohio State, heard the presentation and persuaded Burnett to sign up as a corporate sponsor/client. "Arnold thought about people as human beings," Plummer told me, lighting his third cigarette in twenty minutes. "He thought in people terms."

VALS was just a theory then, Mitchell says: "They were betting on a glimmer in our eye." By 1978 the Values and Lifestyles project had become a separate program at SRI, with a staff of four and thirty-seven clients; since then it has expanded to a two-million-dollar operation with 151 clients and a nineteen-member staff turning out papers on "Values and Lifestyles in Western Europe," "The Emergent Paradigm: Changing Patterns of Thought and Belief," "Societal Expectations of Corporate Performance: Retrospect and Prospect," and other weighty subjects.

What unified these papers was their reliance on the nine life-styles that make up the VALS system. Through the early seventies Mitchell had been working on various models that he hoped would be able to account for the influential "baby-boom" generation's peculiar notions about what constituted success. Finally, during a weekend in 1976, he hit upon the "double hierarchy," a bulb-shaped chart that illustrated two paths to the top of the VALS ladder: the I-Am-Me, Experiential, Societally Conscious (Inner-Directed) route, and the more conventional Belonger, Emulator, Achiever (Outer-Directed) route. Borrowing terms from David Riesman's classic of sociology, *The Lonely Crowd*, and the psychologist Abraham Maslow's five-tiered hierarchy of "needs growth," Mitchell devised elaborate portraits of these nine types, each intended to describe "a unique way of life defined by its distinctive array of values, drives, beliefs, needs, dreams, and special points of view."

The early VALS reports were highly speculative, and drew much of their data from the Bureau of Census, the Department of Labor, and other government agencies. There was no hard evidence that the VALS typology was reliable or that the types even existed. So the people at VALS devised a way to "validate" their hypothesis. The VALS 1980 Field Survey—"based on a national probability sample of households with telephones," according to Mitchell—used a questionnaire eighty-five pages long, on subjects ranging from "Attitudes" to "Media Habits," "Eating and Food Preparation," and "Household Inventory and Product Use." There were questions about respondents' sexual habits ("I like to think I'm a bit of a swinger") and general disposition ("I like myself pretty much the way I am"); how much television they watched and when; what kind of cleaning products they used; which brand of margarine they bought and why. There were questions about credit cards, checking accounts, mortgages, and IRAs; about waterbeds, decorator telephones, lawn furniture, cameras, and pets (did the respondents own "Hamsters, gerbils or mice," "Horses, donkeys, etc."?). Over a million "data points" were developed, Mitchell claims.

Administered to 1,635 subjects, the VALS survey yielded a vast archive of consumer lore: Sustainers drink more instant-breakfast products than any other group. Emulators read more classified ads. Belongers go bowling three times more than I-Am-Mes. Societally Conscious households score high in ownership of dishwashers, garbage disposers, and food processors. Experientials attend fewer high school and college sports events than I-Am-Mes but just as many professional sports events. Achievers play golf, drink cocktails before dinner, and have a lot of credit cards.

Now that it had its own data base, VALS could offer clients not only its numerous reports but also profiles of specific markets. Among the many services listed in its latest brochure are "detailed quantification of VALS types in terms of demographics, attitudes, regional distribution, household inventories, activities, media habits, and consumption patterns for over 700 categories"; "access to special data tapes and print-outs, and VALS on-line computerized data bases"; and "a tailored system for classifying people into VALS's segments in ways relevant to *your* interests." Beginning this year, clients interested in the whole package—and prepared to lay out $26,000—can enroll in the Leading Edge program, which qualifies them to receive the services listed above plus "bonus" reports and services. "We're into geo-demographic research now," Deborah Moroney, the manager of data services for VALS, told me. "Classification by Zip Code. You live on the Upper West Side, right?" (How did she know?) "10024? 10025? You're Bohemian Mix."

Subscribers can also avail themselves of "Getting Started with VALS" (known as "Program Element A"), a day-long "familiarization session" at SRI headquarters, which includes the screening of *American Portrait*, a documentary film about the VALS types. I saw it during a visit to Menlo Park last winter. I had read Mitchell's book and a good many of his papers, so I had a fairly clear idea of the VALS types, but the film enabled me to see actual representatives of each type and made the types more vivid.

American Portrait begins with the need-driven, Survivors and Sustainers, America's marginal classes. Estelle, an old woman shown knitting in her parlor, is a Survivor; she lives in a sparsely furnished apartment, scrapes by on Social Security, and hardly ever goes out. But at least her life possesses a certain dignity—unlike the lives of the Sustainers we see next, a seedy assortment of gamblers and touts interviewed at the race track on what somehow feels like a weekday afternoon. A burly Hispanic confesses that when money comes in he treats himself to a meal in a fancy restaurant; but he isn't going anywhere, and he knows it.

Need-Drivens are an ethnically mixed lot; Outer-Directeds (Belongers, Emulators, and Achievers) are distinctly American. Dave and Donna, a blond Belonger couple, are interviewed standing in front of their local church. Later on, in their kitchen, they explain their choice of neighborhood in theological terms: "This is where the Lord wants us to be." An older Belonger couple, Jessie and Ken (he's a retired career military man), pose before their split-level house and talk about patriotism. Belongers, the largest group in the VALS typology (they make up 38 percent of the population), are traditional, conformist; they're what used to be known as Middle Americans. "They get a job and they stick with it," the narrator says. "They find a product they like and they stick with it."

Emulators, ten percent of the population, are less conventional, and have a mildly dissolute aura about them—like the bartender in a Hawaiian shirt who won big at the craps table the night before and is already making plans to spend his winnings. You won't find him putting the money in an IRA. "Emulators are always on their way," the narrator explains. "They want the Achiever life but they haven't cracked the code." They do seem a pretty bewildered lot. "Where did these people get it?" Lenny, a door-to-door salesman, feels as he drives through a wealthy neighborhood marveling at the posh homes. "I mean, do they own a factory, or what?"

Achievers, 20 percent of the population, are the second-largest group and the richest. Ann-Marie and Steve, interviewed in their hot tub, are a typical Achiever pair. Steve is blunt, athletic, hearty; Ann-Marie, sipping a glass of wine, talks in a quiet, authoritative voice about her theory of interior design, the effort she makes to balance formality with a "personal touch." Ann-Marie and Steve have "the right stuff," according to the narrator; and so does John, an Achiever architect who has a Porsche. John worries that he works too hard and doesn't have many friends, but there's nothing he can do about it; he's driven. "You either win or you lose," he says. "Money is a way of keeping score."

To Rob Noxious, however (the name is Rob's own invention), money means "hatred and anger and resentment." Rob, a guitar-playing punk rocker who goes around in shades and sports an earring, is an I-Am-Me. Together with the Experientials and the Societally Conscious, he belongs in the Inner-Directed category. But Rob is a rebellious youth, angry and maladjusted; his identity, the narrator sums up reprovingly, is "I-Am-Not-My-Parents." Jody the Jogger, interviewed on the run, and Tyrone, a muscular young man engaged in "a search for peak experience," are among the Experientials, a more wholesome group. "I like a little excitement, a little adventure," Jody testifies. "I'm happy," Tyrone declares.

Inner-Directeds seem Californian; they backpack, do yoga, are into holistic medicine. But where Experientials and I-Am-Mes only focus inward, the Societally Conscious (11 percent of the population) are aware of social issues and active in politics. Andy, a bookseller with a penchant for sixties rhetoric about the excessive power of corporations, clearly was once a campus radical. He's still suspicious of politicians, but he's working within the system now, and his shop is doing well. Tom, another representative of the Societally Conscious, lives in a comfortable suburban home with his wife, Sherona, and their infant son; he's a lawyer for the Environmental Defense Fund. (Is it just a coincidence that the two Societally Conscious men depicted in *American Portrait*—dark-haired, bespectacled Andy and balding, bearded Tom—both appear to be Jews?)

The Integrateds, the last group shown in the film, represent the VALS ideal. Chris, a management consultant who wears a tie but keeps his shirt open at the neck, hopes to devote thirty or forty hours a month to "learning." So do Mel and Patricia, a writer and an artist with a lucrative clothing business. Mel wants to paint and compose music too, he says, strolling in a park with his arms around Patricia. Integrateds are both creative and prosperous; no wonder they're the smallest of the VALS groups.

"Essentially what we're trying to do is to understand people," Brooke Warrick, who produced *American Portrait*, told me in Menlo Park. "Our goal is to identify constellations of underlying motives within American society." The atmosphere of the VALS headquarters supports his claim. Housed in the sprawling SRI complex, the corridor of plainly furnished offices has the informal feel of a college English department. The staff prides itself on being "heterarchical"—that is, without a lot of titles on the doors—and Societally Conscious. "Our goal is responsible consumerism," Warrick told me.

Though SRI has annual revenues of some $175 million, it is a not-for-profit organization, and the VALS program benefits from this status. I was curious about what happens to the profits. "Internally we look like a profit-making company," Warrick explained. But there is "an elusive difference." SRI has no stockholders, so profits are invested in research, "for the benefit of our clients." But surely VALS employees must get some share of the profits? SRI does offer "compensation incentives," Warrick admitted, and staff salaries reflect the program's success. Then what does "not-for-profit" mean? "It means we don't pay taxes."

On the wall of every staff member's office is a framed copy of the VALS "Mission Statement":

The mission of the VALS program is to exert a positive and creative force in the evolution of the American culture. VALS aims to do this by acquiring, disseminating, and applying insights into how values can aid institutions and individuals to operate in a more humane, productive, responsive, and ethical way.

Specifically, VALS intends:

- To become a significant part of American business thinking
- To enhance public awareness of the role of values in social change
- To extend applications of VALS to non-business domains
- To contribute to SRI research, remain financially healthy, and operate for the enjoyment and personal growth of the staff.

VALS, then, is more than a market-research outfit; it's a credo, an aesthetic, a way of interpreting contemporary life. "Hegel says somewhere that the philosopher's task is to comprehend his time and thought," James Ogilvy, who gave up a job teaching philosophy at Williams to join VALS, said one afternoon in his office. "In the university I could not comprehend my time and thought. Here I can." The portable radio on his desk was tuned to a classical-music station. In the corner was a Herman Miller chair. "My wife bought it for me," Ogilvy said. "It's supposed to remind me that it's okay to just sit around and read."

Intense and vigilant, with a fondness for quoting the philosophers he used to teach ("My main man is still Hegel"), Ogilvy made it clear that he hasn't given up philosophy; he's only given up the academic world. "I spent ten years in the philosophy department at Yale before I went to Williams," he said, "but I got bored with the technical scholasticism of the academic world. I think it was Leibniz who said, 'To speak with the learned, speak with the vulgar.'"

Ogilvy handed me a book he had written in collaboration with two colleagues in the VALS program, Paul Hawken and Peter Schwartz. It is called *Seven Tomorrows*, and it offers seven possible scenarios for the 1980s and 1990s, ranging from The Official Future, in which America continues to prosper and achieves a "technological triumph," to such bleak prophecies as Chronic Breakdown (the economy worsens, events spin out of control, and "what little economic activity persists has the air of a scramble for better deck chairs on a doomed Titanic"); Beginnings of Sorrow ("Cold weather, crime, hunger, and abandoned institutions leave an angry, weakened, and shocked populace that experiences a psychic death"); and Apocalyptic Transformation (a nuclear war begins in space and culminates in the destruction of Istanbul). In between are more tranquil scenarios: The Center Holds, Mature Calm, and Living Within Our Means. "It's a pluralistic book," Ogilvy said. "What we're trying to show is that there isn't just one god or king. There are lots of ways up the mountain. Our task is to map the evolutionary movement of the human spirit—to know species consciousness."

Robert Kimball, who worked with clients on specific ad campaigns, helping them to understand their target audiences (he has since left SRI), was another fugitive from academe. An anthropologist with an M.A. in Southeast Asian Studies ("I was a total academic"), he returned from Indonesia in the late sixties to find that teaching jobs were scarce, and he ended up working at a research firm in New York. That led to a series of jobs as a high-level marketing executive and eventually to VALS, after a corporate headhunter called and asked if he could recommend any candidates for a job there. "I was going through some dramatic changes," he told me. "I loved my work, but I missed that side of it, analyzing people and society. So I recommended myself."

Kimball, fast-talking and energetic, broke off from a telephone conference that had been going on since 6:30 that morning (my appointment was at ten) to tell me about a campaign he had worked on with Timex to develop a line of three home health-care products: a blood-pressure monitor, a digital electronic scale, and a thermometer that can register a person's temperature in less than twenty seconds. "This was a perfect instance of life-style, VALS-oriented packaging," he said. "We knew that the potential market for these products was Achievers and the Societally Conscious. Why? Because they're more accepting than Belongers of high-tech products. Because they're at the high end of the gift market— and these products make wonderful gifts; I gave away a lot of blood-pressure monitors last Christmas. And because our target audience is into health. This is a group that's comfortable with the concept of prevention."

Kimball recommended a print campaign—"The VALS types we were going after don't watch a lot of TV"—so Timex saturated magazines that are popular among Achievers and the Societally Conscious. The hardest part was coming up with the right image. Timex executives recruited people from shopping centers ("mall intercepts"), assembled them in "focus groups," and talked about the new Timex line. The result was a package for the blood-pressure monitor that featured an "upscale-looking" Achiever couple who had just strode off the tennis court. "Tennis is a popular Achiever sport," Kimball said. "Just right for our usage frame: healthful people engaged in healthful pursuits."

The people at Timex loved the presentation. "We're a new corporate division, so we had to start from scratch," Jim Dean, who directed the marketing campaign for Timex, says. "VALS was integral to our development. We spent a lot of time just kind of hypothesizing about which VALS groups would be receptive to our product categories—and we must have been right, because we sold a lot of Timex products." Within a year Timex had captured 34 percent of the market for electronic blood-pressure monitors; its closest competitor had nine.

Teresa Kersten, a VALS marketing consultant with a B.A. from the humanities honors program at Stanford, told me that *Reader's Digest* uses VALS when advising potential advertisers on how to reach its readership. Clairol was reluctant to advertise in *Reader's Digest*, "because they were convinced its readers were a bunch of stodgy, middle-aged housewives," Kersten said over lunch at the Bay Window, a cozy English tearoom near the SRI complex. "It's definitely an Outer-Directed audience, with a strong Belonger component, and the *Digest* had to show the advertiser how they could address that audience." *Reader's Digest* went to Clairol and interpreted two of its "product executions" for Nice 'n Easy hair coloring according to VALS. One was an Inner-Directed ad, more appropriate for, say, *Cosmopolitan*; the other was Outer-Directed, and fine for *Reader's Digest*. The Inner-Directed ad showed a woman in a slip, feeling her hair, enjoying the softness Clairol gave it. "She was focused inward," Kersten pointed out. "The whole ad was about how good the product makes you feel." The woman in the second ad was a traditional, Outer-Directed type: she was wearing a dress and makeup, and giving a testimonial.

Clairol ultimately decided on "a new creative," as Paula Byrne, the research manager at *Reader's Digest*, describes it, which ran in both magazines. It showed a fully dressed woman in profile, and it had the challenging tone that Inner-Directeds like and the endorsement that Outer-Directeds like. *Color and condition that should have been yours can be*, declares the new creative. *Make it happen. Sells the most. Conditions the most.* Outer-Directeds are reassured that Nice 'n Easy is popular, and Inner-Directeds feel in charge of their own lives. Make it happen.

For most of its clients VALS has done just that. Henderson Advertising, a firm in South Carolina that handles the Folonari wine account, knew that it should be going after Inner-Directeds, because VALS data revealed that they were the kind of people who drink wine and were "first-time users"—that is, willing to buy new brands. "They make their own judgments, take chances," Jack Shimell, Henderson's director of marketing services, says. "They'll go out and try something a little different." And they're casual about the wine they drink—which is why Pernell Roberts, the "spokesman" for Folonari, was shown in a recent Henderson's ad without a tie, grabbing the jug right out of the refrigerator. "ID's will drink jug wine," Shimell says. "They don't care if it has a cork or not."

When Recreational Equipment, Inc., an outdoor-gear retailer in Seattle, wanted to find out more about who was buying its products, it commissioned VALS to do a survey and learned that between 48 percent and 50 percent of its customers were Societally Conscious (versus a mere 11 percent in the country at large). So it designed a catalogue featuring models who bore vestiges of the counterculture—beards, moustaches, longish hair—and conducted an "environmental review" of its stores with an eye toward making them more congenial to those types. "Earth tones appeal to our customer base," Carsten Lien, the vice-president of Recreational Equipment, says, "and we know that Societally Conscious types process information well. They make highly informed purchase decisions, so we tend to offer a lot of information about our products." From VALS reports the retailer's marketing executives also knew, for instance, that skiing, a popular sport among eighteen-to-thirty-four-year-olds, is less popular among those with "maturing life-styles"—people with families. Once they enter what Lien calls "the withdrawal mode," these people tend to buy more camping equipment than sports gear. "What VALS did," Lien says, "was to give us a feel for the phases of people's life-styles as they go through life's conduit toward the grave."

Joseph Plummer, of Young & Rubicam, has used VALS on a number of campaigns. "You remember the 'Jell-O Is Fun' campaign?" he asks. "The woman who tells her family, 'I didn't make dessert. Instead, I made some fun'? Jell-O's a Belonger brand; it shows women in the provider role. So we got some Belonger women in here, and tried it out on them. They loved it." Thus the famous, "Watch that wobble, see that wiggle" campaign.

Where did one come up with Belonger women? I wondered. "We found a town in the New York area that had a good sample of the more consumer-oriented VALS types, and did in-depth interviews. We talked to them, photographed them, photographed their homes. We questioned them about what products they used, and tape-recorded their answers. Then we analyzed our data and put together a series of consumer profiles based on VALS."

One couple Young & Rubicam interviewed were Holly and Bill, a management trainee and a designer who live in a Boise Cascade pre-fab but have put a lot of money into their living room. Holly and Bill are Emulators, and Emulators "spend where it shows," Plummer says (even if their sense of interior design is a little off; they've installed track lighting and a chandelier in the same room). They jog and play tennis, shop at Saks and Bloomingdale's, and read "Achiever life-style" magazines. They'd like to *be* Achievers, but they lack the Achiever style and the money to back it up.

What VALS offered, according to Plummer, was a new way for the "creatives" at Young & Rubicam to visualize the needs of Holly and Bill—or of Ruth, a Belonger who works as a secretary in her local church and has a flamingo on her front lawn; or of Carol, an Achiever executive who lives in a wealthy Connecticut suburb and buys only top-of-the-line brands because she doesn't like "the hassle of shopping around." VALS has made consumers less abstract. It has clarified "their needs, their lives, their life-styles, and their experiences," and gives a sense of them as individuals rather than statistics.

Not everyone in the advertising business is so convinced. One complaint I have heard often is that the VALS types are contrived and artificial. "In reality, all of us have traits common to each of the eight types," John Hadley, the associate research director at Foote, Cone & Belding's Chicago office, wrote in 1982 in *On-Line*, the newsletter of Interactive Market Systems, a distributor of computerized media and marketing data. "One may have Belonger tendencies in a grocery store, Achiever tendencies in an auto showroom, and Emulator tendencies at a stereo dealer. VALS doesn't account for this possibility." For all its sociological complexity—the academic treatises on consumer values, the references to Maslow and Riesman, the fine distinctions among types—the VALS typology is still highly theoretical. It was "built from the top down," Hadley argued, "—developed conceptually by piecing together other theories rather than empirically from consumer data."

Another objection is that VALS isn't really comprehensive. Survivors and Sustainers are largely ignored (they're "extremely downscale typologies," one marketing consultant I spoke with explained). Nor are the main groups original. The affluent types correspond, more or less, to the conventional gradations of middle class (Belongers) and upper-middle class (Achievers and Societally Conscious). These types represent "a jazzed-up version of the all-American status ladder—with a heavy marketing orientation," Joan Kron observes in her book *Home-Psych: The Social Psychology of Home and Decoration.* Or, as Jim Walsh, of Merrill Lynch, puts it, "Some of 'em are ridiculous."

Then there's the matter of statistics. Is the VALS sample large enough to give a sense of the various types? Integrateds, the exalted two percent, are generally discarded as too small a group to consider in any meaningful way, and some of the other categories are marginal: I-Am-Mes constitute three percent of the population, Experientials five percent (though VALS consultants claim they're the fastest-growing type). "The samples suddenly fall apart when you break them down into all those groups," one marketing executive whose firm subscribes to VALS admits. "For the smaller categories you're talking about a few hundred people, and that's just not enough to work with."

To increase the data base, VALS consultants devised what they call the VALS Lifestyle Classification System, a highly abbreviated version of the original survey that consists of thirty statements—"I like to be outrageous"; "Just as the Bible says, the world literally was created in six days"—with which respondents are asked to agree or disagree. Clients can administer the new form to consumers and forward the results to Menlo Park to be classified into VALS types. (How they do it is "proprietary information," but the people at VALS claim that the short form yields virtually the same results as the longer one.) Since 1982 Simmons Market Research Bureau (SMRB) and Mediamark Research Inc. (MRI) have been including the new VALS form in their surveys, which encompass much wider samples than VALS uses; Simmons and MRI each poll 20,000 people annually. VALS clients who put up $12,500 for access to the SMRB/VALS or the MRI/VALS data base get a "VALS-coded" breakdown of which VALS types use their products. Instead of identifying its readers as, say, men from eighteen to thirty-five with incomes of about $25,000, *Penthouse* can say that it has "a strong franchise among Inner-Directed Males." (According to MRI/VALS, 46 percent of *The Atlantic*'s readership are Societally Conscious.)

Advertisers that appeal to an "upscale audience" can assume that Achievers, Experientials, and the Societally Conscious are their primary customers. The average Achiever—to resort to the old demographic profile—is forty-three years old, with 13.7 years of education and a median household income of $37,000; the average Experiential is twenty-seven years old, 14.2 years of education and a median household income of $26,000; the average Societally Conscious is thirty-six, with 14.7 years of education and a median household income of $32,000. For a client interested in advertising a domestic wine, it's worth knowing that these three segments rank highest in domestic-wine consumption and read the most weeklies but are on the low end of the spectrum when it comes to watching television. The conclusion is obvious: forget television and concentrate on magazines.

Still, even agencies that have "gone on-line" with VALS recommend caution. "Magazines don't have those breakouts," Carla Loffredo, a vice-president and the director of media at the Marsteller agency, says. "And even if a magazine is predominantly one type, we still want to reach the other. Say we're marketing an antihistamine, and we know from VALS that more Achievers use antihistamines than any other type. We still have to address the Belonger segment; they're a major marketing type we can't ignore."

VALS is "one of many inputs," Loffredo says. "We use a little bit of everything"—and that seems to be the consensus among media buyers. "We use it along with demographics," Chet Bandes, a vice-president and the director of media research at Doyle Dane Bernbach, says. "Like any tool, you apply it where the marketing data makes sense." Chester Gore, the president of the agency that bears his name, says that VALS is "as good a single measure of who's out there as we have," but his advice to

advertising directors contemplating a print campaign in a specific magazine is to take an issue home for the weekend and read it. "If you can't
figure out who it's trying to reach, talk to the editor—and if you still can't,
advertise somewhere else." VALS isn't the only way to interpret the consumer, John Hadley concluded in his *On-Line* article. "It is just a *different* and *additional* way."

American Portrait ends with a glimpse of the Stars and Stripes whip-
ping in the wind while Aaron Copland's patriotic *Appalachian Spring*
swells in the background and the narrator intones: "VALS helps us to see
the America of tomorrow." Living in that America, at least as it is
depicted in the VALS documentary, will require a good deal of money.
The Societally Conscious Tom and Sherona can afford a big house on a
quiet suburban street (even if he does work for the Environmental Defense Fund); Ann-Marie and Steve, the Achiever couple lolling in their
hot tub, are clearly well off. As for the Integrateds Mel and Patricia,
they're more interested in art than in material possessions—though even
Mel concedes that "money makes things easier."

These couples are in what Carsten Lien, of Recreational Equipment,
Inc., calls "a buying mode." They're young and they have a lot of money
to spend. It is primarily to their generation that VALS has addressed itself.
"Forget the cult of youth," James Ogilvy says. "The Oedipal rebellion of
the sixties is over. We're going from slay the father to protect the
mother." In *The Nine American Lifestyles*, Arnold Mitchell predicts that
Inner-Directeds, now 19 percent of the population, will constitute nearly
a third by 1990. (This figure includes the Integrateds, a category that will
grow from two to four percent.) In the "Renaissance" future, one of four
that Mitchell posits and the one he believes in most, the 1980s will turn
out to be the "Decade of the Real Thing"—a decade characterized by the
quest for "the down-to-earth, the authentic, the direct, the honest, the
unfrilly, the real." The number of Belongers will decline; Achievers and
Emulators will react to the predominance of Inner-Directed values with a
"new conservatism"; Experientials and the Societally Conscious will continue to express themselves through "artistic pursuits and single-issue
politics." In the 1990s a new class of visionary Achievers—"a kind of
person the United States has not yet known"—will emerge and eventually combine with Inner-Directeds to produce a more activist Integrated type.

How will these attitudes affect business in America? Some changes
are visible already: a preference for low-tar cigarettes, decaffeinated
sodas, foreign cars, low-alcohol beers and wines. But products are products, and there's no indication that the "graying counterculturalists," as
William Meyers refers to the Inner-Directeds of the 1980s and 1990s in

The Image-Makers, will be spending any less. The "bottom line," according to the VALS introductory brochure, is "how to apply values and lifestyle information in marketing, planning, product development, and other areas of business"—in other words, how to get across the message that it's okay to be a consumer again.

QUESTIONS FOR READING, RESPONDING, AND WRITING

Summarizing Main Points

1. List the nine American lifestyles that VALS identifies and the three larger categories into which the nine fall. Briefly define each type.
2. What is VALS's "bottom line" or the purpose of its extensive research into and segmentation of the American public? What points do you think Atlas is trying to make about VALS?

Analyzing Methods of Discourse

1. The last sentence of Atlas's essay reads: "The 'bottom line,' according to the VALS introductory brochure, is 'how to apply values and lifestyle information in marketing, planning, product development, and other areas of business'— in other words, how to get across the message that it's okay to be a consumer again." How does Atlas's rephrasing of the VALS statement indicate his attitude toward VALS?
2. Besides the last sentence, where else in the essay does Atlas's attitude become apparent?

Focusing on the Field

1. Atlas introduces several ex-academics and people educated in the humanities who are working for VALS. What reasons do they give for leaving academic jobs or for joining VALS? How do they describe their jobs at VALS? Why do you suppose Atlas makes their backgrounds so prominent?
2. Atlas published this essay in *The Atlantic Monthly*, and parenthetically states in the essay that "according to MRI/VALS, 46 percent of *The Atlantic*'s readership are Societally Conscious." Why do you suppose he provides this information? Why does he include it in parentheses?

Writing Assignments

1. Compare Atlas's essay to Carol Caldwell's "You Haven't Come a Long Way, Baby: Women in Television Commercials," looking specifically at the research techniques each describes and the attitudes each takes toward those techniques.
2. In which of the nine American lifestyle categories do you think that VALS would place you? Write a one-paragraph profile of yourself according to VALS.

Carol Caldwell

YOU HAVEN'T COME A LONG WAY, BABY: WOMEN IN TELEVISION COMMERCIALS

A free-lance writer whose work on popular culture and celebrities has appeared in *Rolling Stone, Esquire,* and *New Times* magazines, Carol Caldwell draws on her own experience in advertising for the following essay on that industry's portrayal of women in television commercials. A former copywriter, Caldwell is highly critical of advertising, and, in this essay, often lampoons her target with its own phraseology— a technique displayed in her very title. Caldwell has also drawn on additional experience before the cameras. When asked to appear with her cat Rayette in a kitty litter commercial, she tells of having arrived "wearing blue jeans and a shirt, my usual at-home ensemble," only to be told by the male art director: first, that her attire was inappropriate, and, then, that filming would have to be "postponed until [they] found something that looked more housewifey."

Caldwell supplements her behind-the-scenes experience with statistical and historical research, interviews with men and women in the ad industry, and perhaps most importantly, with findings that were the results of "four weeks spent in front of daytime TV, logging household product commercials." She brings a wealth of information and personal knowledge to bear on this essay in an effort to answer its perplexing central question: "Why have advertisers, who make their living keeping up with trends, been so slow to get on board with the women's revolution?"

It's the beginning of the age of television, and all around it's black and white. Millions of minuscule scan dots collide in electronic explosion to create Woman in her Immaculate Kitchen. She is Alpha, Omega, eternal and everlasting Mother Video, toasting and frying, cleansing and purifying, perfectly formed of fire and ice. Permanent-waved, magenta-lipped, demurely collared and cuffed, cone-shaped from her tightly cinched waist down through yards and yards of material that brush coquettishly midcalf, she is Betty Furness for Westinghouse; and you can be *sure* if it's Westinghouse.

The year is 1951. On the set of CBS-TV's *Studio One*, Furness has just captured the part to become America's first full-time product spokeswoman on television. Advertising execs at Westinghouse are taking a stab at having someone other than the host sell their product; they reason (and quite correctly) that Furness, with her Brearley School cool and her Broadway glamor, is a figure thousands of women will admire and listen to. During the audition Betty alters the script supplied by the casting director. Later, she tells *Time* magazine that she ad-libbed the refrigerator routine because "it was written like men think women talk!"

1952. While John Daly, Bill Henry, and Walter Cronkite monitor Ike and Adlai at the conventions, Betty Furness opens and shuts forty-nine refrigerators, demonstrates the finer points of forty-two television sets, twenty-three dishwashers and twelve ovens for a total of four-and-a-half hours of air time. General Eisenhower is on the air approximately an hour and twenty minutes; Mr. Stevenson, fifty minutes.

1956. Bright and blondeened, twenty-eight-year-old Julia Meade is the commercial spokeswoman for Lincoln on the *Ed Sullivan Show*, for Richard Hudnut hair products on *Your Hit Parade*, for *Life* magazine on John Daly's news show. She is pulling down a hundred thousand dollars a year, which moves *Time* to comment, "Julia (34–20–34) is one of a dozen or so young women on TV who find self-effacement enormously profitable." Howard Wilson, a vice-president of Kenyon & Eckhardt, Lincoln's ad agency, hired Julia for the spots with trepidation: a woman just couldn't be convincing about such things as high torque, turbo drive, and ball-joint suspensions. His fears, it turns out, were unfounded, and Meade becomes the perky prototype for a whole slew of carefully coiffed women selling cars—selling *anything*—by means other than their technical knowledge. And so Julia Meade begat Bess Myerson, who begat Anita Bryant, who begat Carmelita Pope, who begat Florence Henderson, each wholesome, flawless, clear of eye and enunciation, in short, sixty-second reminders of everything the American woman ought to be.

Times change, however, and eventually infant TV's ideal, untouchable dozen spokeswomen were replaced by hundreds of nameless actresses who portray "the little woman" in scenarios believed, by the agencies who create them, to be honest-to-God, middle-American, slice-of-life situations. As early as 1955, this new wave of commercial realism got a pat on the back by the industry's weekly trade paper, *Advertising Age*. Procter & Gamble had just come out with a revolutionary new way to sell soap on TV: "It is very difficult for a soap commercial to emerge from the mass of suds, with every known variant on the familiar theme of the woman holding up a box of "X" soap powder with a grisly smile pointing to a pile of clothes she has just washed. Cheer has come up with the unique approach of dramatizing an everyday washing problem from the poor woman's point of view with a sound-over technique of stream of consciousness."

That stream of consciousness flowed unchecked until Bill Free's famous National Airlines "Fly Me" faux pas in 1971. Women activists carried signs, stormed Free's and National's offices, read proclamations, and permeated the media with protest. Free talks of this trying and critical time with a humor and stoicism that comes from a six-year perspective, and from no longer handling the account. "The women's movement was identifying itself—and our 'Fly Me' campaign was an opportunity for a public platform. We were deluged with letters and calls. I even got an absurd letter from one of the leaders of the movement (who must go unnamed) demanding that I surely planned the sexual innuendo in the word 'fly'—she meant as in men's trouser pants." He paused. "The ad community continues to demean women, far more subtly than in our campaign."

There are some easy hints at why this is so: Of the seventy-five thousand people currently employed in advertising, only 16.7 percent are women in other than clerical positions—not exactly an overwhelming voice. And, while advertising executives often live in the suburbs of large cities, they just as often tend to have a low regard for anyone who isn't an urbanite. As one New York agency executive quipped, "All I really know about the Middle America I sell to everyday is that it's the place I fly over to get to L.A."

But these notations still don't answer the question: Why have advertisers, who make their living keeping up with trends, been so slow to get on board with the women's revolution? Where was everybody the recent night David Brinkley closed the book on America's traditional homelife structure, citing the fact that a mere seven percent of our nation's homes still maintained the time-honored tradition of the everyday housewife. Mom has officially flown the coop just about everywhere, except on TV in the commercials.

At a roundtable on women's advertising sponsored by the agency trade publication *Madison Avenue*, Harriet Rex, a vice-president at J. Walter Thompson, had this comment to make: "There's always been a lag between what is and what the ad business has codified as what 'is.'" And Rena Bartos, a senior VP at the same agency, said, "Advertising may be a mirror of society but somehow the image in that mirror is a little out of focus. It plays back a 1950s reflection in a 1970s world."

Madison Avenue's "little woman" is hardly new, and only partially improved. When feminists cite advertising that is "acceptable," it's invariably print ads. This isn't surprising, since magazine ads are prepared for specific subscribers whose personal backgrounds and attitudes have been carefully documented by the publication and noted by the agency. Television, on the other hand, commands a much larger and subsequently less definable audience.

So it is left to the advertisers and their agencies to define who television's consuming woman might be and what type of commercial she might like. The reward is compelling: Americans heap a total $9.2 billion every year into the coffers of the nation's top three TV advertisers—Procter & Gamble, Bristol-Myers, and General Foods. Still, the women portrayed aren't always to the customers' liking, and last year agitated viewers marched en masse outside P&G headquarters in Cincinnati, suggesting in rather unladylike terms what to do with Mr. Whipple and his grocery store groupies. Inside, P&G stockholders took little heed, voting down a suggestion that their commercial portrayal of women be reconsidered.

Others in the business did listen. When the National Organization for Women sent all major advertising agencies a position paper on the role of women in commercials, no one was surprised that most of the commercials on the air didn't jibe with the NOW requirements. Several agencies, fearing intervention by the Federal Trade Commission, prodded their own regulatory outfit to consider the matter. The National Advertising Review Board formed a panel, including Patricia Carbine, publisher of *Ms.*; Joyce Synder, coordinator of the task force on the image of women for NOW; the vice-presidents of broadcast standards for ABC and NBC; and a number of officers of sponsoring companies. A twenty-one page directive came out in 1975, in which the panel made a number of suggestions concerning ways in which advertisers could improve their portrayal of women. Here's what came out in the wash: "Advertising must be regarded as one of the forces molding society," the study asserted. "Those who protest that advertising merely reflects society must reckon with the criticism that much of the current reflection of women in advertising is out of date." Before airing a commercial, the panel urged advertisers to run down the NARB checklist, which included the following points:

- Are sexual stereotypes perpetuated in my ads? Do they portray women as weak, silly and over-emotional?
- Are the women portrayed in my ads stupid?
- Do my ads portray women as ecstatically happy over household cleanliness or deeply depressed because of their failure to achieve nearperfection in household tasks?
- Do my ads show women as fearful of not being attractive, of not being able to keep their husbands or lovers, fearful of in-law disapproval?
- Does my copy promise unrealistic psychological rewards for using the product?

Well now, does it? With these self-regulatory commandments in mind, I spent four weeks in front of daytime TV, logging current household product commercials and trying to determine just where women stand in the advertising scheme of things. During that time, Iris dickered with Rachel and Mac's teetering marriage, Beth died, Stacy miscarried, and Jennifer killed John's wife so they could finally be together.

Now a word from our sponsors.

Ring around the collar lives. After eight long years, the little woman is still exposing hubby and the kids to this awful embarrassment. It can strike virtually anywhere—in taxis, at ballgames, even on vacation doing the limbo. Our lady of the laundry is always guilty, always lucky to have a next-door neighbor who knows about Wisk, the washday miracle, and always back in hubby's good, but wary, graces by the happy ending. The Wisk woman faces the same unspoken commercial threat that the Geritol woman faces: "My wife, I think I'll keep her . . ." *if* she keeps in line.

Jim Jordan is president of Batten, Barton, Durstine and Osborn Advertising. Eight years ago, in a fit of cosmic inspiration, he came up with "ring around the collar" for his agency's client, Lever Bros. Since then, Jordan has run check-out-counter surveys on his commercials, asking shoppers who were purchasing Wisk, "You must be buying this product because you like the commercials." The reply he got was always the same: "Why no! I hate those commercials; but why should I hold that against the product?"

Jim Jordan echoes advertising's premier axiom: "The purpose of the commercial is not the aesthetic pleasure of the viewer—it's to sell the product." And Wisk is selling like gangbusters. He doesn't believe "ring around the collar" commercials show women in an embarrassing light; and to assume that, he says, "would be giving commercials more credit than they deserve."

Perhaps. And perhaps his "ring around the collar" campaign is getting more credit than it deserves for selling Wisk. Take any commercial with a simple message, repeat it again and again, and the product, if it's good, will sell, even if the spot is mindless and annoying. It's fixing the name of the product in the consumer's mind with a quick, catchy phrase that's important.

The household slice-of-life commercial is one of the classic offenders of the NARB checklist. (Are sexual stereotypes perpetuated? You'd best believe it. Are the women portrayed stupid? And how.) Crisco's current campaign is a flawless example of this much-imitated genre, which has been developed and designed by Procter & Gamble. In it various long-suffering husbands and condescending neighbors are put through the heartache of greasy, gobby chicken and fries, all because some unthinking corner-cutter spent "a few pennies less" on that mainstay of American cookery, lard. These pound-foolish little women cause their loved ones to live through "disasters" and "catastrophes." At the cue word "catastrophe," our video crumples into wavy electronic spasms and thrusts us back to the scene of the crime: to that excruciating point in the Bicentennial picnic or the backyard cookout when Dad has to wrinkle his upper lip and take Mom aside for a little set-to about her greasy chicken. The moral, delivered by an unseen pedantic male announcer, is plain: "Ladies who've learned—buy Crisco."

These examples are, sad to say, still very much the rule for women's portrayals in thirty- and sixty-second spots. They occur with alarming regularity during the daytime hours, when stations may sell up to sixteen commercial minutes an hour. (The nighttime rate is a mere eight minutes, 40 seconds per hour.) Now, you are probably not the average American who spends some six hours a day in front of the old boob tube (which, when the maximum number of commercials per hour is computed, means over an hour and a half of product propaganda). And you probably are quite sure that commercials have absolutely no effect on you. Maybe they don't. But a shaken agency copywriter told me the first word his child spoke was "McDonald's," and I've stood in a grocery store line and watched while a mother, tired of her child's tears, lets him wander off and return—not with a candy bar, but with a roll of Charmin. Make no mistake about it: the cumulative effects of commercials are awesome. As the NARB study argues: "An endless procession of commercials on the same theme, all showing women using household products in the home, raises very strong implications that women have no other interests except laundry, dishes, waxing floors, and fighting dirt in any form. . . . Seeing a great many such advertisements in succession reinforces the traditional stereotype that a "woman's place is *only* in the home."

There have, in the past few years, been commercials that break the homebody mold. The Fantastik spray commercial, "I'm married to a man, not a house" (which, incidentally was written and produced by men), has reaped much praise, as has L'Oreal's "I'm worth it" campaign. "Ten years ago, it would have been, 'John thinks I'm worth it,'" says Lenore Hershey, editor of *Ladies' Home Journal. Ms'* Pat Carbine thinks United Airlines is flying right when they address women executives, "You're the boss." She also likes the Campbell's soup "working wife" commercial, in which a man scurries around the kitchen, preparing soup for his woman, but adds, "I'm afraid they took the easy route and resorted to total role reversal—making her look good at the expense of the man."

Indeed, Lois Wyse of Wyse Advertising fears that advertisers are not only failing to talk to today's women, but they're missing men as well. The reason for this, as she sees it, is research—the extensive demographic studies done on who buys what product. Last winter Wyse told *Madison Avenue*, "About twenty years ago we were all little Ozzies and Harriets to all the people who do research, and now their idea of contemporizing is to make the Ozzies into Harriets and the Harriets into Ozzies."

Marketing research, with its charts and graphs and scientific jargon, has increased in importance over the last ten years or so, while creativity, the keystone to the Alka-Seltzer, Volkswagen, and Benson & Hedges campaigns of the sixties, has taken the backseat. Ask anybody in advertising why commercials still show the little woman bumbling around in a fearful daze, and you'll find the answer is always the same: "Because our research tells us it is so." Agencies devote hundreds of thousands of dollars to find out who's buying their client's stuff and why. And it's not just Mom up there on the charts and graphs. Marketing researchers dissect and analyze the buying habits, educational and income levels of every member of the family. They even know what we do with our leisure time, and how much God we've got.

This subjective form of research is amorphously titled life-style research, explained by the respected *Journal of Marketing* in the following brave-new-world lingo: "Life-style data—activities, interests, opinions—have proved their importance as a means of *duplicating* the consumer for the marketing researcher. . . ." And more: "Life-style attempts to answer questions like: What do women think about the job of housekeeping? Do they see themselves as homebodies or swingers? Life-style provides definitions like 'housewife role haters,' 'old-fashioned homebodies' and 'active affluent urbanites.'"

But life-style research is still in its infancy and very, very expensive. The trendiest and most attainable form of research going is called focus-group research, the grassroots movement of advertising research. From lairs of hidden cameras and tape-recording devices, agency and client-types, despite the experts' warnings that focus-group samples are far too small to be projected on a national scale, eke out a vision of their consumer that almost invariably fits just the stereotype they had in mind in the first place, and proceed to advertise accordingly.

The theory, quite simply, is to get inside women's heads in order to get inside their pocketbooks. From Satellite Beach to Spokane, fact-finding specialists are retained at grand sums to commune with the natives and document their particular buying habits. For instance:

The canned-meat industry's advertising wasn't paying off in the Southeast. Focus-group researchers were called in and groups of eight women were randomly selected from Memphis neighborhoods. The women fit the product's buyer profile—in this case, all came from families with middle to lower-middle incomes. Each woman was paid ten dollars. On an assigned day each focus group would meet for a two-hour session at the suburban home of the researcher's field representative—a woman who was a veteran of several similar exercises. As the women took their seats around the dining room table, loosening up with coffee and homemade cake, the client and agency folk sat, out of sight, in the rumpus room, carefully scanning the meeting on closed-circuit monitors. This is what they heard.

MODERATOR: Do any of you ever buy canned meats?

VOICES: Oh yes. Yeah. Uh, huh.

MODERATOR: When do you buy them?

ANN: Well, my husband went to New Orleans, so I bought a lot of canned goods. The children enjoy them.

LOU: Well, I bought Vienna sausage the other day 'cause the Giant had a special on it—seventy-nine cents a can—it's usually a dollar nine, a dollar nineteen. You could only get four at a time, so I went back twice that week.

MODERATOR: Do you buy these for particular members of the family?

NORMA: If they didn't like it, I wouldn't buy it.

DELORES: Melvin loves the hot dog chili. And the baby—you can just stick a Vienna sausage in her hand and she'll go 'round happy all day.

MODERATOR: Do you read the labels on canned meats?

VOICES: Oh sure. Yes.

NORMA: The children read the labels first and called my attention to it. When I saw it had things like intestines and things like that, I didn't want to buy potted meat any more.

LOU: Fats, tissues, organs. If you read the labels on this stuff—when they say hearts. . . . I don't know. I don't like hearts.

VIRGINIA: Well, psychologically you're not geared to it.

ALMA: They could lie on the label a little bit. Just don't tell us so much. (Laugh.) It would taste pretty good, but . . . yeah. I'd rather not know.

MODERATOR: What do you think ought to be on the labels?

ANNE: I think you ought to know about the chemicals

NORMA: I love to read calories on the side of a can.

DELORES: I wonder what all's in those preservatives?

IDA: The side of this Hormel can here says that this meat is made by the same company that makes Dial soap. Says Armour-Dial.

NORMA: At least you think it's clean.

DELORES: Some preservatives do taste like soap. . . .

IDA: I wouldn't be eating that stuff with them chemicals.

ANN: Well, if you worry about that, you're going to starve to death.

VIRGINIA: You'd never eat in a restaurant if you ever got back in the kitchen.

MODERATOR: Would you buy a product because of the advertising?

VOICES: No. No. Maybe.

IDA: My children love that Libby's—the one, "Libby's, Libby's, Libby's. . . ."

NORMA: Now, if there's young kids that go to the grocery store with you, everytime they'll pick up something. . . . "Libby's, Libby's, Libby's."

DELORES: Every time I see Hormel chili . . . I think about them people out at a fireside by the beach eating that chili. One of them is playing a guitar and they start singing.

VIRGINIA: Armour has a cute hot dog commercial, that's where they're all marching around, weenies, ketchup and mustard. . . .

IDA: Yeah. That's cute.

MODERATOR: Do any of you ever buy Spam?

IDA: What's Spam?

ANNE: It's chopped something. Or pressed.

LOU: It's beaver board.

MODERATOR: Beaver what?

Most researchers claim that their studies are only as good as the people who interpret them. The interpreters are usually the agency and clients who—many advertising executives will admit, but only off the record—read their own product concerns into the comments of the panelists. Quite often, complaints about daytime commercials ("They're awful!" "Ridiculous!" "Laughable!") are brushed aside. "You can formulate breakthrough approaches in order to reach this new woman," Joan Rothberg, a senior VP at Ted Bates, told *Madison Avenue*, "and yet the traditional 'Ring Around the Collar' approach wins out in terms of creating awareness and motivating people to buy the product."

One of the final research tests a commercial can go through after it's been created and storyboarded is the Burke test. One day up at my old agency, the creative director, a writer, and an art director came blazing through the halls with hats and horns, announcing at 120 decibels, "We Burked twenty-nine! We Burked twenty-nine!" Now this may sound to you as it did to me that day, as if these people were talking in tongues. What having "Burked twenty-nine" actually means is the percentage the commercial scored in recall after one viewing by a large audience. The average number on the Burke scale for the particular product my friends were testing was twenty-five—so you can understand the celebration.

Because the agencies and their clients accept Burke scores as valid, the scores become a powerful factor in what types of commercials will run. It's no accident that the Burke company is located in Cincinnati, since Cincinnati is the birthplace of Crest, Crisco, Comet, Charmin, Cheer, Bonus, Bounce, Bounty, Bold, Lava, Lilt, Pampers, Prell, Downy, Dash, and Duz—in other words, Cincinnati is the home of the King Kong of Household Cleanliness, Procter & Gamble. From high atop magnificent offices, P&G executives control daytime television and a goodly portion of prime time, too. They are the top-dollar spender on TV, having put out $260 million last year alone in commercial time bought. They produce and have editorial control over five of the biggest soap operas on TV: As the World Turns, Another World, Edge of Night, Guiding Light, and Search for Tomorrow, which reach some forty million women every day.

Procter & Gamble is the most blatant offender in perpetuating "the little woman" commercial stereotype. Because of its monopoly on both media and marketplace (it pulls in $3.6 billion every year) and because its research is the most expensive and extensive, P&G is the recognized leader and arbiter of format and content in household product commercials—where P&G goes, others will follow.

This does not spur innovation. In one P&G agency, the creative people have two formulae they use for "concepting" a commercial: regular slice-of-life (problem in the home, solution with the wonderful product) or what the agency guy calls "two C's in a K." The "K" stands for kitchen; the "C" is a four-letter word.

Once a commercial is written, tested, and approved by the client, it's got to be cast and shot. I asked Barbara Claman to talk about what agency people and their clients ask for when they're casting housewife roles. She should know: Barbara's built up one of the largest commercial casting agencies in the country. The day we talked all hell was breaking loose outside her office door. Scores of women and children had come to try out for a McDonald's commercial.

I wondered if agencies ever called for a P&G-type housewife for their commercials.

"Absolutely. She should be blond—or, if brunette, not too brunette. Pretty, but not too pretty. Midwestern in speech, middle-class looking, gentile. If they want to use blacks, they want *waspy* blacks."

"What about P&G-type husbands?"

"Same thing," Claman said. "But you'll find that the husband is getting to play the asshole more and more in American commercials."

"But do you see a change occurring? A trend in women's portrayals away from the traditional P&G type?"

"A little. I think they'd like to be a little more real. They're realizing, very slowly, that the working woman has a lot of money."

"What if they want a Rosie, a Madge or a Cora—one of the Eric Hoffer working-class philosopher-queens?"

Barbara laughed. "They'll say, 'Let's cast a ballsy one.'"

"Are you offended by the roles they want to put women in? Do you try to change their thinking on this?"

"I'm totally offended. I'm tired of seeing women hysterical over dirt spots on their glasses. I get lady producers in here all the time. We've tried to change their minds about the roles. You see how successful we've been."

Jane Green is another casting director in New York. She tells of a friend who was auditioning for a P&G spot in which the agency's creative people were trying to break out of the housewife mold. They'd called interesting faces—real people who wore real clothes. A couple of hours passed and the P&G client was obviously agitated. He turned to the agency producer: "What are you people trying to pull over on me? The woman in this commercial needs to be *my* wife, in *my* bathroom in Cincinnati—not some hip little chickie. Whom do you think we're selling to?"

One wonders. Recently an agency producer asked me and my cat Rayette to be in a kitty litter commercial. I arrived wearing blue jeans and a shirt, my usual at-home ensemble. The art director, who was wearing jeans himself, wasn't pleased: "Where is your shirt-waist? I told the producer I wanted a *housewife* look in this commercial." I tried to explain that most women—housewives and otherwise—had left those McMullans and Villagers back at the Tri Delt house in '66. The shoot was postponed until we found something that looked more housewifey.

Some commercial trends have passed: The damsel in distress has, for the time being, retreated to her tower. (Remember the thundering White Knight? The mystical, spotless Man from Glad? Virile, barrel-chested Mr. Clean?) But others remain, the most blatantly offensive, perhaps, being those commercials using women as sex objects to entice the consumer into buying the product. Most agency people aren't allowed to comment on the scheme of things in such commercials (one slip of the tongue and that multimillion-dollar account might choose another, more circumspect agency). But Dwight Davis, VP and creative director on the Ford dealers' account with J. Walter Thompson in Detroit, says it's no secret Detroit is still the national stronghold of selling with sex. Why? The male is still the decision maker in car buying ("Our research tells us it is so"); and the auto is still an extension of the American male libido. So we've got Catherine Deneuve hawking Lincoln-Mercurys. She circles the car in her long, slinky gown and slips inside to fondle the plush interior. Catherine signs off, sprawled across the hood of the car, with a seductive grrrrr. She is, as Davis describes the phenomenon, the car advertisers' "garnish on the salad."

Commercials like this, and the little woman slice-of-life, are caricatures of themselves. That's precisely why Carol Burnett and the people at *Saturday Night Live* have so much fun with them. Even the new wave of women's commercials isn't spared. In a spoof Anne Beatts wrote for *Saturday Night*, a middle-class Mom, dressed not in a shirtwaist but a polyester pantsuit, rushes into the kitchen, crashing through a café-curtained dutch door. She starts to have a heart-to-heart with the camera: "I'm a nuclear physicist and Commissioner of Consumer Affairs." She starts to put her groceries away.

"In my spare time, I do needlepoint, read, sculpt, take riding lessons, and brush up on my knowledge of current events. Thursday's my day at the day-care center, and then there's my work with the deaf; but I still have time left over to do all my own baking and practice my backhand, even though I'm on call twenty-four hours a day as a legal aid lawyer in Family Court. . . ." Our New-Wave Mom is still running on, all the time very carefully folding the grocery bags and stuffing them into a cabinet where literally hundreds of other carefully folded bags are stacked incredibly neatly, when the omniscient announcer comes in:

"How does Ellen Sherman, Cleveland housewife, do it all? She's smart! She takes Speed. Yes, Speed—the tiny blue diet pill you don't have to be overweight to need."

If the "average" woman is true to her portrayal in commercials, we've got a pretty bitter pill to swallow. But you know, we all know, commercials don't portray real life. Nice Movies' Dick Clark, who's done spots for Coca-Cola, Toyota, and Glade, points out, most commercials are "formula answers to advertising questions—bad rip-offs of someone else's bad commercials." They are bad rip-offs of their viewers too. But, someday, some bright young advertising prodigy will begin a whole new trend of commercials that don't talk down, don't demean or debase, and still sell soap or toothpaste or cars like crazy. And then everyone will be doing it. Double your money back, guaranteed.

Why am I so sure? Because, as Brinkley so neatly points out, only seven percent of our homes have the traditional resident Mom. Because there are more women doctors, engineers, copywriters, jockeys, linesmen, you name it, than ever before. Because women are becoming more selective in their buying habits. Because, quite simply, research tells me it is so.

QUESTIONS FOR READING, RESPONDING, AND WRITING

Summarizing Main Points

1. Carol Caldwell asks, "Why have advertisers, who make their living keeping up with trends, been so slow to get on board with the women's revolution?" Does she answer this question? Is there more than one reason for the delay? If so, list them all in the order of importance that Caldwell would assign them.
2. Do you feel that women were portrayed accurately in the advertising of the fifties and sixties? At what point does it become obvious in Caldwell's essay that women are inaccurately portrayed? To what cause does Caldwell ascribe this inaccuracy?

Analyzing Methods of Discourse

1. Caldwell uses as her major example the advertising from Procter & Gamble. Is this an appropriate company to zero in on? Why or why not?
2. Caldwell points out some examples of inaccuracies in the portrayal of men in

advertising. Do you feel she presents a balanced assessment? Why or why not? If she doesn't, why, then, does she include any examples of masculine stereotyping?

Focusing on the Field

1. It is clear that Caldwell places little faith in "lifestyle" research, mostly because the people who interpret that research "read their own product concerns into the comments of the panelists." What sort of interpretation would *you* make of the interview Caldwell includes?
2. How does Caldwell's last sentence call attention to what she considers the most serious problem in advertising? Do you feel her tone throughout the essay suggests that she is optimistic or pessimistic about the future of advertising?

Writing Assignments

1. In a paragraph or two, construct an advertisement of your own that portrays women more accurately than contemporary commercials do.
2. Martin Esslin, in "Aristotle and the Advertisers: The Television Commercial Considered as a Form of Drama," argues that the participants in television commercials are fictional and merely dramatic characters, but that these commercials form "the religion by which most of us actually live . . . the actual religion that is being absorbed by our children." In a short essay that also considers Caldwell's essay, discuss the possible consequences of Esslin's point.

Peter F. Drucker

THE JOB AS PROPERTY RIGHT

"**N**ine out of ten youngsters who receive a college degree can expect to spend all their working lives as managerial or other professional employees of institutions," asserts Peter F. Drucker in the introduction to his book, *A Society of Organizations* (1981). The following essay constitutes a chapter of that book and typifies its aims: "to give insight into—and an understanding of—this world of the executive" and "to stimulate both thought and action . . . to do a better job and, above all, to welcome and accommodate the new and different." Drucker has rightfully been called the "Mr. Management" of our time. His books prophetically describe the rapidly changing world of not only business enterprises but of other major institutions, such as hospitals, schools, and government agencies as well.

Drucker was born in Vienna, Austria in 1909 and came to America in 1937. He now resides with his wife in Claremont, California, where he is Clarke professor of social science at Claremont Graduate School. He has also taught at Bennington, Sarah Lawrence, and New York University. Drucker studied at both Frankfurt and Hamburg Universities, and, in addition to an LL.D. from Frankfurt, he holds nine honorary degrees from colleges and universities in England, Switzerland, Japan, Belgium, and the United States. His many awards include a Presidential citation from the International Management Congress and the Order of the Sacred Treasure, Japan. His intensive and influential writings, mainly in management, include: *The New Society: the Anatomy of the Industrial Order* (1950), *The Age of Discontinuity: Guidelines to Our Changing Society* (1969), and *The Effective Executive* (1962).

In every developed non-Communist country, jobs are rapidly turning into a kind of property. The mechanism differs from culture to culture; the results are very much the same.

In Japan there is lifetime employment for the permanent (that is, primarily, male) employee in government and large businesses. This means, in effect, that short of bankruptcy the business is run primarily for the employee, whose right to the job has precedence over outside creditors and legal owners alike.

In Europe, increasingly, employees cannot be laid off; they have to be bought out with redundancy payments. In a few countries, such as Belgium and Spain, these payments can be so large as to be equivalent to a full salary or wage over the remainder of an employee's lifetime for a worker with long years of seniority. And the High Court of the European Community, in a decision which is considered binding in all member countries, has ruled that the claim to redundancy payments survives even an employer's bankruptcy and extends to the other assets of the owners of the employing firm.

In the United States recent legislation has given the employee's pension claim a great deal of the protection traditionally reserved for property. Indeed, in the event of bankruptcy or liquidation of the employing firm, employee pension claims take precedence over all other claims (except government taxes) for up to 30 percent of the employing firm's net worth.

The various fair-employment regulations in the United States, whether on behalf of racial minorities, women, the handicapped, or the aged, treat promotion, training, job security, and access to jobs as a matter of rights. It's getting harder to dismiss any employee except "for cause." And there is growing pressure, including a bill before Congress, to make the employer responsible for finding the employee an equivalent job in the event of a layoff.

Jobs, in effect, are being treated as a species of property rather than as contractual claims.

Historically there have been three kinds of property: "real" property such as land; "personal" property such as money, tools, furnishings, and personal possessions; and "intangible" property such as copyrights and patents. It is not too farfetched to speak of the emergence of a fourth—the "property in the job"—closely analogous to property in the land in premodern times.

The property rights in the job, such as pension claims or lifetime employment, cannot be bought or sold, pawned or bequeathed. Nor can they be taken away from their "rightful owner." And this was pretty much the way the law treated property in land in medieval Europe and premodern Japan.

This parallel is no accident, I submit. The emergence of property rights in the job does not result from union pressures or government fiat; neither, for instance, had much to do with Japan's lifetime employment practices. Rather, what a Marxist would call the "objective forces of history" have dictated that first land and now jobs would be accorded the status of real property.

For the great majority of people in most developed countries, land was the true "means of production" until well into this century, often until World War II. It was property in land which gave access to economic effectiveness and with it to social standing and political power. It was therefore rightly called by the law "real" property.

In modern developed societies, by contrast, the overwhelming majority of the people in the labor force are employees of organizations—in the United States the figure is 93 percent—and the "means of production" is therefore the job. The job is not "wealth." It is not "personal property" in the legal sense. But it is a "right" in the means of production, an *ius in rem*, which is the old definition of real property. Today the job is the employee's means of access to social status, to personal opportunity, to achievement, and to power.

For the great majority in the developed countries today the job is also the one avenue of access to personal property. Pension claims are by far the most valuable assets of employees over fifty, more valuable, indeed, than all his other assets taken together—his share in his house, his savings, his automobile, and so on. And the pension claim is, of course, a direct outgrowth of the job, if not part of the job.

The evolution of the job into a species of property can be seen as a genuine opportunity. It might be the right, if not the only, answer to the problem of "alienation," which Marx identified a century and a quarter ago as resulting from the divorce of the "worker" from the "means of production."

But as the long history of land tenure abundantly proves, such a development also carries a real danger of rigidity and immobility. In

Belgium, for instance, the system of redundancy payments may prevent employers from laying off people. But it also keeps them from hiring workers they need, and thus creates more unemployment than it prevents or assuages. Similarly, lifetime employment may be the greatest barrier to the needed shift in Japan from labor-intensive to knowledge-intensive industries.

How can modern economies cope with the emergence of job property rights and still maintain the flexibility and social mobility necessary for adapting quickly to changes? At the very least, employing organizations will have to recognize that jobs have some of the characteristics of property rights and cannot therefore be diminished or taken away without due process. Hiring, firing, promotion, and demotion must be subject to pre-established, objective, public criteria. And there has to be a review, a pre-established right to appeal to a higher judge in all actions affecting rights in and to the job.

Standards and review will, paradoxically, be forced on employers in the United States by the abandonment of fixed-age retirement. To be able to dismiss even the most senile and decrepit oldster, companies will have to develop impersonal standards of performance and systematic personnel procedures for employees of all ages.

The evolution of jobs into a kind of property also demands that there be no "expropriation without compensation," and that employers take responsibility to anticipate redundancies, retrain employees about to be laid off, and find and place them in new jobs. It requires redundancy planning rather than unemployment compensation.

In the emerging "employee society," employees through their pension funds, are beginning to own—and inevitably will also control—the large businesses in the economy. Jobs are becoming a nexus of rights and a species of property. This development is surely not what people mean when they argue about "capitalism," pro or con. But it is compatible with limited government, personal freedom, and the rational allocation of resources through the free market. It may thus be the effective alternative to the "state capitalism" of the totalitarians, which, under the name of "communism," makes government into absolute tyranny and suppresses both freedom and rationality.

QUESTIONS FOR READING, RESPONDING, AND WRITING

Summarizing Main Points

1. According to Drucker, is America ahead or behind the rest of the free world in treating jobs as a kind of property? Support your answer with evidence from Drucker's essay.

2. Drucker suggests that holding a job is a "right." Describe the ways that Drucker turns what seem to be business decisions into ethical decisions.

Analyzing Methods of Discourse

1. How does Drucker signal the change from describing an existing circumstance to advocating a solution?
2. Drucker parallels "job property rights" with the history of land property rights. List the similarities that Drucker demonstrates.

Focusing on the Field

1. According to Drucker, what is the major difficulty that modern economics must face as jobs turn into a kind of property?
2. Drucker is advocating an ethical position that might be considered "anti-capitalist" or "anti-free enterprise." Do you consider his essay "alarming"? Why or why not?

Writing Assignments

1. Compare and contrast the business ethics that Drucker implies here with Michael Korda's in "When Business Becomes Blood Sport" and John Kenneth Galbraith's in "How to Get the Poor Off Our Conscience."
2. Does the computer industry, as described by Tracy Kidder in "How to Make a Lot of Money," treat jobs as property? Using evidence from both Kidder's essay and Drucker's essay, defend your assertion in an essay of your own.

John Kenneth Galbraith

HOW TO GET THE POOR OFF OUR CONSCIENCE

John Kenneth Galbraith wrote his first popular book, *The Great Crash, 1929* (now in its third edition), for a popular audience so that, in his own words, "other economists would have to react to me. My work would not be ignored." Of an earlier book, *A Theory of Price Control* (1952), Galbraith has said, "maybe fifty people read it and it had absolutely zero influence," even though it was to him "the best book I ever wrote in many ways." Galbraith calls himself a writer first and foremost. He generally proceeds through four drafts and on the fifth puts in "that note of spontaneity that everybody likes." Though economics is Galbraith's most frequent topic, a novel called *The Triumph* (1968), chosen as a Book-of-the-Month Club selection, and a work of political commentary, *How to Get Out of Vietnam: A Workable Solution to the Worst Problem of Our Time* (1967), demonstrate Galbraith's ability to move outside of textbook theory. According to Galbraith, "economics, as it is conventionally taught, is in part a system of belief designed less to reveal truth than to reassure its communicants about established social arrangements." As the following essay shows, Galbraith feels that economics should be less concerned with money and more concerned with how society works, who runs it, and how we can learn from our mistakes.

Galbraith, born in Ontario, Canada in 1908, studied at the University of Toronto (B.S. in agriculture, 1931), the University of California (M.S., 1933; Ph.D., 1934), and Cambridge University. He has served as an advisor to two presidents and was American Ambassador Extraordinary and Plenipotentiary in India from 1961 to 1963. Out of his massive output, *The Affluent Society* (1958, 1969) is perhaps his best known and most respected work.

Included in the final section of this book are two student essays that respond to Galbraith's solution to "getting the poor off our conscience."

I would like to reflect on one of the oldest of human exercises, the process by which over the years, and indeed over the centuries, we have undertaken to get the poor off our conscience.

Rich and poor have lived together, always uncomfortably and sometimes perilously, since the beginning of time. Plutarch was led to say: "An imbalance between the rich and poor is the oldest and most fatal ailment of republics." And the problems that arise from the continuing coexistence of affluence and poverty—and particularly the process by which good fortune is justified in the presence of the ill fortune of others—have been an intellectual preoccupation for centuries. They continue to be so in our own time.

One begins with the solution proposed in the Bible: the poor suffer in this world but are wonderfully rewarded in the next. Their poverty is a temporary misfortune; if they are poor and also meek, they eventually will inherit the earth. This is, in some ways, an admirable solution. It allows the rich to enjoy their wealth while envying the poor their future fortune.

Much, much later, in the twenty or thirty years following the publication in 1776 of *The Wealth of Nations*—the late dawn of the Industrial Revolution in Britain—the problem and its solution began to take on their modern form. Jeremy Bentham, a near contemporary of Adam Smith, came up with the formula that for perhaps fifty years was extraordinarily influential in British and, to some degree, American thought. This was utilitarianism. "By the principle of utility," Bentham said in 1789, "is meant the principle which approves or disapproves of every action whatsoever according to the tendency which it appears to have to augment or diminish the happiness of the party whose interest is in question." Virtue is, indeed must be, self-centered. While there were people with great good fortune and many more with great ill fortune, the social problem was solved as long as, again in Bentham's words, there was "the greatest good for the greatest number." Society did its best for the largest possible number of people; one accepted that the result might be sadly unpleasant for the many whose happiness was not served.

In the 1830s a new formula, influential in no slight degree to this day, became available for getting the poor off the public conscience. This is associated with the names of David Ricardo, a stockbroker, and Thomas Robert Malthus, a divine. The essentials are familiar: the poverty of the poor was the fault of the poor. And it was so because it was a product of their excessive fecundity: their grievously uncontrolled lust caused them to breed up to the full limits of the available subsistence.

This was Malthusianism. Poverty being caused in the bed meant that the rich were not responsible for either its creation or its amelioration. However, Malthus was himself not without a certain feeling of responsibility: he urged that the marriage ceremony contain a warning against undue and irresponsible sexual intercourse—a warning, it is fair to say, that has not been accepted as a fully effective method of birth control. In more recent times, Ronald Reagan has said that the best form of population control emerges from the market. (Couples in love should repair to R. H. Macy's, not their bedrooms.) Malthus, it must be said, was at least as relevant.

By the middle of the nineteenth century, a new form of denial achieved great influence, especially in the United States. The new doctrine, associated with the name of Herbert Spencer, was Social Darwinism. In economic life, as in biological development, the overriding rule was survival of the fittest. That phrase—"survival of the fittest"—came, in fact, not from Charles Darwin but from Spencer, and expressed his view of economic life. The elimination of the poor is nature's way of improving the race. The weak and unfortunate being extruded, the quality of the human family is thus strengthened.

One of the most notable American spokespersons of Social Darwinism was John D. Rockefeller—the first Rockefeller—who said in a famous speech: "The American Beauty rose can be produced in the splendor and fragrance which bring cheer to its beholder only by sacrificing the early buds which grow up around it. And so it is in economic life. It is merely the working out of a law of nature and a law of God."

In the course of the present century, however, Social Darwinism came to be considered a bit too cruel. It declined in popularity, and references to it acquired a condemnatory tone. We passed on to the more amorphous denial of poverty associated with Calvin Coolidge and Herbert Hoover. They held that public assistance to the poor interfered with the effective operation of the economic system—that such assistance was inconsistent with the economic design that had come to serve most people very well. The notion that there is something economically damaging about helping the poor remains with us to this day as one of the ways by which we get them off our conscience.

With the Roosevelt revolution (as previously with that of Lloyd George in Britain), a specific responsibility was assumed by the government for the least fortunate people in the republic. Roosevelt and the presidents who followed him accepted a substantial measure of responsibility for the old through Social Security, for the unemployed through unemployment insurance, for the unemployable and the handicapped through direct relief, and for the sick through Medicare and Medicaid. This was a truly great change, and for a time, the age-old tendency to avoid thinking about the poor gave way to the feeling that we didn't need to try—that we were, indeed, doing something about them.

In recent years, however, it has become clear that the search for a way of getting the poor off our conscience was not at an end; it was only suspended. And so we are now again engaged in this search in a highly energetic way. It has again become a major philosophical, literary, and rhetorical preoccupation, and an economically not unrewarding enterprise.

Of the four, maybe five, current designs we have to get the poor off our conscience, the first proceeds from the inescapable fact that most of the things that must be done on behalf of the poor must be done in one way or another by the government. It is then argued that the government is inherently incompetent, except as regards weapons design and procurement and the overall management of the Pentagon. Being incompetent and ineffective, it must not be asked to succor the poor; it will only louse things up or make things worse.

The allegation of government incompetence is associated in our time with the general condemnation of the bureaucrat—again excluding those concerned with national defense. The only form of discrimination that is still permissible—that is, still officially encouraged in the United States today—is discrimination against people who work for the federal government, especially on social welfare activities. We have great corporate bureaucracies replete with corporate bureaucrats, but they are good; only public bureaucracy and government servants are bad. In fact, we have in the United States an extraordinarily good public service—one made up of talented and dedicated people who are overwhelmingly honest and only rarely given to overpaying for monkey wrenches, flashlights, coffee makers, and toilet seats. (When these aberrations have occurred, they have, oddly enough, all been in the Pentagon.) We have nearly abolished poverty among the old, greatly democratized health care, assured minorities of their civil rights, and vastly enhanced educational opportunity. All this would seem a considerable achievement for incompetent and otherwise ineffective people. We must recognize that the present condemnation of government and government administration is really part of the continuing design for avoiding responsibility for the poor.

The second design in this great centuries-old tradition is to argue that any form of public help to the poor only hurts the poor. It destroys morale. It seduces people away from gainful employment. It breaks up marriages, since women can seek welfare for themselves and their children once they are without their husbands.

There is no proof of this—none, certainly, that compares that damage with the damage that would be inflicted by the loss of public assistance. Still, the case is made—and believed—that there is something gravely damaging about aid to the unfortunate. This is perhaps our most highly influential piece of fiction.

The third, and closely related, design for relieving ourselves of responsibility for the poor is the argument that public-assistance measures have an adverse effect on incentive. They transfer income from the diligent to the idle and feckless, thus reducing the effort of the diligent and encouraging the idleness of the idle. The modern manifestation of this is supply-side economics. Supply-side economics holds that the rich in the United States have not been working because they have too little income. So, by taking money from the poor and giving it to the rich, we increase effort and stimulate the economy. Can we really believe that any considerable number of the poor prefer welfare to a good job? Or that business people—corporate executives, the key figures in our time—are idling away their hours because of the insufficiency of their pay? This is a scandalous charge against the American businessperson, notably a hard worker. Belief can be the servant of truth—but even more of convenience.

The fourth design for getting the poor off our conscience is to point to the presumed adverse effect on freedom of taking responsibility for them. Freedom consists of the right to spend a maximum of one's money by one's own choice, and to see a minimum taken and spent by the government. (Again, expenditure on national defense is excepted.) In the enduring words of Professor Milton Friedman, people must be "free to choose."

This is possibly the most transparent of all of the designs; no mention is ordinarily made of the relation of income to the freedom of the poor. (Professor Friedman is here an exception; through the negative income tax, he would assure everyone a basic income.) There is, we can surely agree, no form of oppression that is quite so great, no constriction on thought and effort quite so comprehensive, as that which comes from having no money at all. Though we hear much about the limitation on the freedom of the affluent when their income is reduced through taxes, we hear nothing of the extraordinary enhancement of the freedom of the poor from having some money of their own to spend. Yet the loss of freedom from taxation to the rich is a small thing as compared with the gain in freedom from providing some income to the impoverished. Freedom we rightly cherish. Cherishing it, we should not use it as a cover for denying freedom to those in need.

Finally, when all else fails, we resort to simple psychological denial. This is a psychic tendency that in various manifestations is common to us all. It causes us to avoid thinking about death. It causes a great many people to avoid thought of the arms race and the consequent rush toward a highly probable extinction. By the same process of psychological denial, we decline to think of the poor. Whether they be in Ethiopia, the South Bronx, or even in such an Elysium as Los Angeles, we resolve to keep them off our minds. Think, we are often advised, of something pleasant.

These are the modern designs by which we escape concern for the poor. All, save perhaps the last, are in great inventive descent from Bentham, Malthus, and Spencer. Ronald Reagan and his colleagues are clearly in a notable tradition—at the end of a long history of effort to escape responsibility for one's fellow beings. So are the philosophers now celebrated in Washington: George Gilder, a greatly favored figure of the recent past, who tells to much applause that the poor must have the cruel spur of their own suffering to ensure effort; Charles Murray, who, to greater cheers, contemplates "scrapping the entire federal welfare and income-support structure for working and aged persons, including A.F.D.C., Medicaid, food stamps, unemployment insurance, Workers' Compensation, subsidized housing, disability insurance, and," he adds, "the rest. Cut the knot, for there is no way to untie it." By a triage, the worthy would be selected to survive; the loss of the rest is the penalty we should pay. Murray is the voice of Spencer in our time; he is enjoying, as indicated, unparalleled popularity in high Washington circles.

Compassion, along with the associated public effort, is the least comfortable, the least convenient, course of behavior and action in our time. But it remains the only one that is consistent with a totally civilized life. Also, it is, in the end, the most truly conservative course. There is no paradox here. Civil discontent and its consequences do not come from contented people—an obvious point. To the extent that we can make contentment as nearly universal as possible, we will preserve and enlarge the social and political tranquility for which conservatives, above all, should yearn.

QUESTIONS FOR READING, RESPONDING, AND WRITING

Summarizing Main Points

1. Galbraith centers his essay on various ways "to get the poor off our conscience." What method does Galbraith himself recommend? Do you personally feel that Galbraith's method is the best?
2. Galbraith begins his essay by recounting at least five different historical ways men "have undertaken to get the poor off our conscience." List those ways and the major historical figure or text associated with each.

Analyzing Methods of Discourse

1. Galbraith considers most of the historical methods of getting the poor off our conscience "a bit too cruel." When does his attitude toward these methods first become clear? How does he link the historical methods with contemporary efforts?
2. Galbraith provides many objections to contemporary efforts to get the poor off our conscience. Yet ultimately, any effort to help the poor must employ at least some of the current designs. Where does Galbraith first begin to make clear the distinction between helping the poor and getting the poor off our conscience? List other moments in the essay where that distinction is made either implicitly or explicitly.

Focusing on the Field

1. Galbraith is known for his irony and humor. List two or more specific examples of humor in this essay. Do you feel that his sense of humor makes Galbraith more or less convincing?
2. Galbraith lists—and numbers—the "current designs we have to get the poor off our conscience." Do you feel this technique makes him more or less convincing? If Galbraith were writing only to other economists, do you feel he would organize and substantiate his essay in the same way?

Writing Assignments

1. Choose a particular side to a controversial issue (e.g., pro or con abortion, birth control, capital punishment), and in one paragraph, refute objections to your own position. Demonstrate, as Galbraith does, how those potential objections or difficulties can be overcome or are of little consequence.
2. Galbraith concludes his essay with the claim that "Compassion, along with the associated public effort, is the least comfortable, the least convenient, course of behavior and action in our time. But it remains the only one that is consistent with a totally civilized life. Also, it is, in the end, the most truly conservative course." Write a two- to three-page essay responding to Galbraith's conclusion. (For examples of how other students responded to this assignment, see pp. 747–769.)

Michael Korda

WHEN BUSINESS BECOMES BLOOD SPORT

As the author of *Power! How to Get It, How to Use It* and *Success!,* Michael Korda knows whereof his titles speak. Born in London, England in 1933, Korda received a B.A. from Magdalene College, Cambridge in 1958. That year he also joined on as an editorial assistant with Simon and Schuster publishers, eventually becoming their editor-in-chief. As an editor, Korda has become both famous and infamous for his flamboyance and salesmanship, as well as for an editing talent that enemies and friends alike have termed "brilliant." He parlayed this talent into books of his own, starting with *Male Chauvinism* (1973), which analyzes men *in* society and their effect *on* society, and *Power!* and *Success!,* how-to books on corporate advancement in top and middle management ranks. In 1979, he turned from the self-help mode to write *Charmed Lives,* an account of his own life with his father, Vincent, and with uncles Alexander and Zoltan, two film-industry giants. Korda's tone in this book was less strident than in his previous efforts—judged, in fact, to be appropriately warm and wry by critics—and the book received good reviews. In 1982, Korda joined the ranks of the novelists he had for so long published with *Worldly Goods.*

The following essay, first published in *Playboy* magazine, is written in the self-help mode of *Power!* and *Success!*

The word survival, because of its most recent connotations, has come to be associated with those pessimistic souls who are convinced that a Communist-inspired world economic collapse ("It"), an urban uprising ("Them") or some other catastrophe is going to force middle-class white Americans to the hills, where they will have to live off the land and defend themselves against whoever the enemy turns out to be, domestic or foreign, according to their ideology. Judging from the voluminous literature of "survivalists" (as they call themselves to show they're not just passive survivors), Armageddon is going to be like a homicidal boy-scout outing.

But surviving the eighties may well turn out to be not so very different from surviving the seventies or the sixties, or even the forties. The key weapon will not be a handmade dagger or a roll of gold coins strapped to your waist but, as usual, smarts, quick thinking, a keen sense of competition and the cultivation of basic survival instincts. The battleground will not be in the hills, mountains and urban street, but where it has always been: right here in the office, where you're trying to hold on to your job or work your way up to a better-paying one.

And with good reason. When corporations talk about running lean and cutting out the fat, when interest rates soar and business stagnates, when corporate America hunkers down, *they mean you*, as several million of your fellow citizens have already discovered. As the economy falters, as more women enter the work force, as companies tighten up in the face of foreign competition, the race to the top is going to be harder, tougher and faster. What's more, even those who *do* survive are going to have to get themselves promoted at a rapid rate if they're going to stay ahead of inflation.

It's no longer enough just to do your job. You have to do it better than your competitors or, at any rate, *be seen* as doing it better. Born survivors don't have problems in this area. Nobody has to tell *them* to look out for number one. They've been doing it for a lifetime. They can step into a revolving door behind you and come out ahead. It's in their blood. Nothing personal, but if you're in the way, too bad.

"The fast track is getting faster all the time," my friend Hal Grieff says, as he nurses a Perrier with lime in the grillroom of The Four Seasons, casing the house. Architect Philip Johnson is here; Sy Newhouse, the financier who has just bought Random House, is here; Morton Janklow, the lawyer-agent who represents Judith Krantz, is here; Douglas Fairbanks, Jr., is having lunch with theatrical superlawyer Arnold Weissberger; Irving Lazar is table-hopping from Truman Capote to John Chancellor. Grieff looks content, or as content as a 24-hour-a-day survivor can look. He's among winners.

Actually, Grieff is more at home in "21," where there's a less glitzy group of winners—David Mahoney, reputedly one of the highest-paid corporate C.E.O.s in the country; Roy Cohn, the lawyer whose very name strikes terror in the hearts of opposing counsel; Michael Burke of Madison Square Garden, the Rangers and the Knicks. It's essential to Grieff that he isn't surrounded by losers, nonentities, *schleps*. He can breathe.

Grieff stares at a plump, elderly man seated across from us with a ravishing young woman, pulling on a Davidoff Monte Cristo Individuale, while watching the maître de spoon out caviar. There is a bottle of Dom Pérignon champagne in a silver ice bucket beside the table. The elderly man's eyes resemble the caviar. They are black and very, very cold.

"Gunther Kleinfeld," Grieff says with approval. "A *real* survivor."

Kleinfeld, it so happens, has survived being a concentration-camp inmate, a displaced person, a penniless refugee; he has made and lost several fortunes, survived innumerable bankruptcies, divorces, mergers, acquisitions and lawsuits to emerge as a heavyweight hotel and resort developer. Who else, Grieff asks rhetorically, could have persuaded Saudi investors to put their petrodollars into an Israeli hotel?

Grieff's eyes sparkle with admiration. He relishes survival stories. He himself has danced from network to network and back again, always leaping one step up in salary and title while leaving behind him a trail of disaster. He knows exactly when to ask for a raise (when his numbers are up), when to move to a new job (when he knows his numbers are down but before the company has found out), when to say yes, when to say no; when, as they say, to play his hand and when to fold.

When Grieff worked at CBS ("Black Rock"), he outfitted himself with a dark suit from Morty Sills, black Gucci loafers, capped teeth (a $10,000 investment in success), brown hair—the CBS hard-edged look. At NBC (more *haimish*, particularly under Fred Silverman), he switched to tweed suits from Dunhill Tailors, brown brogues from Peal & Co., knitted ties. At ABC, he adopted what he called his "off-the-rack" look, the fighting underdog image. Grieff's talent for camouflage is impeccable.

He himself is a connoisseur of survival techniques. He tells how he was invited to lunch by the chairman of the board of a major corporation. Grieff was in one of his periodic slumps—"kamikaze time" he calls it— when, every so often, he runs something into the ground. And when he does, he's off to a new job before the news is out on the street. He buys a few new suits, eats out at expensive restaurants, puts on a show. He doesn't believe in waiting around glumly for the ax to fall; he's off and running in time for it to descend on his former subordinates who stayed behind.

The chairman's secretary suggests lunch the next day at one in Biarritz. Grieff knows most of the restaurants in New York, but Biarritz doesn't ring a bell. "Which Biarritz is it, honey?" he asks, hoping to conceal his ignorance.

"Biarritz, France," the secretary says.

A lesser man would express surprise, or ask for a ticket, but Grieff is a survivor. He charges a Concorde round-trip ticket to his American Express card, flies to Paris, rents a car, drives to Biarritz, and at one the next day, he's having lunch with the legendary tycoon, who shows no surprise that Grieff has flown the Atlantic to see him.

"You staying in France long?" he asks Grieff after picking his brain for two hours, between telephone calls.

Grieff doesn't hesitate. "No," he says, "I'm going back to New York tonight. I have a heavy day tomorrow."

"Tomorrow is Saturday."

Grieff shrugs. "I get my best work done on weekends. It's the only time the office is quiet."

A look of respect crosses his host's face. "You flew here just to see me?" he asks.

Grieff nods.

"At your *own* expense?"

Grieff hesitates, but he knows his man. "No," he says, "at *yours*. I'm billing you for the whole thing."

His host smiles with relief and shakes Grieff's hand. "Good!" he says. "You want the job, you got it. For a moment there, I thought you were a schmuck!"

Grieff laughs as he tells the story. Hell, that's nothing. Gunther Kleinfeld once rented an apartment in Aristotle Onassis' building and rode up and down in the elevator for days so that he could meet Ari "by accident" and pitch him a hot investment. What's more, he persuaded Onassis to put up $13,000,000 between the 24th floor and the lobby, and got a lift downtown in Onassis' limousine afterward.

Grieff studies people like that. He's a fast learner for a boy from the Bronx, for a boy from *anywhere*. He has his shoes polished twice a day, at his desk. He carries no money in his pockets. He doesn't own an overcoat, gloves, a raincoat, galoshes or an umbrella. A guy who goes everywhere in a limo doesn't need them, and Grieff knows that owning any one of those objects stamps you as a nonlimo person.

Grieff gets a limo written into his contracts for starters, though he's too shrewd to make a point of it, which might suggest that his limo status was a matter for negotiation. During his discussions, he merely alludes to the world-famous entertainment company that was just about to hire a major executive at $250,000 a year and lost him because it refused to give him a limo. Chintzy!

Everybody laughs; nobody wants to be thought chintzy. Grieff's limo slips in without argument. After all, if a guy is worth a quarter of a mil a year, he's worth a limo. And a cost-of-living clause, and half a mil of life insurance, and first-class travel.

Grieff dismisses those things as unimportant. He knows how to sell himself—he's money in the bank. He talks about what *he* can do for them. In a gentlemanly way, he takes it for granted that they're going to look after him. No demands, no specifics, no shopping list of perks. Grieff talks about profits, bottom line, the dazzling future. He lets *them* suggest what they'll offer him, nodding his head impatiently, almost with embarrassment, as if those details were of no interest to him compared with the challenge and excitement of the job at hand.

They almost think he'd pay them to let him do the job. By the time he's through, they're throwing limos, stock options and health-club memberships at him, and he's shrugging—sure, that's fine, whatever you guys want. I'll take whatever you think is fair. Shit, I don't care if I ride the *subway*, except it's a waste of time, but let me tell you how I can turn this area around for you. . . .

It's easy to overlook the fact that success is not a question of ego, because most successful people are egomaniacs, self-involved to an extraordinary degree. But (and it's the 24-kt. but) they have their ego firmly under control. Survivors know that pride and ego are heavy burdens to carry on the way up. As the late Harry Cohn, the foulmouthed, tough, genius boss of Columbia Studios, used to say, "I need a guy, I'll kiss his ass in Macy's window at high noon. I'm not proud."

You want the deep respect of your peers; you don't want to demean yourself; your self-image is important to you? Congratulations; you're a wonderful human being. But that sudden pain between the shoulder blades just may be a knife. Survivors believe in getting what they want. As one successful executive thoughtfully said, "I need to feel good about myself 24 hours a day. And I feel good about myself when I've *won*."

A scene: The garden of a house in Bel Air, California, survival capital of the Western world. Here is the town where a guy can blow $20,000,000 or $30,000,000 on a movie and get financing for another even as the first one is sinking, because, in the words of one executive, "At least a guy like that *thinks* big, you know. There's always a chance he'll score; whereas some *schlep* who hasn't got the guts for a big failure probably won't ever have a hit."

This is the town where, when David Begelman, the studio boss, was convicted of check forgery, he was sentenced to make a documentary film on drug addiction (in other towns, he probably would have gotten one to ten in the slammer) and given a standing ovation by the "industry" when he went into Ma Maison for lunch after the sentencing. "Look," someone explained, "he made money for Columbia, right?"

In any case, Daren Yegrin, the head of a major studio, is waiting by the pool of his Bel Air home for the arrival of a man he hates, Bobby Dime. Bobby is a film maker who has made at least two expensive flops for Yegrin, who had a much-publicized love affair with Mrs. Yegrin, who divorced her husband to marry Bobby, with even more publicity. Bobby has been in litigation with Yegrin for years. There are lawyers who have bought themselves beach houses in Malibu from the feud between those two men.

The pool is empty. Yegrin is not the kind of guy who wastes time swimming. Just at the moment, he *needs* Bobby Dime. A car door slams, Dime comes up through the lemon groves and topiary bushes, tanned, lean, handsome, shirt open to the waist; his face lights up in a smile. Yegrin stops grinding his teeth with rage, smiles like a maniac, rushes down the steps, throws his arms around Bobby, hugs, pats, feels, strokes, paws.

He virtually drags Dime to the pool, takes his arm as if they are about to be married, raises it high above his shoulder, hand in hand, and says with profound emotion, "This is my boy!"

Bobby looks touched, moved, humbled. He takes Yegrin's hands in his. "You've always been like a father to me, Daren," he says, his voice husky with emotion. "So what's the deal?"

What's the deal? The deal, as it turns out, is pretty much what you'd expect. Bobby will drop his lawsuits against Yegrin. Bobby's wife (Yegrin's ex) will give back the two Maillol bronzes she took with her when she left Yegrin. Yegrin will finance Bobby's new movie. . . .

Bobby walks back to his car. An associate asks Yegrin how he managed to bridge the hostility so quickly. "Schmuck," Yegrin says pleasantly, staring at his empty pool, "I *need* the cocksucker, he needs me. You got to hand it to Bobby. He's a *survivor*."

A touch of affection crosses Yegrin's face. Survivors are a class apart: realists, operators, guys you can trust because you know they can always be relied on to do the best they can for themselves, and at least that's consistent. You can count on them for *something*.

Doesn't Yegrin resent the fact that Bobby ran off with his wife? Yegrin looks pained. As of ten minutes ago, Bobby is his brother, his son, a fabulous guy. Yegrin has little or no patience with people who don't get the message. "That was a long time ago," he says. "Besides, what's a wife compared to a picture?"

Survival is an art. Survivors are artists. The best acting is done in daily life, not on the stage. My late uncle Sir Alexander Korda, the motion-picture producer who could "charm money out of an empty safe," was a gifted survivor. Once, a group of investors called him in to complain that he had lost £5,000,000 of their money. Most men would have tried to defend themselves. Alex did not. He sat there, the living picture of dejection and guilt. They were right, he said quietly; he had been wasteful, careless. He had chosen the wrong scripts, paid too little attention to the budgets. He was too old for this business. He would retire. Perhaps he would be happier living simply in Antibes or Monte Carlo. He might write his memoirs. Possibly a few old friends would visit him, though he doubted it. He only hoped the investors would forgive him.

Within an hour, the investors were busy encouraging Alex, cheering him up. It was out of the question for him to resign; they wouldn't *hear* of it. And by lunchtime, Alex had £2,000,000 more of their money and was back in the action again. When I asked him if he was happy about it, he shook his head, exhaling a cloud of cigar smoke inside his Rolls-Royce. "No," he said, "I let them off too easy. They would have put up three or four million, I think. Still, it's a good lesson for you to learn. Always settle for less than you could get. It doesn't hurt to have a reputation as a gentleman."

Survivors never fall on their faces. They don't show pain, fear, resentment or defeat. They have, to use the basic word, *balls*. Also, *chutzpah*, realism and a sense of self-interest as highly developed as a bat's sonar. Plus a certain degree of inevitable ruthlessness. If you already have all those qualities, and are using them to the maximum degree, you're in good shape for the Eighties, whatever form the apocalypse takes. If there's the slightest fear in your mind that maybe, just *maybe*, you're not moving as fast as you'd like to, or as fast as the guy (or gal) next to you, there are a number of things you should learn about survival. In fact, if your salary isn't increasing by 20 percent a year, given the current rate of inflation, you'd better start learning *fast*.

Survival *can* be learned. Start by recognizing that the days of the organization man (or woman) are gone, partly because organizations themselves are becoming more flexible, less hierarchic, forced to change at a rapid pace because of new technology and unimaginable financial conditions. Organizations no longer "look after" their people. Stay on long enough and you'll find your boss is a man (or woman) 20 years younger than you are, who can't even remember your name. This is not the age for putting in 40 years and retiring with a gold watch. People who put their faith in the Chrysler Corporation for job security, for example, have recently found out (1) that no matter how large a corporation is, it can turn bottoms up in the age of OPEC; and (2) that when a corporation is in big trouble, it doesn't hesitate to shed even its oldest and most loyal employees, while those at the top, who made the original decisions that led to disaster, stay on, with stiff upper lips and six-figure salaries.

In business, the usual practice is to reverse maritime tradition. When the ship hits an iceberg, the captain and the officers take to the boats and the passengers and crew go down with the ship. The lesson to be learned from that is: The higher up you are, the safer your job is. At the *very* top, those who have screwed up go to the International Monetary Fund, or are co-opted into government, or step up to become chairman of the board, or run a foundation. There, it is assumed, since they can do no good, they will find it difficult to do any harm. Even at a less exalted level, the senior executives of a company have the advantage of being better informed (they know when it's time to jump ship) and are in a better position to blame other people (you, for example) for what went wrong.

The trick is to understand the organization the way you understand a woman you love. You don't have to think she's without faults, you may be aware that she has certain secrets in her past, but you have to accept them and understand them. Blindly believing she's perfect is not the best way to survive a love affair or a marriage. It's the employees who are always telling you "This is a great place to work" who usually get canned first in times of trouble. The realists stay on, unless things are so bad it pays to go elsewhere. In the same way, you have to commit yourself to the organization's goals without becoming a company man and trusting that Big Brother, whether it's G.M., Chrysler, CBS or Bankers Trust, will take care of you. Big Brother, you may be sure of it, is looking out for number one.

The first step is to identify the immediate power elite—the men and women who are insiders, who not only participate in the crucial decisions (at whatever level you're involved) but also influence the way in which more senior managers rate their subordinates. This is where survival training pays off. Where there's an "in" group, you have to become part of it, while keeping your eyes open for ways to outflank the group. If the "in" group wears dark-blue suits, buy a dark-blue suit (even if you're a woman). If they're interested in football, learn to talk football (even if you're a woman). The main thing is to be seen as part of the company's basic inner circle, even if it's at some inconvenience to yourself. When the ax falls, it's better to be among those who are busy deciding who gets axed than among the axed. Basic survival.

My friend Dennis Trumbull is a perfect example of what happens when you don't do that. He was hired away at a considerable increase in salary to run a major department in another company. Now, Dennis is bright, make no mistake about it, but he's also a man nursing an over-sized, but fragile, ego—a man obsessed with status.

He fusses over details, over personal prestige—the size of his office, whether or not he's getting engraved stationery and business cards, whether or not his secretary will have a new IBM Selectric. A survivor knows that none of those things matters. Everybody knows you want all of those things and more, but you don't show it—you pretend that you don't care. "Just give me a goddamned desk and a telephone and I'll get to work," as Grieff would say, all the time planning for a corner office with four windows and a sofa.

Dennis worries. Is his office big enough? Is he being invited to the right meetings? Those are not the questions a survivor asks. A survivor's office is just a temporary stopping place on the way to a larger one, and any meeting he attends is made important by the fact that he's there. Also, survivors never worry, or at least they never show they're worried. Or surprised. Or upset. Or upstaged. They don't get mad; they get even.

Give them bad news and they smile or simply nod to suggest that they heard about it before you did and already have it under control.

Survivors don't ask what the limits of their authority are; they simply assume they have all the authority in the world until they reach a stone wall. Dennis spent a lot of time drawing up organization charts and trying to find a way of emphasizing his place in them, without realizing that anybody who does that is simply building a cage for himself. Corporate power players ignore charts. They like to operate *between* the lines and boxes, making other people worry about where they fit in. First-class players, like Grieff, are so good at it that one executive at a network used to complain he couldn't decide whether Grieff reported to him or he reported to Grieff. Of course, by the time he'd worked out that Grieff was his subordinate, Grieff was already his boss.

Not so with Dennis, who was already being written off by the inner circle while his carpet was still being tacked down and his new furniture installed. Dennis wanted things firmly fixed, posted. He was comfortable only when secure. But survivors—and this is of the essence—thrive on insecurity. They operate best in chaos. They thrive on crisis, which is why the present unsettled state of business and the world in general doesn't frighten them a bit. On the contrary, Armand Hammer built his fortune in the aftermath of the Soviet Revolution and civil war. H. L. Hunt made *his* in the wake of the oil-lease crash. Fred Silverman went to NBC-TV when the network was on the skids "because of the challenge." Survivors relish excitement and change, and know how to exploit it.

When my friend Grieff heard about Dennis' organization charts, he laughed. "Dennis is going to be finding out about food stamps soon," he said. "You want to survive, the less you put on paper, the better. I don't even write memos. I phone. No files, no Xeroxes. They have a way of turning against you."

Survivors also know how to put on a show. The survivor tends to be a chameleon—he fits in. An acquaintance of mine was recently hired by a record company in desperate need of his skills as a cost cutter and manager, but he soon found that nobody would take him seriously, not even the president of the company, who had recruited him in the first place. The managers and producers were young, hip, dressed in blue jeans, cowboy boots, turtlenecks, most of them with long hair, beards or mustaches. My friend wore a dark-gray suit, a tie and black Gucci loafers, par for the course at William Morris, whence he came, and to which he reckoned he soon might have to return at a lower salary. He did not change his opinion about what needed to be done in the way of re-organization, but gradually, bit by bit, he changed his appearance: a mustache first, then a pair of Porsche aviator glasses, then a casual jacket and a pair of tailored blue jeans; finally, cowboy boots to replace the Gucci loafers.

Soon, people were listening to him, accepting his recommendations even when it hurt, deferring to him. He had joined the organization, in the sense of adopting its dress and its traditions, and was therefore now criticizing it from the inside, instead of as a hostile stranger. Needless to say, he not only survived but is now running the company. The true survivor always remains an outsider in his secret heart, even when he's inside.

Dennis, of course, failed. He played the game by the rules, not realizing that the rules were there to be ignored. He never understood that survival, in any organization, is a high-stakes game in which everybody wants you to lose. He would have benefited from a conversation with Gunther Kleinfeld.

It is five A.M. and it's dark inside Kleinfeld's plane, as he flies back from Los Angeles, where he has been putting together a deal. Kleinfeld puffs on his cigar as the plane descends toward New York at nearly 600 mph. He is almost, but not quite, relaxed, his legs stretched out with his feet on a leather ottoman, his shoes off. Kleinfeld is in his element.

"What time do we arrive?" he asks, pushing the button on his intercom.

"We'll be landing pretty soon, Mr. Kleinfeld, don't worry," the pilot replies.

A spasm of anger crosses Kleinfeld's plump face. "I didn't *ask* that," he says. "I asked *what time*."

A pause. The pilot clears his throat. "E.T.A. is exactly 5:45, Eastern standard time, Mr. Kleinfeld."

Kleinfeld nods. "Thank you," he says, switching off the intercom. "A new boy," he points out. "He hasn't learned yet. Well, we all learn."

What has Kleinfeld learned?

He stares out the window, thinks for a moment. "To keep moving. When I used to work for other people, I discovered that if you sat for more than a year at the same job or the same salary, you were dead. Get out. Move. Switch jobs. Success is an escalator. If it stops, you're stuck between floors. What do you do if the escalator stops? You get off, take the elevator, take the stairs. Right? You don't just stand there, waiting for it to start up again."

Is that true even when business is bad?

Kleinfeld nods. "Business is bad? So what else is new? There are always problems. Listen, in a plague, you sell coffins, yes? In a drought, you sell water. In a flood?"

"You sell boats."

He smiles. "Or water wings."

How has he always managed to survive?

A moment of thought. "I kept in mind the simple fact that you can only survive by understanding the world as it is. Most people think it ought to be some other way or, worse yet, they hope it really is, despite what they see every day with their own eyes. What you see is what there is. It isn't going to be any better. So you say to yourself, OK, that's the way it is; now"—Kleinfeld pantomimes rolling up his sleeves—"let's get down to it!"

Isn't he ever depressed by that Manichaean point of view?

He laughs. "No. I'm not depressed. Not ever. I survived the Nazis. I survived being a refugee. I survived working for people who were real monsters. I know what matters is to be honest about oneself. I'm ambitious. Fine. I admit it. I'm greedy. OK, so *nu?* I live by my wits. Who doesn't? I'll tell you something. The first time I was ever sent out to negotiate a big deal, I went to England, and I met with these guys in their Savile Row suits and their accents, and I was *impressed*. So we get to dealing, and I realize that I'm brighter than these people, even if they do have old-school ties and handsome shoes. When we get to the end, we settle on two million, and I'm delighted. I was figuring a million five tops. We all shake hands. The guys stand up to leave, and the chief negotiator for the other side suddenly looks as if he'd forgotten something. 'Oh, Mr. Kleinfeld,' he says, 'dollars or pounds? Well, in those days, the pound was worth four bucks. I thought for a moment and I said, 'Pounds.' He nodded as if that was what he expected, and we shook hands. I couldn't believe it. I was willing to settle for $1,500,000, and here I just got $8,000,000 by *keeping my mouth shut!* It taught me a lesson."

What lesson? The plane banks over Manhattan, as the lights begin to turn off in the dark below. The flaps and wheels go down with a subdued hum. Somewhere down there, Kleinfeld's limo is waiting; somewhere in his cooperative apartment, coffee is being brewed for his return. He stares at the SEAT BELTS sign as it lights up and pushes a button to turn it off.

"A guy can land without a seat belt on his own airplane," he says. "I told them to take the sign out. . . . What lesson? If you want to survive in business, even in life, *listen before you talk*. Let the other guy suggest the price. Let the other guy say what he's going to do. Let the other guy mention a number."

The plane lands smoothly, draws to a stop, the stairs descend with a low whine. Outside, Kleinfeld's chauffeur waits in the damp dawn with an umbrella. The limo is parked under the wing. Kleinfeld yawns and makes his way to the door. "Survival," he says, as the copilot helps him into his suit jacket, "is like getting laid—it's just a question of self-confidence and opportunity."

And desire?

Kleinfeld stands on the steps, while the chauffeur holds the umbrella as high as he can to shelter him. "Of course, desire," he says. "The rest you can fake, but the desire to survive—that's the bottom line."

He gets into the car, slams the door, picks up the telephone. Rain is beading the windows. He looks up, pushes a button, his window goes down.

"Hey," he says, "it's raining. You want a lift?"

I nod.

"You know," Kleinfeld remarks, "a real survivor would have stepped into the limo right after me, without asking. I once did that to Onassis, and you know what he said to me? He said, 'You could get shot for that. I have bodyguards.' So I told him, 'I'm not worried.' 'Why not?' he asked. 'Because then you'd never find out what my deal is!'"

Kleinfeld sits back in the limo. He is silent for a moment. "I *liked* Onassis," he says, like a man offering an unpopular opinion. "He was a real survivor." Kleinfeld looks almost sympathetic in the gray dawn light. He is thinking of Onassis. "He taught me another valuable lesson," he remarks in a quiet voice.

I ask what it was.

"Nobody's ever too big to listen to a deal. If you want to survive, you've got to look as if you're *giving*, not getting, *offering*, not asking. A survivor seduces the world. Losers try to rape it, or don't even give it a try, but a survivor believes in *all* the possibilities. He's an eternal optimist about himself—and a pessimist about other people."

Not a bad combination, I suggest.

"Not bad." Kleinfeld looks out at the grimy rows of houses, the rusting el, the potholed streets. "Life teaches you survival," he says. "It's just that most people don't want to learn. They want to believe in organizations, companies, rules, friends, lovers, wives, brothers-in-law. In the end, you want to survive, you got to learn to trust only one person."

He pulls a curtain down to close off his view of Queens—you've seen one pothole, you've seen them all.

"Yourself."

QUESTIONS FOR READING, RESPONDING, AND WRITING

Summarizing Main Points

1. List the traits which, according to Korda, make someone a survivor.
2. Early on, Korda states, "it's no longer enough just to do your job. You have to *be seen* as doing it better." The importance of appearance over substance is a theme that runs through the entire essay. Locate examples of it in Korda's accounts of various survivors and their techniques.

Analyzing Methods of Discourse

1. Gunther Kleinfeld implies that Korda is not a "real survivor" because Korda did not "[step] into the limo right after [him], without asking." Do you agree with Kleinfeld? Checking the list of characteristics Korda has described, try to discover whether or not Korda demonstrates any of them in the course of researching or writing this essay.
2. Korda uses sexual and military terms throughout his essay. Locate several examples of both and their relationship to the subjects under discussion. Do you consider such language appropriate? Why or why not?

Focusing on the Field

1. Korda published this essay in *Playboy* magazine. What sort of reception for this essay would you expect from *Playboy*'s readership? Would you expect a different sort of reception from a different audience—say, readers of *Time* or *Reader's Digest* or your local newspaper? Why?
2. What is Korda's attitude toward survivors? Use evidence from the essay to support your conclusion.

Writing Assignments

1. At the end of the essay, Gunther Kleinfeld tells Korda that he has always "kept in mind the simple fact that you can only survive by understanding the world as it *is*." Korda seems to concur. He refers to survivors as "realists" throughout the essay. Consider both the character of the survivor and the view of the world that a person must hold in order for these statements to be true. Then, write an essay in which you argue for or against the accuracy of both Kleinfeld's and Korda's ideas of what constitutes a "realistic" view of the world.
2. Read Czeslaw Milosz's "On Virtue." Then, write an essay in which you apply Milosz's standards of virtue to Korda's successful executives to determine whether or not they are virtuous.

Thomas J. Peters
Robert H. Waterman, Jr.

SUCCESSFUL AMERICAN COMPANIES

"Successful American Companies" is from the first chapter of Thomas J. Peters's and Robert H. Waterman, Jr.'s recent best-seller, *In Search of Excellence* (1982). The self-avowed reason for the success of their book may be found in its subtitle: *Lessons from America's Best-Run Companies*. Though both Peters and Waterman have long been associated with Stanford University, their book criticizes an "overreliance on analysis from corporate ivory towers and overreliance on financial sleight of hand," in favor of focusing on actual businesses and how they are run. Without ignoring the refined and often removed business thinking of business historians and "theories from academe," Peters and Waterman simply shift the perspective back to the businesses that are themselves already successful.

Both Peters and Waterman are well-established in business, both academically and "in the field." Waterman, after graduating from the Colorado School of Mines as an engineer and gaining his M.B.A. at Stanford, began working for the business consulting firm McKinsey & Company, where he is now director. Peters, a civil engineer, received degrees from both Cornell and Stanford and now runs his own successful business consulting firm. As they tell the reader in "Successful American Companies," *In Search of Excellence* itself began as a business-consulting study.

The Belgian Surrealist René Magritte painted a series of pipes and entitled the series *Ceci n'est pas une pipe* (*This is not a pipe*). The picture of the thing is not the thing. In the same way, an organization chart is not a company, nor a new strategy an automatic answer to corporate grief. We all know this; but like as not, when trouble lurks, we call for a new strategy and probably reorganize. And when we reorganize, we usually stop at rearranging the boxes on the chart. The odds are high that nothing much will change. We will have chaos, even useful chaos for a while, but eventually the old culture will prevail. Old habit patterns persist.

At a gut level, all of us know that much more goes into the process of keeping a large organization vital and responsive than the policy statements, new strategies, plans, budgets, and organization charts can possibly depict. But all too often we behave as though we don't know it. If we want change, we fiddle with the strategy. Or we change the structure. Perhaps the time has come to change our ways.

Early in 1977, a general concern with the problems of management effectiveness, and a particular concern with the nature of the relationship between strategy, structure, and management effectiveness, led us to assemble two internal task forces at McKinsey & Company. One was to review our thinking on strategy, and the other was to go back to the drawing board on organizational effectiveness. It was, if you like, McKinsey's version of applied research. We (the authors) were the leaders of the project on organizational effectiveness.

A natural first step was to talk extensively to executives around the world who were known for their skill, experience, and wisdom on the question of organizational design. We found that they, too, shared our disquiet about conventional approaches. All were uncomfortable with the limitations of the usual structural solutions, especially the latest aberration, the complex matrix form. Yet they were skeptical about the usefulness of any known tools, doubting they were up to the task of revitalizing and redirecting billion-dollar giants.

In fact, the most helpful ideas were coming from the strangest places. Way back in 1962, the business historian Alfred Chandler wrote *Strategy and Structure*, in which he expressed the very powerful notion that structure follows strategy.[1] And the conventional wisdom in 1977, when we started our work, was that Chandler's dictum had the makings of universal truth. Get the strategic plan down on paper and the right organization structure will pop out with ease, grace, and beauty. Chandler's idea *was* important, no doubt about that; but when Chandler conceived it everyone was diversifying, and what Chandler most clearly captured was that a strategy of broad diversification dictates a structure marked by decentralization. Form follows function. For the period following World War II through about 1970, Chandler's advice was enough to cause (or maintain) a revolution in management practice that was directionally correct.

But as we explored the subject, we found that strategy rarely seemed to dictate unique structural solutions. Moreover, the crucial problems in strategy were most often those of execution and continuous adaptation: getting it done, staying flexible. And that to a very large extent meant going far beyond strategy to issues of organizing—structure, people, and the like. So the problem of management effectiveness threatened to prove distressingly circular. The dearth of practical additions to old ways of thought was painfully apparent. It was never so clear as in 1980, when U.S. managers, beset by obvious problems of stagnation, leaped to adopt Japanese management practices, ignoring the cultural difference, so much wider than even the vast expanse of the Pacific would suggest.

Our next step in 1977 was to look beyond practicing businessmen for help. We visited a dozen business schools in the United States and Europe (Japan doesn't have business schools). The theorists from academe, we found, were wrestling with the same concerns. Our timing was good. The state of theory is in refreshing disarray, but moving toward a new consensus; some few researchers continue to write about structure, particularly that latest and most modish variant, the matrix. But primarily the ferment is around another stream of thoughts that follows from some startling ideas about the limited capacity of decision makers to handle information and reach what we usually think of as "rational" decisions, and the even lesser likelihood that large collectives (i.e., organizations) will automatically execute the complex strategic design of the rationalists.

The stream that today's researchers are tapping is an old one, started in the late 1930s by Elton Mayo and Chester Barnard, both at Harvard. In various ways, both challenged ideas put forward by Max Weber, who defined the bureaucratic form of organization, and Frederick Taylor, who implied that management really can be made into an exact science. Weber had pooh-poohed charismatic leadership and doted on bureaucracy; its rule-driven, impersonal form, he said, was the only way to assure long-term survival. Taylor, of course, is the source of the time and motion approach to efficiency: if only you can divide work up into enough discrete, wholly programmed pieces and then put the pieces back together in a truly optimum way, why then you'll have a truly top-performing unit.

Mayo started out four-square in the mainstream of the rationalist school and ended up challenging, de facto, a good bit of it. On the shop floors of Western Electric's Hawthorne plant, he tried to demonstrate that better work place hygiene would have a direct and positive effect on worker productivity.[2] So he turned up the lights. Productivity went up, as predicted. Then, as he prepared to turn his attention to another factor, he routinely turned the lights back down. Productivity went up again! For us, the very important message of the research that these actions spawned, and a theme we shall return to continually in the book, is that it is *attention to employees,* not work conditions per se, that has the dominant impact on productivity. (Many of our best companies, one friend observed, seemed to reduce management to merely creating "an endless stream of Hawthorne effects.") It doesn't fit the rationalist view.

Chester Barnard, speaking from the chief executive's perspective (he had been president of New Jersey Bell), asserted that a leader's role is to harness the social forces in the organization, to shape and guide values. He described good managers as value shapers concerned with the informal social properties of organization.[3] He contrasted them with mere manipulators of formal rewards and systems, who dealt only with the narrower concept of short-term efficiency.

Barnard's concepts, although quickly picked up by Herbert Simon (who subsequently won a Nobel prize for his efforts), lay otherwise dormant for thirty years while the primary management disputes focused on structure attendant to postwar growth, the burning issue of the era.

But then, as the first wave of decentralizing structure proved less than a panacea for all time and its successor, the matrix, ran into continuous troubles born of complexity, Barnard and Simon's ideas triggered a new wave of thinking. On the theory side, the exemplars were Karl Weick of Cornell and James March of Stanford, who attacked the rational model with a vengeance.

Weick suggests that organizations learn and adapt v-e-r-y slowly. They pay obsessive attention to habitual internal cues, long after their practical value has lost all meaning. Important strategic business assumptions (e.g., a control versus a risk-taking bias) are buried deep in the minutiae of management systems and other habitual routines whose origins have long been obscured by time. Our favorite example of the point was provided by a friend who early in his career was receiving instruction as a bank teller. One operation involved hand-sorting 80-column punched cards, and the woman teaching him could do it as fast as lightning. "Bzzzzzzt" went the deck of cards in her hands, and they were all sorted and neatly stacked. Our friend was all thumbs.

"How long have you been doing this?" he asked her.

"About ten years," she estimated.

"Well," said he, anxious to learn, "what's that operation for?"

"To tell you the truth"—Bzzzzzzt, another deck sorted—"I really don't know."

Weick supposes that the inflexibility stems from the mechanical pictures of organizations we carry in our heads; he says, for instance: "Chronic use of the military metaphor leads people repeatedly to overlook a different kind of organization, one that values improvisation rather than forecasting, dwells on opportunities rather than constraints, discovers new actions rather than defends past actions, values arguments more highly than serenity and encourages doubt and contraction rather than belief."

March goes even further than Weick.[4] He has introduced, only slightly facetiously, the garbage can as organizational metaphor. March pictures the way organizations learn and make decisions as streams of problems, solutions, participants, and choice opportunities interacting almost randomly to carry the organization toward the future. His observations about large organizations recall President Truman's wry prophecy about the vexations lying in wait for his successor, as recounted by Richard E. Neustadt. "He'll sit here," Truman would remark (tapping his desk for emphasis), "and he'll say, 'Do this! Do that!' And nothing will happen. Poor Ike—it won't be a bit like the army. He'll find it very frustrating."[5]

Other researchers have recently begun to accumulate data that support these unconventional views. The researcher Henry Mintzberg, of Canada's McGill University, made one of the few rigorous studies of how effective managers use their time.[6] They don't regularly block out large chunks of time for planning, organizing, motivating, and controlling, as most authorities suggest they ought. Their time, on the contrary, is fragmented, the average interval devoted to any one issue being *nine minutes.* Andrew Pettigrew, a British researcher, studied the politics of strategic decision making and was fascinated by the inertial properties of organizations.[7] He showed that companies often hold on to flagrantly faulty assumptions about their world for as long as a decade, despite overwhelming evidence that that world has changed and they probably should too. (A wealth of recent examples of what Pettigrew had in mind is provided by the several American industries currently undergoing deregulation—airlines, trucking, banks, savings and loans, telecommunications.)

Among our early contacts were managers from long-term top-performing companies: IBM, 3M, Procter & Gamble, Delta Airlines. As we reflected on the new school of theoretical thinking, it began to dawn on us that the intangibles that those managers described were much more consistent with Weick and March than with Taylor or Chandler. We heard talk of organizational cultures, the family feeling, small is beautiful, simplicity rather than complexity, hoopla associated with quality products. In short, we found the obvious, that the individual human being still counts. Building up organizations that take note of his or her limits (e.g., information-processing ability) and strengths (e.g., the power flowing from commitment and enthusiasm) was their bread and butter.

CRITERIA FOR SUCCESS

For the first two years we worked mainly on the problem of expanding our diagnostic and remedial kit beyond the traditional tools for business problem solving, which then concentrated on strategy and structural approaches.

Indeed, many friends outside our task force felt that we should simply take a new look at the structural question in organizing. As decentralization has been the wave of the fifties and sixties, they said, and the so-called matrix the modish but quite obviously ineffective structure of the seventies, what then would be the structural form of the eighties? We chose to go another route. As important as the structural issues undoubtedly are, we quickly concluded that they are only a small part of the total issue of management effectiveness. The very word "organizing," for instance, begs the question, "Organize for what?" For the large corporations we were interested in, the answer to that question was almost always to build some sort of major new corporate capability—that is, to become more innovative, to be better marketers, to permanently improve labor relations, or to build some other skill which that corporation did not then possess.

An excellent example is McDonald's. As successful as that corporation was in the United States, doing well abroad meant more than creating an international division. In the case of McDonald's it meant, among other things, teaching the German public what a hamburger is. To become less dependent on government sales, Boeing had to build the skill to sell its wares in the commercial marketplace, a feat most of its competitors never could pull off. Such skill building, adding new muscle, shucking old habits, getting really good at something new to the culture, is difficult. That sort of thing clearly goes beyond structure.

So we needed more to work with than new ideas on structure. A good clue to what we were up to is contained in a remark by Fletcher Byrom, chairman and chief executive of Koppers: "I think an inflexible organization chart which assumes that anyone in a given position will perform exactly the same way his predecessor did, is ridiculous. He won't. Therefore, the organization ought to shift and adjust and adapt to the fact that there's a new person in the spot."[8] There is no such thing as a good structural answer apart from people considerations, and vice versa. We went further. Our research told us that any intelligent approach to organizing had to encompass, and treat as interdependent, at least seven variables: structure, strategy, people, management style, systems and procedures, guiding concepts and shared values (i.e., culture), and the present and hoped-for corporate strengths or skills. We defined this idea more precisely and elaborated what came to be known as the McKinsey 7-S Framework (see figure). With a bit of stretching, cutting, and fitting, we made all seven variables start with the letter S and invented a logo to go with it. Anthony Athos at the Harvard Business School gave us the courage to do it that way, urging that without the memory hooks provided by alliteration, our stuff was just too hard to explain, too easily forgettable.

Hokey as the alliteration first seemed, four years' experience

McKinsey 7-S Framework ©

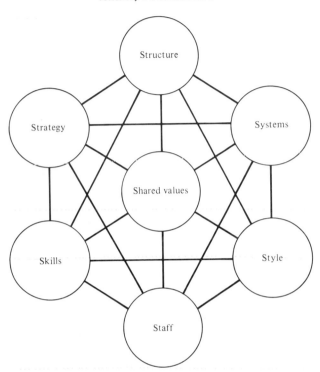

throughout the world has borne out our hunch that the framework would help immeasurably in forcing explicit thought about not only the hardware—strategy and structure—but also about the software of organization—style, systems, staff (people), skills, and shared values. The framework, which some of our waggish colleagues have come to call the happy atom, seems to have caught on around the world as a useful way to think about organizing.* Richard Pascale and Anthony Athos, who assisted us in our concept development, used it as the conceptual underpinning for *The Art of Japanese Management.*[9] Harvey Wagner, a friend at the University of North Carolina and an eminent scholar in the hard-

---

*We were hardly the first to invent a multi-variable framework. Harold Leavitt's "Leavitt's Diamond," for instance (task, structure, people, information and control, environment), has now influenced generations of managers.[10] We were fortunate in enjoying good timing. Managers beset with seemingly intractable problems and years of frustration with strategy and structure shifts were finally ready for a new view by 1980. Moreover, putting the stamp of McKinsey, long known for its hard-nosed approach to management problem solving, behind the new model added immense power.

nosed field of decision sciences, uses the model to teach business policy. He said recently, "You guys have taken all the mystery out of my class. They [his students] use the framework and all the issues in the case pop right to the surface."

In retrospect, what our framework has really done is to remind the world of professional managers that "soft is hard." It has enabled us to say, in effect, "All that stuff you have been dismissing for so long as the intractable, irrational, intuitive, informal organization *can* be managed. Clearly, it has as much or more to do with the way things work (or don't) around your companies as the formal structures and strategies do. Not only are you foolish to ignore it, but here's a way to think about it. Here are some tools for managing it. Here, really, is the way to develop a new skill."

But there was still something missing. True, we had expanded our diagnostic tool kit by quantum steps. True, we had observed managers apparently getting more done because they could *pay attention* with seven S's instead of just two. True, by recognizing that real change in large institutions is a function of at least seven hunks of complexity, we were made appropriately more humble about the difficulty of changing a large institution in any fundamental way. But, at the same time, we were short on practical design ideas, especially for the "soft S's." Building new corporate capability wasn't the simple converse of describing and understanding what's not working, just as designing a good bridge takes more than understanding why some bridges fail. We now had far better mental equipment for pinpointing the cause of organizational malaise, which was good, and we had enhanced our ability to determine what was working despite the structure and ought to be left alone, which was even better. But we needed to enrich our "vocabulary" of design patterns and ideas.

Accordingly, we decided to take a look at management excellence itself. We had put that item on the agenda early in our project, but the real impetus came when the managing directors of Royal Dutch/Shell Group asked us to help them with a one-day seminar on innovation. To fit what we had to offer with Shell's request, we chose a double meaning for the word "innovation." In addition to what might normally be thought of—creative people developing marketable new products and services— we added a twist that is central to our concern with change in big institutions. We asserted that innovative companies not only are unusually good at producing commercially viable new widgets; *innovative companies are especially adroit at continually responding to change of any sort in their environments.* Unlike Andrew Pettigrew's inertial organizations, when the environment changes, these companies change too. As the needs of their customers shift, the skills of their competitors improve, the mood of the public perturbates, the forces of international trade realign, and government regulations shift, these companies tack, revamp, adjust, transform, and adapt. In short, as a whole culture, they innovate.

That concept of innovation seemed to us to define the task of the truly excellent manager or management team. The companies that seemed to us to have achieved that kind of innovative performance were the ones we labeled excellent companies.

We gave our presentation to Royal Dutch/Shell Group on July 4, 1979, and if this research has a birthday, that was it. What fascinated us even more than the effort in The Netherlands, however, was the reaction we subsequently got from a few companies like HP and 3M that we had contacted in preparation for our discussions with Shell. They were intrigued with the subject we were pursuing and urged us on.

Largely because of that, several months later we put together a team and undertook a full-blown project on the subject of excellence as we had defined it—continuously innovative big companies. This was mainly funded by McKinsey, with some support from interested clients. At that point we chose seventy-five highly regarded companies, and in the winter of 1979–80 conducted intense, structured interviews in about half these organizations. The remainder we initially studied through secondary channels, principally press coverage and annual reports for the last twenty-five years; we have since conducted intensive interviews with more than twenty of those companies. (We also studied some underachieving companies for purposes of comparison, but we didn't concentrate much on this, as we felt we had plenty of insight into underachievement through our combined twenty-four years in the management consulting business.)

Our findings were a pleasant surprise. The project showed, more clearly than could have been hoped for, that the excellent companies were, above all, brilliant on the basics. Tools didn't substitute for thinking. Intellect didn't overpower wisdom. Analysis didn't impede action. Rather, these companies worked hard to keep things simple in a complex world. They persisted. They insisted on top quality. They fawned on their customers. They listened to their employees and treated them like adults. They allowed their innovative product and service "champions" long tethers. They allowed some chaos in return for quick action and regular experimentation.

The eight attitudes that emerged to characterize most nearly the distinction of the excellent, innovative companies go as follows:

1. A *bias for action,* for getting on with it. Even though these companies may be analytical in their approach to decision making, they are not paralyzed by that fact (as so many others seem to be). In many of these companies the standard operating procedure is "Do it, fix it, try it." Says a Digital Equipment Corporation senior executive, for example,

"When we've got a big problem here, we grab ten senior guys and stick them in a room for a week. They come up with an answer *and* implement it." Moreover, the companies are experimenters supreme. Instead of allowing 250 engineers and marketers to work on a new product in isolation for fifteen months, they form bands of 5 to 25 and test ideas out on a customer, often with inexpensive prototypes, within a matter of weeks. What is striking is the host of practical devices the excellent companies employ, to maintain corporate fleetness of foot and counter the stultification that almost inevitably comes with size.

2. *Close to the customer.* These companies learn from the people they serve. They provide unparalleled quality, service, and reliability— things that work and last. They succeed in differentiating—*à la* Frito-Lay (potato chips), Maytag (washers), or Tupperware—the most commodity-like products. IBM's marketing vice president, Francis G (Buck) Rodgers, says, "It's a shame that, in so many companies, whenever you get good service, it's an exception."[11] Not so at the excellent companies. Everyone gets into the act. Many of the innovative companies got their best product ideas from customers. That comes from listening, intently and regularly.

3. *Autonomy and entrepreneurship.* The innovative companies foster many leaders and many innovators throughout the organization. They are a hive of what we've come to call champions; 3M has been described as "so intent on innovation that its essential atmosphere seems not like that of a large corporation but rather a loose network of laboratories and cubbyholes populated by feverish inventors and dauntless entrepreneurs who let their imaginations fly in all directions."[12] They don't try to hold everyone on so short a rein that he can't be creative. They encourage practical risk taking, and support good tries. They follow Fletcher Byrom's ninth commandment: "Make sure you generate a reasonable number of mistakes."[13]

4. *Productivity through people.* The excellent companies treat the rank and file as the root source of quality and productivity gain. They do not foster we/they labor attitudes or regard capital investment as the fundamental source of efficiency improvement. As Thomas J. Watson, Jr., said of his company, "IBM's philosophy is largely contained in three simple beliefs. I want to begin with what I think is the most important: *our respect for the individual.* This is a simple concept, but in IBM it occupies a major portion of management time."[14] Texas Instruments' chairman Mark Shepherd talks about it in terms of every worker being "seen as a source of ideas, not just acting as a pair of hands"; each of his more than 9,000 People Involvement Program, or PIP, teams (TI's quality circles) does contribute to the company's sparkling productivity record.[15]

5. *Hands-on, value driven.* Thomas Watson, Jr., said that "the basic

philosophy of an organization has far more to do with its achievements than do technological or economic resources, organizational structure, innovation and timing."[16] Watson and HP's William Hewlett are legendary for walking the plant floors. McDonald's Ray Kroc regularly visits stores and assesses them on the factors the company holds dear, Q.S.C. & V. (Quality, Service, Cleanliness, and Value).

6. *Stick to the knitting.* Robert W. Johnson, former Johnson & Johnson chairman, put it this way: "Never acquire a business you don't know how to run."[17] Or as Edward G. Harness, past chief executive at Procter & Gamble, said, "This company has never left its base. We seek to be anything but a conglomerate."[18] While there were a few exceptions, the odds for excellent performance seem strongly to favor those companies that stay reasonably close to businesses they know.

7. *Simple form, lean staff.* As big as most of the companies we have looked at are, none when we looked at it was formally run with a matrix organization structure, and some which had tried that form had abandoned it. The underlying structural forms and systems in the excellent companies are elegantly simple. Top-level staffs are lean; it is not uncommon to find a corporate staff of fewer than 100 people running multi-billion-dollar enterprises.

8. *Simultaneous loose-tight properties.* The excellent companies are both centralized and decentralized. For the most part, as we have said, they have pushed autonomy down to the shop floor or product development team. On the other hand, they are fanatic centralists around the few core values they hold dear. 3M is marked by barely organized chaos surrounding its product champions. Yet one analyst argues, "The brainwashed members of an extremist political sect are no more conformist in their central beliefs."[19] At Digital the chaos is so rampant that one executive noted, "Damn few people know who they work for." Yet Digital's fetish for reliability is more rigidly adhered to than any outsider could imagine.

Most of these eight attributes are not startling. Some, if not most, are "motherhoods." But as Rene McPherson says, "Almost everybody agrees, 'people are our most important asset.' Yet almost none really lives it." The excellent companies live their commitment to people, as they also do their preference for action—any action—over countless standing committees and endless 500-page studies, their fetish about quality and service standards that others, using optimization techniques, would consider pipe dreams; and their insistence on regular initiative (practical autonomy) from tens of thousands, not just 200 designated $75,000-a-year thinkers.

Above all, the *intensity itself,* stemming from strongly held beliefs, marks these companies. During our first round of interviews, we could "feel it." The language used in talking about people was different. The expectation of regular contributions was different. The love of the product and customer was palpable. And we felt different ourselves, walking around an HP or 3M facility watching groups at work and play, from the way we had in most of the more bureaucratic institutions we have had experience with. It was watching busy bands of engineers, salesmen, and manufacturers casually hammering out problems in a conference room in St. Paul in February; even a customer was there. It was seeing an HP division manager's office ($100 million unit), tiny, wall-less, on the factory floor, shared with a secretary. It was seeing Dana's new chairman, Gerald Mitchell, bearhugging a colleague in the hall after lunch in the Toledo headquarters. It was very far removed from silent board rooms marked by dim lights, somber presentations, rows of staffers lined up along the walls with calculators glowing, and the endless click of the slide projector as analysis after analysis lit up the screen.

We should note that not all eight attributes were present or conspicuous to the same degree in all of the excellent companies we studied. But in every case at least a preponderance of the eight was clearly visible, quite distinctive. We believe, moreover, that the eight are conspicuously absent in most large companies today. Or if they are not absent, they are so well disguised you'd hardly notice them, let alone pick them out as distinguishing traits. Far too many managers have lost sight of the basics, in our opinion: quick action, service to customers, practical innovation, and the fact that you can't get any of these without virtually everyone's commitment.

So, on the one hand, the traits are obvious. Presenting the material to students who have no business experience can lead to yawns. "The customer comes first, second, third," we say. "Doesn't *everyone* know that?" is the implied (or actual) response. On the other hand, seasoned audiences usually react with enthusiasm. They know that this material is important, that Buck Rodgers was right when he said good service is the exception. And they are heartened that the "magic" of a P&G and IBM is simply getting the basics right, not possessing twenty more IQ points per man or woman. (We sometimes urge them not to be so heartened. The process of acquiring or sharpening the basics to anything like the excellent companies' obsessive level, after all, is a lot harder than coming up with a "strategic breakthrough" in one's head.)

American companies are being stymied not only by their staffs but also by their structures and systems, both of which inhibit action. One of our favorite examples is shown in a diagram drawn by a manager of a would-be new venture in a moderately high technology business (see figure).

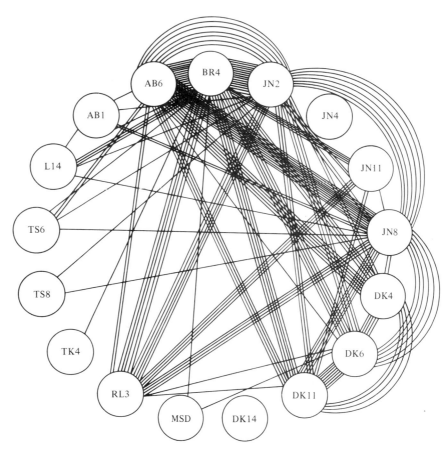

New Product Sign-off.

The circles in this diagram represent organizational units—for example, the one containing MSD is the Management Sciences Division—and the straight lines depict the formal linkages (standing committees) that are involved in launching a new product. There are 223 such formal linkages. Needless to say, the company is hardly first to the marketplace with any new product. The irony, and the tragedy, is that each of the 223 linkages taken by itself makes perfectly good sense. Well-meaning, rational people designed each link for a reason that made sense at the time—for example, a committee was formed to ensure that a glitch between sales and marketing, arising in the last product rollout, is not repeated. The trouble is that the total picture as it inexorably emerged, amusing as it might be to a C. Northcote Parkinson, captures action like a fly in a spider's web and drains the life out of it. The other sad fact is that when we use this diagram in presentations, we don't draw shouts of "Absurd." Instead we draw sighs, nervous laughter, and the occasional volunteer who says, "If you really want a humdinger, you should map our process."

REFERENCES

1. Way back in 1962: Alfred D. Chandler, Jr., *Strategy and Structure: Chapters in the History of the American Industrial Enterprise* (Cambridge, Mass.: MIT Press, 1962).
2. On the shop floors: F. J. Roethlisberger and William J. Dickson, *Management and the Worker* (Cambridge, Mass.: Harvard University Press, 1939).
3. He described good managers: Chester I. Barnard, *The Functions of the Executive* (Cambridge, Mass.: Harvard University Press, 1968), chap. 5.
4. March goes even further: James G. March and Johan P. Olsen, *Ambiguity and Choice in Organizations* (Bergen, Norway: Universitets-forlaget, 1976), p. 26.
5. "He'll sit here": Richard E. Neustadt, *Presidential Power: The Politics of Leadership* (New York: Wiley, 1960), p. 9.
6. The researcher Henry Mintzerg: Henry Mintzberg, *The Nature of Managerial Work* (New York: Harper & Row, 1973), pp. 31–35.
7. Pettigrew, a British researcher: Andrew M. Pettigrew, *The Politics of Organizational Decision Making* (London: Tavistock, 1973).
8. "I think an inflexible organization": William F. Dowling and Fletcher Byrom, "Conversation with Fletcher Byrom," *Organizational Dynamics*, summer 1978, p. 44.
9. *The Art of Japanese Management*: Richard Tanner Pascale and Anthony G. Athos, *The Art of Japanese Management* (New York: Simon & Schuster, 1981).
10. Footnote: "Leavitt's Diamond": Harold J. Leavitt, *Managerial Psychology*, 4th ed. (Chicago: University of Chicago Press, 1978), pp. 282ff.
11. "It's a shame": Robert L. Shook, *Ten Greatest Salespersons: What They Say About Selling* (New York: Harper & Row, 1980), p. 68.
12. "So intent on innovation": Lee Smith, "The Lures and Limits of Innovation: 3M," *Fortune*, Oct. 20, 1980, p. 84.
13. "Make sure you generate": Dowling and Byrom, p. 43.
14. "IBM's philosophy": Thomas J. Watson, Jr., *A Business and Its Beliefs: The Ideas That Helped Build IBM* (New York: McGraw-Hill, 1963), p. 13.
15. "Seen as a source of ideas": Mark Shepherd, Jr., and J. Fred Bucy, "Innovation at Texas Instruments," *Computer*, September 1979, p. 84.
16. "The basic philosophy": Watson, p. 5.
17. "Never acquire a business": "The Ten Best-Managed Companies," *Dun's Review*, December 1970, p. 30.
18. "This company has never left": "P&G's New New-Product Onslaught," *Business Week*, Oct. 1, 1979, p. 79.
19. "The brainwashed members": C. Barron, "British 3M's Multiple Management," *Management Today*, March 1977, p. 56.

QUESTIONS FOR READING, RESPONDING, AND WRITING

Summarizing Main Points

1. What are the "soft S's" in the 7-S Framework? Under what categories do people—workers, management, and top-level executives—fit in the 7-S Framework?
2. How did Waterman and Peters discover that "it is *attention to employees*, not work conditions per se, that has the dominant impact on productivity"? List the ways that discovery influenced their research techniques.

Analyzing Methods of Discourse

1. Under the section entitled "Criteria for Success," Peters and Waterman make the claim that "the very word 'organizing' . . . begs the question, 'Organize for what?'" What do you think they mean by this statement? Do Peters and Waterman provide other examples of question begging?
2. Toward the middle of their essay, Peters and Waterman italicize the words "*pay attention*" in a passage that reflects on both their successful research and their still unfinished application of that research. Why do you suppose they want to underscore these words? What are Peters and Waterman suggesting management pay attention to?

Focusing on the Field

1. What do Peters and Waterman mean by the term "Hawthorne effects"? Describe what you feel "an endless stream of Hawthorne effects" would be like. Why don't "Hawthorne effects" fit the "rationalist view" of business management?
2. Peters and Waterman provide two diagrams: the first they designed and are advocating; the second is already in use "in a moderately high technology business." Why do you suppose Peters and Waterman supply both? Does the second diagram with its intricate and confusing pattern answer any objections to Peters's and Waterman's simpler, yet still weblike diagram?

Writing Assignments

1. Apply the 7-S Framework to an organizational scheme with which you are familiar (e.g., dormitory policies, registration for classes, family decision making, English composition class). In a short essay, summarize your findings.
2. Peters and Waterman cite Andrew Pettigrew, who "studied the politics of strategic decision making and was fascinated by the inertial properties of organizations." In a short essay, demonstrate how the business of television advertising as described by Carol Caldwell in "You Haven't Come a Long Way, Baby: Women in Television Commercials" exemplifies the "inertial properties of organizations." Support your contention with examples from both essays.

Mike Reed

AN ALTERNATIVE VIEW
OF THE UNDERGROUND ECONOMY

Mike Reed's interest in underground economies stems in part from his memories of growing up on a farm. He has said that Volume I of *The Foxfire Book,* which he quotes in the following essay, sounds very much like his own grandparents, who were from the farm country of Arkansas.

Born himself in Selenas, California in 1944, Reed studied first at San Jose State University (B.A., 1963) and later gained his Ph.D. from the University of Utah, Salt Lake City, in 1974. He has been teaching at the University of Nevada at Reno, where since 1972, he has been chairman of the department of economics.

Reed has published other essays on the methodology of economics, and he says he is sometimes accused of being something of a "dinosaur" and of being "stuck in the mud" since his own economic theory reflects a traditional nineteenth-century approach. He describes his writing as a long, laborious process and claims he follows the "soup theory" of writing and research: "read a lot, sit and let it perk a long while."

In the following selection, first delivered before the annual meeting of the Association for Evolutionary Economics, Reed admonishes his fellow economists for taking what he considers a too narrow and too negative view of the "underground economy." He goes on to suggest an alternative view that, like the underground economy itself, "[lies] outside formal market boundaries."

Over the last decade or so, economists and others concerned with the analysis of economic activity have attempted to explain the decline in U.S. growth rates. The slowdown in the U.S. economy has not been confined solely to this country nor has it been solely an economic phenomena.[1] The other industrialized countries, and indeed, the entire world, have experienced these declines, albeit at different rates.

This economic situation has produced a policy crisis with respect to public finances. With the declines in growth, tax revolts, and other "populist" outpourings, governmental sectors have been sorely pressed to discover new revenue sources.

Both economists and politicians have discovered in social life a new element that is both promising and disturbing—one that is not yet a source of revenue, but certainly has such potential: the underground economy. Lying outside formal market boundaries, the set of activities known as the underground economy has been viewed negatively by economists and policy leaders since they see it as basically an avoidance of taxes. While their concern with tax avoidance is legitimate, their blanket assertion that the underground economy is predicated solely on such narrow grounds is simply that: an assertion.

This article argues that there is another aspect to the underground economy, one not so myopically focused but rather that sees the underground economy as part of a historic evolution involving both the increased need for state finances and the "discovery" of very old activities that are now suddenly attractive to policy leaders as a potential revenue source. Household production, I will argue, can serve as a surrogate for much of what constitutes the underground economy. The popular label obviously includes criminal and other negative practices, but to make it a homogenously negative component of our reality is quite simply wrong.

The article first discusses the manner in which economists have analyzed this element of economic life. We will see that their treatment, following the lines of traditional theory, is inadequate to explain the nature of the practices they seek to comprehend. Secondly, we will turn to studies done by family historians and other social scientists that allow us to better understand the practices labelled "underground." In contrast to the work done by traditional economic theorists, we will see that these latter students give us a much better analysis of economic action through their study of social life as evolving and historical.

ECONOMIC ANALYSES

The analyses of the underground economy conducted by economists have generally been macroeconomic in scope. Common to the overarching philosophy of orthodox theory is most economists' concern with *measurement* of this thing called the underground economy. This arithmomorphic approach to economic phenomena will typically lead to the following bifurcation: "To Edgar Feige and Peter Gutmann it [the underground economy] has meant unmeasured GNP, or better, gross national product which, given current conventions, should be measured but is not. On the other hand, to the Internal Revenue Service . . . it has meant income that is not reported to the tax authorities and that may or may not have been included in the estimations of national income."[2] In Vito Tanzi's edited work on the underground economy one notices both the universal concern with measuring an amorphous phenomenon called the underground economy and the equally universal denial of its validity outside of these measurements. That is, economists are more concerned with validating the concept via its precise measurement than by attempting to familiarize themselves with a set of practices that are perhaps not new, just new to economists.

In working within a given institutional framework and given the empiricist methodology within which orthodox economics is bounded, economist Peter Gutmann can make such simplifying assumptions as that the underground economy did not exist prior to the period 1937–1941.[3] In part this assumption coincides with the nature of the data from which he works. Moreover, it accepts necessarily the historic institution guiding the production and distribution of commodities. Within the circular flow model as abstraction, though, such an approach is tenuous at best in its ability to explain the evolution of an economy simply by assuming the constancy of institutions with the following conundrum: using the revenue orientation mentioned above, the underground economy is shown empirically to exist, but to have no well-defined boundaries. On the other hand, using a strictly monetary approach, we can argue just as well that the underground economy does not exist because the ratio of cash to checking accounts does not show enough variation to account for its alleged existence. And even if it does exist, as we know that it does, then it did not exist in an empirically verifiable manner prior to the late 1930s.

As a consequence, economists' attempts to validate the underground economy's existence become grounded in the calls for a data base that more accurately reflects the nature of the current aggregate reality in order to develop a better set of economic policies.[4] While we cannot quarrel with the call for a better collection of data to develop a more complete set of policy prescriptions to handle a difficult age, one must question the call if it is to be based simply on the reach for more and different numbers.

For our purposes, the real problem with the inability of the economic data and the theory that spawned it to grasp the underground economy may best be viewed if we recall for a moment the nature of the circular flow model. In that completed diagram there are the business and household sectors, along with the government and the foreign trade sector, all connected via the market. And we know, too, that it is in the business component where production occurs. The goods and services produced there are sent, again via the market, to the other components, primarily households, where they disappear. And we all know the story of the businessman who marries his typist and thereby decreases the level of GNP.

I would suggest that this model captures the essence of our concern: the household can no longer be analyzed at the material level as an empty set. It must begin to be seen by economists as a productive unit. I am not suggesting that we transfer the ideas of the production function to replace the utility function.[5] Such a move would trap economists once again in the arithmomorphic analysis that they now utilize. In contrast to formal economic study, the evidence that helps us to understand the family as a productive unit, and consequently the underground economy, is found in other social science and historical literature.

FAMILY AND POPULATION STUDIES

The direction we might take is given to us in the first issue of *The Foxfire Book*. The extended statement of Mrs. Marvin Watts can be used to illustrate the productive nature of family life in a manner which predates generalized market activity.

> my dadie raised the stuff we lived one he groed the corn to make our bread   he groed the cane to make our syrup allso groed they Beans and Peas to make the soup beans out of an dried leather Britches beans and dried fruit enough to last all winter   he Killed enough meat to last all winter
> he Killed a beaf and a Sheep and two or three hogs for the winter   he diden have mutch money for anything   we just had our biskets for sunday morning and when mother ran out of coffie she parched chustnuts and ground them one her coffie mill to make coffie out of   and when it rained and the mills coulden grind our bread we ate potatoes for bread   my dad usto make our shoes   I can remember waring them   my mother usto weaved woal cloth to make blankets and cloths our of   I have worn woal dresses and my dad has worn jome made Britches out of woven woal to my mother also knit our Stockings and socks to   have hope my dad Shear Sheep a lot of times to get tat woal my mother would was it and Spen it make it into thread and then weave it one her loom to make her blankets and cloth out of   we usto have corn Shuckings to get our corn all shucked.[6]

This summary of life in the hills of north Georgia in the early years of the twentieth century typifies traditional rural activity. Not only is the market not a dominant force, the lack of specialized and specific tasks is pervasive: Jack-of-all-trades knowledge was required; specialization occurred, as Mrs. Watts hints, with seasonal activity.

So long as this way of life resides in rural sectors and is not the province of urban areas and hence large sections of the population, the underground economy is not noticeable. But we should remind ourselves that Karl Polanyi explained how the market was created out of a similar social structure in England at the end of the eighteenth century, a situation that Ivan Illich has labelled "the subsistence economy" to distinguish it from the shadow, necessary work associated with industrial activity.[7]

The work of historians provides another useful point of departure. John Demos corroborates our notion of family productivity in his work on Plymouth Colony.[8] Concluding his work, he notes that the family was a multifaceted unit, with a complex set of relations encompassing the immediate members of the family and the external world. As these relations changed with time, we may note that they encompassed many of the functions that are now primarily, if not exclusively, external to the present day American family: schooling, production, welfare, and punishment.[9]

Ruth Schwartz Cowan has given us a detailed portrait of family life over the latter half of the nineteenth century that substantiates the view of the family as a resilient and evolving unit responding actively to historical conditions, but in the end requiring that women stay in the home despite the introduction of labor-saving technologies.[10] In the process of this historical change, the family lost its productive character and became a consuming unit. One of the consequences of such a shift was "the transformation of the household from a busy workplace and social center to a private family abode."[11] Particularly "in middle-class families, housework lost its economic and productive value. Since it was not paid for, it had no place in the occupational hierarchy. . . . While historians have generalized upon the basis of middle-class experience, it is now becoming clear that pre-industrial family patterns persisted over longer time periods on the farm and in working-class families."[12]

I would suggest that the area of family studies, then, is an area from which economists may learn. If we are willing to argue that the family has historically grounded origins in which production did, and does, occur, we may begin to understand something of the nature of the underground economy. It is, in some sense, the continuation of pre-industrial activity. Economic theory has obscured this point as it has become obsessed with its formal taxonomy, whose central concept is the market. I do not wish to suggest that the market be denied, only that its place in the social structure not be universal and separate from other elements of social life. That is, the market as a social institution must rely on the practices of real figures and not mythical Robinsonades.

Currently under analysis is the changing nature of the population. Debate on the class character of the population is centered on the existence, or disappearance, of the middle class as a historically meaningful group.[13]

We may certainly expect that class boundaries will change. Some of the more historically secure classes will be displaced, and as this happens, they will be forced to change their economic habits. It is highly likely that they will begin producing rather than only consuming commodities. As more people begin both producing *and* consuming, they take on the older characteristics of the family, although not always in a positive fashion.[14]

Yet to view this historic process as contemporary crisis and not historic evolution is incorrect. What we have argued here requires that the low aggregate growth rates experienced in the United States in recent years has permitted a set of old practices—embodied in household production—to again become visible. The readership surveys of some of the popular magazines support this observation.

The works published by Rodale Press, for example, show not only that people in increasing numbers are doing more tasks that were formerly relegated to the external market, but also that higher income groups are vigorous participants in this process.[15] And with the ability that comes with material practice, a new element has become visible as well: the adoption of a new anticorporate ideology.

The rejection of a corporate-based hegemony as the manner by which income is increased has led to a redirection of money flows in the economic circuits. Money flows that were formerly predictable and traceable now become problematic and external to the formal categories. Income on which businesses had counted now becomes problematic. The loss of tax revenues, which we noted above, reflects the rise of a noticeable underground economy that appears to be not only large, but also growing fairly rapidly. The important thing for us to keep in mind as students and observers of the economy is that these practices constitute a historical and dialectical process by which families have provided for their wants and needs. It is not a new set of relations, but rather the recall of our own biographies.

NOTES

1. Ralf Dahrendorf, *Europe's Economy in Crisis* (New York: Holmes and Meier, 1982). Also see Alan Wolfe, *America's Impasse: The Rise and Fall of the Politics of Growth* (Boston: South End Press, 1981).
2. Vito Tanzi, "A Second (and More Skeptical) Look at the Underground Economy in the United States," in *The Underground Economy in the United States and Abroad*, ed. V. Tanzi (Lexington, Mass.: D. C. Heath, 1982), p. 103.
3. Barry Moletsky, "America's Underground Economy," in Tanzi, *The Underground Economy*, p. 52.
4. Edgar L. Feige, "How Big is the Irregular Economy?" *Challenge* 22 (November/December 1979): 5–13.
5. Gary Becker, *A Treatise on the Family* (Cambridge, Mass.: Harvard University Press, 1981).
6. Eliot Wigginton, ed., *The Foxfire Book* (New York: Anchor Press, 1972), pp. 15–16.
7. Karl Polanyi, *The Great Transformation* (Boston: Beacon Press, 1957). Ivan Illich, *Shadow Work* (Boston: Marion Boyars, 1981).
8. John Demos, *Family Life in Plymouth Colony* (New York: Oxford University Press, 1970).
9. Ibid., pp. 193–98.
10. Ruth Schwartz Cowan, *More Work for Mother* (New York: Basic Books, 1983).
11. Tamara K. Hareven, ed. *Family and Kin in Urban Communities, 1700–1930* (New York: New Viewpoints, 1977).
12. Ibid., pp. 3–4.
13. Victor F. Zonana, "Population Puzzle," *Wall Street Journal*, 20 June 1984. Also see Nona Glazer, "Everyone Needs Three Hands: Doing Unpaid and Paid Work," in *Women and Household Labor*, ed. Sarah Fenstermaker Berk (Beverly Hills: Sage Publications, 1980), pp. 249–73.
14. Alejandro Portes, "The Informal Sector: Definition, Controversy, and Relation to National Development," *Review* 7 (Summer 1983): 151–74.

15. Don Bowdrea Associates, *Organic Gardening Subscriber Study* (Huntington, Conn., 1982). This study was done for the other magazines that Rodale Press also publishes. For our specific interests this would be *New Shelter* and *Prevention*.

QUESTIONS FOR READING, RESPONDING, AND WRITING

Summarizing Main Points

1. Using material from Reed's introductory summary, his "Economic Analysis," and his "Family and Population Studies," provide a definition of the "underground economy."
2. What is Reed advocating in this essay?

Analyzing Methods of Discourse

1. What is the relationship between the first part of Reed's essay and the two sections that follow it?
2. Besides his interest in the information it provides, what other reasons do you suppose Reed might have in quoting from *The Foxfire Book?*

Focusing on the Field

1. Though Reed divides his essay into "Economic Analyses" and "Family and Population Studies," he ties them together by continuing to use economic terminology in the second section. Locate examples. How does this strategy support his main point?
2. This essay was first presented aloud at the annual meeting of the Association for Evolutionary Economics. Do you notice any way in which Reed constructs his essay so that listeners could follow it?

Writing Assignments

1. Choose one of Reed's economic sources and one of his historical sources (or sources like them), and write an essay in which you analyze a portion of the material each presents and compare their respective modes of presentation.
2. Read Willis, Gier, and Smith's "Stepping Aside: Correlates of Displacement in Pedestrians." In that essay, Willis, Gier, and Smith argue that " 'gallantry' may be as important as power in determining displacements." With this statement, they do not so much refute conventional wisdom as suggest a change in its parameters. Write an essay in which you compare their methodology, conclusions, and goals to Reed's. What is the relation of his argument to the conventional economic wisdom about the "underground economy"?

F·I·V·E

MASS COMMUNICATIONS AND POPULAR CULTURE
Media/Travel/Humor/ Americana/Sports

. . . **W**ithout a doubt the biggest handicap they face if they want to get into this business is the lack of writing ability.

Pat Charbonnet, Columbia Records

We sometimes hear that writing is no longer necessary in an age of easy vocal communication. Phones and tape recorders have taken over much of the function of letters and memos. And one can succeed in many professions without being able to write very well. But there is another side. The very advances in communications technology which support the claim that writing is no longer important have in fact increased the power of language.

If technology has reduced the need to write in some areas, it has increased the need in others. More careers in writing probably exist now than ever before—in technical reporting and journalism, for instance (even television news is written before it is spoken).

Raymond A. Dumont and John M. Lannon

Today's leaders are most frequently men and women who have mastered the art of communication. They know how to get their ideas across. And successful people—those who are continually sought for key positions—effectively combine their ability to communicate with a solid foundation of knowledge. For knowledge is the predominant quality in the transmission of ideas.

Robert Sarnoff, Chairman of the Board,
National Broadcasting Company

In producing newspapers and television news programs, journalists are telling stories, and journalists, like everyone else, tell stories according to certain formulae. Newswriting is governed by narrative patterns imposed not by organizational necessity or ideological purpose but by narrative traditions.

Michael Schudson, "Why News Is the Way It Is"

Broadcast newswriting is necessarily brief, and we achieve that brevity by cutting out facts and details. So training yourself to be a careful observer may seem a waste of time. It isn't. As with any art form—and good writing is an art—what you can do within the confines of the medium demonstrates proficiency. To write well for radio, you must help the listener see the scenes you describe. To write well for television, you must know which visual elements of a story are important and how to use words to describe the elements that are missing or difficult to make out on the screen. As a reporter on the scene, you must observe carefully what is happening. As a writer in the studio, you must study the audiotape, videotape, or film material skillfully to select what is most important. So, begin your career as a broadcast news writer by learning how to be a good observer.

Daniel E. Garvey and William L. Rivers,
Newswriting for the Electronic Media

Today we're beginning to realize that the new media aren't just mechanical gimmicks for creating worlds of illusion, but new languages with new and unique powers of expression. Historically, the resources of English have been shaped and expressed in constantly new and changing ways. The printing press changed not only the quantity of writing but also the character of language and the relations between author and public. Radio, film, TV pushed written English toward the spontaneous shifts and freedom of the spoken idiom. They aided us in the recovery of intense awareness of facial language and bodily gesture. If these "mass media" should serve only to weaken or corrupt previously achieved levels of verbal and pictorial culture, it won't be because there's anything inherently wrong with them. It will be because we've failed to master them as new languages in time to assimilate them to our total cultural heritage.

Marshall McLuhen, "Classroom Without Walls"

The study of mass media is so new that there is still some debate about whether it should be housed with arts, humanities, or the social sciences. The creation of effective mass communication via print, radio, television, or film is an art. It involves the efforts of one or more artists. Each medium can point to its best and proudly proclaim it a unique art form. But mass communication is also a branch of human learning and belongs with other humanities, like English and foreign languages. Each medium has a "literature" all its own: In radio, it's sound; in television, pictures.

Edward Jay Whetmore, *Mediamerica:*
Form, Content, and Consequence
of Mass Communication

Maya Angelou

JOE LOUIS: CHAMPION OF THE WORLD

Maya Angelou was born in 1928 in St. Louis, Missouri. She spent her first eleven years helping her grandmother run the only black general store in Stamps, Arkansas. That store provides the setting for the following excerpt on Joe Louis from *I Know Why the Caged Bird Sings* (1970). Angelou left Stamps in 1940 to join her mother in San Francisco, and, though she has lived in many countries, she still considers California her home. A professional stage and screen performer who studied dance with Martha Graham, she received a Tony Award nomination in 1973 for her performance in the play *Look Away*. Nominated for a National Book Award for *I Know Why the Caged Bird Sings* and for a Pulitzer Prize in 1976 for her collection of poetry, *Just Give Me a Drink of Cool Water 'Fore I Diiie,* Angelou has written many books, including *Gather Together in My Name* (1974) and *Singin' and Swingin' and Gettin' Merry like Christmas* (1976).

Angelou has also composed songs, drama, screenplays, and scores, including a revue with Godfrey Cambridge called *Cabaret for Freedom*. A teacher as well as a performer and writer, Angelou helped administer the School of Music and Drama at the University of Ghana from 1963 until 1966. Since then, she has lectured and taught at several schools, including the Universities of Kansas and California. For her diverse talents, Angelou has been awarded honorary degrees by Smith College (1975), Mills College (1975), and Lawrence College (1976).

The last inch of space was filled, yet people continued to wedge themselves along the walls of the Store. Uncle Willie had turned the radio up to its last notch so that youngsters on the porch wouldn't miss a word. Women sat on kitchen chairs, dining-room chairs, stools and upturned wooden boxes. Small children and babies perched on every lap available and men leaned on the shelves or on each other.

The apprehensive mood was shot through with shafts of gaiety, as a black sky is streaked with lightning.

"I ain't worried 'bout this fight. Joe's gonna whip that cracker like it's open season."

"He gone whip him till that white boy call him Momma."

At last the talking was finished and the string-along songs about razor blades were over and the fight began.

"A quick jab to the head." In the Store the crowd grunted. "A left to the head and a right and another left." One of the listeners cackled like a hen and was quieted.

"They're in a clinch, Louis is trying to fight his way out."

Some bitter comedian on the porch said, "That white man don't mind hugging that niggah now, I betcha."

"The referee is moving in to break them up, but Louis finally pushed the contender away and it's an uppercut to the chin. The contender is hanging on, now he's backing away. Louis catches him with a short left to the jaw."

A tide of murmuring assent poured out the doors and into the yard.

"Another left and another left. Louis is saving that mighty right . . ." The mutter in the Store had grown into a baby roar and it was pierced by the clang of a bell and the announcer's "That's the bell for round three, ladies and gentlemen."

As I pushed my way into the Store I wondered if the announcer gave any thought to the fact that he was addressing as "ladies and gentlemen" all the Negroes around the world who sat sweating and praying, glued to their "master's voice."

There were only a few calls for R.C. Colas, Dr. Peppers, and Hires root beer. The real festivities would begin after the fight. Then even the old Christian ladies who taught their children and tried themselves to practice turning the other cheek would buy soft drinks, and if the Brown Bomber's victory was a particularly bloody one they would order peanut patties and Baby Ruths also.

Bailey and I laid the coins on top of the cash register. Uncle Willie didn't allow us to ring up sales during a fight. It was too noisy and might shake up the atmosphere. When the gong rang for the next round we pushed through the near-sacred quiet to the herd of children outside.

"He's got Louis against the ropes and now it's a left to the body and a right to the ribs. Another right to the body, it looks like it was low. . . . Yes, ladies and gentlemen, the referee is signaling but the contender keeps raining the blows on Louis. It's another to the body, and it looks like Louis is going down."

My race groaned. It was our people falling. It was another lynching, yet another Black man hanging on a tree. One more woman ambushed and raped. A Black boy whipped and maimed. It was hounds on the trail of a man running through slimy swamps. It was a white woman slapping her maid for being forgetful.

The men in the Store stood away from the walls and at attention. Women greedily clutched the babes on their laps while on the porch the shufflings and smiles, flirtings and pinching of a few minutes before were gone. This might be the end of the world. If Joe lost we were back in slavery and beyond help. It would all be true, the accusations that we were lower types of human beings. Only a little higher than apes. True that we were stupid and ugly and lazy and dirty and, unlucky and worst of all, that God Himself hated us and ordained us to be hewers of wood and drawers of water, forever and ever, world without end.

We didn't breathe. We didn't hope. We waited.

"He's off the ropes, ladies and gentlemen. He's moving towards the center of the ring." There was no time to be relieved. The worst might still happen.

"And now it looks like Joe is mad. He's caught Carnera with a left hook to the head and a right to the head. It's a left jab to the body and another left to the head. There's a left cross and a right to the head. The contender's right eye is bleeding and he can't seem to keep his block up. Louis is penetrating every block. The referee is moving in, but Louis sends a left to the body and it's an uppercut to the chin and the contender is dropping. He's on the canvas, ladies and gentlemen."

Babies slid to the floor as women stood up and men leaned toward the radio.

"Here's the referee. He's counting. One, two, three, four, five, six, seven . . . Is the contender trying to get up again?"

All the men in the store shouted, "NO."

"—eight, nine, ten." There were a few sounds from the audience, but they seemed to be holding themselves in against tremendous pressure.

"The fight is all over, ladies and gentlemen. Let's get the microphone over to the referee . . . Here he is. He's got the Brown Bomber's hand, he's holding it up . . . Here he is . . . ."

Then the voice, husky and familiar, came to wash over us—"The winnah, and still heavyweight champeen of the world . . . Joe Louis."

Champion of the world. A Black boy. Some Black mother's son. He was the strongest man in the world. People drank Coca-Colas like ambrosia and ate candy bars like Christmas. Some of the men went behind the Store and poured white lightning in their soft-drink bottles, and a few of the bigger boys followed them. Those who were not chased away came back blowing their breath in front of themselves like proud smokers.

It would take an hour or more before the people would leave the

Store and head for home. Those who lived too far had made arrangements to stay in town. It wouldn't do for a Black man and his family to be caught on a lonely country road on a night when Joe Louis had proved that we were the strongest people in the world.

QUESTIONS FOR READING, RESPONDING, AND WRITING

Summarizing Main Points

1. According to Angelou, what would Joe Louis's defeat mean to the assembled listeners?
2. According to Angelou, does his victory have entirely positive consequences for the listeners?

Analyzing Methods of Discourse

1. In the essay, Angelou presents three points of view on the fight: her own, the announcer's, and the people's in her grandmother's store. How does her style reflect these differing points of view?
2. Early in the essay, Angelou "wondered if the announcer gave any thought to the fact that he was addressing as 'ladies and gentlemen' all the Negroes around the world who sat sweating and praying, glued to their 'master's voice.'" Consider the phrase, "his master's voice"—the famous trademark for RCA equipment. While it provides one meaning, Angelou clearly has another in mind as well. How do both meanings support her main point?

Focusing on the Field

1. How does Angelou's point of view and her use of figures of speech, dialogue, brand-names, slang, and colloquialisms create a subjective tone in her essay? Compare her tone to Art Evans's tone in "Joe Louis as a Key Functionary."
2. Who is Angelou's audience? What do you suppose her goal in writing this essay might be?

Writing Assignments

1. Write an essay in which you describe an incident in your life that stood for something beyond itself.
2. In "My Baseball Years," Philip Roth discusses the expectations for "Jewish boys of our lower-middle-class neighborhood." Write an essay in which you discuss the similarities and differences between the expectations to which Roth was subject and those to which Angelou's people were subject. You might look at Art Evans's "Joe Louis as a Key Functionary" in this regard, since Evans details both Jewish and black reactions to Joe Louis and describes the respective place of each in American society.

William H. Pritchard

THE SCHOLAR AND THE SOAP
A Professor's Path to TV Stardom

William Pritchard was born in Binghamton, New York in 1932. He has been a professor of English literature at Amherst College, where he himself spent his undergraduate years, for over three decades. Highly regarded as a teacher, scholar, and critic, Pritchard gained his B.A. in English in 1953 before taking advanced degrees (M.A., 1956; Ph.D., 1960) at Harvard University. He serves as an advisory editor for *Hudson Review* and is a frequent contributor to many major literary publications, including the *New York Times Book Review, The New Republic,* the *Times Literary Supplement, Poetry,* and *The American Scholar.*

In the following essay, Pritchard records his experience with a passion unlikely to be associated with the intellectual credentials that distinguish his life. He tells of his love affair with the soap opera *Search for Tomorrow* and of how it led to a kind of soap-opera series of incidents in his own life—a series that culminated in a moment of soap-opera stardom for the man himself.

Whenever Pritchard has time off from his show business career, he busies himself writing some of the most cogent literary criticism around. His books include *Wyndham Lewis, Seeing Through Everything: English Writers, 1918–1940,* and, most recently, *Frost: A Literary Life Reconsidered.*

Eight years ago, when others had begun to jog, to correct their corrupt diets, to engage—it was rumored—in affairs of various sorts, I had a different response to creeping middle age. A spry 44, I was well settled as a creature of routine—teaching literature classes at the same hours each term, usually in the morning; always finishing essays and reviews before, rather than after, they were due; eating interesting mixtures of canned soups, plus a ham sandwich with mayonnaise for lunch; making a habit of gin and vermouth before dinner; taking a half-hour nap each day, and so forth. A suitable addition to this routine, I felt, might be the cultivation of a less sublime literary form than I held forth about in my classes, so I decided to find a soap opera to watch, preferably one occurring in the middle of the day while I was eating the ham sandwich, and preferably of the half-hour rather than full-hour brand. It was thus I settled on CBS's venerable "Search for Tomorrow."

This show (hereafter referred to as "Search") had been running since 1951 and became the oldest living soap when its competitor, "Love of Life," fell by the wayside. It boasted an actress, Mary Stuart (she plays the heroine, Joanne, and has had many different last names as men have come and gone), who had graced "Search" since its inception. It concerned itself mainly with the small-town scene: hospitals, marriage and divorce, gossip and rumor, worry, worry, worry. As in every good soap, financial ruin or incipient brain tumors were on the horizon for every member of the cast. Yet somehow the contemplation of these and many other daily disasters makes us, the viewers, feel good. A sonnet by David Slavitt concisely accounts, I think, for this paradox; it ends this way:

> Stupid, I used to think, and partly still
> do, deploring the style, the mawkishness.
> And yet, I watch. I cannot get my fill
> of lives as dumb as mine: Pine Valley's
>   mess
> is comforting. I need not wish them ill.
> I watch, and I delight in their distress.

As the years went by, I would from time to time compile lists of characters, all the ones I could remember, present and past. More often than not at the family supper table I would recount, to a not always enraptured wife and children, the depredations that had occurred earlier in the day. My third son began to watch it with me, during vacations and other times off from school, and if, occasionally, I had to be out of town for a few days, he would be waiting at my return, ready to read off his notes on those productions I'd missed. And even though "Search" didn't do much in the ratings and had nowhere near the popularity of such shows as "General Hospital" or "All My Children," it managed just barely to survive. At one point, in the spring of 1982, it moved from CBS to NBC and for a time occupied a slot at 2:30 in the afternoon. This ordinarily would have been an awkward time for me to view it; luckily I was on sabbatical, so I adjusted my schedule, came home later to lunch, and arrived back at the office at the relaxed hour of 3 p.m.

Then one Thursday afternoon last April, just before the beginning of "Search," a local broadcaster on WWLP, the NBC affiliate in Springfield, Massachusetts, announced that beginning the following Monday her talk show would be switched to 2:30 p.m. (the "Search" slot). It took a moment to penetrate, before I began frantically scanning next week's *TV Guide* and, indeed, saw no listing for "Search" on WWLP. The Boston NBC channel had already disdained to carry it; two other stations that still broadcast it could not, to my knowledge, be received on my tube. I watched the show that day and the next, thoroughly distracted by the thought that this might very possibly be the end of the line for me and "Search."

The next morning I fired off letters: one to the station manager, deploring the decision to cancel and urging a reconsideration; one to the college newspaper, asking students to write and protest; a final one to the *Hampshire Gazette*, where my wife was employed. The station manager responded immediately, informing me that "Search" had been, in his words, "fledgling for a long time on the network" and adding, self-righteously, that NBC itself had been thinking of discontinuing it. I wrote back to point out that I understood a fledgling to be a baby bird just learning to use its wings, and that "Search" had been flying for more than 30 years until (I concluded dramatically) "you shot it down." But clearly I was wasting my words—no reconsideration was in the offing.

Meanwhile my wife had mentioned my loss to a reporter at the *Gazette*, who called up for an interview, then ran a clever piece about the distraught professor who didn't know what to do with himself in the middle of the day, having been deprived of his pleasure. Suddenly, the next morning, things began to move. The wire services had picked up the local story and phone calls began. One came from the offending affiliate in Springfield, wanting to do an interview, another from CBS in Hartford, which showed up with the cameras and was to stick with the story through its life. The exciting question seemed to be, as *USA Today* put it, why this "mild-mannered professor" was also an "addict." "And just why should this English scholar, who teaches poetry, fiction, and criticism, be a 'Search' junkie?" they asked, barely staying for an answer.

My mail improved mightily, both at home and in the office. Most of the letters were from women in the western Massachusetts area who commiserated with me, or wanted me to know how outraged they were and that they had written the station manager. And as the wire services beamed the story to various farther-flung localities, letters arrived from California and Washington (state), Bethany, Pennsylvania, and Gadsten, Alabama, Route 2, Box 61, where a Mrs. Arlene Gregg had an interesting proposal. She would tape two weeks' worth of shows, and send them along to me for viewing. Then I would send the tape back to her, at which point she would have a further two-week batch ready for me. I wrote Mrs. Gregg that I would be happy to receive the first two weeks' worth.

The plot thickened a couple of days later when a call came from someone at NBC, inviting me to fly down to New York City, meet the cast of "Search," and in fact play a bit part on that day's show. Let me think this over, I said, and call you back. Five minutes later I called back to accept, asking only that my wife be permitted to accompany me. (Her reportorial skills would be invaluable; she would remain cool and perceptive while I became flushed and excited.) Accordingly we were put up for the night at an East Side hotel, the Berkshire (I could have dinner *free* in the dining room if I wished), and called for by an NBC publicity person early the next morning.

At the studio it was all bewildering, fast moves from one person to the next, and the sudden disconcerting appearance of tube idols in less than heroic identities. For example, I didn't recognize that female having her hair put up in curlers across the makeup room. Introduced to me, she chirped out a "Hi, William, welcome to the show." It took some time before I registered that the figure being worked over was Marcia McCabe, or more significantly, "Sunny Adamson," tireless investigative reporter fresh from subduing a rapist intent on working his will on her and others. And there was the star herself, the venerable Mary Stuart, who was not in the taping that day but who had come over to the studio at lunchtime to say hello and, as it turned out, share some of my Zabar's corned-beef sandwich.

It was time for the rehearsals of different scenes—a hospital bed, a cabin where the kidnapped teenager was tied to a post and trying to escape, another cabin where pregnant Suzi Wyatt suddenly went into premature labor, and, for me most salient, Bigelow's Bar, where my brief moment would come to fulfillment. I was to precede one of the regulars into "Big's" and for a few seconds, until they moved the cameras to her and forgot me forever, it was all mine. No lines, merely an opening and closing of the saloon door, a couple of steps to the bar, a firm, friendly handshake with "Big" the bartender, and an indication that I needed a beer. And lo, there was the beer, a real one, which I proceeded to sip, while knocking back some real potato sticks. The heavy cameras quickly rolled away from me toward Sunny Adamson. While members of the cast fluffed their lines, cursed things out, or made jokes about the dialogue, my own take was boringly perfect. There was evidently no way my ten-second journey from door to bar could be improved.

My episode didn't appear on the air until about nine days later, and I spent some time figuring out how to arrange a viewing for myself of myself. We had talked about renting a motel room near Hartford, say, someplace where we could pick up the show, but then a number of people in the area called or wrote to tell me that I might be able to see it on my own set from a channel in New Britain, Connecticut. So I purchased an ancient, secondhand outdoor antenna and had it installed on the upstairs porch outside the bedroom. The day of my appearance, however, the reception was worse than average, and the viewing was further complicated by the presence of the faithful Hartford TV crew come to join the professor watching himself.

"Prof lathers in the soaps" ran the lead to the AP account in a Rochester newspaper someone sent along. At about that same time I received my first crank call, from a strange, unidentified voice who said he'd been an "activist" all his life (evidently thinking, because of the letter I'd written to the station, that I too was an activist). He was inviting me to address a "Sexual Liberty meeting" that he was organizing for the Fourth of July. I was to put what he called my "Shakespearean mind" to work and give a speech on, oh, perhaps a nuclear freeze, or some topic related to sexual freedom. I quickly declined. More letters poured in, and radio talk-show hosts from Canada to Delaware issued me invitations to join them on the air. (I finally turned down one station that wanted me to arise for a 6:20 a.m. interview.)

Within the space of two weeks I had gone from a private man who cultivated his habit for half an hour a day, five days a week, to someone to whom such gratification was first denied, then to whom unexpected gratifications came in a flurry. Robert Frost liked to muse about his own career that, as with a wedding, "it begins in felicity and ends in publicity." And then, thinking of marriages that go wrong, Frost would add, "And maybe really *ends* there." But my own bit of publicity was felicitous because I knew it would end, fickle creatures that the media have proved themselves to be. So I was eager to squeeze whatever further experiences I could out of the whole affair.

It turned out that I didn't have to do much squeezing, since about a week after the first New York venture at the "Search" studio, courtesy of NBC, CBS called to suggest I might like to come down and occupy a spot on their "Morning News" program, presided over by Bill Kurtis and Diane Sawyer. My classes had just ended, and CBS's offer to pick me up and bring me back in a limousine was irresistible. (CBS puts up its guests at the Essex House, Central Park South, and my room contained a faulty shower and no telephone book.)

I was slotted to appear at approximately 7:50 a.m., and as I arrived at the CBS studio the next morning Cyrus Vance and Strobe Talbott were being ushered out, having concluded their bit of chat about nuclear arms. In fact this was a big mixed-bag day on "CBS Morning News." The English romance novelist Barbara Cartland was to be interviewed (by Bill Kurtis) and so was the redoubtable Louis Farrakhan. Farrakhan was supposed to precede your humble soap-watcher, who was to be the subject of Diane Sawyer's ministrations, but it was almost 7:30 and the minister had not arrived. While anxious phone calls were being made, suddenly in he swept, flanked by a retinue of well-suited (in a sort of Baptist undertaker-ish way) tie-clasped, highly groomed aides (disciples? bodyguards?). Farrakhan shook hands all round, including the professor's, though conversation did not flow freely between the two of us as we proceeded, in our makeup, to the studio.

Mr. Farrakhan's interview went on for quite a while, indeed was judged to be so important that he was let run overtime. As the clock moved toward 7:55, I began to wonder how I was to be gotten on and off in time for the news at eight. A legitimate wonder, for just as I was directed to occupy the throne, another order came through: "Professor, we're *terribly* sorry about this but there's no time to interview you before the news and (we're *really* sorry about this) there's no time during the second hour of the show either—everything is totally scheduled, filled up." I can still feel the pain. Diane Sawyer came over, sympathetically concerned, telling me how much she'd really wanted to do this story—but her sympathy was powerless against the inexorabilities of scheduling.

There was nothing for it, so it seemed, but to head back to Amherst, dragging my tail behind me. How to describe the mixture of feelings—wounded pride, annoyance at the silly waste of time, rage at CBS, at the intolerable Farrakhan, and at Kurtis for letting him go on, then a glimmer of ironic acceptance of the whole thing as somehow my just deserts ("You *will* move out of your accustomed sphere, will you!"). "Would you like to have your makeup removed?" asked my host for the morning, and I told her never mind, figuring I could wear it back to Amherst. A hasty good-bye and I was at curbside, hand out to open the door of the waiting limousine—when suddenly voices were calling to me to come back, come back, they had canceled some boring bit of consumer research in the next hour and were going to slot me in instead.

After such a victory, snatched from total defeat in the nick of time, the interview itself felt a bit anticlimactic. Diane Sawyer was friendly and enthusiastic, but must have thought she had a queer bird on her hands, this "professor" who watched a soap, and she asked me with a rather heavily underlined facetiousness whether I watched it for its "high literary value." I allowed as how she was teasing me, but then obligingly went on to suggest possible reasons why a literary person might be interested in a narrative that is all talk and that never concludes itself, unless forced to by a sponsor. Almost before it began, my moment was over, with Miss Sawyer—under her own steam or that of a clever assistant—concluding that, in the words of Yeats (which poet the professor taught), some people ate "a crazy salad." It was then time for me to depart, truly depart, and, I assumed, to conclude my career as a mild-mannered media event.

One last but very pleasant gasp came at the end of the summer when I received a call from a friend congratulating me on the restoration of "Search" to WWLP Springfield. "Restoration?" was my surprised response, but indeed it had been restored, without my eagle eye catching it in *TV Guide*. My loyal retinue regrouped: the wire services, two or three radio stations, and faithful CBS Hartford called for an interview, asking me—once more—how did I feel *now?* "Ecstatic," was about all I could muster. The station manager of NBC Springfield was quoted in the paper as wondering why, now that the program had been restored, he had heard nothing from me. I wrote him explaining that I thought it was no more than my due, and that usually I wrote such letters only to complain about something.

QUESTIONS FOR READING, RESPONDING, AND WRITING

Summarizing Main Points

1. Describe Pritchard's initial attitude toward his "cultivation of a less sublime literary form": the television soap *Search for Tomorrow*. Does his attitude change? Provide examples that help the reader discover his attitudes.
2. Describe the ways in which Pritchard's own life becomes like a soap opera.

Analyzing Methods of Discourse

1. Pritchard writes his essay chronologically. List the major episodes in that chronology. How does his presentation allow for a "surprise" ending?
2. Early in the essay, Pritchard states that people watch soap operas because "the contemplation of . . . daily disasters makes us . . . feel good." He quotes the end of a sonnet to express this paradox. What other paradoxes in the essay could the sonnet describe? How might it symbolize the essay as a whole?

Focusing on the Field

1. Why does Pritchard become a news story? Could a viewer without Pritchard's academic credentials have made such a media splash? What other credentials might a viewer bring to this situation that would make his or her interest in it equally newsworthy?
2. How do the people at the *CBS Morning News* view Pritchard? Do you think their view of him is accurate? Is their view of him an important issue here? Why or why not?

Writing Assignments

1. Describe a seemingly insignificant circumstance in your own life that became more than you expected.
2. Pritchard gives several examples of how the news media handled his story. Using Pritchard's examples as models, rewrite the entire incident as it might have appeared in *USA Today* or another news publication with which you are familiar.

Joyce Maynard

EUROPE FOR THE FIRST TIME

A true baby-boomer, Joyce Maynard admits to having spent long hours in front of the television during her childhood. Yet, she clearly spent a good deal of time in front of the typewriter as well. By the time she graduated from high school, Maynard had published stories in *Seventeen* and *Women's Day* magazines. As a freshman at Yale, she became a literary sensation with a *New York Times Magazine* piece called "An Eighteen-Year-Old Looks Back on Life"—a wry look at her own jaded TV generation. She expanded that article into a book, *Looking Back: A Chronicle of Growing Up in the Sixties,* which was published two years later in 1974. Her first novel, *Baby Love,* appeared in 1981.

Born in 1953 in Durham, New Hampshire, Maynard now lives in New York City and still contributes essays to the *New York Times,* such as "Europe for the First Time." Maynard identifies herself as a relative latecomer to European travel and describes what, "after having spent 28 years of life avoiding [it]," her trip abroad meant to her.

By the time I made it to Europe (I was 28, and pregnant with my second child) most of my friends were taking off for places like Nepal and Yugoslavia. ("We'd never been to an Eastern European Communist country," said the friend who spent her vacation in Zagreb.) Not that going to Europe is ever likely to become passé, but for members of the middle class, raised in the era of great expectations in which I spent my teens, crossing the Atlantic some time before high school graduation was about as inevitable as lighting up a joint. Nearly everyone I knew in college had spent a summer biking between youth hostels or working as an au pair in the South of France.

Partly it was chance that prevented me from traveling to Europe at an early age—the summer jobs I found, a succession of first gardens, then cats, dogs, a baby. But partly, too, I had been avoiding Europe by design: I belong to the first generation of my family to be born in America, and I'm the only one of us all living in this country still. Grandchild of Russian émigrés who never could pronounce the letter "v" and of British missionaries who wouldn't have known Babe Ruth from Gary Cooper, I had made it a kind of mission since childhood to pursue everything domestic, "normal"—translate MADE IN U.S.A. It wasn't anything like a political stance, for me, or a fear of foreigners. I came from foreigners, felt halfway foreign myself. I was simply traveling in the opposite direction, away from all things European, avoiding almost everything—food, culture, travel—that would take me from my across-the-board efforts at Americanization.

Long before I reached my mid-20's, I'd come to recognize the silliness of my lingering Europe phobia—and had overcome it enough to appreciate a bottle of French wine or a meal of fresh pasta. But I probably wouldn't have gone out of my way to travel there if a book I wrote hadn't found its way into print abroad. I was offered a nearly free trip to England to promote the book, so I went.

Never having been to Europe before makes going there much harder. A kind of stay-home inertia sets in, together with the sense of "How can I ever begin?" Once we had, a little tentatively, set forth our travel plans, our friends (all more well-traveled than my husband and I) were full of suggestions. And there was the feeling: How can we go to England, after so long, and not see France too, and Italy? I plotted extensions to our trip—the classic syndrome of a nontraveler, for whom even a weekend trip is a major production. (Give me passage to Chicago and I'll be cooking up side trips to the Grand Canyon and Mexico, and then end up staying home because I can't manage to fit in Venezuela.) So with our European trip set for early October, I began talking about Christmas in Rome, the winter in Greece, renting a farmhouse in Italy— all unmissable experiences, according to our worldly friends. Of course, when those plans seemed too complicated, I was ready to throw up my hands in defeat over even the original 10 days in London.

It's paralyzing, I think now, to picture a trip, European or otherwise, as the only one you'll ever make. The burden to see everything becomes too great. We ended up with a compromise: A week in London, a week in Paris, and we'd leave our daughter home with a friend. This would be not only our first trip to Europe, but also our last hurrah before the advent of the new baby.

I remember thinking, once we got there, how familiar it all was. So often a long-anticipated experience turns out nothing like the way one pictured it, but London and Paris were just the same as they were in all the movies. I'd witnessed so many dramas set there, on the screen, I felt, as first-time travelers to Europe often must, like a visitor to a film set. Even the sirens on the streets made the same sound, and cafe accordions, filtering out from side streets, and bicycle bells.

Vivien Leigh and Greer Garson and Leslie Howard and Laurence Olivier came back to me, and all the newsreels from World War II that had never seemed wholly real to me. I knew my history well enough, but it was only standing beside the Arc de Triomphe, remembering footage of weeping Frenchmen and of German soldiers marching right past where I stood, that I began to understand the invasion of France and later, in London, the Blitz.

How did we spend our days? Lots of museums, of course. In Paris, we found ourselves over and over replacing our art-history book memories of paintings with images of the originals, discovering paintings and painters we'd passed over in reproduction and colors—Rubens's flesh tones, a Titian red—nothing like the ones in Jansen's "History of Art." I certainly didn't expect there could be anything fresh or exciting for me in the sight of the ubiquitous Venus de Milo in the original, at the Louvre, but there was, as there was with the Rodins at the Rodin Museum and the Impressionist collection at the Jeu de Paume. I'll probably never again look at so much art in such a concentrated space of time—might not even return to some of the museums I visited. That's what you do on your first trip, and it provides a frame of reference for all the trips that follow.

I don't suppose we went anywhere that green Americans haven't been trooping to for years. In London, we visited all the places on the postcards. We took a bus over to the Tower one afternoon—I, at least, feeling a pretty large proportion of duty over genuine interest—and ended up staying until the guards led us out, discovering, in room after room of a suits-of-armor collection such memorable treasures as armor for an elephant and a child's armor of a size that would have fit our 4-year-old daughter back home.

In Paris we walked along the Left Bank, of course, and leaned over the railings of bridges watching boats on the Seine, munching bread and cheese and feeling something like an obligation (not unpleasant) to hold hands . . . I stood in front of the Mona Lisa—or more accurately, 20 feet back, because of the crowds.

One night we bought what seemed to us hugely extravagant tickets to the late show at the Lido. The line outside, on the Champs Elysée, was a long one. But my husband (more out of fun than a real concern that I might pass out on the sidewalk from exhaustion) pointed out my fairly-advanced pregnancy to the man guarding the door who ushered us both in, with great ceremony and elaborate gestures of concern over my condition, and sat us down in what were surely the best seats in the house, where every now and then the odd feather would drift down on us from a nearly naked dancer no more than an arm's length away. Of course it was a pretty unabashedly tourist-directed show—one we're not likely to seek out again, and one that many worldlier than we must positively scorn. But I loved being a quintessential tourist that night and I think, on one's first trip, that's not a bad way to be.

I did a lot of shopping on our trip. Liberty prints in London, chic French baby clothes, tasteful educational toys. A lot of my purchases I can't now even lay a hand on: an umbrella purchased in the middle of a downpour in Paris, a cheap French smock bought in a market one afternoon that turned surprisingly chilly. Shopping is, for me, not so much the way of procuring tangible proof of a trip as one method (and for me probably the most enjoyable) of finding out about a way of life different from mine.

For the most part, on that European trip, I followed a pretty conventional tourist's route of monuments, churches and museums, but in my shopping I tried to be a native—looked for Band-Aids and notebooks, sewing notions and underwear. I bought a delicious brand of toothpaste and cheap plastic buttons in the shapes of rabbits and teddy bears and ducks and a kind of candy a lot like M & M's, but in a wonderful range of colors that would amaze the children at a birthday party six months later.

I bought a stack of books for my daughter—no Strawberry Shortcake or Smurf equivalents visible, except among the imports, but lots of lovable hedgehogs and field mice, visions of underground animal pantries filled with pies and raspberry jam, doll tea parties, children with governesses. And though I didn't buy food in the market, except the occasional piece of fruit or roll, I spent a lot of time looking and imagining the meals I'd prepare with that butter, those fish. Scallops for sale, still in the shell, with glossy salmon-colored roe I'd never seen before.

The week we were in London, Sadat was shot, so of course we bought a lot of newspapers and tuned in to the television news when we had the chance. It was puzzling and disorienting, experiencing an international crisis reported through other than our own familiar anchor people, and I remember sitting on the bed while my husband adjusted the set, telling him to change the channels; I couldn't believe the coverage we were being given was the official, mainstream version, and kept thinking we must have some obscure, low-budget cable station. But changing the channels didn't help. Wherever we turned it was the same: regular programming virtually uninterrupted, with brief, totally unsentimental and understated reports on the situation in Egypt. I felt nostalgic for the impassioned, even maudlin, remarks I knew the American broadcasters would be making. In London, everything said had an edge of skepticism.

My memory of the tone of those newspaper and television reports blends oddly for me with the only other news event of the week that remains clear: It was the British debut of Johnny Carson—shows taped earlier the same day in Lo Angeles, beamed over by satellite—and the British press stood in universal bemusement at this bizarre phenomenon the Americans regarded as humorous. And the truth was, in that London hotel room, Carson's monologues really didn't seem very funny.

In France, too, our American brand of humor often seemed nonexportable. On a train ride from Paris to Chartres, with a copy of The International Herald Tribune in my lap, I struck up a conversation with an uncharacteristically friendly Frenchman who asked me to translate that day's Doonesbury strip. I did, as best I could, and he first looked totally blank and then smiled politely.

Being in Europe made me aware, almost for the first time, of my own Americanness. I saw myself, for good and ill, as part of an often-brash (but also noticeably hearty, friendly), camera-wielding, corn-fed bunch of tanned, casual, healthy Americans. One or two, or even all of those adjectives may not have applied to all of them, but nearly always there was something recognizable, and distinct from tourists of other nationalities, about the Americans we saw abroad. In Europe I found myself aligned with lots of people who would themselves have seemed to me pretty foreign, back home. On the steps of Montmartre, or filing through Westminster Abbey, we were all simply Americans.

Part of what changed me about that first trip to Europe was Europe, and part, of course, was simply the experience of travel—only barely less new to me than the places I was discovering. A friend, born and raised, as I was, in a small New Hampshire town, told me once she spent the first 20 years of her life planning her first trip abroad, dressing her dolls in travel clothes, packing their steamer trunks and creating imaginary itineraries.

For me, having spent the first 28 years of life avoiding Europe, the effects of that brief two weeks abroad show themselves in subtle ways. (No "citizen of the planet" worldliness about me yet.) Traveling—and traveling, specifically, to that classic destination/point of departure that most of us here in America are either trying to get to or get away from, enlightened me about myself, separated my sense of who I am from where I am. In a different setting, new rules apply—I discover I *do* drink wine in the afternoon, I might wear perfume after all, strike up conversations with strangers in bars, or sleep late. Speaking in another language— even badly—I may have a completely different kind of thing to say.

And the world I inhabit, now that I'm back on my familiar turf, seems larger and more variously populated. Once Europe became real to me, the rest of the globe seemed open, accessible. (It's not just some fluke of a travel bonanza that found us, eight months after our return from London and Paris, heading to Peking.) I'm conscious, always now, of Europe being there. I'll think, sometimes, as I'm peeling apples or changing my son's diaper, that right now, at this very moment, there's a man on a bicycle pedaling across a bridge over the Seine, and someone's lighting up a cigarette in a particular corner of a particular cafe, and someone's tossing bread crumbs to the pigeons in Trafalgar Square.

Two days after we got home from our trip, a man flew a small plane through the Arc de Triomphe. I would once have watched the film footage on the news as I'd watch the Starship Enterprise hurtling through space. Home from my travels, I gasp, still, at the spectacle of the plane's wings as they barely cleared the two sides of the Arc. But the Arc itself had shifted in my mind, from a distant landmark to one of those places, like Bloomingdale's or my daughter's school, that I visit sometimes, and know my way around.

QUESTIONS FOR READING, RESPONDING, AND WRITING

Summarizing Main Points

1. What is Maynard's attitude toward Europe before and after her trip?
2. Some of the changes that Maynard experiences as a result of her trip she tells the reader about directly. Other changes are more subtly related. List all the changes that you can find.

Analyzing Methods of Discourse

1. List the items that Maynard buys on her trip to Europe. How does her shopping reflect her own past and her "Americanness"? What might a shopping list of your own tell someone about you?
2. Maynard establishes both a cause-and-effect relationship and a chronology in her narrative. List the ways the two are related.

Focusing on the Field

1. List the details that demonstrate Maynard's familiarity with, and appreciation for, popular cultures, both American and European. How does Maynard's recognition of herself as a tourist allow her greater insight into her own experience? Does that recognition result in a greater understanding of European or American culture?
2. This essay first appeared in the *New York Times*. Do you notice any assumptions that Maynard makes about her audience as a result?

Writing Assignments

1. Write a short essay that describes a trip that you have taken. Be sure to include, as Maynard does, the ways in which the trip helped you discover something about yourself.
2. Write an essay in which you compare and contrast Maynard's view of her "Americanness" to John Kouwenhoven's view of what constitutes "Americanness" in "What's American about Amerca?"

Philip Roth

MY BASEBALL YEARS

Philip Roth gained recognition as a writer while still in his twenties with the publication of *Goodbye, Columbus and Five Short Stories,* for which he won the National Book Award in 1960. Like Neil Klugman, the hero of the title novella, Roth was born in Newark, New Jersey (in 1933) and attended Rutgers University. But while Neil stayed in Newark, Roth, after receiving a B.A. from Bucknell University, went on for an M.A. in 1954 at the University of Chicago, where he studied and taught for another three years. Roth has also taught at the University of Iowa and has been a writer-in-residence at both Princeton and the University of Pennsylvania. He has produced a steady stream of novels since 1959, including *Letting Go* (1962), *When She Was Good* (1967), *My Life as a Man* (1974), and *The Ghost Writer* (1979), the first in a series of novels which all feature protagonist Nathan Zuckerman. In addition to his National Book Award, Roth has received a variety of grants, fellowships, and awards for his writing from the *Paris Review,* the Jewish Book Council of America, the National Institute for Arts and Letters, and the Ford Foundation. He also was nominated for an American Book Award for *The Ghost Writer* in 1980, which he declined.

Though Roth gained early fame with *Goodbye, Columbus,* the novel which gained him real notoriety was *Portnoy's Complaint* (1971). While some critics found its explicit language and scenes vital, others found them merely pornographic and linked this issue to his allegedly two-dimensional portrayal of women. Yet, despite the controversy that continues to rage around his material, Roth's talent, the comic vitality and virtuosity of his style, finds almost universal acknowledgement, allowing him to maintain his position in contemporary American fiction.

In the following essay, he steps out of the line of fire to reminisce about a somewhat safer subject—his love of baseball and literature.

In one of his essays George Orwell writes that, though he was not very good at the game, he had a long, hopeless love affair with cricket until he was sixteen. My relations with baseball were similar. Between the ages of nine and thirteen, I must have put in a forty-hour week during the snowless months over at the neighborhood playfield—softball, hardball, and stickball pick-up games—while simultaneously holding down a full-time job as a pupil at the local grammar school. As I remember it, news of two of the most cataclysmic public events of my childhood—the death of President Roosevelt and the bombing of Hiroshima—reached me while I was out playing ball. My performance was uniformly erratic; generally okay for those easygoing pick-up games, but invariably lacking the calm and the expertise that the naturals displayed in stiff competition. My taste, and my talent, such as it was, was for the flashy, whiz-bang catch rather than the towering fly; running and leaping I loved, all the do-or-die stuff—somehow I lost confidence waiting and waiting for the ball lofted right at me to descend. I could never make the high school team, yet I remember that, in one of the two years I vainly (in both senses of the word) tried out, I did a good enough imitation of a baseball player's *style* to be able to fool (or amuse) the coach right down to the day he cut the last of the dreamers from the squad and gave out the uniforms.

Though my disappointment was keen, my misfortune did not necessitate a change in plans for the future. Playing baseball was not what the Jewish boys of our lower-middle-class neighborhood were expected to do in later life for a living. Had I been cut from the high school itself, *then* there would have been hell to pay in my house, and much confusion and shame in me. As it was, my family took my chagrin in stride and lost no more faith in me than I actually did in myself. They probably would have been shocked if I had made the team.

Maybe I would have been too. Surely it would have put me on a somewhat different footing with this game that I loved with all my heart, not simply for the fun of playing it (fun was secondary, really), but for the mythic and aesthetic dimension that it gave to an American boy's life— particularly to one whose grandparents could hardly speak English. For someone whose roots in America were strong but only inches deep, and who had no experience, such as a Catholic child might, of an awesome hierarchy that was real and felt, baseball was a kind of secular church that reached into every class and region of the nation and bound millions upon millions of us together in common concerns, loyalties, rituals, enthusiasms, and antagonisms. Baseball made me understand what patriotism was about, at its best.

Not that Hitler, the Bataan Death March, the battle for the Solomons, and the Normandy invasion didn't make of me and my contemporaries what may well have been the most patriotic generation of schoolchildren in American history (and the most willingly and successfully propagandized). But the war we entered when I was eight had thrust the country into what seemed to a child—and not only to a child—a struggle to the death between Good and Evil. Fraught with perilous, unthinkable possibilities, it inevitably nourished a patriotism grounded in moral virtue and bloody-minded hate, the patriotism that fixes a bayonet to a Bible. It seems to me that through baseball I was put in touch with a more humane and tender brand of patriotism, lyrical rather than martial or righteous in spirit, and without the reek of saintly zeal, a patriotism that could not so easily be sloganized, or contained in a high-sounding formula to which you had to pledge something vague but all-encompassing called your "allegiance."

To sing the National Anthem in the school auditorium every week, even during the worst of the war years, generally left me cold. The enthusiastic lady teacher waved her arms in the air and we obliged with the words: "See! Light! Proof! Night! There!" But nothing stirred within, strident as we might be—in the end, just another school exercise. It was different, however, on Sundays out at Ruppert Stadium, a green wedge of pasture miraculously walled in among the factories, warehouses, and truck depots of industrial Newark. It would, in fact, have seemed to me an emotional thrill forsaken if, before the Newark Bears took on the hated enemy from across the marshes, the Jersey City Giants, we hadn't first to rise to our feet (my father, my brother, and I—along with our inimical countrymen, the city's Germans, Italians, Irish, Poles, and, out in the Africa of the bleachers, Newark's Negroes) to celebrate the America that had given to this unharmonious mob a game so grand and beautiful.

Just as I first learned the names of the great institutions of higher learning by trafficking in football pools for a neighborhood bookmaker rather than from our high school's college adviser, so my feel for the American landscape came less from what I learned in the classroom about Lewis and Clark than from following the major-league clubs on their road trips and reading about the minor leagues in the back pages of *The Sporting News*. The size of the continent got through to you finally when you had to stay up to 10:30 p.m. in New Jersey to hear via radio "ticker-tape" Cardinal pitcher Mort Cooper throw the first strike of the night to Brooklyn shortstop Pee Wee Reese out in "steamy" Sportsman's Park in St. Louis, Missouri. And however much we might be told by teacher about the stockyards and the Haymarket riot, Chicago only began to exist for me as a real place, and to matter in American history, when I became fearful (as a Dodger fan) of the bat of Phil Cavarretta, first baseman for the Chicago Cubs.

Not until I got to college and was introduced to literature did I find anything with a comparable emotional atmosphere and aesthetic appeal. I don't mean to suggest that it was a simple exchange, one passion for another. Between first discovering the Newark Bears and the Brooklyn Dodgers at seven or eight and first looking into Conrad's *Lord Jim* at age eighteen, I had done some growing up. I am only saying that my discovery of literature, and fiction particularly, and the "love affair"—to some degree hopeless, but still earnest—that has ensued, derives in part from this childhood infatuation with baseball. Or, more accurately perhaps, baseball—with its lore and legends, its cultural power, its seasonal associations, its native authenticity, its simple rules and transparent strategies, its longueurs and thrills, its spaciousness, its suspensefulness, its heroics, its nuances, its lingo, its "characters," its peculiarly hypnotic tedium, its mythic transformation of the immediate—was the literature of my boyhood.

Baseball, as played in the big leagues, was something completely outside my own life that could nonetheless move me to ecstasy and to tears; like fiction it could excite the imagination and hold the attention as much with minutiae as with high drama. Mel Ott's cocked leg striding into the ball, Jackie Robinson's pigeon-toed shuffle as he moved out to second base, each was to be as deeply affecting over the years as that night—"inconceivable," "inscrutable," as any night Conrad's Marlow might struggle to comprehend—the night that Dodger wild man, Rex Barney (who never lived up to "our" expectations, who should have been "our" Koufax), not only went the distance without walking in half a dozen runs, but, of all things, threw a no-hitter. A thrilling mystery, marvelously enriched by the fact that a light rain had fallen during the early evening, and Barney, figuring the game was going to be postponed, had eaten a hot dog just before being told to take the mound.

This detail was passed on to us by Red Barber, the Dodger radio sportscaster of the forties, a respectful, mild Southerner with a subtle rural tanginess to his vocabulary and a soft country-parson tone to his voice. For the adventures of "dem bums" of Brooklyn—a region then the very symbol of urban wackiness and tumult—to be narrated from Red Barber's highly alien but loving perspective constituted a genuine triumph of what my English professors would later teach me to call "point of view." James himself might have admired the implicit cultural ironies and the splendid possibilities for oblique moral and social commentary. And as for the detail about Rex Barney eating his hot dog, it was irresistible, joining as it did the spectacular to the mundane, and furnishing an adolescent boy with a glimpse of an unexpectedly ordinary, even humdrum, side to male heroism.

Of course, in time, neither the flavor and suggestiveness of Red Barber's narration nor "epiphanies" as resonant with meaning as Rex Barney's pre-game hot dog could continue to satisfy a developing literary appetite; nonetheless, it was just this that helped to sustain me until I was ready to begin to respond to the great inventors of narrative detail and masters of narrative voice and perspective like James, Conrad, Dostoevsky, and Bellow.

QUESTIONS FOR READING, RESPONDING, AND WRITING

Summarizing Main Points

1. How does Roth's appreciation of baseball prepare him for his literary studies?
2. Why do you suppose baseball eventually ceases to satisfy his "developing literary appetite"?

Analyzing Methods of Discourse

1. Roth organizes his essay so that his love of baseball and his studies are at first separate, then come together, then separate again. Identify the ways in which Roth creates and manages this arrangement and how it supports his thesis.

2. Throughout the essay, Roth provides us with both a historical time frame and a personal one. What is the effect of each? How does each figure in his thesis?

Focusing on the Field

1. In this essay, Roth makes baseball seem literary. How does he do it?
2. Compare Roth's essay to William Pritchard's "The Scholar and the Soap." Both essays are personal narratives on the relationship between literary study and popular culture. What are the similarities in the two men's views on each subject? What are the differences?

Writing Assignments

1. Write an essay in which you describe a childhood pastime that helped you develop a skill useful later in life.
2. Read Flannery O'Connor's "The Teaching of Literature." In her essay, O'Connor has some disparaging remarks to make about "a generation [of students] that has been made to feel that the aim of learning is to eliminate mystery." Here, Roth describes his life as a student in the forties. Do you think O'Connor's claims hold true for his generation as well? Drawing on material from both essays, write an essay of your own that answers this question.

Simon Barber

THE BOSS DON'T LIKE SWINDLE, MAKE IT ROBBERY
Inside the *National Enquirer*

According to Simon Barber, "every aspect of the [*National*] *Enquirer,* from its management to what it prints, is governed by a surgically precise appreciation of human frailty." Barber should know. Out of work for months after *NOW!,* the British newsweekly for which he had been working as Washington correspondent, folded and with no job prospects in sight, Barber joined on as an articles editor for the *Enquirer* because he "could scarcely afford to go to the supermarket, much less scorn the drivel on its checkout counters."

In the following essay, which first appeared in the *Washington Journalism Review* in 1982, Barber takes the reader on a tour of the *Enquirer* offices, its management, and its route to publication. He describes the newspaper, bought over the counter weekly by over 6 million readers, as a "kind of printed Valium," which like the candy bars and gum with which it shares space, "exists to be consumed." Appealing to moods brought on by "boredom, restlessness, and unfocused dissatisfaction," according to Barber, the *Enquirer* presents the universe as "a bright, uncomplicated, unambiguous place where things either are . . . or are not, [in which] the buyer is told that he is basically good, that the rich and famous are basically miserable, and that the quality of life is improving immeasurably: cancer, obesity, and arthritis can be cured." Though the British-born Barber is quick to separate himself from American journalists who "tend to take a romantic view of their trade, see themselves in the public service," he found his job at the *Enquirer* an "unrewarding task," and left it after five weeks.

The genial Scot at the National Press Club bar in November painted a pleasing picture of *National Enquirer* opulence in the Florida sunshine.

Winter enhanced his plausibility. My visions of having to invade Holly-wood funeral parlors, sift through mountains of celebrity garbage or track Senator Kennedy to see whether he broke the speed limit on the George Washington Parkway were dispelled. "Mythology," he said. And if there was a touch of the hustler in his broad Glasgow accent, it was belied by the half-moon reading glasses, professional tweeds and Mont Blanc fountain pen.

The *Enquirer's* recruiter found me at the vulnerable moment. My previous employer, a British newsweekly, had folded some months previously; the job hunt was going badly; I was broke. I could scarcely afford to go to the supermarket, much less scorn the drivel on its checkout counters. Sympathy for Carol Burnett, whose suit against the *Enquirer* I once cheered, had become a luxury.

He suggested I try my hand as articles editor. It started at a $1,000 a week, carried the responsibility of creating and running a network of reporters, and might, in the event of some really spectacular death or disaster, involve a little travel. Hopelessness, and the rakish idea of building a Smileyesque Circus dedicated to ferreting out the Untold, Amazing and Bizarre, were ample stimuli. I bit, and three days later I was on a prepaid flight to Florida.

The *Enquirer* resides in Lantana, one of those countless ribs of real estate whose primary function is to separate Palm Beach from Fort Lauderdale and I-95 from the Intracoastal Waterway. A bland tract of telegraph poles, tired palm trees and prefabrication, it is remarkable on two counts: it has a large population of Finns and coruscating soullessness.

In the midst of this refugee camp for the cold and old, wedged between a railway line and a crumbling sports facility, the *National Enquirer* makes its one stab at irony and keeps a low profile. Once the visitor has given up trying to figure out the Minoan-style bull's horns that mark the entrance, he is pleasantly surprised by the landscaping. The grounds are thick with hibiscus and other fragrant shrubs, each thoughtfully labelled with its botanical name. The building itself lives up to a more squalid expectation. No bastion of multimillion-dollar publishing this, instead a sleepy single-story sprawl that might serviceably house a small electronics factory. Like everything in Lantana, it exudes the grim quality of being *instant*.

It was perhaps my misfortune to be ushered into the presence of executive editor Mike Hoy at lunchtime. The editorial offices were all but empty, and conveyed, in an efficiently pastel way, a sense of innocent cheerfulness, like an outsized kindergarten. Indeed, one of the newsroom cubicles was stacked with exotic toys. I began to suspect that the people who worked here might be having fun.

Hoy, thirtyish, Australian and modelled on the lines of a hygienic rock star, encouraged this view by offering me a job, on a trial basis, within 15 minutes of our meeting, and by explaining why the company would not, as had once been its practice, rent a car for me. One of my more exuberant predecessors had driven an *Enquirer* Hertz into the Waterway.

Then he said something rather strange. "I want you to know that we really are looking for editors." Having been tracked down by a recruiter and flown in from Washington to be interviewed for such a slot, and having just been offered a month's trial at it, I thought this scarcely needed saying. That impermanence was an institution at the *Enquirer* did not occur to me, nor, as yet, did the connection between its desperation for new blood and whatever had possessed the predecessor to sink his car.

Every aspect of the *Enquirer,* from its management to what it prints, is governed by a surgically precise appreciation of human frailty. This is the great achievement of its owner and publisher, the splendidly named Generoso Pope, Jr., and evidently appreciated by six million supermarket purchasers a week. Pope's relationship with his employees approximates that between the God of the Old Testament and the Children of Israel minus forgiveness. His control is total and awe-inspiring, his ways mysterious, his retribution swift. When he deals with a man, he likes, to use his own very secular phrase, to "have him by the balls," and usually succeeds. Under Hoy's guidance, it was hoped I would quickly learn to divine his will.

Known simply as The Boss or GP, Pope dominates the waking thoughts, and more than a few sleeping ones as well, of all at the *Enquirer.* An authorized account, published in 1978 by the *Miami Herald*, describes Pope as "a tall man, built like a Bronx precinct captain." Fifty-four years have softened that image somewhat, except for the face. Said an editor, one of the few women in the *Enquirer's* higher echelons, "There doesn't seem to be anything behind his eyes." The effect is a mask of staring malevolence, which does little to endear.

He is educated. A top of his class graduate in engineering from MIT, according to the authorized account, he served in the CIA's psychological warfare unit. Further glimpses of his life beyond the *Enquirer,* which he purchased in 1952, are virtually nonexistent. His father was the publisher of the New York Italian-language paper *Il Progresso.* Some see murkiness in the fact that since he moved the operation from New Jersey in 1971, Pope has never left south Florida. He says he hates to fly.

There is an eeriness about him enhanced by gun-toting plainclothes security men who haunt the premises, spot checks on reporters' telephone conversations, and the uniformed Lantana patrolman who escorts Pope to and from his car.

My first day should have taught me more, perhaps, than it did. My initial mistake was to turn up in coat and tie. Higher authority wore shirtsleeves and an increasingly familiar pair of pants, a style, admonished Hoy, that I would do well to emulate. I blundered again by trying to strike up a conversation. Apparently one did not talk to colleagues, be they only six feet away, except by internal telephone and with one's back turned. I needed coffee. "Put a top on it," someone hissed as I carried a cup to my desk. "The Boss don't like stains on his carpet." To atone, I worked through lunch, another miscalculation. "The Boss believes in lunch." Next day I ate, grateful for a temporary escape, only to be informed that I'd been seen leaving the office with the wrong people. My companions were said to be under some form of cloud and best avoided. Besides, what was I doing having lunch? I wondered whether Pope ever specified his desires before punishing those who transgressed them.

The arena in which this curious drama was to be played out might have been a newsroom in any large daily before the electronic age. Its open plan layout was symmetrical about a narrow avenue across which two rows of editors, about nine in all, numbers varied, were occasionally polite to one another. Behind them sat their secretaries, each busily pretending to callers that her boss worked in a private office. Next, pinched into lines of narrow, benchlike desks were 40 or so reporters, each owing allegiance and his job to a particular editor. Finally the writers, who are responsible for the *Enquirer*'s deathless prose and probably the happiest employees. Deemed creative by The Boss, they were left in peace. At the end of the central aisle, rather too close to where I had been stationed, was a series of glass cubicles. Pope had a grander sanctum elsewhere, but it was here he would come when he wished to make his presence felt. Assistants ensured that a pack of Kents and a lighter always awaited his arrival.

As a deracinated Englishman, I should have had some cause to feel at home. A surprising proportion of my new colleagues hailed from Britain and parts of its old empire. A buzz of familiar accents could be heard insinuating charm down various telephones. Having had some success in this department myself, I could imagine the interrogatees being thoroughly disarmed. To their cost.

Pope's predilection for what one American writer has called British Empire Journalists has little to do with the narcotic power of the speech patterns, however, but derives more from their tradition. American reporters tend to take a rather romantic view of their trade, see themselves as somehow in the public service. Their minds are burdened with scruple. Not so the British Empire Journalist. He can report, as in 1978 one imaginative correspondent for the *London Daily Mail* actually did, that President Carter was growing a beard to look more Lincolnesque, and receive a kudogram from his superiors. Rupert Murdoch ranks high in the Pope pantheon, and as publisher of the *Star*, constitutes Pope's most serious opposition.

My first impression was that my fellow editors all looked very ill: exchange their typewriters for oars and they would have made perfect (though, on $60,000 a year and up, very expensive) extras for the sea battle in *Ben Hur*.

Enquirer reporters had the furtive look of kicked and beaten Labrador Retrievers. Foot soldiers, they were at least insulated from The Boss by their editors, whose paranoia-induced savagery was the price of relative security. The reason I had been brought in from outside to be articles editor was that no reporter wanted to risk his neck or his $45,000 a year more than was strictly necessary. Now and then one or two were forcibly promoted—given the option of leaving or climbing—which regularly amounted to the same thing: climbers who failed at editor could expect to be fired, and the chances of making it were no better than those of a World War I subaltern on the Western Front.

One of the luckier ones was the young Englishman sitting to my left. Promoted some months previously, he had begun his career on a small provincial paper outside London, and had been lured to Florida by wealth and warmth. In an earlier age, he might have set out to make his fortune in some tropical outpost of Empire. He seemed to be doing all that was required of him; his file drawer was full of good stories in progress, yet there was an air of doom about him. Colleagues shied away, spoke of him with, of all things in this emotional charnel house, compassion. It turned out he was being executed, *Enquirer*-style.

First they cut his salary, then removed his reporters, forcing him to rely on stringers, finally demanded a massive increase in output. "This is the way Pope always does it," he said one evening towards the end. "They dig you a grave and say climb out if you can. You never can. The grave just gets deeper." Several days later his desk was empty. In this case the editor was allowed to reincarnate himself as a reporter. A rare privilege.

A reason would have been helpful, but my enquiries were about as fruitful as asking a priest to account plausibly for human suffering. The editor's defrocking could be ascribed to no particular commission or omission, it was just the way things worked around here. A sympathetic reporter noticed my puzzlement. "The Boss is a toy train freak," she explained. "I think he likes to see us as a vast toy train set. He throws switches, sets up obstructions, and races us off bridges just for the hell of seeing what happens."

In terms of how they are put together, there is essentially little difference between the *National Enquirer* and, say, *Time*. To the structuralist, anyway. Leads are developed and assigned, reporters and string-ers turn in voluminous files, which are rigorously checked for accuracy, boiled down by writers into the house style, and finally, with luck, printed. There, however, the resemblance ends.

Appearances to the contrary, gungho fabulism is not the *Enquirer's* line of business. Nor indeed is journalism, in any of the accepted senses of the word.

Bear in mind that the *Enquirer* is not designed primarily to inform, amuse, or even, really, to be read. It performs these functions, of course, but they are secondary. It exists to be consumed, much in the same way as premixed peanut butter and jelly. The idea is pretty simple. People enter the supermarket in a buying frame of mind, so let's give them one more brightly packaged object to shove into their shopping bags.

The editorial content addresses itself scientifically to the consuming mood, a condition frequently brought on by boredom, restlessness and unfocused dissatisfaction. The universe depicted is a bright, uncompli-cated, unambiguous place where things either are (in this category we may include metempsychosis, UFOs and psychic fork-bending) or are not (unhappy endings, celibate celebrities, wise government). The buyer is told that he is basically good, that the rich and famous are basically miserable, and that the quality of life is improving immeasurably: cancer, obesity and arthritis can be cured.

In short the *Enquirer* is a kind of printed Valium, its editors little more than pharmacists, cutting each other's throats to combine and recombine a limited number of ingredients which Pope, the master chemist, has determined will have the desired effect. It is a mechanical and, the financial aspect apart, unrewarding task.

The process begins with the lead. Each editor is expected to submit 30 or so to The Boss every Friday, of which perhaps half a dozen may be approved. On the rest he scribbles the ubiquitous initials NG (No Good). The ideas come from reporters and stringers (all of whom receive up to $300 if their offering gets into print), other publications (there is always a race for the new *Omni, Cosmopolitan* and *Self*) and the imagination. Memorable specimens from the latter category include "The Junk Food Diet," "How Brooke Shields, Loni Anderson and Farrah Fawcett are Wrecking Your Marriage" and "Let's Get Accredited as a Salvation Army Fundraiser and Go Knocking on Celebrity Doors to See How Generous the Stars Are." A number of celebrity leads are preemptive. I myself proposed "Wedding Bells for Patti Reagan and Peter [Masada] Strauss." The Elizabeth Taylor-John Warner separation was in the works probably before they had even said their vows, and certainly for months before it occurred. At this very moment at least one editor is contemplating marriage between Robert Wagner, widower of Natalie Wood, and his television co-star Stephanie Powers.

Often, of course, celebrities do dramatic things that even the *Enquirer* cannot foresee, the deaths of Natalie Wood and William Holden for example. In these instances, leads are rushed through under the rubric of "Untold Story," the logic being that there will always be one. In the Wood case, which occurred a few weeks after I arrived, the editor involved went to extraordinary lengths to find something that the voluble Los Angeles coroner Thomas Noguchi had *not* said. What he came up with was the suggestion, ascribed to Top Doctors, that the actress, rather than drowning, had been asphyxiated by a potent mixture of drugs and alcohol. This on the basis of a well-stocked medicine cabinet and the alleged absence of froth on the victim's lips. What I heard of the interviews went as follows: "Doctor, if after consuming such and such a quantity of alcohol, a person were to take drugs x and y, what would be the result?"

Even the most grizzled veteran cannot second guess Pope's taste with any certainty. His notions of what constitutes a contemporary star are quixotic, but seem to derive from movies of the '50s and '60s (hence Sophia Loren, Princess Grace and, by association, her daughter Caroline) and the top ten Nielson-rated shows he happens to watch (not *60 Minutes*). Dudley Moore, of *10* and *Arthur* fame, fails to register on the grounds that he is, and I quote, "Not big enough." The currently lionized Tom Selleck (*Magnum, PI*), did not have the right stuff either, until Pope was persuaded to poll his favorite gauges of gut reaction, the secretaries.

There are, however, some totally predictable NG's, chief among them blacks, except when they practice voodoo, or are child comic Gary Coleman. I presented Hoy with a heart-warming story of a young New Orleans man who had survived a grain elevator explosion and 80 percent burns to become a multimillionaire (a surefire hit under the Rags to Riches category). He immediately asked me what color he was. Black. Kill it. Gays, on the other hand, may be beaten up at will. An outraged account of San Francisco's demographics was headlined "Sick! Sick! Sick!" The *Enquirer*, a self-styled Equal Opportunity Employer, has no minority employees.

Once an approved lead has pleased Story Control, a computer programmed to weed out duplicates, it is ready to be reported, and the ethical mayhem begins.

If celebrities are the potatoes of tabloid journalism, miraculous medicine is the meat. Unfortunately, the medical fraternity likes to be circumspect about describing its advances, and talks of percentages, hopes, possibilities, rarely of anything so definite as a cure. This is too gray for the *Enquirer* which does not recognize the subjunctive mood: a thing either is or it isn't. The trick, therefore, is to get the medical man, who in his right mind would never even talk to the *Enquirer*, to say things that would cost him his shingle if he tried to say them in the *New England*

Journal of Medicine, and on tape. This is known in the trade as Burning Docs.

Technically, the reporter's path is strewn with regulations. Not only must his interviews be taped, but he has signed a waiver binding him to identify himself as working for the *Enquirer* and as using a recorder, thus excusing his employers when, as he must, he sidles past the law. If his editor wants him to get a doctor to say something, he is under considerably more pressure to produce than to be an upright citizen. Refusal to carry out an order is treated with military firmness.

There are many ways to ease on-the-record indiscretion from an interviewee, the most popular being the old 20 Questions ploy. The subject is stroked into a state of trust and then hit with a series of convoluted queries, to which he will answer, if the reporter is adroit enough, merely yes or no. These little words can be made to speak volumes. Critical readers may have wondered how it is that supposedly sophisticated professionals, when quoted in the *Enquirer*, always manage to clutter their remarks with an effusion of amazings, incredibles and fantastics.

This method is openly encouraged by Pope. In a memo distributed to all newcomers he commands bluntly: "Ask leading questions." Lest it be carried too far, reporters are then reminded, "Quotes should not only be appropriate but believable. A Japanese carpenter should not sound like Ernest Hemingway, or vice verse."

Add to this Pope's rather confining taste in vocabulary, and the results can be bizarre. Reporter Byron Lutz had worked hard to produce "The Biggest Swindle in U.S. History," a tale of a computer rip-off within the federal government. He had even persuaded a Justice Department official to agree that it was indeed "the biggest swindle," a questionable assertion by itself. Enter the Evaluator, a character whose task it is to condense finished files into single paragraphs for the benefit of Pope and the writers.

> EVALUATOR: "This won't get through, Lutz. We don't use swindle."
> LUTZ: "But that's what the guy at the Justice Department called it, it's on the tape."
> EVAL.: "It's got to be robbery."
> LUTZ: "But there's a difference."
> EDITOR (INTERVENING): "He's right. Let's look it up in the dictionary."
> EVAL.: "Hey, I don't care. The Boss don't like swindle make it robbery."
> EDITOR (SNAPPING TO WHAT LOOKED SUSPICIOUSLY LIKE ATTENTION): "Get on it, Lutz, get your guy to say robbery. Now."

At least doctors and officials can be made to speak. Celebrities are less obliging with their reputations. To reveal the supposed drama of their lives the reporter must resort to an altogether higher order of guile. In compensation, he is required to offer less in the way of proof. Stars are public property, and consequently vulnerable to the First Amendment.

Much of the information on who is bedding whom, whose career is on the skids and who is currently being detoxified from what, emanates from the thriving gossip industry as a whole. I do not pretend to know how this works. Obviously, however, the *Enquirer* has to delve deeper to satisfy what the commercials call its readers' "Enquiring Minds."

What makes the reporter's mission particularly tough is that he is often covering not a set of circumstances his editor knows or believes to exist, but one that the editor *wishes* to have happen. A new TV series has emerged, perhaps, and The Boss wants an exciting story about its partici- pants. Or an editor may conclude that there has been too striking an absence of Farrah Fawcett. A reconciliation with Lee Majors is needed to fill the gap. Thanks to a large array of "insiders," "friends" and "intimate sources," many of whom are in the *Enquirer's* pay, such things can be arranged.

In some cases, a great deal of old-fashioned shoe-leather reporting does go on, though it has been known to get out of hand. The coffin photographs of Elvis Presley are not an isolated phenomenon. One reporter told me that while tracking the hometown life of a currently popular television actress, he stumbled onto the fact that she had had an abortion. Such was the pressure he was under, he lined up a neigh- borhood hoodlum to steal the records. Getting mixed signals from his editor, he thought better of it.

Celebrity romance stories are frequently the work of reporters whose main activity is to hang around fashionable watering holes. Maitre d's and waiters are also retained. Thus, the *Enquirer* often has a pair of eyes in place when an interesting couple appear in public for the first time, or have a violent quarrel.

Hollywood sex, in the *Enquirer*, is a formulaic affair. The starting assumption is that any physical contact represents romance. At the lower end of the scale, hand holding is described by "insiders," who do not have to be told the *Enquirer* style, as "they looked like a pair of teenagers in love." Any kiss less demure than a peck is evidence that the relationship has turned "hot and heavy."

Equally earnest is the *Enquirer's* attitude towards the paranormal. Cranks are not tolerated, and anyone claiming to have been reborn, sighted UFOs or communicated with the beyond is subjected to hypnotic regression. This is considered sounder evidence than a lie detector be- cause the latter has the unfortunate habit of being accurate.

The reigning exponent of what may be called the "Hey-Martha-Will- You-Get-A-Look-At-This" school is *Enquirer* super-stringer Henry Gris, a former UPI correspondent. His latest find is one "Dr. Victor Azhazha," eminent Soviet scientist. Dr. Azhazha claimed, and there is an artist's conception complete with silhouetted Kremlin to back it up, that a mysterious shining cloud had drifted over Moscow one night causing great consternation. A friend of mine, stationed in Moscow for a well-known British daily, commented, "I didn't see this cloud, which was perhaps careless. It might have started World War III."

A cardinal rule of the information trade is that the more bald and unconvincing a story, the greater the machinery needed to lend it verisimilitude. The *Enquirer* is inordinately proud of its Research Department. A copy of a glowing account in *Editor & Publisher* that appeared in 1978 is compulsory reading for all arrivals.

E&P tells us that Research is staffed by probing professionals, headed by Ruth Annan, a 16-year veteran of *Time*. Her team includes "two medical specialists, two lawyers, a linguist who speaks four languages, a geographer, three with master's degrees in library science, one with a master's degree in educational psychology, and an author."

And yet it regularly lets through palpable inanities. The concept of a "4,000-year-old Stone Age statuette" does not bother it, for example, but this is a quibble. Most of what escapes the tireless fact-checkers is on a grander scale, even in cases where the facts can actually be checked.

Researchers are cunningly paid less than reporters whose work they scrutinize, and thus approach their task with the enthusiasm of inquisitors. That the *Enquirer* is published at all is not their fault.

I have no doubt that Research pursues Truth with genuine vigor, but it is hampered by one major defect: literalmindedness. If the tapes and copy jibe, and sources when contacted agree to what has been reported, the story must, however, reluctantly, be granted the imprimature of accuracy.

One disadvantage of Annan and her staff is that they clog up an already hopelessly slow system—lead time is usually three or four weeks—with haggling that, given the nature of the beast, is utterly unnecessary. On the upside, however, their mere existence enables reporters to tell a suspicious world that, yes, really, the *Enquirer* does strive after fact. As editor Paul Levy told *E&P*, "Today any reporter can say with justifiable pride that he works for the most accurate paper in the country."

QUESTIONS FOR READING, RESPONDING, AND WRITING

Summarizing Main Points

1. According to Barber, what types of stories are most frequently printed in the *Enquirer?* How do the methods of investigating each type differ? How are they the same?

2. Barber describes five different job categories at the *Enquirer*—not including that of "The Boss." List them in order of salary. Which are the most important jobs according to Barber? According to "The Boss"?

Analyzing Methods of Discourse

1. Barber uses many figures of speech (e.g., he likens the *Enquirer* reporters to foot soldiers and Labrador retrievers). List others and describe the ways in which they are appropriate to Barber's main points.
2. In a sense, Barber takes us on a "tour" of the *Enquirer*, showing us its staff and its facilities. What features does he point out along the way? Early on, Barber describes "The Boss." Does that description influence how we see the rest of the newspaper's headquarters and staff?

Focusing on the Field

1. Barber wrote this piece for the *Washington Journalism Review*. What aspects of his presentation would you imagine are most suited to this kind of professional periodical?
2. Barber's essay is at least partially about the ethics of journalism. While Barber admits that the *Enquirer* follows the letter of the law, he presents several ways in which it violates the spirit of the law, of responsible journalism. List those ways. Do you think Barber himself provides a balanced assessment of the *Enquirer*?

Writing Assignments

1. Choose a subject of your own to report on and then write it in two ways: first, for the *Enquirer*, then for a popular news magazine like *Time* or *Newsweek*.
2. Choose an article from the *Enquirer* and one from a magazine like *Time* on similar topics (e.g., diet, fashion, celebrities). Compare and contrast the ways in which the two magazines present their material. Can you make any assumptions about the sources for the two articles from the ways in which they are written?

Stephen King

WHY WE CRAVE HORROR MOVIES

When asked when he writes his best horror fiction, Stephen King answered, "Mornings, always mornings. You think I want to write this stuff at night?" But it is his intense horror, not his ample humor, that makes King the most successful horror writer today. His books have sold well over 10 million copies, and many have been produced as motion pictures.

King was born in 1947 in Portland, Maine and received a B.Sc. from the University of Maine (1970), where, at Orono, he has spent some time as writer-in-residence (1978–1979). As the essay that follows indicates, King not only writes good horror fiction but also understands what makes it good. Though he has received mixed critical attention, King seems very sure of himself as a writer and is, according to one critic, "amazingly good-natured about the fact that many of his most ardent fans suspect that he is probably a madman, or at least a firm believer in the psychic threads that run through his novels." On the contrary, as King himself has said, "the horror writer can give [his readers] a place to put their fears, and it's OK to be afraid then, because nothing is real, and you can blow it all away when it's over."

King cites William Golding's *Lord of the Flies* as the most frightening novel he has ever read, perhaps because it, like many of King's own novels, "has no good guys, just people who are involved." King's fiction includes *Carrie* (1974), *Salem's Lot* (1975), *The Shining* (1977), which was nominated for a Hugo Award from the World Science Fiction Convention, and *The Dead Zone* (1979).

If you're a genuine fan of horror films, you develop the same sort of sophistication that a follower of the ballet develops; you get a feeling for the depth and the texture of the genre. Your ear develops with your eye, and the sound of quality always comes through to the keen ear. There is fine Waterford crystal that rings delicately when struck, no matter how thick and chunky it may look; and then there are Flintstone jelly glasses. You can drink your Dom Perignon out of either one, but, friends, there is a difference.

The difference here is between horror for horror's sake and art. There is art in a horror film when the audience gets more than it gives. Not when our fears are milked just to drive us crazy but when an actual liaison is found between our fantasy fears and our real fears.

Few horror movies are conceived with art in mind; most are conceived for profit. The art is not consciously created but, rather, is thrown off, as an atomic pile throws off radiation. There are films that skate right up to the border where art ceases to be thrown off and exploitation begins, and those films are often the field's most striking successes. *The Texas Chainsaw Massacre* is one of those. I would happily testify to its redeeming social merit in any court in the country. I would not do so for *The Gory Ones*, a 1972 film in which we are treated to the charming sight of a woman being cut open with a two-handed bucksaw; the camera lingers as her intestines spew out onto the floor. The difference is more than the difference between a chain saw and a bucksaw; it is something like 70,000,000 light-years. The *Chainsaw Massacre* is done with taste and conscience. *The Gory Ones* is the work of morons with cameras.

If horror movies have redeeming social merit, it is because of that ability to form liaisons between the real and the unreal. In many cases—particularly in the fifties and then again in the early seventies—the fears expressed are sociopolitical in nature, a fact that gives such disparate pictures as Don Siegel's *Invasion of the Body Snatchers* and William Friedkin's *The Exorcist* a crazily convincing documentary feel. When the horror movies wear their various sociopolitical hats—the B picture as tabloid editorial—they often serve as an extraordinarily accurate barometer of those things that trouble the night thoughts of a whole society.

But horror movies don't always wear a hat that identifies them as disguised comments on the social or political scene (as David Cronenberg's *The Brood* comments on the disintegration of the generational family, or as his *They Came from Within* deals with the more cannibalistic side effects of Erica Jong's "zipless fuck"). More often the horror movie points farther inward, looking for those deep-seated personal fears, those pressure points we all must cope with. This adds an element of universality to the proceedings and may produce an even truer sort of art.

This second kind of horror film has more in common with the Brothers Grimm than with the op-ed pages of tabloid newspapers. It is the B picture as fairy tale. It doesn't want to score political points but, rather, to scare the hell out of us by crossing certain taboo lines. So if my idea about art is correct (it giveth more than it receiveth), this sort of film is of value to the audience by helping it better understand what those taboos and fears are, and why it feels so uneasy about them.

I think we'd all agree that one of the great fears with which all of us must deal on a purely personal level is the fear of dying; without good old death to fall back on, the horror movies would be in bad shape. A corollary to this is that there are "good" deaths and "bad" deaths; most of us would like to die peacefully in our beds at the age of 80 (preferably after a good meal, a bottle of really fine vino and a really super lay), but very few of us are interested in finding out how it might feel to get slowly crushed under an automobile lift while crankcase oil drips slowly onto our foreheads.

Lots of horror films derive their best effects from this fear of the bad death (as in *The Abominable Dr. Phibes*, in which Phibes dispatches his victims one at a time using the 12 plagues of Egypt, slightly updated, a gimmick worthy of the *Batman* comics during their palmiest days). Who can forget the lethal binoculars in *The Black Zoo*, for instance? They came equipped with spring-loaded six-inch prongs, so that when the victim put them to her eyes and then attempted to adjust the field of focus. . . .

Others derive their horror simply from the fact of death itself and the decay that follows death. In a society in which such a great store is placed in the fragile commodities of youth, health and beauty, death and decay become inevitably horrible—and inevitably taboo. If you don't think so, ask yourself why the second grade doesn't get to tour the local mortuary along with the police department, the fire department and the nearest McDonald's. One can imagine—or I can in my more morbid moments—the mortuary and McDonald's combined; the highlight of the tour, of course, would be a viewing of the McCorpse.

No, the funeral parlor is taboo. Morticians are modern priests, working their arcane magic of cosmetics and preservation in rooms that are clearly marked off limits. Who washes the corpse's hair? Are the fingernails and toenails of the dear departed clipped one final time? Is it true that the dead are encoffined sans shoes? Who dresses them for their final star turn in the mortuary viewing room? How is a bullet hole plugged and concealed? How are strangulation bruises hidden?

The answers to all those questions are available, but they are not common knowledge. And if you try to make the answers part of your store of knowledge, people are going to think you a bit peculiar. I know: In the process of researching a forthcoming novel about a father who tries to bring his son back from the dead, I collected a stack of funeral literature a foot high—and any number of peculiar glances from folks who wondered why I was reading *The Funeral: Vestige or Value?*

But this is not to say that people don't have a certain occasional interest in what lies behind the locked door in the basement of the mortuary, or what may transpire in the local graveyard after the mourners have left . . . or at the dark of the moon. *The Body Snatcher* is not really a tale of the supernatural, nor was it pitched that way to its audience; it was pitched as a film (as was that notorious Sixties documentary *Mondo Cane*) that would take us beyond the pale, over that line that marks the edge of taboo ground:

CEMETERIES RAIDED, CHILDREN SLAIN FOR BODIES TO DISSECT! the movie poster drooled. UNTHINKABLE REALITIES AND UNBELIEVABLE FACTS OF THE DARK DAYS OF EARLY SURGICAL RESEARCH EXPOSED IN THE MOST DARING SHRIEK-AND-SHUDDER SHOCK SENSATION EVER BROUGHT TO THE SCREEN! (All of this printed on a leaning tombstone.)

But the poster does not stop there; it goes on specifically to mark out the exact location of the taboo line and to suggest that not everyone may be adventurous enough to transgress that forbidden ground: IF YOU CAN TAKE IT, SEE GRAVES RAIDED! COFFINS ROBBED! CORPSES CARVED! MID-NIGHT MURDER! BODY BLACKMAIL! STALKING GHOULS! MAD REVENGE! MACABRE MYSTERY! AND DON'T SAY WE DIDN'T WARN YOU!

All of it has sort of a pleasant, alliterative ring, doesn't it?

These areas of unease—the political-social-cultural and those of the more mythic, fairy-tale variety—have a tendency to overlap, of course; a good horror picture will put the pressure on at as many points as it can. *They Came from Within*, for instance, is about sexual promiscuity on one level; on another level, it's asking you how you'd like to have a leech jump out of a letter slot and fasten itself onto your face. These are not the same areas of unease at all.

But since we're on the subject of death and decay (a very grave matter, heh-heh-heh), we might look at a couple of films in which this particular area of unease has been used well. The prime example, of course, is *Night of the Living Dead*, in which our horror of these final states is exploited to a point where many audiences found the film well-nigh unbearable. Other taboos are also broken by the film; at one point, a little girl kills her mother with a garden trowel . . . and then begins to eat her. How's that for taboo breaking? Yet the film circles around to its starting point again and again, and the key word in the film's title is not living but dead.

At an early point, the film's female lead, who has barely escaped being killed by a zombie in a graveyard where she and her brother have come to put flowers on their dead father's grave (the brother is not so lucky), stumbles into a lonely farmhouse. As she explores, she hears something dripping . . . dripping . . . dripping. She goes upstairs, sees something, screams . . . and the camera zooms in on the rotting, weeks-old head of a corpse. It is a shocking, memorable moment. Later, a government official tells the watching, beleaguered populace that, although they may not like it (i.e., they will have to cross that taboo line to do it), they must burn their dead; simply soak them with gasoline and light them up. Later still, a local sheriff expresses our own uneasy shock at having come so far over the taboo line. He answers a reporter's question by saying, "Ah, they're dead . . . they're all messed up."

The good horror director must have a clear sense of where the taboo line lies if he is not to lapse into unconscious absurdity, and a gut understanding of what the countryside is like on the far side of it. In *Night of the Living Dead*, George Romero plays a number of instruments, and he plays them like a virtuoso. A lot has been made of this film's graphic violence, but one of the film's most frightening moments comes near the climax, when the heroine's brother makes his reappearance—still wearing his driving gloves and clutching for his sister with the idiotic, implacable single-mindedness of the hungry dead. The film is violent—as is its sequel, *Dawn of the Dead*—but the violence has its own logic, and in the horror genre, logic goes a long way toward proving morality.

The crowning horror in Alfred Hitchcock's *Psycho* comes when Vera Miles touches that chair in the cellar and it spins lazily around to reveal Norman's mother at last—a wizened, shriveled corpse from which hollow eye sockets stare up blankly. She is not only dead; she has been stuffed like one of the birds that decorate Norman's office. Norman's subsequent entrance in dress and make-up is almost an anticlimax.

In A.I.P.'s *The Pit and the Pendulum*, we see another facet of the bad death—perhaps the absolute worst. Vincent Price and his cohorts break into a tomb through its brickwork, using pick and shovel. They discover that the lady, his wife, has, indeed, been entombed alive; for just a moment, the camera shows us her tortured face, frozen in a rictus of terror, her bulging eyes, her clawlike fingers, the skin stretched tight and gray. This is, I think, the most important moment in the post-1960 horror film, signaling a return to an all-out effort to terrify the audience . . . and a willingness to use any means at hand to do it.

Fiction is full of *economic* horror stories, though very few of them are supernatural; *The Crash of '79* comes to mind, as well as *The Money Wolves*, *The Big Company Look* and the wonderful Frank Norris novel *McTeague*. I want to discuss only one movie in this context, *The Amityville Horror*. There may be others, but this one example will serve, I think, to illustrate another idea: that the horror genre is extremely limber, extremely adaptable, extremely useful; the author or film maker can use it as a crowbar to lever open locked doors . . . or as a small, slim pick to tease the tumblers into giving. The genre can thus be used to open almost any lock on the fears that lie behind the door, and *The Amityville Horror* is a dollars-and-cents case in point.

It is simple and straightforward, as most horror tales are. The Lutzes, a young married couple with two or three kids (Kathleen Lutz's by a previous marriage), buy a house in Amityville. Previous to their tenancy, a young man has murdered his whole family at the direction of "voices." For this reason, the Lutzes get the house cheaply.

But they soon discover that it wouldn't have been cheap at half the price, because it's haunted. Manifestations include black goop that comes bubbling out of the toilets (and before the festivities are over, it comes oozing out of the walls and the stairs as well), a roomful of flies, a rocking chair that rocks by itself and something in the cellar that causes the dog to dig everlastingly at the wall. A window crashes down on the little boy's fingers. The little girl develops an "invisible friend" who is apparently really there. Eyes glow outside the window at three in the morning. And so on.

Worst of all, from the audience's standpoint, Lutz himself (James Brolin) apparently falls out of love with his wife (Margot Kidder) and begins to develop a meaningful relationship with his ax. Before things are done, we are drawn to the inescapable conclusion that he is tuning up for something more than splitting wood.

Stripped of its distracting elements (a puking nun, Rod Steiger shamelessly overacting as a priest who is just discovering the Devil after 40 years or so as a man of the cloth, and Margot Kidder doing calisthenics in a pair of bikini panties and one white stocking), *The Amityville Horror* is a perfect example of the tale to be told around the campfire. All the teller really has to do is to keep the catalog of inexplicable events in the correct order, so that unease escalates into outright fear.

All of which brings us around to the real watchspring of *Amityville* and the reason it works as well as it does: The picture's subtext is one of economic unease, and that is a theme that director Stuart Rosenberg plays on constantly. In terms of the times—18 percent inflation, mortgage rates out of sight, gasoline selling at a cool $1.40 a gallon—*The Amityville Horror*, like *The Exorcist*, could not have come along at a more opportune moment.

This breaks through most clearly in a scene that is the film's only moment of true and honest drama, a brief vignette that parts the clouds of hokum like a sunray on a drizzly afternoon. The Lutz family is preparing to go to the wedding of Kathleen Lutz's younger brother (who looks as if he might be all of 17). They are, of course, in the Bad House when the scene takes place. The younger brother has lost the $1500 that is due the caterer and is in an understandable agony of panic and embarrassment.

Brolin says he'll write the caterer a check, which he does, and later he stands off the angry caterer, who has specified cash only in a half-whispered washroom argument while the wedding party whoops it up outside. After the wedding, Lutz turns the living room of the Bad House upside down looking for the lost money, which has now become *his* money, and the only way of backing up the bank paper he has issued the caterer. Brolin's check may not have been 100 percent Goodyear rubber, but in his sunken, purple-pouched eyes, we see a man who doesn't really have the money any more than his hapless brother-in-law does. Here is a man tottering on the brink of his own financial crash.

He finds the only trace under the couch: a bank money band with the numerals $500 stamped on it. The band lies there on the rug, tauntingly empty. "*Where is it?*" Brolin screams, his voice vibrating with anger, frustration and fear. At that one moment, we hear the ring of Waterford, clear and true—or, if you like, we hear that one quiet phrase of pure music in a film that is otherwise all crash and bash.

Everything that *The Amityville Horror* does well is summed up in that scene. Its implications touch on everything about the house's most obvious and insidious effect—and also the only one that seems empirically undeniable: Little by little, it is ruining the Lutz family financially. The movie might as well have been subtitled "The Horror of the Shrinking Bank Account." It's the more prosaic fallout of the place where so many haunted-house stories start. "It's on the market for a song," the realtor says with a big egg-sucking grin. "It's supposed to be haunted."

Well, the house that the Lutzes buy is, indeed, on the market for a song (and there's another good moment—all too short—when Kathleen tells her husband that she will be the first person in her large Catholic family to actually own her own home; "We've always been renters," she says) but it ends up costing them dearly. At the conclusion, the house seems to literally tear itself apart. Windows crash in, black goop comes dribbling out of the walls, the cellar stairs cave in . . . and I found myself wondering not if the Lutz clan would get out alive but if they had adequate homeowner's insurance.

This is a movie for every woman who ever wept over a plugged-up toilet or a spreading water stain on the ceiling from the upstairs shower; for every man who ever did a slow burn when the weight of the snow caused his gutters to give way; for every child who ever jammed his fingers and felt that the door or window that did the jamming was out to get him. As horror goes, *Amityville* is pretty pedestrian. So's beer, but you can get drunk on it.

"Think of the bills," a woman sitting behind me in the theater moaned at one point. I suspect it was her own bills she was thinking about. It was impossible to make a silk purse out of this particular sow's ear, but Rosenberg at least manages to give us Qiana, and the main reason that people went to see it, I think, is that *The Amityville Horror*, beneath its ghost-story exterior, is really a financial demolition derby.

Think of the bills, indeed.

If movies are the dreams of the mass culture—one film critic, in fact, has called watching a movie "dreaming with one's eyes open"—and if horror movies are the nightmares of the mass culture, then many horror movies of recent times express America's coming to terms with the possibility of nuclear annihilation over political differences.

The contemporary political horror films begin, I think, with *The Thing* (1951), directed by Christian Nyby and produced by Howard Hawks (who also had a hand in the direction, one suspects). It stars Margaret Sheridan, Kenneth Tobey and James Arness as the blood-drinking human carrot from Planet X.

A polar encampment of soldiers and scientists discovers a strong magnetic field emanating from an area where there has been a recent meteor fall; the field is strong enough to throw all the electronic gadgets and gizmos off whack. Further, a camera designed to start shooting pictures when and if the normal background-radiation count suddenly goes up has taken photos of an object that dips, swoops and turns at high speeds—strange behavior for a meteor.

An expedition is dispatched to the spot, and it discovers a flying saucer buried in the ice. The saucer, superhot on touchdown, melted its way into the ice, which then refroze, leaving only the tail fin sticking out (thus relieving the special-effects corps of a potentially big-budget item). The Army guys, who demonstrate frostbite of the brain throughout most of the film, promptly destroy the extraterrestrial ship while trying to burn it out of the ice with thermite.

The occupant (Arness) is saved, however, and carted back to the experimental station in a block of ice. He/it is placed in a storage shed, under guard. One of the guards is so freaked out by the thing that he throws a blanket over it. Unlucky man! Quite obviously, all his good stars are in retrograde, his biorhythms low and his mental magnetic poles temporarily reversed. The blanket he's used is of the electric variety, and it miraculously melts the ice without shorting out. The Thing escapes and the fun begins.

The fun ends about 60 minutes later with the creature being roasted medium rare on an electric-sidewalk sort of thing that the scientists have set up. A reporter on the scene sends back the news of humankind's first victory over invaders from space, and the film fades out, not with a THE END title card but with a question mark.

The Thing is a small movie done on a low budget. Like *Alien*, which would come more than a quarter century later, it achieves its best effects from feelings of claustrophobia and xenophobia. But, as I said before, the best horror movies will try to get at you on many different levels, and *The Thing* is also operating on a political level. It has grim things to say about eggheads (and knee-jerk liberals—in the early Fifties, you could have put an equal-sign between the two) who would indulge in the crime of appeasement.

The Thing is the first movie of the Fifties to offer us the scientist in the role of The Appeaser, that creature who for reasons either craven or misguided would open the gates to the Garden of Eden and let all the evils fly in (as opposed, say, to those mad labs proprietors of the Thirties, who were more than willing to open Pandora's box and let all the evils fly out—a major distinction, though the results are the same). That scientists should be so constantly vilified in the technohorror films of the Fifties—a decade that was apparently dedicated to the idea of turning out a whole marching corps of men and women in white lab coats—is perhaps not so surprising when we remember that it was science that opened those same gates so that the atomic bomb could be brought into Eden: first by itself and then trundled on missiles.

The average Jane or Joe during those spooky eight or nine years that followed the surrender of Japan had extremely schizoid feelings about science and scientists—recognizing the need for them and, at the same time, loathing the things they had let in forever. On the one hand, the average Jane or Joe had found a new pal, that neat little all-round guy,

Reddy Kilowatt; on the other hand, before getting into the first reel of *The Thing*, they had to watch newsreel footage as an Army mock-up of a town *just like theirs* was vaporized in a nuclear furnace.

Robert Cornthwaite plays the appeasing scientist in *The Thing*, and we hear from his lips the first verse of a psalm that any filmgoer who grew up in the Fifties and Sixties became familiar with very quickly: "We must preserve this creature for science." The second verse goes: "If it comes from a society more advanced than ours, it must come in peace. If we can only establish communications with it, and find out what it wants——"

Twice, near the film's conclusion, Cornthwaite is hauled away by soldiers; at the climax, he breaks free of his guards and faces the creature with his hands open and empty. He begs it to communicate with him and to see that he means it no harm. The creature stares at him for a long, pregnant moment . . . and then bats him casually aside, as you or I might swat a mosquito. The medium-rare roasting on the electric sidewalk follows.

Now, I'm only a journeyman writer and I will not presume to teach history here. I will point out that the Americans of that time were perhaps more paranoid about the idea of appeasement than at any other time before or since. The dreadful humiliation of Neville Chamberlain and England's resulting close squeak at the beginning of Hitler's war was still very much with those Americans, and why not? It had all happened only 12 years prior to *The Thing*'s release, and even Americans who were just turning 21 in 1951 could remember it all very clearly. The moral was simple—such appeasement doesn't work; you gotta cut 'em if they stand and shoot 'em if they run. Otherwise, they'll take you over a bite at a time (and in the case of the Thing, you could take that literally).

If all this seems much too heavy a cargo for a modest little fright flick like *The Thing* to bear, remember that a man's point of view is shaped by the events he experiences and that his politics is shaped by his point of view. I am only suggesting that, given the political temper of the times and the cataclysmic world events that had occurred only a few years before, the viewpoint of this movie is almost preordained. What do you do with a blood-drinking carrot from outer space? Simple. Cut him if he stands and shoot him if he runs. And if you're an appeasing scientist like Cornthwaite (with a yellow streak up your back as wide as the no-passing line on a highway), you simply get bulldozed under.

By contrast, consider the other end of this telescope. The children of World War Two produced *The Thing*; 26 years later, a child of Vietnam and the self-proclaimed Love Generation, Steven Spielberg, gives us a fitting balance weight to *The Thing* in *Close Encounters of the Third Kind*. In 1951, the soldier standing sentry duty (the one who has foolishly covered the block of ice with an electric blanket) empties his automatic into the alien when he hears it coming; in 1977, a young guy with a happy, spaced-out smile holds up a sign reading STOP AND BE FRIENDLY. Somewhere between the two, John Foster Dulles evolved into Henry Kissinger and the pugnacious politics of confrontation became *détente*.

In *The Thing*, Tobey occupies himself with building an electric boardwalk to kill the creature; in *Close Encounters*, Richard Dreyfuss occupies himself with building a mock-up of Devil's Butte, the creatures' landing place, in his living room. The Thing is a big, hulking brute who grunts; the creatures from the stars in Spielberg's film are small, delicate, childlike. They do not speak, but their mother ship plays lovely harmonic tones—the music of the spheres, we assume. And Dreyfuss, far from wanting to murder these emissaries from space, goes with them.

I'm not saying that Spielberg is or would think of himself as a member of the Love Generation simply because he came to his majority while students were putting daisies in the muzzles of M-1s and Jimmi Hendrix and Janis Joplin were playing at Fillmore West. Neither am I saying that Hawks, Nyby, Charles Lederer (who wrote the screenplay for *The Thing*) and John W. Campbell (whose *novella Who Goes There?* formed the basis for the film) fought their way up the beaches of Anzio or helped raise the Stars and Stripes on Iwo Jima. But events determine point of view and point of view determines politics, and *CE3K* seems to me every bit as preordained as *The Thing*. We can understand that the latter's "Let the military handle this" thesis was a perfectly acceptable one in 1951, because the military had handled the Japs and the Nazis perfectly well in Duke Wayne's Big One, and we can also understand that the former's attitude of "Don't let the military handle this" was a perfectly acceptable one in 1977, following the military's less-than-startling record in Vietnam, or even in 1980 (when *CE3K* was released with additional footage), the year American military personnel lost the chance to free our hostages in Iran following three hours of mechanical fuck-ups.

It may be that nothing in the world is so hard to comprehend as a terror whose time has come and gone—which may be why parents can scold their children for their fear of the bogeyman, when as children themselves, they had to cope with exactly the same fears (and the same sympathetic but uncomprehending parents). That may be why one generation's nightmare becomes the next generation's sociology, and even those who have walked through the fire have trouble remembering exactly what those burning coals felt like.

In the Fifties, the terror of the bomb and of fallout was real, and it left a scar on those children who wanted to be good, just as the Depression of the Thirties had left a scar on their elders. A newer generation—now teenagers, with no memory of either the Cuban Missile Crisis or of the Kennedy assassination in Dallas, raised on the milk of *détente*—may find it hard to comprehend the terror of these things, but they will undoubtedly have a chance to discover it in the years of tightening belts and heightening tensions that lie ahead . . . and the movies will be there to give their vague fears concrete focusing points in the horror movies yet to come.

I can remember, for instance, that in 1968, when I was 21, the issue of long hair was an extremely nasty, extremely explosive one. That seems as hard to believe now as the idea of people killing each other over whether the sun went around the earth or the earth went around the sun, but that happened, too.

I was thrown out of a bar in Brewer, Maine, by a construction worker back in that happy year of 1968. The guy had muscles on his muscles and told me I could come back and finish my beer "after you get a haircut, you faggot fairy." There were the standard catcalls thrown from passing cars (usually old cars with fins and cancer of the rocker panels): Are you a boy or are you a girl? Do you give head, honey? When was the last time you had a bath?

I can remember such things in an intellectual, even analytical way, as I can remember having a dressing that had actually grown into the tissue yanked from the site of a cyst-removal operation that occurred when I was 12. I screamed from the pain and then fainted dead away. I can remember the pulling sensation as the gauze tore free of the new, healthy tissue (the dressing removal was performed by a nurse's aide who apparently had no idea what she was doing), I can remember the scream and I can remember the faint. What I can't remember is the pain itself. It's the same with the hair thing and, in a larger sense, all the other pains associated with coming of age in the decade of napalm and the Nehru jacket.

I've purposely avoided writing a novel with a Sixties time setting because all of that seems, like the pulling of that surgical dressing, very distant to me now—almost as if it had happened to another person. But those things did happen; the hate, paranoia and fear on both sides were all too real. If we doubt it, we need only review that quintessential Sixties counterculture horror film, *Easy Rider*, in which Peter Fonda and Dennis Hopper end up being blown away by a couple of rednecks in a pickup truck as Roger McGuinn sings Bob Dylan's *It's Alright, Ma (I'm Only Bleeding)* on the sound track.

Similarly, it is difficult to remember in any gut way the fears that came with those boom years of atomic technology 25 years ago. The technology itself was srictly Apollonian; as Apollonian as nice guy Larry Talbot, who "said his prayers at night." The atom was not split by a gibbering Colin Clive or Boris Karloff in some eastern European mad lab;

it was not done by alchemy and moonlight in the center of a rune-struck circle; it was done by a lot of little guys at Oak Ridge and White Sands who wore tweed jackets and smoked Luckies, guys who worried about dandruff and psoriasis and whether or not they could afford a new car and how to get rid of the goddamn crab grass. Splitting the atom, producing fission, opening that door on a new world that the old scientist speaks of at the end of *Them!*—these things were accomplished on a business-as-usual basis.

People understood this and could live with it (Fifties science books extolled the wonderful world the friendly atom would produce, a world fueled by nice safe nuclear reactors, and grammar school kids got free comic books produced by the power companies), but they suspected and feared the hairy, simian face on the other side of the coin as well: They feared that the atom might be, for a number of reasons both technological and political, essentially uncontrollable. Those feelings of deep unease came out in movies such as *The Beginning of the End, Them!, Tarantula, The Incredible Shrinking Man* (in which radiation combined with a pesticide causes a very personal horror for one man, Scott Carey), *The H-Men* and *The Four-D Man.* The entire cycle reaches its supreme pinnacle of absurdity with *The Night of the Lepus,* in which the world is menaced by giant bunnies.

All of the foregoing are examples of the horror film with a technological subtext . . . sometimes referred to as the "nature run amuck" sort of horror picture. In all of them, it is mankind and mankind's technology that must bear the blame. "You brought it on yourselves," they all say; a fitting epitaph for the mass grave of mankind, I think, when the big balloon finally goes up and the ICBMs start to fly. It is here, in the technohorror film, that we really strike the mother lode. No more panning for the occasional nugget, as in the case of the economic horror film or the political horror film; pard, we could dig the gold right out of the ground with our bare hands here, if we wanted to. Here is a corner of the old horror-film corral where even such an abysmal little wet fart of a picture as *The Horror of Party Beach* will yield a technological aspect upon analysis—you see, all those beach-blanket boppers in their bikinis and ball huggers are being menaced by monsters that were created when drums of radioactive waste leaked. But not to worry; although a few girls get carved up, all comes right in the end in time for one last wiener roast before school starts again.

The concerns of the technohorror films of the Sixties and Seventies change with the concerns of the people who lived through those times; the Big Bug movies give way to pictures such as *The Forbin Project* ("The Software That Conquered the World") and *2001,* which offer us the possibility of the computer as God, or the even nastier idea (ludicrously executed, I'll readily admit) of the computer as satyr that is laboriously produced in *Demon Seed* and *Saturn 3*. In the Sixties, horror proceeds from a vision of technology as an octopus—perhaps sentient—burying us alive in red tape and information-retrieval systems that are terrible when they work (*The Forbin Project*) and even more terrible when they don't: In *The Andromeda Strain*, for instance, a small scrap of paper gets caught in the striker of a teletype machine, keeps the bell from ringing and thereby (in a fashion Rube Goldberg certainly would have approved of) nearly causes the end of the world.

Finally, there are the Seventies, culminating in John Frankenheimer's not-very-good but certainly well-meant film *Prophecy*, which is so strikingly similar to those Fifties Big Bug movies (only the first cause has changed), and *The China Syndrome*, a horror movie that synthesizes all three of these major technological fears: fear of radiation, fear for the ecology, fear of the machinery gone out of control.

Even such a much-loved American institution as the motor vehicle has not entirely escaped the troubled dreams of Hollywood: before being run out of his mortgaged house in Amityville, James Brolin had to face the terrors of *The Car* (1977), a customized something or other that looked like a squatty airport limo from one of hell's used-car lots. The movie degenerates into a ho-hum piece of hackwork before the end of the second reel (the sort of movie in which you can safely go out for a popcorn refill at certain intervals because you know the car isn't going to strike again for ten minutes or so), but there is a marvelous opening sequence in which the car chases two bicyclists through Utah's Zion National Park, its horn blatting arrhythmically as it gains on them and finally runs them down. There's something working in that opening that calls up a deep, almost primitive unease about the cars we zip ourselves into, thereby becoming anonymous . . . and perhaps homicidal.

There have been a few films that have tried to walk the border line between horror and social satire; one of those that seems to me to tread this border line most successfully is *The Stepford Wives*. The film is based on the novel by Ira Levin, and Levin has actually been able to pull this difficult trick off twice, the other case being that of *Rosemary's Baby*. *The Stepford Wives* has some witty things to say about women's liberation and some disquieting things to say about the American male's response to it.

It is as satiric as the best of Stanley Kubrick's work (though a good deal less elegant), and I defy an audience not to laugh when Katharine Ross and Paula Prentiss step into the home of a neighbor (he's the local druggist, and a Walter Mitty type if ever there were one) and hear his wife moaning upstairs, "Oh, Frank, you're the greatest . . . Frank, you're the best . . . you're the champ. . . ."

The original Levin story avoided the label "horror novel" (something like the label "pariah dog" in the more exalted circles of literary criticism) because most critics saw it as Levin's sly poke at the women's movement. But the scarier implications of Levin's jape are not directed at women at all; they are aimed unerringly at those men who consider it only their due to leave for the golf course on Saturday morning after breakfast has been served to them and to reappear (loaded, more likely than not) in time for their dinner to be served to them. After some uneasy backing and filling—during which it seems unsure of just what it does want to be—the film does, indeed, become a social horror story.

Katharine Ross and her husband (played by Peter Masterson) move from New York City to Stepford, a Connecticut suburb, because they feel it will be better for the children, and themselves as well. Stepford is a perfect little village where children wait good-humoredly for the school bus, where you can see two or three fellows washing their cars on any given day, where (you feel) the yearly United Fund quota is not only met but exceeded.

Yet there's a strangeness in Stepford. A lot of the wives seem a little, well, spacy. Pretty, always attired in flowing dresses that are almost gowns (a place where the movie slips, I think; as a labeling device, it's pretty crude. These women might as well be wearing stickers pasted to their foreheads that read I AM ONE OF THE WEIRD STEPFORD WIVES), they all drive station wagons, discuss housework with an inordinate degree of enthusiasm and seem to spend any spare time at the supermarket.

One of the Stepford wives (one of the *weird* ones) cracks her head in a minor parking-lot fender bender; later, we see her at a lawn party, repeating over and over again, "I simply *must* get that recipe . . . I simply *must* get that recipe . . . I simply *must* . . ." The secret of Stepford becomes clear immediately: These women are *robots*. Freud, in a tone that sounded suspiciously like despair, asked, "Woman . . . what does she want?" Bryan Forbes and company ask the opposite question and come up with a stinging answer. Men, the film says, do not want women; they want robots with sex organs.

There are several funny scenes in the movie; my own favorite comes when, at a women's bitch session that Ross and Prentiss have arranged, the Stepford wives begin discussing cleaning products and laundry soaps with a slow and yet earnest intensity; everyone seems to have walked right into one of those commercials Madison Avenue male execs sometimes refer to as "two Cs in a K"—meaning two cunts in a kitchen.

But the movie waltzes slowly out of this brightly lit room of social satire and into a darker chamber by far. We feel the ring closing, first around Prentiss, then around Ross.

Stepford, a bedroom community serving a number of high-technology software companies, is exactly the wrong place for New Women such as Prentiss and Ross to have landed, we find. Instead of playing poker and drinking beer at the local Men's Association, the Stepford Husbands are creating counterfeit women; the final sellout in which the real women are replaced with their Malibu Barbie counterparts is left for the viewer to grapple with. The fact that we don't actually know the answers to how some of these things are done, or where the bodies are being buried—if there are, indeed, bodies once the change-over is complete—gives the film a grim, surrealist feel that is almost unique in the annals of modern horror films.

The movie reserves its ultimate horror and its most telling social shot for its closing moments when the "new" Ross walks in on the old one . . . perhaps, we think, to murder her. Under her flowing negligee, which might have come from Frederick's of Hollywood, we see Ross's rather small breasts built up to the size of what men discussing women over beers sometimes refer to as "knockers." And, of course, they are no longer the woman's breasts at all; they now belong solely to her husband. The dummy is not quite complete, however; there are two horrible black pools where the eyes should be. The best social horror movies achieve their effect by implication, and *The Stepford Wives*, by showing us only the surface of things and never troubling to explain exactly how these things are done, implies plenty.

Another film that relies on the unease generated by changing mores is William Friedkin's *The Exorcist*, and I'll not bore you by rehashing the plot; I'll simply assume that if your interest in the genre has been sufficient to sustain you this far, you've probably seen it.

If the late Fifties and early Sixties were the curtain raiser on the generation gap, the seven years from 1966 to 1972 were the play itself. Little Richard, who had horrified parents in the Fifties when he leaped atop his piano and began boogieing on it in his lizardskin loafers, looked tame next to John Lennon, who proclaimed that the Beatles were more popular than Jesus—a statement that set off a rash of fundamentalist record burnings.

It was more than a generation gap. The two generations seemed, like the San Andreas Fault, to be moving along opposing plates of social and cultural conscience, commitment and definitions of civilized behavior itself. And with all of this young-*vs.*-old nuttiness as a backdrop, Friedkin's film appeared and became a social phenomenon in itself. Lines stretched around the block in every major city where it played, and even in towns that normally rolled up their sidewalks promptly at 7:30 p.m., midnight shows were scheduled. Church groups picketed; sociologists pontificated; newscasters did back-of-the-book segments for their programs on slow nights. The country, in fact, went on a two-month possession jag.

The movie (and the novel) is nominally about the attempts of two priests to cast a demon out of young Regan MacNeil, of course, a pretty little subteen played by Linda Blair (who later went on to a *High Noon* showdown with a bathroom plunger in the infamous NBC movie *Born Innocent*). Substantively, however, it is a film about explosive social change, a finely honed focusing point for that entire youth explosion that occurred in the late Sixties and early Seventies. It was a movie for all those parents who felt, in a kind of agony and terror, that they were losing their children and could not understand why or how it was happening. It's the face of the Werewolf, a Jekyll-and-Hyde tale in which sweet, lovely and loving Regan turns into a foul-talking monster strapped into her bed and croaking (in the voice of Mercedes McCambridge) such charming homilies as "You're going to let Jesus fuck you, fuck you, fuck you." Religious trappings aside, every adult in America understood what the film's powerful subtext was saying; they understood that the demon in Regan would have responded enthusiastically to the Fish Cheer at Woodstock.

A Warner Bros. executive told me recently that movie surveys show the average filmgoer to be 15 years of age, which may be the biggest reason the movies so often seem afflicted with a terminal case of arrested development. For every film like *Julia* or *The Turning Point*, there are a dozen like *Roller Boogie* and *If You Don't Stop It, You'll Go Blind*. But it is worth noting that when the infrequent blockbusters that every film producer hopes for finally come along—pictures like *Star Wars, Jaws, American Graffiti, The Godfather, Gone with the Wind* and, of course, *The Exorcist*—they always break the demographic hammer lock that is the enemy of intelligent film making. It is comparatively rare for horror movies to do this, but *The Exorcist* is a case in point (and we have already spoken of *The Amityville Horror*, another film that has enjoyed a surprisingly old audience).

A film that appealed directly to the 15-year-olds who provide the spike point for moviegoing audiences—and one with a subtext tailored to match—was the Brian DePalma adaptation of my novel, *Carrie*. While I believe that both the book and the film depend on largely the same social situations to provide a text and a subtext of horror, there's enough difference to make interesting observations on DePalma's film version.

Both novel and movie have a pleasant *High School Confidential* feel, and while there are some superficial changes from the book in the film (Carrie's mother, for instance, seems to be presented in the film as a kind of weird renegade Roman Catholic), the basic story skeleton is pretty much the same. The story deals with a girl named Carrie White, the browbeaten daughter of a religious fanatic. Because of her strange clothes and shy mannerisms, Carrie is the butt of every class joke, the social outsider in every situation. She also has a mild telekinetic ability that intensifies after her first menstrual period, and she finally uses that power to "bring down the house" following a terrible social disaster at her high school prom.

DePalma's approach to the material is lighter and more deft than my own—and a good deal more artistic: the book tries to deal with the loneliness of one girl, her desperate effort to become a part of the peer society in which she must exist, and the failure of that effort. If this deliberate updating of *High School Confidential* has any thesis to offer, it is that high school is a place of almost bottomless conservatism and bigotry, a place where adolescents are no more allowed to rise above their station than a Hindu would be allowed to rise above his caste.

But there's a little more subtext to the book than that—at least, I hope so. If *The Stepford Wives* concerns itself with what men want from women, then *Carrie* is largely about how women find their own channels of power and what men fear about women and women's sexuality—which is only to say that, writing the book in 1973 and out of college only three years, I was fully aware of what women's liberation implied for me and others of my sex. The book is, in its more adult implications, an uneasy masculine shrinking from a future of female equality. For me, Carrie is a sadly misused teenager, an example of the sort of person whose spirit is so often broken for good in that pit of man- and woman-eaters that is your normal suburban high school. But she's also Woman, feeling her powers for the first time, and, like Samson, pulling down the temple on everyone in sight at the end of the book.

Heavy, turgid stuff—but in the novel, it's there only if you want to take it. If you don't, that's OK with me. A subtext works well only if it's unobtrusive (in that, I perhaps succeeded too well; in her review of De Palma's film, Pauline Kael dismissed my novel as "an unassuming pot-boiler"—as depressing a description as one could imagine but not completely inaccurate).

De Palma's film is up to more ambitious things. As in *The Stepford Wives*, humor and horror exist side by side in *Carrie*, playing off each other, and it is only as the film nears its conclusion that horror takes over completely. We see Billy Nolan (well played by John Travolta) giving the cops a big aw-shucks grin as he hides a beer against his crotch early on; it is a moment reminiscent of *American Graffiti*. Not long after, however, we see him swinging a sledge hammer at the head of a pig in a stockyard—the aw-shucks grin has crossed the line into madness, somehow, and that line crossing is what the film as a whole is about.

We see three boys (one of them the film's nominal hero, played by William Katt) trying on tuxedos for the prom in a kind of Gas House Kids routine that includes Donald Duck talk and speeded-up action. We see the girls who have humiliated Carrie in the shower room, by throwing tampons and sanitary napkins at her, doing penance on the exercise field to tootling, lumbering music that is reminiscent of *Baby Elephant Walk*. And yet beyond all these sophomoric and mildly amusing high school cutups, we sense a vacuous, almost unfocused hate, the almost unplanned revenge upon a girl who is trying to rise above her station. Much of De Palma's film is surprisingly jolly, but we sense that his jocoseness is dangerous: Behind it lurks the aw-shucks grin becoming a frozen rictus, and the girls laboring over their calisthenics are the same girls who shouted "Plug it up, plug it up, plug it up!" at Carrie not long before. Most of all, there is that bucket of pig's blood poised on the beam above the place where Carrie and Tommy will eventually be crowned . . . only waiting its time.

The film came along at a time when movie critics were bewailing the fact that there were no movies being made with good, meaty roles for women in them . . . but none of those critics seems to have noticed that in its film incarnation, *Carrie* belongs almost entirely to the ladies. Billy Nolan, a major—and frightening—character in the book, has been reduced to a semisupporting role in the movie. Tommy, the boy who takes Carrie to the prom, is presented in the novel as a boy who is honestly trying to do something manly—in his own way, he is trying to opt out of the caste system. In the film, however, he becomes little more than his girlfriend's cat's-paw, her tool of atonement for her part in the shower-room scene.

"I don't go around with anyone I don't want to," Tommy says patiently. "I'm asking because I want to ask you." Ultimately, he knew this to be the truth.

In the film, however, when Carrie asks Tommy why he is favoring her with an invitation to the prom, he offers her a dizzy sun-'n'-surf grin and says, "Because you liked my poem." Which, by the way, his girlfriend had written.

The novel views high school in a fairly common way: as that pit of man- and woman-eaters already mentioned. De Palma's social stance is more original; he sees this suburban white kids' high school as a kind of matriarchy. No matter where you look, there are girls behind the scenes, pulling invisible wires, rigging elections, using their boyfriends as stalking horses. Against such a backdrop, Carrie becomes doubly pitiful, because she is unable to do any of those things—she can only wait to be saved or damned by the actions of others. Her only power is her telekinetic ability, and both book and movie eventually arrive at the same point: Carrie uses her "wild talent" to pull down the whole rotten society. And one reason for the success of the story in both print and film, I think, lies in this: Carrie's revenge is something that any student who ever had his gym shorts pulled down in phys ed or his glasses thumb-rubbed in study hall could approve of. In Carrie's destruction of the gym (and her destructive walk back home in the book, a sequence left out of the movie because of tight budgeting), we see a dream revolution of the socially downtrodden.

The movies I have been discussing are those that try to link real (if sometimes free-floating) anxieties to the nightmare fears of the horror film. But now, let me put out even this dim light of rationality and discuss a few of those films whose effects go considerably deeper, past the rational and into those fears that seem universal.

Here is where we cross into the taboo lands for sure, and it's best to be frank up front. I think that we're all mentally ill; those of us outside the asylums only hide it a little better—and maybe not all that much better, after all. We've all known people who talk to themselves, people who sometimes squinch their faces into horrible grimaces when they believe no one is watching, people who have some hysterical fear—of snakes, the dark, the tight place, the long drop . . . and, of course, those final worms and grubs that are waiting so patiently underground.

When we pay our four or five bucks and seat ourselves at tenth-row center in a theater showing a horror movie, we are daring the nightmare.

Why? Some of the reasons are simple and obvious. To show that we can, that we are not afraid, that we can ride this roller coaster. Which is not to say that a really good horror movie may not surprise a scream out of us at some point, the way we may scream when the roller coaster twists through a complete 360 or plows through a lake at the bottom of the drop. · And horror movies, like roller coasters, have always been the special province of the young; by the time one turns 40 or 50, one's appetite for double twists or 360-degree loops may be considerably depleted.

We also go to re-establish our feeling of essential normality; the horror movie is innately conservative, even reactionary. Freda Jackson as the horrible melting woman in *Die, Monster, Die!* confirms for us that no matter how far we may be removed from the beauty of a Robert Redford or a Diana Ross, we are still light-years from true ugliness.

And we go to have fun.

Ah, but this is where the ground starts to slope away, isn't it? Because this is a very peculiar sort of fun, indeed. The fun comes from seeing others menaced—sometimes killed. One critic has suggested that if pro football has become the voyeur's version of combat, then the horror film has become the modern version of the public lynching.

It is true that the mythic, "fairy-tale" horror film intends to take away the shades of gray (which is one reason *When a Stranger Calls* doesn't work; the psycho, well and honestly played by Tony Beckley, is a poor schmuck beset by the miseries of his own psychosis; our unwilling sympathy for him dilutes the film's success as surely as water dilutes Scotch); it urges us to put away our more civilized and adult penchant for analysis and to become children again, seeing things in pure blacks and whites. It may be that horror movies provide psychic relief on this level because this invitation to lapse into simplicity, irrationality and even outright madness is extended so rarely. We are told we may allow our emotions a free rein . . . or no rein at all.

If we are all insane, then sanity becomes a matter of degree. If your insanity leads you to carve up women like Jack the Ripper or the Cleveland Torso Murderer, we clap you away in the funny farm (but neither of those two amateur-night surgeons was ever caught, heh-heh-heh); if, on the other hand, your insanity leads you only to talk to yourself when you're under stress or to pick your nose on your morning bus, then you are left alone to go about your business . . . though it is doubtful that you will ever be invited to the best parties.

The potential lyncher is in almost all of us (excluding saints, past and present; but then, most saints have been crazy in their own ways), and every now and then, he has to be let loose to scream and roll around in the grass. Our emotions and our fears form their own body, and we recognize that it demands its own exercise to maintain proper muscle tone. Certain of these emotional muscles are accepted—even exalted—in civilized society; they are, of course, the emotions that tend to maintain the status quo of civilization itself. Love, friendship, loyalty, kindness—these are all the emotions that we applaud, emotions that have been immortalized in the couplets of Hallmark cards and in the verses (I don't dare call it poetry) of Leonard Nimoy.

When we exhibit these emotions, society showers us with positive reinforcement; we learn this even before we get out of diapers. When, as children, we hug our rotten little puke of a sister and give her a kiss, all the aunts and uncles smile and twit and cry, "Isn't he the sweetest little thing?" Such coveted treats as chocolate-covered graham crackers often follow. But if we deliberately slam the rotten little puke of a sister's fingers in the door, sanctions follow—angry remonstrance from parents, aunts and uncles; instead of a chocolate-covered graham cracker, a spanking.

But anticivilization emotions don't go away, and they demand periodic exercise. We have such "sick" jokes as, "What's the difference between a truckload of bowling balls and a truckload of dead babies?" (You can't unload a truckload of bowling balls with a pitchfork . . . a joke, by the way, that I heard originally from a ten-year-old). Such a joke may surprise a laugh or a grin out of us even as we recoil, a possibility that confirms the thesis: If we share a brotherhood of man, then we also share an insanity of man. None of which is intended as a defense of either the sick joke or insanity but merely as an explanation of why the best horror films, like the best fairy tales, manage to be reactionary, anarchistic and revolutionary all at the same time.

The mythic horror movie, like the sick joke, has a dirty job to do. It deliberately appeals to all that is worst in us. It is morbidity unchained, our most base instincts let free, our nastiest fantasies realized . . . and it all happens, fittingly enough, in the dark. For those reasons, good liberals often shy away from horror films. For myself, I like to see the most aggressive of them—*Dawn of the Dead*, for instance—as lifting a trap door in the civilized forebrain and throwing a basket of raw meat to the hungry alligators swimming around in that subterranean river beneath.

Why bother? Because it keeps them from getting out, man. It keeps them down there and me up here. It was Lennon and McCartney who said that all you need is love, and I would agree with that.

As long as you keep the gators fed.

QUESTIONS FOR READING, RESPONDING, AND WRITING

Summarizing Main Points

1. List the different kinds of horror movies that King discusses. Are his categories distinct or do you find areas in which they overlap?
2. King ultimately argues in this essay that the horror movie provides a safe outlet for sharing the "insanity of man." Do you agree?

Analyzing Methods of Discourse

1. King states that "a genuine fan of horror films develops a feeling for the depth and texture of the genre." Does his inclusion of a number of films—e.g., *Close Encounters of the Third Kind, Easy Rider, The Stepford Wives*—that you might not have thought of as horror movies change your view of the genre? Could you briefly analyze the ways in which King defines it?
2. About midway through the essay, King states that "one generation's nightmare becomes the next generation's sociology." Describe in a sentence what this statement means. Identify examples of its application in the essay. Can you think of other examples?

Focusing on the Field

1. Consider the relationships King establishes between the different decades of American culture and the horror movies these periods have spawned. Following his theme, do you think you can predict what horror movies in the nineties will be like?
2. King wrote this essay specifically for *Playboy* magazine. What changes might its publication in another magazine dictate: in one like *Reader's Digest* or *Psychology Today* or an academic journal like the *Journal of Popular Culture* (from which Joan Lynch's "Music Videos: From Performance to Surrealism" is taken)?

Writing Assignments

1. Choose a horror movie that King does not discuss and write an essay in which you (1) fit it into one of his categories or (2) describe its relationship to the decade in which it was made or that which it seems to be about.
2. Read Bruno Bettelheim's "Fairy Tale versus Myth." Write an essay defending the thesis that King's definition of a horror movie fits into either one of Bettelheim's categories—myth or fairy tale.

M. F. K. Fisher

THE INDIGESTIBLE: THE LANGUAGE OF FOOD

Mary Frances Kennedy Fisher was born in 1908 and grew up in Whittier, California. The daughter of an editor, she attended the University of California at Los Angeles and the University of Dijon in France (1929–1932). As the following essay makes clear, Fisher has two consuming interests—food and language. Her many books on gourmets and eating include *Serve It Forth* (1937), *Consider the Oyster* (1941), *How to Cook a Wolf* (1942; 1951), all published under the name Mary Frances Parrish, *The Gastronomical Me* (1943), and *Here Let Us Feast: A Book of Banquets* (1946).

As the titles suggest, Fisher does not necessarily take her gastronomical subjects overly seriously, but she does care about culinary language. In this essay, Fisher warns us that food and the language that describes it are too easily manipulated by advertisers who prey on our base appetite for food and drink in order to sell their products and, in the process, distort and degrade our values and our language. Fisher has said elsewhere that she enjoys "the practice and contemplation of adapting the need to eat to the need to be properly nourished." In much the same way it might be said that she adapts the need to speak to the need to be well-spoken.

Hunger is, to describe it most simply, an urgent need for food. It is a craving, a desire. It is, I would guess, much older than man as we now think of him, and probably synonymous with the beginnings of sex. It is strange that we feel that anything as intrinsic as this must continually be wooed and excited, as if it were an unwilling and capricious part of us. If someone is not hungry, it indicates that his body does not, for a time and a reason, want to be fed. The logical thing, then, is to let him rest. He will either die, which he may have been meant to do, or he will once more feel the craving, the desire, the urgency to *eat*. He will have to do that before he can satisfy most of his other needs. Then he will revive again, which apparently he was meant to do.

It is hard to understand why this instinct to eat must be importuned, since it is so strong in all relatively healthy bodies. But in our present Western world, we face a literal bombardment of cajolery from all the media to eat this or that. It is as if we had been born without appetite, and must be led gently into an introduction to oral satisfaction and its increasingly dubious results, the way nubile maidens in past centuries were prepared for marriage proposals and then their legitimate defloration.

The language that is developing, in this game of making us *want* to eat, is far from subtle. To begin with, we must be made to feel that we really find the whole atavistic process difficult, or embarrassing or boring. We must be coaxed and cajoled to crave one advertised product rather than another, one taste, on presentation of something that we might have chosen anyway if let alone.

The truth is that we are born hungry and in our own ways will die so. But modern food advertising assumes that we are by nature bewildered and listless. As a matter of fact, we come into the world howling for Mother's Milk. We leave it, given a reasonable length of time, satisfied with much the same bland if lusty precursor of "pap and pabulum," tempered perhaps with a brush of wine on our lips to ease the parting of body and spirit. And in between, today, now, we are assaulted with the most insulting distortion of our sensory linguistics that I can imagine. We are treated like innocents and idiots by the advertisers, here in America and in Western Europe. (These are the only two regions I know, even slightly, but I feel sure that this same attack on our innate common sense is going on in the Orient, in India, in Brazil. . . .)

We are told, on radio and television and in widely distributed publications, not only how but what to eat, and when, and where. The pictures are colorful. The prose, often written by famous people, is deliberately persuasive, if often supercilious in a way that makes us out as clumsy louts, gastronomical oafs badly in need of guidance toward the satisfaction of appetites we are unaware of. And by now, with this constant attack on innate desires, an attack that can be either overt or subliminal, we apparently feel fogged-out, bombed, bewildered about whether we really crave some peanut butter on crackers as a post-amour snack, or want to sleep forever. And first, before varied forms of physical dalliance, should we share with our partner a French aperitif that keeps telling us to, or should we lead up to our accomplishments by sipping a tiny glass of Sicilian love potion?

The language for this liquid aphro-cut is familiar to most of us, thanks to lush ads in all the media. It becomes even stronger as we go into solid foods. Sexually the ads are aimed at two main groups—the Doers and the Dones. Either the reader/viewer/listener is out to woo a lover, or has married and acquired at least two children and needs help to keep the machismo-level high. Either way, one person is supposed to feed another so as to get the partner into bed and then, if possible, to pay domestic maintenance—that is, foot the bills.

One full-page color ad, for instance, shows six shots of repellently mingled vegetables, and claims boldly that these combinations "will do almost anything to get a husband's attentions." They will "catch his passing fancy . . . on the first vegetables he might even notice." In short, the ad goes on with skilled persuasion, "they're vegetables your husband can't ignore." This almost promises that he may not ignore the cook either, a heartening if vaguely lewd thought if the pictures in the ad are any intimation of his tastes.

It is plain that if a man must be kept satisfied at table, so must his progeny, and advertisers know how to woo mothers as well as plain sexual companions. Most of their nutritional bids imply somewhat unruly family life, that only food can ease: "No more fights over who gets what," one ad proposes, as it suggests buying not one but three different types of frozen but "crisp hot fried chicken at a price that take-out can't beat": thighs and drumsticks, breast portions and wings, all coated with the same oven-crunchy-golden skin, and fresh from freezer to stove in minutes. In the last quarter of this family ad there is a garishly bright new proposal, the "no-fire, sure-fire, barbecue-sauced" chicken. Personal experience frowns on this daring departure from the national "finger-lickin'" syndrome: with children who fight over who gets what, it would be very messy.

It is easy to continue such ever-loving family-style meals, as suggested by current advertising, all in deceptively alluring color in almost any home-oriented magazine one finds. How about enjoying a "good family western," whatever that may be, by serving a mixture of "redy-rice" and leftover chicken topped with a blenderized sauce of ripe avocado? This is called "love food from California," and it will make us "taste how the West was won." The avocado, the ad goes on, will "open new frontiers of wholesome family enjoyment." And of course the pre-spiced-already-seasoned "instant" rice, combined with cooked chicken, will look yummy packed into the hollowed fruit shells and covered with nutlike green stuff. All this will help greatly to keep the kids from hitting each other about who gets what.

The way to a man's heart is through his stomach, we have been assured for a couple of centuries, and for much longer than that good wives as well as noted courtesans have given their time and thought to keeping the male belly full (and the male liver equally if innocently enlarged). By now this precarious mixture of sex and gastronomy has come out of the pantry, so to speak, and ordinary cookbook shelves show *Cuisine d'amour* and *Venus in the Kitchen* alongside Mrs. Rombauer and Julia Child.

In order to become a classic, which I consider the last two to be, any creation, from a potato soufflé to a marble bust or a skyscraper, must be honest, and that is why most cooks, as well as their methods, are never known. It is also why dishonesty in the kitchen is driving us so fast and successfully to the world of convenience foods and franchised eateries.

If we look at a few of the so-called cookbooks now providing a kind of armchair gastronomy (to read while we wait for the wife and kids to get ready to pile in the car for supper at the nearest drive-in), we understand without either amazement or active nausea some such "homemade" treat as I was brought lately by a generous neighbor. The recipe she proudly passed along to me, as if it were her great-grandmother's secret way to many a heart, was from a best-selling new cookbook, and it included a large package of sweet chocolate bits, a box of "Butter Fudge" chocolate cake mix, a package of instant vanilla pudding, and a cup of imitation mayonnaise. It was to be served with synthetic whipped cream sprayed from an aerosol can. It was called *Old-Fashion Fudge Torte*.

This distortion of values, this insidious numbing of what we once knew without question as either True or False, can be blamed, in part anyway, on the language we hear and read every day and night about the satisfying of such a basic need as hunger. Advertising, especially in magazines and books devoted to such animal satisfaction, twists us deftly into acceptance of the new lingo of gastronomical seduction.

A good example: an impossibly juicy-looking pork chop lies like a Matisse odalisque in an open microwave oven, cooked until "fall-from-the-bone-tender." This is a new word. It still says that the meat is so overcooked that it will fall off its bone (a dubious virtue!), but it is supposed to beguile the reader into thinking that he or she (1) speaks a special streamlined language, and (2) deserves to buy an oven to match, and (3) appreciates all such finer things in life. It takes *know-how*, the ad assures us subliminally, to understand all that "fall-from-the-bone-tender" really means!

This strange need to turn plain descriptive English into hyphenated hyperbole can be found even in the best gastronomical reviews and articles as well as magazine copy. How about "fresh-from-the-oven apple cobbler," as described by one of the more reputable food writers of today? What would be wrong, especially for someone who actually knows syntax and grammar, in saying "apple cobbler, fresh from the oven"? A contemporary answer is that the multiple adjective is more . . . uh . . . contemporary. This implies that it should reach the conditioned brain cells of today's reader in a more understandable, coherent way—or does it?

The vocabulary of our kitchen comes from every part of the planet, sooner or later, because as we live, so we speak. After the Norman Conquest in 1066, England learned countless French nouns and verbs that are now part of both British and American cooking language: *appetite, dinner, salmon, sausage, lemon, fig, almond,* and so on. We all say *roast, fry, boil,* and we make *sauces* and put them in *bowls* or on *plates.* And the German kitchen, the Aztecan: they too gave us words like *cookie* and *chocolate.* We say *borscht* easily (Russian before it was Yiddish). From slavetime Africa there is the word *gumbo,* for okra, and in *benne* biscuits there is the black man's sesame. Some people say that *alcohol* came from the nonalcoholic Arabs.

But what about the new culinary language of the media, the kind we now hear and view and read? What can "freezer-fresh" mean? *Fresh* used to imply new, pure, lively. Now it means, at best, that when a food was packaged, it would qualify as ready to be eaten: "oven-fresh" cookies a year on the shelf, "farm-fresh" eggs laid last spring, "corn-on-the-cob fresh" dehydrated vegetable soup-mix. . . .

Personal feelings and opinions and prejudices (sometimes called skunners) have a lot to do with our reactions to gastronomical words, and other kinds. I know a man who finally divorced his wife because, even by indirection, he could not cure her of "calling up." She called up people, and to her it meant that she used the telephone—that is, she was not calling across a garden or over a fence, but was calling up when she could not *see* her friends. Calling and calling up are entirely different, she and a lot of interested amateur semanticists told her husband. He refused to admit this. "Why not simply *telephone* them? To telephone you don't say *telephone up,*" he would say. Her phrase continued to set his inner teeth, the ones rooted directly in his spiritual jaw, on such an edge that he finally fled. She called up to tell me.

This domestic calamity made me aware, over many years but never with such anguish, how *up* can dangle in our language. And experience has shown me that if a word starts dangling, it is an easy mark for the careless users and the overt rapists of syntax and meaning who write copy for mass-media outlets connected, for instance, with hunger, and its current quasi-satisfactions. Sometimes the grammatical approach is fairly conventional and old-fashioned, and the *up* is tacked onto a verb in a farily comprehensible way. "Perk up your dinner," one magazine headline begs us, with vaguely disgusting suggestions about how to do it. "Brighten up a burger," a full-page lesson in salad-making with an instant powder tells us. (This ad sneaks in another call on home unity with its "unusually delicious . . . bright . . . tasty" offering: "Sit back and listen to the cheers," it says. "Your family will give them to this tasty-zesty easy-to-make salad!")

Of course *up* gets into the adjectives as well as the verbs: *souped up chicken* and *souped up dip* are modish in advertising for canned pudding-like concoctions that fall in their original shapes from tin to saucepan or mixing bowl, to be blended with liquids to make fairly edible "soups," or to serve in prefab sauces as handy vehicles for clams or peanuts or whatever is added to the can-shaped glob to tantalize drinkers to want one more Bloody Mary. They dip up the mixture on specially stiffened pack-aged "chips" made of imitation tortillas or even imitation reconditioned potatoes, guaranteed not to crumble, shatter, or otherwise mess up the landscape. . . .

Verbs are more fun than adjectives, in this game of upmanship. And one of the best/worst of them is creeping into our vocabularies in a thoroughly unsubtle way. It is *to gourmet up*. By now the word *gourmet* has been so distorted, and so overloaded, that to people who know its real meaning it is meaningless. They have never misused it and they refuse to now. To them a gourmet is a person, and perforce the word is a noun. Probably it turned irrevocably into an adjective with descriptive terms like *gourmet-style* and *gourmet-type*. I am not sure. But it has come to mean fancy rather than fastidious. It means expensive, or exotic, or pseudo-elegant and classy and pricey. It rarely describes enjoyment. It describes a style, at best, and at worst a cheap imitation of once-stylish and always costly affectation.

There is gourmet food. There are gourmet restaurants, or gourmet-style eating places. There are packaged frozen cubes of comestibles called gourmet that cost three times as much as plain fast foods because, the cunningly succulent mouth-watering ads propose, their sauces are made by world-famous chefs, whose magical blends of spices and herbs have been touched off by a personalized fillip of rare old Madeira. In other words, at triple the price, they are worth it because they have been gourmeted up. Not long ago I heard a young woman in a supermarket say to a friend who looked almost as gaunt and harried as she, "Oh god . . . why am I here? You ask! Harry calls to say his sales manager is coming to dinner, and I've got to gourmet up the pot roast!"

I slow my trundle down the pushcart aisle.

"I could slice some olives into it, maybe? Pitted. Or maybe dump in a can of mushrooms. Sliced. It's got to be more expensive."

The friend says, "A cup of wine? Red. Or sour cream . . . a kind of Stroganoff . . .?"

I worm my way past them, feeling vaguely worried. I long to tell them something—perhaps not to worry.

There are, of course, even more personal language shocks than the one that drove a man to leave his dear girl because she had to call people up. Each of us has his own, actively or dimly connected with hunger (which only an adamant Freudian could call his!). It becomes a real embarrassment, for example, when a friend or a responsible critic of cookbooks or restaurants uses words like *yummy*, or *scrumptious*. There is no dignity in such infantile evasions of plain words like *good*—or even *delicious* or *excellent*.

My own word aversion is longstanding, and several decades from the first time I heard it I still pull back, like the flanges of a freshly opened oyster. It is the verb *to drool*, when applied to written prose, and especially to anything I myself have written. Very nice people have told me, for a long time now, that some things they have read of mine, in books or magazines, have made them drool. I know they mean to compliment me. They are saying that my use of words makes them oversalivate, like hapless dogs waiting for a bell to say "Meat!" to them. It has made them more alive than they were, more active. They are grateful to me, perhaps, for being reminded that they are still functioning, still aware of some of their hungers.

I too should be grateful, and even humble, that I have reminded people of what fun it is, vicariously or not, to eat/live. Instead I am revolted. I see a slavering slobbering maw. It dribbles helplessly, in a Pavlovian response. It *drools*. And drooling, not over a meaty bone or a warm bowl of slops, is what some people have done over my printed words. This has long worried me. I feel grateful but repelled. They are nice people, and I like them and I like dogs, but dogs *must* drool when they are excited by the prospect of the satisfaction of alerted tastebuds, and two-legged people do not need to, and in general I know that my reaction to the fact that some people slobber like conditioned animals is a personal skunner, and that I should accept it as such instead of meeting it like a stiff-upper-lipped Anglo-Saxon (and conditioned!) nanny.

I continue, however, to be regretfully disgusted by the word *drool* in connection with all writing about food, including my own. And a few fans loyal enough to resist being hurt by this statement may possibly call me up.

It is too easy to be malicious, but certainly the self-styled food experts of our current media sometimes seem overtly silly enough to be fair game. For anyone with half an ear for the English-American language we write and speak, it is almost impossible not to chuckle over the unending flow of insults to our syntax and grammar, not to mention our several levels of intelligence.

How are we supposed to react to descriptive phrases like "crisply crunchy, to snap in your mouth"? We know this was written, and for pay, by one or another of the country's best gastronomical hacks. We should not titter. He is a good fellow. Why then does he permit himself to say that some corn on the cob is so tender that "it dribbles milk down your chin"? He seems, whether or not he means well, to lose a little of the innate dignity that we want from our goumet-judges. He is like a comedian who with one extra grimace becomes coarse instead of funny, or like an otherwise sensitive reader who says that certain writing makes him drool.

Not all our food critics, of course, are as aware of language as the well-known culinary experts who sign magazine articles and syndicated columns. And for one of them, there are a hundred struggling copywriters who care less about mouth-watering prose than about filling ad space with folksy propaganda for "kwik" puddings and suchlike. They say shamelessly, to keep their jobs, that Mom has just told them how to make instant homemade gravy taste "like I could never make before!" "*Believe* me," they beg, "those other gravies just aren't the same! This has a real homemade flavor and a rich brown color. Just add it to your pot drippings." And so on.

Often these unsung kitchen psalmists turn, with probable desperation, to puns and other word games. They write, for instance, that frozen batter-fried fish are so delicious that "one crunch and you're hooked!" Oh, hohoho ha ha. And these same miserable slaves produce millions of words, if they are fortunate enough to find and keep their jobs, about things like synthetic dough that is "pre-formed" into "old-fashioned shapes that taste cooky-fresh and crunchy" in just fifteen minutes from freezer to oven to the kiddies' eager paws and maws.

When the hacks have proved that they can sling such culinary lingo, they are promoted to a special division that deals even more directly with oral satisfaction. They write full-page ads in juicy color, about cocktail nibbles with "a fried-chicken taste that's lip-lickin' good." This, not too indirectly, is aimed to appeal to hungry readers familiar with a franchised fried chicken that is of course known worldwide as finger-lickin good, and even packaged Kitty Krums that are whisker-lickin good. (It is interesting and reassuring, although we must drop a few g's to understand it, that modern gastronomy still encourages us to indulge in public tongueplay.)

Prose by the copywriters usually stays coy, but is somewhat more serious about pet foods than humanoid provender. Perhaps it is assumed that most people who buy kibbles do not bother to read the printed information on all four sides of their sacks, but simply pour the formula into bowls on the floor and hope for the best. Or perhaps animal-food companies recognize that some of their slaves are incurably dedicated to correct word usage. Often the script on a bag of dry pet food is better written than most paperback novels. Possibly some renegade English instructor has been allowed to explain "Why Your Cat Will Enjoy This."

He is permitted tiny professorial jokes, now and then: "As Nutritious As It Is Delicious," one caption says, and another section is called "Some Reading on Feeding," and then the prose goes all out, almost euphorically, with "Some Raving on Saving." The lost academician does have to toss in a few words like *munchy* to keep his job, but in general there is an enjoyably relaxed air about the unread prose on pet-food packages, as opposed to the stressful cuteness of most fashionable critics of our dining habits.

Of course the important thing is to stay abreast of the lingo, it seems. Stylish restaurants go through their phases, with beef Wellington and chocolate mousse high in favor one year and strictly for Oskahoola, Tennessee, the next. We need private dining-out guides as well as smart monthly magazines to tell us what we are eating tonight, as well as what we are paying for it.

A lot of our most modish edibles are dictated by their scarcity, as always in the long history of gastronomy. In 1978, for instance, it became *de rigueur* in California to serve caviar in some guise, usually with baked or boiled potatoes, because shipments from Iran grew almost as limited as they had long been from Russia. (Chilled caviar, regal fare, was paired with the quaintly plebeian potato many years ago, in Switzerland I think, but by 1978 its extravagant whimsy had reached Hollywood and the upper West Coast by way of New York, so that desperate hostesses were buying and even trying to "homemake" caviar from the Sacramento River sturgeons. Results: usually lamentable, but well meant.)

All this shifting of gustatory snobbism should probably have more influence on our language than it does. Writers for both elegant magazines and "in" guides use much the same word-appeal as do the copywriters for popular brands of convenience foods. They may not say "lip-smackin" or "de-lish," but they manage to imply what their words will make readers do. They use their own posh patter, which like the humbler variety seldom bears any kind of scrutiny, whether for original meaning or plain syntax.

How about "unbelievably succulent luscious scallops which boast a nectar-of-the-sea freshness"? Or "a *beurre blanc*, that ethereally light, grandmotherly sauce"? Or "an onion soup, baked *naturellement*, melting its knee-deep crust of cheese and croutons"? Dressings are "teasingly-tart," not teasing or tart or even teasingly tart. They have "breathtakingly visual appeal," instead of looking yummy, and some of them, perhaps fortunately, are "almost too beautiful to describe," "framed in a picture-perfect garnish of utter perfection and exquisiteness," "a pinnacle of gastronomical delight." (Any of these experiences can be found, credit card on the ready, in the bistros-of-the-moment.)

It is somewhat hard to keep one's balance, caught between the three stools of folksy lure, stylish gushing, and a dictionary of word usage. How does one *parse*, as my grandfather would say, a complete sentence like "The very pinkness it was, of mini-slices"? Or "A richly eggy and spiritous Zabaglione, edged in its serving dish with tiny dots of grenadine"? These are not sentences, at least to my grandfather and to me, and I think *spirituous* is a better word in this setting, and I wonder whether the dots of grenadine were wee drops of the sweet syrup made from pomegranates or the glowing seeds of the fruit itself, and how and why anyone would preserve them for a chic restaurant. And were those pink mini-slices from a lamb, a calf? Then there are always verbs to ponder on, in such seductive reports on what and where to dine. One soup "packs chunks" of something or other, to prove its masculine heartiness in a stylish lunchtime brasserie. "Don't forget to special-order!" Is this a verb, a split infinitive, an attempt of the reporter to sound down-to-earth?

Plainly it is as easy to carp, criticize, even dismiss such unworthy verbiage as it is to quibble and shudder about what the other media dictate, that we may subsist. And we continue to carp, criticize, dismiss— and to *eat*, not always as we are told to, and not always well, either! But we were born *hungry*.

QUESTIONS FOR READING, RESPONDING, AND WRITING

Summarizing Main Points

1. According to Fisher, both food and the language that describes it are becoming "indigestible." Point out examples of both and explain why Fisher considers them hard to swallow.
2. Part of the problem that Fisher is describing stems from the contemporary need for time-and-labor-saving meals. Do you think Fisher is too harsh in her assessment of such meals? Or is she more concerned that her readers simply recognize them for what they are? Do you agree with her assessment? Why or why not?

Analyzing Methods of Discourse

1. Fisher defines several words in her essay. List them and their definitions. Why has Fisher chosen to define these particular words?
2. Fisher uses many quotation marks in her essay and not only to indicate a direct quotation from an advertisement. Find several examples of words or phrases in quotation marks and explain why Fisher calls attention to those particular words or phrases with her punctuation. Are there other words or phrases in her essay that might benefit from quotation marks? If so, why has Fisher left them out?

Focusing on the Field

1. Like many good writers, Fisher begins her essay with background material. How is that background material a good introduction for the sorts of paradoxical examples that she later describes?

2. Fisher presents her material in a humorous fashion. Why is this appropriate? Find specific examples of Fisher's humor and describe what is funny about them.

Writing Assignments

1. Fisher points out that "the new culinary language of the media" is, at best, paradoxical and obfuscatory; at worst, contradictory and deceiving. Find examples of advertising language for other products (e.g., automobiles, clothing, electronic equipment) that work the same way. Then expose them as Fisher does here.
2. In his essay, "The Rhetoric of Democracy," Daniel Boorstin claims that "insofar as folk culture becomes advertising, and advertising becomes centralized, it becomes a way of depriving people of their opportunities for individual and small community expression." How is what Fisher's essay describes an example of what Boorstin is worried about? How do Fisher's examples fit into what Boorstin calls the "advertising penumbra"?

Desmond Morris

UNDERSTANDING GESTURES: THE THUMB UP

Desmond Morris comes from a writing family. The son of a writer, Morris married Ramona Baulch Za and has collaborated with her on several books, both juvenile, *Apes and Monkeys* (1964) and *Zoo Time* (1966), and adult, *Men and Apes* (1966) and *Men and Pandas* (1966). Morris, who was born in England in 1928, received his education at Birmingham and Oxford Universities and spent the fifties and sixties working as an animal researcher for Oxford and as curator of mammals for the Zoological Society of London. He remains a research fellow at Oxford's Wolfson College in the department of psychology and contributes to many journals, including *Behavior, New Scientist,* and *Zoo Life.*

His dual interests in animal behavior and psychology led him into the investigation of the behavior of humans *as* animals and resulted in the internationally acclaimed best-seller *The Naked Ape: A Zoologist's Study of the Human Animal* (1967), for which he received an award from the World Organization for Human Potential in 1971. Morris's observations in *The Naked Ape* range from summaries of scientifically accepted studies of human behavior to wilder speculations that describe human behavior in terms of innate animal behaviors. Morris's more recent books— *Intimate Behavior* (1971), *Manwatching: A Field Guide to Human Behavior* (1977), and *Gestures: Their Origins and Distributions* (1979), from which the following selection is taken—examine the varieties of nonverbal communication.

DESCRIPTION

The clenched hand is extended, with the thumb vertically erect. In English it is better known by the popular name 'thumbs up,' despite the fact that the action is commonly performed with only one hand.

ORIGINS

Few gestures can have a stranger history than the familiar 'thumbs up.' There is no doubt in the popular mind as to its origin. Everyone agrees that it hails from the days of gladiatorial combat in ancient Rome, when a decision had to be made concerning the fate of a beaten warrior. Peter Quennell, in his book on *The Colosseum*, describes what has now become the generally accepted scenario:

> In the sovereign's presence, the crowd advised their ruler. Waving cloths and displaying up-turned thumbs, they shouted 'Mitte!' (Let him go free); or, by turning down their thumbs, they vociferated 'Iugula!'—recommending that the fallen man should pay the penalty. When the emperor happened to share their feelings, he confirmed the crowd's verdict . . . and . . . with *pollice verso*, downturned thumb, ordered his immediate execution.

So, if the defeated gladiator had fought well, he could be spared by a thumbs up gesture. If he had fought badly, he could be slain by a thumbs down. From this specific use of the two thumb signals, it is argued, came our modern usage, with the thumbs up meaning 'all's well—O.K.' and the thumbs down meaning 'no good—failure'. This has become the dominant interpretation of the two gestures throughout Europe, and much of the rest of the world.

What could be simpler? The answer is that it would indeed be a simple derivational explanation, if only it happened to be true. But it is not. The ancient Romans did not behave in this manner ascribed to them, and the whole story of the thumbs up 'approval' sign is based on misunderstanding and mistranslation. It is a complete distortion of the facts, and the true basis for our modern usage comes from a different source altogether. What has happened is that, having acquired our modern thumbs up and down meanings from elsewhere, we have then blatantly re-written Roman history to fit in.

There are, in reality, no ancient references to the thumbs going either up *or* down in the Colosseum, at the vital moment of decision. Later authors who have claimed so have simply not understood the Latin phrases. *Pollice verso* does not mean a down-turned thumb—it simply means a turned thumb—one that is moved in some unspecified way. No particular direction can be assumed. The posture of the thumbs of those wishing to spare the gladiator was *pollice compresso*—compressed thumbs. In other words, not thumbs up, but thumbs covered up—thumbs folded away out of sight. What the spectators did, in fact, was to extend their thumbs for a kill and hide their thumbs for an acquittal. The reason for this is not hard to find. If they wanted the victorious man to plunge in his sword, they mimed the act with their hands, their extended thumbs stabbing the air in encouragement. If they wanted to spare the defeated fighter because he proved himself valiant in battle, they did the opposite of sticking out their thumbs—they hid them away. This made sense in an arena as vast as the Colosseum, where the kill/no-kill signals would have to be strongly contrasting to be visible at all.

If this was the true situation, then how has it come to be distorted by later writers? It is not even the case that the truth was completely forgotten. It is recorded both in the *Oxford English Dictionary* and in Brewer's *Dictionary of Phrase and Fable*. Sir James Murray compiled the volume of the O.E.D. dealing with the letter 'T' between 1909 and 1915. Under the entry for phrases connected with the word 'thumb', he includes the following quotation:

> 1880. Lewis and Short. s.v. *Pollex:* To close down the thumb (*premere*) was a sign of approbation; to extend it (*vertere, convertere, pollex infestus*) a sign of disapprobation.

The word *premere* refers to the pressing of the thumb, and the words *vertere, convertere, pollex infestus* refer to the turning and turning around of the 'hostile thumb.' Different words this time, but still the same meanings and still no mention whatever of thumbs going up or down.

Brewer's dictionary was first published in 1870 and has been reprinted many times since then. His entry is just as clear:

> In the ancient Roman combats, when a gladiator was vanquished it rested with the spectators to decide whether he should be slain or not. If they wished him to live, they shut up their thumbs in their fists (*pollice compresso favor judicabatur*); if to be slain, they turned out their thumbs . . . Our popular saying, Thumbs up! expressive of pleasure or approval is probably a perversion of this custom.

Brewer does not hazard a guess as to why anyone should want to pervert so simple a truth. In a moment we shall do so, but first we want to consider some other distortions that occurred. The modern equations: thumbs up = O.K., thumbs down = not O.K., is not the only error that was made. Earlier authors usually made the opposite mistake. This is hard to believe today, but the following quotations should be convincing enough:

R. Garnett, 1887: 'They had unanimously turned their thumbs up. "Sartor," the publisher acquainted him, "excites universal disapprobation."'

J. Dixon, 1896: 'To turn the thumbs up.—To decide against. The Romans in the amphitheatre turned their thumbs up when a combatant was not to be spared.'

R.Y. Tyrrell, 1907: ' "Thumbs down" means "spare him. . . .": the signal for death was "thumbs up."'

What seems to have happened here is that the extended thumb has automatically been thought of as going up, and the hidden thumb as being kept down (rather than pointed down). But as the idea has been passed from author to author, the distortion has hardened. Sadly, it appears that translations from the Latin are often less than scholarly. In one case, we can actually watch the bias change as the years pass. There is a passage in Juvenal's third *Satire*, written at about the beginning of the second century A.D., which, in the original, refers to thumbs being either *verso* or *converso* (according to two different sources). Either way, it means that the thumbs were being turned, but makes no suggestion as to the direction. Juvenal has been translated many times, but if we select just three examples. we can see how the interpretation varies with the period.

Montaigne, in his *Essayes* of 1603 (Second Book, 26th Chapter) translates the Juvenal passage as: 'When people turn their thumbs away, they popularly any slay.' This is very restrained and correct, but he makes it the basis of a comment of his own to the effect that a thumb-sign 'of disfavour or disgrace' is 'to lift them up, and turn them outwards.' Read properly, he is still not badly distorting the original, but the phrase 'lift them up' can easily be taken to mean 'point them up,' and thus is undoubtedly the way many subsequent authors interpreted him.

Dryden, in his translation of Juvenal in 1693, gives the same passage as: 'Where . . . with thumbs bent back, they popularly kill.' Turning away has now become bending back, and again this was taken to mean an erect thumb, even though Dryden was not specific about it.

Coming up to date, in Peter Green's 1967 translation, the passage becomes: '. . . and at the mob's thumbs-down, will butcher a loser for popularity's sake.' Now the meaning has gone the other way, to fit in with modern popular usage.

So, from an ambiguous beginning the distortion has taken off, first in one direction, and then in another. The question we now have to answer is what is it that controls these directions? Are they mere whims, or are there certain pressures being exerted to pull them one way or the other? First, we must consider pressures favouring the idea that thumbs up mean something unpleasant and thumbs down mean something pleasant. Whatever the pressure is, it has not been a particularly strong or

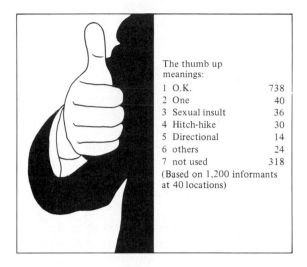

The thumb up
meanings:

1	O.K.	738
2	One	40
3	Sexual insult	36
4	Hitch-hike	30
5	Directional	14
6	others	24
7	not used	318

(Based on 1,200 informants
at 40 locations)

successful one, and has lost out to its rival in modern times. A glance at the list of meanings for the thumbs up gesture, which we obtained from our informants in our present gesture-maps field study, reveals that 738 of them gave the 'O.K.' pleasant meaning, while only 36 gave an unpleasant meaning, namely that of a phallic insult. In the latter case the erect thumb is jerked in the air as a symbolic phallus, and the message is 'to sit on this' or 'up yours.' This appears to be an old usage that has lost ground in the face of the increasingly popular O.K. meaning. If it was once better known than it is today, it could easily have led to the idea that, if an unpleasant thumb gesture was used in the Colosseum, it must have been this one.

Another clue comes from the first century A.D. writings of Pliny. In his great work, *The Historie of the World*, translated into English in 1601 by Philemon Holland, there is a passage in the second chapter of the 28th book, which reads: 'to bend or bow down the thumbs when we give assent unto a thing, or do favour any person, is so usuall, that it is growne into a proverbial speech, to bid a man put down his thumb in token of approbation.' There is no doubt here about the way Pliny viewed the gesture: thumbs down meant O.K. But he was not talking about what happened in the Colosseum. He was referring to ordinary, everyday life, and it is important to make that distinction.

If we now put together these two observations: thumbs up meaning an unpleasant insult, and thumbs down meaning a pleasant form of approval, it is possible to see how these usages, if known about by earlier authors, could have been grafted on, as it were, to the ambiguous statements about what the spectators' thumbs were doing at the gladiatorial combats. This can explain how one kind of distortion developed, but what of the other—the one leading in the opposite direction, to the popular usage of modern times?

To understand this other distortion we have to consider the basic nature of 'up' gestures and 'down' gestures. If we are feeling 'up in the air' we are feeling good, and if we are feeling 'down in the dumps' we are feeling bad. There is something inherently optimistic, positive and dominant about upward movements, and something essentially pessimistic, negative and subordinate about downward movements. This dichotomy pervades the whole of our language and our thinking, and it is obviously going to have an impact on our gestural repertoire as well. So, whatever other, more specific, influences may be at work, there is also going to be a generalized pressure tending to favour a thumbs up gesture as meaning something pleasant and a thumbs down gesture as something unpleasant. We feel that it is this basic influence that has finally favoured the modern interpretation of the thumbs up and down gestures.

There is some evidence that this is not exclusively modern. John Bulwer, in his *Chirologia* of 1644, has this to say about ordinary thumb postures: 'To hold up the thumbe, is the gesture . . . of one shewing his assent or approbation. To hold up both thumbs, is an expression importing a transcendency of praise.' He quotes classical authors to support him in this view, which contradicts the statements made by Pliny. There is no way we can see to reconcile these two views and it looks as though there must have been an early conflict of thumb signals which was eventually resolved by the rise to dominance of the 'up = good' version.

Two other derivational clues exist to help to explain the 'thumbs up = good' equation. There is an old English saying 'Here's my thumb on it!' which was used to seal a bargain. The two people involved each wetted a thumb and then extended it, held upwards, until the two raised thumbs came into contact with one another. It is easy to see how this custom could lead to, or support the idea of holding out a raised thumb as a sign of friendly agreement or approval. Another supportive clue comes from Gérard Brault's study of *French Gestures*, where he says that admiration is expressed when 'the thumb of the right hand is held erect and pushed forward, as if pushing in a thumbtack . . . The thumbs up gesture here signifies "first class," for the French indicate number one with the thumb.'

Summing up, it would be an understatement to say that the origins of the thumbs up gesture are not as simple as most people seem to believe. The whole 'Roman arena' explanation that is so often given, appears to be largely irrelevant. The evidence as to exactly what was happening in ordinary, daily life in ancient times is still not clear and the information is contradictory. But the present-day situation is obvious enough. Everywhere the O.K. message of the thumbs up gesture has come to dominate the scene.

QUESTIONS FOR READING, RESPONDING, AND WRITING

Summarizing Main Points

1. What was the original meaning of the "thumb up," or more precisely, the "*pollice verso*" gesture? How has the physical gesture itself changed over the course of many years?
2. The "thumb up" gesture has paradoxically conveyed both a pleasant and an unpleasant meaning. How does Morris account for this paradox?

Analyzing Methods of Discourse

1. Morris begins his argument by recounting the popularly held misconceptions about the origin of the "thumb up" gesture. How does this help eliminate potential confusion later in his essay?
2. Morris begins several paragraphs by asking questions. Are they always questions that the reader would ask? Does Morris always answer them in the way the reader might expect?

Focusing on the Field

1. Part of Morris's research is "based on 1,200 informants at 40 locations." Why does Morris include this information? Why does he tell his readers that the informants were selected from forty locations?
2. Using several different kinds of sources or authorities, Morris traces the changing meaning of the "thumb up" gesture. List those sources. Are they convincing authorities?

Writing Assignments

1. Make your own survey on the meaning of the "thumb up" gesture or another familiar gesture (e.g., the raised forefinger as "number one," the "V for victory") and report on your results.
2. Morris demonstrates the evolution of the "thumb up" gesture. In "A Biological Homage to Mickey Mouse," Stephen Jay Gould demonstrates the evolution of Mickey Mouse. Compare and contrast the two essays. Is their concept of evolution similar? Explain.

Daniel Boorstin

ADVERTISING: THE RHETORIC OF DEMOCRACY

Daniel J. Boorstin's current prominence among contemporary American historians was neatly foreshadowed by a myriad of early awards and distinctions. Born in 1914 in Atlanta, Georgia, Boorstin graduated summa cum laude from Harvard College in 1934, studied law at Oxford as a Rhodes scholar, and went on to read law at the Inner Temple in London. He received a doctorate in law from Yale University in 1940. In 1944, having taught at both Harvard and Swarthmore, he accepted a position at the University of Chicago, where he was named a Preston and Sterling Morton Distinguished Professor of History. He has also served as the Director of the Smithsonian Institution's National Museum of History and Technology and is currently the Librarian of Congress, a post he assumed in 1975.

A prolific writer, Boorstin is the author of the Pulitzer Prize–winning three-volume history *The Americans* (1958–1973), as well as several other books on American history and culture. Among his other titles are *The Genius of American Politics* (1953), *The Image: A Guide to Pseudo-Events in America* (1962), *The Decline of Radicalism: Reflections on America Today* (1969), and *The Sociology of the Absurd* (1970). Not just eminent, but eminently accessible, Boorstin complements his contributions to professional journals with popular essays in newspapers and periodicals such as *Reader's Digest, Advertising Age,* and *TV Guide.*

Advertising, of course, has been part of the mainstream of American civilization, although you might not know it if you read the most respectable surveys of American history. It has been one of the enticements to the settlement of this New World, it has been a producer of the peopling of the United States, and in its modern form, in its world-wide reach, it has been one of our most characteristic products.

Never was there a more outrageous or more unscrupulous or more ill-informed advertising campaign than that by which the promoters for the American colonies brought settlers here. Brochures published in England in the seventeenth century, some even earlier, were full of hopeful overstatements, half-truths, and downright lies, along with some facts which nowadays surely would be the basis for a restraining order from the Federal Trade Commission. Gold and silver, fountains of youth, plenty of fish, venison without limit, all these were promised, and of course some of them were found. It would be interesting to speculate on how long it might have taken to settle this continent if there had not been such promotion by enterprising advertisers. How has American civilization been shaped by the fact that there was a kind of natural selection here of those people who were willing to believe advertising?

Advertising has taken the lead in promising and exploiting the new. This was a new world, and one of the advertisements for it appears on the dollar bill on the Great Seal of the United States, which reads *novus ordo seclorum*, one of the most effective advertising slogans to come out of this country. "A new order of the centuries"—belief in novelty and in the desirability of opening novelty to everybody has been important in our lives throughout our history and especially in this century. Again and again advertising has been an agency for inducing Americans to try anything and everything—from the continent itself to a new brand of soap. As one of the more literate and poetic of the advertising copywriters, James Kenneth Frazier, a Cornell graduate, wrote in 1900 in "The Doctor's Lament":

> *This lean M.D. is Dr. Brown*
> *Who fares but ill in Spotless Town.*
> *The town is so confounded clean,*
> *It is no wonder he is lean,*
> *He's lost all patients now, you know,*
> *Because they use Sapolio.*

The same literary talent that once was used to retail Sapolio was later used to induce people to try the Edsel or the Mustang, to experiment with Lifebuoy or Body-All, to drink Pepsi-Cola or Royal Crown Cola, or to shave with a Trac II razor.

And as expansion and novelty have become essential to our economy, advertising has played an ever-larger role: in the settling of the continent, in the expansion of the economy, and in the building of an American standard of living. Advertising has expressed the optimism, the hyperbole, and the sense of community, the sense of reaching which has been so important a feature of our civilization.

Here I wish to explore the significance of advertising, not as a force in the economy or in shaping an American standard of living, but rather as a touchstone of the ways in which we Americans have learned about all sorts of things.

The problems of advertising are of course not peculiar to advertising, for they are just one aspect of the problems of democracy. They reflect the rise of what I have called Consumption Communities and Statistical Communities, and many of the special problems of advertising have arisen from our continuously energetic effort to give everybody everything.

If we consider democracy not just as a political system, but as a set of institutions which do aim to make everything available to everybody, it would not be an overstatement to describe advertising as the characteristic rhetoric of democracy. One of the tendencies of democracy, which Plato and other antidemocrats warned against a long time ago, was the danger that rhetoric would displace or at least overshadow epistemology; that is, *the temptation to allow the problem of persuasion to overshadow the problem of knowledge.* Democratic societies tend to become more concerned with what people believe than with what is true, to become more concerned with credibility than with truth. All these problems become accentuated in a large-scale democracy like ours, which possesses all the apparatus of modern industry. And the problems are accentuated still further by universal literacy, by instantaneous communication, and by the daily plague of words and images.

In the early days it was common for advertising men to define advertisements as a kind of news. The best admen, like the best journalists, were supposed to be those who were able to make their news the most interesting and readable. This was natural enough, since the verb to "advertise" originally meant, intransitively, to take note or to consider. For a person to "advertise" meant originally, in the fourteenth and fifteenth centuries, to reflect on something, to think about something. Then it came to mean, transitively, to call the attention of another to do something, to give him notice, to notify, admonish, warn or inform in a formal or impressive manner. And then, by the sixteenth century, it came to mean: to give notice of anything, to make generally known. It was not until the late eighteenth century that the word "advertising" in English came to have a specifically "advertising" connotation as we might say today, and not until the late nineteenth century that it began to have a specifically commercial connotation. By 1879 someone was saying, "don't advertise unless you have something worth advertising." But even into the present century, newspapers continue to call themselves by the title "Advertiser"—for example, the Boston *Daily Advertiser*, which was a newspaper of long tradition and one of the most dignified papers in Boston until William Randolph Hearst took it over in 1917. Newspapers carried "Advertiser" on their mastheads, not because they sold advertisements but because they brought news.

What, then, were some of the main features of modern American advertising—if we consider it as a form of rhetoric? First, and perhaps most obvious, is *repetition*. It is hard for us to realize that the use of repetition in advertising is not an ancient device but a modern one, which actually did not come into common use in American journalism until just past the middle of the nineteenth century.

The development of what came to be called "iteration copy" was a result of a struggle by a courageous man of letters and advertising pioneer, Robert Bonner, who bought the old New York *Merchant's Ledger* in 1851 and turned it into a popular journal. He then had the temerity to try to change the ways of James Gordon Bennett, who of course was one of the most successful of the American newspaper pioneers, and who was both a sensationalist and at the same time an extremely stuffy man when it came to things that he did not consider to be news. Bonner was determined to use advertisements in Bennett's wide-circulating New York *Herald* to sell his own literary product, but he found it difficult to persuade Bennett to allow him to use any but agate type in his advertising. (Agate was the smallest type used by newspapers in that day, only barely legible to the naked eye.) Bennett would not allow advertisers to use larger type, nor would he allow them to use illustrations except stock cuts, because he thought it was undignified. He said, too, that to allow a variation in the format of ads would be undemocratic. He insisted that all advertisers use the same size type so that no one would be allowed to prevail over another simply by presenting his message in a larger, more clever, or more attention-getting form.

Finally Bonner managed to overcome Bennett's rigidity by leasing whole pages of the paper and using the tiny agate type to form larger letters across the top of the page. In this way he produced a message such as "Bring home the New York Ledger tonight." His were unimaginative messages, and when repeated all across the page they technically did not violate Bennett's agate rule. But they opened a new era and presaged a new freedom for advertisers in their use of the newspaper page. Iteration copy—the practice of presenting prosaic content in ingenious, repetitive form—became common, and nowadays of course is commonplace.

A second characteristic of American advertising which is not unrelated to this is the development of *an advertising style*. We have histories of most other kinds of style—including the style of many unread writers who are remembered today only because they have been forgotten—but we have very few accounts of the history of advertising style, which of course is one of the most important forms of our language and one of the most widely influential.

The development of advertising style was the convergence of several very respectable American traditions. One of these was the tradition of the "plain style," which the Puritans made so much of and which accounts for so much of the strength of the Puritan literature. The "plain style" was of course much influenced by the Bible and found its way into the rhetoric of American writers and speakers of great power like Abraham Lincoln. When advertising began to be self-conscious in the early years of this century, the pioneers urged copywriters not to be too clever, and especially not to be fancy. One of the pioneers of the advertising copywriters, John Powers, said, for example, "The commonplace is the proper level for writing in business; where the first virtue is plainness, 'fine writing' is not only intellectual, it is offensive." George P. Rowell, another advertising pioneer, said, "You must write your advertisement to catch damned fools—not college professors." He was a very tactful person. And he added, "And you'll catch just as many college professors as you will of any other sort." In the 1920's, when advertising was beginning to come into its own, Claude Hopkins, whose name is known to all in the trade, said, "Brilliant writing has no place in advertising. A unique style takes attention from the subject. Any apparent effort to sell creates corresponding resistance. . . . One should be natural and simple. His language should not be conspicuous. In fishing for buyers, as in fishing for bass, one should not reveal the hook." So there developed a characteristic advertising style in which plainness, the phrase that anyone could understand, was a distinguishing mark.

At the same time, the American advertising style drew on another, and what might seem an antithetic, tradition—the tradition of hyperbole and tall talk, the language of Davy Crockett and Mike Fink. While advertising could think of itself as 99.44 percent pure, it used the language of "Toronado" and "Cutlass." As I listen to the radio in Washington, I hear a celebration of heroic qualities which would make the characteristics of Mike Fink and Davy Crockett pale, only to discover at the end of the paean that what I have been hearing is a description of the Ford dealers in the District of Columbia neighborhood. And along with the folk tradition of hyperbole and tall talk comes the rhythm of folk music. We hear that Pepsi-Cola hits the spot, that it's for the young generation—and we hear other products celebrated in music which we cannot forget and sometimes don't want to remember.

There grew somehow out of all these contradictory tendencies—combining the commonsense language of the "plain style," and the fantasy language of "tall talk"—an advertising style. This characteristic way of talking about things was especially designed to reach and catch the millions. It created a whole new world of myth. A myth, the dictionary tells us, is a notion based more on tradition or convenience than on facts; it is a received idea. Myth is not just fantasy and not just fact but exists in a limbo, in the world of the "Will to Believe," which William James has written about so eloquently and so perceptively. This is the world of the neither true nor false—of the statement that 60 percent of the physicians who expressed a choice said that our brand of aspirin would be more effective in curing a simple headache than any other leading brand.

That kind of statement exists in a penumbra. I would call this the "advertising penumbra." It is not untrue, and yet, in its connotation it is not exactly true.

Now, there is still another characteristic of advertising so obvious that we are inclined perhaps to overlook it. I call that *ubiquity*. Advertising abhors a vacuum and we discover new vacuums every day. The parable, of course, is the story of the man who thought of putting the advertisement on the other side of the cigarette package. Until then, that was wasted space and a society which aims at a democratic standard of living, at extending the benefits of consumption and all sorts of things and services to everybody, must miss no chances to reach people. The highway billboard and other outdoor advertising, bus and streetcar and subway advertising, and skywriting, radio and TV commercials—all these are of course obvious evidence that advertising abhors a vacuum.

We might reverse the old mousetrap slogan and say that anyone who can devise another place to put another mousetrap to catch a consumer will find people beating a path to his door. "Avoiding advertising will become a little harder next January," the *Wall Street Journal* reported on May 17, 1973, "when a Studio City, California, company launches a venture called Store Vision. Its product is a system of billboards that move on a track across supermarket ceilings. Some 650 supermarkets so far are set to have the system." All of which helps us understand the observation attributed to a French man of letters during his recent visit to Times Square. "What a beautiful place, if only one could not read!" Everywhere is a place to be filled, as we discover in a recent *Publishers Weekly* description of one advertising program: "The $1.95 paperback edition of Dr. Thomas A. Harris' million-copy best seller 'I'm O.K., You're O.K.' is in for full-scale promotion in July by its publisher, Avon Books. Plans range from bumper stickers to airplane streamers, from planes flying above Fire Island, the Hamptons and Malibu. In addition, the $100,000 promotion budget calls for 200,000 bookmarks, plus brochures, buttons, lipcards, floor and counter displays, and advertising in magazines and TV."

The ubiquity of advertising is of course just another effect of our uninhibited efforts to use all the media to get all sorts of information to everybody everywhere. Since the places to be filled are everywhere, the amount of advertising is not determined by the *needs* of advertising, but by the *opportunities* for advertising which become unlimited.

But the most effective advertising, in an energetic, novelty-ridden society like ours, tends to be "self-liquidating." To create a cliché you must offer something which everybody accepts. The most successful advertising therefore self-destructs because it becomes cliché. Examples of this are found in the tendency for copyrighted names of trademarks to enter the vernacular—for the proper names of products which have been made familiar by costly advertising to become common nouns, and so to apply to anybody's products. Kodak becomes a synonym for camera, Kleenex a synonym for facial tissue, when both begin with a small *k*, and

Xerox (now, too, with a small *x*) is used to describe all processes of copying, and so on. These are prototypes of the problem. If you are successful enough, then you will defeat your purpose in the long run—by making the name and the message so familiar that people won't notice them, and then people will cease to distinguish your product from everybody else's.

In a sense, of course, as we will see, the whole of American civilization is an example. When this was a "new" world, if people succeeded in building a civilization here, the New World would survive and would reach the time—in our age—when it would cease to be new. And now we have the oldest written Constitution in use in the world. This is only a parable of which there are many more examples.

The advertising man who is successful in marketing any particular product, then—in our high-technology, well-to-do democratic society, which aims to get everything to everybody—is apt to be diluting the demand for his particular product in the very act of satisfying it. But luckily for him, he is at the very same time creating a fresh demand for his services as advertiser.

And as a consequence, there is yet another role which is assigned to American advertising. This is what I call "erasure." Insofar as advertising is competitive or innovation is widespread, erasure is required in order to persuade consumers that this year's model is superior to last year's. In fact, we consumers learn that we might be risking our lives if we go out on the highway with those very devices that were last year's lifesavers but without whatever special kind of brakes or wipers or seat belt is on this year's model. This is what I mean by "erasure"—and we see it on our advertising pages or our television screen every day. We read in the *New York Times* (May 20, 1973), for example, that "For the price of something small and ugly, you can drive something small and beautiful"—an advertisement for the Fiat 250 Spider. Or another, perhaps more subtle example is the advertisement for shirts under a picture of Oliver Drab: "Oliver Drab. A name to remember in fine designer shirts? No kidding. . . . Because you pay extra money for Oliver Drab. And for all the other superstars of the fashion world. Golden Vee [the name of the brand that is advertised] does not have a designer's label. But we do have designers. . . . By keeping their names *off* our label and simply saying Golden Vee, we can afford to sell our $7 to $12 shirts for just $7 to $12, which should make Golden Vee a name to remember. Golden Vee, you only pay for the shirt."

Having mentioned two special characteristics—the self-liquidating tendency and the need for erasure—which arise from the dynamism of the American economy, I would like to try to place advertising in a larger perspective. The special role of advertising in our life gives a clue to a pervasive oddity in American civilization. A leading feature of past cultures, as anthropologists have explained, is the tendency to distinguish between "high" culture and "low" culture—between the culture of the literate and the learned on the one hand and that of the populace on the other. In other words, between the language of literature and the language of the vernacular. Some of the most useful statements of this distinction have been made by social scientists at the University of Chicago—first by the late Robert Redfield in his several pioneering books on peasant society, and then by Milton Singer in his remarkable study of Indian civilization; When a Great Tradition Modernizes (1972). This distinction between the great tradition and the little tradition, between the high culture and the folk culture, has begun to become a commonplace of modern anthropology.

Some of the obvious features of advertising in modern America offer us an opportunity to note the significance or insignificance of that distinction for us. Elsewhere I have tried to point out some of the peculiarities of the American attitude toward the *high* culture. There is something distinctive about the place of thought in American life, which I think is not quite what it has been in certain Old World cultures.

But what about distinctive American attitudes to *popular* culture? What is our analogue to the folk culture of other peoples? Advertising gives us some clues—to a characteristically American democratic folk culture. Folk culture is a name for the culture which ordinary people everywhere lean on. It is not the writings of Dante and Chaucer and Shakespeare and Milton, the teachings of Machiavelli and Descartes, Locke or Marx. It is, rather, the pattern of slogans, local traditions, tales, songs, dances, and ditties. And of course holiday observances. Popular culture in other civilizations has been for the most part both an area of continuity with the past, a way in which people reach back into the past and out to their community, and at the same time an area of local variations. An area of individual and amateur expression in which a person has his own way of saying, or notes his mother's way of saying or singing, or his own way of dancing, his own view of folk wisdom and the cliché.

And here is an interesting point of contrast. In other societies outside the United States, it is the *high* culture that has generally been an area of centralized, organized control. In Western Europe, for example, universities and churches have tended to be closely allied to the government. The institutions of higher learning have had a relatively limited access to the people as a whole. This was inevitable, of course, in most parts of the world, because there were so few universities. In England, for example, there were only two universities until the early nineteenth century. And there was central control over the printed matter that was used in universities or in the liturgy. The government tended to be close to the high culture, and that was easy because the high culture itself was so centralized and because literacy was relatively limited.

In our society, however, we seem to have turned all of this around. Our high culture is one of the least centralized areas of our culture. And our universities express the atomistic, diffused, chaotic, and individualistic aspect of our life. We have in this country more than twenty-five hundred colleges and universities, institutions of so-called higher learning. We have a vast population in these institutions, somewhere over seven million students.

But when we turn to our popular culture, what do we find? We find that in our nation of Consumption Communities and emphasis on Gross National Product (GNP) and growth rates, advertising has become the heart of the folk culture and even its very prototype. And as we have seen, American advertising shows many characteristics of the folk culture of other societies: repetition, a plain style, hyperbole and tall talk, folk verse, and folk music. Folk culture, wherever it has flourished, has tended to thrive in a limbo between fact and fantasy, and of course, depending on the spoken word and the oral tradition, it spreads easily and tends to be ubiquitous. These are all familiar characteristics of folk culture and they are ways of describing our folk culture, but how do the expressions of our peculiar folk culture come to *us*?

They no longer sprout from the earth, from the village, from the farm, or even from the neighborhood or the city. They come to us primarily from enormous centralized self-consciously *creative* (an overused word, for the overuse of which advertising agencies are in no small part responsible) organizations. They come from advertising agencies, from networks of newspapers, radio, and television, from outdoor-advertising agencies, from the copywriters for ads in the largest-circulation magazines, and so on. These "creators" of folk culture—or pseudo-folk culture—aim at the widest intelligibility and charm and appeal.

But in the United States, we must recall, the advertising folk culture (like all advertising) is also confronted with the problems of self-liquidation and erasure. These are by-products of the expansive, energetic character of our economy. And they, too, distinguish American folk culture from folk cultures elsewhere.

Our folk culture is distinguished from others by being discontinuous, ephemeral, and self-destructive. Where does this leave the common citizen? All of us are qualified to answer.

In our society, then, those who cannot lean on the world of learning, on the high culture of the classics, on the elaborated wisdom of the books, have a new problem. The University of Chicago, for example, in the 1930's and 1940's was the center of a quest for a "common discourse." The champions of that quest, which became a kind of crusade, believed that such a discourse could be found through familiarity with the classics of great literature—and especially of Western European literature. I think they were misled; such works were not, nor are they apt to become, the common discourse of our society. Most people, even in a democracy, and a rich democracy like ours, live in a world of popular culture, our special kind of popular culture.

The characteristic folk culture of our society is a creature of advertising, and in a sense it *is* advertising. But advertising, our own popular culture, is harder to make into a source of continuity than the received wisdom and commonsense slogans and catchy songs of the vivid vernacular. The popular culture of advertising attenuates and is always dissolving before our very eyes. Among the charms, challenges, and tribulations of modern life, we must count this peculiar fluidity, this ephemeral character of that very kind of culture on which other peoples have been able to lean, the kind of culture to which they have looked for the continuity of their traditions, for their ties with the past and with the future.

We are perhaps the first people in history to have a centrally organized mass-produced folk culture. Our kind of popular culture is here today and gone tomorrow—or the day after tomorrow. Or whenever the next semiannual model appears. And insofar as folk culture becomes advertising, and advertising becomes centralized, it becomes a way of depriving people of their opportunities for individual and small-community expression. Our technology and our economy and our democratic ideals have all helped make that possible. Here we have a new test of the problem that is at least as old as Heraclitus—an everyday test of man's ability to find continuity in his experience. And here democratic man has a new opportunity to accommodate himself, if he can, to the unknown.

QUESTIONS FOR READING, RESPONDING, AND WRITING

Summarizing Main Points

1. Do you agree that advertising in America has always promised more than it has delivered? How would Boorstin answer this question?
2. List the main features of modern American advertising and briefly describe them.

Analyzing Methods of Discourse

1. Boorstin provides not only the definition of "advertise," but also its etymology, that is, its historical origin and development. How does that etymology help explain what advertising is today?

2. Boorstin frequently tells his reader what he is about to do or tells them what he has already done. Find examples of these transitional repetitions and explain how they are helpful.

Focusing on the Field

1. Boorstin, in order to describe what he means by "ubiquity," cites statistics from two sources. Find them. How do these statistics and their sources make Boorstin's comments more believable?
2. Boorstin is a noted historian. What part does history play in this essay? A look at other essays by historians (e.g., Alan Bullock's "The Young Adolph Hitler," Barbara Tuchman's "The Trojan Horse," S. E. Morison's "History as a Literary Art") might help you in this regard.

Writing Assignments

1. Boorstin mentions that seventeenth-century English brochures describing America "were full of hopeful overstatements, half-truths, and downright lies." Find contemporary examples of such advertising (e.g., real estate ventures) and prepare a report that supports Boorstin's claims.
2. Boorstin suggests that our Constitution as the "oldest written constitution in the world" is a parable for the "self-liquidating tendency." Comment on how that affects your understanding of the Constitution.

John A. Kouwenhoven

WHAT'S AMERICAN ABOUT AMERICA?

John Kouwenhoven was born in 1909 in Yonkers, New York. He received an M.A. in English from the Harvey School in Hawthorne, New York in 1936 and a Ph.D. in English from Columbia University in 1938. That year, he joined the faculty at Bennington College in Vermont, where he taught literature for three years. In 1947, he became an associate professor at Barnard College, where he has spent a long and distinguished teaching career. For the six years between his appointments at Bennington and Barnard, Kouwenhoven worked as an assistant and associate editor at *Harper's* magazine. Later, he became a contributing editor there.

In addition to devoting himself to his teaching and writing careers, Kouwenhoven has been a trustee of the Rhode Island School of Design, a member of the executive council and advisory council of the Society for the History of Technology, a fellow of Great Britain's Royal Society of Arts, and a member of the American Studies Association, among other organizations. He has also been on the editorial board of *American Quarterly* and has been an advisory editor of *Technology and Culture*.

Kouwenhoven is most well known for his studies in American culture, and has produced several books on the subject. They include *Adventures in America, 1857–1900* (1938), *Made in America: The Arts in Modern Civilization* (1948), *American Panorama* (1957), and *The Beer Can by the Highway* (1961). In the following essay, first published in *Harper's* in 1957, Kouwenhoven sets out to define the quality that makes America American. He takes the reader on a tour of the America he has discovered, one in which, like the Manhattan skyline he finds distinctively American, "an unforeseen unity has evolved" from an "irrational, unplanned, and often infuriating chaos."

The discovery of America has never been a more popular pastime than it is today. Scarcely a week goes by without someone's publishing a new book of travels in the bright continent. The anthropologists, native and foreign, have discovered that the natives of Middletown and Plainville, U. S. A. are as amazing and as interesting as the natives of such better known communities as the Trobriand Islands and Samoa. Magazines here and abroad provide a steady flow of articles by journalists, historians, sociologists, and philosophers who want to explain America to itself, or to themselves, or to others.

The discoverers of America have, of course, been describing their experiences ever since Captain John Smith wrote his first book about America almost 350 years ago. But as Smith himself noted, not everyone "who hath bin at Virginia, understandeth or knowes what Virginia is." Indeed, just a couple of years ago the Carnegie Corporation, which supports a number of college programs in American Studies, entitled its Quarterly Report "Who Knows America?" and went on to imply that nobody does, not even "our lawmakers, journalists, civic leaders, diplomats, teachers, and others."

There is, of course, the possibility that some of the writers who have explored, vicariously or in person, this country's past and present may have come to understand or know what America really is. But how is the lay inquirer and the student to know which accounts to trust? Especially since most of the explorers seem to have found not one but two or more antipodal and irreconcilable Americas. The Americans, we are convincingly told, are the most materialistic of peoples, and, on the other hand, they are the most idealistic; the most revolutionary, and, conversely, the most conservative; the most rampantly individualistic, and, simultaneously, the most gregarious and herd-like; the most irreverent toward their elders, and, contrariwise, the most abject worshipers of "Mom." They have an unbridled admiration of everything big, from bulldozers to bosoms; and they are in love with everything diminutive, from the "small hotel" in the song to the little woman in the kitchen.

Maybe, as Henry James thought when he wrote The American Scene, it is simply that the country is "too large for any human convenience," too diverse in geography and in blood strains to make sense as any sort of unit. Whatever the reason, the conflicting evidence turns up wherever you look, and the observer has to content himself with some sort of pluralistic conception. The philosopher Santayana's way out was to say that the American mind was split in half, one half symbolized by the skyscraper, the other by neat reproductions of Colonial mansions (with surreptitious modern conveniences).

"The American will," he concluded, "inhabits the skyscraper; the American intellect inherits the Colonial mansion." Mark Twain also defined the split in architectural terms, but more succinctly: American houses, he said, had Queen Anne fronts and Mary Ann behinds.

And yet, for all the contrarieties, there remains something which I think we all feel to be distinctively American, some quality or characteristic underlying the polarities which—as Henry James himself went on to say—makes the American way of doing things differ more from any other nation's way than the ways of any two other Western nations differ from each other.

I am aware of the risks in generalizing. And yet it would be silly, I am convinced, to assert that there are not certain things which are more American than others. Take the New York City skyline, for example—that ragged man-made Sierra at the eastern edge of the continent. Clearly, in the minds of immigrants and returning travelers, in the iconography of the ad-men who use it as a backdrop for the bourbon and airplane luggage they are selling, in the eyes of poets and of military strategists, it is one of the prime American symbols.

Let me start, then, with the Manhattan skyline and list a few things which occur to me as distinctively American. Then, when we have the list, let us see what, if anything, these things have in common. Here are a dozen items to consider:

1. The Manhattan skyline
2. The gridiron town plan
3. The skyscraper
4. The Model-T Ford
5. Jazz
6. The Constitution
7. Mark Twain's writing
8. Whitman's *Leaves of Grass*
9. Comic strips
10. Soap operas
11. Assembly-line production
12. Chewing gum

Here we have a round dozen artifacts which are, it seems to me, recognizably American, not likely to have been produced elsewhere. Granted that some of us take more pleasure in some of them than in others—that many people prefer soap opera to *Leaves of Grass* while others think Mark Twain's storytelling is less offensive than chewing gum—all twelve items are, I believe, widely held to be indigenous to our culture. The fact that many people in other lands like them too, and that some of them are nearly as acceptable overseas as they are here at home, does not in any way detract from their obviously American character. It merely serves to remind us that to be American does not mean to be inhuman—a fact which, in certain moods of self-criticism, we are inclined to forget.

What, then, is the "American" quality which these dozen items share? And what can that quality tell us about the character of our culture, about the nature of our civilization?

SKYLINES AND SKYSCRAPERS

Those engaged in discovering America often begin by discovering the Manhattan skyline, and here as well as elsewhere they discover apparently irreconcilable opposites. They notice at once that it doesn't make any sense, in human or aesthetic terms. It is the product of insane politics, greed, competitive ostentation, megalomania, the worship of false gods. Its products, in turn, are traffic jams, bad ventilation, noise, and all the other ills that metropolitan flesh is heir to. And the net result is, illogically enough, one of the most exaltedly beautiful things man has ever made.

Perhaps this paradoxical result will be less bewildering if we look for a moment at the formal and structural principles which are involved in the skyline. It may be helpful to consider the skyline as we might consider a lyric poem, or a novel, if we were trying to analyze its aesthetic quality.

Looked at in this way, it is clear that the total effect which we call "the Manhattan skyline" is made up of almost innumerable buildings, each in competition (for height, or glamor, or efficiency, or respectability) with all of the others. Each goes its own way, as it were, in a carnival of rugged architectural individualism. And yet—as witness the universal feeling of exaltation and aspiration which the skyline as a whole evokes—out of this irrational, unplanned, and often infuriating chaos, an unforeseen unity has evolved. No building ever built in New York was placed where it was, or shaped as it was, because it would contribute to the aesthetic effect of the skyline—lifting it here, giving it mass there, or lending a needed emphasis. Each was built, all those now under construction are being built, with no thought for their subordination to any over-all effect.

What, then, makes possible the fluid and everchanging unity which does, in fact, exist? Quite simply, there are two things, both simple in themselves, which do the job. If they were not simple, they would not work; but they are, and they do.

One is the gridiron pattern of the city's streets—the same basic pattern which accounts for Denver, Houston, Little Rock, Birmingham, and almost any American town you can name, and the same pattern which, in the form of square townships, sections, and quarter sections, was imposed by the Ordinance of 1785 on an almost continental scale. Whatever its shortcomings when compared with the "discontinuous street patterns" of modern planned communities, this artificial geometric grid—imposed upon the land without regard to contours or any preconceived pattern of social zoning—had at least the quality of rational simplicity. And it is this simple gridiron street pattern which, horizontally, controls the spacing and arrangement of the rectangular shafts which go to make up the skyline.

The other thing which holds the skyline's diversity together is the structural principle of the skyscraper. When we think of individual buildings, we tend to think of details of texture, color, and form, of surface ornamentation or the lack of it. But as elements in Manhattan's skyline, these things are of little consequence. What matters there is the vertical thrust, the motion upward; and that is the product of cage or skeleton, construction in steel—a system of construction which is, in effect, merely a three-dimensional variant of the gridiron street plan, extending vertically instead of horizontally.

The aesthetics of cage, or skeleton, construction have never been fully analyzed, nor am I equipped to analyze them. But as a lay observer, I am struck by fundamental differences between the effect created by height in the RCA building at Radio City, for example, and the effect created by height in Chartres cathedral or in Giotto's campanile. In both the latter (as in all the great architecture of the past) proportion and symmetry, the relation of height to width, are constituent to the effect. One can say of a Gothic cathedral, "This tower is too high"; of a Romanesque dome, "This is top-heavy." But there is nothing inherent in cage construction which would invite such judgments. A true skyscraper like the RCA building could be eighteen or twenty stories taller, or ten or a dozen stories shorter without changing its essential aesthetic effect. Once steel cage construction has passed a certain height, the effect of transactive upward motion has been established; from there on, the point at which you cut it off is arbitrary and makes no difference.

Those who are familiar with the history of the skyscraper will remember how slowly this fact was realized. Even Louis Sullivan—greatest of the early skyscraper architects—thought in terms of having to close off and climax the upward motion of the tall building with an "attic" or cornice. His lesser contemporaries worked for years on the blind assumption that the proportion and symmetry of masonry architecture must be preserved in the new technique. If with the steel cage one could go higher than with load-bearing masonry walls, the old aesthetic effects could be counterfeited by dressing the façade as if one or more buildings had been piled on top of another—each retaining the illusion of being complete in itself. You can still see such buildings in New York: the first five stories perhaps a Greco-Roman temple, the next ten a neuter warehouse, and the final five or six an Aztec pyramid. And that Aztec pyramid is simply a cheap and thoughtless equivalent of the more subtle Sullivan cornice. Both structures attempt to close and climax the upward thrust, to provide something similar to the *Katharsis* in Greek tragedy.

But the logic of cage construction requires no such climax. It has less to do with the inner logic of masonry forms than with that of the old Globe-Wernicke sectional bookcases, whose interchangeable units (with glass-flap fronts) anticipated by fifty years the modular unit systems of so-called modern furniture. Those bookcases were advertised in the 'nineties as "always complete but never finished"—a phrase which could with equal propriety have been applied to the Model-T Ford. Many of us remember with affection that admirably simple mechanism, forever susceptible to added gadgets or improved parts, each of which was interchangeable with what you already had.

Here, then, are the two things which serve to tie together the otherwise irrelevant components of the Manhattan skyline: the gridiron ground plan and the three-dimensional vertical grid of steel cage construction. And both of these are closely related to one another. Both are composed of simple and infinitely repeatable units.

THE STRUCTURE OF JAZZ

It was the French architect, Le Corbusier, who described New York's architecture as "hot jazz in stone and steel." At first glance this may sound as if it were merely a slick updating of Schelling's "Architecture . . . is frozen music," but it is more than that if one thinks in terms of the structural principles we have been discussing and the structural principles of jazz.

Let me begin by making clear that I am using the term jazz in its broadest significant application. There are circumstances in which it is important to define the term with considerable precision, as when you are involved in discussion with a disciple of one of the many cults, orthodox or progressive, which devote themselves to some particular subspecies of jazz. But in our present context we need to focus upon what all the subspecies (Dixieland, Bebop, Swing, or Cool Jazz) have in common; in other words, we must neglect the by no means uninteresting qualities which differentiate one from another, since it is what they have in common which can tell us most about the civilization which produced them.

There is no definition of jazz, academic or otherwise, which does not acknowledge that its essential ingredient is a particular kind of rhythm. Improvisation is also frequently mentioned as an essential; but even if it were true that jazz always involves improvisation, that would not distinguish it from a good deal of Western European music of the past. It is the distinctive rhythm which differentiates all types of jazz from all other music and which gives to all of its types a basic family resemblance.

It is not easy to define that distinctive rhythm. Winthrop Sargeant has described it as the product of two superimposed devices: syncopation and polyrhythm, both of which have the effect of constantly upsetting rhythmical expectations. André Hodeir, in his recent analysis, *Jazz: Its Evolution and Essence*, speaks of "an unending alternation" of syncopations and of notes played *on* the beat, which "gives rise to a kind of expectation that is one of jazz's subtlest effects."

As you can readily hear, if you listen to any jazz performance (whether of the Louis Armstrong, Benny Goodman, or Charlie Parker variety), the rhythmical effect depends upon there being a clearly defined basic rhythmic pattern which enforces the expectations which are to be upset. That basic pattern is the ¼ or ¾ beat which underlies all jazz. Hence the importance of the percussive instruments in jazz: the drums, the guitar or banjo, the bull fiddle, the piano. Hence too the insistent thump, thump, thump, thump which is so boring when you only half-hear jazz—either because you are too far away, across the lake or in the next room, or simply because you will not listen attentively. But hence also the delight, the subtle effects, which good jazz provides as the melodic phrases evade, anticipate, and return to, and then again evade the steady basic four-beat pulse which persists, implicitly or explicitly, throughout the performance.

In other words, the structure of a jazz performance is, like that of the New York skyline, a tension of cross-purposes. In jazz at its characteristic best, each player seems to be—and has the sense of being—on his own. Each goes his own way, inventing rhythmic and melodic patterns which, superficially, seem to have as little relevance to one another as the United Nations building does to the Empire State. And yet the outcome is a dazzlingly precise creative unity.

In jazz that unity of effect is, of course, the result of the very thing which each of the players is flouting: namely, the basic ¼ beat—that simple rhythmic gridiron of identical and infinitely extendible units which holds the performance together. As Louis Armstrong once wrote, you would expect that if every man in a band "had his own way and could play as he wanted, all you would get would be a lot of jumbled up, crazy noise." But, as he goes on to say, that does not happen, because the players know "by ear and sheer musical instinct" just when to leave the underlying pattern and when to get back on it.

What it adds up to, as I have argued elsewhere, is that jazz is the first art form to give full expression to Emerson's ideal of a union which is perfect only "when all the uniters are isolated." That Emerson's ideal is deeply rooted in our national experience need not be argued. Frederick Jackson Turner quotes a letter written by a frontier settler to friends back East, which in simple, unself-conscious words expresses the same reconciling of opposites. "It is a universal rule here," the frontiersman wrote, "to help one another, each one keeping an eye single to his own business."

One need only remember that the Constitution itself, by providing for a federation of separate units, became the infinitely extendible framework for the process of reconciling liberty and unity over vast areas and conflicting interests. Its seven brief articles, providing for checks and balances between interests, classes, and branches of the government establish, in effect, the underlying beat which gives momentum and direction to a political process which Richard Hofstadter has called "a harmonious system of mutual frustration"—a description which fits a jazz performance as well as it fits our politics.

The aesthetic effects of jazz, as Winthrop Sargeant long ago suggested, have as little to do with symmetry and proportion as have those of a skyscraper. Like the skyscraper, a jazz performance does not build to an organically required climax; it can simply cease. The "piece" which the musicians are playing may, and often does, have a rudimentary Aristotelian pattern of beginning, middle, and end; but the jazz performance need not. In traditional Western European music, themes are developed. In jazz they are toyed with and dismantled. There is no inherent reason why the jazz performance should not continue for another 12 or 16 or 24 or 32 measures (for these are the rhythmic cages which in jazz correspond to the cages of a steel skeleton in architecture). As in the skyscraper, the aesthetic effect is one of motion, in this case horizontal rather than vertical.

Jazz rhythms create what can only be called momentum. When the rhythm of one voice (say the trumpet, off on a rhythmic and melodic excursion) lags behind the underlying beat, its four-beat measure carries over beyond the end of the underlying beat's measure into the succeeding one, which has already begun. Conversely, when the trumpet anticipates the beat, it starts a new measure before the steady underlying beat has ended one. And the result is an exhilarating forward motion which the jazz trumpeter Wingy Manone once described as "feeling an increase in tempo though you're still playing at the same tempo." Hence the importance in jazz of timing, and hence the delight and amusement of the so-called "break," in which the basic ¼ beat ceases and a soloist goes off on a flight of rhythmic and melodic fancy which nevertheless comes back surprisingly and unerringly to encounter the beat precisely where it would have been if it had kept going.

Once the momentum is established, it can continue until—after an interval dictated by some such external factor as the conventional length of phonograph records or the endurance of dancers—it stops. And as if to guard against any Aristotelian misconceptions about an end, it is likely to stop on an unresolved chord, so that harmonically as well as rhythmically everything is left up in the air. Even the various coda-like devices employed by jazz performers at dances, such as the corny old "without a shirt" phrase of blessed memory, are harmonically unresolved. They are merely conventional ways of saying "we quit," not, like Beethoven's insistent codas, ways of saying, "There now; that ties off all the loose ends; I'm going to stop now; done; finished; concluded; signed, sealed, delivered."

TWAIN AND WHITMAN

Thus far, in our discussion of distinctively "American" things, we have focused chiefly upon twentieth-century items. But the references to the rectangular grid pattern of cities and townships and to the Constitution should remind us that the underlying structural principles with which we are concerned are deeply embedded in our civilization. To shift the emphasis, therefore, let us look at item number 7 on our list: Mark Twain's writing.

Mark's writing was, of course, very largely the product of oral influences. He was a born story-teller, and he always insisted that the oral form of the humorous story was high art. Its essential tool (or weapon), he said, is the pause—which is to say, timing. "If the pause is too long the impressive point is passed," he wrote, "and the audience have had time to divine that a surprise is intended—and then you can't surprise them, of course." In other words, he saw the pause as a device for upsetting expectations, like the jazz "break."

Mark, as you know, was by no means a formal perfectionist. In fact he took delight in being irreverent about literary form. Take, for example, his account of the way *Pudd'nhead Wilson* came into being. It started out to be a story called "Those Extraordinary Twins," about a youthful freak consisting, as he said, of "a combination of two heads and four arms joined to a single body and a single pair of legs and I thought I would write an extravagantly fantastic little story with this freak of nature for hero—or heroes—a silly young miss [named Rowena] for heroine, and two old ladies and two boys for the minor parts."

But as he got writing the tale, it kept spreading along and other people began intruding themselves—among them Pudd'nhead, and a woman named Roxana, and a young fellow named Tom Driscoll, who—before the book was half finished—had taken things almost entirely into their own hands and were "working the whole tale as a private venture of their own."

From this point, I want to quote Mark directly, because in the process of making fun of fiction's formal conventions he employs a technique which is the verbal equivalent of the jazz "break"—a technique of which he was a master.

When the book was finished, and I came to look round to see what had become of the team I had originally started out with—Aunt Patsy Cooper, Aunt Betsy Hale, the two boys, and Rowena, the light-weight heroine—they were nowhere to be seen; they had disappeared from the story some time or other. I hunted about and found them—found them stranded, idle, forgotten, and permanently useless. It was very awkward. It was awkward all around; but more particularly in the case of Rowena, because there was a love match on, between her and one of the twins that constituted the freak, and I had worked it up to a blistering heat and thrown in a quite dramatic love quarrel [now watch Mark take off like a jazz trumpeter flying off on his own in a fantastic break] wherein Rowena scathingly denounced her betrothed for getting drunk, and scoffed at his explanation of how it had happened, and wouldn't listen to it, and had driven him from her in the usual "forever" way; and now here she sat crying and broken-hearted; for she had found that he had spoken only the truth; that it was not he but the other half of the freak, that had drunk the liquor that made him drunk; that her half was a prohibitionist and had never drunk a drop in his life, and, although tight as a brick three days in the week, was wholly innocent of blame; and, indeed, when sober was constantly doing all he could to reform his brother, the other half, who never got any satisfaction out of drinking anyway, because liquor never affected him. [Now he's going to get back on the basic beat again.] Yes, here she was, stranded with that deep injustice of hers torturing her poor heart.

Now I shall have to summarize again. Mark didn't know what to do with her. He couldn't just leave her there, of course, after making such a to-do over her; he'd have to account to the reader for her somehow. So he finally decided that all he could do was "give her the grand bounce." It grieved him, because he'd come to like her after a fashion, "notwithstanding she was such an ass and said such stupid, irritating things and was so nauseatingly sentimental"; but it had to be done. So he started Chapter Seventeen with: "Rowena went out in the back yard after supper to see the fireworks and fell down the well and got drowned."

It seemed abrupt, [Mark went on] but I thought maybe the reader wouldn't notice it, because I changed the subject right away to something else. Anyway, it loosened up Rowena from where she was stuck and got her out of the way, and that was the main thing. It seemed a prompt good way of weeding out people that had got stalled, and a plenty good enough way for those others; so I hunted up the two boys and said they went out back one night to stone the cat and fell down the well and got drowned. Next I searched around and found Aunt Patsy Cooper and Aunt Betsy Hale where they were aground, and said they went out back one night to visit the sick and fell down the well and got drowned. I was going to drown some of the others, but I gave up the idea, partly because I believed that if I kept that up it would arouse attention, . . . and partly because it was not a large well and would not hold any more anyway.

That was a long excursion—but it makes the point: that Mark didn't have much reverence for conventional story structure. Even his greatest book, which is perhaps also the greatest book written on this continent—*Huckleberry Finn*—is troublesome. One can scarcely find a criticism of the book which does not object, for instance, to the final episodes, in which Tom rejoins Huck and they go through that burlesque business of "freeing" the old Negro Jim—who is, it turns out, already free. But, as T. S. Eliot was, I think, the first to observe, the real structure of *Huck Finn* has nothing to do with the traditional form of the novel—with exposition, climax, and resolution. Its structure is like that of the great river itself—without beginning and without end. Its structural units, or "cages," are the episodes of which it is composed. Its momentum is that of the tension between the river's steady flow and the eccentric superimposed rhythms of Huck's flights from, and near recapture by, the restricting forces of routine and convention.

It is not a novel of escape; if it were, it would be Jim's novel, not Huck's. Huck is free at the start, and still free at the end. Looked at in this way, it is clear that *Huckleberry Finn* has as little need of a "conclusion" as has a skyscraper or a jazz performance. Questions of proportion and symmetry are as irrelevant to its structure as they are to the total effect of the New York skyline.

There is not room here for more than brief reference to the other "literary" items on our list: Whitman's *Leaves of Grass*, comic strips, and soap opera. Perhaps it is enough to remind you that *Leaves of Grass* has discomfited many a critic by its lack of symmetry and proportion, and that Whitman himself insisted: "I round and finish little, if anything; and could not, consistently with my scheme." As for the words of true poems, Whitman said in the "Song of the Answerer"—

> They bring none to his or her terminus or to be content and full,
> Whom they take they take into space to behold the birth of stars, to
>   learn one of the meanings,
> To launch off with absolute faith, to sweep through the ceaseless
>   rings and never be quiet again.

Although this is not the place for a detailed analysis of Whitman's verse techniques, it is worth noting in passing how the rhythm of these lines reinforces their logical meaning. The basic rhythmical unit, throughout, is a three-beat phrase of which there are two in the first line (accents falling on *none*, *his*, and *term* . . . *be*, *tent*, and *full*), three in the second and in the third. Superimposed upon the basic three-beat measure there is a flexible, nonmetrical rhythm of colloquial phrasing. That rhythm is controlled in part by the visual effect of the arrangement in long lines, to each of which the reader tends to give equal duration, and in part by the punctuation within the lines.

It is the tension between the flexible, superimposed rhythms of the rhetorical patterns and the basic three-beat measure of the underlying framework which unites with the imagery and the logical meaning of the words to give the passage its restless, sweeping movement. It is this tension, and other analogous aspects of the structure of *Leaves of Grass* which give to the book that "vista" which Whitman himself claimed for it. If I may apply to it T. S. Eliot's idea about *Huckleberry Finn*, the structure of the *Leaves* is open at the end. Its key poem may well be, as D. H. Lawrence believed, the "Song of the Open Road."

As for the comics and soap opera, they too—on their own frequently humdrum level—have devised structures which provide for no ultimate climax, which come to no end demanded by symmetry or proportion. In them both there is a shift in interest away from the "How does it come out?" of traditional story telling to "How are things going?" In a typical installment of Harold Gray's *Orphan Annie*, the final panel shows Annie walking purposefully down a path with her dog, Sandy, saying: "But if we're goin', why horse around? It's a fine night for walkin' . . . C'mon, Sandy . . . Let's go . . ." (It doesn't even end with a period, or full stop, but with the conventional three dots or suspension points, to indicate incompletion.) So too, in the soap operas, *Portia Faces Life*, in one form or another, day after day, over and over again. And the operative word is the verb *faces*. It is the process of facing that matters.

AMERICA IS PROCESS

Here, I think, we are approaching the central quality which all the diverse items on our list have in common. That quality I would define as a concern with process rather than with product—or, to re-use Mark Twain's words, a concern with the manner of handling experience or materials rather than with the experience or materials themselves. Emerson, a century ago, was fascinated by the way "becoming somewhat else is the perpetual game of nature." And this preoccupation with process is, of course, basic to modern science. "Matter" itself is no longer to be thought of as something fixed, but fluid and ever-changing. Similarly, modern economic theory has abandoned the "static equilibrium" analysis of the neo-classic economists, and in philosophy John Dewey's instrumentalism abandoned the classic philosophical interest in final causes for a scientific interest in "the mechanism of occurrences"—that is, process.

It is obvious, I think, that the American system of industrial mass production reflects this same focus of interest in its concern with production rather than products. And it is the mass-production system, *not* machinery, which has been America's contribution to industry.

In that system there is an emphasis different from that which was characteristic of handicraft production or even of machine manufacture. In both of these there was an almost total disregard of the means of production. The aristocratic ideal inevitably relegated interest in the means exclusively to anonymous peasants and slaves; what mattered to those who controlled and administered production was, quite simply, the finished product. In a mass-production system, on the other hand, it is the process of production itself which becomes the center of interest, rather than the product.

If we are aware of this fact, we usually regard it as a misfortune. We hear a lot, for instance, of the notion that our system "dehumanizes" the worker, turning him into a machine and depriving him of the satisfactions of finishing anything, since he performs only some repetitive operation. It is true that the unit of work in mass production is not a product but an operation. But the development of the system, in contrast with Charlie Chaplin's wonderful but wild fantasy of the assembly line, has shown the intermediacy of the stage in which the worker is doomed to frustrating boredom. Merely repetitive work, in the logic of mass production, can and must be done by machine. It is unskilled work which is doomed by it, not the worker. More and more skilled workers are needed to design products, analyze jobs, cut patterns, attend complicated machines, and co-ordinate the processes which comprise the productive system.

The skills required for these jobs are different, of course, from those required to make handmade boots or to carve stone ornament, but they are not in themselves less interesting or less human. Operating a crane in a steel mill, or a turret lathe, is an infinitely more varied and stimulating job than shaping boots day after day by hand. A recent study of a group of workers on an automobile assembly line makes it clear that many of the men object, for a variety of reasons, to those monotonous, repetitive jobs which (as we have already noted) should be—but in many cases are not yet—done by machine; but those who *like* such jobs like them because they enjoy the process. As one of them said: "Repeating the same thing you can catch up and keep ahead of yourself . . . you can get in the swing of it." The report of members of a team of British workers who visited twenty American steel foundries in 1949 includes this description of the technique of "snatching" a steel casting with a magnet, maneuvered by a gantry crane running on overhead rails:

> In its operation, the crane approaches a pile of castings at high speed with the magnet hanging fairly near floor level. The crane comes to a stop somewhere short of the castings, while the magnet swings forward over the pile, is dropped onto it, current switched on, and the hoist begun, at the same moment as the crane starts on its return journey. [And then, in words which might equally be applied to a jazz musician, the report adds:] The

whole operation requires timing of a high order, and the impression gained is that the crane drivers derive a good deal of satisfaction from the swinging rhythm of the process.

This fascination with process has possessed Americans ever since Oliver Evans in 1785 created the first wholly automatic factory: a flour mill in Delaware in which mechanical conveyors—belt conveyors, bucket conveyors, screw conveyors—are interlinked with machines in a continuous process of production. But even if there were no other visible sign of the national preoccupation with process, it would be enough to point out that it was an American who invented chewing gum (in 1869) and that it is the Americans who have spread it—in all senses of the verb—throughout the world. An absolutely nonconsumable confection, its sole appeal is the process of chewing it.

The apprehensions which many people feel about a civilization absorbed with process—about its mobility and wastefulness as well as about the "dehumanizing" effects of its jobs—derive, I suppose, from old habit and the persistence of values and tastes which were indigenous to a very different social and economic system. Whitman pointed out in *Democratic Vistas* more than eighty years ago that America was a stranger in her own house, that many of our social institutions, like our theories of literature and art, had been taken over almost without change from a culture which was not, like ours, the product of political democracy and the machine. Those institutions and theories, and the values implicit in them, are still around, though some (like collegiate gothic, of both the architectural and intellectual variety) are less widely admired than formerly.

Change, or the process of consecutive occurrences, is, we tend to feel, a bewildering and confusing and lonely thing. All of us, in some moods, feel the "preference for the stable over the precarious and un-completed" which, as John Dewey recognized, tempts philosophers to posit their absolutes. We talk fondly of the need for roots—as if man were a vegetable, not an animal with legs whose distinction it is that he can move and "get on with it." We would do well to make ourselves more familiar with the idea that the process of development is universal, that it is "the form and order of nature." As Lancelot Law Whyte has said, in *The Next Development in Man:*

> Man shares the special form of the universal formative process which is common to all organisms, and herein lies the root of his unity with the rest of organic nature. While life is maintained, the component processes in man never attain the relative isolation and static perfection of inorganic pro-cesses . . . The individual may seek, or believe that he seeks, independence, permanence, or perfection, but that is only through his failure to recognize and accept his actual situation.

As an "organic system" man cannot, of course, expect to achieve stability or permanent harmony, though he can create (and in the great arts of the past, has created) the illusion of them. What he can achieve is a continuing development in response to his environment. The factor which gives vitality to all the component processes in the individual and in society is "not permanence but development."

To say this is not to deny the past. It is simply to recognize that for a variety of reasons people living in America have, on the whole, been better able to relish process than those who have lived under the imposing shadow of the arts and institutions which Western man created in his tragic search for permanence and perfection—for a "closed system." They find it easy to understand what that very American philosopher William James meant when he told his sister that his house in Chocorua, New Hampshire, was "the most delightful house you ever saw; it has fourteen doors, all opening outwards." They are used to living in grid-patterned cities and towns whose streets, as Jean-Paul Sartre observed, are not, like those of European cities, "closed at both ends." As Sartre says in his essay on New York, the long straight streets and avenues of a gridiron city do not permit the buildings to "cluster like sheep" and protect one against the sense of space. "They are not sober little walks closed in between houses, but national highways. The moment you set foot on one of them, you understand that it has to go on to Boston or Chicago."

So, too, the past of those who live in the United States, like their future, is open-ended. It does not, like the past of most other people, extend downward into the soil out of which their immediate community or neighborhood has grown. It extends laterally backward across the plains, the mountains, or the sea to somewhere else, just as their future may at any moment lead them down the open road, the endless-vistaed street.

Our history is the process of motion into and out of cities; of westering and the counter-process of return; of motion up and down the social ladder—a long, complex, and sometimes terrifyingly rapid sequence of consecutive change. And it is this sequence, and the attitudes and habits and forms which it has bred, to which the term "America" really refers.

"America" is not a synonym for the United States. It is not an artifact. It is not a fixed and immutable ideal toward which citizens of this nation strive. It has not order or proportion, but neither is it chaos except as that is chaotic whose components no single mind can comprehend or control. America is process. And in so far as people have been "American"—as distinguished from being (as most of us, in at least some of our activities, have been) mere carriers of transplanted cultural traditions—the concern with process has been reflected in the work of their heads and hearts and hands.

QUESTIONS FOR READING, RESPONDING, AND WRITING

Summarizing Main Points

1. Just before he begins his discussion of the items on his list, Kouwenhoven asks two questions: "What, then, is the 'American' quality which these dozen items share? And what can that quality tell us about the character of our culture, about the nature of our civilization?" Locate his answers to these questions. Do you agree with him?

2. What are the "underlying structural principles" that Kouwenhoven thinks are "deeply embedded in our civilization"? List examples of these principles. Does their number and the many forms they take throughout the essay convince you that they are "deeply embedded"? Why or why not?

Analyzing Methods of Discourse

1. Kouwenhoven states that "those engaged in discovering America often begin by discovering the Manhattan skyline." Why do you suppose Kouwenhoven starts with the Manhattan skyline? How does he build his essay on this beginning? Do you think it would have mattered had he begun with his discussion of jazz? Why or why not?

2. Kouwenhoven describes the way in which jazz rhythms create momentum: "When the rhythm of one voice . . . lags behind the underlying beat, its four-beat measure carries over beyond the end of the underlying beat's measure into the succeeding one, which has already begun. Conversely, when the trumpet anticipates the beat, it starts a new measure before the steady underlying beat has ended one." How does Kouwenhoven structure his essay to create this same effect?

Focusing on the Field

1. Kouwenhoven uses a variety of vocabularies in this essay (e.g., architectural, musical, literary) and often overlaps them in the same paragraph. Find such a paragraph and consider how this strategy affects the content of the paragraph, how it supports his main points.

2. Kouwenhoven paints a very positive picture of America as "process." Yet, he published this essay in 1957. From your position in the eighties, evaluate his argument for America as process. Is this same largely positive view possible today? Why or why not?

Writing Assignments

1. Choose an item to add to Kouwenhoven's list and discuss, as he does, the ways in which that item is "distinctly American."

2. Write an essay in which you discuss the ways in which shopping centers, as Joan Didion describes them in "On the Mall," demonstrate the American qualities that Kouwenhoven defines and describes.

Nora Ephron

THE BOSTON PHOTOGRAPHS

Nora Ephron's life has always made good copy and seems often to have been about the production of good copy. Born in 1941 to screenwriter parents, who based a successful play "Take Her, She's Mine" on her letters home from Wellesley College, Ephron went on to pursue her own writing career after college. From 1963 to 1972, she worked as a reporter and free-lancer for the *New York Post,* before becoming a contributing editor and columnist for *Esquire* magazine. She moved to *New York* magazine for a year as a contributing editor, but returned to *Esquire* as a senior editor and columnist. She produced essays on a wide variety of topics, and many of her best have been collected in *Wallflower at the Orgy* (1970), *Crazy Salad* (1975), and *Scribble, Scribble* (1979).

In 1983, Ephron wrote both a screenplay, for which she and coauthor Alice Arden received an Academy Award nomination, and a novel, *Heartburn,* a thinly disguised account of her much publicized breakup with journalist Carl Bernstein over his affair with an ambassador's wife. Though the confessional nature of the novel shocked some critics, it really should have come with little surprise from a writer who had been acclaimed for her acerbic and often autobiographical essays, and who had been taught during childhood to take notes on her life because "everything makes good copy." In the following essay, Ephron takes this rule on copy and applies it to the profession of photojournalism, as she reflects on why various newspapers decided to print "The Boston Photographs."

"I made all kinds of pictures because I thought it would be a good rescue shot over the ladder . . . never dreamed it would be anything else . . . I kept having to move around because of the light set. The sky was bright and they were in deep shadow. I was making pictures with a motor drive and he, the fire fighter, was reaching up and, I don't know, everything started falling. I followed the girl down taking pictures . . . I made three or four frames. I realized what was going on and I completely turned around, because I didn't want to see her hit."

You probably saw the photographs. In most newspapers, there were three of them. The first showed some people on a fire escape—a fireman, a woman and a child. The fireman had a nice strong jaw and looked very brave. The woman was holding the child. Smoke was pouring from the building behind them. A rescue ladder was approaching, just a few feet away, and the fireman had one arm around the woman and one arm reaching out toward the ladder. The second picture showed the fire escape slipping off the building. The child had fallen on the escape and seemed about to slide off the edge. The woman was grasping desperately

Stanley Forman, Pulitzer Prize 1975

at the legs of the fireman, who had managed to grab the ladder. The third picture showed the woman and child in midair, falling to the ground. Their arms and legs were outstretched, horribly distended. A potted plant was falling too. The caption said that the woman, Diana Bryant, nineteen, died in the fall. The child landed on the woman's body and lived.

The pictures were taken by Stanley Forman, thirty, of the *Boston Herald American*. He used a motor-driven Nikon F set at ½₅₀, f5.6-S Because of the motor, the camera can click off three frames a second. More than four hundred newspapers in the United States alone carried the photographs: the tear sheets from overseas are still coming in. The *New York Times* ran them on the first page of its second section; a paper in south Georgia gave them nineteen columns; the *Chicago Tribune*, the *Washington Post* and the *Washington Star* filled almost half their front pages, the *Star* under a somewhat redundant headline that read: SENSATIONAL PHOTOS OF RESCUE ATTEMPT THAT FAILED.

The photographs are indeed sensational. They are pictures of death in action, of that split second when luck runs out, and it is impossible to look at them without feeling their extraordinary impact and remembering, in an almost subconscious way, the morbid fantasy of falling, falling off a building, falling to one's death. Beyond that, the pictures are classics, old-fashioned but perfect examples of photojournalism at its most spectacular. They're throwbacks, really, fire pictures, 1930s tabloid shots; at the same time they're technically superb and thoroughly modern—the sequence could not have been taken at all until the development of the motor-driven camera some sixteen years ago.

Most newspaper editors anticipate some reader reaction to photographs like Forman's; even so, the response around the country was enormous, and almost all of it was negative. I have read hundreds of the letters that were printed in letters-to-the-editor sections, and they repeat the same points. "Invading the privacy of death." "Cheap sensationalism." "I thought I was reading the *National Enquirer*." "Assigning the agony of a human being in terror of imminent death to the status of a side-show act." "A tawdry way to sell newspapers." The *Seattle Times* received sixty letters and calls; its managing editor even got a couple of them at home. A reader wrote the *Philadelphia Inquirer:* "*Jaws* and *Towering Inferno* are playing downtown; don't take business away from people who pay good money to advertise in your own paper." Another reader wrote the *Chicago Sun-Times:* "I shall try to hide my disappointment that Miss Bryant wasn't wearing a skirt when she fell to her death. You could have had some award-winning photographs of her underpants as her skirt billowed over her head, you voyeurs." Several newspaper editors wrote columns defending the pictures: Thomas Keevil of the *Costa Mesa* (California) *Daily Pilot* printed a ballot for readers to vote on whether they would have printed the pictures; Marshall L. Stone of Maine's *Bangor Daily News*, which refused to print the famous assassination picture of the Vietcong prisoner in Saigon, claimed that the Boston pictures showed the dangers of fire escapes and raised questions about slumlords. (The burning building was a five-story brick apartment house on Marlborough Street in the Back Bay section of Boston.)

For the last five years, the *Washington Post* has employed various journalists as ombudsmen, whose job is to monitor the paper on behalf of the public. The *Post*'s current ombudsman is Charles Seib, former managing editor of the *Washington Star*; the day the Boston photographs appeared, the paper received over seventy calls in protest. As Seib later wrote in a column about the pictures, it was "the largest reaction to a published item that I have experienced in eight months as the *Post*'s ombudsman. . . .

"In the *Post*'s newsroom, on the other hand, I found no doubts, no second thoughts . . . the question was not whether they should be printed but how they should be displayed. When I talked to editors . . . they used words like 'interesting' and 'riveting' and 'gripping' to describe them. The pictures told of something about life in the ghetto, they said (although the neighborhood where the tragedy occurred is not a ghetto, I am told). They dramatized the need to check on the safety of fire escapes. They dramatically conveyed something that had happened, and that is the business we're in. They were news. . . .

"Was publication of that [third] picture a bow to the same taste for the morbidly sensational that makes gold mines of disaster movies? Most papers will not print the picture of a dead body except in the most unusual circumstances. Does the fact that the final picture was taken a millisecond before the young woman died make a difference? Most papers will not print a picture of a bare female breast. Is that a more inappropriate subject for display than the picture of a human being's last agonized instant of life?" Seib offered no answers to the questions he raised, but he went on to say that although as an editor he would probably have run the pictures, as a reader he was revolted by them.

In conclusion, Seib wrote: "Any editor who decided to print those pictures without giving at least a moment's thought to what purpose they served and what their effect was likely to be on the reader should ask another question: Have I become so preoccupied with manufacturing a product according to professional traditions and standards that I have forgotten about the consumer, the reader?"

It should be clear that the phone calls and letters and Seib's own reaction were occasioned by one factor alone: the death of the woman. Obviously, had she survived the fall, no one would have protested; the pictures would have had a completely different impact. Equally obviously, had the child died as well—or instead—Seib would undoubtedly have received ten times the phone calls he did. In each case, the pictures would have been exactly the same—only the captions, and thus the responses, would have been different.

But the questions Seib raises are worth discussing—though not exactly for the reasons he mentions. For it may be that the real lesson of the Boston photographs is not the danger that editors will be forgetful of reader reaction, but that they will continue to censor pictures of death precisely because of that reaction. The protests Seib fielded were really a variation on an old theme—and we saw plenty of it during the Nixon-Agnew years—the "Why doesn't the press print the good news?" argument. In this case, of course, the objections were all dressed up and cleverly disguised as righteous indignation about the privacy of death. This is a form of puritanism that is often justifiable; just as often it is merely puritanical.

Seib takes it for granted that the widespread though fairly recent newspaper policy against printing pictures of dead bodies is a sound one; I don't know that it makes any sense at all. I recognize that printing pictures of corpses raises all sorts of problems about taste and titillation and sensationalism; the fact is, however, that people die. Death happens to be one of life's main events. And it is irresponsible—and more than that, inaccurate—for newspapers to fail to show it, or to show it only when an astonishing set of photos comes in over the Associated Press wire. Most papers covering fatal automobile accidents will print pictures of mangled cars. But the significance of fatal automobile accidents is not that a great deal of steel is twisted but that people die. Why not show it? That's what accidents are about. Throughout the Vietnam war, editors were reluctant to print atrocity pictures. Why *not* print them? That's what that war was about. Murder victims are almost never photographed; they are granted their privacy. But their relatives are relentlessly pictured on their way in and out of hospitals and morgues and funerals.

I'm not advocating that newspapers print these things in order to teach their readers a lesson. The *Post* editors justified their printing of the Boston pictures with several arguments in that direction; every one of them is irrelevant. The pictures don't show anything about slum life; the incident could have happened anywhere, and it did. It is extremely unlikely that anyone who saw them rushed out and had his fire escape strengthened. And the pictures were not news—at least they were not national news. It is not news in Washington, or New York, or Los Angeles that a woman was killed in a Boston fire. The only newsworthy thing about the pictures is that they were taken. They deserve to be printed because they are great pictures, breathtaking pictures of something that happened. That they disturb readers is exactly as it should be: that's why photojournalism is often more powerful than written journalism.

QUESTIONS FOR READING, RESPONDING, AND WRITING

Summarizing Main Points

1. Why does Ephron think "the Boston Photographs" should be printed? Do you agree or disagree with her?
2. Ephron provides plenty of objections to printing the photographs. List them. She provides only one paragraph of advocacy. Why might this be?

Analyzing Methods of Discourse

1. In its original version, photographs did not accompany the essay. How does their inclusion here affect Ephron's argument?
2. How does Ephron's presentation of the material work as a form of advocacy for her position? Consider style, content, and organization in your analysis.

Focusing on the Field

1. In the first three paragraphs, Ephron states the circumstances behind the photographs rather matter-of-factly. List the facts. Where does Ephron stray from the facts with opinions of her own?
2. Read Simon Barber's essay on the *National Enquirer*, "The Boss Don't Like Swindle, Make It Robbery." Then, evaluate "The Boston Photographs" according to the *Enquirer*'s criteria for its stories. Would "The Boston Photographs" be suitable for the *Enquirer?* What facts might it suppress? What facts might it highlight? What sort of details might its editors or writers add to the story to make it more appropriate for publication in the *Enquirer?*

Writing Assignments

1. Write the opening paragraph from a pretended *National Enquirer* version of "The Boston Photographs."
2. Both Ephron's and Barber's essays take as their subject journalistic ethics. Write an essay of your own that compares the two essays on this score. Make your own position clear.

Paul Fussell

THE BOY SCOUT HANDBOOK

Born in 1924, Paul Fussell was an undergraduate at Pomona College in California before going into combat in World War II as an army infantry officer. After being wounded, he returned to complete his B.A. at Pomona and his Ph.D. in English at Harvard. Fussell went on to make valuable use of both his early military experience and literary training. An English professor at Rutgers University for many years, he accepted the Donald Regan Chair in English at the University of Pennsylvania in 1983. Known in academic circles for his scholarship on eighteenth-century literature and for *Poetic Meter and Poetic Form* (1965; 1979), Fussell gained a wider audience through essays and book reviews published in *Harper's* and *New Republic* and through *The Great War and Modern Memory,* for which he won the National Book Critics' Circle Award and the National Book Award in 1976. That book was an account of the effect the First World War had on the British and their literature; Fussell is currently working on a study of the "behavior of the imagination during the Second World War."

Whether writing on war, literature, or the class structure, as he does in *Class: A Guide through the American Status System* (1983), Fussell is notably uncompromising. Here, for instance, in the title essay from his 1982 collection, *The Boy Scout Handbook and Other Observations,* Fussell chides his own comrades in "humanist criticism" for their inability to recognize that a "vigorous literary-moral life constantly takes place just below (sometimes above) [their] vision," and proceeds to train his vision on that life as it is counseled in one of the world's most widely read books.

It's amazing how many interesting books humanistic criticism manages not to notice. Staring fixedly at its handful of teachable masterpieces, it seems content not to recognize that a vigorous literary-moral life constantly takes place just below (sometimes above) its vision. What a pity Lionel Trilling or Kenneth Burke never paused to examine the intersection of rhetoric and social motive among, say the Knights of Columbus or the Elks. That these are their fellow citizens is less important than that the desires and rituals of these groups are desires and rituals, and thus of permanent social and psychological consequence. The culture of the Boy Scouts deserves this sort of look-in, especially since the right sort of people don't know much about it.

The right sort consists, of course, of liberal intellectuals. They have often gazed uneasily at the Boy Scout movement. After all, a general, the scourge of the Boers, invented it; Kipling admired it; the Hitlerjugend (and the Soviet Pioneers) aped it. If its insistence that there is a God has not sufficed to alienate the enlightened, its khaki uniforms, lanyards, salutes, badges, and flag-worship have seemed to argue incipient militarism, if not outright fascism. The movement has often seemed its own worst enemy. Its appropriation of Norman Rockwell as its official Apelles has not endeared it to those of exquisite taste. Nor has its cause been promoted by events like the TV appearance a couple of years ago of the Chief Pardoner, Gerald Ford, rigged out in scout neckerchief, assuring us from the teleprompter that a Scout is Reverent. Then there are the leers and giggles triggered by the very word "scoutmaster," which in knowing circles is alone sufficient to promise comic pederastic narrative. "*All* scoutmasters are homosexuals," asserted George Orwell, who also insisted that "*All* tobacconists are Fascists."

But anyone who imagines that the scouting movement is either sinister or stupid or funny should spend a few hours with the latest edition of *The Official Boy Scout Handbook* (1979). Social, cultural, and literary historians could attend to it profitably as well, for after *The Red Cross First Aid Manual, The World Almanac,* and the Gideon Bible, it is probably the best-known book in this country. Since the first edition in 1910, twenty-nine million copies have been read in bed by flashlight. The first printing of this ninth edition is 600,000. We needn't take too seriously the ascription of authorship to William ("Green Bar Bill") Hillcourt, depicted on the title page as an elderly gentleman bare-kneed in scout uniform and identified as Author, Naturalist, and World Scouter. He is clearly the Ann Page or Reddy Kilowatt of the movement, and although he's doubtless contributed to this handbook (by the same author is *Baden-Powell: The Two Lives of a Hero* [1965]), it bears all the marks of composition by committee, or "task force," as it's called here. But for all that, it's admirably written. And although a complex sentence is as rare as a reference to girls, the rhetoric of this new edition has made no compromise with what we are told is the new illiteracy of the young. The book assumes an audience prepared by a very good high-school education, undaunted by terms like *biosphere, ideology,* and *ecosystem.*

The pliability and adaptability of the scout movement explains its remarkable longevity, its capacity to flourish in a world dramatically different from its founder's. Like the Roman Catholic Church, the scout movement knows the difference between cosmetic and real change, and it happily embraces the one to avoid any truck with the other. Witness the new American flag patch, now worn at the top of the right sleeve. It betokens no access of jingoism or threat to a civilized internationalism. It simply conduces to dignity by imitating a similar affectation of police and fire departments in anarchic towns like New York City. The message of the flag patch is not "I am a fascist, straining to become old enough to purchase and wield guns." It is, rather, "I can be put to quasi-official use, and like a fireman or policeman I am trained in first aid and ready to help."

There are other innovations, none of them essential. The breeches of thirty years ago have yielded to trousers, although shorts are still in. The wide-brimmed army field hat of the First World War is a fixture still occasionally seen, but it is now augmented by headwear deriving from succeeding mass patriotic exercises: overseas caps and berets from World War II, and visor caps of the sort worn by General Westmoreland and sunbelt retirees. The scout handclasp has been changed, perhaps because it was discovered in the context of the new internationalism that the former one, in which the little finger was separated from the other three on the right hand, transmitted inappropriate suggestions in the Third World. The handclasp is now the normal civilian one, but given with the left hand. There's now much less emphasis on knots than formerly; as if to signal this change, the neckerchief is no longer religiously knotted at the tips. What used to be known as artificial respiration ("Out goes the bad air, in comes the good") has given way to "rescue breathing." The young are now being familiarized with the metric system. Some bright empiric has discovered that a paste made of meat tenderizer is the best remedy for painful insect stings. Constipation is not the bugbear it was a generation ago. And throughout there is a striking new lyricism. "Feel the wind blowing through your hair," the scout is adjured, just as he is exhorted to perceive that Being Prepared for life means learning "to live happy" and—equally important—"to die happy." There's more emphasis now on fun and less on duty; or rather, duty is validated because, properly viewed, it is a pleasure. (If that sounds like advice useful to grown-ups as well as to sprouts, you're beginning to get the point.)

There are only two possible causes of complaint. The term "free world" surfaces too often, although the phrase is mercifully uncapitalized. And the Deism is a bit insistent. The United States is defined as a country "whose people believe in a supreme being." The words "In God We Trust" on the coinage and currency are taken almost as a constitutional injunction. The camper is told to carry along the "Bible, Testament, or prayer book of your faith," even though, for light backpacking, he is advised to leave behind air mattress, knife and fork, and pancake turner. When the scout finds himself lost in the woods, he is to "stay put and have faith that someone will find you." In aid of this end, "Prayer will help." But the religiosity is so broad that it's harmless. The words "your church" are followed always by the phrase "or synagogue." The writers have done as well as they can considering that they're saddled with the immutable twelve points of Baden-Powell's Scout Law, stating unambiguously that "A Scout is Reverent" and "faithful to his religious duties." But if "You have the right to worship God in your own way," you must see to it that "others retain their right to worship God in their way." Likewise, if "you have the right to speak your mind without fear of prison or punishment," you must "ensure that right for others, even when you do not agree with them." If the book adheres to any politics, they can hardly be described as conservative; they are better described as slightly archaic liberal. It is broadly hinted that industrial corporations are prime threats to clean air and conservation. In every illustration depicting more than three boys, one is black. The section introducing the reader to some Great Americans pays respects not only to Franklin and Edison and John D. Rockefeller and Einstein; it also makes much of Walter Reuther and Samuel Gompers, as well as Harriet Tubman, Martin Luther King, and Whitney Young. There is a post-Watergate awareness that public officials must be watched closely. One's civic duties include the obligation to "keep up on what is going on around you" in order to "get involved" and "help change things that are not good."

Few books these days could be called compendia of good sense. This is one such, and its good sense is not merely about swimming safely and putting campfires "cold out." The good sense is psychological and ethical as well. Indeed, this handbook is among the very few remaining popular repositories of something like classical ethics, deriving from Aristotle and Cicero. Except for the handbook's adhesions to the motif of scenic beauty, it reads as if the Romantic movement had never taken place. The constant moral theme is the inestimable benefits of looking objectively outward and losing consciousness of self in the work to be done. To its young audience vulnerable to invitations to "trips" and trances and anxious self-absorption, the book calmly says: "Forget yourself." What a shame the psychobabblers of Marin County will never read it.

There is other invaluable advice, applicable to adults as well as to scouts. Some is practical, like "Never use flammable fluids to start a charcoal fire. They burn off fast, lighting only a little of the charcoal." Some is civic-moral: "Take a 2-hour walk where you live. Make a list of things that please you, another of things that should be improved." And then the kicker: "Set out to improve them." Some advice is even intellectual, and pleasantly uncompromising: "Reading trash all the time makes it impossible for anyone to be anything but a second-rate person." But the best advice is ethical: "Learn to think." "Gather knowledge." "Have initiative." "Respect the rights of others." Actually, there's hardly a better gauge for measuring the gross official misbehavior of the seventies than the ethics enshrined in this handbook. From its explicit ethics you can infer such propositions as "A scout does not tap his acquaintances' telephones," or "A scout does not bomb and invade a neutral country, and then lie about it," or "A scout does not prosecute war unless, as the Constitution provides, it has been declared by the Congress." Not to mention that because a scout is clean in thought, word, and deed, he does not, like Richard Nixon, designate his fellow citizens "shits" and then both record his filth and lie about the recordings ("A scout tells the truth").

Responding to Orwell's satiric analysis of "Boys' Weeklies" forty years ago, the boys' author Frank Richards, stigmatized by Orwell as a manufacturer of excessively optimistic and falsely wholesome stories, observed that "The writer for young people should . . . endeavor to give his young readers a sense of stability and solid security, because it is good for them, and makes for happiness and peace of mind." Even if it is true, as Orwell objects, that the happiness of youth is a cruel delusion, then, says Richards, "Let youth be happy, or as happy as possible. Happiness is the best preparation for misery, if misery must come. At least the poor kid will have had something." In the current world of Making It and Getting Away with It, there are not many books devoted to associating happiness with virtue. The shelves of the CIA and the State Department must be bare of them. "Horror swells around us like an oil spill," Terrence Des Pres said recently. "Not a day passes without more savagery and harm." He was commenting on Philip Hallie's *Lest Innocent Blood Be Shed*, an account of a whole French village's trustworthiness, loyalty, helpfulness, friendliness, courtesy, kindness, cheerfulness, and bravery in hiding scores of Jews during the Occupation. Des Pres concludes: "*Goodness. When was the last time anyone used that word in earnest, without irony, as anything more than a double cliché?*" The Official Boy Scout Handbook, for all its focus on Axmanship, Backpacking, Cooking, First Aid, Flowers, Hiking, Map and Compass, Semaphore, Trees, and Weather, is another book about goodness. No home, and certainly no government office, should be without a copy. The generously low price of $3.50 is enticing, and so is the place on the back cover where you're invited to inscribe your name.

QUESTIONS FOR READING, RESPONDING, AND WRITING

Summarizing Main Points

1. Summarize the ideals and advice that Fussell claims *The Boy Scout Handbook* offers. What controls these ideals?
2. What is Fussell's attitude toward these ideals? What is your attitude toward these ideals? Do you suppose that Fussell read *The Boy Scout Handbook* as a child?

Analyzing Methods of Discourse

1. Fussell is often funny in this essay. Point to specific examples. How does that humor affect the reader's attitude toward Fussell? Toward the material he presents?
2. Halfway through the essay, Fussell provides a little test for his readers: "If this sounds like advice useful to grown-ups as well as sprouts, you're beginning to get the point." If Fussell had begun his essay by insisting that *The Boy Scout Handbook* was appropriate for adults, do you think he would have been as successful in persuading his audience? Why or why not?

Focusing on the Field

1. Fussell often writes as a social historian. How is *The Boy Scout Handbook* an appropriate artifact for his investigation? According to Fussell, why has the *Handbook* been ignored by humanist critics?
2. Fussell talks about both conservatives and liberals. Do you believe he fits into either camp? Neither camp? How might his political beliefs affect your attitude toward what he has to say?

Writing Assignments

1. Choose a familiar children's book (e.g., *Treasure Island*, a Nancy Drew mystery, a Dr. Seuss book) and, in a short essay, demonstrate how it might be "useful to grown-ups as well as sprouts."
2. Both Fussell here and Philip Roth in "My Baseball Years" find literary-moral worth in popular culture that appeals to young people. Compare and contrast their approaches to popular culture.

Walker Percy

THE LAST DONAHUE SHOW
A Thought Experiment

Novelist Walker Percy discovered his calling by a somewhat circuitous route rather late in life. Born in 1913 in Birmingham, Alabama, he received his B.A. from the University of North Carolina and his M.D. from Columbia University Medical School in 1941. But his internship at New York's Bellevue Hospital signaled the end rather than the beginning of his medical career. As a result of performing routine autopsies on derelicts, Percy contracted pulmonary tuberculosis and was confined for two years of treatment. Returning to medicine as an instructor of pathology, he suffered a relapse, necessitating another prolonged period of rest. His illness, though it effectively sabotaged his first career choice, brought him to his second. Percy spent those periods of forced inactivity in reading, much of it philosophical, and made what he calls the second great intellectual discovery of his life—the first was the beauty of the scientific method—that of "the singular predicament of man in the very world which has been transformed by . . . science." This intellectual and moral dilemma is at the center of his novels and essays, and, seemingly, of his mid-life conversion to Roman Catholicism.

After his second bout with tuberculosis, Percy returned to Louisiana, just outside New Orleans, the scene of much of his fiction. His first novel, *The Moviegoer*, was published in 1961 and won him the National Book Award. Subsequent novels include *The Last Gentleman* (1966), *Love in the Ruins* (1971), *Lancelot* (1977), and *The Second Coming* (1980). He has also written two collections of essays, *The Message in the Bottle* (1975) and *Lost in the Cosmos* (1984), from which the following selection is taken.

His scientific, philosophic, and religious training informs all of Percy's writing. Reviewer Martin Kirby has called his style "quasi-scientific" and has noted that "he seems to be trying to persuade logically, but his insights are essentially emotional and poetic." The following essay demonstrates both sides of this equation. In a stylistic tour de force, Percy creates a "thought experiment" that uses the "last" *Phil Donahue Show* as its singularly absurd setting in order to provide some disturbing insights into contemporary life.

The Donahue show is in progress on what appears at first to be an ordinary weekday morning.

The theme of this morning's show is Donahue's favorite, sex, the extraordinary variety of sexual behavior—"sexual preference," as Donahue would call it—in the country and the embattled attitudes toward it. Although Donahue has been accused of appealing to prurient interest, with a sharp eye cocked on the ratings, he defends himself by saying that he presents these controversial matters in "a mature and tasteful manner"—which he often does. It should also be noted in Donahue's defense that the high ratings of these sex-talk shows are nothing more or less than an index of the public's intense interest in such matters.

The guests today are:

Bill, a homosexual and habitué of Buena Vista Park in San Francisco.

Allen, a heterosexual businessman, married, and a connoisseur of the lunch-hour liaison.

Penny, a pregnant fourteen-year-old.

Dr. Joyce Friday, well-known talk-show sex therapist, or, in media jargon, a psych jockey.

> BILL'S STORY: Yes, I'm gay, and, yes, I cruise Buena Vista. Yes, I've probably had over 500 encounters with lovers, though I didn't keep count. So what? Whose business is it? I'm gainfully employed by a savings-and-loan company, am a trustworthy employee, and do an honest day's work. My recreation is Buena Vista Park and the strangers I meet there. I don't molest children, rape women, snatch purses. I contribute to United Way. Such encounters that I do have are by mutual consent and therefore nobody's business—except my steady live-in friend's. Naturally he's upset, but that's our problem.
>
> DONAHUE (*striding up and down, mike in hand, boyishly inarticulate*): C'mon, Bill. What about the kids who might see you? You know what I mean. I mean—(*Opens his free hand to the audience, soliciting their understanding*)
>
> BILL: Kids don't see me. Nobody sees me.
>
> DONAHUE (*coming close, on the attack but good-naturedly, spoofing himself as prosecutor*): Say, Bill, I've always been curious. Is there some sort of signal? I mean, how do you and the other guy know—Help me out—

BILL: Eye contact, or we show a bit of handkerchief here. *(Demonstrates)* *(Studio audience laughter)*

DONAHUE *(shrugging—Don't blame me, folks—pushes up nose bridge of glasses, swings mike over to Dr. J.F. without looking at her)*: How about it, Doc?

DR. J.F. *(in her non-mincing-words voice)*: I think Bill's behavior is immature and depersonalizing. *(Applause from audience)* I think he ought to return to his steady live-in friend and work out a mature, creative relationship. You might be interested to know that studies have shown that stable gay couples are more creative than straights. *(Applause again, but more tentative)*

DONAHUE *(eyes slightly rolled back, swings mike to Bill)*: How about it, Bill?

BILL: Yeah, right. But I still cruise Buena Vista.

DONAHUE *(pensive, head to one side, strides backward, forward, then over to Allen)*: How about you, Allen?

ALLEN'S STORY: I'm a good person, I think. I work hard, am happily married, love my wife and family, also support United Way, served in the army. I drink very little, don't do drugs, have never been to a porn movie. My idea of R and R—maybe I got it in the army—is to meet an attractive woman. What a delight it is to see a handsome mature woman, maybe in the secretarial pool, maybe in a bar, restaurant, anywhere, exchange eye contact, speak to her in a nice way, respect her as a person, invite her to join me for lunch (no sexual harassment in the office—I hate that!), have a drink, two drinks, enjoy a nice meal, talk about matters of common interest, then simply ask her—by now, both of you know whether you like each other. What a joy to go with her up in the elevator of the downtown Holiday Inn, both of you silent, relaxed, smiling, anticipating . . . The door of the room closes behind you. You look at her, take her hand. There's champagne already there. You stand at the window with her, touch glasses, talk—there's nothing vulgar. No closed-circuit TV. Do you know what we did last time? We turned on *La Bohème* on the FM. She loves Puccini.

DONAHUE: C'mon, Allen, what are ya handing me? What d'ya mean you're happily married? You mean *you're* happy.

ALLEN: No no. Vera's happy too.

AUDIENCE *(mostly women)* groans: Nooooooo.

DONAHUE: Okay okay, ladies, hold it a second. What do you mean, Vera's happy? I mean, how do you manage—Help me out, I'm about to get in trouble—Hold the letters, folks—

ALLEN: Well, actually, Vera has a low sex drive. We've been quite inactive, even at the beginning—

AUDIENCE: Nooooo. *(Groans, jumbled protests)*

DONAHUE *(backing away, holding up a placating free hand, backing around to Dr. J.F.)*: It's all yours, Doc.

DR. J.F.: Studies have shown that open marriages can be growth experiences for both partners, however—*(groans from audience)*—however, it seems to me that Vera may be getting the short end here. I mean, I don't know Vera's side of it. But could I ask you this? Have you and Vera thought about re-energizing your sex life?

ALLEN: Well, ah—

DR. J.F.: Studies have shown, for example, that more stale marriages have been revived by oral sex than any other technique—

DONAHUE: Now, Doc—

DR. J.F.: Other studies have shown that mutual masturbation—

DONAHUE (*eyes rolled back*): We're running long, folks, we'll be right back after this—don't go away. Oh boy. (*Lets mike slide to the hilt through his hand, closes eyes as camera cuts away to a Maxithins commercial*)

DONAHUE: We're back. Thank the good Lord for good sponsors. (*Turns to Penny, a thin, inattentive, moping teenager, even possibly a preteen*) Penny?

PENNY (*chewing something*): Yeah?

DONAHUE: What's with you, sweetheart? (*Solicitous, quite effectively tender*)

PENNY: Well, I liked this boy a lot and he told me there was one way I could prove it—

DONAHUE: Wait a minute, Penny. Now this, your being here, is okay with your parents, right? I mean, let's establish that.

PENNY: Oh sure. They're right over there—you can ask them. (*Camera pans over audience, settling on a couple with mild, pleasant faces. It is evident that on the whole they are not displeased with being on TV*)

DONAHUE: Okay. So you mean you didn't know about taking precautions—

DR. J.F. (*breaking in*): Now that's what I mean, Phil.

DONAHUE: What's that, Doc?

DR. J.F.: About the crying need for sex education in our schools. Now if this child—

PENNY: Oh, I had all that stuff at Ben Franklin.

DONAHUE: You mean you knew about the pill and the other, ah—

PENNY: I had been on the pill for a year.

DONAHUE (*scratching head*). I don't get it. Oh, you mean you slipped up, got careless?

PENNY: No, I did it on purpose.

DONAHUE: Did what on purpose? You mean—

PENNY: I mean I wanted to get pregnant.

DONAHUE: Why was that, Penny?

PENNY: My best friend was pregnant.

(*Audience groans, laughter*)

DR. J.F.: You see, Phil, that's just what I mean. This girl is no more equipped with parenting skills than a child. She is a child. I hope she realizes she still has viable options.

DONAHUE: How about it, Penny?

PENNY: No, I want to have my baby.

DONAHUE: Why?

PENNY: I think babies are neat.

DONAHUE: Oh boy.

DR. J.F.: Studies have shown that unwanted babies suffer 85 percent more child abuse and 150 percent more neuroses later in life

DONAHUE (*striding*): Okay, now what have we got here? Wait. What's going on?

There is an interruption. Confusion at the rear of the studio. Heads turn.

Three strangers, dressed outlandishly, stride down the aisle.

DONAHUE (*smacks his forehead*): What's this? What's this? Holy smoke.

Already the AUDIENCE is smiling, reassured both by Donahue's comic consternation and by the exoticness of the visitors. Clearly, the AUDIENCE thinks, they are part of the act.

The three strangers are indeed outlandish.

One is a tall, thin, bearded man dressed like a sixteenth-century reformer. Indeed he could be John Calvin, in his black cloak, black cap with short bill, and snug earflaps.

The second wears the full-dress uniform of a Confederate officer. Though he is a colonel, he is quite young, surely no more than twenty-five. Clean-shaven and extremely handsome, he looks for all the world like Colonel John Pelham, Jeb Stuart's legendary artillerist. Renowned both for his gallantry in battle and his chivalry toward women, the beau ideal of the South, he engaged in sixty artillery duels, won them all. With a single Napoleon, he held off three of Burnside's divisions in front of Fredericksburg before being ordered by Stuart to retreat.

The third is at once the most ordinary-looking and yet the strangest of all. His dress is both modern and out-of-date. In his light-colored double-breasted suit and bow tie, his two-tone shoes of the sort known in the 1940s as "perforated wing tips," his neat above-the-ears haircut, he looks a bit like the clean old man in the Beatles' movie A *Hard Day's Night*, a bit like Lowell Thomas or perhaps Harry Truman. It is as if he were a visitor from the Cosmos, from a planet ten or so light-years distant, who had formed his notion of earthlings from belated transmissions of 1950 TV, from watching *The Ed Sullivan Show*, old Chester Morris movies, and Morey Amsterdam. Or, to judge from his speaking voice, he could have been an inveterate listener during the golden age of radio and modeled his speech on Harry Von Zell's.

DONAHUE (*backpedaling, smacking his head again*): Holy smoke! Who are these guys? (*Beseeching the audience with a slow comic pan around*)

The AUDIENCE laughs, not believing for a moment that these latecomers are not one of Donahue's surprises. And yet—

DONAHUE (*snapping his fingers*): I got it. Wait'll I get that guy. It's Steve Allen, right? Refugees from the Steve Allen show, "Great Conversations"? Famous historical figures? You know, folks, they do that show in the studio down the hall. Wait'll I get that guy.

General laughter. Everybody remembers it's been done before, an old show-biz trick, like Carson barging in on Rickles during the *C.P.O. Sharkey* taping.

DONAHUE: Okay already. Okay, who we got here? This is Moses? General Robert E. Lee? And who is this guy? Harry Truman? Okay, fellas, let's hear it. (*Donahue, an attractive fellow, is moving about as gracefully as a dancer*)

STRANGER (*speaking first, in his standard radio announcer's voice, which is not as flat as the Chicagoans who say, Hyev a hyeppy new year*): I don't know what these two are doing here, but I came to give you a message. We've been listening to this show.

DONAHUE (*winking at the audience*): And where were you listening to us?

STRANGER: In the green room.

DONAHUE: Where else? Okay. Then what do you think? Let's hear it first from the Reverend here. What did you say your name was, Reverend?

REVEREND: John Calvin.

DONAHUE: Right. Who else? Okay, we got to break here for these messages. Don't go 'way, folks. We're coming right back and sort this out, I promise. (*Cut to Miss Clairol, Land O Lakes margarine, Summer's Eve, and Alpo commercials*)

But when the show returns, JOHN CALVIN, who does not understand commercial breaks, has jumped the gun and is in mid-sentence.

CALVIN (*speaking in a thick French accent not unlike Charles Boyer's*): — of his redemptive sacrifice? What I have heard is licentious talk about deeds which are an abomination before God, meriting eternal damnation unless they repent and throw themselves on God's mercy. Which they are predestined to do or not to do, so why bother to discuss it.

DONAHUE (*gravely*): That's pretty heavy, Reverend.

CALVIN: Heavy? Yes, it's heavy.

DONAHUE (*mulling, scratching*)· Now wait a minute, Reverend. Let's check this out. You're entitled to your religious beliefs. But what if others disagree with you in all good faith? And aside from that (*prosecutory again, using mike like forefinger*) what's wrong with two consenting adults expressing their sexual preference in the privacy of their bedroom, or, ah, under a bush.

CALVIN: Sexual preference? (*Puzzled, he turns for help to the Confederate officer and the Cosmic stranger. They shrug.*)

DONAHUE (*holding mike to the officer*): How about you, sir? Your name is—

CONFEDERATE OFFICER: Colonel John Pelham, C.S.A. commander of the horse artillery under General Stuart.

PENNY: He's cute.

(*Audience laughter*)

DONAHUE: You heard it all in the green room, Colonel. What d'ya think?

COLONEL PELHAM (*in a soft Alabama accent*): What do I think of what, sir?

DONAHUE: Of what you heard in the green room.

PELHAM: Of the way these folks act and talk? Well, I don't think much of it, sir.

DONAHUE: How do you mean, Colonel?

PELHAM: That's not the way people should talk or act. Where I come from we'd call them white trash. That's no way to talk if you're a man or a woman. A gentleman knows how to treat women. He knows because he knows himself, who he is, what his obligations are. And he discharges them. But, after all, you won the war, so if that's the way you want to act, that's your affair. At least we can be sure of one thing.

DONAHUE: What's that, Colonel?

PELHAM: We're not sorry we fought.

DONAHUE: I see. Then you agree with the Reverend, I mean Reverend Calvin here.

PELHAM: Well, I respect his religious beliefs. But I never thought much about religion one way or the other. In fact I don't think religion has much to do with whether a man does right. A West Point man is an officer and a gentleman, religion or no religion. I have nothing against religion. In fact, when we studied medieval history at West Point, I remember admiring Richard Coeur de Lion and his recapturing Acre and the holy places. I remember thinking I would have fought for him just as I fought for Lee and the South.

Applause from the AUDIENCE. CALVIN puts them off, but this handsome officer reminds them of Rhett Butler–Clark Gable, or rather Ashley Wilkes–Leslie Howard.

DONAHUE (*drifting off, frowning—something is amiss, but he can't put his finger on it. What is Steve Allen up to? He shakes his head, blinks*): You said it, Colonel. Okay. Where were we? (*Turning to Cosmic stranger*) We're running a little long. Can you make it brief, Harry—Mr. President, or whoever you are? Oh boy.

The COSMIC STRANGER now stands stiffly, hands at his sides, and begins speaking briskly, very much in the style of the late Raymond Gram Swing:

I will be brief. I have taken this human form through a holographic technique unknown to you in order to make myself understood to you.

Hear this. I have a message. Whether you heed it or not is your affair.

I have nothing to say to you about God or the Confederacy, whatever that is—I assume it is not the G2V Confederacy in this arm of the galaxy—though I could speak about God, but it is too late for you and I am not here to do that.

We are not interested in the varieties of your sexual behavior, except as a symptom of a more important disorder.

It is this disorder which concerns us and which we do not fully understand.

As a consequence of this disorder you are a potential threat to all civilizations in the G2V region of the galaxy. Throughout G2V you are known variously and jokingly as the Ds or the DDs or DLs, that is, the dingalings or the death-dealers or death-lovers. Of all the species here and in all of G2V, you are the only one which is by nature sentimental, murderous, self-hating, and self-destructive.

You are two superpowers here. The other is hopeless, has already succumbed, and is a death society. It is a living death and an agent for the propagation of death.

You are scarcely better—there is a glimmer of hope for you—but that is of no interest to me.

If the two of you destroy each other, as appears likely, it is of no consequence to us. To tell you the truth, G2V will breathe a sigh of relief.

The danger is that you may not destroy each other and that your present crude technology may constitute a threat to G2V in the future.

I am here to tell you three things: what is going to happen, what I am going to do, and what you can do.

Here's what will happen. Within the next twenty-four hours your last war will begin. There will occur a twenty-megaton airburst one mile above the University of Chicago, the very site where your first chain reaction was produced. Every American city and town will be hit. You will lose plus-minus 160 million immediately, plus-minus 50 million later.

Here's what I am going to do. I have been commissioned to collect a specimen of DD and return with it so that we can study it toward the end of determining the nature of your disorder. Accordingly, I propose to take this young person referred to as Penny—for two reasons. One, she is perhaps still young enough not to have become hopeless. Two, she is pregnant, and so we will have a chance to rear a DD in an environment free of your noxious influence. Then perhaps we can determine whether your disorder is a result of some peculiar earth environmental factor or whether you are a malignant sport, a genetic accident, the consequence of what you would have called in an earlier time an MD—*mutatio diabolica*, a diabolical mutation.

Finally, here's what you can do. It is of no consequence to us whether you do it or not because you will no longer be a threat to anyone. This is only a small gesture of good will to a remnant of you who may survive and who may have the chance to start all over—though you will probably repeat the same mistake. We have been students of your climatology for years. I have here a current reading and prediction of the prevailing wind directions and fallout patterns for the next two weeks. It so happens that the place nearest you which will escape all effects of both blast and fallout is the community of Lost Cove, Tennessee. Our projection is that very few of you here and you out there in radioland will attach credibility to this message. But the few of you who do may wish to use this information. There is a cave there, corn, grits, collard greens, and smoked sausage in abundance.

That is the end of my message. Penny—

> DONAHUE: We're long! We're long! Heavy! Steve, I'll get you for this. Oh boy. Don't forget, folks, tomorrow we got surrogate partners and a Kinsey panel—Come back—You can't win 'em all—'Bye! Grits. I dunno.

(Audience applause. Cut to station break, Secure Card 65 commercial, Alpo, and Mentholatum, then The Price Is Right.*)*

QUESTION:

If you heard this Donahue show, would you head for Lost Cove, Tennessee?

(Check one)

☐ **A.** Yes

☐ **B.** No

QUESTIONS FOR READING, RESPONDING, AND WRITING

Summarizing Main Points

1. Percy compares at least two aspects of contemporary society: sexual behavior and the threat of self-annihilation. According to Percy, what is the relation between the two? Do you agree that the two are related in the way Percy suggests?
2. How would you respond to the final question? What does the final question imply about mass communications as a possible cause for the difficulties that the Cosmic Stranger alludes to?

Analyzing Methods of Discourse

1. Percy sets up his essay in the form of a "thought experiment"—that is, he imagines a dialogue on *The Last Donahue Show*. How does Percy allow for the fact that on a real *Donahue Show*, no one would be permitted to walk on and take over as the three strangers do here? Why is the title important?
2. Why has Percy chosen these particular characters as guests on the show and as intruders? How do the intruders comment on particular guests? What is Percy's attitude toward the guests? The intruders? Donahue? The audience?

Focusing on the Field

1. In his essay, Percy glances at a troubling aspect of contemporary society: mass communication. What do you feel his attitude is toward the *Donahue Show*?

Find evidence in the essay to support your position. What is your own attitude toward the *Donahue Show?*
2. Why does the Cosmic Stranger consider his audience to be in "radioland"? Would it make any difference if the Cosmic Stranger knew he was on TV?

Writing Assignments

1. After watching a *Donahue Show* and noting Donahue's mannerisms and speech, compare Percy's presentation of Donahue to the real Donahue, looking at the stage directions Percy provides as well as the show's subject and the way in which he has Donahue handle it.
2. While Percy imitates the format of the *Donahue Show*, he leaves out the audience question-and-answer period that follows Donahue's own interview with his guests. After watching a *Donahue Show* for the actual format, write a question-and-answer session for *"The last Donahue Show."*

Martin Esslin

ARISTOTLE AND THE ADVERTISERS:
The Television Commercial Considered
as a Form of Drama

Martin Esslin has been called the most important critic writing on drama today. His career in this field has been not only long and distinguished, but varied. Born in Budapest, Hungary in 1918, Esslin studied at the University of Vienna and received his degree from the Reinhardt Seminar of Dramatic Art in Vienna in 1938. A year later, he moved to Great Britain, where he worked as a writer and director for the British Broadcasting Corporation from 1940 to 1977. During those years, he also performed a variety of other jobs for the BBC, acting as producer and scriptwriter for European services from 1941 until 1955, when he became an assistant head of European productions. In 1961, he was the assistant head of drama and became head of drama in 1963, a post he held until his departure in 1977 to become a professor of drama at Stanford University in California. In addition to his work in broadcasting, Esslin has written and edited a number of books on controversial playwrights: Bertolt Brecht, Harold Pinter, Antonin Artaud, and Samuel Beckett. In 1963, he published his most famous work, *The Theatre of the Absurd,* a major study of the avant garde playwrights of the fifties and sixties (e.g., Beckett, Jean Genet, and Eugene Ionesco), the title of which became the catchphrase for a genre. Esslin also contributes essays and reviews to numerous periodicals, and is the advisory editor of *Drama Review* and the drama editor of the *Kenyon Review*, where the following essay originally appeared.

We have all seen it a hundred times, and in dozens of variations: that short sequence of images in which a husband expresses disappointment and distress at his wife's inability to provide him with a decent cup of coffee and seems inclined to seek a better tasting potion outside the home, perhaps even on the bosom of another lady; the anxious consultation, which ensues, between the wife and her mother or an experienced and trusted friend, who counsels the use of another brand of coffee; and finally the idyllic tableau of the husband astonished and surprised by the excellence of his wife's new coffee, demanding a second—or even a third!—cup of the miraculously effective product.

A television commercial. And, doubtless, it includes elements of drama. . . . Yet: is it not too short, too trivial, too contemptible altogether to deserve serious consideration? That seems the generally accepted opinion. But in an age when through the newly discovered technologies of mechanical reproduction and dissemination drama has become one of the chief instruments of human expression, communication, and, indeed, thought, all uses of the dramatic form surely deserve study. If the television commercial could be shown to be drama, it would be among the most ubiquitous and the most influential of its forms and hence deserve the attention of the serious critics and theoreticians of that art, most of whom paradoxically still seem to be spellbound by types of drama (such as tragedy) which are hallowed by age and tradition, though practically extinct today. And, surely, in a civilization in which drama, through the mass media, has become an omnipresent, all-pervasive, continuously available, and unending stream of entertainment for the vast majority of individuals in the so-called developed world, a comprehensive theory, morphology, and typology of drama is urgently needed. Such a theory would have to take cognizance of the fact that the bulk of drama today is to be found not on the stage but in the mechanized mass media, the cinema, television, and, in most civilized countries, radio; that both on the stage and in the mass media drama exists in a multitude of new forms which might even deserve to be considered genres unknown to Aristotle—from mime to musicals, from police serials to science fiction, from Westerns to soap opera, from improvisational theatre to happenings—and that among all these the television commercial might well be both unprecedented and highly significant.

The coffee commercial cited above, albeit a mere thirty to fifty seconds in length, certainly exhibits attributes of drama. Yet to what extent is it typical of the television commercial in general? Not all TV commercials use plot, character, and spoken dialogue to the same extent.

Nevertheless, I think it can be shown that most, if not all, TV commercials are essentially dramatic, because basically they use mimetic action to produce a semblance of real life, and the basic ingredients of drama—character and a story line—are present in the great majority of them, either manifestly or by implication.

Take another frequently occurring type: a beautiful girl who tells us that her hair used to be lifeless and stringy, while now, as she proudly displays, it is radiantly vital and fluffy. Is this not just a bare announcement, flat and undramatic? I should argue that, in fact, there is drama in it, implied in the clearly fictitious character who is telling us her story. What captures our interest and imagination is the radiant girl, and what she tells us is an event which marked a turning point in her life. Before she discovered the miraculous new shampoo she was destined to live in obscurity and neglect, but now she has become beautiful and radiant with bliss. Are we not, therefore, here in the presence of that traditional form of drama in which a seemingly static display of character and atmosphere evokes highly charged, decisive events of the past that are now implicit in the present—the type of drama, in fact, of which Ibsen's *Ghosts* is a frequently cited specimen?

What, though, if the lady in question is a well-known show business or sporting personality and hence a *real* rather than a fictitious character? Do we not then enter the realm of reality rather than fictional drama? I feel that there are very strong grounds for arguing the opposite: for film stars, pop singers, and even famous sporting personalities project not their real selves but a carefully tailored fictional image. There has always, throughout the history of drama, been the great actor who essentially displayed no more than a single, continuous personality rather than a series of differing characters (witness the Harlequins and other permanent character types of the commedia dell'arte, great melodrama performers like Frédéric Lemaître, great comics like Chaplin, Buster Keaton, Laurel and Hardy, or the Marx Brothers, or indeed great film stars like Marilyn Monroe or John Wayne—to name but a very few). Such actors do not enact parts so much as lend their highly wrought and artistically crafted fictitious personality to a succession of roles that exist merely to display that splendid artifact. Hence if Bob Hope or John Wayne appear as spokesmen for banking institutions, or Karl Malden as the advocate of a credit card, no one is seriously asked to believe that they are informing us of their real experience with these institutions; we all know that they are speaking a preestablished, carefully polished text which, however brief it may be, has been composed by a team of highly skilled professional writers and that they are merely lending them the charisma of their long-established—and fictional—urbanity, sturdiness, or sincerity.

There remains, admittedly, a residue of nondramatic TV commercials: those which are no more than newspaper advertisements displaying a text and a symbol, with a voice merely reading it out to the less literate members of the audience; and those in which the local car or carpet salesman more or less successfully tries to reel off a folksy appeal to his customers. But these commercials tend to be the local stations' fill-up material. The bulk of the major, nationally shown commercials are profoundly dramatic and exhibit, in their own peculiar way, in minimal length and maximum compression, the basic characteristics of the dramatic mode of expression in a state of particular purity—precisely because here it approaches the point of zero extension, as though the TV commercial were a kind of differential calculus of the aesthetics of drama.

Let us return to our initial example: the coffee playlet. Its three-beat basic structure can be found again and again. In the first beat the exposition is made and the problem posed. Always disaster threatens: persistent headaches endanger the love relationship or success at work of the heroine or hero (or for headaches read constipation, body odor, uncomfortable sanitary pads, ill-fitting dentures, hemorrhoids, lost credit cards, inefficient detergents which bring disgrace on the housewife). In the second beat a wise friend or confidant suggests a solution. And this invariably culminates in a moment of insight, of conversion, in fact the classical anagnorisis that leads to dianoia and thus to the peripeteia, the turning point of the action. The third beat shows the happy conclusion to what was a potentially tragic situation. For it is always and invariably the hero's or heroine's ultimate happiness that is at stake: his health or job or domestic peace. In most cases there is even the equivalent of the chorus of ancient tragedy in the form of an unseen voice, or indeed, a choral song, summing up the moral lesson of the action and generalizing it into a universally applicable principle. And this is, almost invariably, accompanied by a visual epiphany of the product's symbol, container, trademark or logo—in other words the allegorical or symbolic representation of the beneficent power that has brought about the fortunate outcome and averted the ultimate disaster; the close analogy to the *deus ex machina* of classical tragedy is inescapable.

All this is compressed into a span of from thirty to fifty seconds. Moreover such a mini-drama contains distinctly drawn characters, who while representing easily recognizable human types (as so many characters of traditional drama) are yet individualized in subtle ways, through the personalities of the actors portraying them, the way they are dressed, the way they speak. The setting of the action, however briefly it may be glimpsed, also greatly contributes to the solidity of characterization: the tasteful furnishings of the home, not too opulent, but neat, tidy, and pretty enough to evoke admiring sympathy and empathy; the suburban scene visible through the living room or kitchen window, the breakfast table that bears witness to the housewifely skills of the heroine—and all subtly underlined by mood music rising to a dramatic climax at the moment of anagnorisis and swelling to a triumphant coda at the fortunate conclusion of the action. Of all the art forms only drama can communicate such an immense amount of information on so many levels simultaneously within the span of a few seconds. That all this has to be taken in instantaneously, moreover, ensures that most of the impact will be subliminal—tremendously suggestive while hardly ever rising to the level of full consciousness. It is this which explains the great effectiveness of the TV commercial and the inevitability of its increasing employment of dramatic techniques. Drama does not simply translate the abstract idea into concrete terms. It literally incarnates the abstract message by bringing it to life in a human personality and a human situation. Thus it activates powerful subconscious drives and the deep animal magnetisms which dominate the lives of men and women who are always interested in and attracted by other human beings, their looks, their charm, their mystery.

"A message translated into terms of personality"—that, certainly, is one of the focal points around which TV commercials turn: the housewife, attractive but anonymous, who appears in such a commercial, exudes all the hidden attraction and interest she can command. Each of these mini-playlets stands by itself. Each is analogous to a complete play in conventional drama. It can be shown repeatedly, and can have a long run. But then the characters in it are spent. There is another form, however, even more characteristic of television drama—the serial. The series of plays featuring a recurring set of characters is the most successful dramatic format of television. No wonder, then, that the TV commercial mini-drama also resorts to the recurring personality, be he or she fictional; real-life-synthetic, like the film stars or sporting heroes mentioned above; or allegorical, like the sweet little lady who embodies the spirit of relief from stomach acids and miraculously appears with her pills to bring comfort to a succession of truck drivers, longshoremen, or crane operators suffering from upset tummies.

The free interchangeability of real and fictional experts in this context once again underlines the essentially fictitious character even of the "real" people involved and shows clearly that we are dealing with a form of drama. The kindly pharmacist who recommends the headache powder, the thoughtful bespectacled doctor who recounts the successes of a toothpaste, the crusty small-town lady grocer who praises her coffee beans with the air of experience based on decades of wise counseling are manifestly actors, carefully type-cast; yet their authority is not a whit less weighty than that of the rare actual experts who may occasionally appear.

The actor on the stage who plays Faust or Hamlet does not, after all, have to be as wise as the one or as noble as the other: it suffices that he can *appear* as wise or as noble. And the same is true of the dramatized advertisement: since illusion is the essence of drama, the illusion of authority is far more valuable in the dramatized commercial than any real authority. The fact that an actor like Robert Young has established himself as a medical character in an evening series enables him to exude redoubled authority when he appears in a long series of commercials as a doctor recommending caffeine-free coffee. It need not even be mentioned any longer that he is playing a doctor. Everybody recognizes him as a doctor while also remaining completely aware that he is an actor. . . . (It is Genêt, among modern playwrights, who has recognized the role of illusion as a source of authority in our society. His play *The Balcony* deals with precisely that subject: the insignificant people who have merely assumed the trappings of Bishop, Judge, or General in that house of illusions, the brothel, can, in the hour of need, be used to convince the masses that those authorities are still present. Many TV commercials are, in fact, mini-versions of *The Balcony.*)

The creation of authority figures—in a world where they are conspicuously absent in reality—can thus be seen as one of the essential features, and endeavors, of the TV commercial. That these authority figures are essentially creations of fiction gives us another important indication as to the nature of the drama we are dealing with: for these authority figures, whether fictional or not, are perceived as real in a higher sense. Fictions, however, which embody the essential, lived reality of a culture and society, will readily be recognized as falling within the strict definition of *myth*. The TV commercial, no less than Greek tragedy, deals with the myths at the basis of a culture.

This allows us to see the authority figures that populate the world of the TV commercial as analogous to the characters of a mythical universe: they form an ascending series that starts with the wise confidant who imparts to the heroine the secret of better coffee (a Ulysses or Nestor) and leads via the all-knowing initiate (pharmacist, grocer, doctor, or crusty father figure—corresponding to a Tiresias, a Calchas, or the priestess of the Delphic oracle) into the realm of the great film stars and sporting personalities who are not less but even more mythical in their nature, being the true models for the emulation of the society, the incarnation of its ideals of success and the good life, and immensely rich and powerful to boot. The very fact that a bank, a cosmetics firm, or a manufacturer of breakfast foods has been able to buy their services is proof of that corporation's immense wealth and influence. These great figures—Bob Hope, John Wayne, John Travolta, Farrah Fawcett-Majors—on the one hand lend their charisma to the businesses with whom they have become identified, and on the other they prove the power and effectiveness of those concerns. In exactly the same way, a priest derives prestige from the greatness of the deity he serves, while at the same time proving his own potency by his ability to command the effective delivery of the benefits his deity provides to the community. The great personalities of the TV commercial universe can thus be seen as the demigods and mythical heroes of our society, conferring the blessings of their arche-typal fictional personality image upon the products they endorse and through them upon mankind in general, so that John Wayne becomes, as it were, the Hercules, Bob Hope the Ulysses, John Travolta the Dionysos, and Farrah Fawcett-Majors the Aphrodite of our contemporary Pan-theon. Their presence in the TV commercial underlines its basic char-acter as ritual drama (however debased it may appear in comparison to that of earlier civilizations).

From these still partially realistic demigods the next step up the ladder of authority figures is only logical: we now enter the realm of the wholly allegorical characters, either still invested with human form, like the aforementioned Mother Tums, a spirit assuming human shape to help humans as Athene does when she appears as a shepherd or Wotan as the Wanderer; or openly supernatural: the talking salad that longs to be eaten with a certain salad dressing; the syrup bottle that sings the praises of its contents; the little man of dough who incarnates the power of baking powder; the tiny pink and naked figure who projects the living image of the softness of a toilet tissue; or the animated figures of the triumphant knights (drawing on the imagery of St. George and the Dragon) who fight, resplendent in shining armor, endless but ever vic-torious battles against the demons of disease, dirt, or engine corrosion—a nasty crew of ugly devils with leering, malicious faces and corrosive voices.

The superhuman is closely akin to the merely extra-human: the talking and dancing animals who appear in the commercials for dog and cat foods are clearly denizens of a realm of the miraculous and thus also ingredients of myth; so, in a sense, are the objects that merely lure us by their lusciousness and magnetic beauty: the car lit up by flashes of lightning which symbolize its great power, the steaks and pizzas that visibly melt in the mouth. They, too, are like those trees and flowers of mythical forests which lure the traveler ever deeper into their thickets, because they are more splendid, more colorful, more magnetic than any object could ever be in real life.

Into this category, by extension, also fall the enlarged versions of the symbolic representation of products and corporations: those soft drink bottles the size of the Eiffel tower, those trademarks which suddenly assume gigantic three-dimensional shape so that they tower above the landscape and the people inhabiting it like mountain ranges, the long lines of dominoes that collapse in an immense chain reaction to form the logotype of a company. Here the drama of character has been reduced to a minimum and we are at the other end of the spectrum of theatrical expression, the one contained in the word itself—*theatron*—pure spectacle, the dominant element being the production of memorable images.

Like all drama, the TV commercial can be comprehended as lying between the two extremes of a spectrum: at one end the drama of character and at the other the drama of pure image. In traditional drama one extreme might be exemplified by the psychological drama-of-character of playwrights like Molière, Racine, Ibsen, or Chekhov; the other extreme by the drama of pure image like Ionesco's *Amedée*, Beckett's *Happy Days* or *Not I*. On a slightly less ambitious plane, these extremes are represented by the French bedroom comedy and the Broadway spectacular. At one extreme ideas and concepts are translated into personality, at the other the abstract idea itself is being made visible—and audible.

It is significant, in this context, that the more abstract the imagery of the TV commercial becomes the more extensively it relies on music: around the giant soft drink bottle revolves a chorus of dancing singers; the mountain range of a trademark is surrounded by a choir of devoted singing worshippers. The higher the degree of abstraction and pure symbolism, the nearer the spectacle approaches ritual forms. If the Eucharist can be seen as ritual drama combining a high degree of abstraction in the visual sphere with an equally powerful element of music, this type of TV commercial approaches a secular act of worship: often, literally, a dance around the golden calf.

Between the extremes which represent the purest forms at the two ends of the spectrum are ranged, of course, innumerable combinations of both main elements. The character-based mini-drama of the coffee playlet includes important subliminal visual ingredients, and the crowd singing around the super-lifesize symbol contains an immense amount of instantaneous characterization as the faces of the singers come into focus when the camera sweeps over them: they will always be representative of the maximum number of different types—men, women, children, blacks, Asians, the young and the old—and their pleasant appearance will emphasize the desirable effects of being a worshipper of that particular product.

The reliance on character and image as against the two other main ingredients of drama—plot and dialogue—is clearly the consequence of the TV commercial's ineluctable need for brevity. Both character and image are instantly perceived on a multitude of levels, while dialogue and plot—even the simple plot of the coffee-playlet—require time and a certain amount of concentration. Yet the verbal element can never be entirely dispensed with. Still, all possible ways of making it stick in the memory must be employed: foremost among these is the jingle which combines an easily memorized, rhymed, verbal component with a melody, which, if it fulfills its purpose, will fix the words in the brain with compulsive power. Equally important is the spoken catchphrase, which, always emanating from a memorable personality and authority figure, can be briefer than the jingle and will achieve a growing impact by being repeated over and over until the audience is actually conditioned to complete it automatically whenever they see the character or hear the first syllable spoken.

Brecht, the great theoretician of the didactic play *(Lehrstueck)*, was the first to emphasize the need for drama to be "quotable" and to convey its message by easily remembered and reproduced phrases, gestures, and images. His idea that the gist of each scene should be summed up in one memorable *Grundgestus* (a basic, gestural, and visual as well as verbal, instantly reproducible—quotable—compound of sound, vision, and gesture) has found its ideal fulfillment in the dramaturgy of the TV commercial. And no wonder: Brecht was a fervent adherent of behaviorist psychology and the TV commercial is the only form of drama which owes its actual practice to the systematic and scientifically controlled application of the findings of precisely that school of psychological thought. Compared with the TV commercial, Brecht's own effort to create a type of drama which could effectively influence human behavior and contribute to the shaping of society must appear as highly amateurish fumbling. Brecht wanted to turn drama into a powerful tool of social engineering. In that sense the TV commercial, paradoxically and ironically, is the very culmination and triumphant realization of his ideas.

From the point of view of its *form* the range of TV commercial drama can thus be seen as very large indeed: it extends from the chamber play to the grand spectacular musical; from the realistic to the utmost bounds of the allegorical, fantastical, and abstract. It is in the nature of things that as regards content its scope should be far more restricted. The main theme of this mini-species of drama—and I hope that by now the claim that it constitutes such will appear justified—is the attainment of happiness through the use or consumption of specific goods or services. The outcome (with the exception of a few noncommercial commercials, that is, public service commercials warning against the dangers of alcoholism or reckless driving) is always a happy one. But, as I suggested above, there is always an implied element of tragedy. For the absence of the advertised product or service is always seen as fatal to the attainment of peace of mind, well-being, or successful human relationships. The basic genre of TV commercial drama thus seems to be that of melodrama in which a potentially tragic situation is resolved by a last minute miraculous intervention from above. It may seem surprising that there is a relative scarcity of comedy in the world of the TV commercial. Occasionally comedy appears in the form of a witty catchphrase or a mini-drama concentrating on a faintly comic character, like that fisherman who urges his companions to abandon their breakfast cereal lest they miss the best hour for fishing, and who, when induced to taste the cereal, is so overwhelmed by its excellence that he forgets about the fishing altogether. But comedy requires concentration and a certain time span for its development and is thus less instantly perceivable than the simpler melodramatic situation, or the implied tragedy in the mere sight of a character who has already escaped disaster and can merely inform us of his newfound happiness, thus leaving the tragic situation wholly implicit in the past. The worshippers dancing around the gigantic symbol of the product clearly also belong in this category: they have reached a state of ecstatic happiness through the consumption of the drink, the use of the lipstick concerned, and their hymnic incantations show us the degree of tragic misfortune they have thus avoided or escaped. There is even an implication of tragedy in the straight exhortation uttered by one of the tutelary demigods simply to use the product or service in question. For the failure to obey the precepts uttered by mythic deities must inevitably have tragic results. Nonfulfillment of such commandments involves a grave risk of disaster.

And always, behind the action, there hovers the power that can bring it to its satisfactory conclusion, made manifest through its symbol, praised and hymned by unseen voices in prose or verse, speech or song. There can be no doubt about it: the TV commercial, exactly as the oldest known types of theatre, is essentially a religious form of drama which shows us human beings as living in a world controlled by a multitude of powerful forces that shape our lives. We have free will, we can choose whether we follow their precepts or not, but woe betide those who make the wrong choice!

The moral universe, therefore, portrayed in what I for one regard as the most widespread and influential art form of our time, is essentially that of a polytheistic religion. It is a world dominated by a sheer numberless pantheon of powerful forces, which literally reside in every article of use or consumption, in every institution of daily life. If the winds and waters, the trees and brooks of ancient Greece were inhabited by a vast host of nymphs, dryads, satyrs, and other local and specific deities, so is the universe of the TV commercial. The polytheism that confronts us here is thus a fairly primitive one, closely akin to animistic and fetishistic beliefs.

We may not be conscious of it, but this *is* the religion by which most of us actually live, whatever our more consciously and explicitly held beliefs and religious persuasions may be. This is the actual religion that is being absorbed by our children from almost the day of their birth.

And no wonder—if Marshall McLuhan is right, as he surely is, that in the age of the mass media we have turned away from a civilization based on reading, linear rational thought, and chains of logical reasoning; if we have reverted to a nonverbal mode of perception, based on the simultaneous ingestion of subliminally perceived visual and aural images; if the abolition of space has made us live again in the electronic equivalent of the tribal settlement expanded into a global village—then the reversion to a form of animism is merely logical. Nor should we forget that the rational culture of the Gutenberg Galaxy never extended beyond the very narrow confines of an educated minority elite and that the vast majority of mankind, even in the developed countries, and even after the introduction of universal education and literacy, remained on a fairly primitive level of intellectual development. The limits of the rational culture are shown only too clearly in the reliance on pictorial material and highly simplified texts by the popular press that grew up in the period between the spread of literacy and the onset of the electronic mass media. Even the Christianity of more primitive people, relying as it did on a multitude of saints, each specializing in a particular field of rescue, was basically animistic. And so was—and is—the literalism of fundamentalist forms of puritan protestantism.

Television has not created this state of affairs, it has merely made it more visible. For here the operation of the market has, probably for the first time in human history, led to a vast scientific effort to establish, by intensive psychological research, the real reactions, and hence also the implicit mechanisms of belief, displayed by the overwhelming majority of the population. The TV commercial has evolved to its present dramaturgy through a process of empirical research, a constant dialectic of trial and error. Indeed, it would be wrong to blame the individuals who control and operate the advertising industry as wicked manipulators of mass psychology. Ultimately the dramaturgy and content of the TV commercial universe is the outcrop of the fantasies and implied beliefs of those masses themselves; it is they who create the scenarios of the commercials through the continuous feedback of reactions between the makers of the artifacts concerned and the viewers' responses.

It would be wholly erroneous to assume that the populations of countries without TV commercials exist on a higher level of implied religious beliefs. In the countries of the Communist world, for example, where commercials do not exist, the experience of the rulers with the techniques of political persuasion has led to the evolution of a propaganda which, in all details, replicates the universe of the TV commercials. There too the reliance is on incantation, short memorable catchphrases endlessly repeated, the instant visual imagery of symbols and personality portraits (like the icons of Marx, Engels, and other demigods carried in processions; the red flags, the hammer-and-sickle symbolism) and a whole gamut of similarly structured devices that carry the hallmark of a wholly analogous primitive animism and fetishism. It is surely highly significant that a sophisticated philosophical system like Marxism should have had to be translated into the terms of a tribal religion in order to reach and influence the behavior of the mass populations of countries under the domination of parties which were originally, in a dim past, actuated by intellectuals who were able to comprehend such a complex philosophy. It is equally significant that citizens of those countries that are deprived of all commercials except political ones become literally mesmerized and addicted to the Western type of TV commercials when they have a chance to see them. There is a vast, unexpressed, subconscious yearning in these people, not only for the consumer goods concerned but also for the hidden forces and the miraculous action of the spirits inhabiting them.

In the light of the above considerations it appears that not only must the TV commercial be regarded as a species of drama but that, indeed, it comes very close to the most basic forms of the theatre, near its very roots. For the connection between myth and its manifestation and collective incarnation in dramatized ritual has always been recognized as being both close and organic. The myth of a society is collectively experienced in its dramatic rituals. And the TV commercial, it seems to me, is the ritual manifestation of the basic myth of our society and as such not only its most ubiquitous but also its most significant form of folk drama.

What conclusions are we to draw from that insight (if it were granted that it amounts to one)? Can we manipulate the subconscious psyche of the population by trying to raise the level of commercials? Or should we ban them altogether?

Surely the collective subconscious that tends to operate on the level of animistic imagery cannot be transformed by any short-term measures, however drastic. For here we are dealing with the deepest levels of human nature itself that can change only on a secular time-scale—the time-scale of evolutionary progress itself. Nor would the banning of TV commercials contribute anything to such a type of change.

What we can do, however, is to become aware of the fact that we are here in the presence of a phenomenon that is by no means contemptible or unimportant, but, on the contrary, basic to an understanding of the true nature of our civilization and its problems. Awareness of subconscious urges is, in itself, a first step towards liberation or at least control. Education and the systematic cultivation of rational and conscious modes of perception and thought might, over the long run, change the reaction of audiences who have grown more sophisticated and thus raise the visual and conceptual level of this form of folk-drama. A recognition of the impact of such a powerful ritual force and its myths on children should lead to efforts to build an ability to deal with it into the educational process itself. That, at present, is almost wholly neglected.

And a recognition of the true nature of the phenomenon might also lead to a more rational regulation of its application. In those countries where the frequency of use of TV commercials and their positioning in breaks between programs rather than within them is fairly strictly regulated (Germany, Britain, Scandinavia, for instance), TV commercials have lost none of their efficacy and impact but have become less all-pervasive, thus allowing alternative forms of drama—on a higher intellectual, artistic, and moral level—to exercise a counterbalancing impact. Higher forms of drama, which require greater length to develop more individualized character, more rationally devised story lines, more complex and profound imagery might, ultimately, produce a feedback into the world of the commercial. Once the commercial has ceased to be—as it is at present—the best produced, most lavishly financed, technically most perfect ingredient of the whole television package, once it has to compete with material that is more intelligent and more accomplished, it might well raise its own level of intelligence and rationality.

These, admittedly, may be no more than pious hopes, whistling in the dark. Of one thing, however, I am certain: awareness, consciousness, the ability to see a phenomenon for what it is must be an important first step towards solving any problem. Hence the neglect of the truly popular forms of drama—of which the TV commercial is the most obvious and most blatant example—by the serious critics and theoreticians of that immensely important form of human expression seems highly regrettable. The TV commercial—and all the other forms of dramatic mass entertainment and mass manipulation—not only deserve serious study; a theory of drama that neglects them seems to me elitist, pretentious, and out of touch with the reality of its subject matter.

QUESTIONS FOR READING, RESPONDING, AND WRITING

Summarizing Main Points

1. What are the dramatic features of television commercials?
2. Esslin claims that "experts" on television are "essentially fictitious." List the ways he supports this contention.

Analyzing Methods of Discourse

1. Esslin's essay moves from a descriptive argument—what commercials are—to a prescriptive argument—what we should do about them. How do the arguments interconnect?
2. Early in the essay, Esslin argues that television commercials are a form of drama. He supports that argument both deductively—that is, from generally shared assumptions or premises—and inductively—that is, from examples and evidence. Point out the two kinds of support.

Focusing on the Field

1. Esslin uses many technical terms from the dramatic arts. What are those terms? How does Esslin manage to define those terms for the average reader?
2. Esslin claims that the television commercial is "the most widespread and influential art form of our time." Do you agree or disagree?

Writing Assignments

1. Analyze a familiar commercial as a form of drama. Note how it does or does not incorporate the features that Esslin describes.
2. Daniel Boorstin in "Advertising: The Rhetoric of Democracy" writes that advertising in the United States "has been one of our most characteristic products." Compare and contrast his attitude to Esslin's. Which writer is most critical of advertising methods?

Joan D. Lynch

MUSIC VIDEOS:
From Performance to Dada–Surrealism

Joan Lynch, born in Boston, Massachusetts in 1935, spent over six months preparing the following essay. Considered groundbreaking, the piece marks one of the first serious studies of music videos. Because of her position ahead of the field, Lynch had little help from earlier scholars and was forced to consider all kinds of music videos and study many, many tapes—not all of which, as she makes clear, were from the "top twenty" list. Then, starting from scratch, she constructed the categories in which to fit that plethora of videos.

Lynch, who teaches in the film and theater program at Villanova University, began her scholarly career in the English program at Baskin College, where she gained a B.A. in 1957. In 1970, she took an M.A. at Villanova, and in 1980, she received a doctorate in education from Temple. The author of *Film Education in the Secondary Schools,* as well as several articles on film for such publications as the *Journal of the University Film Association* and *Media and Methods,* Lynch analyzes film primarily from a sociological perspective, though her results vary, depending on both the films she studies and the "thesis" she finds in those films. She is currently at work on a study of how "Hollywood Looks at Yuppie Ladies," with a view toward establishing whether Yuppie women are portrayed as having as much integrity as Yuppie men.

The music video is still in its early childhood, born out of necessity in 1980 when the record business slumped for the second year in a row and the lessening appeal of radio was blamed.[1] Its ancestors are music, particularly rock movies both main-stream and avant-garde, television, radio and commercials. In many ways music videos most resemble commercials. They are short, usually three to four minutes, aim to engage the viewer in a direct, immediate experience and their major "raison d'etre" is to sell. Their product is the music, more particularly the record of the music. Since the birth of music videos, the record industry has climbed out of the doldrums and is thriving once again.[2]

The record companies, instead of being grateful to the child prodigies they spawned, are beginning to see them as the albatross in their budgets. The cost of making them has climbed to an average of $40-$50,000.[3] What was once a day's shoot can now extend to three weeks with pre-production time.[4] The record companies' solution to the budget explosion is to propose that television stations pay for the videos as they would any other programming, and alternately to begin brain-storming marketing strategies to sell the videos themselves.[5] Thus far, only Michael Jackson's "Thriller" and a concert video by Fleetwood Mac have sold any appreciable number in the videocassette format.[6]

The economic struggle will continue to be waged as it is in any other industry, but other problems are also cropping up. Directors for whom making a music video was once just another commercial gig are beginning to think of themselves as artists and they sometimes find themselves in conflict with the performers whom they serve. Directorial concept is pitted against the musician's wish to keep the band and the instruments central.[7] The history of music video is becoming a microcosm of that of the movie industry; star and director battle for control. The musician, whose song may sell records regardless of the quality of the video, has, of course, the upper hand.

This conflict points to the central issue in the development of the video as an art form. The video itself, unless the record companies come up with marketing strategies, has no intrinsic commercial value. When one hears of the top twenty music videos, that figure is the result of the audience survey polls taken by stations such as MTV or of record sales, not music video sales. A really amateurish video may stay on the top twenty for weeks; yet an extraordinarily stylish video may never make the list at all. There may not even be any relationship between the way the record sounds and the style of the video. "Eyes Without a Face," by Billy Idol, is a very pleasant ballad when heard on the radio. In the video one is treated to Billy's curled lip, leather and chain costuming and the imagery of Heavy Metal-fire, entrapment and sado-masochism.

There are literally thousands of music videos. Some are worthy of being hailed as examples of a new art form; others deserve being reviled as trash both in form and content. Making generalizations about them is like trying to draw the average American face. Nevertheless, certain common features, formally and thematically, do emerge.

To date, three basic structures can be identified. The most common one by far, with multiple variations, is centered on the performance itself. There are also narrative videos and videos that are strongly influenced by experimental film.

The cinematic processes are heavily used to create visual interest in the performance video. There are dissolves, lap-dissolves, split screens, masked screens, superimpositions, extreme angle shots, backlighting, intercutting, rapid cutting and so on. The repertory of cinematic tricks may be exhausted in the effort to hold the audience's visual attention. There are also other ways to keep the performance intact while giving the audience something to watch. The performance may be done in a setting appropriate to the lyrics. "Almost Over You" is set in the singer's apartment; her lover's face appears in every reflective surface. Unusual settings may be utilized, such as rows of lit candles or a constructivist set that resembles a huge pile of junk.

The performers may work with extras to whom they can relate. Grace Slick's "All the Machines" is set in a primitive environment surrounded by machines. Extras run the machines or become machines themselves. The theme is nature versus technology, a not uncommon one in videos. A much simpler video is The Romantics' "Talking in Your Sleep." The performers move through rows of girls in night clothes; the climax comes with the appearance of a Marilyn Monroe look-alike.

The performance may be intercut with visuals relating to the lyrics or with images that bear little relationship but are there for humor or shock value. Van Halen's "Panama" is an example of the latter. The dominant images are of traveling but occasionally an outrageous one appears, such as a man peaking through a woman's leg in a toilet. Def Leppard's "Bringin' on the Heartbreak" is set in an industrial area dominated by huge oil drums. The pain of heartbreak is concretized for the audience in the image of the lead singer tied Christ-like to the mast of a boat ferried by two medieval-looking masked men.

Dance is a strong element in most videos, and at times the entire performance is choreographed. "The Warrior" by Scandal resembles a modern dance piece far more than a rock concert.

The line between performance and narrative videos becomes thin when the performers tell the story or appear in the setting where the narrative takes place. The group Night Ranger narrates an episode in the life of "Sister Christian," a straight convent girl who longs for the world of cars and boys and succeeds ultimately in breaking away. Liberation from the shackles of a constraining environment is a recurrent theme in videos. The musicians of ZZ Top not only tell the story of the girl they call Legs, they act as the catalysts or fairy godfathers who spring her Cinderella-like from a repressive and even cruel environment, metamorphose her from a plain Jane to a slick chick and give her a pumpkin-coach in the form of a little red sports car to go off with her Prince Charming.

This notion of the performer as a magician or Christ-like power figure is pervasive in the genre. In "Magic" by the Cars, people of all nations reach out to touch Rick Ocasek, who proves his worthiness of this adoration by walking on water. Deniece Williams in "Let's Hear It for the Boy" has the power to turn dunces into slickly outfitted dancers and wimps into athletes, a combination of the performer as power figure motif and the transformation or Cinderella motif. Michael Jackson seems clearly to be a Christ figure in "Beat It." Warring gangs prepare for action, climaxing in a fight in a warehouse. Michael, with a single touch, separates the fighting leaders who join him in a dance as do their followers.

Pure narrative videos are mini-movies with the performers playing the heroes or heroines. In "Love Is a Battlefield," Pat Benatar rejects her working class parents to work as a prostitute. She becomes the leader of a rebellion against the pimp and returns home saddened but wiser. Cyndi Lauper is also the child of working class parents in "Time after Time," as she was in "Girls Just Wanna Have Fun." Her transformation is from plain Jane to Punker. Even her boyfriend finds her partially shaved head and dyed hair hard to accept, so she ends up going off alone presumably to seek others of her kind.

In the hundreds of videos I have watched, the parents were portrayed as lower middle class. The icons of motherhood are an apron and a broom. Fathers typically sit around in undershirts and swill beer. Marriage and a family are traps which the wary and the hip avoid. One exception to this is Tracy Ullman's "They Don't Know." Tracy, the performer, tells the story dressed in a succession of chic outfits. She also plays the heroine who falls in love, marries and ends up like the rest of the lower class parents, pushing the baby in a supermarket dressed in the obligatory shapeless dress and apron with stringy hair and bedroom slippers.

When the upper classes appear in a video they are figures of fun to be mocked and their rituals are set up to be disrupted. In the anarchic "Round and Round," by Ratt, Milton Berle plays both an aristocratic paterfamilias and a well-corseted, snooty dowager. Chaos occurs during a dinner party when the butler serves live rats in a serving dish; the lead Rat at this point crashes through the ceiling onto the table. Exchanging his tux for a Rats costume, the butler joins the band.

Work in videos is something to be avoided, even the glamorous work of the pop star himself. In "Love Somebody," Rick Springfield is engaged in the arduous task of watching his own concert on a studio monitor to which he lip synchs. His eye catches a poster of a tropical island and he imagines himself there with a beautiful girl. The remainder of the video intercuts between studio, concert stage and island until the end when an explosion occurs in the editing room. Rick leaves, grinning happily, film strung around his neck, presumably glad to be freed from the onerous task of editing his own footage.

The most interesting music videos are those influenced by experimental film. Descendants of "Entr'acte," An "Andalusian Dog" and "Ballet Mecanique," they borrow the techniques of Dada, Surrealism and abstract film. Those that opt for pure abstraction are less compelling than the abstract video that builds a pattern that may be discerned in repeated viewings. In "Miss Me Blind" by Culture Club, oriental images dominate. The images, which are very harmonious at the opening, change to violent ones centering on the possibility of one character blinding the other physically. Various blinds (window shades) are pulled up and down. The word "blind" flashes on and off the screen. Intercut with these images are masks, strips of film and oriental letters. The piece ends with Boy George donning a white oriental mask. In the next frame, the mask is empty save for a fake blue eye which drips tears.

Many surrealistic music videos are more confusing than amusing. The best exploit spatial and temporal disjunction to create meaning. In "Harden My Heart" by Quarterflash the lyrics concern a girl's need to leave her lover psychically as well as physically. A narrow corridor symbolizes her confinement and restriction; the desert represents freedom and a third space set in a future time, a garage with the band on motorcycles, will become her means of escape. There is rapid cutting in the piece from one space and time to the other until the final frame when we see that the narrow corridor is in the desert. The heroine walks out the door to freedom and climbs aboard a motorcycle. A bulldozer then collapses the building and a flame thrower burns it.

Freudian imagery, the hallmark of Surrealism, is not found very often in the music video. Sexual symbolism was necessary in an age of censorship; the erotic was suggested in an oblique, indirect way. Today, if there is any one element that characterizes music videos, it is their blatant sexuality, though some censorship still exists. Kevin McVaney, programming director for MTV, claims that his primary concern in choosing the videos that will play is quality of the music; his next greatest concern is compliance with community moral standards.[8] One wonders exactly how explicit material needs to be before it is banned, since some videos such as "Gloria," by The Doors, leave little to the imagination. "Gloria" is the story of a groupie who gets very close to her idol.

A striking exception to the general rule that little Freudian sex symbolism is used in music videos today may be found in "When Doves

Cry," by Prince and the Revolution. The ending of the piece finds Prince and the band dressed in very stylish costumes in what appears to be a concert setting. Very quickly the screen splits and images merge to create highly suggestive sexual symbols. The image of Prince himself splits and then merges to create a phallus. As a woman plays a guitar, there is a cut to a close-up of that musical instrument which then splits creating the female sex symbol.

By far the most effective of the music videos is a piece that is pure Dada, "You Might Think," by The Cars; to give tribute to public taste, it was also number one on the MTV audience survey poll for many weeks. "You Might Think" resembles a painting by Magritte. The colors used are bright pastels. Change of scale, scale dissociation and displacement are the techniques used to create Dadaist surprise and humor. Voyeurism pervades the piece. The lead singer spies on his beloved through her window in which he appears gargantuan and through a periscope in her bathtub. He becomes the lipstick in her tube, then, as a fly, lands on her nose. He perches with her on the sink, and when they fall in, a canoe appears and they row off. Like King Kong, he snatches her from her bed and clinging to a nearby building holds her Fay Wray-like in his hand. He displaces others in her affection, turning into a screen character in a movie she is watching and knocking her current boyfriend out of a photograph, to replace him. The band backs him up. They serenade her while in her medicine chest and from her soap bar. It comes as no surprise that The Car's next video to be released will be directed by Andy Warhol.

Music videos are the strongest and the weakest of pop art. Many are crude, vulgar, offensive or just plain boring. Some few are three-minute masterpieces. In the summer of 1984, the Whitney Museum in New York ran a video art retrospective that showed the full capacities of video as an artistic medium. It is my hope that some archivist is collecting the most artistic of the music videos and that they, too, will someday be shown in a museum setting.

Many predict that credits will soon appear at the end of a video. When the choreographer, art director, scene designer and director are named, the videos will drop their disposable status as commercials and move toward being potentially recognized and collected as art. This would also open the door to videos being anthologized, labelled and sold as representatives of the work of a particular artist other than the performer.

NOTES

1. Jay Cocks, "Sing a Song of Seeing: Rock Videos are Firing up a Revolution," *Time*, 122 (Dec. 26, 1983), p. 54.

2. Ibid., p. 56.
3. "Music Video Director's Symposium," *Variety*, 314 (March 14, 1984), p. 88.
4. Ibid., p. 70.
5. "Beautiful Model Meets Sumo Wrestler," *Forbes*, 132 (Sept. 12, 1983), p. 38.
6. "Music Videos: Growth of a New Art Form," *Rolling Stone*, No. 404 (Sept. 15, 1983), p. 90.
7. *Variety*, p. 70.
8. Symposium on Music Videos held at the Young Filmmakers by the New York Film Council, New York City, New York, June 21, 1984.

QUESTIONS FOR READING, RESPONDING, AND WRITING

Summarizing Main Points

1. List the characteristics that comprise each of the three categories into which Lynch divides music videos. Do you agree with the divisions Lynch makes? Why do you suppose she defines the representation of parents, the upper classes, and work in the narrative category? Do these representations apply to the other categories as well? Note, too, the categories into which she places sex and the performer-as-magician.
2. Describe the "economic struggle" which Lynch suggests the making of a music video presents. What does Lynch see as the solution to this "economic struggle"? How will this solution change the nature or character of music videos?

Analyzing Methods of Discourse

1. Lynch begins her essay with the statement that music videos most resemble commercials and ends it with her description of their potential to become art. Consider the categories she proposes and their arrangement. How does her discussion of the three categories help chart the music video's evolution from commercial to art?
2. In paragraph eleven, Lynch argues that "the line between performance and narrative videos becomes thin when the performers tell the story or appear in the setting where the narrative takes place." Explain the ways in which the next paragraph on the performer as-magician illustrates this type of transition.

Focusing on the Field

1. Lynch presumes her audience's familiarity with the terms "Dada" and "surrealism." Both terms were used to label artistic movements in the early part of the twentieth century which had as their goals the "discovery of a more authentic reality" through the transformation of art and society. Dadaists sought "to abolish traditional cultural and aesthetic forms by techniques of comic derision in which irrationality, chance, and intuition were the guiding principles." Similarly, surrealists sought the "radical transformation of existing social, scientific, and philosophical values through the total liberation of the unconscious." (*American Heritage Dictionary*, pp. 331–332, 1295) Do you think, through her use of these terms, Lynch is making similar claims for music videos? Why or why not?

2. How much familiarity does Lynch presume that her audience has with music videos? Locate evidence in the essay to support your conclusion.

Writing Assignments

1. Analyze and classify several of the more recent music videos according to the categories Lynch provides. Do the categories fit? Is it necessary to ignore any aspects of the videos in order to make them fit? Using all your findings, write an essay that argues that music videos are or are not evolving along the lines Lynch has described.
2. Compare Martin Esslin's "Aristotle and the Advertisers" to Lynch's essay. Then, using material from both essays, write an essay of your own in which you argue that television commercials are or are not like music videos.

Art Evans

JOE LOUIS AS A KEY FUNCTIONARY:
White Reactions toward a Black Champion

Currently an associate professor of sociology at Florida Atlantic University, Art Evans gained his B.A. (1973) from Delaware State College and both his M.A. (1975) and his Ph.D. (1978) from Kansas State University. He has published articles in *Social Science Quarterly, The Professional Geographer,* the *Journal of Black Studies,* and the *Journal of Sport and Social Issues,* where in a 1979 article, "Differences in Recruitment of Blacks and Whites at a Big Eight University," he was able to combine his primary interests in the sociology of sport and in dominant-minority relations.

He is able to combine those interests again here in "Joe Louis as a Key Functionary: White Reactions toward a Black Champion." Though in this essay his focus is on Joe Louis and his 1936 title bout with German fighter Max Schmeling, Evans makes a broader point about white society's treatment of black athletes. According to Evans, sport presents an interesting paradox for the black athlete. It "reflects dominant values, norms, and ideology of society," while at the same time, because of its competitive nature, it allows the chance to achieve a status denied elsewhere in society. This situation leads Evans to argue that athletic ability qualifies blacks to become "key functionaries—'actors performing crucial activities for the total system'—for their sports units, but their performances have little bearing in eradicating white perceptions of their inferior status in a larger society."

Olsen (1978: 25–26) defines "key functionaries" as actors performing crucial activities for the total system. Systems depend on adequate performance from key functionaries for overall survival and operation. Because of their locations and activities, key functionaries are indispensable actors for any system's operations. This article investigates responses of dominants toward racial minorities when the latter occupy key functionary positions traditionally reserved for the former. Specifically, white Americans' responses toward Joe Louis, a black heavyweight boxing champion, are explored. The Joe Louis-Max Schmeling heavyweight title fight of 1938 is the primary focus because this match exemplifies Louis's role as a key functionary for the American system. I argue that Louis's achieved status as the American representative fighting against Nazism did not negate whites' negative perception of him as black. Sport reflects dominant values, norms, and the ideology of society (Edwards, 1973: 84–100; Loy et al., 1978: 297–331; Coakley, 1978: 15–35). Hence one expects institutional discrimination in the general context of American society to exist in athletics. Institutional discriminatory beliefs and practices against blacks during the time of the Louis-Schmeling fight are crucial in understanding whites' responses to Louis.

Hitler had reached the height of his power in Germany by the time of this fight. Many Americans were uneasy with Nazi ideology and the German boxer who vowed to return to his nation with the heavyweight crown. The Louis-Schmeling fight acquired both political and symbolic significance, featuring American democracy and Nazi supremacy as opponents (Orr, 1969: 19–63; Leonard, 1980: 73). Schmeling gained favor among those supporting Nazi ideology because he also was a believer. White Americans, however, felt somewhat ambivalently toward Louis. On the one hand, whites practiced institutional discrimination against all black Americans, relegating them to low status positions in society. On the other hand, Louis was black but had achieved the status of a great fighter and was expected to represent and fight symbolically for American freedom and democracy.

During the 1930s institutional discrimination against blacks was pervasive. Race was the determining variable that denied blacks access to privilege and power. Even talented and educated blacks could not acquire positions of prestige and influence in integrated contexts because of skin pigmentation. These imposed segregational arrangements were supported by the doctrine of white supremacy. Such discriminatory practices had and continue to have an enduring negative effect on the black population. Relations between blacks and whites were strained during the 1930s, resulting in whites solidifying their economic and racial domination through social, judicial, and political discrimination. In general social interactions between whites and blacks during the Louis-Schmeling fight were antagonistic, not harmonious (Wilson, 1978; Sitkoff, 1978). Using this historical background, I suggest that whites perceived Louis in categorical and inferior terms despite his status as a key functionary. However, before discussing examples of white perceptions of Louis, a theoretical framework of racial minorities occupying key functionary positions is needed.

THEORETICAL FRAMEWORK OF RACIAL MINORITIES AS KEY FUNCTIONARIES

Racial stratification often results in an impermeable caste system. Such systems delineate racial minorities by their ascribed status and categorically debar them from preferred roles and statuses. The position of racial minorities is always disadvantageous because salient rewards (e.g., power, privilege, and prestige) are allocated by dominants who formulate and judge rules of that system (Blalock, 1962; Berry and Tischler, 1978; Kinloch, 1979). Almost no escape exists for even qualified members because they, like others in their category, are perceived and responded to by dominants as inferior. Says Kramer (1970: 7):

> race . . . is itself the harshest form of differentiation. Unlike ethnicity, which may be diminished over time, race is never irrelevant under any circumstances; members of different racial groups always respond to each other as representatives of their respective categories rather than as individuals.

Blalock (1967: 74) suggests two resources racial minorities may utilize to help overcome their disadvantaged situation. First, pressure resources (e.g., protest, boycotts, and strikes) can be employed to force concessions from adamant dominants. Pressure resources, however, often prove problematic over time because they necessitate mass organization and diminish in value once tokens gain access to privileged positions.

Second, competitive resources may be used to advance a racial minority's position in society. These resources are especially advantageous in competitive situations where each position functions as a key functionary and individual performances are judged independently and objectively. A competitive system cannot afford to discriminate on the basis of ascribed status because rewards gained depend on that system's performance in relation to other systems. Such systems recruit only the most qualified persons to perform roles because all are crucial. Professional athletics for the most part are a competitive system. Managers and owners recruit only qualified athletes to maximize the sport unit's chances of winning and hence of receiving rewards. Because records are kept on each athlete, it seems unlikely a superior athletic performance will go unnoticed (Blalock, 1967: 92). According to Coakley (1978: 277–313) the competitive aspect of professional sport is key to understanding the overrepresentation of blacks in athletics today.

Blacks' representation in professional sport has proliferated (Olsen, 1968: 10), but racial discrimination directed toward them does exist. Athletic prowess of black athletes is secondary to their race (Boyle, 1963: 100–134; Brown, 1973: 168–173; Edwards, 1969; Eitzen and Sanford, 1975: 948–959; Evans, 1979: 1–10). In other words, athletic ability qualifies blacks to become key functionaries for their sport units when competing in sport systems, but their performances have little bearing in eradicating white perceptions of their inferior status in the larger society. One explanation for this paradox is that professional sport is not only competitive but also functions as entertainment. Of fans who follow sports and pay to observe them, most are white and middle class. Edwards (1973: 214) notes that the dynamics of fan involvement require that they cognitively and affectively identify with the sport unit, but

> This identification is hindered in cases where an athletic unit is composed of members of one race and the population upon which it depends for fan support is composed of another. . . . It was this fact which motivated the movement of the American Basketball Association's Dallas franchise to remove four of the ten blacks from its eleven man 1972–73 roster. According to the team's head coach, "Whites in Dallas are simply not interested in paying to see an all black team and the black population alone cannot support us."

Potentially, all black professional athletes face a conflict between their achieved and ascribed statuses. On the one hand, able athletes are honored and esteemed, but, on the other hand, as blacks, they are treated as inferior (Edwards, 1973: 182). Their ascribed role disvalues them, as their achieved role accords them esteem. In most cases the ascribed status overshadows any achievement and results in inconsistent cognitions (Yinger, 1965: 10–14). Examine, for example, the case of Jackie Robinson, a key functionary for his athletic unit, who nevertheless faced prejudice and discrimination from white fans and teammates despite his objective performance (Robinson and Duckett, 1972). Unlike Robinson, who was a key functionary only for his team, Joe Louis became involved in a sporting event that placed him in a key functionary status for all America. One ex post facto explanation suggests that white Americans placed race prejudice aside to support Louis against the German Schmeling. This article does not support this claim. Instead I suggest that despite Louis's role as a key functionary for American democracy, whites demonstrated an ambivalence toward him. Whites found it difficult to support Louis fully as a national hero because they simultaneously regarded him as inferior because he was black.

WHITES' PERCEPTIONS OF JOHNSON AND LOUIS

Louis was the second black to hold the heavyweight championship. The first was Jack Johnson, who won the title by defeating Tommy Burns in 1908. I believe white Americans' responses toward Louis are linked to the career of Johnson.

Johnson held the heavyweight crown from 1908 to 1915. After Johnson won the crown whites became disillusioned with boxing as a professional sport because the then popular theory of Social Darwinism (which supported the belief of white superiority) was shattered. A central concern of white fans was that a black would permanently reign as champion; this situation they would not tolerate. For example President Roosevelt expressed his concern over the outcome of the Johnson-Burns match by calling for the prohibition of all pugilism in the United States (Gilmore, 1975: 71).

Some whites who believed the Johnson-Burns contest was a fluke and that a white could always easily defeat a black urged Jim Jeffries (a retired white undefeated champion) to return to the ring to fight Johnson. The Johnson-Jeffries fight occurred on Independence Day, 1910, demonstrating the political significance of the match. This fight proved disappointing to white fans when Jeffries was easily defeated.

Negative reactions from whites stemmed not only from the fact that Johnson was a black champion but also because his mannerisms outside and inside the ring defied conventional stereotypes regarding how blacks were supposed to behave. For whites, Johnson's conduct was abominable and arrogant.

> Johnson's activities spurred on several Progressive reform movements from prohibition and anti-vice campaigns to attempts to ban boxing matches. His defeat of Jeffries led to a successful fight to prevent movies of the fight from being shown and convinced Congress to pass a law banning the interstate transportation of fight films. Long after his death laws banning interracial marriages passed in reaction to Johnson's white wives were still enshrined in several state's constitutions . . . Johnson was viewed by whites as too "impudent," he showed so much scorn for his white opponents, and was so unrepentent that for decades after his era whites feared that other black sports figures would do the same [Gilmore, 1975: 6].

The foundation of white fears concerning Johnson was that he would serve as a role model for blacks causing the status quo to be in jeopardy. Immediately after the Jeffries match whites used negative sanctions di-

rected toward all blacks to suggest that their dominance was still intact. For example, fight-related riots and disturbances perpetuated by whites toward blacks occurred in almost every American city. Though some blacks had only a vague familiarity with Johnson they were often the targets of white hostility. Consider the following:

> I was fourteen at the time. Jack Johnson, a Negro, defeated Jim Jeffries, a white man. . . . White men in my county could not take it. A few Negroes were beaten up because a Negro had beaten a white man in far away Nevada. Negroes dared not discuss the outcome of this match in the presence of whites. In fact Johnson's victory was hard on the white man's world . . . Jack Johnson committed two grave blunders as far as whites were concerned: he beat up a white man and he was socializing with a white woman—both deadly sins [Mays, 1971: 19].

On the cognitive level whites did not identify with Johnson as their champion. This feeling led white managers and promoters to search for a "Great White Hope." According to Lardner (1951) promoters traveled to cities and rural towns looking for strong tall white males to oppose Johnson. In some cities "White Hope Tournaments" were staged to determine which white boxer could best oppose the black champion. Certainly these affairs were not openly competitive because all black fighters were barred from participating (Lardner, 1951).

When Johnson lost his title to Jess Willard in 1915, whites were jubilant because they believed the ideology of white superiority was regenerated (Gilmore, 1975). Perhaps the following is indicative of feelings on the part of whites:

> It is a point of pride with the ascendant race not to concede supremacy in anything, not even to a gorilla. The fact the Mr. Willard made it possible for many millions of his fellow citizens to sit down to their dinners last night with renewed confidence in their eight-inch biceps, flexed, and their twenty-eight-inch chests, expanded in his peculiar triumph [Gilmore, 1975: 138].

After Johnson's fall, integrated professional sports became less available to black athletes. Whites were determined, especially within the sport of boxing, that a black (in particular an arrogant one) would never fight for the heavyweight crown again (Lardner, 1951).

Despite institutional segregational arrangements and the reluctance of the white boxing establishment to allow blacks to fight for the crown, Louis's objective competitive boxing record could not be denied. Louis turned professional in 1934 and had won an impressive total of 46 fights (36 of which were by knockout) even before winning the title from Jim Braddock in 1937. His only defeat was to Schmeling in 1935. By any

objective standard his record in the ring was impressive and could not be overlooked, even by racists. If one considers athletic prowess in isolation of other traits, Louis was overly qualified and deserved a chance at the crown.

Another and perhaps more important factor accounting for the change of heart within the white boxing establishment concerning black fighters was Louis's demeanor. I have already noted the entertainment function of sport and the importance of fans identifying with athletes. In contrast to the "arrogant" Johnson, Louis was basically a docile person and therefore less of a threat to whites:

> One of the champion's most likeable traits is an utter lack of snobbishness, and the attention of such notables as few colored products of the Alabama backwoods have ever seen has not upset his equilibrium [Brown, 1940: 50].

At least one writer has suggested that the years during Johnson's reign as champ would have been less problematic for whites if Louis had held the crown:

> Probably the White Hope era of 1908–15 would not have been exactly what it was if Louis had been champion then instead of Johnson. Johnson's character had a strong influence on the temper of the time. He was much that Louis is not—haughty, articulate, stubborn, determined to express his nature openly and to assert all his rights in the face of prejudice [Lardner, 1951: 22–23].

Louis's behavior was carefully structured to meet white expectations. For example, Louis's managers—John Roxborough, Julian Black, and James Blackwell—attempted to package their fighter so that race would be subordinate to his boxing skills. They taught Louis even such details as bathing, hair care, and table manners. They controlled his car driving, airplane riding, and any other behaviors that might offend whites. To fight Braddock for the heavyweight championship Louis needed not only to be overly qualified but to demonstrate behaviors acceptable to the predominantly white fans (Brown, 1940: 52).

Despite Louis's behavioral transformation and his great skills as a fighter, whites still perceived him in negative, categorical, and stereotypical terms. Consider the following description of Louis after winning one of his many fights.

> Probably the most important asset of this kinky-haired, thick-lipped embalmer was the cool, expressionless manner in which he fought. . . . That dead pan has been a potent box-office factor. . . . Never has he aroused revulsion at seeing him tower over a fallen white man [*Literary Digest*, 1936: 36].

There is also some evidence that some white Americans renewed their search for a "Great White Hope" during Louis's reign, though less hysterically than in the days of Johnson (Orr, 1969).

THE LOUIS-SCHMELING FIGHT

Louis's role as a key functionary for America is demonstrated in his second fight with Schmeling. Regardless of what whites felt toward Louis, he had to be accommodated because of his outstanding competitive record. The importance and political nature of the fight can be seen by examining those in attendance at ringside. The following were among the many who attended: Mayor LaGuardia, the postmaster general of the United States, four governors representing Michigan, Connecticut, New Jersey, and Pennsylvania, Supreme Court justice, the secretary of state, and more than 100 fans from as far away as California (Daley, 1938: 15).

Minority group interests were also represented, though many could not afford to attend:

> Indications are that between 8,000 and 10,000 Negroes will attend the fight. . . . The two-and-a-half million Jews in New York are solidly behind Louis and they expect to represent a large quota of the attendance [*The New York Age*, 1938: 1].

It is safe to assume that both blacks and Jews were interested in the fight out of self-interest rather than nationalistic concerns. For blacks a Louis victory would be a symbolic triumph over the notion of white supremacy as expressed by both America and Germany. We have already noted the effects of institutional discrimination on black Americans during the 1930s. Like white Americans, Germans also held racist beliefs that suggested blacks were inferior. For example, even

> Schmeling stated in a recent interview that a Negro had no right with the world's heavyweight championship; that he had returned from Germany to take it away from him. . . . He said that after he had wrested the heavyweight title from Joe Louis, it would be up to the other white fighters to wrest the other championships from all other Negroes holding them [Abbott, 1938: 6].

An article about the first Louis-Schmeling fight appearing in the German publication *Der Weltcampf* is indicative of the racist attitudes Nazis held about blacks. After denouncing the use by France, England, and the United States of black troops in World War I, the article stated:

> These countries cannot thank Schmeling enough for this victory for he checked the arrogance of the Negro race and clearly demonstrated to them

the superiority of white intelligence. He restored the prestige of the white race and in doing so accomplished a cultural achievement. I for one am convinced that Schmeling was fully conscious of this fact and that he fought as a representative of the white race. . . . The victory of Italy in Abyssinia must be regarded in the same light. . . . After the war started there was only one thing left, the fight of a white against a black nation. This has become a racial fight. The same question must be asked: What would have happened if Abyssinia had won? The same answer applies: the whole black world would have risen up against the white race in arrogance and bestial cruelty [Spandau, 1936: 301].

Jewish Americans wanted Louis to beat Schmeling because they strongly identified with German Jews being persecuted under the Nazi regime. In 1937 Jewish groups were helpful in forcing the cancellation of the Braddock-Schmeling championship match by organizing a national boycott. Jews did not make the same attempt for the Louis fight because they feared Gentiles would put the bout over despite their protest (Clark, 1938: 8).

Almost every walk of life was represented in the fight crowd or radio audience. New York City, not expecting such a crowd, ordered 3,000 extra policemen to cover the fight, leaving other parts of the city deserted (Dawson, 1938: 25). On the night of the fight New York welcomed 30,000 visitors and made more than $3,000,000 from them in sales. Hotels, night clubs, and railroads could not meet the demands of the newly arriving people.

For all the publicity and promotion, the fight was a disappointment. It only lasted two minutes and four seconds, with Louis winning by a technical knockout. Within this short time span Schmeling was decked three times and received a fractured vertebra (*Time*, 1938: 19–20).

Events leading up to and after the fight demonstrate how whites failed to support fully or cognitively identify with Louis. For example, Schmeling arrived in the United States to begin training for the fight on May 19, 1938. After recuperating from his journey, he left New York City to train in Spectator, New York. Before boarding the train, however, he received a strong ovation from white Americans (*New York Times*, 1938a: 25). After reviewing the *New York Times* concerning Schmeling's workouts, I found that between May 18 and June 20 an overwhelming amount of attention is devoted to the crowds who came to observe him. On some days Schmeling received up to 8,000 visitors to his camp (*New York Times*, 1938a, 1938b, 1938c, 1938d). It appears safe to assume that the majority of spectators who observed Schmeling were white Americans when one considers the negative views Schmeling expressed toward blacks and Jews. Louis's training sessions were not covered as extensively, but when discussed the writers were quick to point out the racial make-up of his supporters:

So dense was the congestion around his training ring that Louis himself had to fight his way to it. He was surrounded at every step by worshipful admirers, mostly of his own race [Nichols, 1938: 26)].

This does not suggest that whites did not support Louis. However, the racial make-up of the crowds attending both training camps closely parallels the dual existence of most blacks and whites living during these times.

Another indication of what whites felt toward Louis is how they perceived black fighters in general. In some cases the athletic prowess of black fighters was explained as a latent benefit of the institution of slavery:

The Negro race has provided some of the outstanding prize fighters. . . . This leads to the consideration that slavery in the South, while a cause of sorrow to the Negro race, nonetheless physically was a benefit. The 250 years that slaves of the South worked in the cotton fields and on the plantation accounts for the splendid physique of the race today. Life in the open air, away from the congested conditions of the cities has been beneficial to the white and black races. . . . With the influx of the Negro into the industrial North it will not take a generation to stunt their growth and reduce them to the inferior physique of the white factory laborers [Duckett, 1938: 10].

Even on the night of the Louis-Schmeling fight sportswriters demonstrated how they did not contain their racism by referring to all black fighters in the preliminary bouts as "dusky warriors." In particular, one qualified black fighter was described in the following manner:

Dusky Dave Clark carries his mouth protector pushed forward under his upper lip making him look like one of the Ubangi savages from South Africa [Kieran, 1938: 14].

One would expect an athletic victory by Louis would cause much celebration among all Americans if indeed they regarded him as "winning for America." However, I found that for the most part blacks were the only group demonstrating celebrative behaviors. For example, in Chicago,

Shots were fired in the air, firecrackers set off, trolley poles jerked from streetcars and some windows broken. . . . Crowds poured into the street, a few moments after Schmeling's defeat was broadcast from New York. Dancing Negroes covered the pavements and tied up traffic. . . . Special police details were on duty in the district South Loop but no arrests were reported [*The New York Times*, 1938f].

In Harlem blacks were also overjoyed that Louis had won. Extra police were assigned to special duty in Harlem as it celebrated the victory of

Louis. The Harlem streets were almost deserted when the fight began because blacks were indoors, listening to the radio description of the knockout. But,

> No sooner was the Schmeling debacle over than thousands of men and women and children surged out of the tenements and radio stores into the Harlem streets shouting with glee (*The New York Times*, 1938e).

The celebration in Harlem was so enormous that the police commissioner ordered all traffic on Seventh Avenue between 125th and 145th Streets shut off so the celebrants could enjoy themselves. The commissioner reported that "this is their night; let them have their fun" (*The New York Times*, 1938e). In Cleveland, however, police were not so generous to the black celebrants. For example, police used tear gas to quell riotous crowds in the black section. One man was shot to death and two white policemen were knocked unconscious by flying bricks.

For the most part, whites did not celebrate Louis's victory, and if they did it was done quietly and did not receive public notice. The diminutive response from whites toward Louis does not mean they had no interest in the fight or did not support Louis. All evidence suggests whites were as interested in a Louis victory as blacks, though the reasons were different. I argue that whites did not celebrate the Louis victory because they could not cognitively identify with him as a national rather than only a black hero, despite his status as a key functionary for their system.

DISCUSSION

I do not claim as absolute truth that whites supported Louis out of nationalistic concerns, yet perceived him as inferior because he was black. However, when the historical circumstances of racial discrimination against blacks are taken into account and events prior to and after the fight are observed, I believe this inference is justified.

It was impossible for a nation with a history like ours, where the races were separated in every social realm, to judge Joe Louis only on the basis of his individual traits. Steps were taken in this direction, but Louis's race was never forgotten. This was exemplified in the many articles I found that acknowledged Louis's great skill, yet went on to remark on his color, stereotypical physical characteristics, or his lack of intelligence.

This ambivalence is also demonstrated by the fact that only those newspapers and magazines aimed at black audiences made reference to racist Nazi ideology. Publications aimed at the general public played down any reference to Louis as representing America; yet German tabloids clearly saw the fight as a contest between races. Despite denials by

some, press attention and the makeup of the ringside audience indicate that the Louis-Schmeling match was indeed seen as politically important by white Americans. Their failure to acknowledge this publicly demonstrates their failure to identify cognitively with Louis.

I have discussed how Louis succeeded in the competitive aspect of sport, and his status as a key functionary. But these two things do not appear to supersede the entertainment aspect of sport. In order to be successful, entertainment must be socially acceptable to the audience. The social climate of our country precluded the public's cognitively identifying with and thereby lending their full support to Joe Louis. His socially ascribed status transcended his achievements in the competitive realm.

This analysis should not be limited to the specific case of Joe Louis. Are today's black athletes, continually lauded by the press, judged by fans primarily on their individual merits, or does their race still transcend their role as key functionary? Finally, on a broader scale, this analysis can be used in examining minority key functionaries in their organizational settings; for example, in the government, military, business, religion, and entertainment. How do ambivalent responses of dominants affect these individuals socially and psychologically? Does this contribute to marginality?

QUESTIONS FOR READING, RESPONDING, AND WRITING

Summarizing Main Points

1. Evans describes the roles played by Jack Johnson, Joe Louis, and Jackie Robinson in professional athletics. List the differences in their roles and describe the ways in which those differences are a result of both the sports that they played and their personalities.
2. Define both "achieved status" and "ascribed status" as Evans uses the terms.

Analyzing Methods of Discourse

1. Evans begins his essay with both historical and professional background information—that is, he places the facts of Joe Louis's career within a historical perspective for his reader, and he defines certain terms that might be considered technical vocabulary by his reader. List any other ways that Evans helps the reader cope with the material he discusses and the ways in which he discusses it.
2. Evans also provides a thesis sentence very early on. Later, in the section of his essay entitled "Discussion," Evans repeats his thesis. The two sentences are not *exactly* alike. How, exactly, are they different? Why are they different?

Focusing on the Field

1. How does Evans's point of view and his use of authorities, subtitles, footnotes, and word choice create an objective tone in his essay? Cite specific examples.

Compare his tone and approach to the subject to those of Maya Angelou in "Champion of the World."

2. Who is Evans's intended audience? Given the limits of his audience that Evans's professional vocabulary must necessarily create, what would you think the goal of this essay might be?

Writing Assignments

1. Are there "key functionaries" in other areas besides sports? In high school, perhaps? In college? In a short essay, describe the status, both "ascribed" and "achieved," of "key functionaries" you have encountered (e.g., prom queen, class president, football star, band leader).

2. Rewrite the section entitled "Theoretical Framework of Racial Minorities as Key Functionaries" for a wider audience.

A·P·P·E·N·D·I·X

STUDENT WRITERS ON THE
WRITING PROCESS
Essays and Interviews

The following section contains essays written by undergraduates at Rutgers University in response to writing assignment #2 on John Kenneth Galbraith's controversial essay, "How to Get the Poor off Our Conscience," pp. 548–554. Cathy Young, a double major in political science and English, and Daniel Desch, a major in electrical engineering, respond in parallel interviews to questions concerning the ways in which they planned, drafted, and completed their essays. The opening section of Daniel Desch's draft with his analytic comments is also included. You may wish to compare the professional responses of William Tucker to the same issues of writing as seen in his commentary following "Conservation in Deed."

WRITING ASSIGNMENT—GALBRAITH

Galbraith concludes his essay with the claim that "Compassion, along with the associated public effort, is the least comfortable, the least convenient, course of behavior and action in our time. But it remains the only one that is consistent with a totally civilized life. Also, it is, in the end, the most truly conservative course." Write a brief essay responding to Galbraith's conclusion.

FIRST DRAFT—ESSAY #1

HOW TO GET GALBRAITH OFF YOUR CONSCIENCE
Daniel Desch

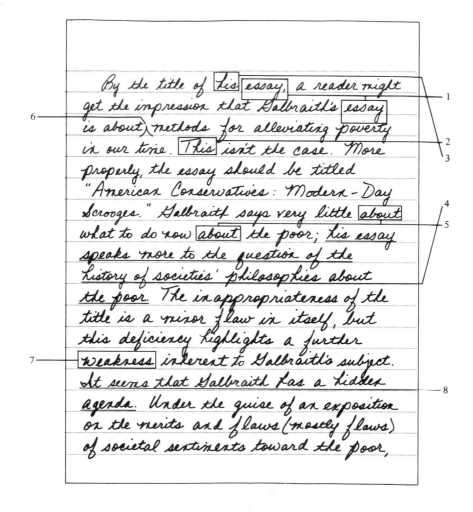

By the title of this essay, a reader might get the impression that Galbraith's essay is about methods for alleviating poverty in our time. This isn't the case. More properly, the essay should be titled "American Conservatives: Modern-Day Scrooges." Galbraith says very little about what to do now about the poor; his essay speaks more to the question of the history of societies' philosophies about the poor. The inappropriateness of the title is a minor flaw in itself, but this deficiency highlights a further weakness inherent to Galbraith's subject. It seems that Galbraith has a hidden agenda. Under the guise of an exposition on the merits and flaws (mostly flaws) of societal sentiments toward the poor,

he is attacking the policies of Ronald
Reagan and a perceived rise in conservatism in the United States. There
is nothing wrong with Galbraith's agenda
as it stands; it is his use of distortions
and misrepresentations to serve his
argument that rankles. If he had
presented a reasoned, considerate indictment of past and present policies, his
essay would have been perhaps less
amusing, less provocative, but certainly
more respectable and more informative.
As it stands Galbraith, while cloaking
his prose in a conservative and intellectual style, makes a number of veiled
yet inflamatory statements and all told
says few things of any importance.
    As his first citation of a historical

solution, Galbraith proposes that the Bible absolves the wealthy of responsibility for the poor by virtue of the great reward the poor will receive in the next life. If he seriously believes that is a lesson in the Bible (Old or New Testament), then Galbraith has pathetically misinterpreted scripture. More likely, he is intimating that this philosophy is the way the wealthy Biblically justify their riches in a world of hunger. Nonetheless, Galbraith is reaching too far here. Does anyone believe that God looks favorably on the Haves when they ignore the plight of the Have-nots? Indeed, if there is one lesson taught consistently throughout Jewish and Christian philosophy, it is charity toward the poor; no

rational interpretation justifies Galbraith's
cynical approach to the Judeo-Christian
ethic.

His next distortion is less glaring but
no less ridiculous. Galbraith criticizes
Bentham for his utilitarianism because
"... the result might be sadly unpleasant
for the many whose happiness was not
served." But Bentham's philosophy is
above all pragmatic, and admirably so.
That is, Bentham recognized that
society (perhaps of the twentieth century
and certainly of the eighteenth century)
is probably not capable of alleviating
everyone's poverty. He quite rightly believed that though society may not be
able to help everyone, it had an
obligation to do as much as possible.

Galbraith implies that Bentham's philosophy is in some way morally deficient. Not so. In fact, utilitarianism is a milestone in the history of humanitarian thought. This philosophy brought about a number of needed social reforms and it has adherents even today.

Later, Galbraith compares Ronald Reagan to Malthus when he paraphrases Reagan's belief that the best form of population control emerges from the market. Galbraith's intent is to criticize Reagan for expressing what — 14 Galbraith considers irrelevant and cruel. Unfortunately for Galbraith, what Reagan said is also undeniably true. Does anyone not know of a couple who practice birth control

because they can not afford a larger
family? Has Galbraith never heard of
Catholics who, despite papal interdiction,
rely on more effective contraception than
the rhythm method so they can one day
send their children to college instead of
to the mine? Is it not more libertarian
and less cruel to allow people to regulate
their own reproduction on the basis of
need than to force birth restrictions on
them? Therefore, is Galbraith
justified in attacking Reagan for
making such an astoundingly truthful
and intelligent observation?

    Further, Galbraith blunders when
he attempts to make the reader believe
that most Americans consider the
Pentagon efficient and corruption-free.

Ask anyone about outrageous expenses in the federal government and nine times out of ten, the response will include an enumeration of thousand-dollar screw drivers, incredible cost overruns for impressive looking antiaircraft guns that don't hit anything and huge over-billing incidents by General Dynamics, the defense department's most important contractor. To suggest that Americans are blind to these incompetencies and crimes is ridiculous and, indeed, rather insulting.

Here is one more example to round off this list of misrepresentations. I do not care much for supply-side economics; it has brought us enormous deficits despite reducing inflation and increasing

employment. Nonetheless, Galbraith's
description of this economic policy rivals
the brothers Grimm. "Supply-side
economics holds that the rich in the
United States have not been working
because they have too little income. So
by taking money from the poor and
giving it to the rich, we increase effort
and stimulate the economy." No, supply-
side economics holds that the rich have
not been investing and thereby broadening
the economy because they are heavily
taxed. The middle class have not been
spending and thereby creating a demand
for products because they too are heavily
taxed. So, by decreasing taxes on
these two groups, more investments
launch more businesses, and more

spending creates a market for new products. Both of these effects create more jobs that "trickle down" money to the poor. Galbraith continues: "Can we really believe ... that business people – corporate executives, the key figures in our time – are idling away their hours because of the insufficiency of their pay? This is a scandalous charge against the American business-person, notably a hard worker." It certainly is a scandalous charge – more so since Galbraith is about the only person making such absurd claims. I do not assert that supply-side economics lives up to its ambitions. But when Galbraith deliberately and facetiously misrepresents its tenets so as to more easily criticize it, he defeats himself. By setting up such obvious straw men, he makes himself look silly and he insults the intelligence of his reader.

Ironically, my objections fail to dissuade me from the truth of Galbraith's fundamental thesis. A civilized society does indeed have an obligation to help its most unfortunate members and through easing the suffering of the poor, that society gains stability and harmony. This essay responds in part to this idea; however, there isn't much to say. That is, Galbraith's opinion is hardly surprising or original; further, it is ridiculous to assert

—16

that only liberals share his beliefs. He implies in his last paragraph that conservatives have no concern for the welfare of the poor and that humanitarian impulses are natural only to liberals. Whether he is motivated by a sense of moral righteousness or by a cynical, calculated desire to draw moderates and conservatives onto the liberal side of the fence, Galbraith accomplishes nothing but alienating the groups he is trying to persuade. What should amaze the reader is that "How to get the Poor off our Conscience" was written by John Kenneth Galbraith and not Gore Vidal. Galbraith

would have been better served
by following a more truly conservative course himself – writing
a temperate, legitimate treatise
instead of a collection of irresponsible
recriminations.

SOME DIFFERENCES BETWEEN ROUGH DRAFT AND FINAL COPY

1. "Essay" used twice sounds bad.
2. Indefinite reference: "this." Does it refer to Galbraith's topic or to the existence of poverty or something else?
3. "His" is ambiguous in first sentence. Does it refer to Galbraith or the reader? The whole first sentence is eliminated.
4. Awkward phrase—sounds clumsy.
5. "About" used twice sounds bad.
6. Putting in the phrase "a compilation of" breaks up the verb "is" and "methods" and makes the sentence sound better for some reason.
7. There is no weakness in Galbraith's subject. The problem is Galbraith's approach to the subject.
8. This sentence is too strong. It makes Galbraith sound like a conspirator in some secret plot.
9. The first mention of Reagan in a formal essay ought, I think, to be formal.
10. It would seem more natural and native to say "this country."
11. Eliminate "As it stands" to enhance the readability of the sentence.
12. "Such an astoundingly" seems to excuse Galbraith for criticizing Reagan's idea. If it were astounding, then maybe Galbraith missed it or didn't understand what Reagan meant.
13. "Ridiculous" is too strong.
14. Inserting "an idea that" clarifies the meaning of the sentence.
15. Things cannot rival people. People rival people. Galbraith must rival the brothers Grimm. Galbraith's decription cannot rival the brothers Grimm.
16. This sentence makes it sound as if I based my essay on the topic I did because I couldn't think of anything else to say.

FINAL DRAFT—ESSAY #1

HOW TO GET GALBRAITH OFF YOUR CONSCIENCE
Daniel Desch

The reader might get the impression from the title of Galbraith's essay that his topic is a compilation of methods for alleviating poverty in our time. This would be the wrong impression. More properly, the essay should be titled "American Conservatives: Modern Day Scrooges." Galbraith says very little about what to do now to help the poor; he speaks more about historical attitudes toward the poor and how these attitudes have evolved to become the political philosophies of today. The inappropriateness of the title is a minor flaw in itself, but this deficiency highlights a further weakness inherent to Galbraith's motivation in writing his essay. Under the guise of an exposition on the merits and flaws (mostly flaws) of societal sentiments toward the poor, he is attacking the policies of President Reagan and a perceived rise in conservativism in this country. There is nothing wrong with Galbraith's agenda as it stands; it is his use of distortions and misrepresentations to serve his argument that rankles. If he had presented a reasoned, considered indictment of past and present policies, his essay would have been perhaps less amusing, less provocative, but certainly more respectable and more informative. Galbraith, while cloaking his prose in a conservative and intellectual style, makes a number of veiled, yet inflammatory statements and, all told, says few things of any importance.

As his first citation of a historical solution, Galbraith proposes that the Bible absolves the wealthy of responsibility for the poor by virtue of the great reward the poor receive in the next life. If he seriously believes that is a lesson in the Bible (Old or New Testament), then Galbraith has pathetically misinterpreted scripture. More likely, he is intimating that this philosophy is the way the wealthy biblically justify their riches in a world of hunger. Nonetheless, Galbraith is reaching too far here. Does anyone believe that God looks favorably on the haves when they ignore the plight of the have-nots? Indeed, if there is one lesson taught consistently throughout Jewish and Christian philosophy, it is charity toward the poor; no rational interpretation justifies Galbraith's cynical approach to the Judeo-Christian ethic.

His next distortion is less glaring but not less erroneous. Galbraith criticizes Bentham for his utilitarianism because ". . . the result might be sadly unpleasant for the many whose happiness was not served." But Bentham's philosophy is, above all, pragmatic, and admirably so. That is, Bentham recognized that society (perhaps of the twentieth century and certainly of the eighteenth century) is probably not capable of alleviating everyone's poverty. He quite rightly believed that though society may not be able to help everyone, it has an obligation to do as much as possible. Galbraith implies that Bentham's philosophy is in some way morally deficient. Not so. In fact utilitarianism is a milestone in the history of humanitarian thought. This philosophy brought about a number of needed social reforms, and it has adherents even today.

Later, Galbraith compares Ronald Reagan to Malthus when he paraphrases Reagan's belief that the best form of population control emerges from the market. Galbraith's intent is to criticize Reagan for expressing an idea that Galbraith considers irrelevant and cruel. Unfortunately for Galbraith, what Reagan said is also undeniably true. Does anyone not know of a couple who practice birth control because they cannot afford a larger family? Has Galbraith never heard of Catholics who, despite papal interdiction, rely on more effective contraception than the rhythm method so they can one day send their children to college instead of to the mine? Is it not more libertarian and less cruel to allow people to regulate their own reproduction on the basis of need than to force birth restrictions on them? Therefore, is Galbraith justified in attacking President Reagan for making a truthful and intelligent observation?

Further, Galbraith blunders when he attempts to make the reader believe that most Americans consider the Pentagon efficient and corruption-free. Ask anyone about outrageous expenses in the federal government, and nine times out of ten, the response will include an enumeration of thousand-dollar screwdrivers, incredible cost overruns for impressive-looking but useless antiaircraft guns, and huge overbilling incidents by General Dynamics, the Defense Department's most important contractor. To suggest that Americans are blind to these incompetencies and crimes is ridiculous and insulting.

Here's one more to round off this list of misrepresentations. I do not care much for supply-side economics; it has brought us enormous deficits despite reducing inflation and increasing employment. Nonetheless, Galbraith, in his description of this economic policy, rivals the brothers Grimm for sheer fantasy. "Supply-side economics holds that the rich in the United States have not been working because they have too little income. So by taking money from the poor and giving it to the rich, we increase effort and stimulate the economy." No, supply-side economics holds that the rich have not been investing and thereby broadening the economy because they are heavily taxed. The middle class has not been spending and thereby creating a demand for products because it too is heavily taxed. So, by decreasing taxes on these two groups, more investments launch more businesses and more spending creates a market for new products. Both of these effects create more jobs that "trickle down" money to the poor. Galbraith continues: "Can we really believe . . . that business people—corporate executives, the key figures in our time—are idling away their hours because of the insufficiency of their pay? This is a scandalous charge against the American businessperson, notably a hard worker." It certainly is a scandalous charge—more so since Galbraith is about the only person making such absurd claims. I do not assert that supply-side economics lives up to its ambitions. But, when Galbraith deliberately and facetiously misrepresents its tenets so as to criticize it more easily, he defeats himself. By setting up such obvious straw men, he makes himself look silly and he insults the intelligence of his reader.

Ironically, my objections fail to dissuade me from the truth of Galbraith's fundamental thesis. A civilized society does indeed have an obligation to help its most unfortunate members, and through easing the suffering of the poor that society gains stability and harmony. This essay responds in part to this idea, if only to say so what? That is, Galbraith's opinion is hardly surprising or original; further, it is ridiculous to assert that only liberals share his beliefs. He implies in his last paragraph that conservatives have no concern for the welfare of the poor and that humanitarian impulses are natural only to liberals. Whether he is motivated by a sense of moral righteousness or by a cynical, calculated desire to draw moderates and conservatives onto the liberal side of the fence, Galbraith accomplishes nothing but alienating the groups he is trying to persuade. What should amaze the reader is that "How to Get the Poor off Our Conscience" was written by John Kenneth Galbraith and not

Gore Vidal. Galbraith would have been better served by following a more truly conservative course himself—writing a temperate, legitimate treatise instead of a collection of irresponsible recriminations.

ANSWERS TO INTERVIEW—ESSAY #1

1. What notes, physical or mental, did you make after reading the essay and the assignment? Could you give an example? I made notes on the parts of the essay that struck me as being particularly wrong. For example: next to the sections concerning the Pentagon and national defense, in the margin I wrote: "WHAT!?"

2. What was your first idea about a way to respond? I first thought I would simply write something about how true Galbraith's theme (compassion, public effort, and all that) is and expand on "preserving and enlarging . . . social and political tranquility."

3. Did the sentence you first wrote down remain in the final draft? Did you try for a lead sentence before beginning the essay? No, I changed my first sentence several times. Yes.

4. What kind of audience did you assume? Was it a hostile one? What educational level did you assume? How much knowledge of the topic? I assumed my audience to be intelligent and educated but not necessarily very well versed in the area of our topic. I did not assume a hostile audience. For example, I assumed the audience to be knowledgeable about the Bible and know something about supply-side economics and current events but not necessarily anything about utilitarianism.

5. How do you go about getting started on an essay? How do you handle distractions? Do you have one place where you always work? If I can, (if I have time) I think about it for a long time (two or three days) before I get ready to sit down and write. I may ask people what they think about my ideas so I can get a fresh perspective.

   Since I have practically no power to ignore distractions, I write in a place with as few of them as possible, but that is not necessarily always the same place.

6. How did you decide how to organize the essay? How would you describe its organization? It was rather simple. When I decided I was going to criticize Galbraith's distortions, the organization laid itself out for me: first paragraph explaining and introducing the slight change in approach to the topic, five internal paragraphs each dealing with one aspect of my objections, and a final paragraph explaining how all of this hurts Galbraith's intent and alienates the reader.

7. What revisions of organization, if any, did you make between drafts? The only revision made was to change the order of two of the internal paragraphs to match the order that the subjects appeared in Galbraith's essay. I had first intended to put the internal paragraphs in order of importance but decided it was unnecessary (especially since I could not decide what that order should be).

8. What sentence-level revisions did you make? What was your reasoning? Please give examples. What techniques of revision do you use? Examples and explanations of revisions are given in the text explaining the difference between the rough draft and the final copy. Usually I reread and rewrite a sentence over and over until it sounds right.

9. Do you use a thesaurus or handbook of style? What other external aids do you commonly use? Thesaurus: yes. Handbook: Strunk and White. I use a dictionary and encyclopedia commonly. Occasionally, I will resort to Corbett's Classical Rhetoric for the Modern Student.

10. Were you blocked at any point? How do you handle writer's block? I was blocked at every sentence in the first paragraph, at the transitions between paragraphs, and at the last sentence of the last paragraph.

   I bang my head against the wall until something comes out. Sometimes, I just have to stop writing and do something entirely different for a while.

11. What parts would you expand were you to make this a longer essay? I would research more of Galbraith's claims: the context of the Rockefeller quote, the real effectiveness and efficiency of current welfare bureaucracies, details about the philosophies of George Gilder and Charles Murray.

12. What was the hardest part about writing the essay? Writing the first paragraph is always the hardest part for me.

13. What part did you like best? Why? I liked the last paragraph the best because it allowed me to vent my annoyance about Galbraith's essay all together in one place.

14. What part did you like least? Why? I have a lot of difficulty getting started. Consequently I liked the first paragraph the least. When I am writing the first paragraph of any essay, I am still in the process of deciding the exact course of the essay. The first paragraph is very tedious and may take hours.

15. What changes of mind, if any, occurred during the writing of the essay? What did you learn in the process of writing itself? What did you discover about what you thought by the need to express a position? Very often, when I am writing something, the exertion of figuring out how to express an idea can change my mind about an issue or it may enable me to see it in a new light. Not so with this essay. In fact, the struggle to find the right word and the best phrasing and, above all, the work to avoid saying irresponsible things and to not make unsubstantial claims cemented my opinion that Galbraith should have done the same.

16. What additional aspects of the process of writing would you like to comment on? What I write down the first time and the second time is usually pretty lousy. But, if I rewrite enough times, I can eventually hit on something that I recognize as being well written. It is a process of trial and error that gets easier with practice. I am not

a good writer, rather I only recognize when something I have
written is good.

GALBRAITH IS WRONG
Cathy Young

There is hardly a better way to crush ideological opponents than to start
by implying that they are uncaring and selfish, while your position is the
only virtuous, compassionate, and decent one. That is exactly what John
Kenneth Galbraith does in his essay on dealing with poverty. He
categorically declares that anyone who opposes the welfare state is
merely seeking "to escape responsibility for one's fellow beings": we, the
affluent, invent rationales for not giving to the poor so we can "get the
poor off our conscience." The speaker's conscience is, presumably, above
reproach in this matter.

One has to marvel at the ease with which Mr. Galbraith dismisses
the negative (perhaps it is better to say ugly) aspects of the modern
welfare state—aspects that even most liberals now half-heartedly acknowledge. More and more often, one hears civil-rights veterans and
architects of the "Great Society" welfare programs say that, for all the
good those programs have achieved, they have also inadvertently caused
much damage and ought to be, not scrapped, but rethought.

Mr. Galbraith, meanwhile, prefers to eulogize the accomplishments of
the social policies he so cherishes: "We have nearly abolished poverty
among the old, greatly democratized health care, assured minorities of
their civil rights, and vastly enhanced educational opportunities." The
reality behind this rhapsody is an almost 80 percent high-school dropout
rate among minority students in some inner-city neighborhoods and an
epidemic of single motherhood among black teenagers. Almost half of all
black females have a baby before the age of twenty, and about a quarter
have two or more. More black girls today drop out of school to have a
baby than go to college (so much for educational opportunity). Over half
of all black babies born today are born to unwed teenagers—with a near-
guaranteed one-way ticket to poverty for a birth certificate. It takes no
more than common sense to link this to the expansion of programs
supporting single mothers, which offer young women a way to make a
living—poor though it be—without studying, working, or getting married.

And so, for all we have done to assure minorities of their civil rights,
the gap between the median income for black and white households is
actually wider now than it was in the 1950s, despite the impressive
gains of the black middle class and the tremendous influx of black men
and women into professional jobs. While male-headed and especially two-
paycheck black families do almost as well financially as their white
counterparts, the average black family income is dragged down by the
millstone of female-headed households. We have created a vast underclass

of uneducated, unqualified people who come from, and go on to form, broken families, transmitting welfare dependency and teenage parenthood from generation to generation.

In the face of all this, Mr. Galbraith makes the staggering assertion that "there is no proof" of the pernicious effect of aid to the poor in its present form on the poor themselves. Perhaps it is affluent liberals like Mr. Galbraith who really "get the poor off their conscience" by bribing them with handouts and contributing a sum of money they will not miss toward welfare checks—so they can tell themselves they have done their part in the virtuous enterprise of compassion.

"Compassion, alongside with the associated public effort," Mr. Galbraith preaches, "is the least comfortable, the least convenient, course of behavior . . . but it remains the only one that is consistent with a totally civilized life. Also, it is . . . the most truly conservative course." True—if "conservative" is taken to mean "dedicated to maintaining the status quo." Let Mr. Galbraith look at the South Bronx he invokes, and decide whether the status quo is worth maintaining. He thus explains the conservative value of "compassion": "Civil discontent and its consequences do not come from contented people," therefore government aid to the poor will "preserve . . . social and political tranquility." When one sees the lack of self-esteem, goals, and hope that is so prevalent among the young of the underclass, pushing so many kids into teenage parenthood, drugs, and crime, one wonders what "contentment" and what "tranquility" Mr. Galbraith is talking about.

The choice is not, as Mr. Galbraith would have us think, between keeping people on dole and letting those who can't fend for themselves starve to death. We do indeed have a responsibility to the less fortunate. But let us not forget that adult, healthy men and women should normally be responsible for themselves; that to be a lifelong unilateral recipient of care, assistance, and compassion is humiliating and infantilizing. We can exercise our responsibility and concern for the poor in ways that will break the vicious cycle of dependency perpetuated by handouts, and enable people to lead normal, self-sufficient, dignified lives. Such a course of action is now being timidly charted by programs in some states that put welfare recipients to work or in job training, and encourage kids from disadvantaged backgrounds to stay in school. Those programs, too, will be costly; but the money and the effort will go toward eliminating poverty, not making it more bearable. Merely subsidizing the poor is—to turn the tables on Mr. Galbraith—a way to escape the responsibility of coming up with a real solution to the problem of long-term poverty.

ANSWERS TO INTERVIEW—ESSAY #2

1. What notes, physical or mental, did you make after reading the essay and the assignment? Could you give an example? I made several mental notes while reading the essay. One: the sanctimonious nature of John K. Galbraith's argument. Also, I noted his blindness to the

human misery created by welfare programs and to the alarming statistics which reflect this misery, and his evasion of the issue of personal responsibility.

2. What was your first idea about a way to respond? My first idea about a way to respond was to point out, and support by data, the harmful effects of the "compassionate" programs advocated by Galbraith, and also to turn around his argument and suggest that perhaps giving handouts to the poor is a way of getting them off one's conscience, without actually having done much to improve their lot.

3. Did the sentence you first wrote down remain in the final draft? Did you try for a lead sentence before beginning the essay? My lead sentence was basically the same in the first draft, but I split it in two. Initially, it read, "In his speech on dealing with the poor, John K. Galbraith follows the time-honored method of crushing his opponents by making them feel guilty and selfish, and presenting his position as the only moral, decent, and compassionate one." I then decided that it would be better to describe Galbraith's method of argument as a general principle, and then to point to Galbraith himself.

4. What kind of audience did you assume? Was it a hostile one? What educational level did you assume? How much knowledge of the topic? I assumed a neutral audience, preferably with at least some college, and with a basic knowledge of what the welfare state is and how welfare programs work.

5. How do you go about getting started on an essay? How do you handle distractions? Do you have one place where you always work? Before getting started on an essay, I usually formulate all the essential points I want to make in it, and then decide in which order I am going to make them and which points should follow from others. Sometimes, I start by formulating my conclusion, and then work my way back to the beginning. Often, I work from a spontaneous good idea—what I hope is a witty rejoinder, for instance.

6. How did you decide how to organize the essay? How would you describe its organization? I decided to organize the essay in the following way: first, attack the self-righteousness behind Galbraith's basic message; then, go on to demonstrate the practical effects of the "compassionate" programs he advocates and his blindness to those effects; then, to suggest real ways of helping the poor that Galbraith does not address.

7. What revisions of organization, if any, did you make between drafts? I did not make any major revisions in organization except by eliminating some repetitive sentences. One change I made was to move the sentence "Perhaps it is affluent liberals . . . who really 'get the poor off their conscience'" from the end of the first paragraph, where it was originally, to the second half of the article, where it is now. I decided that the accusation would work far more effectively if it followed my description of the harmful consequences of the welfare

state and of the social pathologies it has created. The description itself is meant to make the reader feel that Galbraith's defense of aid to the poor is somewhat hypocritical. This feeling would reinforce the effect of the conclusion. Having been exposed to the facts I list, the reader, I thought, would be more receptive to my charge against Galbraith than he or she would have been to an unfounded accusation. In other words, I decided that the charge should follow the damaging evidence and not the other way round.

I also added a sentence, at the end of the third paragraph, explicitly linking the social pathologies I had just described to the welfare programs defended by Galbraith.

8. What sentence-level revisions did you make? What was your reasoning? Please give examples. What techniques of revision do you use? My principle in revising sentences is to strive for greater brevity and clarity. Sometimes, I also revise a sentence to give it an ironic twist. For example, the quote from Galbraith in the third paragraph was originally followed by: "We have also created a situation in which the dropout rate for minority students in some inner-city high-schools is almost 80 percent, and more black girls have a baby while in high school than go to college—for all the vastly enhanced educational opportunity. We have also created an epidemic of teenage pregnancy, a situation where over half of all black babies born today are born to unwed teenage mothers. . . ." When I read these sentences over, I realized they were somewhat repetitive, long, and a little confusing. I also thought that, before saying that "we have created" the situation I described, I should demonstrate the cause-and-effect relationship between social programs and teenage motherhood. Finally, I thought "the reality behind the rhapsody" was a good, sarcastic way to sum up the gist of what I was saying, and would underline the contrast between Galbraith's assessment of the results of social programs and the grim statistics I was citing.

9. Do you use a thesaurus or handbook of style? What other external aids do you commonly use? Occasionally, I use a thesaurus and also an Oxford American dictionary, to make sure of the precise meaning of a word.

10. Were you blocked at any point? How do you handle writer's block? I did not get blocked while working on this article, but when I do get blocked, I usually skip the sentence or paragraph that I'm having a problem with, write down its basic idea without working on the style or a satisfactory formulation of the idea, and go on to the next part. Then, later, I return to the hard part and work on it. By then, the block is usually gone; or sometimes I get a spontaneous inspiration on how to do it while working on something else.

11. What parts would you expand were you to make this a longer essay? If I were to make this essay longer, I would explain in greater detail the connection between welfare programs and the cycle of poverty and teenage motherhood. I would also explore the links between the

"welfare culture" and crime. The other topic to which I would give more space is possible solutions to this crisis—new ways to help the poor help themselves. I could also focus more on the criticism of welfare programs and of their consequences that has come, in recent times, from some black intellectuals and leaders.

12. What was the hardest part about writing the essay? The hardest part about writing the essay was to effectively sum up my conclusion without sounding preachy.

13. What part did you like best? Why? The part I liked best about writing the essay was debunking Galbraith's pretensions to a monopoly on compassion—for himself and for liberals in general. It was a pleasure because Galbraith himself made it so easy by blatantly skirting all the difficult questions.

14. What part did you like least? Why? I can't really say there was any part I liked least—writing, especially writing a polemic, and on a topic I'm interested in, is always fun as far as I'm concerned. If I absolutely have to give an answer, it was probably the part with all the statistics on high-school dropout rates, teenage motherhood, average family incomes, etc. In a sense, you can't get too creative with statistics, and at the same time you have to choose the ones that will hit the hardest and describe the facts in the most effective way you can. Still, I can't say I didn't enjoy working on that part.

15. What changes of mind, if any, occurred during the writing of the essay? What did you learn in the process of writing itself? What did you discover about what you thought by the need to express a position? No changes of mind because my views on this matter are already well thought out, and I've given it a lot of attention in the past. No discoveries about what I thought, either—for the same reason.

16. What additional aspects of the process of writing would you like to comment on? When you are writing a polemic, one thing to avoid, I believe, is moralizing. Above all, don't just name your opponent's faults and errors—show them, on the basis of fact. It is better, I believe (as I have said before) to first list the facts that prove your point, and then to make the point when the reader's ready for it. On the other hand, sometimes there can be an opposite approach: If the point you are making is likely to amaze or shock the reader, it might be a good idea to first state the idea—jolting the reader into greater attention toward, and awareness of, the issue you're discussing, and then proceed with the proof.

A TABLE
OF LINKED SELECTIONS

A. COMPOSITIONAL TECHNIQUES

I. Cause and Effect

1. Russell Baker, "The Making of a Writer"
2. Richard Rodriguez, "Memories of a Bilingual Childhood"
3. Ada Louise Huxtable, "Houston"
4. Alan Bullock, "The Young Adolph Hitler"
5. Samuel Eliot Morison, "History as a Literary Art"
6. Flannery O'Connor, "The Teaching of Literature"
7. Reuben Brower, "Reading in Slow Motion"
8. Margaret Mead, "New Superstitions for Old"
9. Anne Hollander, "Dressed to Thrill"
10. Dorothy Wickenden, "Bowdlerizing the Bard: How to Protect Your Kids from Shakespeare"
11. Irving R. Kaufman, "The Insanity Plea on Trial"
12. George F. Kennan, "Cease This Madness: The Nuclear Arms Race"
13. Frank Willis, Jr., Joseph A. Gier, and David E. Smith, "Stepping Aside: Correlates of Displacement in Pedestrians"
14. Horace Freeland Judson, "Scientific Investigation: The Rage to Know"
15. Sheila Tobias, "Who's Afraid of Math, and Why?"
16. Dennis Avery, "U.S. Farm Dilemma: The Global Bad News Is Wrong"
17. Thomas J. Peters and Robert H. Waterman, Jr., "Successful American Companies"
18. Stephen King, "Why We Crave Horror Movies"
19. Daniel Boorstin, "Advertising: The Rhetoric of Democracy"
20. Paul Fussell, "The Boy Scout Handbook"

IV. Definition

II. Biography and Autobiography

III. Ethics and Behavior

IV. Humor and Satire

ACKNOWLEDGMENTS

John Anderson, "The Heartbreak of Cyberphobia." Reprinted from *Creative Computing*, August 1983. Copyright © 1983 by Ziff-Davis Publishing Company. Reprinted by permission of Ziff-Davis Publishing Company and Wayne Kaneshiro.

Maya Angelou, "Joe Louis: Champion of the World." From *I Know Why the Caged Bird Sings*. Copyright © 1969 by Maya Angelou. Reprinted by permission of Random House, Inc.

Isaac Asimov, "Pure and Impure: The Interplay of Science and Technology." Reprinted by permission of Saturday Review Magazine, copyright © 1979.

James Atlas, "Beyond Demographics: How Madison Avenue Knows Who You Are and What You Want." From *The Atlantic Monthly*, October 1984. Reprinted by permission of the author.

Dennis Avery, "U.S. Farm Dilemma: The Global Bad News Is Wrong." Copyright © American Association for the Advancement of Science, 1985. From *Science Magazine*, October 25, 1985. Reprinted by permission of Science Magazine and the author.

Russell Baker, "The Making of a Writer." From *Growing Up*. Copyright © 1982 by Russell Baker. Reprinted by permission of Congdon & Weed, Inc.

James Baldwin, "If Black English Isn't a Language, Then Tell Me, What Is?" Copyright © 1979 by The New York Times Company. Reprinted by permission.

Simon Barber, "The Boss Don't Like Swindle, Make It Robbery—Inside the *National Enquirer*." From the *Washington Journalism Review*, July/August 1982. Copyright © 1982 by author. Reprinted by permission of Simon Barber.

Roland Barthes, "The Brain of Einstein." From *Mythologies*, selected and translated by Annette Lavers, 13th printing. English translation copyright © 1972 by Jonathan Cape Ltd. Reprinted by permission of Farrar, Straus & Giroux, Inc.

Louise Bernikow, "Trivia, Inc.: A Simple Multimillion-Dollar Board Game." Copyright © 1985 by author. Reprinted from *Esquire* magazine, March 1985, with permission of Louise Bernikow.

Bruno Bettelheim, "Fairy Tale versus Myth: Optimism versus Pessimism." From *The Uses of Enchantment: The Meaning and Importance of Fairy Tales*, copyright © 1975, 1976 by Bruno Bettelheim. Vintage Books edition, May 1977. Published in U.S.A. by Random House. Reprinted by permission of Random House, Inc.

Daniel Boorstin, "Advertising: The Rhetoric of Democracy." From *Democracy and Its Discontents*. Copyright © 1974 by Daniel Boorstin. Reprinted by permission of Random House, Inc.

Reuben Brower, "Reading in Slow Motion." From *Reading for Life*, edited by Jacob Price. Copyright © 1959 by The University of Michigan. Reprinted by permission of The University of Michigan Press.

Thumb: More Reflections in Natural History. Reprinted by permission of W. W. Norton and Company, Inc. and Stephen Jay Gould. Copyright © 1980 by Stephen Jay Gould.

Stephen Jay Gould, "Darwin and the Expansion of Evolutionary Theory." From *Science Magazine*, April 1983. Reprinted by permission of Science Magazine and the author.

Jay Haley, "The Art of Psychoanalysis." Reprinted from *ETC.*, Vol. XV, Number 3, by permission of International Society for General Semantics. Copyright © 1958.

Ernest Hartmann, "What Is a Nightmare?" From *The Nightmare: The Psychology and Biology of Terrifying Dreams*. Copyright © 1984 by Ernest Hartmann. Reprinted by permission of Basic Books, Inc., Publishers.

Margaret Hennig and Anne Jardim, "The Middle Management Career Path." From *The Managerial Woman*. Copyright © 1976, 1977 by Margaret Hennig and Anne Jardim. Reprinted by permission of Doubleday and Company, Inc.

Anne Hollander, "Dressed to Thrill." From *The New Republic*, January 26, 1985. Reprinted by permission of The New Republic, Inc. Copyright © 1985 by The New Republic, Inc.

Langston Hughes, "Salvation." From *The Big Sea*. Copyright © 1940 by Langston Hughes. Copyright renewed © 1968 by Arna Bontemps and George Houston Bass. Reprinted by permission of Farrar, Straus & Giroux, Inc.

Ada Louise Huxtable, "Houston." From *Kicked a Building Lately?* Copyright © 1976 by The New York Times Company. Reprinted by permission.

Robert Jastrow, "The Law of the Expanding Universe." From *God and the Astronomers*. Published by W. W. Norton & Company, Inc. Copyright © 1978 by Robert Jastrow. Reprinted by permission of the author.

Horace F. Judson, "Scientific Investigation: The Rage to Know." Reprinted by permission of the author.

Irving R. Kaufman. "The Insanity Plea on Trial." Copyright © 1982 by The New York Times Company. Reprinted by permission.

George F. Kennan, "Cease This Madness: The Nuclear Arms Race." From *The Atlantic Monthly*. January 1981. Reprinted by permission of Harriet Wasserman Literary Agency, Inc., as agents for the author. Copyright © 1981 by George F. Kennan.

Tracy Kidder, "How to Make a Lot of Money." From *The Soul of a New Machine*. Copyright © 1981 by John Tracy Kidder. Reprinted by permission of Little, Brown and Company, in association with The Atlantic Monthly Press.

Stephen King, "Why We Crave Horror Movies." Copyright © 1981 by Stephen King. Reprinted by permission of the author and Kirby McCauley Ltd. This article first appeared in *Playboy*, December 1981.

Michael Korda, "When Business Becomes Blood Sport." Originally appeared in *Playboy*, June 1981. Copyright © 1981 by Michael Korda. Reprinted by permission of Playboy Magazine and International Creative Management, Inc.

John A. Kouwenhoven, "What's American about America." Copyright © 1956 by Harper's Magazine. All rights reserved. Reprinted from the July 1956 issue by special permission.

Steven Levy, "My Search for Einstein's Brain." Copyright © 1978 by Steven Levy. Reprinted by permission of The Sterling Lord Agency, Inc.

Konrad Lorenz, illustrations in "A Biological Homage to Mickey Mouse." From *Studies in Animal and Human Behavior*, copyright © 1971. Reprinted by permission of Harvard University Press and by Walt Disney Productions.

Stan Luxenberg, "McDonald's: The Franchise Factory." From *Roadside Empires*. Copyright © 1985 by Stan Luxenberg. Reprinted by permission of Viking Penguin, Inc.

Joan D. Lynch, "Music Videos: From Performance to Dada-Surrealism." From the *Journal of Popular Culture*, Summer 1984. Reprinted with permission of the editor.